SOFTWARE DEVELOPMENT IN PASCAL

SARTAJ SAHNI

University of Minnesota

THE CAMELOT PUBLISHING COMPANY
FRIDLEY, MINNESOTA

The Camelot Publishing Co.
1551 Camelot Lane NE
Fridley
Minnesota 55432

First Printing

Library of Congress Cataloging in Publication Data

Sahni, Sartaj
   Software Development In Pascal

   Includes bibliographies and index.
   1. Software development in Pascal

ISBN: 0-942450-01-9
Library of Congress: 85-070519

DEDICATION

to

my wife: Neeta

and

my children: Agam and Neha

PREFACE

The objective of this book is to provide an introduction to all aspects of the software development task. The length of this book is, perhaps, a testimony to the difficulties encountered in software development. The topics covered in this book represent this author's attempt to define software engineering. These topics include traditional software engineering topics such as: problem specification, human interface design, modularization, aesthetic programming, stepwise refinement, testing, and documentation. In addition, material on program verification, performance analysis and measurement, data structures, and algorithms is also included. It is my opinion that these topics are as important to software development as are the topics in the first set.

This text can be used in a variety of courses currently taught in undergraduate programs. It is necessary to cover the book in its entirety to get a good feel for all aspects of software development. An introductory software engineering course can be based on the material in Chapters 1 through 9. An introductory data structures and algorithms course can be based on Chapters 10 through 14. A second course in programming (commonly called advanced programming) can be taught using material from Chapters 1 through 7, and 9 through 12. For a thorough coverage of the material in this book, a two semester sequence is recommended.

ACKNOWLEDGEMENTS

I am deeply indebted to several of my colleagues who have helped make this book possible. First of all, I wish to acknowledge the efforts of Jayaram Bhasker, Jim Cohoon, Eliezer Dekel, Ten-Hwang Lai, Mark Luker, and Lou Rosier. Their careful and timely reading of this manuscript has resulted in several enhancements. Thanks are due to John Jelatis for his assistance with the typesetting software. Finally, I wish to thank the University of Minnesota for providing a work environment that has made this book possible.

BUGS

It is my belief that there isn't (and probably never will be) a bug free book of reasonable size on the market today. Consequently, I am confident that this book contains several bugs. I will appreciate any correspondence from the readers regarding bugs (or suspected bugs) that they might find. I will attempt to correct these in subsequent printings of this book.

Sartaj Sahni
Minneapolis
March 1985

CONTENTS

CHAPTER 1

SOFTWARE DEVELOPMENT

1.1. DEVELOPMENT ACTIVITIES

The term *software development* encompasses all the activities involved in going from a problem statement to a working and well documented computer program that solves this problem. One difficulty in obtaining a complete list of these activities is that programming is as much an art as it is a science. As such, there are many creative aspects to it. Furthermore, the science of programming is continually changing and a sufficient degree of maturity has not as yet been achieved. Another difficulty is that the development of good, reliable software is a sufficiently complex task that some aspects of it continue over the entire life of the resulting software system. For example, it is impossible to guarantee the correctness of reasonably large and complex programs such as operating systems, compilers, and database management systems. As a result, errors in these programs are discovered even after they have been in use for several years. So, program maintenance continues over the life of the program. Another aspect is program enhancement. User needs change in time and it becomes necessary to modify or enhance the program as needs change.

Despite these difficulties, one can come up with a list of activities that are generally performed during the software development process. Our list is:

1

2 Software Development

(1) Specification

(2) Design

(3) Modularization

(4) Selection of a programming language or languages

(5) Program development

(6) Validation

(7) Performance analysis and measurement

(8) Documentation

(9) Maintenance

(10) Enhancement

We illustrate each of these activities by considering as an example the problem of developing a text processor. In discussing software development, it is useful to keep in mind the different categories of individuals involved in the process. The following categories are relevant to our discussion:

(1) *The problem originator*. This is the person (or persons) who poses the problem that is to be solved by the resulting software system.

(2) *Designers*. These are the individuals who design the software system.

(3) *Programmers*. These are the individuals charged with the duty of implementing the design.

(4) *Maintenance Staff*. This staff has the responsibility of discovering and correcting the cause of any errors that may be discovered in the software after it has been released for use. We shall assume that this group also has the responsibility of providing any and all product enhancements that may be called for during the life of the software system.

(5) *Users*. This is the community that actually uses the software system after it has been released for use.

In some software development projects, all the above categories may consist of the same individual. For example, you may pose the problem, design and implement its solution yourself, and be the sole user of the system. Further, having used the system, you may discard the resulting program. In this situation, the need for maintenance and enhancement will not arise. When the software project involves the development of a large and complex piece of software, each of the above categories is generally comprised of different individuals. Our discussion of the software development activities assumes that the programming environment is an interactive one and that the standard input device is a keyboard and the standard output device a monitor (referred to as the screen).

1.2. SPECIFICATION

In this step, we are concerned mainly with trying to understand what the problem is. Without a thorough and precise understanding of the problem, it is unlikely that a satisfactory program can be arrived at. Generally, the person who originates the problem and the one (or ones) who develop the resulting software system are different people. So, it is not surprising that when the problem is first posed, the would be programmer may have an incomplete understanding of exactly what the program is supposed to do. This may be the case even when the programmer and problem originator are the same person. Often, the originator of the problem has not thought the problem through sufficiently to have a precise set of requirements available.

The following statements are often heard in programming classrooms across the world and provide evidence of the truth of our earlier statements:

A disgruntled programmer on receiving his graded program back...

> *But you didn't say it was to be done this way. I thought this is what you wanted.*

An instructor on being asked whether the text processor to be written should contain a screen or line editor ....

> *Oh, you decide for yourself and do whatever you think is best.*

(Of course, after you have made the decision and spent innumerable hours designing and programming your text processor, the instructor has finally thought over the problem and determined that the decision you made is inappropriate for the environment he has in mind. So, your efforts have gone to waste and you need to restart from scratch.)

In the text processor specification stage, we would like to get answers to questions such as:

(1)   What is the text processor supposed to do? Generally speaking, it should provide for the editing (i.e., entry and correction) and formatting (i.e., alignment of left and right margins; setting of paragraphs, type fonts, point sizes, etc.) of text. What are the needs of the targeted user community? Should it also allow for the handling of mathematical equations?

(2)   Are the editing and formatting functions to be separated or done in parallel? If the functions are done in parallel, then each time a change is made, it may be necessary to reformat the entire text. On the other hand, if the functions are separated the user does not know what the formatted text is going to look like while he/she is entering the text.

It may even be necessary to have a combination of both as typically, text being entered from a keyboard will be displayed only on a screen with limited capability. For example, it may not be possible to display boldface or italic characters on the screen, or it may not be possible to display characters of varying size on the screen, etc. All these could, of course, be possible on another display (i.e., output) device such as a dot matrix printer or phototypesetter. So, it may be desirable to design the text processor in such a way that it formats for the screen during text editing (of course taking the limitations of the screen into account) and then reformats for other devices later as needed.

(3)   Is the editor to be screen oriented? I.e., are we to display a screenfull of text at any time and allow the user to move to any part of this screen and edit that part? Or, is it a line editor in which the user must specify the line numbers of the lines of text that are to be edited? Or, is it a combination of the two in which the user can switch between screen and line modes as he/she sees fit?

1.3. DESIGN

Having understood what the problem is, we need to develop a top level design for the software system that will meet the specifications. This level of design is concerned primarily with the functional behavior of the system and not with the implementation details of the various functional blocks. We are concerned with those aspects of the software system that affect its external behavior, i.e., the user interface.

Exactly what takes place in the design step depends on the degree to which the problem has been specified. The problem specification may be so precise as to require little or nothing to be done by way of design. In the case of our text processor example, however, much needs to be done. Assume that the specifications call for a text processor with the following characteristics:

(1) It is to handle text only. No provision for mathematical equations or graphic symbols is required.

(2) It is to format on the screen during editing and is also to provide advanced formatting features for other display devices.

(3) It should support both line editing and screen editing modes.

In the design step, we need to determine such things as:

(1) What edit functions are to be provided in screen and line mode? Some obvious functions for screen mode are: insert new text above or below the line the cursor is presently at; delete present line; change word beginning at cursor; delete character pointed at by cursor; insert new text to the left of the cursor; insert new text to the right of the cursor; move cursor up (down) one line; move cursor forward (backward) one screen (or page); move cursor left (right) one character (word); and move cursor to the left (right) end of the line the cursor is at.

Some desirable functions for line mode editing are: delete lines numbered n through m; move cursor to line numbered n; search for the next line that contains a particular string pattern; replace all occurences of pattern x occurring in lines n through m by the string y.

(2)   Having determined the functions, we need to determine what keystrokes the user must use to perform each of these functions. Let us consider the screen edit mode. This mode itself may be subdivided into two modes: command and insert. Every keyboard entry while in command mode is regarded as a command to the editor. Figure 1.1 shows a possible set of editor commands. The ^ sign that appears in some of the command names is the control key. This key is to be depressed at the same time as the next key in the command name. The command ^→, for instance, is invoked by depressing the ^ and → keys simultaneously. The editor command names are kept short so as to minimize user effort. At the same time, an attempt is made to design command names such that they relate closely to the functions they perform. For example, the command ↑ means move the cursor up one line. The design of the command names of Figure 1.1 assumes that the editor is to be used on a computer or computer terminal that has an extended keyboard (such as the one on the IBM-PC). In particular, the keyboard must have the keys <PgUp>, <PgDn>, etc. that are nonstandard. This aspect of the design is therefore dependent on the target computer. It is necessary at this time to return to the problem originator and determine whether the assumption made regarding the extended keyboard is valid.

When in insert mode, every keyboard entry (but one) is regarded as new text. The exception is the entry that switches us out of insert mode and back into command mode. In Figure 1.1, the escape key (<esc>) is used for this purpose.

(3)   Should the processor be menu driven? I.e., when the processor is invoked, is a list of processor capabilities displayed as in Figure 1.2, or do we get a blank screen and require the user to remember what the processor can do and how to get it to do this? A menu driven program is much easier to use and relieves the user of the burden of having to remember the details of how to use the program. Can the software design assume the presence of pointing devices such as mice, touch pads, and touch screens? If so, we can consider the use of icons. We also have the option of permitting other modes of selecting from a menu. For example, instead of selecting by number as in Figure 1.2, we could use a mouse to move the cursor to the desired selection.

Command	Function
→	move cursor one character right
←	move cursor one character left
^→	move cursor one word right
^←	move cursor one word left
L	move cursor to left end of line
R	move cursor to right end of line
↑	move cursor up one line
↓	move cursor down one line
<PgUp>	move cursor back one screen
<PgDn>	move cursor forward one screen
^X	delete character at cursor
^L	delete word left of cursor
^R	delete word right of cursor
^D	delete line at cursor
U	insert text above cursor line
D	insert text below cursor line
I	insert left of cursor
A	insert right of cursor
^U	undo last command
^M	change mode to line edit
<esc>	switch to command mode

Figure 1.1 Screen editor commands.

(4) Should there be an on-line help facility so that the user can at any time request information on how to use the text processor? If so, how is this help facility to be invoked? One possibility is to use part of the screen to display important processor commands as in Figure 1.3. Another is to provide this information on a second screen that the user can display at any time. With this approach, the user must switch from the text screen to the command screen and back as needed.

We may also provide a more detailed help facility that

FRIENDLY TEXT PROCESSOR

FUNCTIONS

1. Edit
2. Format
3. Exit from text processor

SELECT FUNCTION BY ENTERING NUMBER

Figure 1.2 Startup menu for text processor

can be invoked by the user as needed. This facility could provide a complete description of the commands and could also include examples illustrating the use of each command. So, we may have a command H for help. When H is entered in command mode, the screen display could change to the one shown in Figure 1.4. If L is entered in response to the question of Figure 1.4, then the screen display could be as shown in Figure 1.5.

It is not difficult to see that everything listed above in the design step could very well have been provided to us as a specification. The real difference between specification and design is that the programmer must design the software system to conform to the specification. So, if certain edit functions are part of the specification, these must be provided for and must work as specified. Functions that are not part of the specification can be designed to work in a manner the designer deems best. This distinction between specification and design is

Friendly Screen Editor Commands			
cursor	**delete**	**insert**	**misc.**
→char right	^Xchar	Uline up	^Uundo
←char left	^Lword left	Dlines down	^Mline mode
⌐→word right	^Rword right	Awords right	
⌐←word left	^Dline	Iwords left	
Lleft end of line			^Qquit
Rright end of line			Ssave file
↑ line up			Hhelp
↓ line down			
Fscreen forward		^ is control key. Depress with next character.	
Bscreen back			

SPACE FOR USER TEXT DISPLAY

Figure 1.3 Permanent help display on screen

important as all too often, programmers design a program that does not conform to the specifications but which they believe is better than what could be achieved if they had adhered to the specifications. This practice is intolerable. The specifications dictate what is required. If your program does not satisfy the requirements in every respect, you have not solved the problem that was posed.

Since, you will often feel that what you are doing in the design step should perhaps have been part of the specifications or that particular design decisions will materially affect the resulting program, it is a good idea to go back to the problem originator and discuss the various

---

Friendly Screen Editor ... On Line Help

Which Command?

Figure 1.4 Response to request for help

design alternatives. This may result in a modification or refinement of the problem specifications. When this process is carried out to its extreme, the entire design will become part of the specifications.

1.4. MODULARIZATION

Modularization is a technique that is used to decompose a large and complex task into a collection of smaller less complex tasks. This technique may be applied to many of the activities of software development. The objective is to divide the software system into many functionally independent parts or *modules* so that each can be developed relatively independently. This will reduce the overall software development time as it is much easier to solve several small problems than one large one. Additionally, different modules can be developed by different persons, in parallel. If necessary, each module may be further decomposed so as to obtain a hierarchy of modules as shown in Figure 1.6.

At the top level, the text processor has been split into two modules. The first of these is the editor and the second the formatter. The editor does editing as well as screen formatting while text is being entered. The formatter formats the text for display on a device other than a screen. The specification, design, and development of each of these modules can be carried out in a relatively independent manner once the interface between the two has been fully specified. In Figure 1.6, the editor itself has been split into two modules: the screen editor

---

Friendly Screen Editor ... Help for command *L*

The command L moves the cursor to the leftmost position on the line the cursor is presently at. If the cursor is already at the leftmost position on that line, it remains there.

Example L transforms the situation:

This is a ⬚l ine of text.

Into the situation:

⬚T his is a line of text.

The remainder of the screen is unchanged.

Enter <esc> to return to editor

Figure 1.5 Help for command L.

and the line editor. Each of these modules can be specified, designed, and developed independently. The functions of the screen editor include cursor movement, formatting the text for on screen display as it is entered, text movement, text deletion, etc. These functions may also be specified, designed, and developed in a relatively independent manner.

Each box in Figure 1.6 is called a *node*. The *children* of a node *x* are the nodes immediately below and connected to *x*. *x* is the *parent* of its children. A node that has no children is called a *leaf* and the unique node with no parent is called the *root*. The line connecting

1.6. PROGRAM DEVELOPMENT

In all but the simplest of cases, the program code corresponding to a module is arrived at by going through a sequence of development steps. We begin with a very high level description of the module and successively refine it to the lowest level, which is the Pascal code. During this refinement process, we will need to determine the data structures as well as the algorithms to be used to accomplish the objectives of the module. The data structures will generally be determined in a top down manner by beginning at the highest level of the modularization hierarchy and determining the structures that are to be shared by the modules at the next level. Thus all modules that share data must work with the same structure for that data. If modules A and B use some data that is not shared, then they need not know how each is structuring it. While a module is being coded, further modularization may take place.

1.7. VALIDATION

Validation and verification are two activities that are carried out to establish correctness of the software system. These activities may be performed at each stage of the software development process. In *validation*, the correctness of the result of each stage is established with respect to the initial problem specification. In *verification*, correctness is established with respect to the specification for that stage.

Since the cost of correcting errors in a software system is considerably less when they are detected early in the development process, validation and verification are to be performed at each step of the software development process rather than just upon completion. This means that the problem specifications should be validated/verified for consistency, completeness, and correctness before one proceeds to the design of the software. In case the specifications are found to be inconsistent, incomplete, or incorrect in any way, they should be modified so as to achieve consistency, completeness, and correctness before beginning the design step. The conformance of the design with the given specifications should be validated/verified before one formulates a program plan. The program plan itself should be verified before coding commences. Each coded module and the final software system should be verified before the system is released for use.

Despite the existence of fairly sophisticated software tools to assist in validation and verification, inconsistencies in one step of the development process are discovered after the next has begun. In practice, therefore, software development is an iterative process with several steps being repeated to correct errors.

In the remainder of this section, we shall specifically deal with program validation only. The ideas presented apply equally to the validation/verification that is to be performed at all steps of the development process. There are essentially two approaches to validation: static analysis and testing.

In a *static analysis* of a program the code is not executed. It is however analyzed for correctness using automatic or manual methods. The most common forms of static analysis are:

(1)   Use of a compiler to detect the presence of syntactic errors.

(2)   Use of flow graphs.

(3)   Symbolic execution.

(4)   Desk checks, walk-throughs, and inspections.

(5)   Simulation.

(6)   Correctness proofs.

Most compilers, in addition to detecting errors in the syntax of the program will detect the following errors:

(1)   Undefined variables.

(2)   Variables that have been defined but not used. Such variables indicate the possible presence of spelling or logic errors.

(3)   Variables that get redefined before use as in the program fragment:

$$x := 2; y := 3; z := 5; x := y + z;$$

The presence of such variables also indicates the possible presence of errors in the program.

(4)   Unreachable segments of code.

(5)   Mismatch in data types between formal and actual parameters of procedures and functions.

Since the problems of determining whether a variable is actually used in any execution of a program or whether a segment of program code is executed in any execution of a program are undecidable (i.e., these problems are not solvable by any program that terminates on all inputs), compilers cannot detect all such occurrences. However, they can detect most such occurrences.

Traditionally, compilers check only if the syntax of the program permits variable use (i.e., it appears on the right hand side of at least one assignment statement or appears in at least one Boolean expression that forms the conditional of an **if**, **while**, or **until** statement, or is used in the parameters of a procedure or function call, or is used in the parameters of a **for** statement. Code reachability is determined only from syntactic considerations. For example, in the following code fragment:

```
goto 10
20: x := 2;
```

the statement labeled 20 is unreachable if there is no statement of the form **goto** 20 in the program.

The semantics of the program may be such that even though the syntax permits use of a variable and allows for code reachability, neither of these may occur. Problems of this type can often be detected using flow graphs. In the flow graph approach, one obtains a diagram (called a flow graph) that represents the flow of control in the program. As an example, consider the code:

```
x :=2; y:=3;
if x > y then z :=4
        else x := 2 * y;
y := z;
```

The flow graph for this is shown in Figure 1.7. By examining the paths ABCE and ABDE in this graph, one sees that whenever the path ABDE is taken, the variable x is redefined before use and that the variable z is undefined at statement E.

In a symbolic execution of the code, the program is executed without assigning values to the input variables. Even though the program of Figure 1.7 has no input variables, a symbolic execution will

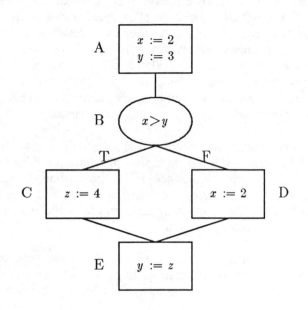

Figure 1.7 Flow graph

reveal that the statement C is unreachable. x and y are assigned the values 2 and 3, respectively, in A. Since the conditional in B evaluates to false, the statement in C is unreachable. Hence, x is always redefined before use in this program. Further, z is always undefined at statement E.

If the code in A is changed to:

$x := 2;$ **read**(y);

then the result of a symbolic execution is:

if $2 > y$ **then** $[x := 2; y := 4; z := 4]$
else $[x := 2y; y$ and z are undefined$]$

The traditional way to analyze a program is for the programmer to sit at a desk and go through his/her program manually. A manual program analysis can be an effective way to check the correctness of the logic of a program. Since most people cannot detect their own errors, it is best to have someone other than the programmer perform this manual desk check. *Walk-throughs* and *inspections* are two disciplined manual techniques for validation. In both of these, a team that includes the software developers and several persons not associated with the development reviews the software. The team goes through the specifications, design, code, etc. manually.

In an inspection, the specifications, design, or code are read out aloud, step by step. A list of common pitfalls is used to assist in the detection of errors and inconsistencies. The ensuing discussion generally results in the discovery of existing errors and inconsistencies. In a walk-through, the team manually simulates the execution of the program on one or more test data.

In a simulation, one constructs models of the program and the environment in which the program is to be used. The models are then analyzed to determine if the program will work to specifications.

None of the static analysis methods discussed so far can conclusively establish the validity of the program. Several mathematically rigorous methods have been proposed for this. We shall elaborate on these in a later chapter. These methods are too cumbersome to be applied on any reasonably large programs. Further, the possibility of automating the proof process is ruled out by a result from the theory of computing. This result states that there is no algorithm (i.e., a program that is guaranteed to terminate on all inputs) to establish the correctness of all programs.

No amount of static analysis can actually establish that the constructed software system will work in the target environment. This statement is true even if one can formally prove the correctness of the program. This is so because correctness proofs never account for the target environment. Code that passes through inspections and walk-throughs may fail to work correctly. This may be caused by some idiosyncracies in the compilers used, or in the operating system of the target computer, etc, or even because the reviews failed to uncover all the errors.

To gain any confidence at all that the program will work in the target hardware/software environment, the program must be run against real data in this environment. *Testing* is the process of actually executing the code in the target environment and comparing the performance of the software system with the specifications. The results obtained from test data are compared with the expected results from a correct system. Testing provides us with some confidence that the program works correctly. Our degree of confidence increases with the number and variance of the tests (provided, of course, that these tests show that the program is working as expected).

A naive approach to provide a correctness proof is to test the program on all possible inputs and compare the results with the expected or "correct" results. If these match on all inputs, then the program is correct. This exhaustive testing of a program is impractical for the following reasons:

(1)   The number of input data to be tested is usually infinite or astronomical. So, testing will never terminate.

(2)   The correct results are often known only for certain inputs.

So, no practical amount of testing can establish correctness. Hence, the real objective of testing is to expose the presence of errors (if any). A good test data is one that causes an incorrect program to malfunction.

Testing may proceed bottom up or top down. In the bottom up approach, we begin by testing the leaf modules independently and then work our way up the module hierarchy validating collections of modules that comprise a module at a higher level. When the bottom up approach is used, we need to write a *driver* program that sets up the appropriate test environment (eg., data structures created by other modules that are needed by the module being tested).

If we use the bottom up approach on our text processor example of Figure 1.6, the modules for the screen editor functions ($\leftarrow$, $\uparrow$, $\downarrow$, etc.) will be tested before the screen editor module is tested; the editor module will be tested only after both the screen and line editor modules are tested; the root module (text processor) gets tested only after the editor, formatter, and quit modules have been tested.

output, data structure, data derivation, system size and volume, system dynamics, system properties, and system management. The PSA is capable of automatically generating reports from the system database. This database itself is created by entering information about the software system using PSL. The categories of reports that can be produced are: database modification reports, reference reports, summary reports, and analysis reports.

(2) *SADT (Structured Analysis and Design Technique).* This system attempts to provide methods to think in a structured and modular way about large complex problems; work as a team with effective division and coordination of effort and roles; communicate interview, analysis, and design results in a clear and precise notation; document results and decisions in such a way as to provide a complete audit of history; control accuracy, completeness, and quality through frequent a review and approval procedure; and plan, manage, and assess the progress of the development project.

(3) *EPOS, SREM, RDL, PDL*, etc.

A formal treatment of the available software development support systems is beyond the scope of this book. The interested reader may follow up on these systems by reading some of the articles referenced at the end of this chapter.

1.13. SUMMARY

Software development may be regarded as a three phase activity: requirements, implementation, and post-release. Specification and design define the *requirements phase.* Coding, verification, testing, and performance analysis and measurement define the *implementation phase.* Maintenance and enhancement define the *post-release phase.* Modularization is used during both the requirements and implementation phase while documentation is created during all three phases.

Even though an ordered list of software development activities has been provided, some of these activities are often performed interactively. As mentioned above, there is often a need during the design step to go back to the problem originator for further guidance and specification. Needs for additional specification and design may be discovered during the implementation phase; results from the performance evaluation step may force a reconsideration of the earlier steps; etc. The need for continued dialogue with the problem originator during all phases of the development process cannot be overemphasized.

The development of reasonably complex software is greatly facilitated by the use of computer aids such as PSL/PSA, SADT, etc.

1.14. REFERENCES AND SELECTED READINGS

The December 1974 issue of Computing Surveys (published by the Association of Computing Machinery) is a special issue on the subject of programming. This issue provides good general material for many of the topics dealt with in this book. The papers:

Programming and documenting software projects, by P. J. Brown

and

An overview of programming practices, by J. M. Yohe

are of particular interest for Chapter 1. The remaining three papers that appear in this issue are relevant to the discussion of later chapters. For a comparative evaluation of different approaches to software development, see the article:

The operational vs the conventional approach to software development, by P. Zave, *Communications of the ACM*, Vol. 27, No. 2, Feb. 1984, pp. 104-118.

The subject of computer aids for software development is covered well in the May 1982 issue of Computer (Published by the IEEE). The PSL/PSA and SADT systems are, respectively, described in the articles:

PSL/PSA: A computer-aided technique for structured documentation and analysis of information processing systems, by D. Teichroew and E. Hershey, III, *IEEE Transactions on Software Engineering*, Vol. SE-3, No. 1, Jan. 1977, pp. 41-48.

and

> Structured analysis for requirements definition, by D. Ross and K. Schoman, Jr., *IEEE Transactions on Software Engineering*, Vol. SE-3, No. 1, Jan. 1977, pp. 6-15.

Our description of the capabilities of PSL/PSA and SADT are actually quotes from the above two articles. References to the remaining software development support systems mentioned in this chapter can be found in:

> Development support systems, by R. Lauber, *IEEE Computer*, Vol. 15, No. 5, May 1982, pp. 36-49.

A good overview of validation methods appears in the paper:

> Validation, verification, and testing of computer software, by W. R. Adrion, M. Branstad, and J. Cherniavsky, *ACM Computing Surveys*, Vol. 14, No. 2, June 1982, pp. 159-192.

CHAPTER 2

SPECIFICATION

2.1. INTRODUCTION

The problem originator must provide an accurate specification or definition of the problem for which a computer program is to be written. Likewise, the programmer must ensure that the resulting program meets this specification in every way. This chapter examines the specification of problems from different domains.

Different software development support systems have different requirement specification languages. These languages range from informal English narrative to a formal programming language-like notation. Some support systems even allow for formal mathematical constructs involving quantifiers and Boolean operators. While we shall not favor any particular development system here, our examples will attempt to span the range of possible specification notations.

For some of our examples, a precise mathematical specification can be provided. For others, it is more practical to provide English narrative only. In some instances, a specification using programming language-like notation is possible and in yet others, a combination of mathematical language and English narrative will be used. We defer the use of programming language like notation to the next chapter.

The need for documenting each step of the specification process cannot be overemphasized. A record of all discussions with the problem originator (especially those that result in a change in the specification) must be kept. Computer assisted documentation tools are very effective for this. If the problem is initially specified verbally (as in a phone call from the problem originator ... "write me a program to ..."), you must first write down your understanding of the problem. Then take this written version to the problem originator and make sure that it agrees with what he/she has in mind. Further dialogue may be called for as you begin to develop the program. Whenever you reach a point where a decision will restrict the problem instances that your program can handle, you must go back to the problem originator and confirm the acceptability of that decision. This will result in a refinement of the problem specification.

Remember, it is much easier to incorporate changes in the specifications and resolve any ambiguities and inconsistencies before any design and implementation work has been done than afterwards. So, every effort should be made in the specification stage to ensure that one has a complete and consistent specification of the problem for which the software system is to be developed.

2.2. MATHEMATICAL PROBLEMS

Problems with a precise mathematical formulation are often the easiest to specify. Here too an inadequate specification is often provided by problem originators who are not too familiar with programming. For example, consider the problem of finding the larger of two elements x and y. The problem is very nicely defined in terms of the input/output specification:

Input x, y

Output $\max\{x, y\}$

While this completely captures the essence of the problem to be solved, there isn't enough information present to write a program for it's solution. We need to know whether x and y are strings, polynomials, vectors, numbers, etc. In programming languages such as Pascal, we need even more detailed information. If x and y are numbers, are they real or integer?

A problem originator unfamiliar with the limitations of contemporary programming languages will be unaware of the need to provide data type information in the problem specification. Moreover, most programmers on seeing the original specification will immediately obtain a "complete understanding" of the problem and realize the deficiency in the specification only when they sit down to write the program. At this time more dialogue between originator and programmer will take place (hopefully). Failure to carry out this dialogue can very well result in a program that finds the larger of two integers (the easy solution) while the problem originator envisioned a general purpose program that could find the larger of two elements regardless of their type. It is better to know that your assumption on the type of x and y is incorrect before you have written, tested, and documented your program than after.

Let us consider further examples of the specification of mathematical problems and the refinements in specification needed before programming can proceed.

Example 2.1: [Searching] We are required to write a program that searches a list $a[1]$, $a[2]$, ..., $a[n]$ of n elements for the element x. The input/output specification for this problem is:

Input n, $a[i]$, $1 \leq i \leq n$, x

Output If $a[i] \neq x$, $1 \leq i \leq n$, then 0. Otherwise, an integer i such that $1 \leq i \leq n$ and $a[i] = x$.

Refinements in the specification are needed to answer the following questions.

(1) What is the user environment? Is the program to be used as a procedure by another program or is it to be a stand alone product? In the latter case, where do the $a[i]$'s come from? Are they to be obtained interactively from the user?

(2) How large can the list of elements get? I.e., what is the maximum value for n? If n is too large, then the element list will have to be read into memory piecemeal from a storage device such as a disk. In this case, the search program will need to know the name and/or characteristics of the file that contains the list. If n is sufficiently small, all n elements can be resident in memory when the search is being carried out.

(3) Is the list ordered in any way? If, for example, $a[1] \leq a[2] \leq \ldots \leq a[n]$, then the program can use this information to arrive at a faster search program than would otherwise be possible.

(4) What is the data type of the elements in the list? This information is needed so that variables of the appropriate type can be declared. If the data type is not one of the standard data types (eg., integer, real, Boolean) provided by the programming language, then it will be necessary to write our own code to test for the equality of two elements (eg., the elements may be vectors or polynomials). For standard data types, the Boolean expression $x = y$ can be used to determine if x equals y.

The refined specification might take the form:

Input n, an unordered list $a[i]$, $1 \leq i \leq n$, and x where n is in the range [0, 200] and the elements are integer.

Output If $a[i] \neq x$, $1 \leq i \leq n$, then 0. Otherwise, an integer i such that $1 \leq i \leq n$ and $a[i] = x$.

In addition, the user environment needs to be specified. □

Example 2.2: [Sorting] The initial input/output specification of this problem may take the form:

Input n, $a[i]$, $1 \leq i \leq n$

Output A reordered list of elements such that $a[1] \leq a[2] \leq \ldots \leq a[n]$.

Refinements are needed in the specification to answer the same questions as posed in Example 2.1. □

Example 2.3: [Thirsty Baby] A very thirsty, but intelligent baby wants to quench her thirst. She has access to a glass of water, a bottle of wine, a can of beer, a carton of milk, cans of a variety of juices, and bottles and cans of various sodas. In all there are n different liquids available to the baby. From past experience with these n liquids, the baby knows that some are more satisfying than others. In fact, the baby has assigned satisfaction values to each liquid. s_i units of satisfaction are obtained by drinking one ounce of the ith liquid.

Ordinarily, the baby would just drink enough of the liquid that gives her greatest satisfaction per ounce and thereby quench her thirst in the most satisfying way. Unfortunately, there isn't enough of this most satisfying liquid available. Let a_i be the amount in ounces of liquid i that is available. The baby needs to drink a total of t ounces to quench her thirst. How much of each available liquid should she drink?

We may assume that satisfaction is additive. Let x_i denote the amount of liquid i that the baby should drink. The solution to her problem is obtained by finding real numbers x_i, $1 \le i \le n$ that maximize

$$\sum_{i=1}^{n} s_i x_i$$

subject to the constraints

$$\sum_{i=1}^{n} x_i = t$$

$$0 \le x_i \le a_i, \ 1 \le i \le n$$

Note that if $\sum_{1}^{n} a_i < t$, then there is no solution to the baby's problem. Even if she drinks all the liquids available, she will be unable to quench her thirst.

This precise mathematical formulation of the problem provides an unambiguous specification of what the program is to do. Having obtained this formulation, we are now in a position to provide the input/output specification. This takes the form:

Input n, t, s_i, a_i, $1 \le i \le n$. n is an integer and the remaining numbers are positive reals.

Output Real numbers x_i, $1 \le i \le n$, such that $\sum_{i=1}^{n} s_i x_i$ is maximum, $\sum_{i=1}^{n} x_i = t$, and $0 \le x_i \le a_i$, $1 \le i \le n$. Output a suitable message if $\sum_{i=1}^{n} a_i < t$. $\square$

A mathematical formulation for many problems can be obtained without too much difficulty. These formulations are generally the clearest ones to work with. However, the normal mathematical formulation of problems is usually not sufficiently refined to enable us to write a program for its solution. Further dialogue with the problem originator will result in a sufficiently refined specification.

2.3. PROGRAMMING LANGUAGES

A *compiler* is a program that translates programs written in a high level programming language such as Pascal, Ada, COBOL, PL/I, FORTRAN, Basic, etc. into the machine language of the computer that the program is to be run on. In order to write a compiler for a language such as Pascal, we need a complete and precise specification of both the high level and the machine language.

Machine languages can be adequately specified by providing a table of the available instructions and a mathematical description of the function performed by each. High level languages, on the other hand, are generally more complex and their specification requires the use of more sophisticated tools. The specification of a programming language has two components: specification of syntax and specification of semantics.

We may draw an analogy between natural languages and programming languages. A book written in English consists of chapters. Each chapter consists of sections. Sections themselves are made up of sentences which in turn are made up of words, punctuation marks and numerals. The words are composed of letters and hyphens. Likewise, a Pascal program contains **procedures**, **functions**, and blocks which may be regarded as the chapters, sections or paragraphs of the

program. These in turn are composed of statements such as the assignment, **for**, **case**, **begin**, and **end** statements. These are like the sentences of a natural language. Each statement is composed of words
that may be reserved words in the language such as **begin** and **end**,
programmer defined names such as *InterestRate* and *Profit*, numbers
such as 1.2 and -50, operators such as "+", "−", and "/", or punctuation marks such as "." and ";". Programmer defined names and
numbers are composed of lower level entities such as letters and
digits. The lowest level entities in a programming language define the
vocabulary of the language. Each element of this vocabulary is called
a *symbol* of the language.

Syntax is concerned with the legal ways of combining symbols
from the vocabulary of the language to obtain programs. Some of the
symbols in the Pascal vocabulary are *A*, *b*, 1, 9, +, ., **end**, **var**,
until, and **begin**. Not all ways of putting these symbols together
result in a syntactically correct Pascal program. For instance

end; 1; r; **begin**; /)

is not a valid Pascal program.

Semantics is concerned with the meaning of the syntactically
correct constructs of the language (i.e., of the sentences, paragraphs,
etc.). What does the expression $a+b$ mean? What is the meaning of
the statement:

for $i := 1$ **to** n **do**
    $a[i] := b[i] + c[i]$;

The syntax of a programming language such as Pascal can be
specified using a formal and precise mathematical notation called BNF
(Backus-Naur Form) notation. The semantics of a language, on the
other hand, are provided in a somewhat informal manner using English
prose and examples.

We shall examine the use of BNF (or more precisely Extended
BNF) notation to specify the syntax of Pascal. The vocabulary of
BNF notation includes the following symbols:

words These are used to denote syntactic elements of the programming language such as statements, expressions, names, and numbers. So that there is no confusion between the words of the BNF notation and those of Pascal, we shall enclose the BNF words in angle brackets as in <Integer>.

| This symbol denotes "or". Thus, $a \mid b$ means a or b.

[ ] These are used to enclose optional items.

{ } These are used to enclose syntactic elements that may be repeated 0 or more times.

= $x = y$ means that x is by definition equal to y. x is a BNF word and y is an expression that consists of the BNF symbols defined above and the symbols of the programming language being specified.

To avoid confusion between the symbols "{}[] |" which are used in both BNF and in the programming language, we shall enclose these common programming language symbols in quotes as in "[".

With these formalities taken care of, we proceed to examples that illustrate how the BNF notation may be used to specify the syntax of a programming language. We may define <Zero> to denote 0 using the notation:

<Zero> = 0

The syntactic entity <NonZeroDigit> is defined as:

<NonZeroDigit> = 1 | 2 | 3 | 4 | 5 | 6 | 7 | 8 | 9

This is to be read as "a nonzero digit is a 1 or a 2 or a ... or a 9". A <Digit> whether zero or not can be defined as:

<Digit> = 0 | 1 | 2 | 3 | 4 | 5 | 6 | 7 | 8 | 9

Or we may use the shorter form:

<Digit> = <Zero> | <NonZeroDigit>

A natural number can now be defined as:

<NaturalNumber> = <Digit> {<Digit>}

This has the interpretation: "A natural number is a digit followed by zero or more digits". Some examples of valid natural numbers are given below:

1   234   000189   456666660   0707000

If we remove the first digit from a natural number that has more than one digit, then the remaining digits also form a natural number. This leads us to the following recursive definition of the entity <Natural-Number>:

<NaturalNumber> = <Digit> | <Digit> <NaturalNumber>

This is read as: "A natural number is either a digit or a digit followed by a natural number". Another recursive definition of a natural number is:

<NaturalNumber> = <Digit> | <NaturalNumber> <Digit>

If we do not wish to allow natural number representations that have leading zeroes (except for the representation of the number zero itself), then we may use the definition:

<NatNum> = <Digit> | <NonZeroDigit> <NaturalNumber>

An integer may be defined as:

<Integer> = <NaturalNumber> | +<NaturalNumber>
            | −<NaturalNumber>

Alternatively, we may define a syntactic entity <Sign> as:

<Sign> = + | −

and then define integer as:

<Integer> = [<Sign>] <NaturalNumber>

which has the interpretation: "An integer is a natural number preceded by an optional sign". If statement labels are to be at most five digits long and the first digit is to be nonzero, then the following definition can be used:

<Label> = <NonZeroDigit> [<Digit>] [<Digit>] [<Digit>] [<Digit>]

The following defines a <Label> to be any natural number:

<Label> = <NaturalNumber>

In the original language specification for Pascal, any natural number can be a label. So, the definition just given corresponds to standard Pascal. The label declaration part of a Pascal program is defined as:

<LabelDeclarationPart> = **label** <Label> {, <Label>}

This is read as: "the label declaration part consists of the reserved word **label** followed by one or more labels". The labels are separated by commas. Some other simple definitions are:

<Exponent> = E<Integer>

<RealNumber> = <Integer>.<NaturalNumber> [<Exponent>]
         | <Integer> <Exponent>

<UpperCase> = *A* | *B* | *C* | *D* | *E* | *F* | *G* | *H* | *I* | *J* | *K* | *L* | *M* |
         N | *O* | *P* | *Q* | *R* | *S* | *T* | *U* | *V* | *W* | *X* | *Y* | *Z*

<LowerCase> = *a* | *b* | *c* | *d* | *e* | *f* | *g* | *h* | *i* | *j* | *k* | *l* | *m* |
         n | *o* | *p* | *q* | *r* | *s* | *t* | *u* | *v* | *w* | *x* | *y* | *z*

<Letter> = <UpperCase> | <LowerCase>

<AlphaNumeric> = <Letter> | <Digit>

<Identifier> = <Letter> {<AlphaNumeric>}

<GoToStatement> = **goto** <Label>

<ArithmeticOperator> = + | − | * | /

<RelationalOperator> = < | <= | = | > | >= | <>

<Operator> = <ArithmeticOperator> | <RelationalOperator>

Now, let us tackle the problem of specifying all legal variable names. First, let us see the different types of such names that are permitted in Pascal. The simplest of these is, quite naturally, called a simple variable. Any <Identifier> as defined above is a candidate for a simple variable name. Some examples are *maximum*, *balance*, and *InterestRate*. Names such as *a*[2], *student.age*, and *f* ↑ where *f* is a file name are clearly not simple variables. These are, respectively, examples of indexed variables, field designators, and file buffers. Collectively, these are termed *component variables*. The third and last category of variables includes all referenced variables (eg., *x* ↑). Syntactically, these are similar to file buffers. We may define the syntactic entity <Variable> to be:

<Variable> = <Identifier> | <ComponentVariable>
     | <ReferencedVariable>

We have already defined the entity <Identifier>. As remarked above, a component variable is defined as:

<ComponentVariable> = <IndexedVariable> | <FieldDesignator>
     | <FileBuffer>

An indexed variable is any variable which uses an array index at its right end. Some syntactically valid indexed variables are:

    a[2]   *boy*[2,5+*j*].*name*[5]   *link* ↑ .*address*[2,6]

From these examples, it becomes evident that an indexed variable is really any array variable followed by an index into the array. In BNF, this takes the form:

<IndexedVariable> = <ArrayVariable> "[" <Expression>
                           {,<Expression>} "]"

<ArrayVariable> = <Variable>

This definition asserts that syntactically, an indexed variable is a variable followed by a left bracket ([), followed by one or more expressions, followed by a right bracket (]). The expressions provide the indices into the <Variable>. While syntactically any variable can be an array variable, the semantics of the language dictate that only those variables that have been declared to be of type **array** are array variables. This restriction cannot be incorporated into the BNF specification.

Notice the recursive nature of the preceding definition. The entity <Variable> is defined in terms of the entity <ComponentVariable> which in turn is defined in terms of <IndexedVariable>. But this entity is itself defined in terms of the entity <Variable>. Recursion is a very powerful tool that can be used to provide compact BNF definitions. The following BNF statements together with a specification of the entities <Expression> and <FileVariable> complete the specification of the entity <Variable>.

<FieldDesignator> = <RecordVariable>.<FieldIdentifier>

<RecordVariable> = <Variable>

<FieldIdentifier> = <Identifier>

<FileBuffer> = <FileVariable> ↑

<ReferencedVariable> = <PointerVariable> ↑

<PointerVariable> = <Variable>

AMBIGUITY

Let us now turn our attention to the syntactic entity <Expression>. For simplicity, we restrict ourselves to the operators +, −, *, and /. In addition, we permit the delimiters "(" and ")". All legal expressions that are composed of constants, variables, and these operators and delimiters are described by the definition:

<Operator> = + | − | * | /

<Expression> = <Integer> | <RealNumber>
           | [<Sign>] <Variable>
           | <Expression><Operator><Expression>
           | (<Expression>)

Once again, we have a recursive definition. We readily see that all integers, reals, and signed and unsigned variables are expressions. From the definition, it follows that any of these combined by an operator is also an expression.   So, $x+y$, $-a/b$, etc. are expressions. Similarly, enclosing any expression in parenthesis yields a valid expression. We may reapply the definition to this expanded class of expressions and obtain yet other expressions and so on. So, we may use the definition to generate all expressions that satisfy the definition.

Now suppose we are given some arbitrary expression e and we wish to show that it satisfies the definition. If it is of the form (f), then we need merely show that f is a valid expression. If e is an integer, real, or a signed or unsigned variable, then it satisfies the definition. The only possibility left is that e is of the form f *operator* g where *operator* is one of $+$, $-$, $*$, and $/$. If we can show that f and g are valid expressions, then it will follow that e is a valid expression. Repeating this process (which is called *parsing*), we may establish that e is a valid expression.

Some expressions together with their parsings are given in Figure 2.1. As can be seen, the parsing of an expression may not be unique. A specification that permits multiple parsings is *ambiguous*.

Ambiguity in specifications is sometimes no cause for concern. For instance, the specification:

<Number> = <Digit> | <Digit> [<Number>]
           | [<Number>] <Digit>

is ambiguous as any number with more than one digit can be parsed in more than one way. However, this ambiguity is inconsequential as it does not, in any way, affect the semantics of the number.

In other instances, ambiguity in specification is highly undesirable. The entity <Expression> is an instance where this is so. Different parsings of an expression result in different evaluations of the expression and different evaluations can produce different results. As an example, consider the expression $a+b*c$. Two parsings are given in Figures 2.1 (a) and (b). The parsing of Figure 2.1 (a) is equivalent to the expression $(a+b)*c$ while that of Figure 2.1 (b) is equivalent to the expression $a+(b*c)$. If $a = 2$, $b = 3$, and $c = 4$, then the evaluation of $a+b*c$ using the parsing of Figure 2.1 (a) will yield the result 20 while the result is 24 when the parsing of Figure 2.1 (b) is used.

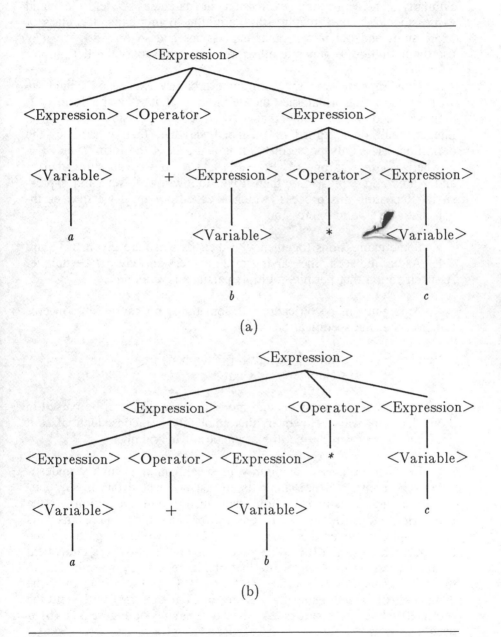

(a)

(b)

Figure 2.1 Expressions and their parsings

As another example of the undesirableness of ambiguity in the specification of a language, consider the following specification of <IfStatement>:

<IfStatement> = **if** <BooleanExpression> **then** <Statement>
       | **if** <BooleanExpression> **then** <Statement>
              else <Statement>

The following **if** statement can be parsed in the two ways given in Figure 2.2. The parsing of this figure assumes that <Statement> is define to include both assignment statements and **if** statements (i.e., <IfStatement> and that <BooleanExpression> is defined to include simple variables.

if *x* **then if** *y* **then** *a* := 2 **else** *a* := 3

The different parsings will result in programs with different meanings. This problem with determining which **if** the **else** clause associates with is called the *dangling else problem*

How can we modify the BNF specification of an expression so that each expression can be parsed in exactly one way? First, we need to decide how the unique evaluation of an expression is to proceed. This decision is specified by providing priorities for the evaluation of operators. For our limited operator set, the convention is:

$*$ and $/$ have priority over $+$ and $-$. $*$ and $/$ have the same priority and $+$ and $-$ have the same priority. Adjacent operators that have the same priority are evaluated left to right. Parenthesis explicitly demarcate subexpression boundaries.

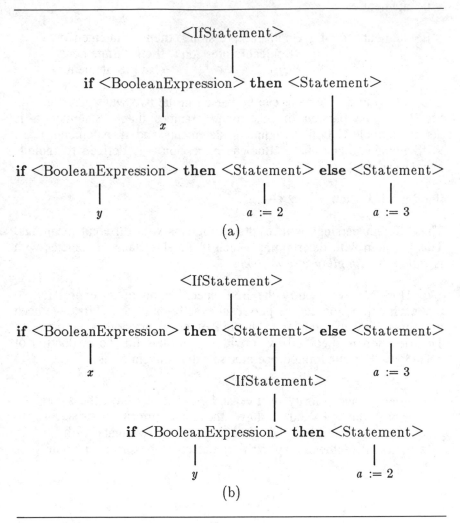

Figure 2.2 Two parsings of an **if** statement

Example 2.4: The expressions $x/y/z+a-b*z$ and $(((x/y)/z)+a)-(b*z)$ are equivalent. According to the priority rules, the expression $x/y/z$ must be parsed as in $(x/y)/z$. Further, since / has a higher priority than $+$, $(x/y)/z+a-b*z$ is to be parsed as $((x/y)/z)+a-b*z$. Now, since $+$ and $-$ have the same priority, we get $(((x/y)/z)+a)-b*z$ as the only possible parse. Finally, since $*$ has a higher priority than $-$, the parse is completed as $(((x/y)/z)+a)-(b*z)$. $\square$

The following sequence of definitions ensures that there is exactly one way to parse each expression. In addition, it conforms to the priority scheme given above.

<UnsignedConstant>
= <NaturalNumber>
| <NaturalNumber>.[<NaturalNumber>] [<Exponent>]
| <ConstantIdentifier>

<AddOp> = + | −

<MultOp> = * | /

<Expression> = [<Sign>] <Term>
| <Expression> <AddOp> <Term>

<Term> = <Factor> | <Term> <MultOp> <Factor>

<Factor> = <Variable> | <UnsignedConstant>
| "("<Expression>")"

Example 2.5: Consider the expression $a+b*c$. Replacing the operators and operands by BNF syntactic quantities, we see that this expression is of the form:

<Variable><AddOp><Variable><MultOp><Variable>

There is only way to parse this to get the syntactic entity <Expression>. This unique parse is given in Figure 2.3. $\square$

We can specify the complete set of valid Pascal expressions by the following set of BNF definitions:

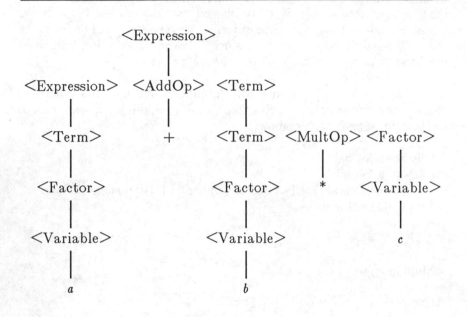

Figure 2.3 Unique parsings

<UnsignedConstant>
  = <NaturalNumber>
  | <NaturalNumber>.[<NaturalNumber>] [<Exponent>]
  | <ConstantIdentifier> | <String> | **nil**

<AddOp> = + | − | **or**

<MultOp> = * | / | **and** | **div** | **mod**

<RelationalOp> = < | > | <= | >= | <> | "=" | **in**

<Expression>
  = <SimpleExpression>
    | <SimpleExpression> <RelationalOp> <SimpleExpression>

<SimpleExpression> = [<Sign>] <Term>
                      | <SimpleExpression><AddOp> <Term>

$<Term> = <Factor> \mid <Term> <MultOp> <Factor>$

$<Factor> = <Variable> \mid <UnsignedConstant> \mid (<Expression>)$
$\mid <Set> \mid \textbf{not} <Factor> \mid <FunctionDesignator>$

The entities $<String>$, $<Set>$, and $<FunctionDesignator>$ have yet to be defined. These and other definitions are considered in the exercises.

While many BNF definitions are needed to specify the syntax of a programming language such as Pascal (it takes about five pages to list all of them), once we have these definitions, there can be no doubt as to which "Pascal programs" are syntactically correct and which aren't. With this specification in hand, it is possible to develop a compiler for the language.

2.4. SPREAD SHEET

This time, the problem originator has asked us to write a program to provide all normal spread sheet capabilities. This appears to be a sufficiently short problem description. However, not much can be done until we discover what a spread sheet is and which operations are considered normal.

Let us go back to the originator and see if we can learn something about the problem. The originator might refer us to the library or to the user manual for an existing spread sheet program or he/she might actually spend some time with us and explain the problem some more. Regardless of the route taken by the originator, we will be in a better position to go about the task of developing a software system for the spread sheet problem following this meeting.

Assume that the originator decides to give us an example of a spread sheet together with it's use. We learn that a spread sheet is just that .. A spread sheet. It is a large sheet of paper with some entries on it. An example is given in Figure 2.4. This spread sheet was created by a real estate investor who owns several large apartment complexes. This investor is toying with the idea of acquiring the "Sleepy Eye Apartment Complex". Being a prudent business woman, she wishes to analyze the financial feasibility of the acquisition before she buys the complex. So, she pulls out a large sheet of paper and begins to write down the anticipated expenses and earnings from the project. Since this is a laborious task, she does this for only the first three months of ownership. Figure 2.4 is the result of her labors.

As we can see, a spread sheet is nothing but a matrix of *cells*. Some cells have labels in them, some have numeric quantities, and others are empty (corresponding to the blank lines). Now, let us learn some more about spread sheets by examining what our investor is going to do when she looks at the cash flow figures (figures in parenthesis are negative amounts).

The first thing that might strike our investor is that she has forgotten to include the income from the coin operated laundary machines and the vending machines located all over the complex. So, she wishes to insert two additional rows in the income section of the spread sheet. But after doing this, the total income and cash flow rows as well as the last column entries change. These are to be recomputed to obtain the spread sheet of Figure 2.5.

Some other functions the investor might wish to perform on this spread sheet are:

(1) Increase the analysis period to one year and determine the effects of increased rents. This would entail the inclusion of additional columns. It would be nice if the spread sheet could automatically update the entries for the rows and column that contain totals.

(2) Change the apartment rental income using various vacancy factors and various per unit rents. This task becomes easy if the rental income had been defined by a formula such as:

MonthlyAptIncome
    $= MonthlyVacancyRate * NumberOfUnits * MonthlyRent$

Now if we had one row that contains the anticipated monthly vacancy rate and another that contains the projected monthly income from apartment rents, then by adjusting the entries in these rows, we could see the impact of changing these quantities on the income from apartment rents. Better yet, if the entries in the totals rows and column had been defined by formulas such as:

TotalMonthlyIncome $=$ *SumOfMonthlyIncomesInIncomeSection*

TotalColumnEntry $=$ *SumOfRowEntries*

	April	May	June	Total
Sleepy Eye Apartment Complex Project				
All Figures In Thousands				
Income				
Apartments	20	20	20.2	60.2
Garages	2.0	1.8	1.7	5.5
Interest On Deposits	.5	.5	.5	1.5
Total Income	22.5	22.3	22.4	67.2
Expenses				
Debt Service				
Mortgage	12	12	12	36
Contract For Deed	5	5	5	15
Total Debt Service	17	17	17	51
Administrative				
Manager	1.1	1.1	1.2	3.4
Caretaker	.9	1.0	1.0	2.9
Accountant	.5	.5	.5	1.5
Total	2.5	2.6	2.7	7.8
Taxes				
Real Estate	2	2	2.2	6.2
Workmen's Comp	.5	.6	.7	1.8
Total	2.5	2.6	2.9	8
Operating				
Utilities	1	.9	.5	2.4
Lawn Care	0	.2	.4	.6
Snow Removal	.3	0	0	.3
Misc.	.2	.2	.2	.6
Total	1.5	1.3	1.1	3.9
Maintenance	.5	.5	.5	1.5
Insurance	.2	.2	.2	.6
Total Expenses	24.2	24.2	24.4	72.8
Cash Flow	(1.7)	(1.9)	(2.0)	(5.6)

Figure 2.4 Sleepy Eye Spread Sheet

Sleepy Eye Apartment Complex Project
All Figures In Thousands

	April	May	June	Total
Income				
Apartments	20	20	20.2	60.2
Garages	2.0	1.8	1.7	5.5
Interest On Deposits	.5	.5	.5	1.5
Laundary Machines	.2	.2	.2	.6
Vending Machines	.4	.4	.4	1.2
Total Income	223.1	22.9	23	69
Expenses				
Debt Service				
Mortgage	12	12	12	36
Contract For Deed	5	5	5	15
Total Debt Service	17	17	17	51
Administrative				
Manager	1.1	1.1	1.2	3.4
Caretaker	.9	1.0	1.0	2.9
Accountant	.5	.5	.5	1.5
Total	2.5	2.6	2.7	7.8
Taxes				
Real Estate	2	2	2.2	6.2
Workmen's Comp	.5	.6	.7	1.8
Total	2.5	2.6	2.9	8
Operating				
Utilities	1	.9	.5	2.4
Lawn Care	0	.2	.4	.6
Snow Removal	.3	0	0	.3
Misc.	.2	.2	.2	.6
Total	1.5	1.3	1.1	3.9
Maintenance	.5	.5	.5	1.5
Insurance	.2	.2	.2	.6
Total Expenses	24.2	24.2	24.4	72.8
Cash Flow	(1.1)	(1.3)	(1.4)	(3.8)

Figure 2.5 Sleepy Eye Spread Sheet

etc.

then all entries in the sheet that are affected by the change in vacancy factors and monthly rent per unit can be recomputed automatically.

(3) Perhaps, the investor wishes to study the effects of a larger down payment or of a change in interest rate. This is easily done if she has cells in the upper left corner of the sheet that contain the purchase price, down payment, amount of mortgage available, its interest rate, amount of CD (contract for deed) available, and its interest rate. Using these values, one may devise formulas for all the debt service entries. Now, by simply changing some entries in the upper left corner of the spread sheet and an automatic reevaluation of the sheet, we can study the effects of various alternatives.

The brief example above has hopefully convinced you that a spread sheet is a very powerful financial tool. If not, the list of required capabilities given below will. This list was provided to us during our most recent discovery session with the originator.

(1) Each cell should be able to hold either a value or a label. The value in a cell (if any) may be of type $, real, or integer. It should be possible to specify a formula for each value cell. These formulas must be able to use values from other cells in the spread sheet.

(2) If a cell value is changed, then all cells affected by this change must also be changed.

(3) It must be possible to print the entire spread sheet as well as to print segments of it.

(4) The insertion (deletion) of new (old) rows and columns must be provided for. Any formulas affected by this insertion (deletion) must be updated.

(5) The spread sheet software system must allow for the automatic drawing of pie charts, bar charts (histograms), stacked graphs and line graphs using spread sheet data. In addition, it should be possible to write sophisticated reports that use data from several different spread sheets.

For some of you, this brief session with the problem originator might have been adequate to get a good understanding of the spread sheet problem. For the rest of you, it will be necessary to practice with existing spread sheet programs. We shall see the capabilities of spread sheet programs in greater detail when we attempt to design one.

The specification provided for the spread sheet problem is both very informal and very incomplete. It leaves the designer with a significant number of decisions. However, this level of specification is not unusual in the "real world". When the problem is first conceived, it is posed in somewhat ambiguous and informal terms. It is left to the system designer to explore the problem further and develop a sufficiently flexible and easy to use system. When specifications of this type are provided, it is very important that the designer keep in touch with the problem originator throughout the design phase.

2.5. DATABASE MANAGEMENT

In a relational database, data are organized into a collection of relations, tables or files. For our purposes here, each of these terms is synonymous. Our objective is to write a software system to facilitate the management of data so organized. As in the case of the initial specification of the spread sheet problem, the specification for the database problem is informal and concise. However, it is quite incomplete. To begin with, the system designer may not know what a database system is.

Rather than dwell upon the theory of relational databases and formal definitions, we illustrate the concept using an example. Consider the Maverick Publishing Company. This company serves as the "middle man (or woman)" between the authors and the vendors of books. It does no printing of its own but merely contracts out to different printing presses depending on the type of book. This company has the following data that is to be managed:

(1) Employee data including names, addresses, salary, department, skill, and seniority data.

(2) Inventory data. This includes the inventory of all books published by the company. It also includes the addresses of the printers used for each book.

(3) Sales data. This includes the quantity of each book sold.

(4) Expense data. All expenses incurred by the company.

The expense data is organized into a table as in Figure 2.6. Each row of this table is a *record*. Each record of this table has the six fields: *Date, Category, Vendor, Invoice, Amount, Paid*. The only fields that need explanation are *Invoice* and *Paid*. *Invoice* is the invoice (or bill) number provided by the *Vendor*. *Paid* is a Boolean valued field which is true iff the company has paid the *Vendor* the stated amount. We shall call this table the *Expense* relation.

Date	Category	Vendor	Invoice	Amount	Paid
070484	shipping	UPS	2001	124.34	T
072384	supplies	Nelsons	1000987	56.95	F
022284	shipping	Emery	141423	321.87	T
091984	printing	Viking	ABC54C6	15023.45	F
010684	supplies	K-Mart	1698C	234.72	T
082284	utilities	NSP	787898	234.76	T

Figure 2.6 Expense relation.

In order to pay vendors, we need vendor addresses. These can be maintained in the expense relation by adding an address field to each record. If this is done, then we have to enter this information each time we receive a bill from a vendor. Further, if a vendor's address changes, we will need to reflect this change in all the records that correspond to this vendor. It is better to define a new relation called *VendorAddress*. Each record in this relation has the fields: *Name, Street, City, State, ZIP, Country*. An example is given in Figure 2.7.

Name	Street	City	State	ZIP	Country
UPS	2200 Broadway	Minneapolis	MN	55412	USA
K-Mart	5725 Central Ave.	Col. Hgts.	MN	55422	USA
Franks	2929 Mtn View Rd	Chicago	IL	63210	USA

Figure 2.7 The relation *VendorAddress*

Some other relations that will be useful for the Maverick Publishing Company are:

Sales = (*Date*, *Invoice*, *Book*, *Quantity*, *PO*, *Buyer*, *Amount*, *Recd*)

BuyerAddress = (*Buyer*, *Street*, *City*, *State*, *ZIP*, *Country*)

Inventory = (*Book*, *Quantity*, *Printer*, *OnOrder*)

Employee = (*Name*, *JoinDate*, *Department*, *Salary*, *Skill*)

The relations *EmployeeAddress* and *PrinterAddress* are also needed and they have the same fields as *VendorAddress* and *BuyerAddress*. Some of the fields used above need explanation. In the *Sales* relation, *Invoice* is the publishing company's invoice number; *PO* is the buyer's purchase order number; and *Recd* is a Boolean valued field that is true iff the stated amount has been received by the company. In the *Inventory* relation, *OnOrder* is the quantity of books that have been ordered from the printers and which haven't yet been received.

The above definitions by no means represent the ultimate way for a publishing company to organize its data. We can think of several improvements. For example, in the relation *Inventory*, we should probably have a field *Due* that tells us when the ordered books are expected. All the address relations should probably also have a phone number field. These definitions should, however, be adequate to convince you that the data of large complex organizations can be effectively organized into a collection of relations, i.e., into a relational database.

What are the capabilities that a relational database management system must provide? We list the most obvious ones here and present additional ones as part of the system design.

(1) *Create:* A capability to define new relations as needed.

(2) *Entry:* It must be possible to enter new records into the relations.

(3) *Update:* We should be able to modify the records in a relation

(4) *Output:* Print or display the contents of a relation.

(5)   *Destroy:* Remove all trace of a relation.

(6)   *Select:* Select all records that satisfy some requirements from a given relation. For example, we may wish to select all records in the *Sales* relation that have *Recd* = F and *Date* < (today's *Date* − 6 months). Following this, we would probably get on the phone and demand payment (at the very least, a gentle reminder will be sent to the buyer).

(7)   *Join:* This operation combines records from two relations. In the previous paragraph, we selected the records corresponding to sales that were made at least six months ago and for which payment has not as yet been received. The selected records themselves form a new relation (called *Result*). Once this has been done, we can proceed to combine these records with the *BuyerAddress* relation to get records of the type:

(*Date*, *Invoice*, *Book*, *Quantity*, *PO*, *Buyer*, *Amount*, *Recd*, *Street*, *City*, *State*, *ZIP*, *Country*)

The *join* of two relations $R1$ and $R2$ is a new relation whose fields are the union of the fields of the two relations. The records in this new relation are obtained by combining together all pairs (*a*, *b*) of records where *a* is in $R1$, *b* is in $R2$, and *a* and *b* agree on the fields that are common to $R1$ and $R2$.

(8)   *Projection:* This operation is useful when one wishes to strip certain fields from a relation. For example, the relation that results from the above join contains some fields that are not needed when a reminder to the buyer is being sent. These are: *Recd*, *Book*, and *Quantity*. These fields can be eliminated by projecting the result of the join on the fields that are to be retained as in:

project *Result* **by** *Date*, *Invoice*, *PO*, *Buyer*, *Amount*, *Street*,
                                City, *State*, *ZIP*, *Country*

The same relation can also be produced using the following sequence of database operations:

select *Sales* **where not** *Recd*
project *Result* **by** *Date*, *Invoice*, *PO*, *Buyer*, *Amount*
join *Result* *BuyerAddress*

Even though some of the desirable capabilities of a database system have been informally specified above, we are still left with the task of specifying the actual format of the individual instructions that will accomplish these tasks. When one sits down to design the database system, several other desirable capabilities will come to mind. At that time, we might wish to return to the problem originator and see if these are to be implemented.

2.6. SUMMARY

A problem specification is simply a definition of the problem for which we are to write a program. Some problems can be easily and precisely stated (eg., searching and sorting). For other problems, a complete specification is quite cumbersome but essential, if we are to obtain a satisfactory program. For example, the formal specification of the syntax of the Pascal language runs into several pages of BNF definitions. Without this specification, of course, we will not be able to tell which Pascal programs are syntactically correct. So, it will not be possible to write a compiler for the language. In some cases where a complete and formal specification is possible, the effort needed to arrive at this mathematically rigorous specification may not be justifiable. Some experience with the problem may be adequate to lead to a complete understanding. Text processors, spread sheet programs, and database management systems are examples of these.

2.7. EXERCISES

1. Obtain input/output specifications for the following problems:
   (a) Area of a rectangle.
   (b) Roots of a quadratic.
   (c) Mean and standard deviation of n numbers.
   (d) Largest and smallest of n numbers.
   (e) Substring of a string.

2. Let L be a language of strings. The symbols in the strings are taken from the vocabulary V. For example, $\{a, aa, aaa, aaaa, \ldots\}$ is the set of all strings of length at least one that can be formed from the vocabulary $\{a\}$. The set $\{aa, aaaa, aaaaaaaa, \ldots\}$ defines the language that consists of strings of even length.

For each of the language and vocabulary pairs given below, obtain a BNF specification for the language. In each case, you may assume that the language contains no string of zero length.

(a) $V = \{a\}$, L = all strings of even length

(b) $V = \{a, b\}$, L = all strings that contain an equal number of a's and b's.

(c) $V = \{a, b\}$, L = all strings with $n \geq 0$ a's followed by $m \geq 0$ b's.

(d) $V = \{a, b\}$, L = same as in (c) except that the number of a's and b's is the same.

(e) $V = \{0, X\}$, L = all strings of the form ZXY where Z and Y are strings of 0's. The number of 0's in Z and Y is the same.

(f) $V = \{0, 1\}$, L = all strings Y such that Y is a palindrome.

(g) $V = \{0, 1\}$, L = all strings that are the binary representation of an even number.

(h) $V = \{0, 1\}$, L = all strings that are the binary representation of an odd number.

3. Obtain the BNF definitions for the following Pascal entities. You may use the syntactic entities already defined in the text.

(a) \<ReservedWord\>

(b) \<Comment\>

(c) \<ConstantDeclarationPart\>

(d) \<VariableDeclarationPart\>

(e) \<TypeDeclarationPart\>

(f) \<CaseStatement\>

(g) \<ForStatement\>

(h) \<WhileStatement\>

(i) \<RepeatUntilStatement\>

(j) \<IfStatement\>

(k) \<String\>

(l) \<Set\>

(m) <FunctionDesignator>

4. Use the BNF definition of an expression provided in Section 2.3
    and obtain the unique parsings for the following expressions:
    (a) $x+y+z/x/a-b$
    (b) $(x-y)*(c-d)+a-b/c$
    (c) $(a/b)-(c+d-f/g)/(s+t)/(e/f+h)$
    (d) $a+b-c+d*e*f/g*(a+c)/k$

5. For the restricted operator set $\{+, -, *, /\}$, obtain an unambigu-
    ous BNF specification for expressions in which $*$ and $/$ have
    priority over $+$ and $-$ and in which equal priority operators are
    evaluated right to left.

6. Study any commercially available spread sheet program that you
    have access to. Obtain a list of all the functions and capabilities
    provided by it. Write a brief specification, in English, of what
    each of these functions does.

7. Repeat the previous exercise for a relational database system.

8. Repeat Exercise 6 for a word processing system.

9. Write an informal specification for each of the following games.
    The way the game is played and the win/lose conditions should
    be clear from your specification. Some research in a library may
    be needed to get the complete rules.
    (a) Tic-tac-toe
    (b) Hangman
    (c) Blackjack
    (d) Slot machine
    (e) Checkers

10. [Dekel] Write an informal specification for a personal record
    keeping program. This program should provide the user with the
    following capabilities: a)Track financial transactions according
    to user specification. b) Get financial reports c) Print checks d)
    Track inventory. e) Reconcile money accounts. f) Organize tax

records.

11. [Dekel] As you could understand from the text, the job of software design is quite complex. Write an informal specification for a program that will help the software designer with his job. The program should facilitate the top down design process and help the designer track the different parts of the design.

CHAPTER 3

DESIGN

3.1. INTRODUCTION

Many decisions are made during the process of software development. Some of these directly affect how the program is to be used. Typically, these decisions involve the nature of the user interface provided. Answers to questions such as the ones listed below are sought.

(1) What capabilities should the program provide? Clearly, at least those mentioned in the problem specification are to be provided. There may be others whose inclusion will make the program more desirable from the users' point of view.

(2) Should the program be interactive or batch or both?

(3) Is the program to be menu driven?

(4) What level of on-line help is to be provided?

(5) What should the exact format of user level commands be?

Other decisions made during the programming process affect such things as performance, program comprehensibility, maintainability, and ease of enhancement. Typically, these decisions involve the choice of data structures and algorithms, program aesthetics, level of modularization, and quality of documentation. While the choice of data structures and algorithms will generally be noticed by the user in terms of a change in performance, these changes do not materially affect the usage of the program (except to the extent these decisions limit the range of problem sizes that can be handled using a reasonable amount of computer time and memory and the extent to which a good real time response is desired).

In the *design phase* of software development, we are concerned primarily with those decisions that affect the user interface. In some cases, the problem specification may be so detailed that all decisions of this type have already been made. Generally, however, this will not be the case. In fact, even for the simplest of problems, some design work may be called for.

The objective of the design phase of programming is to refine the problem specification to the point where the only decisions that remain are those that do not affect the users' perception of the program. We are concerned with a user level design as opposed to the more detailed and well hidden design decisions that relate to the implementation of the design as a computer program.

The five questions listed above state the major considerations for design. While we have already made the assumption that our programming environment is interactive, the issue of interactive vs batch still arises in the design of user commands. We shall address this issue as it arises in our discussion of the remaining four questions.

Since in the design phase we are really refining the problem specification, it is a good practice to take the completed design to the problem originator for approval. Perhaps the design is too ambitious or not ambitious enough.

3.2. CAPABILITIES

When designing the capabilities to be provided by the program, one needs to be very sensitive to the needs of the user community. A user survey is generally called for. The users surveyed should themselves be very knowledgeable about the application for which the program is being designed. If programs for this application already exist, one can ask questions such as:

(1)   What do you like about the existing programs?

(2)   What don't you like about them?

(3)   Which additional features would make it easier for you to accomplish your task?

When no programs for the given application exist, one can survey practitioners in this application area and attempt to learn what the useful functions are.

The design examples to be studied at the end of this chapter will give you a good idea of the richness of capabilities one can provide.

3.3. MENUS

In the context of computer programming, a *menu* is an itemized list of selections provided by a program. The use of a menu frees the user from the burden of remembering all the selections provided as well as from remembering how these selections are to be made. As an example, consider a program called *games* that permits you to play any one of the following games on your computer:

Bandit	Paratroopers
Blackjack	Pac Man
Cosmic Crusaders	Space Invaders
Donkey	Spider
Frenzy	Tic Tac Toe
Hangman	Wumpus

When designing the user interface for the games program, we can assume the user already knows the selections available (he/she has the user manual open in front of him/her). In this case, the user may be required to type something like:

games bandit

from the keyboard in order to play the game Bandit. Using this approach, the user must either remember details such as "bandit" is to be typed and not Bandit or he/she must constantly refer to another source (such as a user manual or an on-line help facility) for this information.

GAMES

SELECTIONS AVAILABLE

A. Bandit
B. Blackjack
C. Cosmic Crusaders
D. Donkey
E. Frenzy
F. Hangman
G. Paratroopers
H. Pac Man
I. Space Invaders
J. Spider
K. Tic Tac Toe
L. Wumpus

SELECT GAME BY ENTERING LETTER
PRESS <esc> TO EXIT

Figure 3.1 Menu for games program

A more enterprising designer might require the user to just enter the command *games* from the keyboard. Following this, a menu such as the one shown in Figure 3.1 might be displayed. To use the games program when the menu route is taken, the user need only know that the command is *games*. There is no need for the user to remember which games are available or to remember the "computer name" for each of these.

Some of the salient features of the menu of Figure 3.1 are:

(1) The selections have been listed in alphabetical order. This makes it easier for the user to locate a particular selection. When the number of selections is small (say at most four), it may be preferable to list the selections in order of the anticipated frequency of use as in Figure 1.2.

(2) The task of locating a particular selection has also been facilitated by listing only one selection per line. When there are more
selections than available lines on the display screen, then the
selections can be displayed using two or more columns as in Figure 3.2. This format is less readable than the one selection per
line format but is clearly preferable to having the top part of the
menu disappear from the screen before the user has had a chance
to make the selection.

A.	Bandit	G.	Paratroopers
B.	Blackjack	H.	Pac Man
C.	Cosmic Crusaders	I.	Space Invaders
D.	Donkey	J.	Spider
E.	Frenzy	K.	Tic Tac Toe
F.	Hangman	L.	Wumpus

**SELECT GAME BY ENTERING LETTER
PRESS \<esc\> TO EXIT**.

Figure 3.2 Two column menu for games program

(3) By using letters rather than numerals, we have reduced the
number of key strokes necessary for game selection from 3 (to
select Wumpus, the user has to enter 12\<return\>) to 1 (pressing
the \<Return\> key is no longer required as the first key pressed
makes the selection). Upto 26 selections can be listed using this
selection scheme. This is probably about all one should have on
a screen at one time. The use of letters has, however, introduced an element of confusion. Must the selection be made by
typing in upper case letters or will lower case letters do? The
menu clearly has upper case letters. So, it is reasonable to
expect that these will work. However, to type an upper case
letter one has to press the "shift" key as well as the appropriate
letter key on the keyboard. Life would be so much easier if
lower case letters had been used. But this leads to a less pretty
menu and then there is always the possibility that the "caps lock"
key has been pressed and the user is unaware of this. All problems go away if both lower and upper case letters are accepted.

(4)   A provision has been made to exit from the game program. The style used is different from that used in Figure 1.2 where "Exit" was listed as one of these selections. The style of Figure 1.2 is recommended only when the number of selections is small. An advantage of following the style of Figure 3.2 to exit is that this can be standardized on over all menus. Following the style of Figure 1.2, a different numeral or letter is required to exit from each menu unless the exit option is consistently made the first option.

Other Considerations

The readability of the menu can be significantly enhanced through the use of color. The selections can, for instance, be displayed in green and the remaining lines in blue. This option is, of course, available only if the user has a color display.

Selecting from a menu can be made more convenient through the use of appropriate hardware devices. For instance, a natural way to select from a menu is to simply touch the selection on the screen. So, if we wish to select the game "Paratroopers" from the menu of Figure 3.1, we could place a finger anywhere on the screen line labeled "G". This method of menu selection is possible when the user has a touch sensitive display monitor.

Another useful hardware device for making selections is a mouse. This is essentially a pointing device that permits the user to refer to any part of the screen. When a mouse is available, the menu may be displayed as in Figure 3.3 with an arrow pointing to (say) the first selection. The desired selection is made by moving the arrow (using the mouse) to the desired game and then pressing the mouse control key. A variation in this design style is to eliminate the arrow of Figure 3.3 and enclose the present selection by a box that may be moved up or down.

In the absence of a mouse, the selection style just described may be implemented via software. The arrow or box may be moved using the cursor up, down, left, and right keys on the keyboard. When the arrow or box has been correctly positioned, the return key is pressed.

GAMES

SELECTIONS AVAILABLE

A.   Bandit $<===$
B.   Blackjack
C.   Cosmic Crusaders
D.   Donkey
E.   Frenzy
F.   Hangman
G.   Paratroopers
H.   Pac Man
I.   Space Invaders
J.   Spider
K.   Tic Tac Toe
L.   Wumpus

SELECT GAME BY POSITIONING $<===$
PRESS <return> WHEN DONE
PRESS <esc> TO EXIT

Figure 3.3 Menu for games program

Hierarchically Structured Menus

In a *flat* menu, all selections are provided on the screen simultaneously as in the examples seen so far. At times, it is desirable to organize the selections into a hierarchy of menus. This is particularly the case when the number of selections available is such that all cannot be displayed on the screen conveniently or when the available selections do not form a logically coherent set of selections. In these cases, a natural hierarchical partitioning of the selections is to be used.

As an example, consider the program *entertainment* which provides the user interface for all available entertainment programs. Suppose that there are 200 such programs. We might partition these into the categories listed in the menu of Figure 3.4. A further partitioning into logical components may be both possible and desirable. Figure 3.5 shows a menu that can be displayed if the selection "Games" is

---

ENTERTAINMENT

SELECTIONS AVAILABLE

A.   Games
B.   Music
C.   Graphics

SELECT CATEGORY BY ENTERING LETTER
PRESS \<esc\> TO EXIT

Figure 3.4 Root level menu for entertainment program.

made from the menu of Figure 3.4. Alternatively, if the number of games (both joystick and keyboard) is small, the menu of Figure 3.1 or 3.2 can be displayed when the selection "Games" is made from the root level menu. Figure 3.6 shows a possible hierarchical organization for the entertainment menu.

GAMES

SELECTIONS AVAILABLE

A.   Joystick Games
B.   Keyboard Games

SELECT CATEGORY BY ENTERING LETTER
PRESS \<esc\> TO RETURN TO PREVIOUS MENU

Figure 3.5 A level 2 menu for the entertainment program

If the number of joystick games is too large to be incorporated into one menu, we could artificially partition these into the categories:

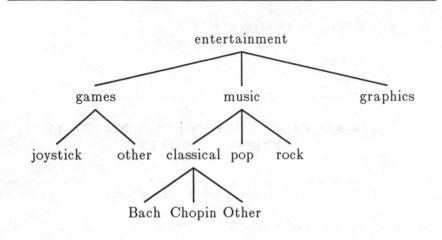

Figure 3.6 Hierarchical structure of entertainment menu

(1) Joystick Games I
(2) Joystick Games II
(3) Joystick Games III

Another possibility is to simply display as many selections as will fit on the screen and provide a capability to see more as in Figure 3.7.

One disadvantage of using a hierarchical menu is that it can take forever to get down to a leaf in the hierarchy and actually begin to play a game. This problem can be overcome by designing the entertainment command so that it accepts a parameter as in:

entertainment parameter

If no parameter is specified, then the root level menu is displayed. Otherwise the menu or leaf program specified by "parameter" is invoked. So, if parameter = "joystick games", then the joystick games menu is displayed bypassing two levels of the menu hierarchy. If parameter = "Cosmic Crusaders", then the game Cosmic Crusaders

---

GAMES

SELECTIONS AVAILABLE

A.   Army
B.   Bushwack
C.   Cosmic Crusaders
D.   Chariots
E.   Dragons
F.   Guns
G.   MORE SELECTIONS

SELECT GAME BY ENTERING LETTER
PRESS <esc> TO EXIT

Figure 3.7 Menu for joystick games

is begun immediately.

Another possibility is to collapse the number of levels in the menu heirarchy. For example, the root level menu for the entertainment command could take the form shown in Figure 3.8.

The use of menus to organize entertainment programs or functions of a text processor can naturally be extended to organize all the software supported by a computer system. It would be so much nicer if after one logged into a computer, a display such as the one in Figure 3.9 is seen rather than the customary blank screen or the prompt symbols ":", "?", "%", or ">".

Horizontal Menu Display Style

Let us briefly examine an alternate style for the display of both flat and hierarchical menus. This style is exemplified in Figure 3.10. The menu shown here is the spread sheet menu from the program 123 developed by Lotus Corp. In this style, a portion of the screen (in this case the top few lines) is reserved for the display of menus. The remainder of the screen is used to display user data. As a result, the user can simultaneously view his/her spread sheet and select the next

---

ENTERTAINMENT

SELECTIONS AVAILABLE

    A.   Joystick Games
    B.   Keyboard Games
    C.   Bach
    D.   Chopin
    E.   Other tunes
    F.   Graphics

**SELECT CATEGORY BY ENTERING LETTER
PRESS <esc> TO EXIT**

Figure 3.8 Alternate root level menu for entertainment program

---

WELCOME TO THE UNIVERSITY COMPUTER

SOFTWARE SELECTIONS AVAILABLE

    A.   CAD/CAM Tools
    B.   Entertainment
    C.   Databases
    D.   Financial Tools
    E.   Graphics Aids
    F.   Language Translators
    G.   Mail
    H.   Text Processors
    I.   Statistical Packages

**SELECT CATEGORY BY ENTERING LETTER
PRESS <esc> TO EXIT**

Figure 3.9 Welcome menu from user friendly computer

function to perform.

|Worksheet| Range Copy Move File Print Graph Data Quit
Global Insert Delete Column-Width Erase Titles Window Status

REST OF SCREEN USED TO DISPLAY SPREAD SHEET

Figure 3.10 Horizontal menu organization.

The menu of Figure 3.10 uses the first line to display the available selections. The second line displays the menu selections available at the next level in the menu hierarchy. The spread sheet functions have been divided into the eight categories (plus Quit) shown on line 1. Each of these eight entries may be regarded as a menu name. The box around "Worksheet" indicates that this selection will be made if the <Return> key is pressed. The selections available from the Worksheet menu are displayed on line 2. This menu will be displayed on line 1 if the return key is pressed at this time. I.e., line 2 will become line 1; the box will be around Global; and the selections available from the Global menu will be displayed on line 2. When the box is moved to (say) Copy, the selections from this menu will be displayed on line 2. So, line 2 is a one level look ahead for the hierarchical menu.

The appropriate selection can be made by moving the box using either a mouse (this feature is not provided in 123) or the cursor movement keys (each time the key → is pressed, the box moves one selection right; from the rightmost one, it moves to the leftmost one). Alternatively, the selection can be made by typing the first letter of the selection (notice that the selection names have been chosen so that different selections begin with a different letter). So, if the key W (or w) is pressed, the Worksheet selection is made.

Summary

Menus can be effectively used to create user friendly programs or systems. Some of the advantages of using menus are summarized below:

(1) The user need not remember the selections available. A byproduct of this is that if additional selections become available, these can be added to the menu and the user will become aware of the additions the next time he/she accesses the relevant menu in the hierarchy.

(2) Since all selections are made by pressing a single key, the possibility of spelling errors has been eliminated. Of course now the user might press the wrong key. But since each menu (except the root) provides an escape to its parent menu, it is easy to recover from this error.

3.4. COMMAND FORMAT

The user is going to interact with the program through the use of commands. It is imperative that the commands are designed such that they perform meaningful functions and are easy to use. The function performed by each command should be precisely documented. In addition, the command format must be chosen so as to facilitate its use. We illustrate these three points through a series of examples.

Consider the text editor command "move cursor one character left". This is clearly a meaningful task for a text editor. This task is sufficiently primitive that one might expect that no design work is needed. However, we need to decide the outcome of this command when the cursor is already at the left end of the line. From this point, does the cursor move to the right end of the preceding line or does it remain at its present position? What if there is no preceding line? What must the user do to effect a "move cursor one character left". Must he/she press the backspace key or the key "←"? Or, can she press either? Must the return key also be pressed?

How about the command to delete a word? Is it to delete only the characters beginning at the cursor and going upto (but not including) the next blank or punctuation mark or end of line? Should the characters on the left of the cursor and upto (but not including) the nearest (on the left) blank or punctuation mark or begin of line also be deleted? If we opt for the latter, then the cursor can be positioned anywhere in a word and the word deleted. If we opt for the former, then to delete an entire word, the cursor has to first be moved to the start of that word. But this option has the advantage that we can delete the right end of the word without deleting the entire word. Regardless of the option we choose, we may still be unsatisfied with the result. Deleting the word "axe" from the sentence:

He came with hammer, axe, spoon, and fork.

will leave behind the sentence:

He came with hammer, spoon, , and fork.

So, perhaps the comma and one blank should also have been deleted. How is the word delete command invoked? Should the user type "D", or "^D" (i.e., he/she must simultaneously press the control and "D" keys)?

Next, consider some high level file operations. Suppose we wish to make a copy of the file $c1$ under the name *chapter*1. Should we name this function "copy" or "cp" or should both names be recognized? Should the command be designed to provide interactive operation as in the following dialogue between user and program:

user: *copy*
program: Copy From:
user: *c*1
program: Copy To:
user: *chapter*1
program: *c*1 copied to *chapter*1

Another possiblity for the last response is:

program: Not enough space to copy

Or, the dialogue might take the course:

program: *chapter*1 already exists. Should I overwrite (Y/N)?
user: N

program: Copy aborted

Even for a function as primitive as a file copy, several design options exist. Should existing files be overwritten without user confirmation? Should the user be notified if there isn't enough space to copy the file? While this latter question might evoke the answer "But surely", it is surprising as to the number of commercial file manipulation systems that don't give you any indication that only part of your file could be copied.

The file copy example illustrates a very good programming attitude. This is to protect the user from himself/herself. Let's face it, everyone makes a *boo boo* once in a while. To the extent possible, the penalty for these *boo boos* should be minimized. There is a good chance that if the destination file already exists, the user does not want to overwrite it. So, give the user the opportunity to correct his/her mistakes. Confirm the overwrite before actually overwriting.

The erase file operation is another example of a command that leaves users with a hand on their forehead or with a lost expression shortly after execution. Perhaps, you have already experienced this yourself. Shortly after erasing a file, you realize that you still need it. Or perhaps a spelling error caused the wrong file to get erased. The erase command should also be designed to request confirmation before actually erasing.

Clearly, all commands can be designed to protect the user from himself/herself. When this is carried out to an extreme, the resulting program is very tedious to use. Imagine the frustration of someone trying to use a text editor which responds "Are you sure?" each time a command is entered. The secret is to ask for confirmation only when it will be difficult for the user to recover from an erroneously entered command. For example, it doesn't matter if the user erroneously moves the cursor to any part of his file. He can get it back to the original spot without too much effort.

Even in situations where recovery is difficult, it is often more desirable to provide an "undo" command to undo whatever was done by the last command. The confirmation technique should be used only when it is impractical to undo the command. To undo a copy onto an existing file, it is necessary to save the existing file under a different name. This requires extra space and also leaves us with the problem of erasing the saved copy after a suitable period of time. If there is enough space, we can maintain a backup copy of each file. The backup copy represents the previous incarnation (if any) of that file. So, corresponding to the file *chapter*1 we have its previous incarnation in *chapter*1.*bak*. When *chapter*1 is rewritten, *chapter*1.*bak* is also rewritten. The command "*copy c*1 *chapter*1" results in the following file changes (in practice, the first line is effected by simply renaming the file *chapter*1, *chapter*1.*bak*).

*chapter*1.*bak* ← *chapter*1;
*chapter*1 ← *c*1;

The choice of command names is often a difficult one. While it is obvious that names that convey some idea of the function being performed are to be preferred over those that do not, the tradeoff between the clarity of longer names and the ease of entering shorter ones is difficult to resolve. Another difficulty is that many functions are referred to by different names. Which of the names: remove, erase, delete, and rm is the best choice for the command to delete (or erase or remove) a file? Is "rename" to be preferred over "ren" and "ChangeName" for the command that changes the name of an existing file? Should the command to display the contents of a file on a screen be called *display*, *list*, *show*, or just *l*?

The decisions are clearly difficult to make. Even if we surveyed a group of users and picked the most popular choices, we would still not satisfy everyone. A nice way out of this dilemma is to provide the user with the ability to rename all the commands. In the case of a text editor, for example, we might provide a renaming program that sequences through each editor command and queries the user if he/she wishes to rename it. If so, the new name is recorded. The new names must be checked for possible ambiguity. For example, the name "←" might have been assigned to all three of the commands: "move cursor one character left", "move cursor one word left", and "move cursor to left end of line". Once errors of this kind have been resolved, the text editor can work with the new set of names. Another possibility is to allow synonyms for command names.

Summary

We may summarize the lessons of this section by the following recommendations:

(1) Design commands so that they perform tasks that are logically meaningful to the user.

(2) Where possible, design commands to be interactive. If the answer to one of the program queries has a limited set of responses, these can be provided in a menu and the user asked to select the desired response. To accomodate the experienced user, these commands should allow for the specification of all options on the command line itself. This allows for bypassing several levels of interrogation and menus.

(3) Document each command precisely. The documentation must be very specific about what the command does at boundaries such as end of line, start of line, first line, last line, etc.

(4) Don't split up logically meaningful tasks into two or more commands.

(5) Design commands so as to protect the user from himself/herself. When following this recommendation, avoid making the system too tedious to use.

(6) Choose command names that are both meaningful and easy to type. Avoid very long names that cannot be typed without error.

(7) Provide the user with the ability to use his/her own command names.

3.5. ON-LINE HELP

An often overlooked aspect of program design is the need to design some on-line help capability into the program. Since, it is unreasonable to expect a casual user of a program to remember all command names and the precise manner in which they work, a facility that enables the user to get this information while he/she is using the program is desirable. Even frequent users may have a need for this help facility. After sitting in front of a computer for several hours, anyone is capable of briefly forgetting the subtleties of a command.

The traditional solution to this problem is to refer the user to the "user documentation". This is unsatisfying as the user may be working at a site different from where the documentation is located, or perhaps someone else is using it at the time. Another problem is that it takes too much time to find exactly what one is looking for in an "on paper" documentation. The difficulties cited above with the "on paper" user documentation can be overcome by providing an on-line help facility. Whenever the user is in trouble, he/she can request help from the program itself.

In order to be really useful, the help facility must be an integral part of the program. It should be possible to invoke this facility no matter which level of the program hierarchy we are at. In particular, it should not be necessary to terminate the program before one can seek help. For example, suppose we are editing a piece of text and wish to determine the exact specification of the "move cursor one line down" command. It would indeed be tedious if we have to first save our work file, then exit from the text editor and processor, then invoke the help program, and then resume editing. When the help facility is integrated into the text processor, we can get the needed help by directly invoking the help facility as in Figure 1.3.

There are essentially two levels of on-line integrated help that can be provided: abbreviated and detailed.

Abbreviated Help

Abbreviated help facilities are designed to take up minimal screen space and are displayed at all times. Typically, such a facility will simply list all (or at least the more frequently used) available command names and provide a very terse description of the function performed by each. An example of such a help facility for a text processor is provided in Figure 1.3. In this case, all the commands listed in Figure 1.1 have been included. With each command name (such as ←), there is enough information provided that anyone who is reasonably familiar with a screen editor will know what outcome to expect from the command (except for boundary situations like when the cursor is at the end of a line or at the first or last line, etc.).

The abbreviated help display of Figure 1.3 is quite similar to the one provided by the text processor "Wordstar" (developed by MicroPro). Two additional examples of abbreviated help facilities provided by existing commercially available programs are provided in Figures 3.11 and 3.12.

Even though you may never have seen the programs from which these examples have been drawn, you can easily see how to go about using these programs. The abbreviated help facilities of both the Basic editor (copyright IBM) and the communications program PC-

TOP OF SCREEN IS USED TO DISPLAY USER PROGRAM

1 LIST 2 RUN 3 LOAD 4 SAVE 5 CONT 6 LPT1 7 TRON 8 TROFF 9 KEY 0 SCREEN

Figure 3.11 Abbreviated help file for Basic on the IBM-PC

TALK III (developed by FREEWARE) use the bottom line of the screen only. In the case of the Basic editor, the help line tells us what the ten available function keys on the IBM-PC keyboard do. F1 lists part of the program, F2 will run the program that is currently in memory, F3 is used to load a program into memory, and so on. The help line for PC-TALK III lists only the more frequently used communication functions. If a file is to be transmitted, the two keys Alt and T are to be simultaneously pressed; to receive a file, we need to press the keys Alt and R; to dial a number, the keys Alt and D are pressed; etc.

At this point, you may be confused about the difference between a help line and a menu. The menu of Figure 3.10 and the help lines of Figures 3.11 and 3.12 certainly look similar. The difference is that when a menu is displayed, the user **must** make a selection from it. A help line is passive. It is just using up part of the screen and providing valuable information to the user. But, the program is not waiting for the user to make a selection from the help line. In fact, at times, help lines may not even provide information about commands in the present program. For example, the abbreviated help facility for our

---

^PrtSc = prnt Alt-T = tran R = recv D = dial E = echo M = msg X = exit <Home> = help

---

Figure 3.12 Abbreviated help screen for PC-TALK III on the IBM-PC

text processor may also list some formatter commands that can be inserted into the text.

Detailed Help

Ideally, the detailed help facility will provide all the information needed to use the program. In general, this information will also include examples as in Figure 1.5. There are, however, some practical limitations to how detailed a help facility one can provide on-line. These limitations are imposed by both the amount of memory available to the program and the disk space available. The more detailed the help facility, the more the memory and disk space needed by the help facility. One should also note that a more detailed help facility isn't necessarily a more usable help facility. The detailed help facility should be crisp, concise, and precise. The user should be able to get the desired information quickly and accurately.

In designing the detailed help facility, you should keep in mind that this facility is not a substitute for the user documentation. It is not intended for the person who wants to learn how to use the program but for the person who already has some knowledge about this and merely needs to refresh his/her memory occasionally. People who have no knowledge at all about the program should look into the user documentation which could also be kept on-line. This on-line documentation need not be integrated into the program and can be written as an interactive tutorial to the program. The Lotus tutorial for 123 cited in the references is a good example of an on-line interactive tutorial for a program.

When the abbreviated help facility does not list all available commands, the detailed help facility should at least provide such a list with bare bones information on how to use them. An example of such a bare bones detailed help facility is the help display obtained when the <Home> key is pressed on an IBM-PC executing PC-TALK III. This is shown in Figure 3.13. The abbreviated help facility (Figure 3.12) tells us how to get to the detailed help display. This summary of commands does provide us additional information. For example, file transmission is both started and terminated by pressing Alt-T. This command and others are toggled commands. Since all the commands in PC-TALK III are menu driven, the information provided in Figure 3.13 is adequate for a reasonably knowledgeable user.

The command summary of Figure 3.13 is displayed on the right side of the screen. This overwrites whatever was on this part of the screen before. Once the command summary has been written, the program returns to command mode. While at first, we might regard the unavailability of a command to restore the screen to its original content a serious shortcoming, there isn't much need for this in the communications application for which PC-TALK III is designed.

The detailed help facility for a program can be anywhere from a few lines long to several thousands of lines. When designing this facility, one should strive to provide as much information as is possible in the given memory and disk space limitations. The information

===PC-TALK III COMMAND SUMMARY===	
PrtSc	print screen contents
^PrtSc	contin. printout (or ^PgUp)
Alt-R	Receive a file (or PgDn)
Alt-T	Transmit a file (or PgUp)
	transmit: pacing '=p' binary '=b'
	tran/recv: XMODEM '=x'
Alt-V	View file Alt-Y = delete
Alt-D	Dialing directory
Alt-Q	redial last number
Alt-K	set/clear Func keys (Alt-J)
Alt-=	set/clear temp Alt keys
Alt-E	Echo toggle Alt-M = Message
Alt-S	Screendump Alt-C = Clearsc
Alt-P	communications Parameters
Alt-F	set program deFaults
Alt-L	change Logged drive
Alt-W	set margin Width alarm
Alt-Z	elapsed time/current call
Alt-X	eXit to DOS
Ctrl-End	send sustained Break signal

Figure 3.13 Detailed help file of PC-TALK III

should be provided in a crisp and concise form.

3.6. DESIGN EXAMPLES

3.6.1. TEXT PROCESSORS

We elaborate on the screen editor design of Chapter 1. We must first consider whether there are any functions besides those listed in Figure 1.1 that a screen editor should provide? Let's begin by looking at features that don't directly relate to the task of editing but which will make the editor easier to use.

File management capabilities immediately come to mind. A sampler of desirable commands that relate to this is given below.

FS   Save the current workfile on a disk. To facilitate easy recovery to the previous generation of this workfile, the save should be implemented so as to first rename the previous generation workfile and then write the new version out under the proper name.

FW   Write a portion (or block) of the current workfile on a disk. The portion to be written out can be designated by placing block begin and end markers around the block. We shall discuss this in greater detail later. The write operation should be menu driven. The user should be interrogated as to the name of the destination file. In case this file already exists, an overwrite, append, or cancel confirmation should be sought.

FE   Erase a file. Again, the user is to be interrogated regarding the name of the file to be erased. In case no file by that name exists, the user should be notified. Perhaps a spelling error was made.

FN   Rename a file. The old and new names are to be obtained from the user. If the old name does not exist or a file having the new name already exists, confirmation procedures should be initiated.

FR   Read a file and insert its contents into the current workfile beginning at the line where the cursor is positioned. Once again, the user needs to provide the name of the file that is to be inserted and confirmation procedures initiated in case no file with this name exists or if the file is not a text file.

FD   This command lists the names of all files in the default directory.

With the exception of the commands FS and FD, all others have been described as interactive commands. For instance, all the information needed to erase a file is obtained interactively from the user. One may also want to provide a batch option as in:

FE chap1

which results in the file "chap1" being erased and:

FN chap1 chap2

which results in chap1 being renamed chap2. If chap2 already exists, the user should be asked to confirm the loss of the existing version of chap2.

Next, let us turn our attention to tasks that are directly related to editing. We have already seen a need to mark the begin and end of a block of text (i.e., to write it out). In text processing, there is often a need to move blocks of text from one part of the workfile to another. This task is also easily accomplished by first marking the begin and end of the block and then specifying where the block is to be moved. So, there is a need for the following commands:

BB Place a block begin marker immediately to the left of the present cursor position.

BE Place a block end marker immediately to the left of the present cursor position.

BM Move the block of text between the begin and end markers to the position immediately to the left of the current cursor position.

BC Make a copy of the block of text between the begin and end markers and insert it immediately to the left of the current marker position. This differs from a BM in that the marked block of text is now at two places (the original as well as the new).

In case a color monitor is being used, the marked block of text can be displayed in a color different from that used for the rest of the text. On a monochrome monitor, the block may be displayed in high intensity video. This provides the user with a visual check that the block to be moved has been correctly marked. In case the end marker precedes the begin marker, no text shows up in the different color. When a block move or copy is requested, the user must be notified if the command failed because the end marker preceded the begin marker. To ascertain that the user has become aware of this failure, the move and copy commands can insist on a user response such as depressing the <esc> key after reading the failure message.

An alternate to requiring that blocks be marked before a block move or copy can be performed, is to make these commands interactive. For instance, the block move command can carry out the following dialogue:

user: BM
editor: Move a block of text
　　　　Move cursor to first character of block to be moved.
　　　　Press <Return> when done.
user: (sequence of cursor moves) <Return>
editor: {highlight this character using a different color, etc.}
　　　　Move cursor to last character of block to be moved.
　　　　Press <Return> when done.
user: (sequence of cursor moves) <Return>
editor: {highlight all characters in block to be moved}
　　　　Is block OK? (Y/N)
user: Y
editor: Move cursor to position block is to move to.
　　　　Press <Return> when done.
user: (sequence of cursor moves) <Return>
editor: {Block is moved and displayed highlighted at new position}

　　Figure 1.1 contains a fairly rich set of cursor movement commands. Despite this, it is very tedious to move back and forth in a large document using these commands alone. It is very desirable to permit the user to place markers at various points in the document and specify a direct cursor movement to any of the marked points. The necessary commands are:

PPxxx　　Here xxx is a label used as a place marker. The label is to be placed immediately to the left of the present cursor position. After it has been placed, it can be displayed in the text using a different color or by enclosing it in symbols such as "[" and "]" or "<" and ">". The user should be asked to provide a different label in case the label xxx is still in use. A command abort option should also be available.

PMxxx　　Move cursor to the point marked xxx. If no such marker has been placed, the user should be interrogated as to a possible error in entering the label. The option to cancel the command should be available.

PExxx　　Erase the marker xxx. Notify the user in case the marker xxx does not exist in the text.

　　Another useful capability for a text editor is the ability to search for (and possibly replace) specified text. For instance, a user may wish to replace all occurrences of the string "calculator" in a marked block by the string "computer". We see the need for the two string find/replace commands:

SF   Find the next occurrence of a specified string. Next could mean either forward or backward from the current location of the cursor.

SR   Find a specified string and replace it with another. Several options are possible here. We may wish to replace all occurrences of the specified string, the next *n* occurrences, only those occurrences in which the string is a whole word (rather than a prefix or suffix of another word), etc. Further, we may wish to ignore case when finding and replacing the string. In the example cited above, we may wish to replace all occurrences of Calculator by Computer, of Calculators by Computers, of calculator by computer, and of calculators by computers.

In order to facilitate good formatting on different output devices, it is also desirable to provide a rich collection of commands that are to be used by the text formatter for this purpose. In our design, each such command begins withe a "". in column 1. Hence, we shall call these commands "dot commands". Since every input line with a period in column 1 is interpreted as a dot command by the editor and formatter, it is necessary to provide a mechanism to have a genuine period (i.e., one that does not signify a dot command) in column 1. One possibility is to have the user type \. in columns 1 and 2 to get a period in column 1 and to type \\. to get \. in columns 1 and 2 of the formatted output.

A sampler of useful dot commands is provided below:

PG   Begin a new page.

DS   Start double spacing of lines.

SS   Start single line spacing.

OT   This command has three parameters as in:

.OT L C R

L, C, and R are, respectively, the titles to be put on the top left, center, and right of every odd numbered page.

ET   Titles for even numbered pages.

BB   Begin a block of text that is not to be split over pages (unless the block is longer than a page).

EB   End the block of text.

At this time, we have a preliminary list of requirements for our text editor. A complete requirements list for a sophisticated and flexible text editor is much larger. As the number of command names increases, it becomes quite difficult to manage them and ensure that all command names are different. These difficulties are alleviated by adopting a top-down modular design methodology. This methodology is discussed in the next chapter.

We are ready to design the help files for the editor. The total number of editor commands is so large that we can't possibly display them all in our abbreviated help facility of Figure 1.3. The abbreviated help facility can be restructured into a hierarchical facility. We add the entries "F Files", "B Blocks", "P Place Markers", "S Strings", and ". Dot Commands" under the heading "Misc". When the user selects F, B, P, S, and ".", the help lines of Figure 1.3 are replaced by those for the file, block, place marker, string commands, and dot commands respectively. We leave the design of the abbreviated help files for each of these as an exercise.

It is now time to design each of the editor and formatter (i.e., dot commands) commands listed. The design should be sufficiently precise that a computer program for the command can be written. In particular, the action performed by the command at all boundary conditions must be specified. Some sample designs are provided below. Some of these designs use a programming language-like notation while others rely merely on English.

Command ←
if *CursorColumn* > 1
then *CursorColumn* = *CursorColumn* − 1;

If *CursorColumn* is a program variable that denotes the current column position of the cursor, then the above specification can actually be used as Pascal code for this function. The specification clearly states the behavior of the "move character left" function both at the left boundary (*CursorColumn* = 1) as well as at other positions. In this case, an English language specification will be less compact and not any clearer.

Command *FS*
if workfile has no name **then**
begin
  loop
     ask user for workfile name;
     if name is legal or command canceled **then exit** from loop
     else provide user with a description of legal names;
   repeat;
   if cancel **then** abort command;
end;
if there is already a file with the workfile name
then save this file under the name "name.bak";
write workfile under the specified name;
if no error
then write success message and terminate command
else begin
     write failure message and ask user to press <esc>;
    wait until <esc> has been pressed;
     abort command;
   end

The above specification of the file save command is quite specific. It covers all possibilities and tells us precisely what will happen under these different possiblities. However, obtaining the specification in this precise form is almost as much work as writing a computer program for the function. A version that uses only English may, however, be ambiguous. To complete the design of the file save command, we need to specify the exact form of the program prompt that asks for the file name and the exact text used to notify the user of errors.

Command *FW*
if no marked block
then begin
     write an error message;
     ask user to press <esc> key after reading the message;
     wait until <esc> key has been pressed;
     abort command;
   end;
{There is a marked block.}

loop
    ask user for a name to write to;
    if name is legal or command canceled **then exit** from loop
    else provide user with a description of legal names;
repeat;
if cancel **then** abort command;
{Does file with this name exist?}
if file exists
then begin
        ask user if he wishes to overwrite, append, or cancel;
        keep asking until one of the above three responses is obtained;
        perform the requested option;
        if error **then** write message and abort;
    end
else begin {new name}
    write the block out; {Note block may be null}
    if no error
    then write success message and terminate command
    else begin
        write failure message and ask user to press <esc>;
        wait until <esc> has been pressed;
         abort command;
      end;
      end;

Once again, the use of programming language notation mixed with English enables us to arrive at a precise and easy to read specification.

Command *.DS*
This dot command is best specified in English. The specification is: "Change to double line spacing". If we are already in this spacing mode, then this dot command has no effect.

3.6.2. PASCAL PROGRAMMING ENVIRONMENT

At first, one might think there isn't much one can do by way of user interface design for a Pascal programmer. Perhaps all that is needed is to design the structure of the command that invokes the Pascal compiler. If the user wishes to compile the Pascal program *test*, should he have to type:

pascal test

or should the command just be *pascal*? In the latter case the compiler will interrogate the user:

Which Program?

When one thinks about the needs of a Pascal programmer, one comes to the realization that Pascal programmers really need more than just a program that translates their Pascal code into machine language code. They need an environment that supports programming in Pascal. The language translator is only one aspect of this environment. Let us elaborate on the needs of the Pascal programmer.

First, the program to be compiled has to be entered into the computer. During this entry process, one can expect to make mistakes that will need to be corrected. So, the programming environment must support the entry and editing of Pascal programs. Our instinctive reaction to this need is that it can be met by using any text editor that is available on the host computer. In fact, this is often the only route available to most Pascal programmers.

If we study Pascal programs, we will realize that the editing (including initial entry) needs are better met by providing editor features that are specialized to this application. For example, the editor could provide automatic indentation of program lines. This could be done by providing special commands to begin a new indentation level and to revert to the previous indentation level. The user could set the degree of indentation (2, 3, or 4 spaces) as part of the initialization procedure for the editor.

The editor could also provide templates for the entry of statements such as **if**, **while**, **case**, etc. For example, to enter a **while** statement, the user might type the command ^W. Following this, the editor will ask for the conditional and body of the **while** statement. Once these have been obtained, these will be properly displayed in the program using the selected indentation rules.

In addition, the compiler and editor should be well interfaced. For example, the compiler may invoke the editor when an error is discovered and display the errorneous line for correction.

When we put our mind to it, we can come up with many edit tasks that are specialized to programs and even to the particular programming language (in our case Pascal) used. These can and should be incorporated into the editor for programs written in that language.

In order to save the user from the task of having to learn the idiosyncrasies of many different editors, the additional features should be built on top of an existing and commonly used editor. For example, the Turbo Pascal programming environment (developed by Borland International) provides an editor built on top of Wordstar (actually, it just uses the same command names as used in Wordstar for the common capabilities) that provides automatic indentation during program entry.

There is also a need for specialized program formatters. These could automatically set the reserved words in the language in bold face, the variable names in italics, and the comments in Roman. In case the print device available does not support these type fonts, then the reserved words could be underlined. In addition, all program lines can be automatically numbered for easy reference. The formatter might automatically print different procedures on a different page or print many small ones on the same page.

The programming environment for Pascal could support file management tasks too. These could include the automatic retention of up to two or three generations of the user program. The programming environment could additionally provide for the saving and future execution of compiled or object code.

With these ideas in our mind, we can envision a startup menu for our Pascal programming environment that has the form given in Figure 3.14.

There are other design considerations that pertain more directly to the compiler (or translator) part of the environment. Is the compiler going to be a one pass or two pass compiler? What limitations will the compiler impose on programs? Can variable names be arbitrarily long? Or are they to be limited to 32 characters? Should the compiler handle certain extensions to standard Pascal? Which ones? When these decisions are made, the language being compiled may no longer be pure Pascal and a new language specification will be required.

Pascal Programming Environment

FUNCTIONS

1. Edit
2. Print Program
3. Generate Object Code Only
4. Execute Object Code
5. Compile And Execute

Press <esc> to exit

Figure 3.14 Startup menu for Pascal programming environment

3.6.3. SPREAD SHEETS

A spread sheet is a matrix of cells. Each cell can contain either a label (i.e., textual information) or a value (i.e., numeric information). The value in a cell (if any) is computed using some formula which may involve the values in other cells of the sheet. The design of a spread sheet environment involves the design of the following components:

(1) A file manager that saves, retrieves, renames, and deletes spread sheets. It should also be able to display the contents of a file directory.

(2) A display formatter that formats the spread sheet for display on various display devices. At a minimum this should provide for display on a screen and on a sheet of paper via a printer.

(3) A sufficiently rich set of sheet manipulation commands.

(4) Abbreviated and detailed on-line help facilities.

(5) Editor to edit formulas and labels. The requirements for this editor are far more restricted than those of a general purpose text processor. This editor has to handle at most one line of characters at any time and need only provide elementary cursor control and character delete and insert commands.

(6)   Menus for menu driven portions of the environment.

(7)   Interface to other useful programs such as programs to draw graphs and prepare documents using spread sheet data. These programs could also be an integral part of the spread sheet environment and be customized to accept data directly from the spread sheet.

The design of the file manger is essentially the same as that for our programming environment and text processor examples. Customizing the text processor to allow for documents that use data from one or more spread sheets involves the addition of a mechanism to reference relevant cells of spread sheets from within a document. The text processor can extract the appropriate values and labels from the specified spread sheets and insert them into the text. Similarly, the graph drawing program should accept spread sheet input.

We shall not dwell further on the text processor and graph customization or interface issues. Instead, let us devote our energies to the design of the display formatter, command set, menus, and on-line help facilities. In the sequel, we shall need a mechanism to address any cell in the sheet. A convenient one results by labeling the columns of the sheet using letters and the rows using digits (Figure 3.16). Thus, the first 26 columns are indexed using a single letter, the next 26×26 columns are indexed using two letters, etc. A cell may now be addressed by providing its column and row index as in: A3, A23, X15, AB21, ABT12, etc.

Display Formatter

We begin with the interactive screen display. This is what the user will use when creating, modifying, and viewing the spread sheet. The remaining display devices are used to get paper (or film) copies of final versions of spread sheets for distribution.

The designed screen display consists of three parts. The first part uses the top few lines of the screen to display menus and status information. When a menu is being displayed, it will be displayed using the horizontal format of Figure 3.10. Cell status information will be displayed whenever an entry into a cell is being made. At this time, the cell address (given by its column and row index); the type of entry being made (or already made) into the cell (label or value); cell contents; and formula (if any) will be displayed (Figure 3.16). The box containing "Value" is called the status box. Other possible contents for this box are "Edit" (displayed when a cell content is being edited); "Help" (when in the detailed help menu); "Wait" (when formula values are being computed or the spread sheet is being printed or saved); and "Ready" (when the program is ready for the user to initiate a new action).

B4: +B2+B3 $\boxed{\text{Value}}$ 22.5

	A	B	C	D	E	F
1		Jan	Feb	March	April	May
2	Expenses	10.25	25.97	55.89	121.98	
3	Losses	12.25	21.25	31.45	0	131.29
4	Total	$\boxed{22.50}$				
5						
6						
7						

F1 Help F2 Commands F3 Edit F4 Calc Mode F5 Calc F6 Goto cell

---

Figure 3.16 Display screen for spread sheet

The second part of the display shows as large a portion of the spread sheet as will fit on the available screen. The current cell is highlighted by surrounding it with a box or by shading it some color. This box or shaded rectangle is called the cell pointer. The values of all cells in the present screen display are also shown. The formula in a particular cell is displayed on the status line by moving the cell pointer to the desired cell.

The third part of the display is the on-line abbreviated help facility. In Figure 3.16, only the bottom line of the screen is used for this purpose. The current settings of the function keys are displayed.

Having designed the basic display, we need to provide a facility to move the cell pointer around the display. A suitably rich set of commands for this is described below.

←	Move pointer one cell left. If the cell pointer is presently in the leftmost column, then provide an audio signal and do nothing. If the column on the left is presently not part of the screen display, then shift all columns rightward to bring in the column on the left. This will result in some of the rightmost display columns dissappearing from the screen.
→	Move pointer one cell right. Operates in a manner similar to ←.
↓	Move pointer one cell down. Similar to ←.
↑	Up one cell. Similar to ←.
<Home>	Move to first cell in first row of spread sheet.
<PgUp>	The spread sheet may be visualized as consisting of many pages where each page is large enough to fit on the screen (Figure 3.17). The notion of a page is defined relative to the current screen. <PgUp> displays the page above the current page. If there is no page above the current one, then an audio signal is provided and no action is taken. If there is an upper page, this page is displayed and the pointer is positioned at the cell in the current column and last row of the new page.
<PgDn>	Display the page below the current one. Similar to <PgUp> except that the pointer is positioned at the cell in the same column and first row of the new page.
<Tab>	Display page at right. Pointer moves to cell in first column of new page. It remains in the same row as before.
<BackTab>	Display page at left; move pointer to rightmost column in the new page; do not change the row position of the pointer.
F6	Move pointer to the designated cell. This is menu driven. When the function key F6 is pressed the user is prompted:

Move to which cell?

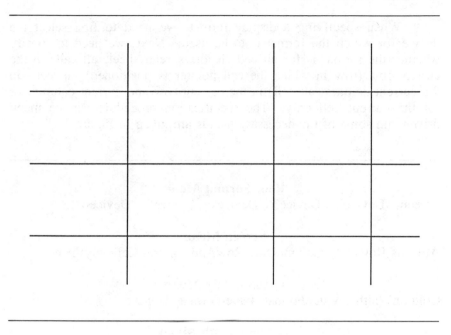

Figure 3.17 Pages

> If the specified cell is in the presently displayed page, the pointer is simply moved there. Otherwise, a sequence of page moves is initiated to get to the right page.

As we can see, some of the pointer movement commands required for the spread sheet application are different from those required for text processing.

Another desirable display feature is the ability to select display formats. For instance, some labels may be very long, but we may wish to display just the first few characters so that more columns will fit onto a page. Similarly, some computed values may have many decimal digits in them and we might wish that only two digits after the decimal point be displayed on the screen. Also, we might wish a different display format to be used for different display devices (screen,

80 column printer, 132 column printer, 256 column printer, typesetter, color film recorder, dot matrix printer, etc.).

When specifying a display format, we need to first select the device for which the format is to be used. Next, we need to specify whether the format is for all cells in the spread sheet, all cells in the current row (row in which the cell pointer is positioned), all cells in the current column, all cells in the current row and current column, or for the current cell only. The specification procedure can be menu driven and some of the necessary menus are given in Figure 3.18.

Root Format Menu
Screen Device2 Device3 Device4 Device5 Device6

Screen Menu
AllCells RowOnly ColumnOnly RowAndColumn CellOnly Done

ColumnOnly Menu
ColumnWidth   ValueFormat LabelFormat Done

ColumnWidth Menu
Enter Column Width (1-40):

LabelFormat Menu
NumberOfCharacters Centered LeftJustify RightJustify Done

ValueFormat Menu
$ Integer FixedDecimal Real

Figure 3.18 Format Menus

As can be seen, the format menu is hierarchically structured. Some menus permit multiple choices. For example, from the screen menu, one can set the format for the present row, then move the pointer to a new column and set the format for that column, then move to yet another cell and set the format for that cell alone. From the column-only menu, one can set the formats for many columns one at a time. The column-width menu, on the other hand, permits you to set the width of just one column and then returns to the parent menu. The look ahead feature of Figure 3.10 may be used to give the user advance information about the selections available from the succeeding menu.

When in any multiple step command, it will sometimes be necessary to cancel the command and revert to the original state, or to undo just the last step. These options should be provided for and the abbreviated help line can display how to accomplish these tasks. For example, whenever any of the format menus is displayed, the help line can read:

F1   Cancel And Return To Ready Status   F2   Undo Last Step

While much design work remains for the display formatter, we shall terminate our discussion of it now and move on to the sheet manipulation commands.

Sheet Manipulation Commands

We shall design only some of the more important commands here. Some others will be considered in the exercises. The commands we consider and their designs are given below. All commands are menu driven and use the selection mechanisms of Figure 3.10. When the function key F2 is pressed, the overall root menu for all commands is displayed. The selections here will list the names of the next level menus (egs., spread sheet, format, files, print, etc.). Some desirable commands that are to be incorporated into the spread sheet menu are given below.

C   This copies an entry from one cell to a range of cells. If the entry is a label or a constant, it is copied as is. If it is a formula, then the copying is quite intricate and depends on how the formula was originally entered. An example will illustrate this. Consider the formula +B2+B3 entered into cell B4 of Figure 3.16. The formulas for the remaining cells in row 4 are essentially the same (i.e., add the values in the two cells immediately above). So, the B2 and B3 in the formula for cell B4 are to be interpreted as the cell one above and the cell two above. We say that the cell addresses are relative. When this formula is copied across row 4, we want the B's replaced by C's, then by D's, then by E's, etc., to get the formulas:

C4 = +C2+C3
D4 = +D2+D3
E4 = +E2+E3
etc.

However, we might want some cell addresses to be copied as is (example, cells containing global constants such as interest rate, etc.). Whether a cell address is to be relative or absolute can be specified at the time the formula is first entered into the cell.

The formula to be copied is assumed to reside in the current cell. When the copy command is invoked, it first determines from the user the range of cells the formula, label, or constant is to be copied into. A "from" cell and a "to" cell are provided by the user. These define a rectangle with the specified cells at two of its corners. If a label or constant is being copied, then it is simply replicated in all the cells in this rectangle. If a formula is being copied, each relative cell address in this formula is changed as necessary for each cell in the rectangle. The remaining components of the formula are copied as is.

IR Insert a row above the row the pointer is in. Update formulas in affected cells.

IC Insert a column to the left of the column the pointer is in.

DR Delete row pointer is in.

DC Delete column containing pointer.

To enable the selection of the above commands, the entries Insert, Delete, and Copy can be added to the spread sheet command menu.

Formulas

Formulas can be permitted to contain constants, relative and absolute cell addresses, predefined functions such as *sum*, *average*, *sqrt*, *log*, etc., cell ranges as in:

sum($B1..B20,C1..C5$)

which causes the sum of the values in the cells B1 through B20 and C1 through C5 to be computed; arithmetic, logical, and relational operators, and parentheses. Since most addresses can be expected to

be relative addresses, we can require that absolute addresses be pre-
fixed by a special symbol (such as $ or ! or %). This imposes a one
character typing penalty on absolute addresses only. We might also
wish to allow the user to enter cell addresses by moving the cell
pointer to them. The edit feature discussed earlier will allow for the
correction of any errors introduced during entry.

The complete design of the user interface for a sophisticated
spread sheet environment can take weeks (if not months) to complete.
The Lotus spread sheet environment for example contains over 100
commands, more than 50 menus, a very detailed on-line help facility,
and an interactive tutorial. The interactive tutorial is not integrated
into the rest of the program as the integrated help facility is adequate
for anyone reasonably familiar with spread sheets. This environment
also supports database management and sophisticated graph drawing.

With over 100 commands, ensuring that each command has a
unique name; writing down the design of each command and being
able to locate it in the documentation; etc. are difficult tasks. Completing the design of a complex software system is made much easier
if we adopt the top down modular approach of the next chapter.

We shall have to content ourselves here with the level of design
provided thus far. This is adequate to give you a flavor for what is
involved in designing a spread sheet environment.

3.7. REFERENCES AND SELECTED READINGS

Several of the example menus of this chapter has been taken from the
following software systems:

Wordstar, by MicroPro, MicroPro International Corporation,
San Rafael, California.

IBM-Basic, by Microsoft, IBM Corporation, Boca Raton,
Florida.

PC-TALK III, by Freeware, Tiburon, California.

Turbo Pascal, by Borland International, Scotts Valley, California.

and

Lotus 123, by Lotus Corporation.

Much of the development of this chapter has been significantly influenced by these software systems. Exposure to the above systems as well as to the Lotus interactive tutorial will give you a good insight into the capabilities one can provide in different types of software systems. Advanced material on specification of editor and formatter commands using a programming language like notation appears in the papers:

Program specification applied to a text formatter, by M. Feather, *IEEE Trans. On Software Engineering*, Vol. SE-8, No. 5, 1982.

and

Combining testing with formal specifications: A case study, by P. McMullin and J. Gannon, *IEEE Trans. On Software Engineering*, Vol. SE-9, No. 3, 1983.

3.8. EXERCISES

1. List some additional file manipulation commands that are desirable in a text editor environment. For each, provide an informal description as in Section 3.6.1.

2. List some additional dot commands that will be useful during text formatting. For each of these, provide an informal description.

3. Design the abbreviated help files for the categories F, B, P, S, and "." of the editor design of Section 3.6.1.

4. Provide a design specification for each of the editor commands of Figure 1.3. Use a combination of English and programming language constructs.

5.   Do the previous exercise for the editor file commands listed in Section 3.6.1. Do not repeat the specifications for FS and FW. Use a combination of English and programming language constructs.

6.   Repeat Exercise 4 for the case of the editor block commands listed in Section 3.6.1.

7.   Repeat Exercise 4 for the case of the editor place marker commands listed in Section 3.6.1.

8.   Repeat Exercise 4 for the case of the editor string commands listed in Section 3.6.1. Design these commands to be interactive.

9.   Repeat Exercise 4 for the case of the dot commands listed in Section 3.6.1.

10.   Complete the design of the interactive block move command that was begun in Section 3.6.1. You need to specify the dialogue that is needed for the remaining possibilities.

11.   Design the interactive dialogues needed by the print, generate object code, execute object code, and compile and execute options provided in the menu of Figure 3.14. For example, to generate object code, thc system must determine the name of the Pascal source file and that of the object file to be created.

12.   List some additional capabilities that are desirable in an editor of Pascal programs. These capabilities should be specialized to thc needs of Pascal programmers and should not include any capabilities mentioned in Section 3.6.2. Describe each of these capabilities in sufficient detail and include appropriate computer/user dialogues for interactive commands.

13.   Assume that we have decided to provide menu driven functions to enter various Pascal statements. Design and describe how these functions work on the following statements:

   a.   **const**

     b.   **var**

     c.   **while**

     d.   **case**

     e.   **program**

     f.   **procedure**

     g.   **begin**

14. List some useful extensions to standard Pascal. Explain why each of the suggested extensions is considered useful.

15. Extend the Pascal programming language with a sufficiently rich set of language constructs to permit color graphics. Describe the desirable capabilities.

16. You are to design a windowing capability for use with Pascal programs. This capability should allow the user to define a possibly overlapping set of windows on the screen and to send output to or receive input from any point in any one of these windows. Design a set of useful capabilities in connection with this problem. You may find it instructive to first study an existing windowing package.

17. For the editor design of Section 3.6.1, develop a notation to permit the importing of data from spread sheets into the text document.

18. Design additional cursor control commands that may be useful in a spread sheet environment.

19. Spread sheet users often find it useful to freeze certain label columns and rows so that these do not scroll off the screen as one moves to distant parts of the sheet. Design this capability.

20. Design an interactive command to copy a block of spread sheet cells.

21. Design spread sheet commands to add and delete rows and columns. Your commands are to be interactive and should allow the experienced user to bypass any or all levels of the interrogation. Carefully specify all changes made by the commands to the spread sheet.

22. Obtain a complete design for software systems for each of the following games. Your design must include a list of all user commands together with a specification of each; a design of all display formats to be used; and a design for all menus. Any other features related to the user interface should also be included.

    (a) Tic-tac-toe

    (b) Hangman

    (c) Blackjack

    (d) Slot machine

    (e) Checkers

23. Design a software system that allows for the entry and display of textual slides. These slides are to be used in conjunction with a lecture. Provision for at least the following must be made:

    a. Multicolored slides.

    b. Characters of different size.

    c. Display of characters in italics, bold, and roman fonts.

    d. Importing of preformatted figures from other files.

    e. The sequential display of slides with each slide being displayed for a prespecified length of time.

    f. Ability to interrupt the sequential display with the display of an arbitrary slide. This interruption should be followed by a resumption of the normal sequence.

CHAPTER 4

MODULARIZATION

4.1. INTRODUCTION

The divide-and-conquer strategy has been used successfully by many conquering kings and emperors. If you wish to defeat a formiddable enemy and you have but a small army, then a good strategy is to divide the enemy into small factions and defeat each faction separately. The key realization here is that it is often easier to deal with the components of the whole than with the whole itself.

One can provide many examples of the successful application of this strategy. The administration of a large country is carried out by dividing the country into many smaller and more easily administered modules or units. These modules are called states. Each state is further subdivided into counties. Counties are subdivided into cities and cities into communities. This division of the entire country into modules is best described pictorially by a modularization tree as in Figure 4.1.

The entire administrative module is the country. This is represented at the root of the modularization tree. The state modules are represented at the next level of the tree. Each state module is comprised of several county modules. These are represented at the next level. Counties are subdivided into cities and cities into communities.

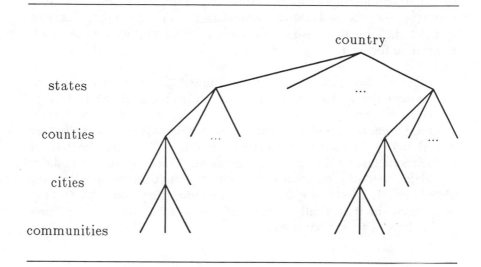

Figure 4.1 Administrative modules in a country

Each module in this tree has its own administrative body that has well defined administrative tasks. The country is administered by the federal government. This administrative module is concerned with only those issues that are of importance to the country as a whole (eg., defense). Other administrative issues are delegated to the administrative modules at the next level. State administrative modules, in turn, concern themselves with only those issues that are of importance to the entire state. They do not concern themselves with the administrative problems of other states (so, there is an independence of function amongst modules at the same level). In addition, the state administrative module does not delve into matters that may be considered internal to its lower level modules (the counties).

The administrative modules of Figure 4.1 are logically viable (the modules deal with geographically contiguous pieces of territory). There is a degree of independence in the administrative tasks assigned to each module and there is also a well defined channel for information flow. Information can flow up and down the administrative hierarchy via the established links only. The modularization of the administrative functions has made the governing of the entire country a more manageable task. One can only imagine the chaos that would prevail if one attempted to administer a country by a single unstructured (or flat) administrative organization. For example, consider administering the USA using two million administrators who are each responsible for everything.

The functions of some of the administrative modules of Figure 4.1 are sufficiently simple that a further refinement of the module is unnecessary. For example, a community can be administered by a community council. Other modules are more complex and are further refined into a hierarchy of modules. Figure 4.2 shows the refined modular structure of the federal government. Once again, the modules are logically coherent in that all administrative functions that are related are lumped into the same module; they are functionally independent in that ideally one module will not delve into the functions delegated to another module.

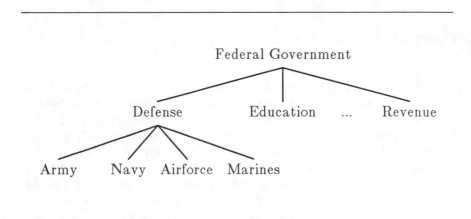

Figure 4.2 Modules of the federal government

The hierarchical organization of the administrative structure of a country is quite similar to that of many other organizations. The administrative structure of a large corporation is shown in Figure 4.3. The modules in this organization enjoy the same characteristics of coherence, independence, and manageability of function as do those in our earlier example.

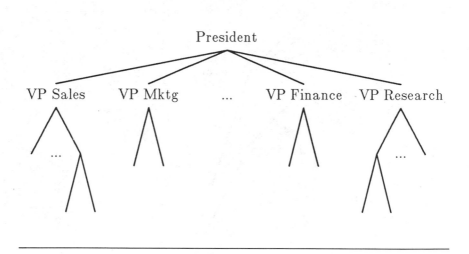

Figure 4.3 Hierarchical administrative structure of a corporation

While our discussion thus far suggests that the way to achieve a hierarchical decomposition is to begin at the top and successively refine modules into lower level modules, it is also possible to begin at the bottom and combine lower level modules to get higher level modules. Thus, in organizing the administrative units in a country, we can begin with the communities and group them into cities. Groups of cities can be combined into counties, and neighboring counties into states. The two different approaches to modularization are respectively referred to as *top-down* and *bottom-up* modularization. The top-down approach is intuitively more appealing and we shall develop this further.

The essential principle underlying the top-down modularization strategy is to divide an otherwise unmanageable task into several smaller tasks that are more easily managed. This division process may be iterated upon as needed to obtain a multilevel hierarchy of tasks that is best depicted as a tree. A further refinement of the tasks in this tree may be necessary. This refinement is also modular and represented by one tree for each task that is so refined. We may visualize the organization as comprising of trees in two planes. The tree

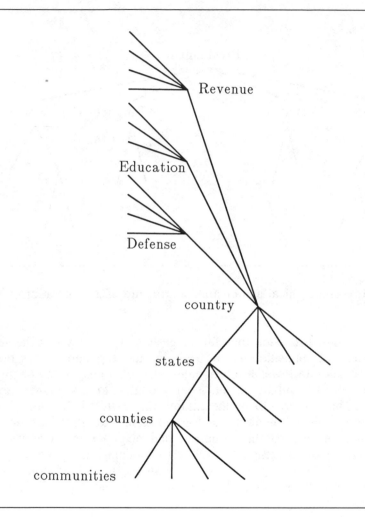

Figure 4.4 Multiplanar modularization tree

of Figure 4.1 is in one plane. The tree of Figure 4.2 which represents a refinement of the root of Figure 4.1 may be visualized as being attached to the root of Figure 4.1 but growing in a second plane as in Figure 4.4. Some of the nodes in this plane may themselves get refined into trees in yet another plane and so on. So, the divide-and-conquer methodology really results in a multiplanar tree modularization. The key characteristics of the modules are:

(1) *Logical Coherence* Each module serves a logically coherent function.

(2) *Independence* Each module is relatively independent of the others. Ideally, inter-module communication is carried out via the links in the modularization tree only.

(3) *Manageability* Each module is sufficiently refined so that it is manageable.

The top-down modularization strategy is very useful in the programming environment. Consider the "Sleepy Eye Apartment Complex" spread sheet of Figure 2.4. It is evident that our investor used the top-down modular approach to arrive at this. The contributions to the financial analysis have first been divided into the two logically coherent categories (or modules): income and expenses. Income itself has been partitioned into the categories: income from apartments, from garages, and deposits. If it were not for this partitioning, it is unlikely that our investor would have discovered the absence of income from vending machines. The income from apartments can further be partitioned into the categories: income from studio apartments, one bedroom apartments, two bedroom apartments, and three bedroom apartments. Evidently, our investor did not see the need to have this fine a modularization. Expenses have been partitioned into the categories debt service, administrative, taxes, operation, maintenance, and insurance. With this modularization, it is easier to detect missed expenses than when all expenses are bunched together into a single module.

Top down modularization may be effectively used to improve the intellectual manageability of several steps of the programming process. We have already seen one use of this technique in the design phase. There, we used it effectively to manage large menus.

Another aspect of the design step that will benefit from the use of modularization is the capabilties design. The number of different commands needed in a text processor and a spread sheet is quite large. Consequently, it is quite difficult for even the designer to remember all and it is quite likely that he will find himself designing essentially the same command more than once. The manageability of the capabilities design is significantly enhanced if the designer uses the top-down modular approach. You have probably already noticed that the capabilities design for our text editor and spread sheet systems were getting out of hand. The number of capabilities that have to be managed is such that the intellectual manageability of the design is difficult using a flat organization. A hierarchical organization is called for.

4.2. TEXT EDITOR

Let us apply the top-down modularization methodology to the task of designing the command set for our text editor. We begin by first determining the basic categories of commands that are needed. These are:

(1) cursor control

(2) insert text

(3) delete text

(4) place markers

(5) block movement

(6) search for and replace strings

(7) files

(8) help

(9) quit

(10) undo

At this time it is possible for us to do something that could not be done when we attempted to design the commands directly. We can sit back and look at the commands at a much higher level (i.e., by category) of granularity. We can ask whether there is any general capability that is lacking rather than ask whether we need another cursor control command. It is possible to concentrate on generalities rather than details. This is difficult to do when our first opportunity for reflection is after thirty editor commands have been listed in a disorganized manner.

Having determined the basic categories, we can proceed to design the commands in each category. Since the number of commands in each category is sufficiently small, there is no need for further division into subcategories. It is now possible for us to look at all the commands within a category and answer questions such as:

(1) Is the command set for this category sufficiently rich? Am I missing some commands?

(2) Have some commands been duplicated?

(3) Are some unnecessary?

It is much harder to answer these design questions when all commands are lumped together into a single category.

This enhancement in the intellectual manageability of the command design task can be passed along to the user in the form of command names that are easy to remember. This is done by prefixing the command names with a category selector. As a result, command names can be duplicated across categories. The immediate implication of this is that command names in one category can be selected independent of the names selected in another category. As a result, we can expect to have command names that are more suggestive of the function they perform. So, it will be easier for the user to remember these names and he/she will need to refer to the abbreviated help facility less often. Note that if some command category has only one command in it (as in undo), then this command need not be assigned a name. The category selector is adequate.

Another advantage of using a category selector for command names is that if we later discover that a command category has been inadvertently omitted, then the new command category can be designed as an independent module and added to the remainder of the design. We need only ensure that the category selector for this is different from the other category selectors.

Since the cursor control commands will be used most often and use special keyboard characters such as ← and →, we shall give them the null prefix and not assign them a name that is a prefix for the other command categories. Thus, cursor control is done by simply entering the cursor control command. A reasonable choice of prefixes for the remaining categories is the first letter in the category name. Notice that each category name begins with a different letter. With this choice we can reasonably expect the user to have no difficulty remembering the category selector. The only anticipated source of confusion is whether the selector is an upper or lower case letter. This possible source of confusion is eliminated by allowing the use of both. So, all file commands begin with F (or f), all block commands with B (or b), etc.

Some of the text editor command names are listed by category in Figure 4.5. Notice that the modular design makes it easier for us to locate a command in this list. We can expect the benefits of the modular design methodology to also be reflected in the user documentation. A modular documentation is a natural consequence of a modular design.

4.3. SPREAD SHEET

The benefits of using the top-down modularization methodology are even greater when applied to the command set of a spread sheet program. The number of commands here can well exceed a hundred. When all of these are considered for design as one module, it is quite difficult to ensure that each has been assigned a different name. Determining whether we have an adequate set of commands requires Herculean effort. Our task becomes much simpler if we partition the command set into logically coherent subsets. A possible partitioning is:

(1) cursor control

(2) insert (rows and columns)

(3) delete (rows and columns)

(4) copy cells

(5) move cells

(6) display format

(7) edit

(8) files

(9) recompute

(10) windows

(11) titles

Once this division of commands into categories has been done, we can more easily design an adequate set of commands. The design of a particular category of commands may be further facilitated by dividing it into logically coherent subcategories. For example, the display formatter commands can be divided into the subcategories:

Cursor control
→	move cursor one character right
←	move cursor one character left
ˆ→	move cursor one word right
ˆ←	move cursor one word left
L	move cursor to left end of line
R	move cursor to right end of line
↑	move cursor up one line
↓	move cursor down one line
<PgUp>	move cursor back one screen
<PgDn>	move cursor forward one screen

Insert text
IU	insert above cursor line
ID	insert below cursor line
IL	insert left of cursor
IR	insert right of cursor

Delete text
DX	delete character at cursor
DL	delete word left of cursor
DR	delete word right of cursor
DD	delete line at cursor

Place markers
PP	place marker
PM	move marker
PE	erase marker

Block movement
BB	begin block
BE	end block
BM	move block
BC	copy block

...

Figure 4.5 Modularized commands for the text editor

(1)   monochrome screen

(2)   color screen

(3)   printer

(4)   typesetter

As is the case of the text editor, decomposing the command set into logically coherent modules makes it easier for us to determine whether any class of commands is absent. It also enables us to design commands in smaller and functionally related groups. This should result in a richer, consistent, and better designed command set.

4.4. DATABASE MANAGEMENT

The concept of a relational database was introduced in Chapter 2. Let us explore the design of a software system that enables one to manage a database (i.e., a collection of relations). First, we need to know something about the environment in which this database management system is to be used. Suppose that the following requirements are placed on the system:

(1)   It is to be used in an interactive environment.

(2)   It should be possible to create reports using data from the relations.

(3)   The system should allow for the writing, storing, and running of programs that consist of command sequences that are often used.

(4)   Compounding of commands should be allowed for. So, for example, it should be possible to select all records in a relation that meet some criterion and display only certain fields (i.e., a projection) by using a single command.

Certainly, the above requirements leave us with much freedom in the design of the system. Following in a modular manner, we may decompose the database system into the following modules:

(1)   COMMAND: This module consists of all the commands that will be available to the user when he/she is working in interactive mode.

(2)   PROGRAM: This module provides all programming support to the user. In particular, a program editor and programming statements in addition to normal database command statements are to be designed in this module.

(3)   REPORT: The report module will consist of all capabilities provided to facilitate the generation of reports.

At this time, we have three functional categories to deal with.
We can devote some time now to see if any other functional categories
are called for. If we discover some now or later, these may be added
to the module set and designed relatively independent of the other
modules. Let us proceed with the command module. We need commands for each of the following functions:

(1)   Create a relation.

(2)   Insert new records into an existing relation.

(3)   Delete records and relations.

(4)   Display records and relations.

(5)   Copy records and relations.

(6)   Modify records and relations.

(7)   Join two relations.

(8)   Compute functions over values of record fields.

(9)   Sort records in a relation.

(10) Invoke and exit from help facilities.

(11) Exit from the database system.

While we have quite a long list of command categories, this list
is still a manageable one. At this point, it is still possible for us to
determine if any command category is missing or has been replicated.
One feature that is often provided in a relational database system is the
ability to index a relation on one or several of its fields. This is done
primarily to provide better performance. We shall not consider this
feature in our discussion.

Assume that we are unable to think of any additional command
categories at this time. Our next step in the design is to consider each
of the above command categories (one by one). This is done below.

CREATE
In this category, we can think of just one command. This command
will permit the user to define a new relation. The following information is needed for this:

(a)   The name of the new relation.

(b)   Number of fields in a record.

(c)   Name of each field. In this connection, we need to develop naming rules. How long can a name be? Must it begin with a character from the English alphabet? Are upper and lower case characters distinguished? What are the allowable characters in a name?

(d)   Type of each field. I.e., are the values assignable to the field integers, real numbers, dollar amounts, dates, phone numbers, social security numbers, character strings, etc.? At this time, we see a need to determine the allowable field types. Perhaps, in addition to certain system defined types (such as the ones just stated), a provision for user defined types is needed. The characteristics of each field type need to be accounted for in the remaining commands. For example, a date has associated with it a month, day, and year; a dollar amount consists of a dollar value and a cent value; etc. These characteristics may be used to check for input errors. The system may refuse to accept date data in which the month is not in the range 1 through 12. Similarly, dollar amounts in which the number of cents exceeds 99 may be ragarded as invalid.

(e)   Is there a default value associated with any of the fields? If so, what is it? We need to decide whether the system will permit only defaults that are constants or will also accept expressions composed of values of other fields in the record.

(f)   Are there any data integrity constraints in addition to those that are part of the data type characteristics? For example, in a particular application it may be required that a certain dollar amount field never have value in excess of $1000.

In addition to designing the exact format used by the CREATE command to get all the above information, we need to decide what action is to be taken when any of the following situations is detected:

(a)   A relation with the specified name already exists in the database.

(b)   A field name has been repeated in the record.

(c)   An unknown data type has been specified.

With the above discussion in mind, we can visualize our command to create a relation taking the interactive form specified in Program 4.1. Here, we have used programming language constructs to specify our design. Further refinement of this is needed to arrive at a program that implements the command. In addition to some of the obvious details, help files (both detailed and abbreviated) need to be designed. The abbreviated help file will provide such information as how to abort the command, back up to an earlier part of the interrogative process, and how to make changes in a response.

---

command *CREATE*
{Design specification of the command: *CREATE*}
begin
    if no relation name has been specified with the command
    then ask for a name;

    while name is illegal **and** command not aborted **do**
      provide user with naming rules and ask for a new name;

    if command not aborted
    then if name already exists
        then notify user that name exists and reinitiate
            name getting process
        else begin {creation process}
Determine whether record structure is to be obtained from some existing relation. If so, get the structure from this relation. Note that the relation may not exist and appropriate error recovery must be provided for.

if this is a new record structure **then** obtain for each field, its name, type, default, and integrity constraints;

Create an empty relation (i.e., a relation with zero records) having this record structure;
        end;
end.

Program 4.1

INSERT
The user may wish to insert records at a particular point in a relation. This requires the ability to specify both the relation and the position. We could require these to be part of the insert command as in:

INSERT INTO XX AFTER n

which has the interpretation: insert records into the relation *XX* after the *n*th record. In addition to the *AFTER* clause, we may wish to provide a *BEFORE* clause. Another desirable feature comes from the realization that users often do several things with one relation before going to another relation. Rather than require the user to specify the relation name on each command, we could permit the user to specify a default name. This is used whenever a name is not explicitly provided. For this purpose, we introduce a new command: DEFAULT to be used as in:

DEFAULT XX

This command can be implemented so that if *XX* is not provided, then the user is interrogated for the default relation name. Another useful feature is to allow insertion from another relation. With this, the syntax of the insert command becomes:

INSERT [INTO XX] [AFTER n | BEFORE n] [FROM YY]

In case there is no *INTO* clause, then the default relation (if any) is used. If there is no *AFTER* or *BEFORE* clause, then the insertion is made after the last record accessed by the user. When the *FROM* clause is absent, the new records are to be obtained interactively. We can free the user from remembering the order in which the *INTO*, *AFTER*, etc. clauses are to specified by accepting them in all possible orders.

The discussion of the insert command has brought up the concept of position in a relation. To manipulate this position, we need to define a set of position commands. We may add this category to our earlier list of command categories. Notice that in designing the command *INSERT*, we have actually combined several types of inserts into a generic command. The abbreviated help for this command will, at a minimum, display the above mentioned syntax as soon as the command *INSERT* has been typed by the user.

DELETE
This command category is to provide for the deletion of both records and relations. To delete a relation, we could use the format

DELETE XX

which causes the relation *XX* to be removed from the database. To facilitate the deletion of several relations with a single command, we could permit the use of wildcards in the name specification *XX*. For instance, if ? and * are two characters that are not permitted in legal names, then A??B would mean all names that are four characters long, begin with A, and end in B; A*B, on the other hand, could represent all names that begin with an A and end in a B (regardless of length). We leave the design of a suitably flexible wildcard scheme as an exercise.

To delete records, the following format may be used:

DELETE [FROM XX] [<Selector>]

where <Selector> is used to identify the records to be deleted. If the *FROM* clause is absent, the default relation (if any) is used. Useful forms of selectors are:

1.   Last *n*. Delete the last *n* records beginning at the present record.
2.   Next *n*. Delete the next *n* records beginning at the present record.
3.   Where *B*. *B* is a boolean expression involving the values of some or all of the fields in the records. All records for which *B* is true are deleted.

DISPLAY
The user may wish to display only certain fields (i.e., a projection) of certain records (i.e., a selection) of a relation. In addition, the display may be desired on the screen and/or on other display devices (eg., a printer). A possible syntax for the display command is:

DISPLAY [FROM XX] [*TO* device list] [<Selector>] [<Fields>]

where device list includes all the devices on which the records are to be displayed; <Selector> is as defined above for the delete command; and <Fields> has the format:

FIELDS <FieldName> {,<FieldName>}

A clause that we may consider adding to the display command is a *FORMAT* clause which permits the user to specify his own display format. When this is not specified, a default format is to be used. Hence, we need to design a default display format.

JOIN
The records from two relations are to be combined. The general format for this command can be:

JOIN [<Relation>] *TO XX* [<Selector>] [<Fields>]

If <Relation> is not specified, the default relation (if any) is used. *XX* is the second relation in the join. <Selector> controls the join. If this is not specified, then every record in one relation is paired (or joined) with each record in *XX*. If <Selector> is specified, then record *A* from the first relation is paired with a record *B* from the second relation iff (if and only if) the <Selector> is true for this pair. The resultant relation contains all the fields in the two input relations unless <Fields> is specified. In this latter case, only the specified fields are contained in the result.

Since it is possible for the two input relations to have fields with the same name, the syntax for <Selector> and <Fields> should permit the user to designate which relation he/she has in mind. An easy solution to this is to use the syntax:

XX.FF

to designate field *FF* of the relation *XX*. So, <Fields> takes the form:

<Fields> = *FIELDS* [<RelationName>.] <FieldName>
            {, [<RelationName>.] <FieldName>}

The above discussion should give you a good feel for the merits of the modular approach to designing the commands. We now proceed to the categories: PROGRAM and REPORT.

PROGRAM
The user programs will utilize the commands described above. In order to provide complete flexibility in programming, it is best to extend a programming language such as Pascal so that it recognizes

the database commands and performs these in an appropriate way. Thus, *CREATE, DEFAULT, DELETE, DISPLAY, JOIN, POSITION*, etc. become reserved words of the extended Pascal language in much the same way that **repeat, while**, and **end** are reserved words in standard Pascal.

To support the programming task, a program editor is also desirable. In addition, a command such as:

RUN XX

which causes the program *XX* to be run needs to be added to the set of interactive commands.

REPORT
To support the report generating needs, a text editor and formatter that support the importing of data from the database is needed. The formatter will recognize database commands, cause these to be executed, and put the results into the appropriate place in the report.

4.5. PROGRAMS

We have said much about the applicability of the top-down modularization methodology to the task of designing the user interface of a program but nothing about its applicability to the actual writing of a program. It is natural to expect the final program to mirror the methodology used in the design phase. If we have a flat design, then the resulting program is usually one long piece of code. The modularity of a hierarchical design translates into a modular program. The modularization efforts of the design phase compel us to develop the program itself in a modular manner.

Assume that the design phase has been completed and we are ready to write a computer program that implements this design. Having already spent much time refining the problem specifications and coming up with a satisfactory design, we are probably just itching to get our hands on a computer keyboard and begin coding a program that implements our design. If we are to have any chance of coming up with a program that will work eventually, we must exercise great restraint at this time and plan out the program before we begin to implement it in any programming language.

Consider our text processor design. At the root level, the text processor has been partitioned into the three modules: editor, formatter, and quit (Figure 1.2). It is natural to develop our program so that it reflects this modularization in the design. Hence, our program will contain at least four modules. One of these will correspond to the root module of the design. This module's primary function is to interrogate the user and determine which processor function he/she wishes to perform; verify that the choice is a legitimate one; and then invoke the program module corresponding to this selection. The remaining three program modules correspond to the three children of the root.

At this time, we can make implementation decisions that are global to these four modules without getting concerned about the implementation details of the lower level modules. We can make decisions about the data structures that are to be shared by the various modules. The text editor and formatter share the text file. If the formatter is to be able to perform its task, it must know the precise format in which the editor saves the text file created by the user.

All four modules can be expected to change the screen display. This is true for even the quit module which will clear the screen before exiting from the text processor to the higher level module (perhaps the operating system) that invoked it. We can identify useful screen manipulation functions such as: clear screen, turn screen scroll on, turn screen scroll off, locate the cursor, write a piece of text beginning at a particular position of the screen, clear rows i through j of the screen, etc.. Rather than write these for each module separately, we can lump them together into a fifth module called "screen utilities".

The program modules for the root, editor, and formatter will each have a need to get characters from the keyboard as these are entered. In fact, these characters may actually be entered faster than they can be used by the program. For example, a user who is very familiar with the editor might key in the selection

fr myfile<return>

without waiting for the abbreviated help menu for the file category of editor commands to be displayed. The user still expects the editor to read in the file "myfile". So, there is a need for a keyboard utility that accepts and saves characters as they are keyed in. Another useful utility is one that translates all upper case letters into lower case or all lower case letters into upper case. This will clearly make our menus and command selections easier. However, this translation should not be carried out during text entry. So, a capability to turn the translation on/off is needed. All keyboard utilities can be lumped together into a sixth module called "keyboard utilities".

The input/output specifications for each module must be provided. This is necessary as some modules will be used by others. For this, the precise function performed by the module being used must be known.

Now, we are ready to go deeper into the hierarchical design. Let us examine the editor module. This module itself is decomposed into several modules. The root module for the editor has the task of determining the command category and then invoking the appropriate command category module. If we identify functions that are common to the command modules (but not to the formatter and quit modules), then these can be put together into a new program module at this level. We should also make decisions about data structures that are common to the children modules of the editor. The deliberations that take place at this time might cause us to reconsider the more global decisions made at a higher level in the design hierarchy. Once, these decisions have been made, we can proceed to the next level in the editor hierarchy. Upon completing the program plan for the editor, we can continue with the formatter and so on.

Obtaining the program plan involves the following steps:

(1)   Determine the program modules for each level of the design hierarchy. We will, in general, have at least one program module for each design module. Additional modules that provide a service function to other modules may also be needed. These can be added to the design hierarchy to obtain the structure of Figure 4.6.

(2)   Determine the data structures and data representations that are common to the children of each node.

(3)   Obtain a precise input/output specification of each module.

Obtaining the program plan involves going up and down the design tree many times. Using the top-down approach, we will begin at the root and proceed downwards. However, some decisions made at a higher level may make lower level decisions impossible. So, it

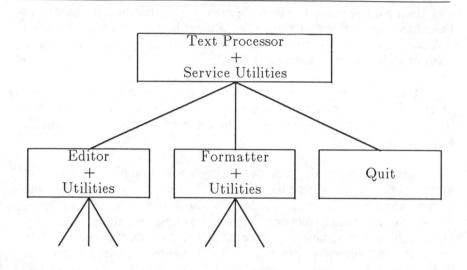

Figure 4.6 Module hierarchy with service modules included

will be necessary to backtrack up the tree and change earlier decisions.

Having completed the program plan, we can proceed to develop the program. At this point, we will be faced with the problem of deciding what syntactic form each program module is to take. Should the module be implemented as a procedure, a function, a block of code, or a collection of procedures? Consider the root module of Figure 4.6. We have several syntactic possibilities for this module. One possibility is to implement it as a single procedure *TextProcessor* that is itself comprised of one procedure for each module in the service modules and one procedure for each of the children modules. This will result in the program structure shown in Program 4.2.

Another possibility is to write the *RootModule* directly as the body of the *TextProcessor* as in Program 4.3. In this program, the function *Number* converts character information into its numeric code. In this program, *WriteMenu* is a screen utility that writes the specified menu onto the screen. Whether such a utility is useful or not will depend on the degree of homogeniety in the menus being used. We may need separate utilities for single column menus, multiple column

---

procedure *TextProcessor*;
[Declaration part of procedure]

{Screen utilities}
procedure *ClearScreen*;
procedure *WriteScreen*(...);
  ...

{Keyboard utilities}
procedure *ReadKeyboard*(**var** *x*);
  ...

{Functional modules}
procedure *RootModule*;
procedure *Editor*;
procedure *Formatter*;
procedure *Quit*;

begin {body of *TextProcessor*}
  RootModule;
end; {of *TextProcessor*}

Program 4.2

menus, and horizontal menus.

Yet another possibility results when we take note of the fact that the *Quit* module is sufficiently simple that it may be written as a block of code that is directly inserted into case 3 of Program 4.3. When this is done, we get Program 4.4.

The program modules corresponding to the editor and formatter are expected to be sufficiently complex and long that integrating them directly into the body of *TextProcessor* will significantly impair the readability of the program. So, these must be implemented as separate procedures. The option of coding a module as a block of code to be directly inserted as needed into a program should be considered only for short modules that are invoked from only a single point in the program. This option should be taken only if it results in an improvement in program readability.

```
procedure TextProcessor;
var x: char; done: boolean;

{Screen utilities}
procedure ClearScreen;
procedure WriteScreen(...);
procedure WriteMenu(x);
  ...

{Keyboard utilities}
procedure ReadKeyboard(var x: char);
  ...

{Functional modules}
procedure Editor;
procedure Formatter;
procedure Quit;

begin {body of TextProcessor}
    done := false;
    while not done do
    begin
      ClearScreen;
      WriteMenu(RootMenu);
      repeat
        ReadKeyboard(x); {Get menu selection}
      until (Number(x)>0) and (Number(x)<4); {Until valid selection}
      case x of
        '1': Editor;
        '2': Formatter;
        '3': Quit; {Quit sets done to true}
      end; {of case}
    end; {of while}
end; {of TextProcessor}
```

Program 4.3

```
procedure TextProcessor;
var x: char; done: boolean;

{Screen utilities}
procedure ClearScreen;
procedure WriteScreen(...);
   ...

{Keyboard utilities}
procedure ReadKeyboard(var x);
   ...

{Functional modules}
procedure Editor;
procedure Formatter;

begin {body of TextProcessor}
   done := false;
   while not done do
   begin
      ClearScreen;
      WriteMenu(RootMenu);
      repeat
         ReadKeyboard(x); {Get menu selection}
      until (Number(x)>0) and (Number(x)<4));  {Until valid selection}
      case x of
         '1': Editor;
         '2': Formatter;
         '3': begin ClearScreen; done := true; end;
      end; {of case}
   end; {of while}
end; {of TextProcessor}
```

Program 4.4

When writing the editor module, it is best to implement all command modules (except the cursor control module) as separate procedures to get the program structure of Program 4.5. The cursor control command module has been written as a block of code that is directly integrated into the editor body. Since there is no category selector for a cursor command, we will have to list all cursor commands in a case selector if the cursor control command module is written as a separate procedure.

---

procedure *Editor*;
var *WorkFile*: **file**; *done*: **boolean**;
    CommandSelectors, *CursorCommands*, *selections*: **set of char**;
procedure *SelectWorkFile*;

{Command and cursor control modules}
   ...

begin {body of *Editor*}
  done := **false**;
  SelectWorkFile;
  while not *done* **do**
  begin
    CommandSelectors := [I,i,D,d,P,p,B,b,S,s,F,f,H,h,Q,q,U,u];
    CursorCommands := [↑ , ↓ , ←, →, ...];
    selections := *CommandSelectors* + *CursorCommands*;
    {Clear portion of screen reserved for abbreviated help facility}
    ClearScreenTop;
    WriteEditorHelp;
    repeat
      GetKeyboard(x);
    until (x **in** *selection*);
    case x **of**
      'I','i': *InsertText*;
      'D','d': *DeleteText*;
      'P','p': *PlaceMarkers*;

       ...
      ' ↑ ': *CursorLineUp*;
      ' ↓ ': *CursorLineDown*;
       ...

    end; {of **case**}
  end; {of **while**}
end; {of *Editor*}

Program 4.5 Editor module

Generally, the readability of a program is enhanced by using the style of Program 4.3. The characeristics of this style that lead to this enhancement in readability are:

(1) The root module is implemented as the body of the program.

(2) Service modules that are placed in the root are implemented as a collection of procedures and functions.

(3) The children of the root are each implemented as a single procedure or function. The syntactic style is then applied recursively to these children.

Two exceptions to the general syntactic rule exist. These are:

(1) The root module itself may be further modularized in a second plane as in Figure 4.4. In this case, readability is enhanced by collapsing all the planes in the modularization hierarchy into a single plane as shown in Figure 4.7. The style of Program 4.3 can now be used on this single plane modularization.

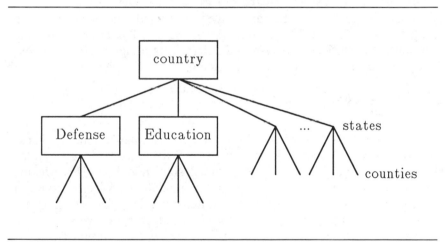

Figure 4.7 Single plane representation of Figure 4.4

(2) Directly coding very short modules into the parent module often enhances readability. This is especially true when these modules cause a "loop" in the parent module to terminate (eg., the *Quit* module of *TextProcessor*). Note, however, that a module that is invoked from several places in a program should never be

directly coded into each of these places. Doing this, severely hampers maintenance, as a change to the module requires changes to be made in many parts of the program.

Adopting a hierarchical modular program plan significantly improves the intellectual manageability of a program. It allows us to concern ourselves with coding details only as the need for these details arises. In order for this strategy to succeed, it is essential that the input/output specification of each program module be done in as precise a manner as possible. Further, each module must be implemented so that it strictly conforms to this specification. Any deviation from this can lead to disaster when the modules are put together to obtain the complete program. Modules that worked independently may fail to work as a team.

The modular program plan also suggests an organization for a team of programmers who might have been assigned the programming task. This team can be split into subteams with one being assigned the utilities and root module and the others each assigned a child module of the root. Each subteam can further split itself into subteams in a similar way. So long as each subteam rigidly adheres to the input/output specifications of the module(s) it is assigned, the independently coded modules will work as a team when put together.

4.6. SUMMARY

Well, we are at the end of our discussion on modularization. Perhaps, the concept of a module is still fuzzy. What exactly is a module? How does one partition a problem into design modules? How do the design modules translate into program modules? When should a module be further partitioned into children modules? These are questions to which one cannot provide formal satisfactory answers. All we can say is that a module is an entity that enjoys the following properties:

(1)   logical coherence

(2)   independence of functionality relative to other modules

(3)   intellectual manageability

There will generally be many ways to modularize a complex problem or program. One way may be more natural to one set of designers and another modularization may be more natural to another set of designers. So, it is not very meaningful to ask "which is the best modularization?". When modularizing, our objective should be to obtain modules that score high on the three criteria listed above.

4.7. REFERENCES AND SELECTED READINGS

The references for this chapter are generally the same as those for Chapter 3. Two relational database systems that you might wish to study are:

> dBASE-II, Ashton-Tate, Culver City, California

and

> Condor, Condor Computer Corporation, Ann Arbor, Michigan.

The query language QUEL of the relational database system INGRES can be embedded into many popular programming languages. This allows the user to utilize the full power of the database management system within his/her application. Information about this system may be obtained from INGRES, Relational Technology Corp., Berkeley, California.

4.8. EXERCISES

1. Complete the design of the text editor begun in Chapter 3. Proceed in a modular manner. You must produce a typewritten design document that contains at least the following:

   (a) Brief statement of the environment for which the editor is being designed.

   (b) A modularization tree for the command set. This should include all command names.

   (c) A description of each command. The descriptions should be organized by command modules.

   (d) Abbreviated help files for all command modules.

   (e) Description of any user install capabilities (eg. capability to rename commands or command categories, capability to set display colors for text and help files).

   Notice that the design document you are required to prepare is not the complete design document as discussed in Chapter 1. A complete document will include computer program listings, details of algorithms and data structures, test data, etc. Since you have not been asked to develop the complete program, this information is not available as yet.

2. Do the previous exercise for the case of the command set of a spread sheet program. In designing the commands, you may find it helpful to study some existing spread sheet programs.

3. Produce a design document similar to that of Exercise 1 for the case of a program that simulates a hand calculator. The minimal requirements for this program are:

   (a) It is to work in an interactive environment.

   (b) The calculator face (i.e., keys and display) must be displayed on the users screen at all times. The display part of this face must emulate normal calculator behavior.

   (c) The program must permit the user to select both function (+, −, *, etc.) and data keys (0, 1, 2, ..., 9) by pressing the appropriate keys on the keyboard of the computer (or terminal) in use.

   (d) You should add additional functionality to the calculator. Some possibilities are keys to find means, standard deviations, areas of common shapes, mortgage calculations, etc.

   (e) Help files must be provided.

   (f) An install program that enables the user to select different colors for different parts of the display must be provided.

   Your design document must contain complete details of all capabilities. Before beginning the design, you should study the behavior of some existing calculators.

4. Repeat the previous exercise for a programmable calculator. Once again, you may wish to study such a calculator before commencing with the design.

5. Design a software system that maintains an appointment calendar. In addition to the following, your system must provide at least two additional useful capabilities.

   (a) Your system must allow for entry, deletion, and editing of appointments for any date in the future.

(b) It should be possible to view the appointments for any day in the past, present, or future.

(c) A query capability that permits retrieval of appointments by content should be provided for. For example, it should be possible to ask questions such as "When is the next appointment with Mr. Joseph?".

(d) An on line help capability is to be provided.

(e) User installation of commands, colors, etc. is to be provided for.

6. Design a wildcard scheme to be used in specifying relation names. In addition to the capabilities mentioned in the text, this scheme should allow for the specification of names such as: any number of As followed by a C, XY(any number of CD's)ZETA, etc.

7. For the interactive database environment of Section 4.4, design a suitably rich set of commands for each of the following categories. Provide a BNF specification in cases where you elect to combine several functionally different commands into a single format.

(a) Copy records and relations. This should permit the copying of records and relations into new relations. The old version (if any) of the relation copied to is to be destroyed. As a precaution, you may wish to ask for confirmation before you destroy the old version. Copying of selected records and selected fields should be provided for.

(b) Modify records and relations. Record modification should be permitted on an individual basis as well as by a selection function. Record modification on an individual basis requires some primitive editing capabilities. Modification of a relation might include such things as: add a new field, delete an old field, change a default value or an integrity constraint, etc.

(c) Compute functions over values of record fields. Some useful functions are: mean, standard deviation, and sum.

(d) Sort records in a relation. Sorting may be into increasing or decreasing order of a field. Alternatively, a lexicographic sort on several fields may be desired. Another possibility is to sort on some function of the fields of a record.

(e) Invoke and exit from help facilities. This is generic for all commands.

(f) Exit from the database system.

(g) Positioning in a relation. The user may wish to reposition to the *n*th record, or to a record *n* records ahead or behind the current position, or position to the next or previous record that meets some criterion, or position to the last record in the relation.

8.   Design and provide a complete BNF specification for <Selector> (see Section 4.4 for details).

9.   Design a default display format for a relational database. You may choose a different default for screen and printer display. The primary difference arises when a record is too long to fit on a screen line or when the number of records is too large for simultaneous display on a screen. In this case, you may wish to provide the user with a capability to shift lines left, right, up, and down. In the case of a printer, all selected records must be printed in some suitable format.

10. Design a software system that develops and monitors basic vocabulary skills. You may assume that the target computer has a speech synthesizer that is capable of speaking out text and numeric strings. Your system should include the following components:

a)   A memory game in which the user is asked to repeat a sequence of letters. Begin with a sequence of size 1 and expand until the user makes an error.

b)   A spelling game that speaks out words and asks for the spelling.

c)   A pronunciation program that requests words or text and speaks it.

11. [Dekel] Design the human interface for the data entry function of a relational database. The main objectives should be to minimize the number of key strokes and hiding the complexity of the data base from the data entry clerk. By nature, in a relational database the same field entry can belong in several

tables or in several records. You can use the database example of Chapter 2 in your design.

12. [Rosier] Design a file migration/archival system for a computer system with many users. Seldomly used files are to be archived on realtively inexpensive storage media. Frequently used files are stored on on-line disk units. The user is to have the ability to cause a file to migrate to the on-line media or to archive it. Your system must provide a good user interface for this. In particular, you must have available a catalog of all user files. For each file, you must be able to tell the user whether it is currently stored on the on-line storage.

CHAPTER 5

AESTHETIC PROGRAMS

5.1. PROGRAM BEAUTY

Consider the following problem that is being faced by Mary.

> Mary intends to open a bank account with an initial deposit of $100. She intends to deposit an additional $100 into this account on the first day of each of the next 19 months for a total of 20 deposits (including the initial deposit). The account pays interest at the rate of 5% per annum compounded monthly. Her initial deposit is also at the first of the month. Mary would like to know what the balance in her account will be at the end of each of the 20 months in which she will be making a deposit.

Two Pascal programs to solve this problem are given in Programs 5.1 and 5.2, respectively. The corresponding computer outputs are, respectively, given in Figures 5.1 and 5.2. Even though the output from Program 5.1 can be verified as being correct, this program is aesthetically unsatisfying. In fact, if we were to wear our artistic programmer hat and look at this program, we would probably rate it very ugly.

```
line  program x(input, output);
  1   label 1,2;
  2   var x: real; y: integer;
  3   begin
  4   x := 100;y := 1;
  5   1: x := 241*x/240;
  6   writeln(y, x);
  7   if y = 20 then goto 2;
  8   y :=y+1;
  9   x := x+100;
 10   goto 1;
 11   2: end.
```

Program 5.1

The adage:
Beauty is in the eyes of the beholder.

is as valid for computer programs as it is for anything else. So, there are probably many programmers who will regard Program 5.1 as being at least as beautiful as Program 5.2. But then, these same programmers would probably pay $2 million for my art work of Figure 5.3. (Checks may be sent to me, care of The Camelot Publishing Company. In return, an original and signed version will be sent to you.)

In order that we may all start with some common notions of program beauty, let us simply agree that program beauty is measured by the following factors:

(1) ease of use

(2) comprehensibility

(3) aesthetics of the input and output.

Clearly, all of these are subjective measures and it is going to be extremely difficult to take a program and assign it a scientifically sound numeric score on beauty. Nonetheless, we can provide guidelines as to how to arrive at programs that will generally be regarded as beautiful. First, let us list below some of the reasons why Program 5.1 is dissatisfying while Program 5.2 is not.

```
line  program account(input, output);
 1    {compute the account balance at the end of each month}
 2    const  InitialBalance = 100;
 3           MonthlyDeposit = 100; {additional deposit per month}
 4           TotalMonths = 20;
 5           AnnualInterestRate = 5;  {percent rate}
 6    var balance, interest, MonthlyRate: real; month: integer;
 7    begin
 8        MonthlyRate := AnnualInterestRate/1200; {rate per $}
 9        balance := InitialBalance;
10        writeln('     Month     Balance');
11        for month := 1 to TotalMonths do
12        begin
13          interest := balance*MonthlyRate;
14          balance := balance+interest;
15          writeln(month:10,'    ', balance:10:2);
16          balance := balance+MonthlyDeposit;
17        end;
18        writeln;
19        writeln('Balance is balance at end of month');
20    end.
```

Program 5.2 Aesthetic account balance program

(1)   The chosen program name x for Program 5.1 gives us no information at all about what problem the program solves. On the other hand, the name *account* given to Program 5.2 at least tells us the program has something to do with an account. We could have been more obvious and called it *MarysProblem*, or *Marys-MonthlyBalance*, etc.

(2)   The comment immediately following the **program** statement for Program 5.2 makes clear exactly what the program does. No such statement exists in the ugly program.

(3)   None of the variable names used in the ugly program give any indication as to what they signify. For example, the variable x represents the account balance. But there is no way to guess this from the name x. On the other hand, the significance of each of the names used in the beautiful program is apparent from the

1	1.0041666667E+02
2	2.0125173611E+02
3	3.0250695168E+02
4	4.0418406398E+02
5	5.0628483091E+02
6	6.0881101770E+02
7	7.1176439694E+02
8	8.1514674859E+02
9	9.1895986004E+02
10	1.0232055261E+03
11	1.1278855491E+03
12	1.2330017389E+03
13	1.3385559128E+03
14	1.4445498958E+03
15	1.5509855204E+03
16	1.6578646267E+03
17	1.7651890626E+03
18	1.8729606837E+03
19	1.9811813533E+03
20	2.0898529422E+03

Figure 5.1 Output from ugly program

name. In case of possible ambiguity, a comment has been added (lines 3, 5, and 8).

(4)   The logic of the ugly program is relatively harder to discern because of the use of **goto**'s. The use of the control construct **for** in the beautiful program makes the logic of the program transparent.

(5)   By indenting the lines of code within the block of lines 7 through 20 (beautiful program), we have made it visually easy to identify the main body of the program. Furthermore, by indenting the lines of code that fall within the **for**, we have made it easy to visually determine the start and end of the **for** construct. No such visual aids have been used in the ugly program.

Month	Balance
1	100.42
2	201.25
3	302.51
4	404.18
5	506.28
6	608.81
7	711.76
8	815.15
9	918.96
10	1023.21
11	1127.89
12	1233.00
13	1338.56
14	1444.55
15	1550.99
16	1657.86
17	1765.19
18	1872.96
19	1981.18
20	2089.85

Balance is balance at end of month

Figure 5.2 Output from beautiful program

(6) Line 5 of the ugly program computes the new balance. Its correctness is not immediately apparent. This can cause difficulties in program comprehension. We may verify its correctness by noting that the monthly interest rate is 5/12% or 5/1200 = 1/240 per dollar. Consequently, if the balance at the start of the month is x, then after adding in that months interest, it will be $x + x/240 = 241 \times x/240$. In the beautiful program, the interest is clearly computed in a separate step (line 13) and then added to the previous balance (line 14). The correctness of these lines is immediate.

On the negative side, this improved clarity has been obtained by sacrificing some amount of efficiency. Computing

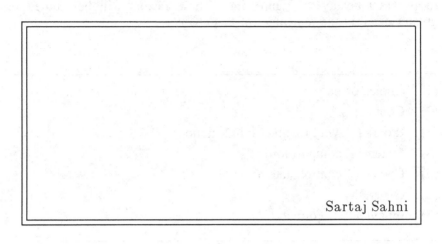

Sartaj Sahni

Figure 5.3 Untitled (and also blank) abstract by Sartaj Sahni

the new balance as in line 5 of the ugly program takes less computer time than computing it using lines 13 and 14 of the beautiful program. So, at times beauty might come at the expense of efficiency and we will have to evaluate this trade off. In this particular example, the expected difference in the computing times of the two programs is insignificant.

(7) The output from the beautiful program is easier to read. The output is clearly labeled and the balance is given in dollars and cents rather than as a decimal number with many meaningless digits of significance (Figure 5.1).

(8) The beautiful program uses constant names such as *InitialBalance*, *MonthlyDeposit*, *InterestRate*, *TotalMonths*. This introduces a certain degree of versatility (or generality) into the program. Perhaps after running the program, Mary determines that she can actually open her account with an initial balance of $200 but the additional monthly deposits will remain $100. To determine the new monthly balances, one needs to merely change the constant *InitialBalance*. In the case of the ugly program, we would have to go into the program body and determine where the

changes are to be made. This is considerably harder to do.

We summarize our observations about the factors that contribute to program beauty in Figure 5.4. These factors will be studied in greater detail in the remainder of this chapter.

---

(1)   Choice of names

(2)   Comments

(3)   Program layout (including indentation)

(4)   Statement composition

(5)   Choice of control statements

(6)   Generality

(7)   Input/Output Formats

Figure 5.4   Factors contributing to program beauty

5.2. CHOICE OF NAMES

As we have already seen, the choice of names significantly affects the comprehensibility of a program. By carefully choosing the names that we use for variables, constants, procedures, functions, etc., we can provide a great deal of information to the reader of the program. In fact, the names in use can be regarded as a form of in-line (though, perhaps, implicit) documentation of the program. Some guidelines for choosing names are:

(1)   **Choose meaningful names.** From the name it should be evident what quantity the name signifies. Some good names for commonly used quantities are:

average	*maximum*	*minimum*
profit	*loss*	*gain*
integral	*gradient*	*derivative*
InitialBalance	*InterestRate*	*FinalBalance*
deposit	*withdrawal*	*ServiceCharge*

Notice that the use of upper and lower case letters in the name *InitialBalance* has made this name considerably more readable than if we had used the almost equivalent name *initialbalance*. This more readable style can, of course, be adopted only if your Pascal compiler accepts both upper and lower case letters. In this book, we shall assume that your compiler permits the mixing of upper and lower case letters in names. Some more examples of improved readability using this style are:

CapSize	*vs*	*capsize*
LastIn	*vs*	*lastin*
NewEdge	*vs*	*newedge*
MergeSort	*vs*	*mergesort*

Notice that in the first example, we have some difficulty determining if *capsize* is to be read as the single word "capsize" or as two words "cap size". The correct interpretation will probably be obvious when the name is placed in the context of the problem being solved. Yet, it is much clearer to use the form *CapSize*.

(2) **Use easily recognized acronyms.** In other words, avoid the use of unneccesarily long names. The longer the name, the greater the chance of a spelling error. In addition, typing in a long name that appears 100 times in a program will be quite a bit more annoying and cumbersome than if an equally (or even slightly less) meaningful but shorter acronym had been used.

So, for example, the following acronyms may be preferred to the corresponding longer forms shown:

acronym	longer form
max	*maximum*
min	*minimum*
TotalInterest	*YearToDateInterest*
MortgageAt1203	*MortgageBalanceAt1203CheeryLane*
AverageScore	*AverageScoreOnTestConductedInRoom203*

(3) **Don't use similar and confusing names.** So, if we wish to compute the maximum age, weight, and height of the members of the Dallas Cowboys, then we can use the set {*MaxAge*, *MaxWeight*, *MaxHeight*}, or {*MaximumAge*, *MaximumWeight*, *MaximumHeight*}, or {*MaxAge*, *MaxHt*, *MaxWt*}. The set {*max*1, *max*2, *max*3} would be without immediate meaning and also be quite confusing because of the similarity.

(4) **It is allright to use short meaningless names at times.** Suppose we wish to sum the values in the array $a[1..100]$. The program fragment:

```
sum := 0;
for i := 1 to 100 do
   sum := sum + a[i];
```

is infinitely preferable to the program fragment:

```
sum := 0;
for LoopIndex := 1 to 100 do
   sum := sum + a[LoopIndex];
```

This is so even though the name *LoopIndex* is more meaningful than the name i. The use of the longer name *LoopIndex* is not justified as it is accepted programming practice to use short names such as i, j, k, etc. for loop indices when the loop index does not carry any significance to the problem. When the loop index does signify a quantity of relevance to the problem, the use of a meaningful name is to be preferred. This, in fact, is the case in Program 5.2 where we used the name *month* as the loop index.

Similarly, in a program, we might compute partial results for which we could have a very hard time developing meaningful names. In these situations, it is perfectly alright to use such names as x, y, z, etc. As an example, consider the problem of determining the roots of a quadratic equation. We are given an equation of the form:

$$ax^2 + bx + c = 0, \, a \neq 0$$

where the values of a, b, and c are known and we wish to determine the values of x for which the equations is satisfied. These values are called the *roots* of the quadratic. It is well known that there are exactly two (not necessarily distinct) roots which are given by the formula:

$$\frac{-b \pm \sqrt{b^2 - 4ac}}{2a}$$

Since $b^2 - 4ac$ can be less than 0, it is necessary to test for this before computing the square root. The use of the name x in the roots program given in Program 5.3 is quite acceptable.

(5) **Don't use names that are meaningful only to you** (because of your individual experience). Use names that are meaningful to the most general audience.

5.3. COMMENTS

As remarked in the previous section, implicit in-line documentation is provided by the very choice of names used in the program. The explicit in-line documentation of a program is comprised of its comment statements.

In Pascal, comments are provided by enclosing them in braces as below:

{This is a comment in Pascal}

Since many keyboards do not have the symbols "{" and "}", an alternate way to designate comments is provided. This consists of using "(*" and "*)", respectively, in place of "{" and "}". We shall use braces throughout this book as they are easier to use and cleaner than the alternate form.

line	program *QuadraticRoots*(input, output);
1	{Compute the roots of a quadratic}
2	**var** *a*, *b*, *c*, *root*1, *root*2, *RealPart*, *ImagPart*, *x* : **real**;
3	**begin**
4	**writeln**('Program to compute the roots of a quadratic');
5	**writeln**('Enter the values of *a*, *b*, *c*');
6	**readln**(*a*, *b*, *c*);
7	*x* := *b* * *b* − 4 * *a* * *c*;
8	**if** *x* < 0
9	**then begin** {complex roots}
10	*RealPart* := −*b*/(2*a*);
11	*ImagPart* := *sqrt*(−*x*)/(2*a*);
12	**writeln**('Quadratic has complex conjugate roots');
13	**writeln**('Real part is ', *RealPart*);
14	**writeln**('Imaginary part is ', *ImagPart*);
15	**end**
16	**else if** *x* = 0
17	**then begin** {one distinct root}
18	*root*1 := −*b*/(2*a*);
19	**writeln**('Only one distinct root', *root*1);
20	**end**
21	**else begin** {two real roots}
22	*x* := *sqrt*(*x*);
23	*root*1 := (−*b* + *x*)/(2*a*);
24	*root*2 := (−*b* − *x*)/(2*a*);
25	**writeln**('Quadratic has two real roots');
26	**writeln**('root1 is ', *root*1, ' root2 is ', *root*2);
27	**end**;
28	**end**.

Program 5.3 Quadratic roots program

Comments should be used throughout a program to improve its readability. If the answer to any one of the following questions is "No", then additional comments are called for. The additional comments should, of course, move us closer to being able to answer all these questions in the affirmative.

(1)   Is the task being performed by each program, procedure, function, block, and statement clear?

(2)   Is the meaning of every name (except possibly for those used for intermediate results that have no significance relative to the problem being solved and those used as indices of **for** loops) clear?

(3)   Is the computational strategy to be used clear?

If we ask these questions of Program 5.1, the answer is "No" to all three. Since this program solves a rather simple problem, the answer to question 3 will become yes as soon as we provide adequate comments to cause the answers to the first two questions to become yes. After adding appropriate comments, we get Program 5.4. Its readability is significantly better than that of the uncommented version Program 5.1.

```
line   program x(input, output);
  1    {Compute the balance in Mary's account for each of 20 months}
  2    label 1,2;
  3    var x: real; {account balance}
  4        y: integer; {month}
  5    begin
  6    x := 100; {initial balance}
  7    y := 1;
  8    {The annual interest rate is 5%. So the monthly interest
  9     on $x is $x/120. After adding in interest, the balance
 10     becomes $241*x/240}
 11    1: x := 241*x/240;
 12    writeln(y, x);
 13    if y = 20 then goto 2;
 14    y := y + 1;
 15    x := x + 100;
 16    goto 1;
 17    2: end.
```

Program 5.4 Program 5.1 with comments added

The readability of this program can be further improved by using blank lines to separate the logically different parts as well as the congested parts of the program (see Program 5.5). The use of blank lines for this purpose is recommended so long as this does not make the difference between that logical part fitting on one page and being split over two. It is much easier to comprehend a logical constituent of a program when you can see it in its entirety than when you have to keep turning pages.

```
line  program x(input, output);
  1   {Compute the balance in Mary's account for each of 20 months}

  2   label 1,2;
  3   var x: real;  {account balance}
  4       y: integer;  {month}

  5   begin
  6   x := 100;  {initial balance}
  7   y := 1;

  8   {The annual interest rate is 5%.  So the monthly interest
  9    on $x is $x/120.  After adding in interest, the balance
 10    becomes $241*x/240}

 11   1: x := 241*x/240;
 12   writeln(y, x);
 13   if y = 20 then goto 2;
 14   y := y + 1;
 15   x := x + 100;
 16   goto 1;
 17   2: end.
```

Program 5.5 Program 5.4 with blank lines added

Programs 5.2 and 5.3 are quite easy to read and the answers to the above three questions are affirmative for each. Yet, we can add more comments. This would be an overkill and doing so might even impair readability by introducing increased clutter as in Program 5.6. The comments added to the names simply restate the names and are totally redundant. Similarly, the comments added in lines 10, 12, 13, 18, 22, 24, and 25 are of no value as even without them it is obvious that this is what the corresponding line does. The comments added in lines 15 and 19 are of marginal value.

```
line  program account(input, output);
 1    {compute the account balance at the end of each month}
 2    const InitialBalance = 100; {initial balance}
 3          MonthlyDeposit = 100; {additional deposit per month}
 4          TotalMonths = 20; {total months}
 5          AnnualInterestRate = 5; {percent rate}
 6    var balance : real; {monthly balance}
 7        interest : real; {monthly interest}
 8        MonthlyRate : real; {interest rate per month per dollar}
 9        month : integer; {present month}
10    begin {program body}
11      MonthlyRate := AnnualInterestRate/1200; {rate per $}
12      balance := InitialBalance; {initialize}
13      writeln('      Month      Balance'); {Table header}
15      {compute table entries for each month}
16      for month := 1 to TotalMonths do
17      begin
18        interest := balance * MonthlyRate; {interest for month}
19        balance := balance + interest; {balance at end of month}
20        {output table entries for this month}
21        writeln(month:10,'      ', balance:10:2);
22        balance := balance + MonthlyDeposit; {add in this month's deposit}
23      end; {of for loop}
24      writeln; {blank line}
25      {output table footer}
26      writeln('Balance is balance at end of month')
27    end. {of account}
```

Program 5.6 Heavily commented version of Program 5.2

While the comments added at the end of lines 23 and 27 may appear to be of little value in this program, it is generally a good idea to clearly state what each **end** statement is ending. This is particularly useful when the corresponding **begin** or **case** statement is physically distant from the **end** statement and when the nesting pattern is such as to make it visually difficult to see the corresponding **begin** or **case** statement. When the nesting of **begin** and **case** blocks exceeds 3 or 4, it is common to have unmatched **end** statements the first time the program is written. Correcting this kind of error and even avoiding it completely becomes possible if all the **end** statements are properly commented with their corresponding **begin** or **case** statements. We shall see many examples of this as we go through this book.

When writing comments, be absolutely certain that the comment is, in fact, useful. We have already seen several examples of worthless comments. Let us look at the following additional one:

$i := i + 1$; {add one to i}

While we might all sit back and chuckle at this one, it is frequently found in programs. Coming up with suitable and informative comments is more an art than a science. When programs are developed using the top down programming methodology (to be discussed in a later chapter), many of the needed comments become available as a byproduct.

Before concluding this section, let us look at one more example of the subtleties involved in the choice of comments. The comment in the procedure:

procedure *CursorCharLeft*;
{Move the cursor one positon left if not already at left end of line}
.
.
.
end;

adequately describes the task performed by the procedure *CursorCharLeft*. For the procedure:

procedure *PolynomialAdd*(*a*, *b* : *polynomial*, **var** *c* : *polynomial*);
{Add polynomials *a* and *b* and return the sum as polynomial *c*}
.
.
.

end;

the comment adequately describes the task performed by this procedure. However, since the names in use are quite descriptive, the
shorter comment {$c = a + b$} is just as good.

In summary, comments are essential if a program is to be readable. When evaluating the adequacy of the comments in any given
program, one has to consider both the explicit as well as implicit comments present. It is just as easy to go overboard with ones comments
as it is to provide too few comments. Both being too generous as well
as being too stingy with comments impair program readability. If one
has to err, one should err in favor of generosity.

Finally, comments in a program are intended both for the author
of the program as well as for anyone else who may have to read it.
So, comments should be introduced the first time the program is written and not after the program has been debugged and is ready to be
released for use (or grading).

5.4. PROGRAM LAYOUT

By the layout of a program, we mean precisely where on a line does
each statement or statement component begin. Let us begin with the
convention that the **program** statement begins in column 1. Should
the comment (if any) that describes the program begin under the **p** of
the program statement as in Program 5.6 or under the **g** of **program**
as below?

line **program** *account*(input, output);
  1   {compute the account balance at the end of each month}

Indenting lines in a program, as above, may or may not improve the
readability of the program. Several experimental studies on the effects
of indentation on program comprehensibility have been carried out.

Some of these studies are cited in the list of references and selected readings that appears at the end of this chapter.

In this section, we shall examine some of the more common program layout (including indenting) practices and point out those that we feel are most likely to result in programs that are easy to read. First, we do not feel that indenting comments beyond the current indentation level improves readability. So, the positioning of comments as in Program 5.6 is to be preferred to the positioning suggested by the above indented example.

Next, consider the **label**, **const**, **type**, and **var** declaration parts of a program, procedure, or function. When labels are in use, the following layout is usually adequate:

label 10, 20, 25, 30, 40;

If the labels are used at parts of the program that have conceptual significance, the following layout is to be preferred:

label 10 {error trap for bad input},
        20, 30,
        40 {end of program};

Some Pascal implementations permit the use of alphanumeric labels. In this case labels such as *BadInput* and *ProgramEnd* can be used. These may be declared on a single line as no comments are needed to explain their significance. An alternate layout has the name **label** on one line and the actual labels on succeeding lines as below:

label
        10 {error trap for bad input},
        20, 30,
        40 {end of program};

This style uses one extra line and isn't any more readable than the one presented earlier. In case the label list is too long to fit on one line, then succeeding lines should be adequately indented so as to make it visually obvious that these are continuations of the label declaration part. An example is:

label 10, 20, 30, 40, 50, 60, 70,
        80, 90;

Generally, the same recommendations apply to the other declaration parts. Some examples appear in Programs 5.2 through 5.6. We shall see many other examples as we proceed through this book.

The statements within a **begin-end** block should be indented. An indentation of between 2 and 4 spaces gives the best results. Using a 0 or 1 space indentation makes it difficult to identify the start and end of the block (see Program 5.1). Using an indentation much larger than 4 spaces makes it difficult to locate the code within the block. As an example of this, consider the following layout:

begin

$$x := x + 1;$$
$$y := y - x;$$
$$z := z - x;$$

end

Another argument against indenting by too many spaces is that when the level of nesting increases, even short program statements no longer fit on a line. To avoid splitting program statements over lines at deep levels of nesting, one needs to indent using as few spaces as needed to get good readability. Otherwise, the negative effects of splitting statements over lines and of having the program snake too far to the right will outweigh the advantages of indentation. This is illustrated in Programs 5.7 and 5.8.

There are many acceptable layout styles for the **if-then-else** construct. These are illustrated below:

---

begin
        while *condition* 1 **do**
        begin
                while *condition* 2 **do**
                begin
                        while *condition* 3 **do**
                        begin

Program 5.7 Using a large indentation

---

begin
    while *condition* 1 **do**
    begin
        while *condition* 2 **do**
        begin
            while *condition* 3 **do**
            begin

Program 5.8 Program 5.7 with a smaller indentation

if x **then** $s1$ **else** $s2$;

This is a clear compact form to be used only when $s1$ and $s2$ are short simple statements such that the entire **if** statement fits on one line at the present level of indentation. Other possibilities when $s1$ and $s2$ are simple statements are:

if x **then** $s1$
else $s2$;

if x **then** $s1$
    else $s2$;

and

if x
then $s1$
else $s2$;

When $s1$ and/or $s2$ are compound statements with a **begin** and an **end**, some good layouts to use are:

if x **then begin**	**if** x	**if** x
.	**then begin**	**then**
.	.	**begin**
.	.	.
end	.	.
else begin	**end**	.
.	**else begin**	**end**
.	.	**else**
.	.	**begin**
end;	.	.
	end;	.
		end;

The first of these layouts uses the least number of lines but strings the **then** and **else** clauses farthest to the right. The third layout uses the maximum number of lines but keeps the **then** and **else** clauses as far to the left as possible (while still providing the needed indentation). The second layout falls between the first and third in terms of both horizontal and vertical spread. Depending upon the individual circumstances, it may be more desirable to conserve horizontal spread than vertical spread or vice versa. Or, conserving both might be equally desirable. So, there is a right time to use each of the three layouts shown above.

When the level of nesting is such that using the preceding indentation rules, it becomes necessary to split statements over lines, readability can be enhanced by using a temporary negative indentation as below:

```
                                        if x
                                        then
            begin
                .
                .
                .
            end
                                        else
            begin
                .
                .
                .
            end;
```

Finally, let us consider the practice of writing multiple statements on a single line as below:

$i := i + 1; j := j + 1; k := k+1;$

Is this any less or more readable than the layout:

$i := i + 1;$
$j := j + 1;$
$k := k+1;$

When the incrementing of i, j, and k forms a logically meaningful step in the program, this is more clearly represented by the one line layout. Even when the three statements do not form a logically meaningful step, the one line layout may be preferred as it is two lines shorter and just as clear. However, if the practice of writing as many statements as will fit on a line is carried to its extreme, we will end up with vertically compact but totally unreadable programs. As an example, consider the program fragment:

```
a := i + 1; b := j + 1; c := k+1;
i := i + 1; j := j + 1; k := k+1;
d := i + 1; a := j + 1; d := k+1;
i := i + 1; j := d + 1; c := k+1;
b := i + 1; j := a + 1; d := k+1;
```

When the program is very dense, as above, only a courageous programmer will wade through it. Further, writing multiple statements on a single line often inhibits the use of comments (as, if comments are introduced, then fewer statements will fit on the line).

To summarize, program layout affects the readability of a program. Readability can be improved by following the indentation guidelines provided. The value of indentation as a method to enhance readability diminishes when the nesting levels become large unless the program's horizontal spread is controlled by a temporary decrease in the degree of indentation. In particular, we should avoid the splitting of statements over lines that may result from excessive indentation.

Writing multiple statements on a line is an effective way to reduce the vertical spread of a program or program fragment. This is especially desirable when the program or fragment would otherwise cross a page boundary. However, this should not be done to the point where program readability suffers because of density and clutter.

5.5. Statement Composition

Each program statement should represent a logical piece of computation for the problem being solved. Line 7 of Program 5.3 is easily recognized by one familiar with the quadratic roots formula. Decomposing this into the seemingly simpler statements:

```
y := b*b;
z := 4*a*c;
x := y − z;
```

does not improve readability. It actually results in a program that is harder to comprehend. Similarly, consider the following program fragment:

```
x := n*n;
y := n+1;
z := y*y;
SumOfCubes := x*z/4;
```

This computes the sum of the cubes of the integers 1 through n, $n > 0$, using the well known formula:

$$\sum_{i=1}^{n} i^3 = n^2(n+1)^2/4$$

It is much clearer to write:

SumOfCubes := $n*n*(n+1)*(n+1)/4$;

As another example, consider the following statement which computes max$\{x, y\}$:

if $x - y < 0$ **then** max := y
        else max := x;

It takes some thought to verify that it is correct. The correctness of the following version is immediate:

if $x > y$ **then** max := x
        else max := y;

Often, one is tempted to combine several logical steps into one. The motivations for this include a desire to have a "shorter program" and a desire to have a program that runs "marginally faster". Suppose that the second quarter yield from a farm is known to be twice the first quarter yield; the third quarter yield is 1.5 times the second quarter yield; and the fourth quarter yield is the average of the second and third quarter yields. If the first quarter yield is *FirstQtrYield*, what is the total yield for four quarters? An easily comprehended program to compute this quantity includes the following sequence of statements:

SecondQtrYield := 2*FirstQtrYield*;
ThirdQtrYield := 1.5*SecondQtrYield*;
FourthQtrYield := (*SecondQtrYield* + *ThirdQtrYield*)/2;
TotalYield := *FirstQtrYield* + *SecondQtrYield* + *ThirdQtrYield*
                 + *FourthQtrYield*;

A one line program that computes the same total yield is:

TotalYield := 8.5*FirstQtrYield*;

It is much harder to see that this one line does, in fact, compute the correct yield.   Indeed it runs faster than the four line version and is much shorter.   If we choose to use the one line version, then its derivation from the problem statement must be well documented.

Parenthesize your expressions so that their meaning is clear. For example, the following statement:

x := *a*/*b**c;

will be evaluated by first dividing *a* by *b* and then multiplying the result with *c*.   This follows from the precedence rules of the programming language.   While rewriting this statement as:

x := (*a*/*b*)*c;

does not change the order of evaluation, it removes any doubt a reader of the program might have concerning exactly how the statement will be evaluated.   The inclusion of the parentheses has improved the readability of the statement.   Care must be taken not to go to the extreme of parenthesizing fully as below:

x := (((((*a*+*b*)+*c*)+*d*)+*e*);

This statement while leaving no doubt as to the order of computation is less readable than the equivalent statement:

x := *a*+*b*+*c*+*d*+*e*;

5.6. CHOICE OF CONTROL STATEMENTS

5.6.1. Control Statements

If a program consists solely of assignment statements, then execution begins at the first, proceeds to the second, to the third, and so on, until the last such statement is executed. So, when only assignment statements are present, the flow of control (or execution control) is sequential. The presence of input/output statements does not affect this sequential flow. A departure from this sequential flow of control can be affected by the use of *control statements*. In Pascal, the flow of control is affected by the following statement types:

(1) **if-then-else**

(2) **for-do**

(3) **while-do**

(4) **repeat-until**

(5) **case-end**

(6) **goto**

The control of flow patterns resulting from the first five of these control statements is best illustrated by means of flow charts. This is done in Figure 5.5. While the presence of procedure and function calls in a program causes control to temporarily shift to another part of the program, these statements are not considered control statements.

The control patterns shown in Figure 5.5 can be obtained by various combinations of other control statements. Some examples are shown in Figure 5.6. In fact, one can easily show that the two control statements: **if-then-else** and **goto** are sufficient to implement any control sequence possible. One can also show that the **while** construct is sufficient to implement the remaining five control constructs listed above. So, why bother with the other control statements? One answer to this question is that the readability of a program is significantly enhanced when the other control statements are used in place of their **if-then-else/goto** equivalents. Another is that it is easier to prove programs correct when the **goto** statement is not used. Notice that in the absence of **goto** statements within the body of the remaining control statements, each has a single entry point and each exits to the same statement. When all flow of control is performed by single entry

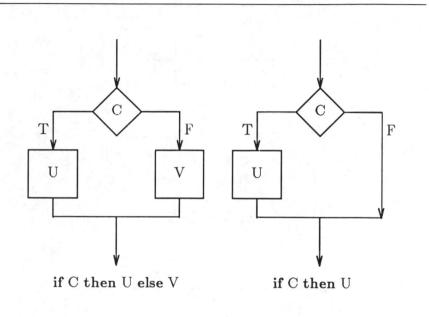

if C then U else V   if C then U

Figure 5.5 Flow charts

single exit statements, program readability and the ability to establish
correctness are enhanced.

Each of the control statements listed above has its place in the
writing of aesthetically pleasing programs. It is essential to use each
where each fits best and not attempt to replace the use of one by a
cumbersome use of another.

In the remainder of this section, we give examples to illustrate
the improvement in readability that results when the right control statement is used at the right place. There is no subsection on the use of
if's as we consider this a sufficiently primitive structure that everyone
might automatically turn to. This is also true of the **goto**. However,
indiscriminate use of the **goto** results in programs that look like a dish
of spaghetti. The flow of control is so interwoven that it is impossible
to determine what the program is doing. For this reason, we provide
guidelines for the proper use of this statement.

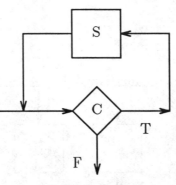

while C do S;

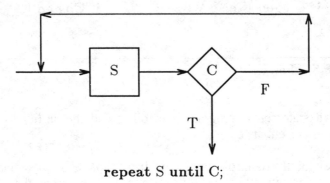

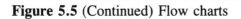

repeat S until C;

Figure 5.5 (Continued) Flow charts

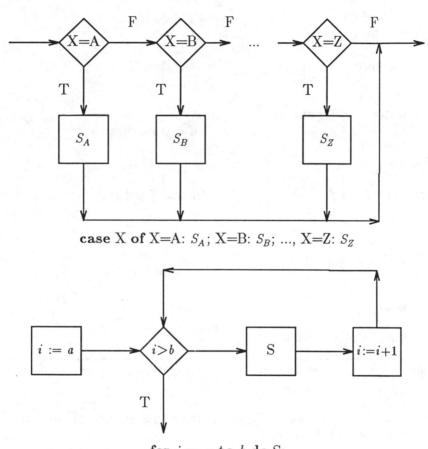

case X of X=A: S_A; X=B: S_B; ..., X=Z: S_Z

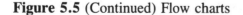

for $i := a$ **to** b **do** S;

Figure 5.5 (Continued) Flow charts

5.6.2. Using The for Statement

The **for** statement repeatedly executes a statement (or compound statement) for certain specific values of a variable (called the loop index). The specific values must be well ordered and the notion of next and

---

$Z := C$;
while Z **do** U;
while Z **do** V;

$Z := C$;
while Z **do** U;

(a) **if** C **then** U **else** V;

(b) **if** C **then** U;

10: **if not** C **then goto** 20;
    S;
    goto 10;
20:

10: S;
    if C **then goto** 10;

(c) **while** C **do** S;

(d) **repeat** S **until** C;

$i := a$;
10: **if** $i > a$ **then goto** 20;
    S;
    $i := i + 1$;
    goto 10;

(e) **for** $i := a$ **to** b **do** S;

Figure 5.6 Implementing one control statement using others

previous value must exist. Typically, the values are integers or values in some enumerated data type.

As an example, consider Mary's account problem of Section 5.1. The flow structure of the resulting program is well suited to the **for** statement. The use of **goto**'s to implement this flow structure results in a less readable program than when the **for** statement is used (see Programs 5.1 and 5.2). If the **while** or **repeat** constructs had been used, the programs of Programs 5.9 and 5.10 would have been obtained. Both of these are almost (though not quite) as easy to comprehend as Program 5.2. The efficiency conscious programmer might still find some virtue in Program 5.1. It is the only version in which the balance is not incremented by $100 an extra time in the end.

It is, however, better to perform this one extra addition than to incur the loss in readability.

```
line  program account(input, output);
 1    {compute the account balance at the end of each month}
 2    const  InitialBalance = 100;
 3           MonthlyDeposit = 100; {additional deposit per month}
 4           TotalMonths = 20;
 5           AnnualInterestRate = 5;  {percent rate}
 6    var balance, interest, MonthlyRate: real; month: integer;
 7    begin
 8      MonthlyRate := AnnualInterestRate/1200; {rate per $}
 9      balance := InitialBalance;
10      writeln('     Month     Balance');
11      month := 1;
12      while month <= TotalMonths do
13      begin
14        interest := balance * MonthlyRate;
15        balance := balance + interest;
16        writeln(month:10,'    ', balance:10:2);
17        balance := balance + MonthlyDeposit;
18        month := month + 1;
19      end;
20      writeln;
21      writeln('Balance is balance at end of month')
22    end.
```

Program 5.9 Account balance program using **while**

5.6.3. Using The while Statement

The **while** statement is to be used when we wish to repeatedly execute a statement (or compound statement) so long as a certain condition is true.

Suppose we wish to search the array elements $a[1]$, ..., $a[n]$ for the occurrence of the element x. Further assume that the position 0 is available in the array for use as we see fit. So, the array has been

```
line  program account(input, output);
 1    {compute the account balance at the end of each month}
 2    const  InitialBalance = 100;
 3           MonthlyDeposit = 100; {additional deposit per month}
 4           TotalMonths = 20;
 5           AnnualInterestRate = 5; {percent rate}
 6    var balance, interest, MonthlyRate: real; month: integer;
 7    begin
 8      MonthlyRate := AnnualInterestRate/1200; {rate per $}
 9      balance := InitialBalance;
10       writeln('     Month     Balance');
11       month := 1;
12      repeat
13         interest := balance * MonthlyRate;
14         balance := balance + interest;
15         writeln(month:10,'     ', balance:10:2);
16         balance := balance + MonthlyDeposit;
17         month := month + 1;
18      until month > TotalMonths;
19      writeln;
20      writeln('Balance is balance at end of month')
21    end.
```

Program 5.10 Account balance program using **repeat**

declared as $a[0..n]$. We are interested in writing a Pascal function that returns the value 0 iff x is not one of the elements in the array. If x is one of the values, then the function returns an index i such that $1 \leq i \leq n$ and $a[i] = x$.

We can simplify the problem somewhat by placing x at position $a[0]$ at the outset. Now, x is guaranteed to be one of the elements $a[0], \ldots, a[n]$. Everything works fine if we begin the search at n and work our way down to position 1. This might seem a natural place to use the **for** statement. Program 5.11 is a solution that uses the **for** statement and **goto**'s. A cleaner program (Program 5.12) results if we use the **while** statement instead. Using the **repeat** statement in place of the **while** results in a program (Program 5.13) that is almost as easy to comprehend but is somewhat less natural to develop.

line	
	function *search(a:elementlist*; *n*: **integer**; *x*: *element*):**integer**;
1	{search *a*[1..*n*] for *x*}
2	**label** 1;
3	**var** *i* : **integer**;
4	**begin**
5	*a*[0] := *x*; {initialize}
6	**for** *i* := *n* **downto** 0 **do**
7	**if** *a*[*i*] = *x* **then goto** 1;
8	1: *search* := *i*;
9	**end**;

Program 5.11   Search program using the **for** and **goto** statements

line	
	function *search(a:elementlist*; *n*: **integer**; *x*: *element*):**integer**;
1	{search *a*[1..*n*] for *x*}
2	**var** *i* : **integer**;
3	**begin**
4	*a*[0] := *x*; *i* := *n*; {initialize}
5	**while** *a*[*i*] <> *x* **do**
6	*i* := *i* − 1;
7	*search* := *i*;
8	**end**;

Program 5.12   Search program using the **while** statement

Next, suppose we wish to compute the squares and cubes of x for values of x ranging from a to b in increments of c. If $a = 2.0$, $b = 3.0$, and $c = 0.1$, then the values of x for which the squares and cubes are desired are: 2.0, 2.1, 2.2, ..., 2.9, and 3.0. A nice program results if a **while** statement is used as in the program fragment of Program 5.14. There is a great initial temptation to solve this problem using a **for** loop. To do this, we need to know how many values

---

```
line   function search(a:elementlist; n: integer; x: element):integer;
1        {search a[1..n] for x}
2        var i : integer;
3        begin
4          a[0] := x; i := n+1;  {initialize}
5          repeat
6              i := i - 1;
7          until a[i] = x;
8          search := i;
9        end;
```

Program 5.13 Search program using the **repeat** statement

there are in the range a to b. This is given by the formula $trunc((b - a)/c)$. Once we have figured this out, we can obtain the program fragment shown in Program 5.15.

```
{Pascal code to input a, b, c, and verify that a≤b precedes this line}
x := a;
while x <= b do
begin
    xsquare := x*x;
    xcube := xsquare*x;
    writeln(x, xsquare, xcube);
    x := x + c;
end;
```

Program 5.14

As a final example, consider the following problem:

> *Joe has taken out a mortgage on his house. The amount of the mortgage, interest rate, and monthly payments are known. The mortgage balance decreases by*

{Pascal code to input a, b, c, and verify that $a \le b$ precedes this line}
$iterations := trunc((b-a)/c) + 1;$
$x := a;$
for $i := 1$ **to** $iterations$ **do**
begin
  $xsquare := x*x;$
  $xcube := xsquare*x;$
  writeln$(x, xsquare, xcube);$
  $x := x + c;$
end;

Program 5.15

*the amount the payment exceeds the interest due. Joe
wishes to get a table that gives him the status of his
mortgage following each payment upto the time the
mortgage is paid off. This table should list the monthly
payment and the amount going towards principal pay off
and interest pay off, and the mortgage balance each
month.*

The most natural way to write the program for this problem is to
use a **while** statement to implement the iterative part as in Program
5.16. In order to use a **for** loop, we must know beforehand how
many iterations of the **while** loop body are needed. Alternatively, we
can set the loop for the maximum possible number of iterations as in:

for $month := 1$ **to maxint do**

and then exit the loop using an **if-goto** construct as in:

if $balance <= 0$ **then goto** 1;

Neither of these alternatives is appealing. The **repeat** statement could
be effectively used in place of the **while** in this example too. But, its
use here is less natural.

line	program *mortgage (input , output)*;
1	{Joe's mortgage problem}
2	**const** *InitialAmount* = 95000;
3	*InterestRate* = 10;
4	*MonthlyPayment* = 1000;
5	**var** *balance, interest, principal, MonthlyRate* : **real**;
6	*month* : **integer**;
7	**begin**
8	*MonthlyRate* := *InterestRate*/1200; {rate per dollar}
9	*balance* := *InitialAmount*; *month* := 1;
10	*interest* := *balance*∗*MonthlyRate*;
11	**if** *interest* >= *MonthlyPayment*
12	**then writeln**('Monthly payment not sufficient')
13	**else begin**
14	**writeln**('month':10, 'Principal':12, 'Interest':12, 'Balance':12);
15	**while** *balance* > 0 **do**
16	**begin**
17	*interest* := *balance*∗*MonthlyRate*;
18	*principal* := *MonthlyPayment* − *interest*;
19	*balance* := *balance* − *principal*;
20	**writeln**(*month*:10, *principal*:12, *interest*:12, *balance*:12);
21	*month* := *month* + 1;
22	**end**;
23	**writeln**
24	**write**('Your last payment should be less');
25	**writeln**(' by the amount shown as the last balance');
26	**end**;
27	**end**.

Program 5.16 Mortgage program

5.6.4. Using The repeat Statement

The **repeat** and **while** statements are quite similar. In fact, the following construct:

repeat
  S;
until *cond*;

is almost identical to the construct:

while not *cond* **do**
  S;

The only difference is that in the **repeat** construct, the statement (or compound statement) S is executed at least once whereas in the **while** construct it may not be executed even once. When S is executed at least once in the **while** construct, the **while** and **repeat** constructs are equivalent. Further, there is no significant difference in the readability of the two constructs and the choice becomes merely one of taste or which appears to be more natural in the given circumstances. Sometimes, it is more natural to think of doing something repeatedly until some condition is met. At other times, it is more natural to think in terms of doing something so long as a certain condition is satisfied.

The difference between the two constructs becomes important when it is legitimate for the program to not execute S even once.

5.6.5. Using The case Statement

The case statement is used when we wish to perform one of several actions based upon the value of some expression. Consider our text processor example of Chapter 1. Suppose that *command* is an enumerated data type with values being the screen editor commands (↑ , ↓ , →, ←, ˆ←, ˆ→, L, R, H, Q, etc.). After a new command has been read in, we need to perform the corresponding action. Assume that the new command is in the variable *c*. The necessary selection of action can be performed by using nested **if**'s as in:

if c = ' ← 'then *CursorCharLeft*
else if c = '→'**then** *CursorCharRight*
else if c = ' ↑ ' **then** *CursorLineUp*
else if c = ' ↓ ' **then** *CursorLineDown*
else if (c = 'H') **or** (c = 'h') **then** *help*
else ...

A much cleaner way to perform the selection is to use the **case** construct as in:

case *c* **of**
    '←': *CursorCharLeft*;
    '→': *CursorCharRight*;
    '↑': *CursorLineUp*;
    '↓': *CursorLineDown*;
    'H','h': *help*;
    .
    .
    .

end

The **case** statement of Pascal is not sufficiently general to permit its use in all situations where we wish to select one of several actions. A highly desirable extension to this statement is one which permits the **case** limb labels to be Boolean expressions as below:

case
    e1: S1
    e2: S2
    e3: S3
    .
    .
    .
    en: Sn
    else: Sn+1
end case

The **else** limb is optional (note that even the **else** limb is unavailable in standard Pascal). The corresponding flow of control is given by the flow chart in Figure 5.7.

As an example of improved readability resulting from the use of this form of the **case** statement, consider Program 5.17 which is a rewrite of the quadratic roots program (Program 5.3). This version is far more readable. The extended **case** is not available in standard Pascal, so we will have to be content with the less readable form of Program 5.3 which uses nested **if**'s.

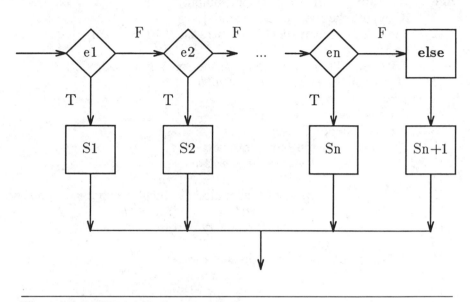

Figure 5.7 Flow chart for extended **case**.

5.6.6. Using The goto Statement

The **goto** statement has been at the center of programming controversy
for many years. As remarked earlier, its indiscriminate use results in
programs whose control structure is so intertwined as to resemble a
dish of spaghetti. This intertwining of the control structure makes it
excessively difficult to comprehend the program. Programs are most
easily comprehended when the flow of control is altered from the
sequential mode only by single entry, single exit statements. This
happens if we eliminate the **goto** from our list of control statements.

There are, however, exceptions to this. The **goto** is a very effective and transparent way to transfer control out of a position that is
buried in several levels of nesting to a position forward in the program
that is at a much smaller level of nesting. The use of the **goto** to
effect a forward move of this type is quite acceptable and will generally lead to programs that are easier to comprehend. This kind of

line	
	program *QuadraticRoots*(input, output);
1	{Compute the roots of a quadratic}
2	**var** *a*, *b*, *c*, *root*1, *root*2, *RealPart*, *ImagPart*, *x* : **real**;
3	**begin**
4	**writeln**('Program to compute the roots of a quadratic');
5	**writeln**('Enter the values of *a*, *b*, *c*');
6	**readln**(*a*, *b*, *c*);
7	*x* := *b* * *b* − 4 * *a* * *c*;
8	**case** {extended **case**}
9	*x* < 0: **begin** {complex roots}
10	*RealPart* := −*b*/(2**a*);
11	*ImagPart* := *sqrt*(−*x*)/(2**a*);
12	**writeln**('Quadratic has complex conjugate roots');
13	**writeln**('Real part is ', *RealPart*);
14	**writeln**('Imaginary part is ', *ImagPart*);
15	**end**;
16	*x* = 0: **begin** {one distinct root}
17	*root*1 := −*b*/(2**a*);
18	**writeln**('Only one distinct root ', *root*1);
19	**end**;
20	*x* > 0: **begin** {two real roots}
21	*x* := *sqrt*(*x*);
22	*root*1 := (−*b* + *x*)/(2**a*);
23	*root*2 := (−*b* − *x*)/(2**a*);
24	**writeln**('Quadratic has two real roots');
25	**writeln**('root1 is ', *root*1, ' root2 is ', *root*2);
26	**end**;
27	**end**; {of extended **case**}
28	**end**.

Program 5.17 Quadratic roots program

forward move is often desired when handling run time error conditions. This is illustrated by the example of Program 5.18.

The fanatic anti-**goto** programmer might attempt to restructure the program by introducing a Boolean variable *error* which is set to **false** initially and to **true** when an error is detected. This programmer would

---

```
program ErrorProne(input, output);
      .
      .
      .
   while condition1 do
   begin
      ...
      while condition2 do
      begin
         ...
         while conditionZ do
         begin
            .
            .
            if x<y
            then begin
                    writeln('Error ... x has become less than y');
                    goto 1;
                 end;
      .
      .
      .
1:end.
```

Program 5.18

then change all the conditionals in the **while** loops to:

(*condition*1 **and not** *error*)
(*condition*2 **and not** *error*)
      .
      .
      .

In addition, the **if-then-goto** statements that detect errors and cause termination will all be rewritten to include **else** clauses in which we will do what was previously being done when no error was detected. This will, of course, increase the nesting levels of the **if** statements and thereby reduce the overall readability of the program. Other changes may also be called for.

Consider the following program fragment (written in pseudo code):

```
if a then [write error; goto 1];
S1
if b then [write error; goto 1];
S2
if c then [write error; goto 1];
S3
if d then [write error; goto 1];
S4
if e then [write error; goto 1];
S5
if f then [write error; goto 1];
S6
```

If we attempt to avoid goto's, this code will take the form:

```
if a then write error
else
 [S1
if b then write error
else
 [S2
if c then write error
else
 [S3
if d then write error
else
 [S4
if e then write error
else
 [S5
if f then write error
else
 [S6]]]]]]
```

which is certainly less pleasing.

At times, we might wish to simply terminate the execution of the current **while** or **until** while we are in the middle of the loop. In this situation, our program fragment might take the form:

```
    .
    .
    .
while condition 1 do
begin
    .
    .
    .
    if condition 2 then goto 1 {exit loop}
    .
    .
    .
end; {of while}
1: S
```

Introducing the Boolean variable *done*, we can obtain the equivalent **goto** free version:

```
    .
    .
    .
done := false;
while condition 1 and not done do
    .
    .
    .
    if condition 2 then done := true
    else begin
        .
        .
        .
        end;
end;
 S
```

The use of the variable *done* in the **while** condition doesn't really tell us anything about what causes the loop to get *done*. It does, however, provide a signal that when we exit from the loop it is quite possible that *condition*1 is still true. So, both versions appear to be equally readable. The latter version is more amenable to standard program verification techniques as it does not contain a **goto**. Choosing between the two forms is purely a matter of taste. The prevalent trend among Pascal programmers is to prefer the latter form over the former.

The **goto** statement should be used with extreme caution. Its use is generally warranted only in the handling of exceptions such as errors and abnormal termination of loops and in cases where it is necessary to move forward out of several levels of nesting.

5.7. GENERALITY

"Generality" is concerned with the writing of programs in such a way that "minor" changes in the problem specification can be accommodated by "minor" changes in the program. Most often, generality is obtained by the generous use of constant names rather than constant values. Some examples will illustrate this.

Accommodating a change in the initial balance, or monthly deposit, or interest rate, or number of months in Mary's problem (cf. Section 5.1) is much harder when Program 5.1 is used than when Program 5.2 is used. In the latter case, the initial values assigned to the respective constant names have to be changed. In the former case, one has to examine the logic of the entire program to determine the necessary changes.

In programming a screen editor, one needs to know the number of characters per line and lines per screen on the display device in use. We have the option of using the numbers 40 and 25 for these quantities wherever they are needed in the program or using the constant names *LineWidth* and *NumberOfLines* instead. Using constant names (properly initialized in the constant declaration part of the program) is preferable as little change need be made when the display device changes to one with a line width of 80 (say).

Another place where program generality is enhanced through the use of constant names is the specification of array sizes. The size of various arrays in use is generally some function of quantities such as the maximum instance size to be solved, the amount of memory available, etc. It is better to use constant names for these quantities and then compute the appropriate functions that determine array sizes. This makes it easier to accommodate changes in the factors that affect array sizes. Ideally, a mechanism to determine array sizes at run time is called for (dynamic allocation of arrays). Thus, when 100 numbers are to be sorted, an array of size 100 will be established. When 300 numbers are to be sorted, the array size will be changed to 300. Unfortunately, Pascal does not support the dynamic allocation of arrays.

The key to generality is to parameterize to the extent possible. Use parameters (constant or variable names) where possible in place of numeric values.

5.8. INPUT / OUTPUT FORMATS

In designing the formats in which the program will accept input and provide output, one must know whether the source of the input and the destination of the output is a human or a machine. For example, if the input is coming directly from a human sitting at the keyboard, then informative prompts should be provided. Suppose we wish to input a social security number, the user should be informed that this is the input required at this time. All too often, the user simply sees the prompt "?" and has no idea what data the program expects at this time. Specifically, the line:

readln(*SSN*);

should be preceded by the line:

writeln('Enter Social Security Number');

Additional information, relating to input format is also desirable in some situations. In the case of a social security number, the user may wonder whether the number is to be entered with dashes as in 123-45-6789 or without dashes as in 123456789. Perhaps, a template with the dashes in place can be provided on the screen. Another useful piece of information to provide the user is the allowable range for the input. For example, suppose we are asking for the number of elements to be sorted. If our sort array has a capacity of 100 elements, then the user should be informed that only values in the range 0 to 100 are acceptable for the number of elements to be sorted.

When the source of the input is the program itself (as in the parameter inputs to a procedure), providing prompts is of little value as no one will see them. Another useful point to keep in mind when designing input formats, is to make these formats as natural for the user as possible. This should be done even if additional work is required of the program to change the format into one more suitable for internal processing. As an example, consider the thirsty baby problem of Example 2.3. Our solution to this problem may require the baby to drink the fluids in nonincreasing order of s_i/a_i until her thirst has been quenched. The resulting program becomes easy if we require the fluids to be initially ordered such that

$$s_1/a_1 \geq s_2/a_2 \geq s_3/a_3 \geq \cdots$$

This requirement shifts the burden of ordering the fluids onto the user as it is unlikely that the fluids will be so ordered in the original problem formulation.

You must avoid placing undue burden on the user to provide input in a form suited to your program. Rather, your program must request input in a form suited (or natural) to the user and then transform it into the form required by your program. So, in the thirsty baby example, your program should do the desired sorting.

When designing output formats, the difference between a human and machine destination is also important. It makes little sense to design easily read tabular output formats if the output is not to be read by a human. When the output destination is a human, the output must be neatly labeled so that its significance is easy to decipher. For example, the output of Figure 5.2 is easier to understand than that of Figure 5.1. Program 5.3 will create output that is easy to read.

It is often desirable to display the input as part of the output. This is particularly true when the output is being generated on a device (such as a printer or a disk) that permits the user to review it later. Since, the output will be read at some later time, the user may potentially have forgotten the input that was provided.

The design of good input and output formats is an art and often more time is required for this activity than for the development of the rest of the program.

5.9. REFERENCES AND SELECTED READINGS

Several rules of thumb that result in aesthetically pleasing programs can be found in the books:

The elements of programming style, by B. Kernighan and P. Plauger, McGraw Hill, New York, 1974.

Programming proverbs, by H. Ledgard, Hayden Book Co., New Jersey, 1975.

and

The programmer's book of rules, by Ledin and Ledin, Lifetime Learning Publications, California, 1979.

Three other articles of relevance to this chapter are:

On the composition of well structured programs, by N. Wirth, *ACM Computing Surveys*, pp. 247-260, Dec. 1974.

Structured programming with goto statements, by D. Knuth, *ACM Computing Surveys*, pp. 261-302, Dec. 1974.

and

Programming style: Examples and counterexamples, by B. Kernighan and P. Plauger, *ACM Computing Surveys*, pp. 303-319, Dec. 1974.

The results of some experimental studies of the effects of various forms of indentation on program readability are reported in the paper:

Program indentation and comprehensibility, by R. Miara, J. Musselman, J. Navarro, and B. Schneiderman, *Communications of the ACM*, Vol. 26, No. 11, Nov. 1983, pp. 861-867.

This paper also contains several references to papers that report on the effects of indentation on program readability.

5.10. EXERCISES

1.   Rewrite Program 5.19 so that it is aesthetically pleasing. This
     program solves the following problem:

> Let $a[1:m]$ and $b[1:n]$ be two nondecreasing
> sequences of numbers, $m \geq 0$ and $n \geq 0$. Let x be a
> third number. We wish to find a pair (i,j),
> $1 \leq i \leq m$ and $1 \leq j \leq n$ such that $a[i]+b[j] = x$.

Program 5.19 returns $(0,0)$ iff there is no pair (i,j) such that $a[i]+b[j]$
$= x$; otherwise it returns (i,j) such that $a[i]+b[j] = x$.

```
procedure GuessWhatIDo(a, b: ElementList; m, n, x:integer; var i, j:integer);
var done: boolean;
begin
i := 1; j := n; done := false;
while (i<=m) and (j>=1) and not done do
if a[i]+b[j] = x then done := true
else if a[i]+b[j] < x then i := i+1
else j := j-1;
if not done then begin
i := 0; j := 0;
end;
end. {of GuessWhatIDo}
```

Program 5.19

---

2.   Rewrite Program 5.20 so that it is aesthetically pleasing. This
     program generates all permutations of the characters in the string
     a. n is the length of a. $zap(a, k, i)$ swaps the kth and ith char-
     acters of a. The initial call is $mystery(a, 1, n)$.

3.   Show how each of the following control constructs may be simu-
     lated using only **while** statements:
     a)   **for-do**
     b)   **while-do**

```
procedure mystery(a: CharList; k, n:integer);
var i: integer;
begin
if k=n then WriteOut(a)
else
for i := k to n do
begin
zap(a, k, i);
mystery(a, k+1, n);
end;
end; {of mystery}
```

Program 5.20 Recursive permutation generator

    c) **repeat-until**

    d) **case-end**

4.   Use the guidelines of this chapter to obtain an aesthetically pleasing Pascal program for each of the following tasks. You will need to use the principles of the earlier chapters to design the program.

    a) Input numbers and compute their average.

    b) Input numbers and compute their standard deviation.

    c) Play the word game: hangman. In this game, the computer selects a word and tells the player the number of letters in this word. The player has to guess the word. At any time, the player can guess either a single letter or the entire word. The player is allowed to make at most 10 erroneous letter guesses before he/she is hanged.

    d) Input data for the thirsty baby problem (Example 2.3) and provide a solution as suggested in Section 5.8.

    e) Input a date and output the day of the week this date falls (or fell) on.

    f) Input two dates and output the number of days between them.

g)   Input the lengths of the three sides of a triangle and output
its area as computed by the formula:

$$area = \sqrt{s(s-a)(s-b)(s-c)}$$

where a, b, and c are the three lengths and s is
$(a + b + c)/2$.

5.   Write an aesthetic program that inputs an integer and writes it out
in words in one of three languages. The output language should
be user selectable. For example, if the selected output language
is English and the input is 25, the output is "twenty five".

6.   Use the guidelines developed so far in this book to obtain a program that translates between roman and arabic numerals.

7.   Repeat the previous exercise for a program to translate the time
of day between the 12 hour and 24 hour systems.

CHAPTER 6

DEFENSIVE PROGRAMMING

6.1. INTRODUCTION

A program is said to terminate *gracefully* on a given set of inputs iff the following arc valid.

(a) It terminates

(b) If the program is successful, the correct answers are output

(c) If the program is unsuccessful, appropriate messages as to the cause of failure are output.

Good programs terminate gracefully no matter what data the user might subject them to.

Even experienced programmers often write programs that terminate gracefully only when "normal" input data is presented to the program. For example, a procedure to sort numbers might work whenever at least 2 numbers are to be sorted. When this procedure is asked to sort 0 or 1 numbers, then the results are catastrophic. Since the procedure will seldom be invoked when fewer than two numbers are to be sorted, its catastrophic behavior on this kind of input will rarely be observed.

Many programs that are logically sound fail once in a while. There are three common causes for this occasional aberrant behavior of otherwise "healthy" programs. These are:

(1)   Input errors

(2)   Numerical errors

(3)   Boundary errors

These causes and methods to defend against them are the subject of this chapter.

6.2.   Input Errors

Often, programs work well so long as the user makes no mistakes in entering the data. Unfortunately, incorrect input will be presented to the program once in a while.

Some examples of incorrect input being provided to a program are:

(1)   Our text editor in command mode might get the input "ZZ" which corresponds to no valid command.

(2)   A search program might be asked to search for x in a list containing -5 elements.

(3)   A procedure to input a vector of size n may be given a value of n that exceeds the size of the input array.

(4)   When inputting a numeric quantity, an alphanumeric quantity might be provided.

(5)   There may be insufficient input.

(6)   The program expects input in a different order from the one in which it is provided.

The arrogant programmer is a staunch supporter of the GIGO (garbage in garbage out) philosophy. This kind of programmer is often overheard repeating the following quote to his/her users:

If you can't give me valid input, you deserve what my program does to you.

In fact the arrogant programmer's program might do any one of the following when presented with bad input:

(1) The text editor on getting the command ZZ might simply erase the users work file (or at the very least insert some lines of garbage) and then abort.

(2) On getting the invalid command ZZ, the text processor might cause the computer to hang. The only way to recover from this may be to reboot the system.

(3) The search program might run indefinitely whenever the size of the element list is negative. Or, the run time error capabilities of the compiler used might cause an error such as "array subscript out of range" to be generated.

(4) The vector input program might proceed to read in n values. This could cause an array subscript error to be generated. If run time checking of array subscripts is not being performed, the extra elements will get read into memory spaces assigned to other arrays and variables. Perhaps even some of the memory assigned to the program instructions will get overwritten leading to more catastrophic conditions.

(5) When the program gets alphanumeric data in place of the expected numeric data, it might generate an obscure error and then abort. If integer input is expected and real data is provided, it might round or truncate the input.

(6) If there are insufficient data, the program might just sit there and wait indefinitely for more data to be entered. Or, if an end of file has been sensed, it might assume that the remaining values are 0 and proceed. Alternatively, the problem size might be scaled down so that the presented data is sufficient for the smaller problem. Of course, all this will be done without informing the user.

The arrogant programmer's objective in taking each of the above actions is to surprise the user as much as the user has surprised his/her program. Several medieval quotes can be used to describe this attitude:

(1) Tit for tat

(2) An eye for an eye

(3) A tooth for a tooth

Medieval programmers are following the path of medieval ways into extinction. Medieval programming practices were the norm when programming was in its infancy. During this period, users were by and large themselves programmers. The "do unto others as they do unto you" adage was used to justify arrogant programming attitudes. With a significant increase in the number of nonprogrammers who use computers and with the ever increasing complexity of programs, the medieval programmer has steadily lost his/her user base. There is no place in the software market for software produced by arrogant medieval programmers.

Contemporary successful programmers need to be humble and strict believers of the principle "to forgive is divine". Programs written by a humble programmer will respond to the above input error situations as below:

(1) When the text processor gets the invalid command ZZ, it first causes the user's terminal or microcomputer to beep (i.e., an audio signal to alert the user is generated). An error message such as:

   *** ERROR ... ZZ is not a valid editor command ***

   PRESS <esc> key when you have read this message

is displayed. The message is displayed prominantly. This is accomplished by displaying the message in a different color from that used in the remainder of the screen (this option is possible only on a color display), or by using a higher intensity (only possible on displays that have different levels of display intensity), or by blanking out the screen and just displaying the message, or by flashing the message on and off, etc.

   By insisting that the user respond by pressing the escape key, one can ensure that the user has, in fact, read the message and is aware that the command entered did not succeed. Introducing this defense into the text editor program, Program 4.5, is quite easy. Most of the work has already been done. All that remains is to add in Pascal code to write out the error message and provide an audio alert signal.

   It is good programming practice to perform a case selector check before each **case** statement. These checks can be omitted only when the logic of the program is such that an invalid case selector value is impossible. For example, the case selector might be computed by a procedure that generates valid selector values only.

(2) The vector read program inputs n and then verifies that it is in the right range. If not, the program asks for a new value or authorization to abort. So, the vector read program contains code such as in Program 6.1. Requiring a specific input like -5 to abort is better than simply accepting any negative value for this purpose. The chances of the user entering a -5 by mistake are much smaller than his/her entering any negative number by mistake. Better still, the program can ask the user to enter $<esc>$ to abort. This certainly carries greater significance.

Another possibility is to limit the number of times the user can try to input a valid value for n to something like 5 or 10. Following this many attempts, the program aborts.

```
done := false;
writeln('Enter the vector size and press return when done');
while not done do
begin
    writeln('Vector size must be between 0 and ', maxsize);
    writeln('Enter a vector size of −5 to abort');
    readln(n);
    if ((n = −5) or ((n >= 0) and (n <= maxsize))
    then done := true
    else
    begin
        beep(1.0);  {1 second audio signal}
        writeln(n, ' is an invalid value for the vector size');
    end;  {of else and if}
end;  {of while}
if n = −5 then goto 999;  {999 is end of program}
```

Program 6.1 Verifying Input

(3) When programming in a language such as Pascal, it is difficult to handle an error caused by a difference in the type of input and type of input variable. Ideally, we would like to be able to say something like:

```
ErrorFlag := false;
OnInputError Set ErrorFlag = true;
                and writeln(x, y, 'Invalid input');
repeat
   readln(x, y);
until (not ErrorFlag);
```

We shall have to be content with the run time error diagnostics provided by the Pascal system in use or read all inputs as text and make our own translations.

(4)   When insufficient data have been provided, the program beeps the user and requests more data. An indication of how much more data is required is provided and the user is given the option of aborting while saving any results obtained so far.

(5)   To prevent errors resulting from data being input in the wrong order, the program requests data by providing a description of the data to be input. For example, rather than request a social security number and phone number by simply using the statement:

```
readln(SSN, PHONE);
```

we could use the sequence:

```
writeln('Enter social security number');
readln(SSN);
writeln('Enter phone number');
readln(PHONE);
```

As in the case of in-line documentation, one can go overboard in protecting against input errors. All our examples have dealt with explicit errors in the input only. There may be errors in the input that can be detected only after some computation has been performed. For example, a divisor might become zero. To guard against this, it is necessary to check the divisor before the division is performed. When this practice is carried to its natural extreme, every subscript is checked before it is used, every value computed in the program is checked before being assigned to another variable, every division is preceded by a check for a zero divisor, etc. The result is a program that is many times longer than is necessary; that runs several times slower than it would without these checks; and that is of diminished comprehensibility. So, it is necessary to find a happy balance between the two extremes of checking for input errors. At a minimum, input

errors that are detectable with little computation should be checked for.
One example of this is verifying that $a \neq 0$ in the quadratic roots program (Program 5.3). While $a \neq 0$ is part of the problem specification,
it is quite possible for the user to erroneously provide this value for
a. Program 5.3 will terminate ungracefully when this happens. This
ungraceful termination can be avoided at little expense.

6.3. Numerical Errors

6.3.1. Introduction

Programs that are known to terminate on a variety of test data may fail
to terminate once in a while because of *numerical errors* caused by the
computer's inability to represent real numbers with complete accuracy.
While virtually all computers represent numbers using the binary system (the only digits used are 0 and 1), we shall illustrate the causes
and effects of numerical errors using the more familiar decimal system.

6.3.2. Representational Errors

In the *decimal system*, numbers are represented as a sequence of digits
in the range 0 through 9. These digits are called *decimal digits*. The
number "six hundred and twenty five" has the representation 625.
This representation is a sequence of three digits 6, 2, and 5. The
number represented by 625 is obtained by adding together the least
significant digit (5), ten times the next significant digit (2), and one
hundred times the most significant digit (6). Numbers represented in
the decimal system generally include a *decimal point* and have the
form:

$$i_j i_{j-1} \cdots i_0 . f_1 f_2 \cdots$$

where the i_k's and f_k's are decimal digits.

We shall explicitly consider nonnegative numbers only. Negative
numbers just require the addition of the symbol "$-$" in front of the
representation of their magnitude. The number represented by the
above sequence of decimal digits is given by the formula:

$$\sum_{k=0}^{j} i_k 10^k + \sum_{k \geq 1} f_k 10^{-k}$$

10 is called the *base* or *radix* of the decimal number system. $\sum_{k=0}^{j} i_k 10^k$ is the *integer* part of the number represented and $\sum_{k\geq1} f_k 10^{-k}$ is the *fractional* part.

There is nothing sacred about using the decimal system to represent numbers. Numbers can be represented just as well using other bases or radices. If the base b is used, then the digits 0 through $(b-1)$ are used in the representation. In the *binary system* which is employed by most computers, the base $b = 2$ is used.

$(i_j i_{j-1} \cdots i_0 . f_1 f_2 ...)_b$ is the base b representation of the number:

$$\sum_{k=0}^{j} i_k b^k + \sum_{k\geq1} f_k b^{-k}$$

For example, $(123)_{16}$ represents the number $16^2 + 2*16 + 3 = $ "two hundred and ninety one" $= (291)_{10}$; $(123)_8 = 8^2 + 2*8 + 3 = $ "eighty three" $= (83)_{10}$; $(1011)_2 = 2^3 + 0*2^2 + 2 + 1 = $ "eleven" $= (11)_{10}$; and $(10.1)_2 = 2 + 0 + 1/2 = $ "two and a half" $= (2.5)_{10}$.

$(i_j i_{j-1} \cdots i_0 . f_1 f_2 ...)_b$ is the *floating point* representation base b of the number it represents. "." is called the *base b point*. When $b = 10$, it is a decimal point; when $b = 2$, it is a binary point; etc.

Personkind has used many different number systems over its history. Some vestiges of these remain today. For instance, the use of the base 60 is manifested in the division of hours into minutes and minutes into seconds. The base 60 number system (*sexagesimal* system) was used by the Babylonians as early as the year 2250 BC.

In a computer, real numbers are typically represented using the *normalized floating point representation*. In this representation, each number (except zero) has the format:

$$\pm .d_1 d_2 \cdots \text{E} \pm e_j e_{j-1} \cdots e_0$$

where $d_1 \neq 0$ (unless $d_1 = d_2 = \cdots = 0$), each d_k and e_k is in the range 0 through $(b-1)$, $d_1 d_2 \cdots$ is called the *mantissa*, and $\pm e_j e_{j-1} \cdots e_0$ is the *exponent*. The number represented is:

$$\pm (\sum_{k\geq1} d_k b^{-k}) * b^e$$

where e is the exponent:

$$\pm \sum_{k=0}^{j} e_k b^k$$

The normalized floating point representation base 10 of several numbers is given below.

one hundred twenty five	$+.125 \text{ E} +3$
minus six point nine	$-.69 \text{ E} +1$
zero point zero four two	$+.42 \text{ E} -1$
minus fifty four point two	$-.542 \text{ E} +2$
minus one over 20	$-.5 \text{ E} -1$

One should have no difficulty in obtaining the normalized floating point representation of a number from its unnormalized representation.

Let us consider the question: "Does every number have a normalized floating point representation base b that contains a finite number of digits in the mantissa?". Numbers that can be so represented are said to have an *exact finite represenation base b*. For every base b, the answer to the preceding question is "No". Consider the representation of fractions by decimal numbers. Some fractions that can be represented exactly using a finite number of decimal digits are:

$1/2 = 0.5$
$1/4 = 0.25$
$1/5 = 0.2$
$1/8 = 0.125$
$12345678/100000000 = 0.12345678$

The fractions below have no exact representation using a finite number of decimal digits:

$1/3 = 0.333333333333...$
$1/6 = 0.166666666666...$
$1/7 = 0.142857142857...$
$1/9 = 0.111111111111...$

Note also that fractions that have an exact finite representation in one number system may not have such a representation in another number system. For example, $1/10 = (.1)_{10} = (.0\,0011\,0011\,\cdots)_2$.

The very fact that a floating point representation is used for numbers implies that there will be inaccuracies in the representation of certain numbers. The results of computations such as:

$x := 1/3;$
$y := sqrt(2);$

will be stored inaccurately. This representational problem is compounded by the fact that a computer represents only a fixed number, δ, of digits from the mantissa. While these digits will generally be binary digits, suppose for a moment that we have a decimal computer. Further assume that this computer keeps only eight decimal digits in the mantissa The fractions $1/2$, $1/4$, $1/5$, $1/8$, $12345678/100000000$ can all be stored accurately. The fractions $1/3$, $1/6$, $1/7$, and $1/9$ cannot. We can only store an approximation to these numbers.

There are two common ways to arrive at the approximation to use. The first of these is called *truncation*. In this method, the excess digits are simply discarded. Figure 6.1 shows the representation of various fractions on a decimal computer that has 1, 2, 4, and 8 digits in the mantissa. Trailing zeroes are omitted for clarity. In addition, we have omitted the sign and exponent parts. All signs are "+" and all exponents are "0". As can be seen, the accuracy of representation decreases with the number of digits. When only one digit is used, the representation of even fractions such as $1/4$ has an inaccuracy.

How much error is introduced when truncation is used? We are generally interested in two measures of the error: *absolute* and *relative*. Let r denote the number we wish to represent and let r' denote its approximation. So, when $r = 1/9$ and $\delta = 2$, $r' = .11$. The absolute error in the representation of r is defined to be $|r - r'|$. We can see that when truncation is used, the absolute error is no more than $|r|*b^{1-\delta}$. The relative error in the representation of r is given by the ratio:

$$\frac{|r - r'|}{|r|}$$

When truncation is used, this error is no more than $b^{1-\delta}$.

Fraction	Truncated representation			
	Number of digits			
	1	2	4	8
1/2	.5	.5	.5	.5
1/3	.3	.33	.3333	.33333333
1/4	.2	.25	.25	.25
1/5	.2	.2	.2	.2
1/6	.1	.16	.1666	.16666666
1/7	.1	.14	.1428	.14285714
1/8	.1	.12	.125	.125
1/9	.1	.11	.111	.11111111
12345678/100000000	.1	.12	.1234	.12345678

Figure 6.1 Truncated representations of fractions

So, if $b = 10$ and $\delta = 5$, the relative error in the representation of a number is at most $.0001 = .01\%$. The absolute error is no more than $.0001*|r|$.

The second approximation method is *rounding*. In this method, we add $0.5E-\delta$ to the mantissa and then truncate the excess digits. This addition might require us to increase the exponent by 1. So, if we are going to keep only two digits, then $.125$ will round to $.13$ and $.14285$ will round to $.14$. $.995$ will round to $.1$ and the exponent will increase by 1. Figure 6.2 shows the representations of the fractions of Figure 6.1 when rounding is used. One may verify that the bounds on the absolute and relative errors in the representation of a number when rounding is used are one half of the corresponding bounds when truncation is used.

The effect of representational errors on the results from our programs is best seen by an example. Consider Program 6.2. This program starts with $x = 0$ and repeatedly adds 0.2 to it. The value of x is written out after each set of 10 such additions. Elementary mathematics tells us that adding 0.2 to x 10 times should increase its value by 2.0. So, we "expect" 20 lines of output from within the **for** loops. The ith line is expected to look like:

Fraction	Rounded representation			
	Number of digits			
	1	2	4	8
1/2	.5	.5	.5	.5
1/3	.3	.33	.3333	.33333333
1/4	.3	.25	.25	.25
1/5	.2	.2	.2	.2
1/6	.2	.17	.1667	.16666667
1/7	.1	.14	.1429	.14285714
1/8	.1	.13	.125	.125
1/9	.1	.11	.111	.11111111
12345678/100000000	.1	.12	.1235	.12345678

Figure 6.2 Rounded representations of fractions

i	$2i$	$2i$	Equal

Surprise! Surprise! When this program was run on an IBM PC, the output of Figure 6.3 was produced. Even the result of adding 0.2 ten times is not the same as 2.0. This surprising output from our program is explained by the observation that .2 does not have an exact finite binary floating point representation. In fact, $(.2)_{10} = (.0\,0110\,0110 \cdots)_2$. If we change 0.2 to 0.5 and $2*i$ to $5*i$ in Program 6.2, the output:

i	$5i$	$5i$	Equal

is obtained for every i. This is so because $(.5)_{10} = (.1)_2$ and so, .5 is represented exactly in our binary computer.

6.3.3. Arithmetic Errors

Even when there are no errors in the representation of our input data, the answers from a computer execution of a program may not obey well established laws of mathematics. This is because the results of performing arithmetic operations on exactly represented numbers may not be exactly representable in our computer. For example, 1 and 3

```
program NumericalErrors(input,output);
var x,y: real; i,j: integer;
begin
   writeln(' i ', '       x    ',' '        y    ',' '     x=y');
   writeln;
   x := 0;
   for i := 1 to 20 do
   begin
     for j := 1 to 10 do
       x := x + 0.2;
     y := 2*i;
     if (x = y) then writeln(i:3, x, y, '   Equal')
                 else writeln(i:3, x, y, '   NotEqual');
   end;
end.
```

Program 6.2

can be represented exactly but 1/3 cannot. Even though .5 is exactly representable as a binary floating point number, $sqrt(.5)$ is not. So, one should not be surprised if $sqrt(.5) * sqrt(.5) \neq .5$ on a computer.

```
program Innocent(input, output);
{Innocent program}
var x, z: real;
begin
   readln(x);
   z := x + 0.5;
   if z=x then writeln('Equal')
          else writeln('Not Equal');
end. {of Innocent}
```

Program 6.3 Innocent program

Computational errors exhibit themselves in more subtle and less exotic circumstances too. Consider Program 6.3. This is about as

i	x	y	x=y
1	2.0000000000E+00	2.0000000000E+00	NotEqual
2	4.0000000000E+00	4.0000000000E+00	NotEqual
3	5.9999999999E+00	6.0000000000E+00	NotEqual
4	7.9999999999E+00	8.0000000000E+00	NotEqual
5	9.9999999999E+00	1.0000000000E+01	NotEqual
6	1.2000000000E+01	1.2000000000E+01	NotEqual
7	1.4000000000E+01	1.4000000000E+01	NotEqual
8	1.6000000000E+01	1.6000000000E+01	NotEqual
9	1.8000000000E+01	1.8000000000E+01	NotEqual
10	1.9999999999E+01	2.0000000000E+01	NotEqual
11	2.1999999999E+01	2.2000000000E+01	NotEqual
12	2.3999999999E+01	2.4000000000E+01	NotEqual
13	2.5999999999E+01	2.6000000000E+01	NotEqual
14	2.7999999999E+01	2.8000000000E+01	NotEqual
15	2.9999999999E+01	3.0000000000E+01	NotEqual
16	3.1999999998E+01	3.2000000000E+01	NotEqual
17	3.3999999998E+01	3.4000000000E+01	NotEqual
18	3.5999999997E+01	3.6000000000E+01	NotEqual
19	3.7999999997E+01	3.8000000000E+01	NotEqual
20	3.9999999997E+01	4.0000000000E+01	NotEqual

Figure 6.3 Output from Program 6.2

innocent looking a program as you can expect to come across. We know that .5 can be represented exactly on every binary computer that has mantissas at least one digit long. Is it too unreasonable to expect that for every x that is exactly representable, the program will output "Not Equal"? To understand why "Equal" can be output even when x is exactly representable, we need to realize that the number of digits in the mantissa of $x + .5$ may exceed the number the computer saves. In this case, the .5 that is added can vanish during truncation or rounding. Thus, there is a loss of *significant digits*. Program 6.3 was run on an IBM PC for different inputs x. The results are summarized below.

x	Output	x	Output
1.0	Not Equal	10.0	Not Equal
2.0	Not Equal	2E10	Not Equal
2E12	Equal	2E14	Equal

The loss of significant digits in Program 6.3 is caused by the tremendous difference between the magnitude of x and that of .5. A loss of significant digits can arise even when the two numbers involved in the arithmetic operation are of comparable magnitude. For instance, suppose that x = .1234610 and y = .1235699. Suppose that we can retain only mantissas with five decimal digits. Using truncation, we get the approximations x' = .12346 and y' = .12356. These approximations are quite acceptable as the relative errors are small. In fact, the approximations are accurate to five digits of significance. If we compute z = $y - x$ using the approximations, we get the approximation z' = .10000$E - 3$. The exact value of z is, however, .10790$E - 3$. So, z has been computed to only two significant digits of accuracy! The relative error in the computation of z is more than 73% even though the relative errors in x and y are less than .008% !

Relative errors magnify very rapidly when we subtract numbers that agree on one or more significant digits.

6.3.4. Living With Numerical Errors

Don't test real numbers for equality

Our first lesson is that *two real numbers will almost never be equal in a computer*. So, we should avoid testing for equality.

As an example of the difficulties we can get into by not following this advice, consider Program 6.4 which computes the square of x for x in the range 0.2 through 2.0 in steps of 0.2. From the output of Program 6.2, we know that if this program is run on an IBM PC, it will not terminate. This is so as x will never exactly equal 2.0. As proof of this, the first 21 lines of output generated by this program are displayed in Figure 6.4. Figure 6.5 displays the output that would have been generated if there were no numerical errors.

```
program squares(input, output);
var x,y: real;
begin
   writeln('     x    ','    x*x    ');
   writeln;
   x := 0;
   while (x <> 2.0) do
   begin
      x := x + 0.2;
      y := x*x;
      writeln(x, y);
   end;
end. {of squares}
```

Program 6.4 Nonterminating program to compute squares

How can the program be made to terminate after producing the desired 10 squares? If we change the conditional in the **while** to $x < 2.0$, the program will surely terminate. But, it might give us 11 lines of output. We can anticipate this from Figure 6.3. After 10 lines of output, x will be slightly smaller than 2.0 and an eleventh line (corresponding to $x = 2.2$) will be generated. Thus, the conditional should be changed to $x < 2.0 - \epsilon$ for some suitably small ϵ. $\epsilon = 0.05$ can be expected to work just fine. This results in the conditional $x < 1.95$.

Well now, 1.95 certainly has no easily seen relation to the problem parameters and its presence in our program is guaranteed to confuse any reader. We might toy with the idea of changing it to $x <= 1.8$. While this will do the job on this example, we cannot be sure that the numerical errors will always result in a value smaller than the true value. What if when the true value of x is 1.8, the value represented in our computer is slightly more than 1.8? In this case, no output line corresponding to $x = 2$ will be generated! To avoid the confusion that results from the use of 1.95, we shall introduce an appropriate comment in the program. Another way to avoid this confusion is to define a constant *epsilon* with value .005. This constant will be used to denote the ϵ used above. The conditional of the **while**

x	x*x
2.0000000000E-01	4.0000000000E-02
4.0000000000E-01	1.6000000000E-01
6.0000000000E-01	3.6000000000E-01
8.0000000000E-01	6.4000000000E-01
1.0000000000E+00	1.0000000000E+00
1.2000000000E+00	1.4400000000E+00
1.4000000000E+00	1.9600000000E+00
1.6000000000E+00	2.5600000000E+00
1.8000000000E+00	3.2400000000E+00
2.0000000000E+00	4.0000000000E+00
2.2000000000E+00	4.8400000000E+00
2.4000000000E+00	5.7600000000E+00
2.6000000000E+00	6.7599999999E+00
2.8000000000E+00	7.8399999999E+00
3.0000000000E+00	8.9999999999E+00
3.2000000000E+00	1.0240000000E+01
3.4000000000E+00	1.1560000000E+01
3.6000000000E+00	1.2960000000E+01
3.8000000000E+00	1.4440000000E+01
4.0000000000E+00	1.6000000000E+01
4.2000000000E+00	1.7640000000E+01

Figure 6.4 First 21 lines of output from Program 6.4

is then written as $x < (2\text{-}epsilon)$.

An alternate solution is to replace the **while** construct with a **for** construct that iterates the statements exactly ten times. While this is possible in this simple example, in other situations (see the mortgage balance example of Program 5.16) it is very difficult to determine the number of iterations that will take place before the **while** loop will terminate.

We are still left with the reality that the output will not be quite accurate. We know that if the squares are computed accurately, they will contain no more than two nonzero decimal digits in the fractional part (see Figure 6.5). So, we might as well get only two fractional

x	x*x
0.2	0.04
0.4	0.16
0.6	0.36
0.8	0.64
1.0	1.00
1.2	1.44
1.4	1.96
1.6	2.56
1.8	3.24
2.0	4.00

Figure 6.5 Output from Program 6.5

```
program squares(input, output);
{This version will terminate on an IBM PC}
var x,y: real;
begin
   writeln('   x   ',' x*x ');
   writeln;
   x := 0;
   {1.95 is used below in place of 2.0 to guard
   against numerical errors}
   while (x < 1.95) do
   begin
      x := x + 0.2;
      y := x*x;
      writeln(x:5:1, y:6:2);
   end;
end. {of squares}
```

Program 6.5 Program 6.4 modified to account for numerical errors digits and hope that the rounding that takes place during output will work in our favor and that the correct results will be output. When these changes are incorporated into Program 6.4, Program 6.5 results. The output generated by the IBM PC is, in fact, what we have displayed in Figure 6.5.

Often, one accounts for numerical errors by measuring the relative difference, $abs(x-d)/d$ (where abs is the absolute value function), between x and the desired value d rather than the absolute difference, $abs(x-d)$. In this case, the **while** loop conditional of Program 6.5 will be changed to $abs(x-d)/d > epsilon$.

Reorganize Computations

When dealing with problems that involve real numbers, it is essential to organize the computations so as to minimize the effects of a loss in significant digits. This is often a difficult objective. On the one hand, one must avoid adding together large and small numbers. On the other, one must avoid subtracting numbers that agree on any number of significant digits. To see the difficulties involved in attempting to meet both requirements, consider the problem of finding the sum of n real numbers that are stored in the real array $x[1..n]$.

This can be done using the straightforward code:

```
sum := 0;
for i := 1 to n do
  sum := sum + x[i];
```

This computes the sum with the least possible relative error so long as the $x[i]$'s are of the same sign and are of comparable magnitude. When all $x[i]$'s have the same sign but are of widely varying magnitude, more accurate results are obtained by adding numbers in increasing order of magnitude. This gives the small numbers a chance to get large enough to make a difference when added to the larger numbers. For instance, if $x[1] = 2E12$ and $x[i] = .5$, $2 \leq i \leq 1001$, then adding these 1001 $x[i]$'s together in the order 1 through 1001 produces the result $sum = 2E12$ on an IBM PC. Adding them together in the reverse order produces the result $sum = 2.0000000005E12$ which is the exact answer.

This technique clearly doesn't do much good if the sum of the small numbers isn't near enough in magnitude to the larger numbers to affect the final value of *sum*. For instance, if $n = 3$, and $x[1..3] = (2E12, .5, .5)$, then regardless of the order in which we add the three numbers on an IBM PC, we shall still get *sum* = 2E12. This is the best we can do given the mantissa size the IBM PC keeps. The result isn't too alarming as the relative error is negligible. It is only $(1/2)E-12 = .5E-12$. Of course, if absolute error is our concern, then the smallness of the relative error is little consolation. The absolute error in *sum* is 1.

Now, suppose that we have both positive and negative numbers. If we sort the numbers in order of increasing magnitude and then add them together as suggested above, then there is a good chance that we will be adding together numbers of different sign that agree on some significant digits. This can be expected to magnify the relative errors that already exist. A good strategy to control this growth in the relative error is to compute the sums of the positive and negative numbers separately and then add these two sums together. Each individual sum can be computed in the order suggested above.

The preceding strategy has a shortcoming of its own. Let us apply it to the numbers $(2E12, .5, .5, -2E12)$. The resulting sum on an IBM PC is 0. However, if we add 2E12 and -2E12 first, and then add the two .5's, we get the answer 1.0. We need to strike a balance between the two causes of a loss of significant digits.

As another example, consider the problem of computing the average of n positive real numbers $x[i]$, $1 \leq i \leq n$. This average is given by the formula:

$$average := \frac{1}{n} \sum_{i=1}^{n} x[i]$$

The program code of Program 6.6 computes the average. Observe the defense introduced in the code to handle the case $n \leq 0$. When $n \leq 0$, the average is zero.

When the $x[i]$'s are large, the sum $\sum_{i=1}^{n} x[i]$ can be larger than the largest real number that can be stored in the computer. In this case, an "overflow" error will be generated during the execution of the **for**

---

if $n<=0$ **then** *average* := 0
else begin
      sum := $x[1]$;
      for i := 2 **to** n **do**
        sum := *sum* + $x[i]$;
      average := *sum*/n;
    end; {of **if**}

Program 6.6

loop and the program will terminate unsuccessfully (and also ungracefully) even though the average itself isn't too large for the computer.

    Program 6.6 was run an IBM PC with $n = 9$ and $x[i] = 2E37$,
$1 \le i \le n$. A run time overflow error that caused the program to terminate unsuccessfully was generated after the first eight $x[i]$'s were
added together.

---

if $n<=0$ **then** *average* := 0
else begin
      average := $x[1]/n$;
      for i := 2 **to** n **do**
        average := *average* + $x[i]/n$;
    end; {of **if**}

Program 6.7

    In an attempt to resolve this difficulty, we might try to compute
the average using the code of Program 6.7. This code runs into difficulties when $x[i]/n$ is too small and has the truncated or rounded
representation .0. These difficulties in computing the average of n
positive numbers can be overcome by suitably scaling the $x[i]$'s and
then unscaling after the average has been computed. For instance, the
average of $x[i] = 2.iE37$, $1 \le i \le 9$ can be computed on an IBM PC by

first dividing all the $x[i]$'s by (say) 10 and then multiplying the resultant average by 10. In order to avoid possible loss of significant digits, it is better to scale by a power of two as this just affects the exponent part of the real number's binary representation.

Avoiding errors caused by a loss of significant digits is generally quite hard to do. Often, one needs to change the formula that is used to compute the results. At times, a simple rearrangement of the order of computations provides satisfactory results.

A more thorough investigation into methods to avoid numerical errors is beyond the scope of this text. Those of you who wish to pursue this topic more seriously should study one of the references on numerical methods that are cited at the end of this chapter.

6.4. Boundary Errors

Programs often fail when they are operating on data that represents a boundary of the problem. We shall use several examples to illustrate what we mean by the boundary of a problem and why these are potential sources of error.

Text Editor

Let us implement two of the cursor control commands as Pascal procedures. First, we assume that the screen is a grid with 40 rows and 80 columns. Each grid position can hold exactly one character. The current position of the cursor is saved in the global variables *CursorRow* and *CursorColumn*. A screen utility *PositionCursor(Row, Column)* is available for use by all procedures that need to reposition the cursor. This utility simply moves the cursor to the specified row and column. The usage of the screen has been set so that the first 15 rows (numbered 1 through 15) are reserved for abbreviated help menus. The remaining rows (i.e., rows 16 through 40) are available for the display of text. The columns are numbered 1 through 80.

Let us begin with procedure *CursorCharLeft* which implements the command "←". Our first attempt at writing this procedure results in the code of Program 6.8. It appears to be correct. Even the value of *CursorColumn* is updated. This procedure produces the desired outcome only when the cursor isn't already positioned at the left boundary (i.e., column 1) of the screen. It fails to work correctly when *CursorColumn* is 1.

```
procedure CursorCharLeft;
{ ← }
begin
    PositionCursor(CursorRow, CursorColumn − 1);
    CursorColumn := CursorColumn − 1;
end; {of CursorCharLeft}
```

Program 6.8

For 79 of the possible 80 different values of *CursorColumn*, the procedure is correct. It doesn't work correctly on the boundary value 1 of *CursorColumn* because a different action is needed here. This is typical of many problems. Accounting for the boundary condition results in the code of Program 6.9 which works correctly for all possible values of *CursorColumn*.

```
procedure CursorCharLeft;
{ ← }
begin
    if CursorColumn > 1 then
    begin
        PositionCursor(CursorRow, CursorColumn − 1);
        CursorColumn := CursorColumn − 1;
    end
    else beep(1.0); {1 second audio signal}
end; {of CursorCharLeft}
```

Program 6.9

Next, let us consider the command " ↑ ". This is supposed to move the cursor one line up. Again, our first attempt at the Pascal code might result in Program 6.10 which works correctly most (but not all) of the time.

---

procedure *CursorRowUp*;
{ ↑ }
begin
   PositionCursor(*CursorRow* −1, *CursorColumn*);
   CursorRow := *CursorRow* − 1;
end; {of *CursorRowUp*}

Program 6.10

     Program 6.10 has two flaws in it. The first is that when *Cursor-Row* is 16, it causes the cursor to move into the abbreviated help facility. The correct action at this time depnds on whether or not we are presently at line 1 of the text. If we are, then there is no preceding line to move the cursor to. If we aren't at line 1 of the text, then we need to scroll rows 16 through 39 of the screen one row down (thereby losing row 40) and then insert into row 16 the preceding line of text. The second flaw has to do with the column position of the cursor. If the preceding line has fewer characters than *CursorColumn*, then the cursor needs to be moved to the last column in the preceding line. So, we have three boundaries to deal with here:

(1)   the cursor is at a text display boundary (row 16)

(2)   the first row of text displayed is line 1 of the text

(3)   the right end of the preceding line (if any) does not extend as far as *CursorColumn*.

     When we account for all of these boundary conditions, we obtain the code of Program 6.11. This program makes use of the constants *DisplayTop* and *DisplayBottom*. *DisplayTop* is the first screen row used to display text (in our case 16). Using the constant *DisplayTop* is preferable to the explicit use of the number 16, for two reasons. The first is that during the implementation of the text editor, we might decide to change the number of rows allocated to the help facility. This change is easier to implement when the first row of the text display is referenced via the constant *DisplayTop*. The second reason is that the constant name *DisplayTop* conveys more meaning than the number 16. Hence, program comprehensibility is enhanced. Similarly, the use of the constant *DisplayBottom* is preferred to the use of the number 40 (the number of rows in a screen may vary from one physical screen to the next).

The program also uses the global variable *TextLine*. This is the line number of the text line the cursor is presently positioned at. The function *LineLength* returns the length (in columns) of the specified line of text. The procedures *ScrollDown* and *InsertLine* are screen utilities whose function you can easily decipher from their usage in procedure *CursorRowUp*.

The course of action we have opted to take at the boundaries must be well documented.

Program 6.11 is quite a bit more complex than Program 6.10. This additional complexity is unavoidable as the boundaries must be accounted for. A program (no matter how simple) that works only part of the time is totally unacceptable. In some situations, it is possible to avoid the inclusion of explicit code to handle boundary conditions by suitably modifying the data structures in use so that boundary conditions cannot arise. Our next example does this. Another example, Rat In A Maze, where we take this path is studied in the next chapter. For the text editor, however, we need to account for boundary conditions explicitly.

Insertion

Consider the problem of inserting an element x into a nondecreasing sequence $a[1] \leq a[2] \leq \ldots \leq a[n]$. Following the insertion, the new sequence of $n + 1$ elements is also to be nondecreasing. So, if $x = 3$ and the sequence is 1, 4, 5, 6, 6, 8 before the insertion, then following the insertion it is 1, 3, 4, 5, 6, 6, 8.

It is easily verified that the Pascal code of Program 6.12 performs this insertion. We can try out some examples with $n = 1, 2, 3,$ 4, etc. In all cases the Pascal code of Program 6.12 performs the insertion correctly. What happens when $n = 0$? We are inserting into an empty sequence. The program fails to work. Depending on the Pascal compiler in use and the compiler options in effect, any one of the following can happen:

(1) If the array a does not have a position 0, a subscript out of range error is produced.

```
procedure CursorRowUp;
{  ↑  }
var length, col: integer;
begin
  if CursorRow > DisplayTop then
  begin
    length := LineLength(TextLine − 1);
    if CursorColumn > length then col := length
                             else col := CursorColumn;
    PositionCursor(CursorRow − 1, col);
    TextLine := TextLine − 1;
    CursorColumn := col;
  end {of then}
  else
  begin {at top of display}
    if TextLine = 1 then beep(1.0)
    else
    begin {there is a preceding line}
      length := LineLength(TextLine − 1);
      if CursorColumn > length then col := length
                               else col := CursorColumn;
      ScrollDown(DisplayTop, DisplayBottom − 1, 1);
      InsertLine(TextLine − 1, DisplayTop);
      PositionCursor(CursorRow, col);
      TextLine := TextLine − 1;
      CursorColumn := col;
    end;
  end;
end; {of CursorRowUp}
```

Program 6.11

(2) The error "$a[0]$ is undefined" is generated.

(3) Since i cannot become 1, the program runs for a long time. Eventually i will be so small that an attempt to address $a[i]$ will cause the system to generate a memory protection error. This will occur since typically the location of $a[i]$ will be computed using the formula:

```
i := n; done := false;
while (a[i] > x) and not done do
begin
   a[i + 1] := a[i];
   if i = 1 then done = true
           else i := i - 1;
end;
a[i] := x;
```

Program 6.12

$$location(a[i]) = location(a[1]) + i - 1$$

Program 6.12 fails to work correctly when presented with the boundary data: "empty list". Another time it fails to work is when the array is full. If *a* has been declared as:

type *ElementList* = **array** [1..*MaxListLength*] **of** *element*;
var *a*: *ElementList*;

then when *n* = *MaxListLength*, the program attempts to create a list one size too big. Program 6.12 fails to work at both of the boundaries: "empty list" and "full list". This is something we would not have discovered unless we explicitly checked the program using boundary data.

Program 6.13 is the insertion procedure that results when we account for the problem boundaries. This implementation assumes that *ElementList* has been defined as:

type *ElementList* = **array** [0..*MaxListLength*] **of** *element*;

and that position zero of the array *a* is available to be used by any procedure as it sees fit. Providing such a position zero greatly simplifies the resulting procedure and also reduces the run time (see Chapter 11).

```
procedure insert(var a: ElementList; var n: integer; x: element);
{Insert x into the ordered list a[1..n]}
var i: integer;
begin
  if n = MaxListLength
  then begin
          writeln('Size of list exceeds ', MaxListLength);
          goto 999;  {end of program}
        end;
  if n < 0 then n := 0;
  a[0] := x;
  i := n;
  while a[i] > x do
  begin
    {move a[i] up one position}
    a[i+1] := a[i];
    i := i - 1;
  end;
  a[i+1] := x; n := n + 1;
end;  {of insert}
```

Program 6.13

It is worth noting that Program 6.13 terminates the execution of
the entire program when it detects an error. In many situations, the
error message provided by this procedure will not be very meaningful
to the user. This is particularly true when the user is unaware that an
insert was even part of the solution process. In these situations, it is
desirable for *insert* to transmit the fact that it was unsuccessful back to
the calling procedure and let the calling procedure output a more
meaningful error message or even attempt to recover from the error.
This can be done by adding another parameter *success* to the procedure. If an error occurs, *success* is set to **false**, otherwise *success* is
set to **true**.

Stacks

Let us examine another problem where our first attempt at a solution fails to work at the boundaries but works everywhere else. We consider the problem of adding and deleting elements from a stack.

A *stack* is an ordered list of elements. One end of this list is designated the *bottom* and the other is called the *top*. A stack with four elements is shown in Figure 6.6(a). New elements are always added at the top of the stack. Suppose we wish to add the element "E" to the stack of Figure 6.6(a). This element will have to be placed on top of the element "D" giving us the configuration of Figure 6.6(b). Deletions from a stack also take place from the top only. Hence if we are to delete an element from the stack of Figure 6.6(b), it will be the element "E". Following the deletion, the configuration of Figure 6.6(a) results. If three successive deletions are performed on the stack of Figure 6.6(b), the stack of Figure 6.6(c) results.

	E←*top*	
D←*top*	D	
C	C	
B	B	B←*top*
A←*bottom*	A←*bottom*	A←*bottom*
(a)	(b)	(c)

Figure 6.6 Stack configurations

From the preceding discussion, we see that a stack is a LIFO (last in first out) list. Lists of this type appear frequently in computing and we shall make use of stacks frequently in later chapters.

A stack can be represented using an array *stack*[1..*MaxStackSize*] and an integer variable *top*. The bottommost element of the stack is placed in position 1, the next element in position 2, and so on. The topmost element is in position *top*. Initially, the stack is empty and we have *top* = 0.

To add the element x to the stack, we need to execute the code:

```
top := top + 1;
stack[top] := x;
```

This works fine so long as the stack is not already full (i.e., so long as $top < MaxStackSize$).

To delete an element and place the deleted element in the variable x we need to execute the code:

```
x := stack[top];
top := top - 1;
```

Again, this works fine only when the stack is not empty (i.e., when $top \neq 0$). The obvious solutions work for all stacks except the empty and full ones. The solutions fail at the boundaries (empty and full)!

```
procedure AddToStack(x: element);
{Add element x to the global stack stack;
 top is the current top of stack;
 and MaxStackSize is the capacity of the stack.}
begin
  if top = MaxStackSize
  then begin
          writeln('Stack overflow');
          goto 999; {go to end of program}
       end;
  top := top + 1;
  stack[top] := x;
end; {of AddToStack}
```

Program 6.14 Add to a stack

The stack add and delete procedures given in Programs 6.14 and 6.15 take the problem boundaries into account and work properly at all times.   Both procedures terminate execution upon detection of an error.   As in the case of *insert*, it may be possible for the invoking procedure to recover from the error or to at least provide an error message that is more meaningful to the user.   In this case, the stack add and delete procedures should be modified to transmit an error signal back to the invoking procedure.

```
procedure DeleteFromStack(var x: element);
{Delete top element from the stack stack;
 return it in x}
begin
   if top = 0
   then begin
            writeln('Attempt to delete from an empty stack');
            goto 999; {go to end of program}
        end;
   x := stack[top];
   top := top - 1;
end; {of DeleteFromStack}
```

Program 6.15 Deletion from a stack

6.5. MISCELLANEOUS CAUSES

Uninitialized Variables

Some compilers set the initial values of all variables not explicitly initialized by the program to zero. Other compilers generate an error message when a program attempts to use a variable that has not been explicitly initialized. Yet others permit the computation to proceed using whatever value the preceding program left in the memory word allocated to the uninitialized variable. This difference in the handling of variables that are not explicitly initialized causes a program to behave differently at different times even on the same input data. To ensure that the program exhibits the correct behavior each time, all variables must be explicitly initialized.

Global And Local Variables

The improper use of global variables is a common source of errors in a syntactically correct program. Global variables should be used only for data that are shared by several procedures, functions, and blocks of code. Other variables (most notably variables used for temporary results and loop indices) should be declared local to the program block in which they are used.

When global variables are in use, the function of each should be well documented. Each block of program code should ensure that the integrity of global data is preserved before relinquishing execution control to another block.

For example, the variables *CursorRow*, *CursorColumn*, and *Text-Line* are global to the procedures *PositionCursor*, *CursorCharLeft*, and *CursorRowUp* (and also to many other editor modules). Suppose that Program 6.8 is modified as in Program 6.16. In addition to difficulties at the boundary, a potential difficulty is created by the fact that at the time *PositionCursor* is invoked, *CursorColumn* does not give the correct column position of the cursor. This difficulty is evidenced when the movement of the cursor is implemented by the following steps:

> Erase cursor from present position
> Illuminate cursor at new position

```
procedure CursorCharLeft;
{ ← }
begin
    CursorColumn := CursorColumn − 1;
    PositionCursor(CursorRow, CursorColumn);
end; {of CursorCharLeft}
```

Program 6.16

Variable And Value Parameters

Pascal supports the following classes of formal parameters:
(1) variable parameters
(2) value parameters
(3) procedure parameters
(4) function parameters

Using variable parameters in place of value parameters and vice versa is another common cause of malfunction in programs. Consider the procedure $X2PlusY2$ of Program 6.17. This procedure computes $x = x^2 + y^2$.

```
procedure X2PlusY2(var x: integer; y: integer);
begin
  x := x*x; y := y*y;
  x := x + y;
end; {of X2PlusY2}
```

Program 6.17

x and y are the *formal* parameters of the procedure $X2PlusY2$. x is a *variable parameter* and y a *value parameter*. Suppose that this procedure is invoked by the statement:

$X2PlusY2(a, b)$;

where a and b are of type **integer**. For this invokation of $X2PlusY2$, a and b are the *actual* parameters.

Formal parameters that are value parameters are equivalent to local variables that are declared within the procedure/function. At the time the procedure/function is invoked, the values of all value parameters are initialized to the values of the corresponding actual parameters. So, in the above example the value of y is initialized to the value of b.

Formal parameters that are variable parameters are equivalent to variables that are global to the procedure/function. Every reference within a procedure/function to a variable formal parameter becomes a reference to the actual parameter. This is equivalent to changing the names of all variable formal parameters to the names of the corresponding actual parameters.

Executing the procedure of Program 6.17 is therefore equivalent to executing the code:

$y := b;$
$a := a*a; y := y*y;$
$a := a + y;$

If $a = 2$ and $b = 3$ at the time $X2PlusY2$ is invoked, then following the execution of $X2PlusY2$, $a = 13$ and $b = 3$.

The values of actual parameters that correspond to value formal parameters do not change when the procedure/function is executed (except when the actual parameter also corresponds to a variable formal parameter). This is true even when the procedure/function changes the value of the value formal parameter. The values of actual parameters that correspond to variable formal parameters change each time the procedure/function changes the value of the variable formal parameters.

If both x and y are declared as variable parameters, then executing $X2PlusY2$ is equivalent to executing the code:

$a := a*a; b := b*b;$
$a := a + b;$

Suppose that $a = 2$ and $b = 3$ when $X2PlusY2$ is invoked and that both formal parameters are variable parameters. When $X2PlusY2$ terminates, $a = 13$ and $b = 9$.

Next, suppose that $X2PlusY2$ is invoked by the statement:

$X2PlusY2(a, a);$

Suppose that $a = 2$ initially and that x is a variable parameter and y is a value parameter as declared in Program 6.17. The execution of

Program 6.17 is equivalent to executing the code:

$y := a$;
$a := a*a$; $y := y*y$;
$a := a + y$;

and following the execution of *X2PlusY2*, we have $a = 8$. If both x and y were variable parameters instead, then the equivalent code is:
$a := a*a$; $a := a*a$;
$a := a + a$;

and $a = 32$ when *X2PlusY2* terminates. So, when both x and y are variable parameters, *X2PlusY2* works correctly only if the actual parameters are not the same. Even when they are not the same, it has the undesired side effect of altering the value of the actual parameter that corresponds to y.

When writing a procedure/function, one must keep the following in mind:

(1) Formal parameters that are not used to transmit results back to the invoking procedure/function/program must be declared as value parameters. An important exception to this is when the formal parameter is a large data structure such as an array. In this case, it is often desirable to make the parameter a variable parameter as doing this significantly improves the run time performance of the program. This is elaborated upon in Chapter 11.

(2) Formal parameters that transmit results back are to be declared as variable parameters.

(3) Make sure that the procedure/function works correctly when the same actual parameter corresponds to two or more variable formal parameters.

6.6. REFERENCES AND SELECTED READINGS

Two interesting readings on the origins of number systems are:

Episodes from the early history of mathematics, by A. Aaboe, Random House, New York, 1964.

and

Ancient Babylonian algorithms, by D. Knuth, *Comm. ACM*, Vol 15, No. 7, July 1972, pp. 671-677.

For a further discussion on numerical errors, see the books:

Elementary numerical analysis: an algorithmic approach, second edition, by S. Conte and C. de Boor, Mc. Graw Hill, New York, 1972.

Numerical Methods, A Software Approach, by Johnston, John Wiley, New York, 1982.

and

Numerical Methods, Software and Analysis, by Rice, McGraw Hill, New York, 1983.

6.7. EXERCISES

1. Obtain the normalized binary floating point representation of the following decimal numbers:

    (a)   .3

    (b)   .4

    (c)   .6

    (d)   .7

    (e)   2.5

    (f)   9.6

    (g)   19.42

2. Show that:

    $$0 \leq |r-r'| < |r|*b^{1-\delta}$$

    when truncation is used and that:

    $$0 \leq |r-r'| < \frac{1}{2}|r|*b^{1-\delta}$$

    when rounding is used. See Section 6.3.2 for a definition of the terms used.

3. Use the ideas introduced in this chapter to introduce all appropriate defenses into Program 6.18.

```
program ThirstyBaby(input, output);
{Thirsty baby solution, see Example 2.3 and Section 5.8}
var s: array[1..10] of real;
    a: array[1..10] of real;
    t: real;
    n, i: integer;

begin
  readln(n, t);

  {input liquids in nonincreasing order of sᵢ/aᵢ}
  for i := 1 to n do
    readln(s[i], a[i]);

  writeln('Liquid', '    Amount');

  {find solution}
  i := 1;
  while t <> 0 do
    if t < a[i] then begin
                  writeln(i, t);
                  t := 0;
                end
              else begin
                  writeln(i, a[i]);
                  i := i + 1;
                  t :=t - a[i];
                end;
end. {of ThirstyBaby}
```

Program 6.18

4. Write a Pascal procedure for each of the following text editor cursor control commands (see Figure 4.5 for an explanation). In each case make sure that your procedure accounts for the problem boundaries. Specify the action to be taken at each boundary. You may avoid getting bogged down with irrelevant details by using screen, keyboard, and text file utilities as needed.

    (a)   ↓

    (b)   →

    (c)   <PgUp>

    (d)   <PgDn>

    (e)   ^→

    (f)   ^←

    (f)   L

    (g)   R

5. Rewrite the stack add and delete programs so that they transmit error conditions back to the calling procedure/function via a parameter *success*. Notice that in this case you can easily avoid the use of **goto** statements.

6. Write defensive and aesthetic Pascal programs for each of the following tasks:

    a)   Input numbers and compute their average.

    b)   Input numbers and compute their standard deviation.

    c)   Play the word game: hangman. In this game, the computer selects a word and tells the player the number of letters in this word. The player has to guess the word. At any time, the player can guess either a single letter or the entire word. The player is allowed to make at most 10 erroneous letter guesses before he/she is hanged.

    d)   Input data for the thirsty baby problem (Example 2.3) and provide a solution as suggested in Section 5.8.

7. Write a defensive and aesthetic Pascal program to simulate a hand calculator as described in Exercise 4.3.

8. Design and implement (in Pascal) a computer program that tests arithmetic (addition, subtraction, multiplication, and division) skills. Your design must be modular and be menu driven. Appropriate on-line help should be available and your program must keep performance scores for all users.

9. Do the previous exercise for the case of a metric conversion program. Your program should convert between the metric and English system and should handle weights, distances, areas, and volumes.

10. Design and implement a computer program for a cash register machine. This program accepts as input a list of items (quantity, description, price, taxable, etc.) and the amount of money tendered and its form (check, cash, credit card). It outputs a list of the purchases, the total amount, tax, etc. In addition, it tells the cashier (in the case of your program, it does this via a second output list) the amount of change (in terms of $20, $10, $5, $1 bills and coin denominations of quarters, dimes, nickels, and cents). Note that to do the latter, your program must know the current contents of the cash register. Your program must be aesthetic, user friendly, and contain all appropriate defenses.

11. [Luker] Write a Pascal program that inputs numbers as text and then translates them into their numeric representations. Your program should be able to handle both real number and integer input. In case of error in input, an appropriate error message or a request for data correction should be generated.

CHAPTER 7

STEPWISE REFINEMENT

7.1. INTRODUCTION

Stepwise refinement is the technique of arriving at a program module through a series of steps. We begin with a program that is written in Pascal pseudocode (a mixture of Pascal and English statements) that is easily seen to be a correct solution to the problem. This version of the program is successively refined (i.e., the pseudocode gets closer to a Pascal program with each refinement) until eventually a Pascal program is obtained. Each refinement is sufficiently close to the previous refinement that its correctness is an immediate consequence of the correctness of the previous refinement. Further, data structure and algorithm decisions are made as the need for these arises.

This method should be contrasted with the alternate approach to programming in which one attempts to obtain the final Pascal code directly. This method is useful only on very small modules. The coding of larger modules is much easier if one adopts the stepwise methodology. When the stepwise refinement method is used, we program *into* Pascal. When we obtain the Pascal program in a single step, we program *in* Pascal. Programming *into* Pascal is to be preferred to programming *in* Pascal whenever the module being programmed isn't trivially small and simple. We shall illustrate the stepwise refinement method using several examples. In each case, program development is preceded by specification, design, and modularization.

7.2. RAT IN A MAZE

Specification

A *maze* (Figure 7.1) is a rectangular area with an entrance and an exit. The interior of the maze contains walls or obstacles that one cannot walk through. The mazes we shall be dealing with have these obstacles placed along rows and columns that are parallel to the rectangular boundary of the maze. The entrance is at the upper left corner and the exit is at the lower right corner.

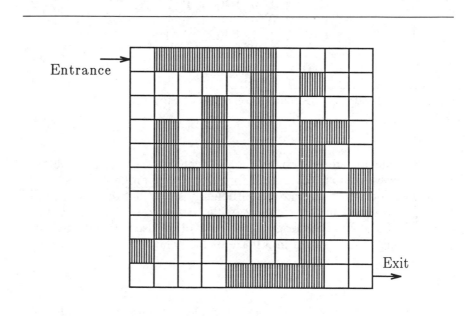

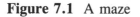

Figure 7.1 A maze

Suppose that the maze is to be modeled as an $n \times m$ matrix with position $(1,1)$ of the matrix representing the entrance and position (n, m) representing the exit. n and m are, respectively, the number of rows and columns in the maze. Each maze position is described by the row and column intersection that it is at. The matrix has a one in position (i, j) iff there is an obstacle at the corresponding maze position. Otherwise, there is a zero at this matrix position. Figure 7.2 shows the matrix representation of the maze of Figure 7.1. The classical *rat in a maze* problem is to find a path from the entrance to the exit of a maze.

```
0 1 1 1 1 1 0 0 0 0
0 0 0 0 0 1 0 1 0 0
0 0 0 1 0 1 0 0 0 0
0 1 0 1 0 1 0 1 1 0
0 1 0 1 0 1 0 1 0 0
0 1 1 1 0 1 0 1 0 1
0 1 0 0 0 1 0 1 0 1
0 1 0 1 1 1 0 1 0 0
1 0 0 0 0 0 0 1 0 0
0 0 0 0 1 1 1 1 0 0
```

Figure 7.2 Matrix representation of maze of Figure 7.1

You are to write a program to solve the rat in a maze problem. You may assume that the mazes for which your program is to work are square (i.e., *m = n*) and are sufficiently small that the entire maze can be represented in the memory of the target computer. Your program will be a stand-alone product that will be used directly by persons wishing to find a path in a maze of their choice.

Design

We shall design the program using the top down modular methodology. It is not too difficult to see that there are three aspects to the problem: input the maze; find a path; output the path. There will be one program module for each of these. A fourth module that displays a welcome message and identifies the program and its author is also desirable. While this module is not directly related to the problem at hand, the use of such a module enhances the "user friendliness" of the program.

The module that finds the path does not interact directly with the user and will therefore contain no help facility and will not be menu driven. The remaining three modules do interact with the user and we need to expend some effort designing the user interface for these. The user interface is to be designed so as to make the user want to use your program over other competing programs.

Let us begin with the "welcome module". We wish to display a message such as:

Welcome To
RAT IN A MAZE
© Joe Bloe, 1985

While this might seem a trivial task, much can be done to obtain a pleasing effect. The message can be multicolored in case the user has a color display. The three lines need to be positioned on the display and the character size used can change from one line to the next (or even from character to character). The welcome message can be introduced on the display with a reasonable time lapse between the introduction of one character and the next. Alternatively, the time lapse can be very small. In addition one might consider the use of sound effects. We also need to determine the duration for which the message is to be displayed. It should be displayed long enough so that it can be read. But not so long as to leave the user yawning.

As we can see, the design of the welcome message (and the whole user interface in general) requires skills that are more closely associated with Hollywood than with traditional Computer Science.

The input module needs to inform thc uscr that the input is expected as a matrix of ones and zeroes. We need to decide whether this matrix is to be provided by rows or by columns. It is perhaps more natural to ask for this matrix by rows. So, let us decide to do it this way. The user must first provide us with the number of rows (which is also the number of columns). This information can be asked for by displaying the message shown in Figure 7.3. The choice of -1 to terminate the program is not as nice as <esc> but since most Pascal impementations will get upset reading this value into an integer valued variable, we have little choice about this. An alternative is to read in the number of rows as a character string. Then determine if the input string has an <esc> in it. If it doesn't, then the string can be translated into its numeric form. In fact, defensive programming requires that all inputs be read as text when one cannot trust the system or the user to be kind to the program.

```
Please Enter The Number Of Rows In The Maze

I Work On Square Mazes With At Most 20 Rows

Enter -1 To Terminate Program

Press <Return> when done
```

Figure 7.3

Next, we may ask for the rows one by one as in:

Please Enter Row 1
Press <Return> when done

As each row is entered, we can display the row on the screen and ask the user to verify the entries. An edit facility to correct errors will be quite helpful. This is certainly preferable (from the users standpoint) to reentering the entire row. The input module can also verify that the entrance and exit of the maze are not blocked. If they are, then no path exists. In all likelihood, the user made an error in input. In the following discussion, we assume that the input module performs this verification and that the entrance and exit are not blocked.

Some other issues in the design of the user interface for the input module are: use of color and sound; size of characters in request messages; positioning of request messages on the display screen; whether the screen should scroll up as we go from one row to the next or whether we should erase the previous row from the display and show the next row at the same place.

Once again, we see that what initially appeared to be a simple task (read in a matrix) is actually quite complex if one wants to do it in a user friendly way.

The output module design involves essentially the same considerations as the design of the input module.

Program Plan

The design phase has already pointed out the need for four program modules. An additional root module that invokes these in the sequence: welcome module; input module; find path module; output module; is also needed. The task of writing the welcome, input, and output modules is simplified by the availability of modules that clear the screen; turn scrolling on and off; position the cursor at a particular point on the screen; and display characters on the screen in different colors and sizes. So, a module comprising a collection of screen utilities is also needed.

Our program will have the modular structure of Figure 7.4. Each program module can be coded independently. The root module will be coded as the body of the overall program; the screen utilities will be a collection of procedures; the welcome, input, find path, and output path modules will each be a single procedure.

At this point, we see that our program is going to have the form given in Program 7.1.

Program Development

Substantial data structure and algorithm issues arise in the development of the path finding module only. Consequently, we shall develop just this module here. The development of the remaining modules is left as an exercise. Without thinking too much about the coding of the module, we can arrive at the Pascal pseudocode given in Program 7.2. This code is readily seen to be correct. Unfortunately, it cannot be presented to a computer in this form and we need to refine it into pure Pascal code.

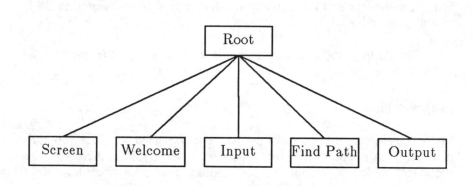

Figure 7.4 Modular structure of rat in a maze program

program *RatInAMaze*(input, output);

{Declaration section}

{Screen utilities}

{Functional Modules}
procedure *welcome*;
procedure *InputMaze*;
procedure *FindPath*;
procedure *OutputPath*;

begin {body of *RatInAMaze*}
  welcome;
  InputMaze;
  FindPath;
  OutputPath;
end. {of *RatInAMaze*}

Program 7.1 Form of rat in a maze program

---

procedure *FindPath*;
begin

Search the maze for a path from the entrance to the exit;

if a path is found **then** set *found* to **true**
else set *found* to **false**;

end; {of *FindPath*}

Program 7.2 First version of *FindPath*

First, let us figure out how we are to search the maze for a path. We begin at the entrance. This is our present position. If the present position is the exit, then we have found a path and we are done. In case we are not at the exit, then we block the present position (i.e., place an obstacle there) so as to prevent the search from returning here. Next, we see if there is an adjacent maze position that is not blocked. If so, we move to this new adjacent position and attempt to find a path from here to the exit. In case we are unsuccessful, we attempt to move to some other unblocked adjacent maze position and try to find a path from there. If all adjacent unblocked positions have been tried and no path is found, there is no path from entrance to exit in the maze. The recursive nature of our maze search translates into the recursive refinement of Program 7.3.

To refine Program 7.3, we need representations for the maze which is a matrix of zeroes and ones, each maze position, and the path from entrance to exit. We can use the upper left corner of a square array, *maze*, to represent the maze. So, if the largest square array we can define (given the memory available to us) has a number of rows equal to *MaxRows* and the user's matrix has only *MazeRows*, *MazeRows* ≤ *MaxRows*, rows, then this matrix can be stored using rows 1 through *MazeSize* and columns 1 through *MazeSize* of *maze*.

Each maze position is described by its row and column index. These are, respectively, called the row and column coordinates of the position. The data type *position* may be defined as:

---

procedure *FindPath*;

procedure *RealPathFinder*(*PresentPosition*: *position*);
begin
   if we are at the exit **then** *found* := **true**;
   else {not at exit}
     block *PresentPosition*;
     while there are unblocked adjacent positions
                    and not *found* **do**
     begin
       RealPathFinder(*NewPosition*);
       if *found* **then** add *PresentPosition* to path;
     end; {of **while**}
end; {of *RealPathFinder*}

begin {body of *FindPath*}
   found := **false**;
   RealPathFinder(*Entrance*);
end; {of *FindPath*}

Program 7.3 Refined version of Program 7.2

type *position* = **record**
                row: **integer**;
                col: **integer**;
            end;

    Next, a representation for the path (if any) from the entrance to the exit is needed. A simple representation results from the use of a one dimensional array *path*[1..*MaxPathLength*] whose values are maze positions. The path to the exit is stored as a sequence of maze positions. An examination of Program 7.3 reveals that the position corresponding to the exit is not added to the path and that the remaining positions are added from exit to entrance (rather than from entrance to exit). So, if the exit is at (10,10) and the tail of the path is: ... (8,9), (9,9), (9,10), (10,10), then we shall have:

$path[1].row = 9$ $path[1].col = 10$
$path[2].row = 9$ $path[2].col = 9$
$path[3].row = 8$ $path[3].col = 9$

How long can the path from entrance to exit in a maze be? We know that the mazes we are to deal with are at most *MaxRows* long and wide and that no path contains an initially blocked position. Also, the path (if any) that we shall find will not go through a maze position more than once as each new position that we move to gets blocked. This prevents us from going in circles. Hence, no path contains more positions than the number of initially unblocked positions. This number is no more than *MaxRows∗MaxRows* (including the entrance and exit positions). We also see that a maze that has no obstacles in it has paths that are *MaxRows∗MaxRows* positions long (see Figure 7.5(a)). It also has paths that are $2MaxRows - 1$ long (see Figure 7.5(b)).

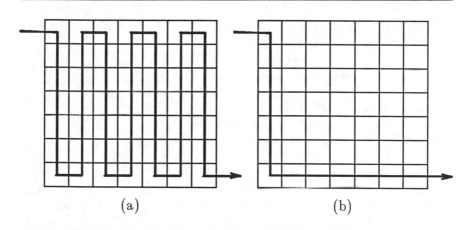

(a)   (b)

Figure 7.5

At this time, we do not know if our path finder will always find the shortest path in a maze. So, let us prepare for the worst and declare *MaxPathLength* to be a constant with value *MaxRows∗MaxRows* $- 1$ (recall that the exit coordinates are not placed in the array *path*). We can later change the value of the constant

MaxPathLength if we discover that our path finder never finds paths that are this long.

The data structures needed so far are two arrays defined as below:

var *maze*: **array** [1..*MaxRows*, 1..*MaxRows*] **of** 0..1;
    path: **array** [1..*MaxPathLength*] **of** *position*;

Since the path length will generally be less than *MaxPathLength* we need a variable *PathLength* that tells us the length of the path found. The variables *maze*, *path*, *MazeSize*, *PathLength*, and *found* will be global to all the functional modules. Let us assume that the largest possible value for *MaxRows*, given the memory available on the target computer, is 50. The declaration section of *RatInAMaze* can now be refined to:

constant *MaxRows* = 50;
    MaxPathLength = 2499; {*MaxRows*∗*MaxRows* − 1}

type *position* = **record**
                row: **integer**;
                col: **integer**;
        end;

var *maze*: **array** [1..*MaxRows*, 1..*MaxRows*] **of** 0..1;
    path: **array** [1..*MaxPathLength*] **of** *position*;
    MazeRows, *PathLength*: **integer**; *found*: **boolean**;

An alternate to saving the path in the array *path* is to save it in the array *maze* itself. In this case, each position in *maze* can have the value 0, 1, or 2. A 2 means that the position is on the path. The development of *FindPath* when this approach is taken is left as an exercise.

To find a path in the maze, we begin at position (1, 1). From here we can move to position (1, 2) if there is no obstacle there (*maze*[1,2] = 0) or we can move to position (2, 1) if there is no obstacle there. Since we can follow only one of these options at a time, we need to select one to try out. The second option can be tried in case the first option does not lead to the exit. Suppose that both options from (1, 1) are available and we elect to move to (1, 2). The problem is now that of finding a path from (1, 2) to the exit.

Before refining our procedure further, let us examine the options available from (1, 2). There are three options: move to any one of (1, 3), (2, 2), and (1, 1) (provided, of course, that no obstacle is present at these positions). The option of moving to (1, 1) is clearly not a desirable one as it gets us back to a position we have already been at. We can prevent moving back to positions that we have already gone through by placing obstacles there. While this destroys the user's maze, we will generally have no use for the maze after the search for a path has been completed. In case we wish to save the maze, then a copy can be made initially and the search procedure can use this copy. Alternatively, we can use the number "2" to block a previously unblocked maze position rather than "1" as is being done at present. Following the search for a path, all "2"'s in the maze can be reset to 0.

Our next refinement is Program 7.4. The program is beginning to look a lot like a Pascal program. It should not be too difficult to see that if Program 7.3 is correct then Program 7.4 is also correct. Adding a position to *path* is much like adding to a stack. However, because of the size of *path*, there is no need to check for space availability before adding a position to it. Notice how the English statements of Program 7.3 have become the comments of Program 7.4. Coming up with meaningful comments is easy when the program is developed in steps.

Before a further refinement can be made we need to resolve some issues. First, let us tackle the problem of determining the options available from any position (*RowNow*, *ColNow*).

From interior positions of the maze (i.e., those not on row 1, row *MazeSize*, column 1, and column *MazeSize*), there are four possibilities: right, down, left, and up. From positions on the boundary of the maze, there are either two or three possibilities. To avoid having to handle positions on the boundaries of the maze differently from interior positions, we shall surround the maze with a wall of obstacles. This wall will occupy rows 0 and *MazeSize* +1 and columns 0 and *MazeSize* +1 of the array *maze* (see Figure 7.6).

Now, all positions in the maze are within the boundary of the surrounding wall and there are four possible positions one can move to

---

procedure *FindPath*;

procedure *RealPathFinder*(*RowNow*, *ColNow*: **integer**);
{Find a path from (*x*, *y*) to the exit}
var *NewRow*, *NewCol*: **integer**;

begin {body of *RealPathFinder*}
   if [*RowNow*, *ColNow*] is the exit **then** *found* := **true**
   else {not at exit}
   begin
      {block present position}
      maze[*RowNow*, *ColNow*] := 1;

      {move from this position}
      while more options from [*RowNow*, *ColNow*] **and not** *found* **do**
      begin {try a new option}
         Let [*NewRow*, *NewCol*] be the position we are trying to move to;
         if *maze*[*NewRow*, *NewCol*] = 0
         then begin
               {search from new position}
               RealPathFinder(*NewRow*, *NewCol*);
               if *found* **then**
               begin
                  {add present position to *path*}
                  PathLength := *PathLength* + 1;
                  path[*PathLength*].*row* := *RowNow*;
                  path[*PathLength*].*col* := *ColNow*;
               end; {of **if** *found*}
             end; {of **if** *maze* = 0}
      end; {of **while**}
   end; {of **else** not at exit}
end; {of *RealPathFinder*}

Program 7.4 Refined version of Program 7.3
(Continued on next page)

```
begin {body of FindPath}
  found := false;
  PathLength := 0;
  RealPathFinder(1,1);
end; {of FindPath}
```

Program 7.4 Refined version of Program 7.3 (continued)

```
1 1 1 1 1 1 1 1 1 1 1 1
1 0 1 1 1 1 1 0 0 0 0 1
1 0 0 0 0 0 1 0 1 0 0 1
1 0 0 0 1 0 1 0 0 0 0 1
1 0 1 0 1 0 1 0 1 1 0 1
1 0 1 0 1 0 1 0 1 0 0 1
1 0 1 1 1 0 1 0 1 0 1 1
1 0 1 0 0 0 1 0 1 0 1 1
1 0 1 0 1 1 1 0 1 0 0 1
1 1 0 0 0 0 0 0 1 0 0 1
1 0 0 0 0 1 1 1 1 0 0 1
1 1 1 1 1 1 1 1 1 1 1 1
```

Figure 7.6 Maze of Figure 7.2 with wall of 1's around it

from each (some of these cannot be moved to because of the obstacles). By surrounding the maze with our own boundary, we have eliminated the need for our program to handle boundary conditions! This results in a significant simplification of the code. This simplification is achieved at the cost of some positions in the array *maze*. *maze* must now be declared as an array with indices in the range [0..*MaxRowsPlus1*, 0..*MaxRowsPlus1*].

The task of trying out alternate paths is simplified if we select from the options available at any position in some systematic way. One such way is to first attempt to move right, then down, then left, and lastly up (see Figure 7.7).

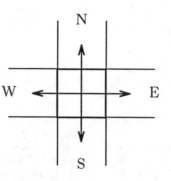

Figure 7.7 The four options from any position in the maze

move	direction	*offset*[*move*].*row*	*offset*[*move*].*col*
1	right	0	1
2	down	1	0
3	left	0	-1
4	up	-1	0

Figure 7.8 Table of offsets

Once an option has been selected, we need to know the coordinates of the position to move to. These are easily computed by maintaining a table of offsets as in Figure 7.8. The four moves right, down, left, and up have, respectively, been numbered 1, 2, 3, and 4. While Pascal permits us to use the array indices right, down, left, and up, the use of names rather than numerals for the four moves causes difficulties later in writing the program as up has no successor and down has no predecessor. In the table of Figure 7.8, *offset*[*i*].*row* and *offset*[*i*].*col*, respectively, give the amounts to be added to the *row* and *col* coordinates of the present position to move to the adjacent position in the direction *i*. For example, if we are presently at the position (3, 4), then the position on the right has *row* coordinate 3+*offset*[1].*row* = 3, and *col* coordinate 4+*offset*[1].*col* = 5.

Incorporating these refinements into the code of Program 7.4 results in the Pascal code of Program 7.5.

Iterative Version

It is interesting to investigate the course our program for the *FindPath* module would have taken if we had not realized the recursive nature of the problem. We begin with the version given in Program 7.2. From the present position [*RowNow*, *ColNow*], we attempt to move forward in the maze. If we are successful, then we move to the new position and from here we attempt to move yet further. In case we are unsuccessful, we need to move back to the previous position. In order to do this, we must remember all positions that we have moved forward from. This can be done by adding a position to *path* before we move forward from it. In this case, *path* records the path we have taken from the entrance to the present position. In case there is no previous position to move back to, all options have been tried and there is no path from the entrance of the maze to its exit. Program 7.6 is the resulting refinement of Program 7.2.

We should note the difference in the structure of *path* between the iterative and recursive versions. When the recursive program terminates, the path from entrance to maze is in reverse order whereas when the iterative version terminates, it is not. Further, we see that in Program 7.6, *path* operates as a stack. Old positions are removed from the same end of *path* as new positions are added to. The generality of the stack add and delete procedures of Chapter 6 is, however, not needed here. We know that the stack (i.e., *path*) will never be full at the time we wish to add a new position to it. Further, when a position is removed we do not care what the coordinates of this position are.

The development of a systematic way to try out options is the same as for the recursive version. The only additional development needed here is a method to determine the next option to try from the position that we are backing up to. A straightforward way to do this

---

```
procedure FindPath;
type displacements = record
                         row: −1..1;
                         col: −1..1;
                     end;
var offset: array [1..4] of displacements; i: integer;

procedure RealPathFinder(RowNow, ColNow: integer);
{Find a path from (RowNow, ColNow) to the exit}

var NewRow, NewCol, option: integer;

begin {body of RealPathFinder}
   if (RowNow = MazeSize) and (ColNow = MazeSize) then found := true
   else {not at exit}
   begin
      {block present position}
      maze[RowNow, ColNow] := 1;
      option := 1;
      while (option<5) and not found do
      begin {try a new option}
         NewRow := RowNow + offset[option].row;
         NewCol := ColNow + offset[option].col;
         if maze[NewRow, NewCol] = 0
         then begin
                 {search from new position}
                 RealPathFinder(NewRow, NewCol);
                 if found then
                 begin
                    {add present position to path}
                    PathLength := PathLength + 1;
                    path[PathLength].row := RowNow;
                    path[PathLength].col := ColNow;
                 end; {of if found}
              end; {of if maze = 0}
```

Program 7.5 Pascal version of Program 7.4
(Continued on next page)

```
      option := option + 1;
    end; {of while}
  end; {of else not at exit}
end; {of RealPathFinder}
begin {body of FindPath}
  found := false;
  PathLength := 0;

  {initialize maze boundary}
  for i := 0 to MazeSize + 1 do
  begin
    maze[0, i] := 1; maze[MazeSize + 1, i] := 1;
    maze[i, 0] := 1; maze[i, MazeSize + 1] := 1;
  end;

  {initialize offsets}
  offset[1].row := 0; offset[1].col := 1; {right}
  offset[2].row := 1; offset[2].col := 0; {down}
  offset[3].row := 0; offset[3].col := -1; {left}
  offset[4].row := -1; offset[4].col := 0; {up}

  {search for path}
  RealPathFinder(1,1);
end; {of FindPath}
```

Program 7.5 Pascal version of Program 7.4 (continued)

is to save the last option used along with the coordinates of the position on the path stack. Saving the last option used is unnecessary as the next option can be computed using information that is already on the path stack. One can verify that if [*RowNow*, *ColNow*] is the position we are presently at and *path*[*PathLength*] is the position we are backing up to, then the next option (*option*) to try is correctly computed by the statement:

```
if path[PathLength].row = RowNow
then option := 3+path[PathLength].col-ColNow
else option := 4+path[PathLength].row-RowNow;
```

The preceding computation yields a value of 5 for *option* iff all four

---

```
procedure FindPath;
var done: boolean;
begin {body of FindPath}

   {initialize variables}
   done := false;
   Initialize path empty;
   Set present position to maze entrance;
   Place an obstacle at the entrance;

   {search for path}
   repeat
      if we are at the exit then done := true
      else
      begin {not at exit}
         if we can move forward from the present position
         then begin
                 Put present position on path;
                 Move to new position;
                 Block new position;
              end
         else {back up to previous position}
            if path empty then done := true
            else begin
               Move to last position on path;
               Take this position off path;
            end; {of back up}
      end; {of not at exit}
   until done;
   if exit is blocked {exit is initially unblocked}
   then found := true {reached exit}
   else found := false; {did not reach exit}
end; {of FindPath}
```

Program 7.6 Iterative refinement of Program 7.2

options from the previous position have been tried. At this point, we can refine Program 7.6 to obtain the Pascal procedure given in Program 7.7.

```
procedure FindPath;
type displacements = record row: −1..1; col: −1..1; end;

var offset: array [1..4] of displacements;
    yes, done: boolean; i: integer;
    RowNow, ColNow, NewRow, NewCol, option: integer;

begin {body of FindPath}

    {Initialize variables}
    PathLength := 0; {path empty}
    done := false;
    RowNow := 1; ColNow := 1; {maze entrance}
    option := 1; maze[1,1] := 1; {obstacle at entrance}

    {Initialize maze boundary}
    for i := 0 to MazeSize + 1 do
    begin
        maze[0, i] := 1; maze[MazeSize + 1, i] := 1;
        maze[i, 0] := 1; maze[i, MazeSize + 1] := 1;
    end;

    {Initialize offsets}
    offset[1].row := 0; offset[1].col := 1; {right}
    offset[2].row := 1; offset[2].col := 0; {down}
    offset[3].row := 0; offset[3].col := −1; {left}
    offset[4].row := −1; offset[4].col := 0; {up}

    repeat {search for path}
        if (RowNow = MazeSize) and (ColNow = MazeSize) then
            {we are at the exit}
            done := true
        else begin {not at exit}
            {can we move forward?}
            yes := false;
```

Program 7.7 Final refinement of Program 7.6
(Continued on next page)

```
    while (option < 5) and not yes do
    begin
        NewRow := RowNow + offset[option].row;
        NewCol := ColNow + offset[option].col;
        if maze[NewRow, NewCol] = 0 then yes := true
        else option := option + 1;
    end; {of while not yes}

    if yes then begin
        {put present position on path}
        PathLength := PathLength +1;
        path[PathLength].row := RowNow;
        path[PathLength].col := ColNow;

        {move to new position}
        RowNow := NewRow; ColNow := NewCol; option := 1;

        {place obstacle at new position}
        maze[RowNow, ColNow] := 1;
    end
    else begin  {back up on path}
        if PathLength = 0 then done := true
        else begin
            {compute next option to try from previous position}
            if path[PathLength].row = RowNow
            then option := 3+path[PathLength].col−ColNow
            else option := 4+path[PathLength].row−RowNow;

            {move to last position on path}
            RowNow := path[PathLength].row; ColNow := path[PathLength].col;
            PathLength := PathLength−1; {take off path}
        end; {of if PathLength = 0}
    end; {of if yes}
  end; {of if not at exit}
until done;
```

Program 7.7 Final refinement of Program 7.6
(Continued on next page)

---

if *maze* [*MazeSize*, *MazeSize*] = 1 **then** *found* := **true**
                      else *found* := **false**;
end; {of *FindPath*}

Program 7.7 Final refinement of Program 7.6 (continued)

The iterative version of *FindPath* is somewhat longer than the recursive version and is also somewhat harder to follow. Recursion is a very important tool that can be effectively used to enhance program comprehensibility. It should, however, be used only in situations where a recursive formulation is natural.

In a later chapter, we shall see that the computer memory required by the recursive version is larger than that required by the iterative version. Also, the iterative version can be expected to run slightly faster than the recursive version. So, on the performance criteria, the iterative version is preferable.

Whether the recursive or the iterative version should be used depends on whether comprehensibility is more important than performance in our particular environment.

Summary

A very short (say upto 10 lines) and logically straightforward procedure can often be written correctly in one pass. For longer and more complex procedures, it is best to first write them in a language closer to English and then successively refine this version of the procedure into Pascal code. So, coding *into* Pascal is to be preferred to coding *in* Pascal when we are coding reasonably complex modules. The advantages of this approach are:

(1)   It is easier to see that the initial English version is correct. By keeping each successive refinement small, one can ensure that the refined version is correct provided the previous version is correct. So, we can have greater confidence in the correctness of the final Pascal code than if we had arrived at it in one step.

(2)   Data structure and algorithm decisions are made as the need for these arises. In contrast, when we program *in* Pascal all data structure and algorithm decisions need to be made at once.

(3) It is easier to identify common tasks that should be coded as procedures/functions.

(4) The problem of developing meaningful comments is alleviated. The high level English statements of one version become the comments of the refined version.

While the discussion of this section suggests a sequential development process, it will often be necessary to go back and revise decisions made earlier. Program development, like the entire programming process, is an iterative process.

7.3. SORTING

Specification

Write a Pascal procedure to sort n elements of type *element* which are stored in an array $a[0..MaxSize]$ of type *ElementList*. The elements themselves occupy positions 1 through n of this array. Obviously, $n \leq MaxSize$ as otherwise we can't fit this many elements in the array. The procedure is to have exactly two parameters. One of type *ElementList* (for the elements to be sorted) and the other of type **integer** (for the number of elements). The data type *element* is a record with an as yet undetermined number of fields. However, it has at least the field *key* which is the field on which the records are to be sorted. This key is of type **integer**. The purpose of the sort is to rearrange the n elements so that $a[1].key \leq a[2].key \leq \dots \leq a[n].key$. You may assume that n is sufficiently small that the sort can be completed in memory and no accesses to an external storage device such as a disk are needed.

Design

The problem specification is sufficiently detailed that very little design work is needed. The only issue to resolve is whether the sort procedure is to be designed for use by other parts of the program or by an interactive user. If the latter is the case, then we might wish to make the procedure menu driven and also include help facilities. Since the environment in which the sort procedure is to be used has not been specified by the problem originator, we may seek a clarification from him/her. Assume that the problem originator tells us that the sort procedure is to be used by other parts of the program. So, it is pointless to design a menu driven procedure with a help facility.

The problem specification is such that no capabilities design is called for either.

Program Plan

At this point the problem appears to be sufficiently small that no modularization to improve intellectual manageability is called for. The program plan is to simply obtain a single module that accomplishes the sort. This module will have the form given in Program 7.8.

---

procedure *sort*(**var** *a*: *ElementList*; *n*: **integer**);

begin
    sort *a*[1..*n*] into nondecreasing order of *a*[*i*].*key*;
end; {of *sort*}

Program 7.8 First version of sort module

Program Development

The data representation of the elements has already been determined. The sort algorithm, however, has not been determined. Before attempting to design our own sort algorithm, we should go to the library and check if this problem has been previously studied. We will discover a wealth of information on this problem. In fact, if we come across the book:

> *The Art Of Computer Programming: Sorting and Searching*,
> Vol. 3, by D. E. Knuth, Addison Wesley, 1973.

we shall see a multitude of sort algorithms presented in a form suitable for easy coding into Pascal. If we come across the book:

> *Fundamentals Of Data Structures In Pascal*, by E. Horowitz
> and S. Sahni, Computer Science Press, 1984.

our task will be even easier as this book contains Pascal procedures for sorting. We now need to simply decide which of these to use. Since this book contains guidelines on when to use each procedure, another consultation with the problem originator to further define the problem environment will enable us to make the selection.

The strategy suggested above is in sharp contrast to the attitude of many programmers. This attitude is best described by the phrase *Not Invented Here* (NIH). Programmers with this attitude find it necessary to develop everything from scratch. Nothing done by others is good enough for them. This attitude results in significantly longer program development time and doesn't necessarily result in better software. It is good practice to see what already exists and evaluate its suitability for the application at hand. If existing software and/or algorithms are found to be suitable, these should be used.

Unfortunately, in a book of this type we are compelled to take the NIH attitude. The reason for this is that the objective of this book is to illustrate the mechanics of program development.

Having just seen the insertion problem in Chapter 6, we might immediately see that n elements can be sorted by beginning with a list of size one (which is clearly sorted) and then inserting the remaining elements into this list one at a time. Suppose we begin with the key sequence:

20 18 15 17 5

These are respectively the key values in positions 1 through 5 of the element list. We begin by inserting the element with key 18 into the sorted list (20) and obtain the sorted list (18, 20). The key sequence in the entire five element list is now:

18 20 15 17 5

Next, the element with key 15 is inserted into the sorted list (18, 20). The resulting key sequence is:

15 18 20 17 5

Inserting the element with key 17 into the sorted sequence (15, 18, 20) yields the key sequence:

15 17 18 20 5

Finally, the fifth element is inserted and we get the sorted sequence:

5 15 17 18 20

---

procedure *sort*(**var** *a*: *ElementList*, *n*: **integer**);
{sort *a*[1..*n*] into nondecreasing order of *a*[*i*].*key*}
{The insertion method is used}

var *i*: **integer**;

begin
  for *i* := 2 **to** *n* **do**
    Insert *a*[*i*] into the sorted sequence *a*[1..*i* − 1];
end; {of *sort*}

Program 7.9 Insertion sort algorithm

Program 7.8 can now be refined to obtain Program 7.9. Since, we already have a procedure (procedure *insert*, Program 6.13) that performs the task specified in the **for** loop of procedure *sort*, we proceed to determine the suitability of this for our application. We can make the following observations about the suitability of this procedure:

(1) The defense mechanism against the element list getting too large (i.e., the test *n* = *MaxSize*) may be dropped as we are guaranteed that the total number of elements is at most *MaxSize*.

(2) Since the keys are of type integer, we can simply set *a*[0].*key* to −**maxint** in procedure *sort* and eliminate the initialization of *a*[0] from procedure *insert*.

(3) Where should *insert* be physically placed? Should it be placed within procedure *sort* or should we provide two modules: *insert* and *sort*. The advantage of doing the latter is that *insert* can then be used by other procedures if needed. However, after we have customized it taking the above observations into account, it may not be suitable for use by other procedures. Another argument against providing two modules is that if the sort is part of a very large program, then the name *insert* may have been assigned to some other module.

Once we have made the decision to place *insert* within *sort*, additional issues arise. Should the element list be passed to *insert* as a parameter or should it be a global variable? How about the element to be inserted and the current size of the sorted segment of the element list? In Chapter 11, we shall see that the decisions made here will affect the performance of the sort procedure. For now, let us simply decide to make all these variables global to *insert*.

Taking these observations into consideration, we arrive at the refinement given in Program 7.10.

At this time, the efficiency conscious programmer may decide that he/she can get some improvement in performance by directly writing the code for *insert* into the body of *sort*. This avoids the run time overhead of calling the procedure *insert*. In this particular example, this is not too bad a thing to do as the overall sort algorithm is sufficiently simple that the resulting loss in program readability is quite negligible. The sort module that results from this action is given in Program 7.11.

It is important to note the subjective nature of many of the decisions made here. The questions asked in observation (3) above and the question "Is Program 7.11 to be preferred over 7.10?" cannot be answered in any mathematically precise way. In both cases, the answers involve a tradeoff between a subjective quantity (program readability) and an objective quantity (performance). The performance gain is quite marginal when global variables are used in place of parameters. Also, the performance gain in going from Program 7.10 to 7.11 is also quite marginal. At the same time, the loss in readability is also quite small.

We will return to the sorting problem in subsequent chapters. There, we shall develop sort methods that are significantly faster than insertion sort.

7.4. NETS

Specification

This problem arises in the design of electronic circuits. These circuits consist of components, pins, and wires. A sample circuit is shown in

```
procedure sort(var a: ElementList; n: integer);
{sort a[1..n] into nondecreasing order of the integer field key}
{Position 0 of a is available}
{The insertion method is used}

var i: integer; x: element;

procedure insert;
{insert x into a[1..i−1]}

var j: integer;

begin {body of insert}
    j := i−1;
    while a[j].key > x.key do
    begin
        a[j+1] := a[j];
        j := j−1;
    end;
    a[j+1] := x;
end; {of insert}

begin {body of sort}
    a[0].key := − maxint; {boundary condition for insert}
    for i := 2 to n do
    begin
        x := a[i];
        insert;
    end;
end; {of sort}
```

Program 7.10 Insertion sort

Figure 7.9. Each wire connects a pair of pins. Two pins i and j are *electrically equivalent* iff there is a (possibly empty) sequence i_1, i_2, ... i_k of pins such that i, i_1; i_1, i_2; i_2, i_3; ..., i_{k-1}, i_k; and i_k, j are all connected by wires. A *net* is a maximal set of electrically equivalent pins. By maximal, we mean that there is no pin outside the net which is electrically equivalent to a pin in the net.

```
procedure sort(var a: ElementList; n: integer);
{sort a[1..n] into nondecreasing order of the integer field key}
{Position 0 of a is available}
{The insertion method is used}

var i, j: integer; x: element;

begin {body of sort}
    a[0].key := − maxint; {boundary condition}
    for i := 2 to n do
    begin
        x := a[i];

        {insert x into a[1..i−1]}
        j := i−1;
        while a[j].key > x.key do
        begin
            a[j+1] := a[j];
            j := j−1;
        end; {of while loop}
        a[j+1] := x;
    end; {of for loop}
end; {of sort}
```

Program 7.11 Insertion sort

Example 7.1: Consider the circuit shown in Figure 7.10. In this figure only the pins and wires have been shown. There are fourteen pins numbered 1 through 14. Each wire may be described by the two pins that it connects. For instance, the wire connecting pins 1 and 11 is described by the pair (1,11) which is equivalent to the pair (11,1). The set of wires is {(1,11), (7,11), (2,12), (12,8), (11,12), (3,13), (4,13), (13,14), (14,9), (5,14), (6,10)}.

Since, pins 1 and 11, and pins 11 and 12 are connected by wires, pins 1, 11, and 12 are electrically equivalent. They are therefore in the same net. These three pins do not, however, form a net as there are other pins that they are electrically equivalent to (e.g., pin 7). So, {1, 11, 12} is not a maximal set of electrically equivalent pins. The set {1, 2, 7, 8, 11, 12} of pins is a net. The circuit of Figure 7.10 has

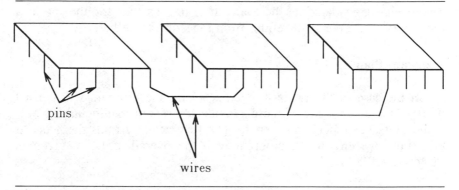

Figure 7.9 A 3 chip circuit on a printed circuit board

two other nets. These are {3, 4, 5, 9, 13, 14} and {6, 10}. □

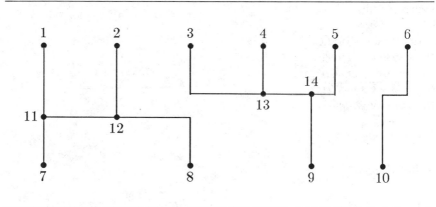

Figure 7.10 Circuit for Example 7.1

You are to write a program that determines the nets in any given circuit. You may assume that the circuits your program has to deal with are sufficiently small that all relevant data can be held in memory.

Design

The design considerations here are the same as that for the rat in a maze problem. We shall refrain from repeating these here.

Program Plan

As in the case of the rat in a maze problem, the program will consist of five modules. Four of these provide for screen manipulation, welcome message, input, and output. The fifth actually finds the nets. At this time, we envision a program with the overall structure given in Program 7.12.

---

program *Nets*(input, output);

{Declaration section}

{Screen utilities}

{Functional Modules}
procedure *welcome*;
procedure *InputCircuit*;
procedure *FindNets*;
procedure *OutputNets*;

begin {body of *Nets*}
  welcome;
  InputCircuit;
  FindNets;
  OutputNets;
end. {of *Nets*}

Program 7.12 Form of net finding program

Program Development

Input Module

The input to the program consists of the number of pins (*NumberOf-Pins*) and the end points of the wires in the circuit. These end points are in the range 1 through *NumberOfPins*. The input module must verify that *NumberOfPins*>0 as otherwise there are no nets to be found. In addition, it should protect itself from bad input by verifying that the end points of each wire are in the specified range. The input module, in addition to accepting the input in a user friendly way must store the wires in memory in a form suitable for use by the net finding module. So, before we can discuss the input module further, we need to determine how the net finding module will work.

Net Finding Module

All nets in a circuit may be found by following the strategy:

> *look at the pins one at a time; if a pin hasn't yet been placed in a net, then begin a new net with this pin in it and determine all other pins in the same net as this pin.*

If we try this strategy out on the circuit of Figure 7.10, we shall first obtain the net containing pin 1, then the net containing pin 3, and finally the net containing pin 6. It is clear that this strategy is guaranteed to work on all circuits. Program 7.13 is the version of *FindNets* that we obtain when this strategy is used.

At this point, we see that the nets are being generated one by one and we might as well output them as they are generated. To do this, we need to revise the form of our overall program (Program 7.12). This revision involves realizing that the output module must now be able to output nets one at a time and that this module will be invoked from *FindNets* rather than from the body of *Nets*. The revised version of Program 7.12 is given as Program 7.14.

The decision to output nets one at a time may also be incorporated into Program 7.13. Before writing a new refinement of this program, we shall make some additional decisions. Let us examine

---

```
procedure FindNets;
var i: integer;

begin
   for i := 1 to n do
      if pin i hasn't been placed in a net yet then
      begin {i is in a new net}
         begin a new net with pin i in it;
         find all pins in this net;
      end; {of if and for}
end; {of FindNets}
```

Program 7.13 First version of *FindNets*

```
program Nets(input, output);

{Declaration section}

{Screen utilities}

{Functional Modules}
procedure welcome;
procedure InputCircuit;
procedure OutputANet;
procedure FindNets;

begin {body of Nets}
   welcome;
   InputCircuit;
   FindNets;
end. {of Nets}
```

Program 7.14 Revised version of Program 7.12

how we can find all pins that are in the same net as another pin i. An obvious way to do this is to begin at pin i and include all pins that are directly connected to this pin by a wire. These directly connected pins are saved on a list called "new pin list" for further processing.

Next, we look at pin that is on the new pin list. All pins that are directly connected to this and which haven't yet been assigned to this net are now assigned to this net. These newly assigned pins are added to the new pin list. This process is iterated until the new pin list becomes empty.

We illustrate this method on the circuit of Figure 7.10. Let us begin with pin 1. This pin is directly connected to pin 11. So, pin 11 is in the same net as pin 1. Pin 11 is added to the initially empty new pin list. Next, we see that pin 11 is directly connected to the pins 1, 7, and 12. Of these, pin 1 has already been assigned to this net. So, only pins 7 and 12 are added to the net. At this time, the new pin list contains the pins 7 and 12. Suppose that pin 7 is removed from this list for further processing. All the pins that pin 7 is directly connected to have already been assigned to this net. So, no additions are made to either the net or the new pin list. Next, pin 12 is removed from the new pin list. Pin 12 gets us two additional pins for this net. These are pins 2 and 8. These are added to the net and the new pin list. Further processing of the pins on the new pin list does not yield any additional pins for this net.

Since the above procedure finds the pins in a net one by one, we can output the pins in a net as they are generated rather than wait for the entire net to be generated. This requires us to revise the output module so that it consists of three procedures. One begins a net, the second continues the output of the net being generated, and the third finishes the output of the current net. The first two procedures will have a parameter that is a pin number. The third procedure has no parameters. We may revise Program 7.14 and get Program 7.15.

In order to keep track of pins that have already been output, we shall use the Boolean array *out*. *out*[i] = **true** iff pin i has already been output. Our net determination and output strategy can now be incorporated into Program 7.13 to obtain the refinement given in Program 7.16. Notice that the new pin list is initialized just once rather than each time a new net is begun. This is so as this list is left empty following the output of each net.

For each pin we need to know the pins that it is directly connected to. With each pin, we shall keep an explicit list of all pins that are directly connected to it. These lists will be created by the input module as it reads in the wires. Since there is no advance information

---

program *Nets*(input, output);

{Declaration section}

{Screen utilities}

{Functional Modules}
procedure *welcome*;
procedure *InputCircuit*;
procedure *BeginNet*(*OutputPin*: **integer**);
procedure *ContinueNet*(*OutputPin*: **integer**);
procedure *FinishNet*;
procedure *FindNets*;

begin {body of *Nets*}
  welcome;
  InputCircuit;
  FindNets;
end. {of *Nets*}

Program 7.15 Revised version of Program 7.13

about the number of pins that can be expected to be on each of these lists, we shall set these up as linked lists (if you haven't used Pascal pointers yet, see Section 12.3.1 for a quick introduction). The nodes on the lists will have two fields: *pin* and *link*. Each node on a list links to the next node via the field *link*. The last node on the list has *link* = **nil**. Linked lists of this type are called *chains*.

An example seven pin circuit is shown in Figure 7.11(a). This circuit has six wires and two nets ({1, 2, 3} and {4, 5, 6, 7}). The input to the input module consists of the number of pins (i.e., 7) and a list of wires. The wires are input as pairs of pins. For our example, six pin pairs are input as we have six wires. These six pairs are shown in Figure 7.11(b). The list structure created by the input module is shown in Figure 7.11(c).

The structure of Figure 7.11(c) uses an array, *PinList*, of pointers to the first node in each list. This is used to keep track of the lists of directly connected pins. The data type and variable declarations

```
procedure FindNets;
var out: array [1..MaxPins] of boolean; i: integer;

begin
  {initialize out}
  for i := 1 to NumberOfPins do
    out[i] := false;
  initialize new pin list to be empty;

  {examine pins one by one and output nets}
  for i := 1 to NumberOfPins do
    if not out[i] then begin
      BeginNet(i);
      out[i] := true;

      {Determine all pins in net containing pin i and output}
      NewPin := i; done := false;
      repeat {until new pin list is empty}
        All pins directly connected to NewPin but not yet output
        are part of the new net.
        So, output these, set out to true for these, and
        put them on the list of new pins;
        if new pin list is empty then done := true
                else take a pin off this list and assign it to NewPin;
      until done;
    end; {of if and for}
end; {of FindNets}
```

Program 7.16 Refinement of Program 7.13

needed are:

```
type NodePtr = ↑ node;
     node = record
                 pin: integer;
                 link: NodePtr;
              end;
var PinList: array [1..MaxPins] of NodePtr;
```

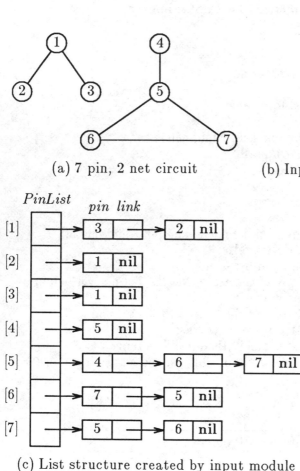

(a) 7 pin, 2 net circuit

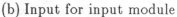

(1,2)
(1,3)
(4,5)
(5,6)
(5,7)
(6,7)

(b) Input for input module

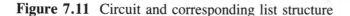

(c) List structure created by input module

Figure 7.11 Circuit and corresponding list structure

Another data structure that is needed is one that maintains the list of new pins. This list can be maintained as a linked list of *nodes* with the variable *front* pointing to the first node in the list. Each node links to the next through the field *link*. The last node on the list has *link* = **nil**. So, the list of new pins is also maintained as a chain. When the chain becomes empty (i.e., has no nodes on it), *front* = **nil**. We shall add new nodes at the front of the chain. Also, nodes will be removed from the front of the chain. So, the list of new pins operates as a stack.

With these decisions made, we can refine Program 7.16 into the Pascal code of Program 7.17.

```
procedure FindNets;
var out: array [1..MaxPins] of boolean; i, j: integer;
    front, k, ptr: NodePtr;

begin
  {initialize out}
  for i := 1 to NumberOfPins do
    out[i] := false;
  front := nil; {initialize new pin list}

  {examine pins one by one and output nets}
  for i := 1 to NumberOfPins do
    if not out[i] then begin
      BeginNet(i);
      out[i] := true;
```

Program 7.17 Final version of FindNets
          (Continued on next page)

Input Module (resumed)

From the discussion and development of the module to find nets, we see that the input module will have the form given in Program 7.18. The refinement of this module into pure Pascal code is left as an exercise.

7.5. ASSEMBLY LINE ORDERING

Specification

On an assembly line, a product such as an automobile is assembled by a sequence of workers. Each performs his/her task after the preceding

---

```
{Determine all pins in net containing pin i and output}
NewPin := i; done := false;
repeat {until new pin list is empty}
    {Process all pins directly connected to NewPin}
    ptr := PinList[NewPin];
    while ptr <> nil do
    begin
        j := ptr ↑ .pin;
        if not out[j] then
        begin
            ContinueNet(j);  {output j}
            out[j] := true;
            k := ptr ↑ .link;

            {add j to list of new pins}
            ptr ↑ .link := front; front := ptr;

            ptr := k;
        end
        else ptr := ptr ↑ .link;
    end; {of while}
    if front = nil then done := true
    else begin
            NewPin := front ↑ .pin;
            front := front ↑ .link;
        end; {of if front = nil}
until done;
FinishNet;
  end; {of if and for}
end; {of FindNets}
```

Program 7.17 Final version of *FindNets* (continued)

---

task on the line has been completed. An assembly line may therefore be viewed as a straight line with work stations located along this line as in Figure 7.12. At each station, a specific task is performed. The materials needed for this task are available at the station. The assembly begins at the left end and the assembled product rolls off the right end of the line.

---

procedure *InputCircuit*;
begin
    Display message describing program and problem size limits;
    Input *NumberOfPins*;
    Initialize *PinList*[*i*] to **nil**, $1 \le i \le n$;
    Ask for wires;
    while more wires **do**
    begin
        Input wire (i, j);
        Put pin *i* on the list *PinList*[*j*];
        Put pin *j* on the list *PinList*[*i*];
    end;
end; {of *InputCircuit*}

Program 7.18 First version of input module

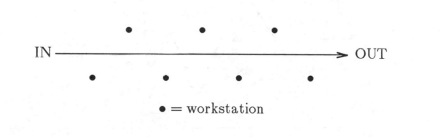

Figure 7.12 An assembly line

    The assembly line ordering problem is to order the assembly tasks to be performed so that they can be assigned to the stations left to right. This ordering must satisfy a prespecified precedence relation between the tasks. This relation consists of a set of pairs (i, j) with the interpretation that task *i* must complete before task *j* can begin. Hence, the workstation for *i* must be to the left of the workstation for *j*.

As an example, suppose we have an assembly problem that requires eight tasks to be performed. Assume that these have been numbered 1−8. The precedence relation is given by the set of pairs:

{(1, 2), (2, 3), (2, 5), (2, 7), (5, 6), (7, 6), (8, 3), (8, 4), (4, 7)}

This set may be drawn pictorially as in Figure 7.13. In this figure, each task is represented by a circle (called a vertex) and each pair by a directed line (called an edge). Task *i* is an *immediate predecessor* of task *j* iff there is a directed edge from *i* to *j* (i.e., iff (*i*, *j*) is a pair in the precedence relation). *j* is an *immediate successor* of *i* iff *i* is an immediate predecessor of *j*. A precedence relation is a special case of the more general structure *graph*. This is studied in Chapter 13.

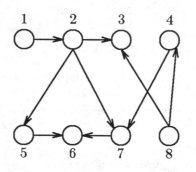

Figure 7.13 Pictorial representation of a precedence relation

For the example assembly problem, there are several linear orderings of the tasks that satisfy the precedence constraints. Some of these are:

1 2 5 8 3 4 7 6
8 4 1 2 3 7 5 6
1 2 8 3 4 5 7 6
8 1 4 2 7 5 6 3

You are to design and implement a Pascal program for the assembly line ordering problem.

Design

Proceeding in a top down modular fashion, we see the need for the following modules: welcome, input, find a linear order, output the linear order. The welcome module will provide the user with a functional description of the capabilities of the program and also provide the version number and any other identifying information associated with the program.

The input module will determine the number of tasks and input the pairs that constitute the precedence relation. This module will check for consistency in data and detect obvious input errors such as the number of tasks being smaller than 1 or larger than the program's capacity, and a pair (i, j) in which either i or j is not in the range [1, *NumberOfTasks*]. In designing the input format, one should keep in mind that it is unreasonable to ask the user to present the pairs in any particular order. So, the input module should accept these pairs in any order the user chooses and create the desired internal representation.

The output module is quite straightforward. It simply outputs the tasks in the left to right order found. Some messages to explain the output may be added.

The module that actually finds the linear order does not interact with the user and there is no user interface design work involved here.

Program Plan

The program plan is quite similar to that for the net finding problem. We envision a program such as the one shown in Program 7.19.

As in the case of the net finding program, we shall find it convenient to output the linear order as it is generated. So, the procedure *OutputOrder* will not be invoked from the body of *AssemblyLine* as it currently is in Program 7.19.

---

program *AssemblyLine*(input, output);

{Declaration section}

{Screen utilities}

{Functional Modules}
procedure *welcome*;
procedure *InputRelation*;
procedure *LinearOrder*;
procedure *OutputOrder*;

begin {body of *AssemblyLine*}
   welcome;
   InputRelation;
   LinearOrder;
   OutputOrder;
end. {of *AssemblyLine*}

Program 7.19 Form of assembly line ordering program

Program Development

Substantial developmental issues arise only in the case of the *LinearOrder* module. Hence, we shall discuss this module only. Once this has been designed, the input and output modules can be designed. Let us begin with Figure 7.13 and try to develop an algorithm to obtain a linear order. We see that tasks that have no immediate predecessors are the only candidates for the first position in this order. So, the first task must be either 1 or 8. Does it matter which we select for this position? We don't know the answer at this time. But, let us continue with either and see if it leads to any difficulties later on. For the sake of definiteness, suppose that we opt for task 8 in position 1 of the linear order.

    Since task 8 has been assigned, the precedence edges (8, 3) and (8, 4) may be removed from Figure 7.13. We can do this as no matter where we subsequently decide to place tasks 3 and 4, these cannot appear before task 8. So the precedence with respect to this task must be satisfied. In addition, task 8 may also be removed. When this is done, we get the graph of Figure 7.14 (a).

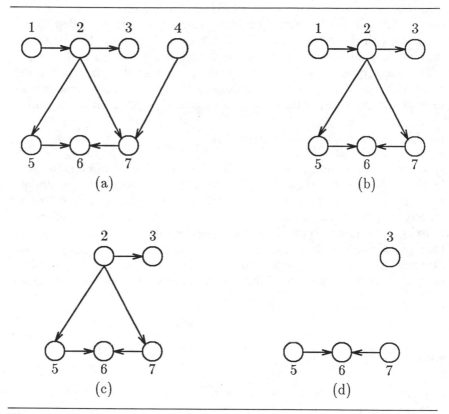

Figure 7.14

From Figure 7.14 (a), it is evident that either of the tasks 1 and 4 can occupy the second position in the linear order. If task 4 is chosen for this position, then Figure 7.14 (b) results from the deletion of this task and the edge (4, 7). At this time, either of the tasks 1 and 7 may be added to the linear order. Suppose that task 1 is added. Deleting this task and the edge (1, 2) results in the graph of Figure 7.14 (c). Now, either of 2 and 7 may be added to the linear order. If 2 is added, the resulting graph is as in Figure 7.14 (d) and the linear order built to this point is 8, 4, 1, 2. Next, we may choose any one of the tasks 3, 5, and 7. Proceeding in this way, a linear order can be generated.

Can anything cause the procedure described above to fail to produce a linear order? As can be seen, a new task can be added to the order at each step provided that there is at least one task with no immediate predecessor. If at any step this is not the case, then there is no linear order possible. To see this, suppose that there are tasks remaining and that each one of these has at least one immediate predecessor. In this case, there must be a sequence of edges of the form:

$$(i_1, i_2), (i_2, i_3), (i_3, i_4), ..., (i_k, i_1)$$

where k is some integer. This is so as the number of remaining tasks is finite. From this sequence, we see that the precedence constraints require that task i_1 must precede itself on the assembly line. This is clearly impossible and no linear order that satisfies the constraints exists. This is the only time the algorithm discussed above fails to produce a linear order. Hence, the outcome of the algorithm is not affected by the choice from amongst the tasks with no immediate predecessors at any step. The above discussion leads to Program 7.20.

```
procedure LinearOrder;
begin
    {create the linear order one task at a time}
    while at least one task with no immediate
                    predecessors remains do
        output any one of the remaining tasks with no immediate
        predecessors as the next task in the linear order;
        delete this task and all precedence pairs it is in;
    end;

    if some tasks remain then  output error
                        else output success;
end; {of LinearOrder}
```

Program 7.20 First version of *LinearOrder*

In order to refine Program 7.20 into a Pascal procedure, we need to decide on a representation for the precedence relation. This representation should facilitate the following tasks:

(1)   Determine if there is at least one remaining task with no immediate predecessor.

(2)   Select one such task.

(3)   Delete a selected task with no immediate predecessor and also delete all the pairs it is in.

(4)   Creation of the representation from an unordered list of precedence pairs.

The linked representation of Figure 7.15 meets our requirements. In this representation, each task is represented by a linked list. This is a list of all the immediate successors of the task. The head node of each list keeps a count of the number of immediate predecessors of the task.   This representation is easily created from the unordered input pairs (see the exercises).   Tasks with zero immediate predecessors can be easily determined.   To delete a task and its associated pairs, we need merely go down the successor list and decrement the predecessor count of each of the tasks on this list.

The data types needed to implement this representation are:

```
type link =  ↑ node;
     node = record
                  task : integer;
                  next : link;
             end;
     HeadNodes = record
                       count : integer;
                       next: link;
                  end;

var list: array [1..MaxTasks] of HeadNodes;
```

In order to facilitate the easy identification of a task with zero immediate predecessors, we shall maintain a list of all such tasks. This list will be a linked list of the task head nodes. This list will operate as a stack and the variable *top* will point to the top task on the list.   We can now refine Program 7.20 to get Program 7.21.   This may be further refined to get the Pascal code of Program 7.22.

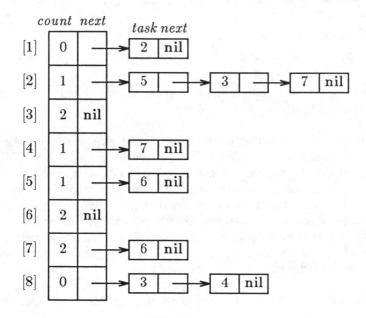

Figure 7.15 Representation for the relation of Figure 7.13

7.6. REFERENCES AND SELECTED READINGS

The following texts are a good source of further material and examples on stepwise program development:

The science of programming, by D. Gries, Springer-Verlag, New York, 1981.

A discipline of programming, by E. Dijkstra, Prentice-Hall, New Jersey, 1976.

Structured Programming, by O. Dahl, E. Dijkstra, and C. Hoare, Academic Press, New York, 1972.

Software engineering: A practitioner's approach, by R.

---

procedure *LinearOrder*;
begin
    initialize the stack of tasks with zero immediate predecessors;

    {create the linear order one task at a time}
    while stack not empty **do**
        remove the top task on the stack;
        output this as the next task in the linear order;
        go down the list for this task and decrement counts;
        if any task's count becomes zero, add it to the stack;
    end;
    if fewer than *NumberOfTasks* tasks have been ouput
    then output error
    else output sucess;
end; {of *LinearOrder*}

Program 7.21 Refinement of Program 7.20

Pressman, McGraw Hill, New York, 1982.

Principles of software engineering and design, by M. Zelkowitz, A. Shaw, and J. Gannon, Prentice-Hall, New Jersey, 1979.

7.7. EXERCISES

1. Develop the *welcome* module of the *RatInAMaze* program. Do this using stepwise refinement.

2. Develop the *InputMaze* module of the *RatInAMaze* program. Do this using stepwise refinement.

3. Develop the *OutputMaze* module of the *RatInAMaze* program. Do this using stepwise refinement.

---

procedure *LinearOrder*;

var *top*, {top of stack}
    NumberOut, NextTask,
    i : **integer**;
    pointer : *link*;

begin
    {initialize stack of tasks with no immediate predecessors}
    top := 0;
    for *i* := 1 **to** *NumberOfTasks* **do**
      if *list*[*i*].*count* = **0** **then begin** {add to stack}
                         list[*i*].*count* := *top*;
                         top := *i*;
                   end; {of **if** and **for**}

Program 7.22 Pascal version of Program 7.21
                    (Continued on next page)

4.   Develop a Pascal program for the Rat-In-A-Maze problem under the assumption that *maze* is a three valued array (0, 1, and 2). Do not use a separate array *path*. Your output should be the maze with the path shown in place (possibly using a different color).

5.   [Count Sort] For the sorting problem of Section 7.3, develop a different sort module. This time use the sort method known as count sort. This is a two phase process. In the first, we determine the number of records that will appear to the left of each record. This is done by simply determining the sum of the number of records with smaller key and the number already to the left with equal key. In the second phase, each record is located at its proper place as determined in the first phase.

6.   [Bubble Sort] Repeat the preceding exercise using the sort method "bubble sort". In this method, we begin at the left end and compare pairs of adjacent records. The left and right records of the pair are swapped in case the left record has a larger key. After one complete left to right pass, the record with largest key

```
{create the linear order one task at a time}
NumberOut := 0;
while top <> 0 do
begin
   {remove top task}
   NextTask := top; top := list[top].count;

   OutputTask(NextTask); NumberOut := NumberOut + 1;

   {process task list}
   pointer := list[NextTask].next;
   while pointer <> nil do
   begin {decrement successor counts}
      i := pointer ↑ .task;
      list[i].count := list[i].count − 1;
      if list[i].count = 0 then begin {add to stack}
                                 list[i].count := top;
                                 top := i;
                               end; {of add to stack}

      pointer := pointer ↑ .next; {go to next successor task}
   end; {of while pointer <> nil}
end; {of while top <> 0}

{check if complete linear order generated}
if NumberOut < NumberOfTasks then Error
else Success;
end; {of LinearOrder}
```

Program 7.22 Pascal version of Program 7.21 (continued)

is at the rightmost position. This is repeated until all records are in order.

7.   [Selection Sort] Repeat Exercise 5 for selection sort. In this method, the record with the largest key is determined and moved to position n. Then the process is repeated on the remaining $n-1$ records. This differs from bubble sort in that only one pair

of records is exchanged in each pass.

8.   Refine the declaration part of Program 7.15 to contain the declarations of all the global variables in program *Nets*.

9.   Refine program 7.18 into a Pascal procedure using the stepwise refinement method.

10. Develop the *BeginNet* module of the *Nets* program. Do this using stepwise refinement.

11. Develop the *ContinueNet* module of the *Nets* program. Do this using stepwise refinement.

12. Develop the *FinishNet* module of the *Nets* program. Do this using stepwise refinement.

13. Write an input module for the assembly line ordering problem. This must create the representation of Figure 7.15.

14. Write a welcome module for the assembly line ordering problem.

15. In connection with the output from *LinearOrder* (Program 7.22), write the modules: *OutputNext*, *Error*, and *Success*.

16. [Flight Reservations] In this programming project, you are required to carry out a complete design and implementation of a software system to handle flight reservations. This system is to be menu driven and the startup menu should provide at least the following options:

   a.   Add a flight

   b.   Cancel a flight

   c.   Determine if any seats are available on a particular flight

   d.   Make a reservation

   e.   Cancel a reservation

f.   Maintain waiting lists

g.   Determine if a particular passenger has a reservation on a particular flight.

You may add any other capabilities that you think will be useful for this environment.

17.   [Machine Shop] This project is concerned with automating a general production or machine shop. Such a shop has three major components: the available machines, the work force, and the jobs to be performed (also called the set of open jobs). The facts of life dictate that all three components are dynamic: new machines are acquired in time and old ones retired; machines become inactive and need maintenance; workers are hired and fired as economic conditions dictate; jobs (or orders) are received in real time; already placed orders may get cancelled; etc. The success of such a machine shop relies heavily on its ability to utilize its resources effectively. This entails being able to schedule the open jobs, the work force, and the machines efficiently. In addition, it is necessary to be able to predict with reasonable accuracy the completion date of each of the open jobs as well as be able to inform potential customers of the expected turnaound date on their orders.

Many machine shops perform all of the above tasks manually. However, automation becomes necessary when the number of machines, workers, and open jobs becomes reasonably large. It is not uncommon to find shops with several hundred machines, a few hundred workers, and several thousand open jobs.

Before describing the programming project, it is necessary to learn some more details about how a machine shop operates. A machine shop consists of several work stations (eg., milling, drill, paint, packaging, shipping, etc.). Each work station has a certain number of machines. For example, the milling station might have 5 milling machines. For simplicity, we shall assume that the machines in a work station have similar characteristics (speed, capacity, setup time, etc.). At any given time, however, a machine may be in need of maintenance and so be unusable.

The work force in this machine shop is divided into

shifts. Each shift has a start time and a finish time associated with it. Each worker is able to operate only machines from certain stations. Safety regulations require that each machine in operation be attended by a qualified worker. So, one person cannot run two or more machines simultaneously. Also, if worker i is presently working on machine j and is to work on machine k next, then it takes him/her $t(j,k)$ time to make the transition (this accounts for the time needed by the worker to go from machine i to machine j).

When a job arrives at the machine shop, it first goes to the "costing department". Here, it is broken down into many tasks. In general, there will be a one-to-one correspondence between tasks and the work stations at which they can be performed. Each task will have a work station assignment and an estimated time (i.e., the time needed to complete the task at this station). For simplicity, we assume that the set of tasks constituting a job is linearly ordered. In general, of course, this set will only constitute a partial order. In addition, a priority is assigned to the job. This priority allows for the handling of "rush" jobs as well as for different cost structures that might be available.

At any instance in time, there may be several jobs ready for execution at each of the work stations. When a worker becomes free, it is necessary to assign him/her to perform a task on an available machine. This involves determining the set of stations with idle machines and waiting jobs at which he/she is qualified to work. Next, one of the possible jobs is to be selected for execution. This is where the priority and due date of the jobs become important. We might simply select the job with the earliest due date; or the highest priority; or the one with least slack time (difference between due date and amount of processing yet to be done); etc. For this project, you may select according to the product of priority and slacktime. Further, you may assume that the shop works two shifts a day. The first begins at 8:00 am and ends at 6:00 pm and the second begins at 7:00 pm and ends at 2:00 am. New jobs enter the system only at the start of the first shift.

You are to design and implement, in Pascal, a menu driven system that provides at least the following capabilities:

a. Add a new job.

b. Delete an existing job. Existing jobs cannot be deleted once processing has begun.

c. Determine when an existing job is expected to complete (under the assumption that no jobs of higher priority enter the system).

d. Determine when a new job may be expected to complete.

e. Add a new worker.

f. Delete an existing worker.

g. Change the characteristics of an existing worker (eg. the set of machines he/she is qualified to work).

h. Add a machine.

i. Delete a machine.

j. Add a work station.

k. Delete a work station.

You will need to keep an event list. This list tells us when each scheduled task will complete. It will be necessary to add new task completion times to this list and to delete the earliest time from the list. To get an efficient implementation, you will need to use the data structure "heap". This is introduced in Chapter 13. For the time being, you may borrow the required heap procedures from this chapter or use a less efficient data structure to keep track of events.

18. [Spelling Checker] Develop a software system that accepts English text as input and outputs all incorrectly spelled words.

CHAPTER 8

PROGRAM CORRECTNESS

8.1. INTRODUCTION

In this chapter, we develop two techniques to establish the correctness of a program. The first of these relies on a proof method known as *mathematical induction* and the second technique is called the *predicate transformer method*.

Let π be any program. In order to prove that π is correct, we need a specification of what a correct version of π is supposed to do. For the most part, we shall provide this specification in an informal manner using English. Later when we get to the predicate transformer method of program correctness, we shall become more formal about this and also about what we mean by correctness.

The term *program state* is used to refer to the values of all variables in a program. A program begins in an *initial* state and is to terminate in a *result* (or *final*) state that describes the solution to the problem the program was designed to solve. A program is *correct* iff it behaves in this way for every legal initial state.

In establishing correctness, we assume that the programs do not meet any abnormal conditions such as: word overflow, insufficient memory, ran out of time, etc. during execution.

Let us review the notation and terminology to be used in this chapter.

A *predicate* $P(x_1, x_2, \ldots, x_n)$, $n \geq 0$, is a mapping from x_1, x_2, ..., x_n to the values **true** and **false**. n is the degree of the predicate. P is the predicate name and the x_i's are *parameters* or *variables*. The set of values assignable to the parameter x_i is called the *domain* of x_i. When the number of parameters is 0, the predicate is called a *proposition*. Some example predicates are provided below. The domain of each of the parameters is the set of all real numbers.

(a) $GREATER(x,y) = \begin{cases} \textbf{true} & \text{if } x > y \\ \textbf{false} & \text{if } x \leq y \end{cases}$

(b) $PRIME(x) = \begin{cases} \textbf{true} & \text{if } x \text{ is a prime number} \\ \textbf{false} & \text{otherwise} \end{cases}$

(c) $SUM(x,y,z) = \begin{cases} \textbf{true} & \text{if } x + y = z \\ \textbf{false} & \text{otherwise} \end{cases}$

(d) $LESS(x,y) = \begin{cases} \textbf{true} & \text{if } x < y \\ \textbf{false} & \text{otherwise} \end{cases}$

$ = GREATER(y,x)$

The logical connectives **and, or, not** , and **implies** are, respectively, denoted by the symbols $\wedge$, $\vee$, $\sim$, and $\implies$. The following defines a predicate that is the **and** of two other predicates.

(e) $GL(x,y,z) = \begin{cases} \textbf{true} & \text{if } x < y < z \\ \textbf{false} & \text{otherwise} \end{cases}$

$ = LESS(x,y) \wedge LESS(y,z)$

For brevity, future predicate definitions will often be made by providing only the condition under which the predicate is true. In addition, when no confusion arises, we shall omit the parameter list from the predicate. For example, the predicates (a), (b), and (c) are equivalent to:

(a) *GREATER*: $x > y$
(b) *PRIME*: x is a prime number
(c) *SUM*: $x + y = z$

Two types of quantifiers: universal ($\forall$) and existential ($\exists$) will be used. $\forall x\, P(x)$ (read: for all $x\, P(x)$) states that $P(x)$ is true for all x in the domain of x. $\exists x\, P(x)$ (read: there exists an $x\, P(x)$) states that $P(x)$ is true for at least one x in the domain of x. When we deal with predicates whose parameters have different domains, we can avoid some confusion by using the notation $\forall x \in D(x)\, P(x)$ which is to be read as "for all x in the domain of x, $P(x)$". A similar notation with respect to $\exists$ may also be used.

A *formula* consists of predicates, domains, quantifiers, logical connectives, the constants **true** and **false**, parentheses, and brackets. While all syntactically correct formulas can be specified using BNF, we shall rely on our intuitive understanding of a syntactically correct formula.

An *inference rule* has the form:

$\{F1, F2, \cdots\} \models G$

where $F1, F2, \ldots$ and G are formulas. The semantics of an inference rule are: If we know the the formulas $F1, F2, \ldots$ are valid, then we can infer that the formula G is valid.

Finally, we shall make reference to three proof methods: direct proof, proof by contradiction, and proof by generalization. A direct proof is used to show the validity of a formula that has the form $F1 \Longrightarrow F2$ where $F1$ and $F2$ are themselves formulas. In a direct proof, we begin by assuming that $F1$ is true and then show that the truth of $F2$ follows from this assumption. To show that a formula $F1$ is true using a proof by contradiction, we begin with the assumption that $F1$ is false. Then, we show that this assumption leads to a contradiction (i.e., some formula G is both true and false). A proof by generalization can be used to show that $P(x)$ is true for all x in $D(x)$. In this proof method, we let a be an arbitrary member of $D(x)$ and show that $P(a)$ is true. Since a could have been any element of $D(x)$, the proof works on all $x \in D(x)$.

8.2. MATHEMATICAL INDUCTION

8.2.1. THE PROOF METHOD

Mathematical induction is an exceptionally powerful proof method. It can be used to establish that a predicate P is true whenever its parameters are assigned values from some given domains. Let us consider a single parameter predicate $P(x)$ and a domain $D(x)$ such that $D(x)$ is the set of all values assignable to x. We shall assume that the members of D are labeled a, $a+1$, $a+2$, ... (i.e., we assume that the elements of the domain can be ordered and each element assigned a unique label, in this order, as indicated). Henceforth, we shall simply refer to an element of $D(x)$ by its label (i.e., a or $a+1$ or $a+2$ or ...). The set $\{0, 1, 2, ... \}$, of natural numbers is an example of a domain that can be so labeled.

Mathematical induction relies on the following inference rule:

MI. $\{P(a),\ \forall x,x+1 \in D(x)\ (P(x) \Rightarrow P(x+1))\} \models \forall x \in D(x)\ P(x)$

Before attempting to use the above inference rule to prove statements of the form $\forall x \in D(x)\ P(x)$, let us establish its correctness.

Theorem 8.1: Inference rule MI is correct.

Proof: We need to show that the following formula is valid:

$$[P(a) \wedge \forall x,x+1 \in D(P(x) \Rightarrow P(x+1))] \Rightarrow \forall x \in D\ P(x)$$

Assume that $[P(a) \wedge \forall x,x+1 \in D(P(x) \Rightarrow P(x+1))]$ is true. Call this assumption, assumption 1 or A1.

Now, we need to show that $\forall x \in D(x)\ P(x)$ follows from A1. The truth of $\forall x \in D(x)\ P(x)$ will be established by contradiction. We begin with the assumption (A2) that $\forall x \in D(x)\ P(x)$ is false (i.e., $\sim\forall x \in D(x)\ P(x)$ is true). We see that A2 is equivalent to $\exists x \in D(x)$

$\bar{P}(x)$. So, $P(x)$ is false for some x in $D(x)$. Because of the nature of $D(x)$, there must therefore exist a least x in $D(x)$ for which $P(x)$ is false. Let this least x be c.

There are two possibilities for c. Either $c=a$ or $c>a$. If $c=a$, then from A1 we obtain $P(c)$. But, by choice of c, $\bar{P}(c)$. So, we have a contradiction.

If $c>a$, then from the choice of c, it follows that $P(c-1)$ is true. From A1, we obtain $P(c-1) \Longrightarrow P(c)$. From this and the knowledge that $P(c-1)$ is true, we obtain $P(c)$. But, c was chosen such that $\bar{P}(c)$ is true. Once again, we have a contradiction.

Hence, there is no x, $x \in D(x)$ such that $P(x)$ is false. I.e., $\forall x \in D(x)\ P(x)$. This concludes the proof. $\square$

A proof by mathematical induction (abbreviated: proof by induction) can be divided into two distinct parts. The first part of the proof establishes the truth of $P(a)$. This part of the proof is called the *induction base* (IB). In the second part of the proof it is shown that $\forall x, x+1 \in D(x)\ (P(x) \Longrightarrow P(x+1))$. From parts one and two of the proof and the inference rule MI, the truth of $\forall x \in D(x)\ P(x)$ is inferred.

The second part of the proof generally proceeds in the following manner. We begin by assuming that $P(x)$ is true for an arbitrary x such that x and $x+1$ are in $D(x)$. This is called the *induction hypothesis* (IH). Next, it is shown that the truth of $P(x+1)$ follows from the induction hypothesis. This part of the proof is referred to as the *induction step* (IS).

Example 8.1: We shall show that $\sum_{i=0}^{n} i = n(n+1)/2$ for all natural numbers n. Inference rule MI will be used. The predicate P in this case is:

$$P(n): \sum_{i=0}^{n} i = n(n+1)/2$$

and $D(x) = (0,1,2,\ldots)$ is the ordered set of natural numbers. In the induction base, we have to prove that $P(0)$ is true. The induction hypothesis will be $\sum_{i=0}^{m} i = m(m+1)/2$ for some arbitrary natural number

m. In the induction step we shall show that the induction hypothesis implies the truth of $P(m+1)$. I.e., $\sum_{i=0}^{m+1} i = (m+1)(m+2)/2$. The complete proof is given below. We use LHS (left hand side) to denote

$\sum_{i=0}^{n} i$ and RHS (right hand side) to denote $n(n+1)/2$.

Proof:

Induction Base: When $n=0$, $\sum_{i=0}^{n} i = 0$ and $n(n+1)/2 = 0$. So, $P(0)$ is true.

Induction Hypothesis: Let m be any arbitrary natural number. Assume that $\sum_{i=0}^{m} i = m(m+1)/2$.

Induction Step: When $n = m+1$, we get

$$\text{LHS} = \sum_{i=0}^{m+1} i = m+1+ \sum_{i=0}^{m} i$$
$$= m+1+m(m+1)/2 \text{ (from the IH)}$$
$$= (m+1)(m+2)/2$$
$$= \text{RHS}$$

Note that since m is an arbitrary natural number, the induction hypothesis and induction step together provide a direct proof of $\forall m \in N \ (P(m) \implies P(m+1))$ where N denotes the set of all natural numbers. $\square$

Example 8.2: Inference rule MI can also be used to show that $\sum_{i=0}^{n} a^i = (a^{n+1}-1)/(a-1)$ for all natural numbers n and $a \neq 1$. The proof is:

Induction Base: When $n = 0$, $\sum_{i=0}^{n} a^i = 1$ and $(a^{n+1}-1)/(a-1) = 1$.

Induction Hypothesis: Let m be any arbitrary natural number. Assume that $\sum_{i=0}^{m} a^i = (a^{m+1}-1)/(a-1)$.

Induction Step: When $n = m+1$,
$$\text{LHS} = \sum_{i=0}^{m+1} a^i = a^{m+1} + \sum_{i=0}^{m} a^i$$

$$= a^{m+1} + (a^{m+1}-1)/(a-1) \text{ (from the IH)}$$
$$= (a^{m+2}-a^{m+1}+a^{m+1}-1)/(a-1)$$
$$= (a^{m+2}-1)/(a-1)$$
$$= \text{RHS} \quad \square$$

Weak Mathematical Induction[1] Weak mathematical induction differs from the mathematical induction discussed so far (called strong mathematical induction) only in the nature of the induction hypothesis. When weak mathematical induction is used, $P(x)$ is assumed true for all values of x, $a \leq x \leq m$. In the induction step, it is proved that $P(m+1)$ is true. In the induction base, $P(a)$ is shown true.

Theorem 8.2: Weak mathematical induction is a valid proof method.
Proof: In weak mathematical induction, the truth of $P(x)$ for all x in $D(x) = \{a, a+1, a+2, ...\}$ is established by showing that:

$$(8.1) \; P(a) \bigwedge \forall m, m+1 \in D(x) \; (\forall x, a \leq x \leq m \; P(x) \Longrightarrow P(m+1))$$

is true. We shall proceed to show that if (8.1) is true, then there is no $j \in D(x)$ for which $P(j)$ is false. The proof is by contradiction. Suppose there exists a $j \in D(x)$ for which $P(j)$ is false. Since the elements of $D(x)$ are a, $a+1$, ..., the existence of a j for which $P(j)$ is false, implies the existence of a least j (say r) for which $P(r)$ is false. If $r = a$, then we have a contradiction with (8.1) as the truth of (8.1) implies that $P(a)$ is true. So, r must be greater than a and $P(a)$, ..., $P(r-1)$ are all true. Hence, $\forall x, a \leq x \leq r-1 \; P(x)$ is true. From (8.1) we can now conclude that $P(r)$ is also true. This contradicts the assumption that $P(r)$ is false. Hence, if (8.1) is true, there can be no $j \in D(x)$ for which $P(j)$ is false. $\square$

The proof of Example 8.1 becomes a proof by weak mathematical induction if the induction hypothesis is changed to:

Assume that $\displaystyle\sum_{i=0}^{n} i = n(n+1)/2$ for $0 \leq n \leq m$ for some arbitrary natural number m.

---

1. A word of caution regarding the terminology used is in order. In some texts, the use of the terms weak and strong mathematical induction is reversed from our use here. So, what we call weak induction here is called strong induction in some other texts.

No other changes in the proof are needed. While every proof by mathematical induction is easily changed to a proof by weak mathematical induction, the reverse is not true. It should be pointed out that in a strict mathematical sense, both forms of induction are equivalent as each form is derivable from the other.

As pointed out in the proof of Theorem 8.2, the inference rule on which weak mathematical induction is based is:

$$\text{WM: } \{P(a),\ \forall m, m+1 \in D(x)[\forall x, a \leq x \leq m\ P(x) \implies P(m+1)]\}$$
$$\models \forall x \in D(x)\ P(x)$$

Example 8.3: Assume that $T(n)$ is defined as:

$$T(n) = \begin{cases} 0 & n=0 \\ T(n/3) + T(n/5) + 2T(n/7) + n & n>0 \end{cases}$$

We shall use WM to show that $T(n) \leq 6n$, $n \geq 0$.

Induction Base: When $n=0$, $T(n) = 0 \leq 6n$.

Induction Hypothesis: Let m be an arbitrary natural number. Assume that $T(n) \leq 6n$ for $0 \leq n \leq m$.

Induction Step: When $n = m+1$, the definition of $T(n)$ yields:

$$T(m+1) = T(\frac{m+1}{3}) + T(\frac{m+1}{5}) + 2T(\frac{m+1}{7}) + m + 1$$

Since, $\dfrac{m+1}{3}$, $\dfrac{m+1}{5}$, and $\dfrac{m+1}{7}$ are all less than or equal to m, the induction hypothesis may be used to obtain:

$$T(m+1) \leq 6\frac{m+1}{3} + 6\frac{m+1}{5} + 12\frac{m+1}{7} + m + 1$$

$$\leq 2(m+1) + 6(m+1)/5 + 12(m+1)/7 + m + 1$$

$$= (2 + 6/5 + 12/7 + 1)(m+1)$$

$$= 207(m+1)/35$$

$$< 6(m+1) \quad \square$$

Example 8.4: Suppose that:

$$T(n) \leq \begin{cases} b & 0 \leq n \leq 1 \\ cn + \dfrac{2}{n} \sum_{j=0}^{n-1} T(j) & n > 1 \end{cases}$$

We wish to show that $T(n) \leq 2(b+c)n\log_e n$, $n \geq 2$. This can be done using WM as below:

Induction Base: When $n=2$, we see that $T(2) \leq 2c + T(0) + T(1)$ $\leq 2c + 2b \leq 2(b+c)*2*\log_e 2$.

Induction Hypothesis: Let m be an arbitrary natural number greater than 1. Assume that $T(n) \leq 2(b+c)n\log_e n$ for $2 \leq n \leq m$.

Induction Step: When $n=m+1$, we get:

$T(m+1)$

$$\leq c(m+1) + \frac{2}{m+1} \sum_{j=0}^{m} T(j)$$

$$\leq c(m+1) + \frac{4b}{m+1} + \frac{2}{m+1} \sum_{j=2}^{m} T(j)$$

$$\leq c(m+1) + \frac{4b}{m+1} + \frac{4(b+c)}{m+1} \sum_{j=2}^{m} j\log_e j \quad \text{(from IH)}$$

$$\leq c(m+1) + \frac{4b}{m+1} + \frac{4(b+c)}{m+1} \int_{2}^{m+1} x\log_e x \, dx$$

$$\leq c(m+1) + \frac{4b}{m+1}$$

$$+ \frac{4(b+c)}{m+1} \left[\frac{(m+1)^2 \log_e(m+1)}{2} - \frac{(m+1)^2}{4} \right]$$

$$= c(m+1) + \frac{4b}{m+1} + 2(b+c)(m+1)\log_e(m+1) - (b+c)(m+1)$$

$$\leq 2(b+c)(m+1)\log_e(m+1) \quad \square$$

Mathematical induction can be used to prove predicates with several parameters. The extension to multiple parameter predicates is not required here and the interested reader is referred to the text by S. Sahni cited at the end of this chapter.

We turn our attention now to the use of induction in establishing the correctness of programs. Our discussion of this is divided into three parts. These three parts, respectively, deal with inductive proofs for recursive programs, inductive proofs for iterative programs that resemble recursive ones, and inductive proofs using assertions or loop invariants.

8.2.2. RECURSIVE PROGRAMS

Induction can often be used to provide simple correctness proofs for recursive programs. No ideas beyond those introduced in Section 8.2.1 are needed to obtain these proofs. So, we shall directly proceed to some examples. The example programs considered here correspond to problems that are normally not solved by recursive programs. However, we intend to use these same problems as examples in subsequent sections in which we shall examine the iterative programs for these problems. The techniques used here do, however, apply to recursive programs in general. In the remainder of this chapter, we use $a[i:j]$, $i \leq j$, as an abbreviation for $a[i]$, $a[i+1]$, ..., $a[j]$.

Example 8.5: [Sequential Search] Let x, n, and $a[1:n]$ be $n+2$ integers. We wish to determine an i such that $i = 0$ iff x is not any of the $a[j]$'s. If x is one of the $a[j]$'s, then i is such that $a[i] = x$. We shall refer to i as the answer to the search problem. So, if $n=4$ and $a[1:4] = [10, 8, 12, 14]$, and $x = 8$, then the answer to the search problem is 2. If $x = 7$, then the answer is 0.

In a sequential search, one compares x with $a[n]$. If x is equal to $a[n]$, then the search terminates successfully with n as the answer. Otherwise, we search $a[1:n-1]$ for x.

A recursive function that solves the search problem is given in Program 8.1. The formal parameter a is defined to be a variable parameter even though *search* does not need to return any values in it. If a is defined as a value parameter, then each recursive call to *search* will make a new copy of a and soon we shall run out of space. For example, if $n = 1000$, then space for 1,000,000 elements are needed to complete the search when *a* is a value parameter. We shall discuss this in greater detail in Chapters 10 and 11.

---

line	function *search*(var *a*: *ElementList*; *n*, *x*: **integer**): **integer**;
1	**begin**
2	**if** $n <= 0$ **then** *search* := 0
3	**else if** $a[n] = x$ **then** *search* := *n*
4	**else** *search* := *search*(*a*, $n-1$, *x*);
5	**end**; {of *search*}

Program 8.1 Recursive sequential search

The correctness of procedure *search* may be established by generalization on the values $a[1]$, $a[2]$, $\cdots$, and x, and by induction on n. In the induction base, we shall show that *search* works correctly when $n = 0$. The induction hypothesis will be the assumption that *search* works correctly for all sequences $a[1..m]$ of size m and for all x. Here m is some arbitrary natural number. In the induction step it will be shown that the program works correctly when $n = m+1$. Now, the correctness of the program for all natural numbers n, all a, and all x follows from MI.

Proof:
Induction Base: When $n = 0$, there are no numbers in $a[1..n]$ and so regardless of the value of x, the answer to the search problem is 0. We see that procedure *search* always returns 0 when $n = 0$ (line 2). So, procedure *search* works correctly for all a, and all x, when $n = 0$.

Induction Hypothesis: Let m be an arbitrary natural number. Assume that procedure *search* works correctly for all $a[1:n]$ and all x when $n = m$.

Induction Step: We need to show that procedure *search* works correctly for all $a[1:n]$, and all x when $n = m+1$. Let $a[1:m+1]$ and x be arbitrary. If $a[m+1] = x$, then $m+1$ is an answer to the search problem (Note that x may occur several times in $a[1:m+1]$. So, the answer to the search problem may not be unique.). As can be seen from line 3, the procedure works correctly in this case. If

$a[m+1] \neq x$, then the answer to the search problem with $n = m+1$ is the same as that to the search problem defined by $a[1:m]$ and x. From the induction hypothesis, this answer is found in line 4 of *search*. This completes the proof of the induction step.

Observe that *search* works correctly even when $n<0$. Our proof, of course, does not establish this. Our proof will remain unchanged if the condition of line 2 is changed to $n=0$. □

Example 8.6: [Insertion] This problem was introduced in Chapter 7. Let $a[1..MaxSize]$ be a sorted array that presently contains n, $n < MaxSize$ integers. So, $a[1] \leq a[2] \leq \cdots \leq a[n]$. We wish to insert the integer x into $a[1:n]$ in such a way that following the insertion the resulting array $a[1:n+1]$ is also sorted. Since n is known to be less than *MaxSize*, the element being inserted can be accomodated in the array a. We may assume that the incrementing of n by 1 will be done external to the *insert* procedure following the insertion.

```
line   procedure insert(var a: ElementList; n, x:integer);
  1    {Insert x into the sorted array a[1:n]}
  2    begin
  3      if n=0 then a[1] := x
  4      else if a[n]>x then begin
  5                              a[n+1] := a[n];
  6                              insert(a, n-1, x);
  7                          end
  8      else a[n+1] := x;
  9    end; {of insert}
```

Program 8.2 Recursive procedure to insert x

A recursive procedure to accomplish this insertion is given in Program 8.2. Notice that if n is a negative integer (say -5), then *insert* terminates abnormally as $a[-5]$ is undefined. The correctness of this procedure for all natural numbers n, all sorted sequences $a[1..n]$, and all x may be established by using generalization on a and x, and induction on n as below.

Proof:

Induction Base: When $n = 0$, the insertion should simply result in x occupying position 1 of the array a. This is precisely what happens in line 3 of procedure *insert*. So, this procedure works correctly when $n = 0$.

Induction Hypothesis: Let m be an arbitrary natural number. Assume that *insert* works correctly for all $a[1..n]$ and all x when $n = m$.

Induction Step: We need to show that *insert* works correctly when $n = m+1$. Let $a[1:m+1]$ and x be arbitrary. If $a[m+1] > x$, then $a[m+1]$ will be in position $m+2$ following the insert. In addition, the position of the remaining numbers is correctly obtained by inserting x into $a[1:m]$. When $a[m+1] > x$, lines 5 and 6 of *insert* are executed. In line 5, $a[m+1]$ is moved to position $m+2$ and in line 6, a recursive call to *insert* made. From the induction hypothesis, it follows that this recursive call correctly inserts x into $a[1:m]$. So, the procedure works correctly for the case $a[m+1] > x$.

The case that remains is $a[m+1] \leq x$. A valid result of the insertion for this case has all the $a[i]$'s in their original positions for $1 \leq i \leq m+1$ and $a[m+2] = x$. The procedure handles this case in line 8 and as can be seen, exactly this configuration is produced. □

Example 8.7: [Binary Search] Binary search is a fast search method to determine if a given number x is present in a sequence $a[i:n]$, $i > 0$, of numbers that is sorted in nondecreasing order. For example, the sequence $a[1:5] = (3, 5, 5, 6, 8)$ is in nondecreasing order.

The basic idea is to compare x with the middle number $a[mid]$ where $mid = (i+n)/2$. If $x = a[mid]$, then x has been found. If $x < a[mid]$, then only the sequence $a[i:mid-1]$ needs to be searched and if $x > a[mid]$, then only $a[mid+1:n]$ needs to be searched. Function *bsearch* (Program 8.3) is the resulting program. If x is in $a[i:n]$, then *bsearch* returns an index j such that $a[j] = x$. It returns 0 iff x is not in $a[i:n]$.

In Program 8.3, a is a value parameter. The decision to make a a value parameter was made on the grounds that a is not changed by the search function. This decision has a severe adverse effect on the performance of the function (see Chapter 11). In practice, one would not program binary search as a recursive function nor would one make *a* a value parameter.

---

line	function *bsearch*(*a*: *ElementList*; *i*, *n*, *x*:**integer**): **integer**;
1	**var** *mid*: **integer**;
2	**begin**
3	*mid* := (*i*+*n*) **div** 2;
4	**if** *i*>*n* **then** *bsearch* := 0 {not found}
5	**else if** *x*=*a*[*mid*] **then** *bsearch* := *mid* {found}
6	**else if** *x*<*a*[*mid*] **then** *bsearch* := *bsearch*(*a*, *i*, *mid*−1, *x*)
7	**else** *bsearch* := *bsearch*(*a*, *mid*+1, *n*, *x*);
8	**end**; { of *bsearch*}

Program 8.3 Recursive binary search

The correctness of *bsearch* may be established using weak mathematical induction on the number of elements $n-i+1$ in $a[i:n]$.

Proof:
Induction Base: When the number of elements in $a[i:n]$ is 0, the answer to the search problem should be 0. In this case, $n = i-1$ and *bsearch* executes only lines 3 and 4. The value 0 is the result.

Induction Hypothesis: Let m be an arbitrary natural number. Assume that *bsearch* works correctly for all sorted $a[i:n]$ and all x whenever $i>0$ and $i-1 \leq n \leq i+m-1$ (i.e., whenever the number of elements is no more than m).

Induction Step: Let $a[i:n]$ be an arbitrary sorted array with $m+1$ elements. So, $n = i+m$. Assume that $i>0$. Let x be arbitrary. In addition to executing the statement of line 3, *bsearch* will now execute the statements corresponding to exactly one of the cases of lines 5, 6, and 7. It is clear that if $x = a[mid]$, then the correct answer is produced. If $x<a[mid]$, then x is in $a[i:i+m]$ iff x is in $a[i:mid-1]$. Since the number of elements in $a[i:mid-1]$ is less than $m+1$, the induction hypothesis guarantees that the result from line 6 is correct. The proof for the case $x>a[mid]$ (line 7) is similar. □

8.2.3. ITERATIVE PROGRAMS

Many iterative programs are actually based on recursive programs. For example, the programs given in Programs 8.1 - 8.3 are seldom written recursively. Instead, they are written iteratively as in this section. We shall reexamine the problems of Examples 8.5 - 8.7 and prove the correctness of the iterative versions of these programs. In addition, a new example is also introduced.

All the proofs of this section explicitly use the fact that following the first iteration of the loop in each of the programs, the program behaves exactly as it would if started with a smaller problem instance. So, in effect, we use the fact that these programs are a restatement of recursive programs!

Example 8.8: [Sequential Search] The problem being solved is the same as that described in Example 8.5. The iterative procedure for sequential search is given in Program 8.4. This procedure avoids an explicit test for x not being in $a[1:n]$ by setting $a[0]$ to x (this, of course, is possible only when *ElementList* has been defined as **array** $[0..MaxSize]$). As a result, x is always one of $a[0:n]$. The answer 0 is, however, returned only if x is not one of $a[1:n]$.

```
line  function seqsearch(a: ElementList; n,x:integer): integer;
 1      var i: integer;
 2      begin
 3        i := n; a[0] := x;
 4        while a[i] <> x do
 5          i := i-1;
 6        seqsearch := i;
 7    end; {of seqsearch}
```

Program 8.4 Iterative sequential search

This procedure may be proved correct for all natural numbers n using induction on n as below.

Proof:
Induction Base: When $n = 0$, i is set to 0 and $a[0]$ to x in line 3. Since $a[0] = x$ and $i = 0$ the first time line 4 is reached, the **while** loop is not entered and *seqsearch* terminates with the answer *seqsearch* $= 0$. This is the correct answer for the case $n = 0$.

Induction Hypothesis: Let m be an arbitrary natural number. Assume that *seqsearch* works correctly for all $a[1:n]$ and all x when $n = m$.

Induction Step: Let $n = m+1$. Let $a[1:m+1]$ and x be arbitrary. The first time line 4 is reached, $i = m+1$. If $a[m+1] = x$, then the answer $m+1$ is returned. This is correct. Otherwise, the **while** loop is entered and i is decremented by 1. So, its value becomes m. From this point on, the procedure behaves exactly as it would if started with $n = m$. From the induction hypothesis, therefore, subsequent iterations of the **while** loop will correctly search $a[1:m]$ for x. $\square$

Example 8.9: [Insertion] An iterative version of Program 8.2 (Example 8.6) is given in Program 8.5. This program assumes that position 0 of a is available. It is essentially the same as Program 6.13 except that all defenses have been stripped from Program 8.5. Under the assumptions of Example 8.6, these defenses are unneccessary. We shall establish the correctness of this procedure by induction on the size, n, of the sorted sequence a.

---

line	**procedure** *insert*(**var** a: *ElementList*; n,x: **integer**);
1	**var** i: **integer**;
2	**begin**
3	$\quad i := n$; $a[0] := x$;
4	$\quad$ **while** $a[i] > x$ **do**
5	$\quad$ **begin**
6	$\quad\quad a[i+1] := a[i]$;
7	$\quad\quad i := i-1$;
8	$\quad$ **end**; {of **while**}
9	$\quad a[i+1] := x$;
10	**end**; {of *insert*}

Program 8.5 Iterative insertion

Proof:
Induction Base: When $n = 0$, x is to be inserted into position $a[1]$. In line 3 of *insert*, i is set to 0 and $a[0]$ is set to x. The conditional (or predicate) $a[i]>x$ of line 4 is false (as $a[i] = a[0] = x$) and so lines 6 and 7 do not get executed. The next line to be executed is line 9 and here, $a[1]$ is set to x. So, the program works correctly when $n = 0$.

Induction Hypothesis: Let m be any arbitrary natural number. Assume that the program works correctly for all nondecreasing sequences of size m and all x.

Induction Step: Let $a[1:m+1]$ be any nondecreasing sequence of $m+1$ numbers. Let x be an arbitrary number. In line 3, i is set to $m+1$ and $a[0]$ is set to x. If $a[m+1]\leq x$ then the **while** loop is not entered and $a[m+2]$ is set to x in line 9. The resulting sequence $a[1:m+2]$ is clearly in nondecreasing order. Hence, *insert* works correctly when $a[m+1]\leq x$.

If $a[m+1]>x$, then the **while** loop is entered and $a[m+2]$ is set to $a[m+1]$ and i decreased to m. From this point on the program behaves exactly as it would if started with the sequence $a[1:m]$ and with $n = m$. From the induction hypothesis, it follows that when line 9 is reached, $a[1:m+1]$ will be in nondecreasing order. Since $a[m+2]\geq a[j]$, $1\leq j\leq m+1$, the sequence $a[1:m+2]$ is also in nondecreasing order. So, *insert* works correctly when $n = m+1$. $\square$

Example 8.10: [Binary search] The binary search method was described in Example 8.7. An iterative procedure corresponding to this search method is given in Program 8.6. Its correctness may be established by weak induction on the number of elements in a.

Proof:
Induction Base: When the number of elements in a is zero, $n = i-1$. In this case, d is set to i and u to $i-1$ in line 3. Since $d>u$, the conditional of line 4 has value **false** and the **while** loop is not entered. The value 0 is returned in line 14. So, the program works correctly when a contains zero elements.

Induction Hypothesis: Let m be any arbitrary natural number. Assume the program works correctly for all x, all $i>0$, and all nondecreasing sequences $a[i:n]$, whenever $i-1\leq n\leq i+m-1$. I.e., whenever

line	
	function *bsearch*(*a*: *ElementList*; *i*,*n*,*x*: **integer**): **integer**;
1	**var** *d*, *u*, *mid*: **integer**; *found*: **boolean**;
2	**begin**
3	*d* := *i*; *u* := *n*; *found* := **false**;
4	**while** (*d*<=*u*) **and not** *found* **do**
5	**begin**
6	*mid* := (*d*+*u*) **div** 2;
7	**if** *x*<*a*[*mid*] **then** *u* := *mid*−1{look in lower half}
8	**else if** *x*=*a*[*mid*] **then begin**
9	*bsearch* := *mid*; {found *x*}
10	*found* := **true**;
11	**end**
12	**else** *d* := *mid*+1; {look in upper half}
13	**end**; {of **while**}
14	**if not** *found* **then** *bsearch* := 0; {*x* not found}
15	**end**; {of *bsearch*}

Program 8.6: Iterative binary search

the number of elements in *a* is no more that *m*.

Induction Step: Let *a*[*i*:*i*+*m*] be any nondecreasing sequence of *m*+1 numbers. Let *x* be any number. *bsearch* begins, in line 3, by setting *d* = *i* and *u* = *i*+*m*. Since *m*≥0, *d*≤*u* and the **while** loop is entered. *mid* is set to (*d*+*u*)/2 = (2*i*+*m*)/2. If *x*<*a*[*mid*], then *x* cannot be one of *a*[*mid*:*i*+*m*]. After having set *u* to *mid*−1, the program behaves exactly as it would if started with the input *a*[*i*:*mid*−1]. Since the number of elements in this sequence is fewer than *m*+1, the induction hypothesis can be used. It follows that the program will work correctly on *a*[*i*:*mid*−1] and so the correct value is returned.

If *x* = *a*[*mid*], then *bsearch* is set to *mid* in line 9 and *found* to **true** in line 10. Following this, the **while** loop terminates and the correct value of *bsearch* is returned. When *x*>*a*[*mid*], *d* is set to *mid*+1 in line 12. From this point on the program behaves exactly as it would if started with input *a*[*mid*+1:*i*+*m*]. The number of elements in this sequence is fewer than *m*+1 and so from the induction hypothesis it follows that the correct value is returned in this case too. This completes the proof of the induction step. □

Example 8.11: [Euclid's GCD program] Let m and n be two positive integers. The *greatest common divisor* (gcd) of m and n (written as $gcd(m,n)$) is the largest natural number that divides both m and n. For example, $gcd(21,14) = 7$; $gcd(18,9) = 9$; $gcd(33,44) = 11$; $gcd(75,30) = 15$; etc.

Euclid's program to compute the gcd of m and n is given as the function *euclid* (Program 8.7). It assumes that $m \geq n > 0$.

line	
	function *euclid*(m, n: **integer**): **integer**;
1	$\{m \geq n > 0\}$
2	**var** r: **integer**; *done*: **boolean**;
3	**begin**
4	*done* := **false**;
5	**repeat**
6	r := m **mod** n;
7	**if** $r = 0$ **then** *done* := **true**;
8	m := n; n := r;
9	**until** *done*;
10	*euclid* := n;
11	**end**; {of *euclid*}

Program 8.7 Euclid's gcd program

The correctness of *euclid* may be established by induction on m. Let *euclid*(m,n) be the value computed by *euclid*. We wish to show that *euclid*$(m,n) = $ gcd (m,n) for all m and n such that $m \geq n > 0$.

Proof:
Induction Base: When $m=1$, there is only one possible value for n, i.e., $n=1$. It is easily seen that *euclid*$(1,1) = 1$ and that $gcd(1,1) = 1$.

Induction Hypothesis: Let m' be an arbitrary natural number such that $m' \geq 1$. Assume that *euclid*$(m,n) = gcd(m,n)$, $1 \leq n \leq m$, $1 \leq m \leq m'$.

Induction Step: We need to show that *euclid*$(m'+1,n) = gcd(m'+1,n)$, $1 \leq n \leq m'+1$. We shall do this by generalization on n. Let b be an arbitrary integer value for n, $1 \leq b \leq m'+1$. If b divides

$m'+1$, then $(m'+1)\bmod b = 0$ and $euclid(m'+1, b) = b = \gcd(m'+1, b)$. If b does not divide $m'+1$, then $r \neq 0$ and following the first iteration of the loop, the program proceeds to compute $euclid(b, (m'+1)\bmod b)$. Since $b < m'+1$ (as if $b = m'+1$ then b divides $m'+1$) and $0 < (m'+1)\bmod b < b$, it follows from the induction hypothesis that $euclid(b, (m'+1)b) = \gcd(b, (m'+1)\bmod b)$. In the exercises, it is shown that $\gcd(m'+1,b) = \gcd(b, (m'+1)\bmod b)$. So, $euclid(m'+1, b) = \gcd(m'+1,b)$. □

8.2.4. LOOP INVARIANTS

Often, simpler correctness proofs for programs that contain loops can be obtained by performing induction on the number of iterations of these loops. When this approach is taken, one associates a predicate with a certain point in the loop (generally the start or end of the loop) and shows that this predicate is true each time program execution reaches this point of the loop. If the program has already been shown to terminate, then we know that this loop invariant is true the last time the loop is executed (there must be a last iteration as the program terminates). This fact is used to establish the correctness of the program.

A predicate whose truth value does not change over successive iterations of a loop is called a *loop invariant*. The following examples illustrate the method of loop invariants and also demonstrate that this approach results in simpler proofs.

Example 8.12: [Binary Search] In this example, we shall present an alternate correctness proof for *bsearch* (Program 8.6). Consider any arbitrary nondecreasing sequence $a[i:n]$, arbitrary integer n, $n \geq i-1$, and arbitrary x. Since the number of elements in $a[d:u]$ decreases following each iteration of the **while** loop, it follows that *bsearch* will terminate after at most $n-i+1$ iterations of this loop (in a later chapter, we shall show that the number of iterations is actually far fewer).

If by the time the program reaches line 14 *found* = **true**, then the right answer is obtained. So, we need only show that line 14 is reached with *found* = **false** iff x is not one of $a[i:n]$. This is established by showing that each time the conditional of line 4 is tested, the predicate P:

P: x is one of $a[i:n]$ iff x is one of $a[d:u]$

is true. MI can be used to show that P is true each time line 4 is reached. The proof is:

Proof:
Induction Base: The first time line 4 is reached, $d = i$ and $u = n$. The predicate P is trivially true.

Induction Hypothesis: Let m be an arbitrary positive integer. Assume that if line 4 is reached an mth time, then P is true.

Induction Step: We shall show that if line 4 is reached for the $m+1$st time, then also P is true. Assume that line 4 is reached for the $m+1$st time. Then, it must also have been reached an mth time. At this time, $d \leq u$ (as line 4 is reached at least one more time) and P is true (from the IH). Only the clauses of lines 7 and 12 are possible for this iteration of the **while** loop. No matter which is executed, the fact that the numbers in a are sorted ensures that P will be true when line 4 is reached next.

So, the predicate P is a loop invariant for the **while** loop of *bsearch*.

If line 14 is reached with *found* = **false**, then the last time line 4 is reached, $d > u$. From the truth of P, and the observation that $a[d:u]$ is an empty sequence when $d > u$, it follows that x is not one of $a[i:i+n-1]$. Once again, the correct answer is returned. $\square$

Example 8.13: [Euclid] As in the case of *bsearch*, an alternate correctness proof (using a loop invariant) can be provided for procedure *euclid* (Program 8.7). Let m' and n' be two arbitrary positive integers such that $m' \geq n'$. Let these, respectively, be the initial values for m and n. We observe that if $r = 0$, then *done* is set to **true** in line 7. If $r \neq 0$, then $1 \leq r < n'$. Hence, the next time line 6 is reached, the new value of n is smaller than the old one. Consequently, line 6 can be reached at most n' times (as by then n would have dropped to 1 and r will become 0). So, *euclid* terminates for all m and n such that $m \geq n > 0$.

We are left with the problem of proving that the value returned from line 10 is in fact $\gcd(m',n')$. Consider the predicate P:

P: $\gcd(m',n') = \gcd(m,n)$

Using MI and the proof provided by Exercise 6, we may show that P is true whenever line 6 is reached. Hence, P is true the last time line 6 is reached. At this time, $r = 0$ and $n = \gcd(m,n) = \gcd(m',n')$. □

8.3. THE PREDICATE TRANSFORMER METHOD

The *predicate transformer* method of proving programs correct was proposed by E. Dijkstra in 1975.

We shall use the term *program* to denote any sequence of Pascal statements. Program 8.8 shows a four line program. Line 1 contains three statements joined together by the connective ";". Lines 2, 3 and 4 each contain 1 statement. Line 3 itself is a one line one statement program while line 1 is a one line three statement program. Line 4 is a one line one statement program.

---

line
1     $x := 2; y := 4; z := 6;$
2     $x := x * y;$
3     $y := y + z;$
4     $z := y - x;$

Program 8.8

A *program state* is described by the values of the variables in the program. Let π be a program that contains the variables x, y, and z. The states π can be in are given by all possible values for the triple (x, y, z). Consider the program π of Program 8.8. The program state after the execution of line 1 is (2, 4, 6). After the execution of line 2, it is (8, 4, 6), after the execution of line 3, it is (8, 10, 6), and after the execution of line 4, it is (8, 10, 2).

We shall restrict our discussion to *deterministic* programs. These programs have the property that every execution of the program that begins in the same state proceeds in exactly the same manner. Programs that do not enjoy this property are called *nondeterministic*. As an example, consider the one line program:

$x := [1, 2];$

which has the interpretation x is assigned the value 1 or 2. The computer executing this program may assign either of these values to x. In particular, one execution of this program might result in $x = 1$ and another in $x = 2$. (Since we shall be dealing with deterministic programs only, it is not very important for you to understand nondeterminism well at this point. This concept is introduced here only because most treatments of the predicate transformer method consider nondeterminism.)

Let I and R be two predicates defined on the program variables. We use the notation:

$$\{I\} \; \pi \; \{R\}$$

to mean the following:

> If the execution of program π begins in a state that satisfies I, then π terminates (i.e., terminates in a finite amount of time) in a state that satisfies R.

I and R are, respectively, called the *precondition* (or *initial assertion*) and *postcondition* (or *result assertion*) of π. Note that we use the term *terminates* as an abbreviation for *terminates in a finite amount of time*.

Example 8.13: Let α, β, γ, and δ, respectively, be the programs that consist solely of line 1, line 2, line 3, and line 4 of Program 8.8. The following are valid statements. (T and F, respectively, denote the predicates that are always true or false.)

(a) $\{T\} \; \alpha \; \{x = 2, y = 4, z = 6\}$

(b) $\{x = 5, y = 6\} \; \beta \; \{x = 30\}$

(c) $\{x = 2, y = 4\} \; \beta \; \{x = 8\}$

(d) $\{x = 5, y = 6\} \; \beta \; \{x = 30, y = 6\}$

(e) $\{y = 10, z = 8\} \; \gamma \; \{y = 18\}$

(f) $\{x = 10, y = 30\} \; \delta \; \{z = 20\}$

(g) $\{x = 10, y = 30\} \; \delta \; \{x = 10, y = 30, z = 20\}$

(h) $\{T\} \; \pi \; \{x = 8, y = 10, z = 2\}$

(i) $\{y > 10, z > 20\} \; \gamma \; \{y > 30, z > 20\}$

The above statements may be restated in English as below:

(a)   No matter what the values of x, y, and z before the program consisting solely of line 1 is executed, the execution of this program will terminate and upon termination, the values of x, y, and z will, respectively, be 2, 4, and 6.

(b)   If $x = 5$ and $y = 6$ before line 2 is executed, then the execution of this line terminates and upon termination, $x = 30$.

(c)   If $x = 2$ and $y = 4$ before line 2 is executed, then the execution of this line terminates and upon termination, $x = 8$.

(d)   If $x = 5$ and $y = 6$ before line 2 is executed, then the execution of this line terminates and upon termination, $x = 30$ and $y = 6$.

(e)   If $y = 10$ and $z = 8$ before line 3 is executed, then the execution of this line terminates and upon termination, $y = 18$.

(f)   If $x = 10$ and $y = 30$ before line 4 is executed, then the execution of this line terminates and upon termination, $z = 20$.

(g)   If $x = 10$ and $y = 30$ before line 4 is executed, then the execution of this line terminates and upon termination, $x = 10$, $y = 30$, and $z = 20$.

(h)   When the program π consisting of line 1-4 is executed, it terminates with $x = 8$, $y = 10$, and $z = 2$.

(i)   If $y > 10$ and $z > 20$ before line 3 is executed, then the execution of this line terminates and upon termination, $y > 30$ and $z > 20$. $\square$

A program π is said to be *totally correct* (or *strongly verifiable*) with respect to the initial and result assertions I and R iff $\{I\} \; \pi \; \{R\}$ is valid. The program π of Program 8.8 is readily seen to be totally correct with respect to the initial assertion $I = T$ and the result assertion $R = (x = 8, y = 10, z = 2)$.

The notation:

$I \; \{\pi\} \; R$

is used to mean the following:

> If program π begins execution in a state for which the initial assertion I is true and if the execution of

π terminates, then on termination, the program
state satisfies the result assertion R.

A program π is said to be *partially correct* (or *consistent*) with
respect to the initial and result assertions I and R iff $I \{\pi\} R$ is valid.
The program given in Program 8.9 is partially correct with respect to
every initial and result assertion as it never terminates. The program
of Program 8.10 is partially correct with respect to the initial assertion
$x > 0$ and the result assertion $x = 2$.

---

while true do
   $x := 2;$
	10: **if** $x = 3$ **then** $x := 2$
	           else goto 10;

Program 8.9   **Program 8.10**

Partial correctness makes a statement about a program only for
those initial states that both satisfy the initial assertion I and lead to
termination. It does not guarantee that the program will terminate
whenever execution begins in a state that satisfies the initial assertion.
Total correctness, on the other hand, states that if a program is begun
in a state that satisfies the initial assertion I, then termination is
guaranteed. Both notions of correctness assert that upon termination,
the program state satisfies the result assertion R.

Note that if a program is totally correct with respect to I and R,
then it is also partially correct with respect to I and R. The reverse is
not true for all programs. In further discussion, we shall be concerned
only with the notion of total correctness. We shall therefore use the
term correct as an abbreviation for total correctness.

Let P and Q be two predicates defined on the states of a program
π. We say that Q is *weaker* than P iff $P \Longrightarrow Q$ is true. I.e., Q is
true for every state for which P is true. For example, the predicate
$x \geq 0$ is weaker than the predicate $x = 0$. The predicate $x + y > 2$ is
weaker than the predicate $x + y > 8$. Observe that "T" (true) is weaker
than all predicates and that every predicate is weaker than "F" (false).

A *predicate transformer* is a function that transforms one predicate into another. Define *WP* to be a predicate transformer which for

every program π and every postcondition Q, yields the weakest precondition P for which $\{P\}$ π $\{Q\}$ is true. Hence, if $\{S\}$ π $\{R\}$ for some predicate R, then $S \implies WP(\pi, R)$. WP is called the *weakest precondition predicate transformer*. $WP(\pi, R)$ transforms the postcondition R into the weakest precondition P for which $\{P\}$ π $\{R\}$ is true.

Alternatively, we may say that $WP(\pi, R)$ is a predicate P which is true for every program state with the property that if π begins execution from this state then π terminates in a state that satisfies R. P is true for no other states.

Example 8.14: Let α, β, γ, and δ be the one line programs defined in Example 8.13. Let π be the four line program of Program 8.8. The following equalities are readily seen to be true:

(a) $WP(\alpha, (x = 2, y = 4, z = 6)) = T$
I.e., every initial state leads to a state that satisfies the given result predicate.

(b) $WP(\alpha, (x = 4)) = F$
I.e., there is no initial state that causes program α to terminate in a state that satisfies the result condition $x = 4$.

(c) $WP(\beta, x = 6) = (xy = 6)$
The weakest precondition on β in order that $x = 6$ be satisfied on termination is that $xy = 6$ before the execution of β begins.

(d) $WP(\beta, x > 10) = x > 10/y$
In order for x to be greater than 10 following the execution of β, x must be greater than $10/y$ before execution begins.

(e) $WP(\gamma, 0 \le y \le 10) = -z \le y \le 10 - z$

(f) $WP(\delta, z > 0) = y > x$

(g) $WP(\delta, (x = 2, z \ge 4)) = (x = 2, y \ge 6)$

(h) $WP(\pi, x = 8) = T$

(i) $WP(\pi, (x = 8, y = 10)) = T$ □

In the predicate transformer method, to prove that a program π is correct with respect to the initial and result assertions I and R, we show that $I \implies WP(\pi, R)$. Theorem 8.3 establishes the validity of the predicate transformer method.

Theorem 8.3: Program π is correct with respect to the initial and result assertions I and R iff $I \implies WP(\pi, R)$.

Proof: From the definition of WP, we see that if the truth of I does not imply the truth of $WP(\pi, R)$, then $\{I\}\ \pi\ \{R\}$ cannot be true. Furthermore, if $I \implies WP(\pi, R)$, then $\{I\}\ \pi\ \{R\}$ is true. Hence, program π is correct with respect to I and R iff $I \implies WP(\pi, R)$. $\square$

The predicate transformer permits a clean definition of program equivalence. Two programs α and β are *equivalent* iff for every result assertion R, $WP(\alpha, R) = WP(\beta, R)$.

Before we can use the predicate transformer method to prove programs correct, we need to develop some expertise in obtaining $WP(\pi, R)$ from π and R. In developing this expertise, it is helpful to study some properties of the predicate transformer WP and also study the form of WP for some of the commonly occurring program statement types.

Theorem 8.4: [Properties of WP] In the following, R and S are predicates and π is a program. Since, R, S, and π occur as free variables, universal quantification is implied by default. So, the following statements are true for every program π (recall that we are dealing with deterministic programs only), every R, and every S.

(a) $WP(\pi, F) = F$

(b) $WP(\pi, R) \lor WP(\pi, S) = WP(\pi, R \lor S)$

(c) $WP(\pi, R) \land WP(\pi, S) = WP(\pi, R \land S)$

(d) $[R \implies S] \implies [WP(\pi, R) \implies WP(\pi, S)]$

Proof:

(a) Observe that there can be no initial state such that π begins execution in this state and terminates in a state that satisfies F (recall that F is false for every state). Hence, the weakest precondition for the postcondition F is a predicate that is true for no state. Consequently, $WP(\pi, F) = F$.

(b) [Distributivity of **or**] Let s be any state for which the left hand side of the equality is true. So, s is a state for which either $WP(\pi, R)$ or $WP(\pi, S)$ or both are true. Suppose that $WP(\pi, R)$ is true for s. This means that program π begun in state s always terminates in a state for which R is true. Consequently, program π begun in state s terminates in a state satisfying $R \lor S$. So, s

satisfies $WP(\pi, R \lor S)$. Similarly, if $WP(\pi, S)$ is true for s, then $WP(\pi, R \lor S)$ is true for s. Consequently, $WP(\pi, R) \lor WP(\pi, S) \Rightarrow WP(\pi, R \lor S)$ is true.

To complete the proof, we need to show the implication in the other direction. Let s be a state for which $WP(\pi, R \lor S)$ is true. Since the program π is assumed to be deterministic, every execution of π beginning in the state s must result in π terminating in the same state t. For this state t, $R \lor S$ is true. If t satisfies R, then s satisfies $WP(\pi, R)$. If t satisfies S, then s satisfies $WP(\pi, S)$. So, s satisfies $WP(\pi, R) \lor WP(\pi, S)$.

Remark: The proof of the preceding paragraph is not valid when π is nondeterministic. Since the execution of a nondeterministic program need not be the same each time it begins from a given initial state, the result state may vary from one execution to the next. As an example, consider the nondeterministic program:

$x := [1, 2]$

which is to be interpreted as x is assigned the value 1 or 2. As mentioned earlier, no rule is specified as to how the selection between 1 and 2 is carried out. In some executions of this program the postcondition $x = 1$ is true while in others $x = 2$ is true. For every execution, however, the postcondition $x = 1 \lor x = 2$ is true. Therefore, $WP(\pi, x = 1) = WP(\pi, x = 2) = F$ and $WP(\pi, x = 1 \lor x = 2) = T$. So, the implication $WP(\pi, R \lor S) \Rightarrow WP(\pi, R) \lor WP(\pi, S)$ is not true for this nondeterministic program.

We leave the proofs of (c) and (d) as exercises. $\square$

Theorem 8.5: Let I be an initial assertion for program π. π terminates whenever execution begins in a state satisfying I iff $I \Rightarrow WP(\pi, T)$.

Proof: When the result assertion is T then the meaning of the predicate transformer becomes: $WP(\pi, T)$ is the weakest precondition such that execution of π begun in a state that satisfies this precondition terminates. The theorem follows from this and the meaning of *weakest*. $\square$

Now that we have studied some of the properties of the predicate transformer *WP*, we turn our attention to the calculus of *WP*. Specifically, we consider the program statements: assignment, **if-then**, **if-then-else**, and **while** and show how to obtain the weakest preconditions for these statements given any postcondition. From these, the weakest preconditions for the other statements of Pascal can be obtained. We also consider the composition of several statements. In what follows, we shall often use "," in place of the connective $\wedge$. This will provide us with a slightly clearer notation.

Assignment Statements

Consider the assignment statement:

$x := exp;$

where *exp* is an expression. Let *R* be any postcondition for this assignment statement and let R_{exp}^x be the predicate obtained by substituting the expression *exp* for every occurrence of *x* in *R* and then simplifying the resulting predicate.

Example 8.15: Consider the assignment statement:

$x := x + 2;$

and the postcondition $R = (x = 10)$. Substituting $x + 2$ for *x* in *R*, we get $x + 2 = 10$. Simplifying, we get $R_{x+2}^x = (x = 8)$.

For the statement:

$x := x+y;$

and the postcondition $R = x>y$, we get $R_{x+y}^x = x+y>y = x>0$.

Finally, consider the statement:

$z := y-x;$

and the postcondition $R = (x = 10, y = 30, z = 20)$. Substituting $y-x$ for z, we get $(x = 10, y = 30, y-x =20)$. Simplifying, we get $R_{y-x}^z = (x = 10, y = 30)$.   Note   that R_{y-x}^z is   true   iff

$(x = 10, y = 30, y-x = 20)$ is true. $\square$

From the definitions provided above, it follows that:

(8.2) $WP(x := exp, R) = R_{exp}^{x}$

If-then

In the program statement:

if B **then** α;

B is a Boolean expression (i.e., it has value **true** or **false**), and α is a program. Let R be any postcondition for this **if** statement. When B is true, the program α is executed. So, for the postcondition R to be true following the execution of this statement, $WP(\alpha, R)$ must be true preceding the execution. When B is false, the postcondition R must be true before execution in order for it to be true following execution. So, we obtain:

(8.3) $WP(\textbf{if } B \textbf{ then } \alpha, R) = [B \wedge WP(\alpha, R)] \vee [\bar{B} \wedge R]$

Example 8.16: Let π be the program:

if $x>0$ **then** $z := 3$;

If R is the predicate $z = 6$, $R_3^z = (3=6) = F$. So, $WP(\pi, R) = [x>0 \wedge R_3^z] \vee [x\leq0 \wedge R] = [x>0 \wedge F] \vee [x\leq0 \wedge z=6] = [x\leq0 \wedge z=6]$.

Next, consider the program δ:

if $x = 2$ **then** $y := z+w$;

Let R be the predicate $x+y = 4$. We see that $R_{z+w}^{y} = (x+z+w = 4)$. So, $WP(\delta, R) = [x=2 \wedge x+z+w=4] \vee [x\neq2 \wedge x+y=4] = [x=2 \wedge z+w=2] \vee [x\neq2 \wedge x+y=4]$. $\square$

If-then-else

Consider the program statement:

if B **then** α
  else β;

where B is a Boolean expression and α and β are programs. Let R be any postcondition for this statement. When B is true, α is executed and for R to be true following execution, it must be the case that $WP(\alpha, R)$ is true before execution. When B is false, $WP(\beta, R)$ must be true before execution in order for R to be true after the execution of this statement. So, we get:

(8.4) $WP(\textbf{if } B \textbf{ then } \alpha \textbf{ else } \beta, R)$
    $= [B \wedge WP(\alpha, R)] \vee [\bar{B} \wedge WP(\beta, R)]$

Example 8.17: Let π be the program:

if $x>0$ **then** $y := 3$
    else $z := 2$;

For the postcondition $R = (y=10, z=6)$, we have $WP(y := 3, R) = (3=10, z=6) = F$, and $WP(z := 2, R) = (y=10, 2=6) = F$. So, $WP(\pi, R) = [x>0 \wedge F] \vee [x\leq 0 \wedge F] = F$.

For the postcondition $R = (y=3, z=5)$, $WP(y := 3, R) = (3=3, z=5) = (z=5)$ and $WP(z := 2, R) = (y=3, 2=5) = F$. Hence, $WP(\pi, R) = [x>0 \wedge z=5] \vee [x\leq 0 \wedge F] = [x>0 \wedge z=5]$.

Finally, consider the postcondition $R = (y>0, z>1)$. $WP(y := 3, R) = (3>0, z>1) = (T, z>1) = (z>1)$ and $WP(z := 2, R) = (y>0, 2>1) = (y>0, T) = (y>0)$. Therefore, $WP(\pi, R) = [x>0 \wedge z>1] \vee [x\leq 0 \wedge y>0]$.

Now, consider the program π:

if $x > y$ **then** $z := x$
    else $z := y$;

Let R be the postcondition $z = \max(x, y)$. From equalities (8.4) and (8.2), we get:

$WP(\pi, R) = [x>y \wedge WP(z := x, R)] \vee [x\leq y \wedge WP(z := x, R)]$

$$= [x>y \wedge x=\max(x,y)] \vee [x\leq y \wedge y=\max(x,y)]$$

$$= \text{true} \ \square$$

While

In the program π:

while B **do**
  α;

B is a Boolean expression and α is a program. Because of the specific instruction set we are considering, it is not possible for one to exit from within this loop. The program α is repeatedly executed so long as B remains true. Let R be any postcondition for this statement. Define $DO(\alpha, R, i)$ as below:

$$DO(\alpha, R, i) = \begin{cases} \bar{B} \wedge R & i=0 \\ B \wedge WP(\alpha, DO(\alpha, R, i-1)) & i>0 \end{cases}$$

Intuitively, $DO(\alpha, R, i)$ is the weakest precondition on π so that π begun in a state that satisfies this predicate will enter its **while** loop exactly i times and terminate in a state that satisfies R.

Theorem 8.6: The following equality is correct:

(8.5) $WP(\pi, R) = [\exists i, i\geq 0\ DO(\alpha, R, i)]$

Proof: We explicitly establish the implication:

(8.6) $WP(\pi, R) \Longrightarrow [\exists i, i\geq 0\ DO(\alpha, R, i)]$

The proof that:

(8.7) $[\exists i, i\geq 0\ DO(\alpha, R, i)] \Longrightarrow WP(\pi, R)$

is left as an exercise.

The proof is by induction on the number of iterations of the **while** loop of π. Let s be any initial state that satisfies $WP(\pi, R)$. Consider the execution of π beginning in this state.

If the **while** loop is executed zero times, then B is false and $WP(\pi, R) = R$. So, $\overline{B} \wedge R$ is true. Hence, $DO(\alpha, R, 0)$ is true and the implication follows.

For the induction hypothesis, let j be an arbitrary natural number. Assume that the implication is correct whenever j iterations of the **while** loop are made.

We shall now show that the implication is correct whenever $j+1$ iterations of the **while** loop are made. Observe that in this case the execution of π is equivalent to the execution of the program δ given in Program 8.11.

α;
while B **do**
   α;

Program 8.11

By assumption on s, s satisfies $WP(\pi, R)$. Further assume that π begun in state s makes exactly $j+1$ iterations of the **while** loop. It is clear that s also satisfies B, and $WP(\delta, R)$, and that program δ begun in the state s will have exactly j iterations of its **while** loop. Let t be the state of program δ after the execution of line 1 (i.e., after the execution of α). Note that the execution of this line must terminate as π begun in the state s terminates. Let γ represent the **while** loop of Program 8.11. Clearly, t satisfies $WP(\gamma, R)$. From the induction hypothesis, it follows that t satisfies $DO(\alpha, R, j)$. Consequently, s satisfies $B \wedge WP(\alpha, DO(\alpha, R, j))$ which is equal to $DO(\alpha, R, j+1)$. So, the implication is valid when $j+1$ iterations are made. $\square$

Example 8.18: Consider the program π:

while $x \leq 0$ **do**
   $x := x + 1$;

Let R be the postcondition $x > 0$. From Theorem 8.6, we obtain:

$WP(\pi, R) = [\exists i, i \geq 0, DO(x := x + 1, R, i)]$

It is not too difficult to see that $DO(x := x + 1, R, j)$ is true for $j = 0$ when $x > 0$ in the initial state and $j = -x$ when $x \leq 0$ in the initial state. So, $WP(\pi, R) = $ **true**. $\square$

Statement Composition

Program 8.8 is the composition of the statements in lines 1 - 4. The program of Program 8.11 is the composition of the program α and the succeeding **while** loop. In general, a program π may be the composition $\alpha; \beta; \gamma; ...; \delta$ of several programs.

The equality:

(8.8) $WP(\alpha; \beta, R) = WP(\alpha, WP(\beta, R))$

is easily proved correct.

Example 8.19: Let π be the composition of the programs α and β given below:

α: $x := x + y$;
β: $y := 2 * x$;

Let R be the predicate $(x > 0, y > 0)$.
$WP(\pi, R) = WP(\alpha, WP(\beta, R))$ (equality 8.8)

$\qquad = WP(\alpha, R^y_{2x})$ (equality 8.2)

$\qquad = WP(\alpha, (x > 0, 2x > 0))$

$\qquad = WP(\alpha, x > 0)$

$\qquad = (x > 0)^x_{x+y}$ (equality 8.2)

$\qquad = (x + y > 0)$ $\square$

Example 8.20: Consider the program π:

α: **if** $x > 3$ **then** $x := 3$;
β: $y := 6 - x$;
γ: $z := x + y$;

Let R be the postcondition $(x \leq 3, y \geq 0, z = 6)$. For program π and R, we get:

$$WP(\pi, R) = WP(\alpha, WP(\beta, WP(\gamma, R)))$$

$$= WP(\alpha, WP(\beta, R^z_{x+y}))$$

$$= WP(\alpha, WP(\beta, (x \leq 3, y \geq 0, x+y=6)))$$

$$= WP(\alpha, (x \leq 3, y \geq 0, x+y=6)^y_{6-x})$$

$$= WP(\alpha, (x \leq 3, 6-x \geq 0, x+6-x=6))$$

$$= WP(\alpha, (x \leq 3, x \leq 6, 6=6))$$

$$= WP(\alpha, (x \leq 3))$$

$$= [(x>3 \wedge WP(x := 3, x \leq 3)) \vee (x \leq 3 \wedge x \leq 3)]$$

$$= [(x>3 \wedge x \leq 3) \vee (x \leq 3)]$$

$$= [x>3 \vee x \leq 3]$$

$$= \textbf{true} \quad \square$$

The next few examples provide program correctness proofs. From Theorem 8.3, we see that to prove that a program π is correct with respect to the initial and result assertions I and R, we need merely prove that $I \Longrightarrow WP(\pi, R)$. In our examples, we first compute $WP(\pi, R)$ and then show that $I \Longrightarrow WP(\pi, R)$.

Example 8.21:   We wish to establish the correctness of the following program π. This program finds the largest and smallest of three numbers x, y, and z.

α: $b := x$;
β: $s := x$;
γ: **if** $y>b$ **then** $b := y$
　　　　else if $y<s$ **then** $s := y$;
δ: **if** $z>b$ **then** $b := z$
　　　　else if $z<s$ **then** $s := z$;

The result assertion R is the conjunction $V \bigwedge W$ of the two clauses $V = [b = \max\{x, y, z\}]$ and $W = [s = \min\{x, y, z\}]$. Since the program is supposed to work properly for all initial values of x, y, and z, the initial assertion is $I = $ **true**. From Theorem 8.4 part (c), we see that it is sufficient to prove $I \implies WP(\pi, V) \bigwedge WP(\pi, W)$. So, let us proceed to determine $WP(\pi, V)$ and $WP(\pi, W)$.

Let γ' and δ', respectively, denote the **else** clauses of the statements labeled γ and δ.

$WP(\pi, V)$ will be obtained using statement composition. First, we compute $WP(\delta, V)$ in two steps as below.

$$WP(\delta', V) = [z<s \bigwedge V_z^s] \bigvee [z \geq s \bigwedge V]$$

$$= [z<s \bigwedge V] \bigvee [z \geq s \bigwedge V]$$

$$= V$$

$$WP(\delta, V) = [z>b \bigwedge V_z^b] \bigvee [z \leq b \bigwedge WP(\delta', V)]$$

$$= [z>b \bigwedge z = \max\{x, y, z\}] \bigvee [z \leq b \bigwedge (b = \max\{x, y, z\}]$$

Next, we obtain $WP(\gamma;\delta, V)$.

$$WP(\gamma', WP(\delta, V)) = [y<s \bigwedge WP(\delta, V)_y^s] \bigvee [y \geq s \bigwedge WP(\delta, V)]$$

$$= WP(\delta, V)$$

$WP(\gamma;\delta, V)$

$$= WP(\gamma, WP(\delta, V))$$

$$= [y>b \bigwedge WP(\delta, V)_y^b] \bigvee [y \leq b \bigwedge WP(\gamma', WP(\delta, V))]$$

$$= [y>b \wedge z>y \wedge z=\max\{x, y, z\}] \vee [y>b \wedge z\leq y \wedge y=\max\{x, y, z\}]$$
$$\vee [y\leq b \wedge z>b \wedge z=\max\{x, y, z\}] \vee [y\leq b \wedge z\leq b \wedge b=\max\{x, y, z\}]$$

Now, $WP(\beta;\gamma;\delta, V)$ is easily obtained.

$$WP(\beta;\gamma;\delta, V) = WP(\gamma;\delta, V)_x^s$$

$$= WP(\gamma;\delta, V)$$

Finally, we obtain:

$WP(\pi, V)$

$$= WP(\beta;\gamma;\delta, V)_x^b$$

$$=[y>x \wedge z>y \wedge z=\max\{x, y, z\}] \vee [y>x \wedge z\leq y \wedge y=\max\{x, y, z\}]$$
$$\vee [y\leq x \wedge z>x \wedge z=\max\{x, y, z\}] \vee [y\leq x \wedge z\leq x \wedge x=\max\{x, y, z\}]$$

$$= [y>x \wedge z>y] \vee [y>x \wedge z\leq y] \vee [y\leq x \wedge z>x] \vee [y\leq x \wedge z\leq x]$$

$$= [y>x \wedge (z>y \vee z\leq y)] \vee [y\leq x \wedge (z>x \vee z\leq x)]$$

$$= [y>x] \vee [y\leq x]$$

$$= \textbf{true}$$

We leave the proof that $WP(\pi, W) = \textbf{true}$ as an exercise. Once this has been established, we obtain $WP(\pi, R) = \textbf{true}$. Consequently, $I \implies WP(\pi, R)$ and the program is correct. $\square$

Example 8.22: In this example, we consider a simple program π that contains a **while** loop. This program is:

α: $x := 0$;
β: **while** $x\leq y$ **do**
    $x := x + 2$;

This program computes the smallest even number (i.e., natural number divisible by 2) that is larger than y. In this example, we shall only prove that on termination, $R = EVEN(x) \wedge x\geq y$. The initial assertion I is **true**.

Let γ denote the body of the **while** loop. We may obtain $DO(\gamma, R, i)$ for the first few values of i as below.

$$DO(\gamma, R, 0) = x>y \wedge EVEN(x) \wedge x \geq y$$

$$= x>y \wedge EVEN(x)$$

$$DO(\gamma, R, 1) = x \leq y \wedge WP(\gamma, DO(\gamma, R, 0))$$

$$= x \leq y \wedge DO(\gamma, R, 0)_{x+2}^{x}$$

$$= x \leq y \wedge x+2>y \wedge EVEN(x+2)$$

$$DO(\gamma, R, 2) = x \leq y \wedge WP(\gamma, DO(\gamma, R, 1))$$

$$= x \leq y \wedge DO(\gamma, R, 1)_{x+2}^{x}$$

$$= x \leq y \wedge x+2 \leq y \wedge x+4>y \wedge EVEN(x+4)$$

$$= x+2 \leq y \wedge x+4>y \wedge EVEN(x+4)$$

At this time, we might suspect that:

$$DO(\gamma, R, i) = \begin{cases} x>y \wedge EVEN(x) & i=0 \\ x+2(i-1) \leq y \wedge x+2i>y \wedge EVEN(x+2i) & i>0 \end{cases}$$

We can verify the correctness of this equality by induction on i. Once this has been done, we can obtain the equality:

$$WP(\beta, R) = [x>y \wedge EVEN(x)]$$
$$\vee \exists i, i \geq 1 \ [x+2(i-1) \leq y \wedge x+2i>y \wedge EVEN(x+2i)]$$

For the complete program π, we obtain:

$$WP(\pi, R) = WP(\alpha;\beta, R)$$

$$= WP(\alpha, WP(\beta, R))$$

$$= WP(\beta, R)_0^x$$

$$= [0>y \wedge EVEN(0)]$$
$$\vee \exists i, i \geq 1 \ [2(i-1) \leq y \wedge 2i>y \wedge EVEN(2i)]$$

$$= [0>y] \lor \exists i, i \geq 1 \ [2(i-1) \leq y \land 2i > y]$$

$$= \textbf{true}$$

The implication $I \implies WP(\pi, R)$ is therefore valid. Consequently, the program is correct with respect to the given initial and result assertions. □

Example 8.23: Consider the recursive function *search* of Program 8.1. Let i denote the result computed by this procedure. The desired result assertion R is $[0 \leq i \leq n] \land [i=0 \implies a[j] \neq x, 1 \leq j \leq n] \land [i \neq 0 \implies a[i]=x]$. While R does not explicitly require that i be an integer, this is implied as we assume that all array indices are integer. Hence, the condition $0 \leq i \leq n$ really means that i is an integer in the range $[0,n]$.

The initial assertion is "n is a natural number" as procedure *search* is supposed to terminate in a state satisfying R for all initial states in which n is a natural number. Note that when $n<0$ initially, R cannot be satisfied on termination as there is no i such that $0 \leq i \leq n$. The correctness of *search* will be established by first determining $WP(search, R)$ and then showing $I \implies WP(search, R)$.

Let U, V, and W, respectively denote the predicates: $[0 \leq i \leq n]$, $[i=0 \implies a[j] \neq x, 1 \leq j \leq n]$, and $[i \neq 0 \implies a[i]=x]$. It is easy to see that $R = U \land V \land W$. In order to simplify matters, we shall use property (c) of Theorem 8.4 (i.e., distributivity of $\land$) and obtain $WP(search, U)$, $WP(search, V)$, and $WP(search, W)$. The conjunction of these three predicates is $WP(search, R)$.

Let β denote the **if** statement:

if $a[n]=x$ **then** *search* := n;
        else *search* := *search*$(a, n-1, x)$;

We are ready to obtain the weakest preconditions for U, V, and W.

$WP(search(a, n, X), U)$

$$= [n \leq 0 \land WP(i := 0, U)] \lor [n>0 \land WP(\beta, U)]$$

$$= [n \leq 0 \land 0 \leq 0 \leq n]$$
$$\lor [n>0 \land [(a[n]=x \land WP(i := n, U)]$$

$$\bigvee (a[n]\neq x \wedge WP(search(a, n-1, x), U))]]$$

$$= [n=0] \vee [n>0 \wedge [(a[n]=x \wedge 0\leq n\leq n]$$
$$\bigvee (a[n]\neq x \wedge WP(search(a, n-1, x), U))]]$$

$$= [n=0] \vee [n>0 \wedge [(a[n]=x \wedge n\geq 0]$$
$$\bigvee (a[n]\neq x \wedge WP(search(a, n-1, x), U))]]$$

$$= [n=0] \vee [n>0 \wedge a[n]=x)$$
$$\bigvee [n>0 \wedge a[n]\neq x \wedge WP(search(a, n-1, x), U)] \quad (8.9)$$

Equations such as (8.9) which define a function in terms of itself are called *recurrence equations*. Methods to solve these equations can be found in the reference cited at the end of this chapter. The simplest of these methods, *substitution*, will be used here to solve (8.9).

The occurrence of *search* on the right hand side of (8.9) may be eliminated by noting that (8.9) is valid for all n. So by substituting $n-1$ for n in (8.9) we obtain $WP(search(a, n-1, x), U)$ in terms of $WP(search(a, n-2, x), U)$. Now, by substituting $n-2$ for n in (8.9), we obtain $WP(search(a, n-2, x), U)$ in terms of $WP(search(a, n-3, x), U)$. By carrying out this substitution n times as below, the value of $WP(search, U)$ is obtained.

$WP(search(a, n, x), U)$

$$= [n=0]$$
$$\bigvee [n>0 \wedge a[n]=x]$$
$$\bigvee [n>0 \wedge a[n]\neq x \wedge [[n-1=0] \vee [n-1>0 \wedge a[n-1]=x]$$
$$\bigvee [n-1>0 \wedge a[n-1]\neq x \wedge WP(search(a, n-2, x), U)]]]$$

$$= [n=0]$$
$$\bigvee [n>0 \wedge a[n]=x]$$
$$\bigvee [n=1 \wedge a[n]\neq x]$$
$$\bigvee [n>1 \wedge a[n]\neq x \wedge a[n-1]=x]$$
$$\bigvee [n>1 \wedge a[n]\neq x \wedge a[n-1]\neq x \wedge WP(search(a, n-2, x), U)]$$

$$= [n=0]$$
$$\bigvee [n>0 \wedge a[n]=x]$$
$$\bigvee [n=1 \wedge a[n]\neq x]$$
$$\bigvee [n>1 \wedge a[n]\neq x \wedge a[n-1]=x]$$
$$\bigvee [n>1 \wedge a[n]\neq x \wedge a[n-1]\neq x \wedge$$

$$[[n-2=0] \lor [n-2>0 \land a[n-2]=x]$$
$$\lor [n-2>0 \land a[n-2]\neq x \land WP(search(a, n-3, x), U)]]]$$

$= [n=0]$
$\lor [n>0 \land a[n]=x]$
$\lor [n=1 \land a[n]\neq x]$
$\lor [n>1 \land a[n]\neq x \land a[n-1]=x]$
$\lor [n=2 \land a[n]\neq x \land a[n-1]\neq x]$
$\lor [n>2 \land a[n]\neq x \land a[n-1]\neq x \land a[n-2]=x]$
$\lor [n>2 \land a[n]\neq x \land a[n\text{--}1]\neq x \land a[n-2]\neq x$
$\quad \land WP(search(a, n-3, x), U)]$

.

.

.

$= [n=0]$
$\lor [n>0 \land a[n]=x]$
$\lor [n=1 \land a[n]\neq x]$
$\lor [n>1 \land a[n]\neq x \land a[n-1]=x]$
$\lor [n=2 \land a[n]\neq x \land a[n-1]\neq x]$
$\lor [n>2 \land a[n]\neq x \land a[n-1]\neq x \land a[n-2]=x]$
$\lor [n=3 \land a[n]\neq x \land a[n-1]\neq x \land a[n-2]\neq x]$
$\lor [n>3 \land a[n]\neq x \land a[n-1]\neq x \land a[n-2]\neq x \land a[n-3]=x]$
$\lor [n=4 \land a[n]\neq x \land a[n-1]\neq x \land a[n-2]\neq x \land a[n-3]\neq x]$
$\lor [n>4 \land a[n]\neq x \land a[n-1]\neq x \land a[n-2]\neq x \land a[n-3]\neq x$
$\quad\quad\quad\quad\quad \land a[n-4]=x]$

$\lor \ldots$

$$= \bigvee_{j=0}^{\infty} [n=j]$$

Hence, procedure *search* terminates in a state with $0\leq i\leq n$ (i.e., returns a value in this range) whenever it is started in a state in which n is a natural number.

Next, let us determine $WP(search, V)$. We use the symbol Q to denote the predicate $[a[j]\neq x, 1\leq j\leq n]$.

$WP(search(a, n, x), V)$

$= [n\leq 0 \land WP(i := 0, V)] \lor [n>0 \land WP(\beta, V)]$

$= [n\leq 0 \land 0=0 \Rightarrow Q]$
$\quad \lor [n>0 \land [a[n]=x \land WP(i := n, V)]$

$$\bigvee [a[n]\neq x \bigwedge WP(search(a, n-1, x), V))]]$$

$$
\begin{aligned}
= [&n\leq 0 \bigwedge Q] \\
&\bigvee [n>0 \bigwedge [a[n]=x \bigwedge (n=0 \Longrightarrow Q)] \\
&\qquad \bigvee [a[n]\neq x \bigwedge WP(search(a, n-1, x), V))]]
\end{aligned}
$$

$$
\begin{aligned}
= [&n\leq 0] \\
&\bigvee [n>0 \bigwedge a[n]=x] \\
&\bigvee [n>0 \bigwedge a[n]\neq x \bigwedge WP(search(a, n-1, x), V)]
\end{aligned}
$$

$$
\begin{aligned}
= [&n\leq 0] \\
&\bigvee [n>0 \bigwedge a[n]=x] \\
&\bigvee [n>0 \bigwedge a[n]\neq x \bigwedge [[n-1\leq 0] \bigvee [n-1>0 \bigwedge a[n-1]=x] \\
&\qquad \bigvee [n-1>0 \bigwedge a[n-1]\neq x \bigwedge WP(search(a, n-2, x), V)]]
\end{aligned}
$$

$$
\begin{aligned}
= [&n\leq 0] \\
&\bigvee [n>0 \bigwedge a[n]=x] \\
&\bigvee [n=1 \bigwedge a[n]\neq x] \\
&\bigvee [n>1 \bigwedge a[n]\neq x \bigwedge a[n-1]=x] \\
&\bigvee [n>1 \bigwedge a[n]\neq x \bigwedge a[n-1]\neq x \bigwedge WP(search(a, n-2, x), V)]
\end{aligned}
$$

$$
\begin{aligned}
= [&n\leq 0] \\
&\bigvee [n>0 \bigwedge a[n]=x] \\
&\bigvee [n=1 \bigwedge a[n]\neq x] \\
&\bigvee [n>1 \bigwedge a[n]\neq x \bigwedge a[n-1]-x] \\
&\bigvee [n>1 \bigwedge a[n]\neq x \bigwedge a[n-1]\neq x \bigwedge \\
&\qquad [[n-2\leq 0] \bigvee [n-2>0 \bigwedge a[n-2]=x] \\
&\qquad \bigvee [n-2>0 \bigwedge a[n-2]\neq x \bigwedge WP(search(a, n-3, x), V)]]
\end{aligned}
$$

$$
\begin{aligned}
= [&n\leq 0] \\
&\bigvee [n>0 \bigwedge a[n]=x] \\
&\bigvee [n=1 \bigwedge a[n]\neq x] \\
&\bigvee [n>1 \bigwedge a[n]\neq x \bigwedge a[n-1]=x] \\
&\bigvee [n=2 \bigwedge a[n]\neq x \bigwedge a[n-1]\neq x] \\
&\bigvee [n>2 \bigwedge a[n]\neq x \bigwedge a[n-1]\neq x \bigwedge a[n-2]=x] \\
&\bigvee [n>2 \bigwedge a[n]\neq x \bigwedge a[n-1]\neq x \bigwedge a[n-2]\neq x \\
&\qquad \bigwedge WP(search(a, n-3, x), V)]
\end{aligned}
$$

$$\vdots$$

$$
\begin{aligned}
= [&n\leq 0] \\
&\bigvee [n>0 \bigwedge a[n]=x]
\end{aligned}
$$

$$\bigvee [n=1 \wedge a[n] \neq x]$$
$$\bigvee [n>1 \wedge a[n] \neq x \wedge a[n-1]=x]$$
$$\bigvee [n=2 \wedge a[n] \neq x \wedge a[n-1] \neq x]$$
$$\bigvee [n>2 \wedge a[n] \neq x \wedge a[n-1] \neq x \wedge a[n-2]=x]$$
$$\bigvee [n=3 \wedge a[n] \neq x \wedge a[n-1] \neq x \wedge a[n-2] \neq x]$$
$$\bigvee [n>3 \wedge a[n] \neq x \wedge a[n-1] \neq x \wedge a[n-2] \neq x \wedge a[n-3]=x]$$
$$\bigvee [n=4 \wedge a[n] \neq x \wedge a[n-1] \neq x \wedge a[n-2] \neq x \wedge a[n-3] \neq x]$$
$$\bigvee [n>4 \wedge a[n] \neq x \wedge a[n-1] \neq x \wedge a[n-2] \neq x \wedge a[n-3] \neq x$$
$$\wedge a[n-4]=x]$$
$$\bigvee \dots$$

$$= \bigvee_{j=-\infty}^{\infty} [n=j]$$

Hence, $WP(search, V) =$ "n is an integer". The proof that $WP(search, W) =$ "n is an integer" is left as an exercise. It follows that $WP(search, R) =$ "n is a natural number". Since, this is also the initial assertion, it follows that procedure $search$ is correct with respect to the given initial and result assertions. $\square$

Remarks The predicate transformer method gets quite unmanageable when one is dealing with complex programs. In particular, computing the weakest precondition for programs with nested loops is quite laborious. So, there are severe limitations to the use of this method in practice. These limitations are greatly reduced if one places assertions at the start and end of blocks of the program and uses the predicate transformer method to show that if the given precondition is true, then the specified postcondition is also true. An alternative is to construct the correctness proof while one is building the program. The text *The Science of Programming*, by David Gries provides an indepth account of how programs and their proofs can be built hand in hand.

8.4. REFERENCES AND SELECTED READINGS

A more detailed treatment of mathematical induction and predicate transformers can be found in the book:

Concepts in discrete mathematics, 2nd Edition, by S. Sahni, Camelot Publishing, Fridley, Minnesota, 1985.

Some advanced readings on the subject of proving programs correct are:

A discipline of programming, by E.W. Dijkstra, Prentice-Hall Inc., Englewood Cliffs, New Jersey, 1976.

The Science of Programming, by D. Gries, Springer Verlag, 1981.

and

A programming logic, by R.L. Constable and M.J. O'Donnell, Winthrop Publishers, Massachusetts, 1978.

8.5. EXERCISES

1. Prove the following using the inference rule MI. In each case, n is a natural number.

   (a) $\sum_{i=0}^{n} i^2 = n(n+1)(2n+1)/6$

   (b) $\sum_{i=0}^{n} i^3 = n^2(n+1)^2/4$

   (c) $\sum_{i=0}^{n} (2i-1)^2 = n(2n-1)(2n+1)/3 + 1$

   (d) $\sum_{i=0}^{n} 2^i = 2^{n+1} - 1$

   (e) $\sum_{i=0}^{n} (x+i*a] = (n+1)x + an(n+1)/2$

   (f) $\sum_{i=1}^{n} \frac{1}{i(i+1)} = \frac{n}{(n+1)}$

   (g) $\sum_{i=0}^{n} \frac{1}{2^i} = 2 - \frac{1}{2^n}$

   (h) $\sum_{i=0}^{n} \frac{i}{2^i} = 2 - \frac{n}{2^n} - \frac{2}{2^n}$

2. [Harmonic Numbers] Let $H_n = \sum_{i=1}^{n} \frac{1}{i}$, $n \geq 1$. H_n is the nth *Harmonic* number. Show that:

   (a) $H_{2^m} \geq 1 + m/2$, $m \geq 0$.

   (b) $(m+1)H_m - m = \sum_{i=1}^{m} H_i$, $m \geq 1$.

   (c) $\sum_{i=2}^{m} \frac{1}{i(i-1)} H_i = 2 - \frac{H_{m+1}}{m} - \frac{1}{m+1}$, $m \geq 2$.

   (d) $\sum_{i=0}^{m} \frac{1}{2i+1} = H_{2m+1} - \frac{1}{2} H_m$, $m \geq 0$.

(e) $\sum_{i=1}^{m} H_i^2 = (m+1)H_m^2 - (2m+1)H_m + 2m$, $m \geq 1$.

3. Let m_i, $1 \leq i \leq n$ be n positive integers. Let $p = \sum_{i=1}^{n} m_i$. Show that:

$$\sum_{i=1}^{n} (m_i / \sum_{j=i}^{n} m_j) \leq \sum_{i=1}^{p} 1/i$$

Use induction on n.

4. Prove the following (n is a natural number and c is a positive constant):

(a) If $T(n) = \begin{cases} T(n/5) + T(3n/4) + cn & n>0 \\ 0 & n=0 \end{cases}$

then $T(n) \leq 20cn$, $n \geq 0$.

(b) If $T(n) = \begin{cases} T(n/9) + T(63n/72) + cn & n>0 \\ 0 & n=0 \end{cases}$

then $T(n) \leq 72cn$, $n \geq 0$.

(c) If $f(n) = \begin{cases} 2f(n/2) + 3 & n>2 \\ 2 & n=2 \end{cases}$

then $f(n) = 5n/2 - 3$ for $n = 2^k$, $k \geq 1$.

(d) If $R(1) = c$, $R(2) = 8.5c$, $R(n) = cn + \dfrac{2}{n} \sum_{i=n/2}^{n-1} R(i)$ when n is even and greater than 2, and $R(n) = cn + \dfrac{2}{n} \sum_{i=(n+1)/2}^{n-1} R(i)$ when n is odd and greater than 2, then $R(n) \leq 4cn$, $n \geq 1$.

5. Prove that $\gcd(m'+1, b) = \gcd(b, (m'+1) \bmod b)$ in the proof of Example 8.10.

6. Use MI to prove that predicate P of Example 8.12 is true each

time line 6 of procedure *euclid* is reached.

7. Write a recursive program corresponding to the iterative version of Euclid's gcd program given in Program 8.7. Prove the correctness of your program using the method of Section 8.2.2.

8. Use the method of loop invariants to show that Program 8.4 is correct.

9. Use the method of loop invariants to show that Program 8.5 is correct.

10 Let $a[1:m]$ and $b[1:n]$ be two nondecreasing sequences of numbers, $m \geq 0$ and $n \geq 0$. Let x be a third number. We wish to find a pair (i,j), $1 \leq i \leq m$ and $1 \leq j \leq n$ such that $a[i]+b[j] = x$. Show that procedure *sum* (Program 8.12) returns (0,0) iff there is no pair (i,j) such that $a[i]+b[j] = x$; otherwise *sum* returns (i,j) such that $a[i]+b[j] = x$. Do this using a loop invariant.

```
line  procedure sum(a, b: ElementList; m, n, x:integer; var i, j:integer);
1       var done: boolean;
2       begin
3         i := 1; j := n; done := false;
4         while (i<=m) and (j>=1) and not done do
5           if a[i]+b[j] = x then done := true
6           else if a[i]+b[j] < x then i := i+1
7                               else j := j-1;
8         if not done then begin
9                           i := 0; j := 0;
10                        end;
11      end. {of sum}
```

Program 8.12

11. Procedure *perm* (Program 8.13) generates all permutations of the characters in the string a. n is the length of a. The initial call is $perm(a, 1, n)$. $interchange(a, k, i)$ swaps the kth and ith characters of a. Prove that this procedure is correct for all natural numbers n. Use induction on n.

line	
	procedure *perm*(*a*: *CharList*; *k*, *n*:**integer**);
1	{Generate all permutations of characters *k* through *n* of string *a*}
2	**var** *i*: **integer**;
3	**begin**
4	**if** *k*=*n* **then** *WriteOut*(*a*)
5	**else**
6	**for** *i* := *k* **to** *n* **do**
7	**begin**
8	*interchange*(*a*, *k*, *i*);
9	*perm*(*a*, *k*+1, *n*);
10	**end**; {of **for**}
11	**end**; {of *perm*}

Program 8.13   Recursive permutation generator

12. Let α, β, γ, and δ be the following program statements:

α: $x := u + v$;
β: $y := x + u$;
γ: **if** $y<0$ **then** $x := y - v$;
δ: **if** $u \geq 5$ **then** $y := x - 6$
              else $y := x + 4$;

Obtain the following weakest preconditions:

(a) $WP(\alpha, x>0)$
(b) $WP(\alpha, x>3 \wedge u<5)$
(c) $WP(\beta, 5 \leq y \leq 10 \wedge x=3)$
(d) $WP(\gamma, x>3)$
(e) $WP(\gamma, x=y-v \wedge y>0)$
(f) $WP(\delta, y=x-6 \vee y=x+4)$
(g) $WP(\gamma, 4 \leq y \leq 25)$
(h) $WP(\alpha;\beta, x=4 \wedge y=6)$
(i) $WP(\beta;\gamma, x>0 \wedge y>0)$
(j) $WP(\gamma;\delta, x>0 \wedge y>0)$
(k) $WP(\alpha;\beta;\gamma;\delta, u=3 \wedge x>2 \wedge y>3)$
(l) $WP(\alpha;\beta;\gamma;\delta, u<0 \wedge x>0 \wedge y<0)$
(m) $WP(\alpha;\beta;\gamma;\delta, v=6 \wedge x<0 \wedge y<5)$

13. Prove parts (c) and (d) of Theorem 8.4.

14. Prove the implication (8.7).

15. Show that $WP(\pi, W) = $ **true** where π and W are as defined in Example 8.21.

16. Use the predicate transformer method to show that the program of Example 8.22 does, in fact, find the smallest even number that is larger than y.

17. Consider the following program:

    α: $x := 1$;
    β: **while** $x<=y$ **do**
        $x := x * 2$;

    Show the on termination, x is the smallest power of two that is larger than y. Use the predicate transformer method.

18. Let π be the following program:

    $i := 2$; $b := a[1]$;
    while $i<-n$ **do**
       if $b<a[i]$ **then** $b := a[i]$;

    Let $R = [b = \max_{1\leq i\leq n} \{a[i]\}]$. Obtain $WP(\pi, R)$.

19. Let π be as below:

    $i := 2$; $b := a[1]$; $s := a[1]$;
    while $i<=n$ **do**
       if $b<a[i]$ **then** $b := a[i]$
               else if $s>a[i]$ **then** $s := a[i]$;

    Let $U = [b = \max_{1\leq j\leq n} \{a[j]\}$, $V = [s = \min_{1\leq j\leq n} \{a[j]\}]$, and $R = U \wedge V$. Obtain $WP(\pi, R)$.

20. Use the predicate transformer method to prove that Program 8.2 is correct. Formulate appropriate initial and result assertions.

21. Use the predicate transformer method to prove that procedure

euclid (Program 8.7) is correct with respect to the initial assertion $m \geq n > 0$ and the result assertion $v = \gcd(m,n)$. v denotes the value returned by the procedure.

22. (a) Obtain a formula similar to (8.5) for the weakest precondition of the **for** statement:

   for $i := n$ **downto** 0 **do**
   $\quad \alpha;$

   (b) Obtain a formula for the weakest precondition of the Pascal **case** statement.

   (c) Obtain a formula for the weakest precondition of the Pascal **repeat** statement.

CHAPTER 9

TESTING

9.1. INTRODUCTION

Test data is a set of inputs that may be provided to a program to check its behavior. For example, each run of the quadratic roots program, Program 5.3, requires values for the three variables: a, b, and c. A possible set of inputs that can be used to test this program is (2, 3, 4) (i.e., $a = 2$, $b = 3$, and $c = 4$). So, (2, 3, 4) may be used as test data for this program. A *test data set* (often abbreviated *test set*) is a collection of test data. For the quadratic roots program, {(2, 3, 4), (1, 5, −2), (3.2, 4.5, 8.2), (−2.6, −9.1, 8.4)} is a possible test set. If this test set is used, the program will be executed four times; once with each of the four sets of inputs in the test set.

Testing is the process of executing the program code in the target environment using test data. The behavior of the program on this test data is compared with that predicted by the program specifications. Hence, for a set of inputs to be used as test data, it is essential that the behavior of a correct program run with that set of inputs be known. Thus, to use the above test set for Program 5.3, we must know the roots of each of the four quadratic equations defined by the four sets of input data.

As remarked in Chapter 1, the number of different inputs that can be provided to a program is generally so large that no practical amount of testing can establish the correctness of the program. For

325

the quadratic roots problem, the number of different quadratic equations that can be input is infinite in theory. In practice, this number is finite though very large. If 16 bits are used to represent each of the inputs a, b, c (including sign, magnitude, and exponent), then only 2^{16} different values are possible for each. Hence, the number of different sets of inputs is only 2^{48}. If our target computer can run Program 5.3 $2^{20} = 1$, 048, 576 times a second, it will take 2^{28} seconds $\cong 8.5$ years to try out all 2^{48} sets of inputs. It is impractical to test Program 5.3 on all possible inputs that may be provided to it. Hence, testing must often be limited to a (very small) subset of all possible inputs. Testing with this subset cannot conclusively establish the correctness of the program. As a result, *the objective of testing is not to establish correctness but to expose the presence of errors.* The test set must be chosen in such a way as to expose any errors that may be present in the program.

To test a program, we need the following:

(1) Access to the target environment. This environment consists of both the hardware and software environment under which the program is to work.

    a. The hardware environment is clearly important. A program that runs correctly on an IBM PC may malfunction on an Apple IIe (or the reverse). A program may function correctly on an IBM PC that has 512K of memory but fail on one that has only 256K of memory. The screen utilities may work correctly on an IBM PC with a medium resolution monitor but incorrectly on the same computer with a high resolution monitor. The output routines may work properly when the printer in use can print 132 columns per line but not when only 80 columns of output can be placed on a single line.

    b. The software environment includes the operating system under which the program is to run. It is quite possible for a program to function correctly under one operating system on a particular computer and fail to run under a different operating system on the same computer. For example, a program that runs correctly under DOS on an IBM PC may fail to run correctly when the operating system is changed to CPM. This may occur even though no change is made to the hardware environment. In fact, it is quite possible for a program to run correctly under one version of an operating system (say DOS 2.1) and to produce errors on another version of the same operating system (say DOS 1.1). A Pascal program may compile correctly using one compiler but may generate compiler errors when another compiler is used.

For the above reasons, it is essential to test the program in the environment in which it is to be eventually used.

(2) When testing a program that consists of several modules (e.g., Figure 9.1), a *test strategy* is needed. There are essentially three different strategies we can follow to test this program. These are, respectively, called big bang testing, big bang integration testing, and incremental testing. In big bang testing, one attempts to test the entire program all at once. In big bang integration testing, the modules A-J are tested separately. When this testing is complete, all modules are put together and tested as a whole. In incremental testing, modules are integrated as they are tested.

(3) Since testing involves the execution of the program (or program module) in the target environment, we need test data. Generally, the test data will consist of several sets of input data. Each set of input data is used on a different execution of the program. This data must be designed with care so as to have a high probability of exposing the errors that may exist in the program being tested. Our goal is to design as small a set of test data as needed to expose all the errors in the program. In order for an input data set to be usable as test data, we must know the behavior of a correct program on this data. This correct behavior can then be compared with the observed behavior. Any deviations from the correct behavior will signal the presence of errors in the program.

9.2. MODULE TESTING STRATEGIES

9.2.1. Big Bang Testing

In *big bang testing*, all testing is performed on the program as a whole. When this approach is used on the program of Figure 9.1, the entire program is compiled and executed with test data. If the behavior of the program disagrees with the expected behavior on any one of the test data, then the cause of this discrepency may be in any of the modules A-J. To detect this cause, one has to check the logic and interface of each of the modules in some systematic order. Once

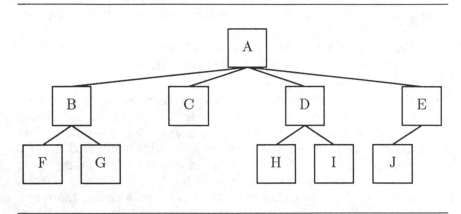

Figure 9.1

the cause of the error has been identified and removed, the program is recompiled and run on the test data.

Some of the disadvantages of big bang testing are:

(1) One has to handle module interfacing problems as well as logic errors within a module at the same time. Module interfacing problems include such things as a discrepency between the number and/or type of formal and actual parameters, discrepency in the form in which a module expects data (say sorted) and the form in which it is actually provided (say unordered) by the invoking module, formal parameters that need to pass computed values back to the invoking module may not have been identified as being of type **var** in the module declaration, etc.

(2) When the behavior of the program on a test run differs from the expected behavior, the cause of the error could be in any of the modules. Finding this cause requires the tester to trace through the entire program. Hence, debugging is expensive.

(3) Big bang testing is expensive in terms of the computer time and memory required. Each time a bug is found and "fixed", the entire program gets recompiled (unless an incremental compiler is in use). For large programs, this recompilation is very expensive. When an incremental compiler is in use, only the module (or part of the module) that has been changed needs to be recompiled. Still, to test the corrected program, the entire program is

loaded into memory and run. The result may be the detection of another bug in the same module as earlier. It would be cheaper to get as many bugs as possible out of each of the modules by testing them separately and then testing the program as a whole.

9.2.2. Big Bang Integration Testing

In *big bang integration*, one tests each of the modules independently. Each of the 10 modules A-J of Figure 9.1 are tested independent of the others. When this testing has been completed, the modules are put together and the entire program tested. Since the individual modules have been tested before being integrated together, one expects that all logic errors within the modules have been detected and corrected before the testing of the integrated program commences. Consequently, when the integrated program is tested, one only expects to discover problems related to the interfaces. In practice, because testing is limited to a subset of all possible inputs, logic errors within a module may be detected even when the integrated program is being tested.

The big bang integration testing strategy clearly overcomes some of the difficulties associated with big bang testing. We make the following observations with regard to this test strategy:

(1) Ideally, all logic errors in a module will be detected when the module is being tested independent of the others. Debugging is easier as it is localized to the module under test.

(2) Module interface problems have to be dealt with only after individual modules have been tested. In the ideal case, all bugs found when the integrated program is being tested will be related to module interface problems alone.

(3) The testing of large programs using this approach is expected to require less computer time. The full memory requirements of the program are needed only when the integrated program is being tested.

(4) There is significant potential for parallel testing. To test one module, we need not wait for the testing of another to complete. Given enough personnel, all modules can be tested in parallel. So, this phase of the testing can be completed quickly.

Big bang integration testing, however, has problems of its own. One of these is a left over from big bang testing. All problems associated with integrating the modules are tackled simultaneously. Thus, while resolving the interface problems between modules B and F, the entire program is being repeatedly compiled and executed. It is cheaper to resolve these problems independent of the problems between the remaining interfaces.

A more subtle difficulty with this approach is one that doesn't exist when the big bang approach is used. This has to do with actually testing one module independent of the others. For example, to test the module B of Figure 9.1, we need to write three modules. First, we need to write a module that invokes B. This module is called a *driver*. In some cases, it is sufficient for the driver module to simply contain a statement to invoke B. In other cases, the driver needs to first set up the environment that B is to work with and then when B has completed, it is necessary for the driver to output the results (if any) for comparison with the expected results.

In addition to the driver for B, we need modules that simulate the modules F and G. These modules are called *stubs*. The stub modules need to provide the results that would otherwise have been provided by modules F and G.

As a concrete example of the difficulties associated in arriving at drivers and stubs, consider the rat in a maze program (Program 7.1). To test the root module, we need stubs for the modules: *welcome*, *InputMaze*, *FindPath*, and *OutputPath*. It is sufficient if these stubs simply write out a message such as "Reached module X". Hence, we may test the root module using the stubs given in Program 9.1. No driver is needed to test the root module.

To test the *welcome* module, we need a driver to invoke this module. This may take the form:

```
begin
    welcome;
end.
```

Since the results of the *welcome* module are displayed on the screen, it is not necessary for additional code to be incorporated into the driver to determine the correctness of *welcome*. Stubs are needed for each

---

```
procedure welcome;
{stub for welcome}
begin
    writeln('Reached procedure welcome');
end; {of stub}


procedure InputMaze;
{stub for InputMaze}
begin
    writeln('Reached procedure InputMaze');
end; {of stub}


procedure FindPath;
{stub for FindPath}
begin
    writeln('Reached procedure FindPath');
end; {of stub}


procedure OutputPath;
{stub for OutputPath}
begin
    writeln('Reached procedure OutputPath');
end; {of stub}
```

Program 9.1 Stubs used when testing root of Program 7.1

screen utility module invoked by the *welcome* module. This time, it is not sufficient to write stubs that simply state that the appropriate module has been reached (as we did in Program 9.1). Suppose that the *welcome* module has the form:

ClearScreen;
WriteScreen('WELCOME TO RAT IN A MAZE', 'blue', 'green');
Delay(25);
ClearScreen;

A stub for *Delay* that simply writes the message "Reached module

Delay", doesn't do us much good. We cannot test whether a 25 second delay is too much or too little time to read the screen. To do this, the stub must actually provide a delay of 25 seconds and for this, the stub will probably have to be the full module for *Delay*! Similarly, a *WriteScreen* stub, to be useful, should actually select the foreground color (blue), background color (green), and write out the desired message. Unless it does this, the testing of *welcome* is of little value. We cannot determine whether the choice of the foreground and background colors is good or whether the message fits on a single line. Unless this is done at this time, then when we test the integrated program we will find ourselves resolving problems other than those associated with module interfaces.

To underscore the need for stubs that faithfully simulate their respective modules, consider the module fragment:

$ModuleA(x, y)$;
$z := x + y*y$;
$ModuleB(x/z, r)$;
$p := q/r$;
$ModuleC(p, q, r, x/y)$;

If the stub for *ModuleA* is like those in Program 9.1 and simply proclaims that it has been reached, an error such as x (or y) undefined may be obtained from line 2. This error may be spurious in that it might be *ModuleA*'s function to appropriately define these variables. Similarly, a division by zero error that may be produced at line 3 may be the result of not simulating *ModuleA* properly. Errors involved with invoking *ModuleC* from line 5 may be caused solely by deficiencies in the stubs for *ModuleA* and *ModuleB*. Drivers and modules are to be written in such a way that all run time errors that are produced (whether they be errors that cause abnormal termination of the program or whether they result in incorrect output) be attributable to causes other than the drivers and stubs.

To test the *FindPath* module, we shall need a driver that sets up the input maze in the form expected by *FindPath*. Writing this driver may not be as difficult as writing the *InputMaze* module. For example, something like:

for $i := 1$ **to** *MazeSize* **do**
  for $j := 1$ **to** *MazeSize* **do**
    read(*maze*$[i,j]$);

will suffice. In addition, a stub for the *OutputPath* module is required so that the path may be output for verification purposes. Once again, it is not sufficient for this stub to simply state that it has been reached. To be useful, it must actually output the path (if any) that has been found.

Finally, let us consider the testing of the *InputPath* module. No stubs are needed. However, we need a driver. The driver has no work to do with respect to setting up the environment needed by *Input-Path*. However, the driver must output the internal representation of the maze input by *InputMaze* so that this can be compared with the expected representation. So, the driver for *InputMaze* may take the form given in Program 9.2.

InputMaze;
{output maze}
for $i := 1$ **to** *MazeSize* **do**
begin
  for $j := 1$ **to** *MazeSize* **do**
    write(*maze*$[i,j]$);
    writeln;
  end;

Program 9.2 Driver for *InputPath*

9.2.3. Incremental Testing

In *incremental testing*, module integration is carried out in parallel with module testing. Further, individual modules are not tested independent of all other modules. Rather, when testing a particular module we make use of already tested modules that may either invoke or be invoked by the module currently being tested. So, for example, if modules A and B (Figure 9.1) have been tested and integrated and modules H and I tested by the time we are ready to test module D, then we do not need a driver module for module D. Rather, the tested module A is used to invoke D (in case the output modules haven't yet been tested and integrated, it may be necessary to add some code to A to output results). Stubs for C and E may be needed but not for H and I. In place of stubs for H and I, we use the tested modules H and I. During the testing of D, we shall be concerned primarily with logic errors in D as well as with integration problems between A and D, D and H, and D and I.

Incremental testing has some advantages over big bang integration testing. Using this approach, the problems related to some of the module interfaces are detected earlier and so are easier to correct. Further, modules that get tested early are included in all further tests. Hence, these modules get exercised more than they would otherwise. Consequently, the degree of testing is greater for these modules. A possible disadvantage of incremental testing is some loss in ability to test modules in parallel. This is more than compensated for by the advantages stated earlier. Incremental testing is generally to be preferred over the other two test strategies.

When carrying out an incremental test of a program, one has to determine the order in which the modules are to be tested and integrated. Two popular strategies for this are: top down and bottom up. These are discussed below:

Top Down Incremental Testing

In *top down incremental* testing, one begins by testing the root module. To do this for the program of Figure 9.1, one needs stubs for modules B, C, D, and E. These stubs replace the corresponding modules in Figure 9.1, and the program of Figure 9.2 is tested. Once the program of Figure 9.2 has been tested, we may replace any one of the stubs B, C, D, and E by its corresponding module and test the resulting program. If we choose to replace stub D, then we test the program shown in Figure 9.3. Notice that this test requires us to write two additional stubs (those for H and I). When the program of Figure 9.3 has been tested, we may replace any of the stubs in this program by the corresponding module and perform tests on the resulting program. This process is continued until all stubs have been replaced by modules and the fully integrated program tested.

Notice that in the top down approach, no drivers are to be written. Only stubs are needed. When deciding which of several stubs to replace by its corresponding module, one may use the following guidelines:

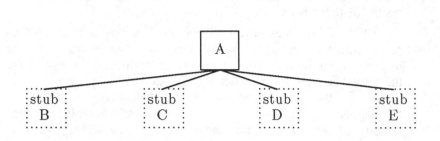

Figure 9.2 Testing module A in the top down approach

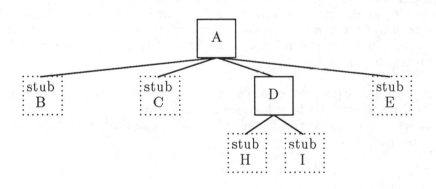

Figure 9.3 Testing module D in the top down approach

(1) Choose a stub replacement sequence that allows you to bring in the I/O (input/output) modules as soon as possible. This will make it easier to input further test cases and also to see the results of these tests.

(2) Once the I/O modules have been included, choose a stub replacement sequence that allows you to bring in modules that have the highest probability of containing errors or those that may have the errors that are most difficult to fix as early as possible. This results in the most error prone modules being tested more thoroughly than the less error prone ones. Additionally, the probability of detecting serious errors early in the testing phase is enhanced.

Our guidelines favor the early testing of I/O modules as once these have been tested and integrated, the testing of the other modules becomes easier.

Bottom Up Incremental Testing

This approach is the reverse of the top down approach. Here, we begin with the leaf modules. Any of the modules F-J of Figure 9.1 may be tested first. In fact, if parallel testing of modules is possible, then all of these may be tested in parallel (by possibly different persons). To test a leaf module, a driver module is needed. However, no stub is required.

In the bottom up approach, a module can be tested only after all its children modules have been tested. Some of the possible sequences in which the modules of Figure 9.1 may be tested using the bottom up approach are:

F, G, H, I, J, B, C, D, E, A
H, I, D, F, G, B, J, C, E, A
G, F, C, B, H, I, D, J, E, A
etc.

When any of the above sequences is used, we need to write driver modules but no stub modules. Like the top down approach, the bottom up approach requires us to choose the next module to be tested. The guidelines for this choice are the same as those for the top down approach. I.e., test the I/O modules, the modules that have the highest probability of containing errors, and those modules that may contain the most difficult to fix errors as early as possible.

In comparing the two incremental testing approaches, we note that stubs are generally harder to write than drivers (especially if the I/O modules get tested first in the bottom up approach). This is a strong reason to favor the bottom up approach over the top down approach. When most errors are expected to be in the higher level modules, one may favor the top down approach. The top down approach has the advantage that as each module gets tested and integrated, more of the program becomes available for use. In the bottom up approach, the root module is tested last. As a result, the tested portions of the program cannot be released for use until all testing is complete.

Using the bottom up approach, a good module test sequence for the rat in a maze program (Program 7.1) is: first test the screen utilities, then test the remaining modules in the order: *welcome*, *Input-Maze*, *OutputPath*, *FindPath*. This order results from the guidelines provided above. We have favored the I/O modules over the most error prone one (*FindPath*) because testing *FindPath* is much easier when we have our I/O modules working.

9.3. GENERATION OF TEST DATA

9.3.1. INTRODUCTION

When developing test data, one should keep in mind that the objective of testing is to expose the presence of errors. This is so as no practical amount of testing can assure us of their absence. If data designed to expose errors fails to expose any errors, then we may have confidence in the correctness of the program. In order to be able to tell whether or not a program malfunctions on a given test data, we must know what the correct response to this data is. Hence, we may evaluate any candidate test data on the following criteria:

1.   What is this data's potential to expose errors?

2.   Do we know what the correct response to this data is?

The techniques available for test data generation fall into two categories: black box methods, and white box methods. In a black box method, test data is developed by considering only the function served by the program (or program module) to be tested. The development of the test data is done without regard to the actual code that realizes the program (or module). Hence, test data that results from a black box method is obtained from a functional analysis of the program (or module).

One can make a distinction between a requirements based black box method and a design based one. In the former, the test data is arrived at by analyzing the problem specifications alone. In the latter, the resulting design (but not the code) is analyzed. We shall not make this distinction here.

The most popular black box methods are: defensive programming methods, I/O partitioning, and cause - effect graphing. These will be studied in detail in subsequent sections.

In a white box method, a structural analysis of the program (or module) is performed. The code is examined and an attempt is made to develop test data whose execution results in a "good" coverage of the program instructions. What we mean by good coverage will be elaborated on in a subsequent section.

9.3.2. BLACK BOX METHODS

9.3.2.1. Defensive Programming Methods

In the chapter on defensive programming, we pointed out the most common causes of failure of a program known to be generally healthy. These are: input errors, numerical errors, and boundary errors. Our test set should include input that will expose program failure in the presence of errors of each of these types.

Some examples of testing for program correctness in the face of input errors are:

(1) When testing a text editor, enter invalid command names. For example, suppose that the valid commands are as in Figure 4.5. We should test the editor with the following inputs:

    a.   XX, this has an invalid command prefix

    b.   IX, invalid insert command

    c.   DZ, invalid delete command

    d.   PZ, invalid place marker command

    e.   BZ, invalid block command

This set of test data is easily constructed as soon as the design of the editor commands has been completed. We need not wait for the code to be written.

(2)   If a program expects to input n data items, see what happens when fewer or more items are made available.

(3)   If the program expects input in a particular order, see what happens when input is provided in a different order.

(4)   The test set for the quadratic roots program (Program 5.3) should include at least one test data in which $a = 0$. Even though this corresponds to invalid input (as per the specifications), the program should terminate gracefully. Unfortunately, Program 5.3 does not do this. A division by zero error results rather than a message such as "This program does not handle the case $a = 0$".

Remember that the objective of testing a program with intentional input errors is to ensure that it either terminates gracefully or it succesfully recovers from these errors. One can be sure that at some time or other, incorrect data will be provided to the program. It is essential that the program not crash when this happens. Even more important, the program should not behave as if all is well and produce results that appear correct but which, in fact, are not.

Testing for the presence of numerical errors is to be done whenever the program uses real-valued data. For this, the general rules are:

(1)   Use data with an inexact representation in the target computer.

(2)   Use data with a wide range of magnitude and also with sign changes.

Often, a program works correctly so long as it is not asked to operate on a problem boundary. To expose errors resulting from program operation at a boundary, one must specifically design test data to exercise the program at the boundary. Some examples of this are:

(1)   When testing the cursor control functions of Figure 4.5 do the following (once again, "^" denotes the "<ctrl>" (control) key):

a. Test → when the cursor is at the rightmost position of a line.

b. Test ← when the cursor is at the leftmost position of a line.

c. Test ^→ when the cursor is at the rightmost word on a line.

d. Test ^← when the cursor is at the leftmost word on a line.

e. Test L when you are already at the left end of a line.

f. Test R from the right end of a line.

g. Test ↑ when the cursor is at the first line of the display. Do this both when the first display line is also the first line of the document and when it is not.

h. Test ↓ when the cursor is at the last line of the display. Do this both when the last display line is also the last line of the document and when it is not.

i. Test <PgUp> when the current display contains the first screenfull of text.

j. Test <PgDn> when the current display contains the last screenfull of text.

Each of the tests a-f should be done both on empty lines as well as on nonempty lines.

(2) A procedure to insert x into a nondecreasing sequence $a[1] \leq a[2] \leq ... \leq a[n]$ should be tested at the following boundaries:

a. $n = 0$. I.e., insertion into an empty sequence.

b. $n = $ maximum size of list. I.e., insertion into a full sequence.

c. $x < a[1]$. I.e., insertion at the left end.

d. $x > a[n]$. I.e., insertion at the right end.

(3) A procedure to add to a stack should be tested on a full stack.

(4) A procedure to delete from a stack should be tested on an empty stack and also on a stack with one element. The latter test will verify that deletion from a one element stack actually leaves behind a proper empty stack.

9.3.2.2. I/O Partitioning

The total number of different inputs that can be given to a program is usually too large to permit an exhaustive testing of the program. To arrive at a reasonably small number of test cases, one can partition the input domain into a set of classes with the following properties:

(1) Every member of the input domain is in some class.

(2) The classes are disjoint. I.e., no member of the input domain is in two or more classes.

(3) If an error is detected by one member of a class, then the same error will be detected by all other members of that class.

From criterion (3), we conclude that a test set need include only one member from each of the created input classes. In practice, it is impossible to ensure criterion (3) without a careful and expensive examination of the code. Since we are using I/O partitioning as a black box method, examination of the code is not permitted. Consequently, we relax criterion (3) to:

(3') If an error is detected by one member of a class, then there is a good likelihood that it will be detected by any other member of the class.

Intuitively, criterion (3') calls for us to group together members of the input domain that we expect will be handled in more or less the same way by the program. Implicit in this is the requirement that inputs that produce materially different output be placed in different classes. Hence, input partitioning also results in a partitioning of the output space. In fact, the partitioning of the input domain is often obtained by first partitioning the output domain. We shall soon see several examples of this.

Because of the relaxation (3'), we cannot be sure that a program that works correctly on one member of each partition will work correctly on all inputs. So, we change our requirement on the test set from exactly one member from each partition to at least one member from each partition.

Several examples of I/O partitioning are given below. As we shall see, I/O partitioning often results in a separate partition for the boundary data. In situations where this is the case, there is an overlap between the effort expended in developing test data when using the defensive programming methods and the I/O partitioning method. In other cases, the test data developed when identifying problem boundaries may actually correspond to data on the boundary of one or more partitions rather than data in a separate partition.

(1) Suppose that we are to test a program to find max{ x, y, z } where x, y, and z are distinct integers. In case x, y, and z are not distinct, an error is to be generated. From the problem specifications, the following partitioning of the output space is obtained:

    a. x

    b. y

    c. z

    d.   Error

We can reasonably expect any program that solves this problem to handle inputs that result in outputs that are in different output partitions differently. Hence, the input domain may be partitioned as below:

    a.   {all distinct integers x, y, and z such that x is the maximum}

    b.   {all distinct integers x, y, and z such that y is the maximum}

    c.   {all distinct integers x, y, and z such that z is the maximum}

    d.   {all integers x, y, and z such that at least two are the same}
Hence, our test set should include at least one member of each of these four classes. For instance, we could try the four data sets: (8, 2, 3), (1, 7, 2), (2, 1, 3), (8, 1, 8). In case we expect some input instances in any one of the above partitions to be handled differently from others in the same partition, then this partition should be further partitioned.

(2) We wish to test a menu that has the five options: A, B, C, D, and E. The input domain is partitioned into the six partitions: {A}, {B}, {C}, {D}, {E}, {all other inputs}. The last partition contains all the invalid inputs that might be provided. If there is reason to suspect that the menu module handles members of the invalid partition differently, then this partition must be further partitioned.

(3) Consider the root finding program (Program 5.3). From the problem specification, we see that there are three possible different outcomes from the resulting program:

    a.   The quadratic has only one distinct real root ($b^2-4ac = 0$).

    b.   There are two distinct real roots ($b^2-4ac > 0$).

    c.   There are two distinct complex roots ($b^2-4ac < 0$).

This results in a partitioning of the inputs into three partitions; one for each of three possible outcomes. In addition, we should add one partition for invalid inputs. This partition consists of all inputs (a, b, c) with $a = 0$. Our test set should contain at least one member of each of these four partitions. Notice that a division by zero error is produced when Program 5.3 is run with any member of the invalid set as input.

(4) Suppose we wish to test the text editor module for the command $\uparrow$. The I/O domain can be partitioned as below:

    a.   Cursor is presently at the first line of the display and this line is not the first line of text.

    b.   Cursor is presently at the first line of text.

    c.   Cursor is not at the first line of the display and the preceding display line does not extend as far as the cursor.

    d.   Cursor is not at the first line of the display and the preceding display line extends at least as far as the cursor.

We can reasonably expect any implementation of $\uparrow$ to handle all instances that fall in each of the above partitions in much the same way. Also, we have good reason to expect that each partition is handled different from the others. So, our test set should include at least one test from each partition.

(5) When partitioning the I/O domain for the stack add module, we get the two partitions: full stack, and nonfull stack. We expect the module to handle additions to all nonfull stacks in the same way. So, we need to test the add module with a full stack and with at least one nonfull stack.

(6) Suppose that a sort module has been written to sort n numbers for n in the range [1, 1000]. The input domain is naturally partitioned into the partitions: $n < 1$, $1 \le n \le 1000$, and $n > 1000$. Notice that the valid inputs are in one partition and the invalid inputs have been partitioned into two. If we suspect that the program may handle the cases $n = 1$ and $n = 1000$ differently, then the partition for the valid inputs should be further partitioned into

three. Observe that the cases $n = 1$ and $n = 1000$ correspond to the boundaries of the partition $1 \leq n \leq 1000$ and will be isolated for testing by one of the defensive programming test methods. Our test set should include at least one member from each of the partitions.

(7) Consider the thirsty baby problem of Section 2.2. From the output specifications, we see that the program is expected to perform differently when $\sum_{i=1}^{n} a_i < t$ and when this sum is $\geq t$. So, the input domain may be partitioned into two: {instances with $\sum_{i=1}^{n} a_i < t$}, and {instances with $\sum_{i=1}^{n} a_i \geq t$}. From both of these partitions, we can separate the invalid instances (i.e., those in which one or more of the a_i's, or the s_i's, or the t are negative or zero. This results in a third partition for the invalid inputs.

9.3.2.3. Cause-Effect Graphing

Cause-effect graphing is a systematic way to arrive at a test set that has a good chance of revealing errors. It is quite similar to I/O partitioning and may be regarded as a formal approach to this. It is particularly useful in arriving at test data that incorporates a combination of input conditions. Cause-effect graphing generally results in a finer partitioning of the input domain than obtained by ad hoc methods.

For the program or module to be tested, we need to first identify the following:

(1) A set of causes. This is a set of Boolean expressions involving input values. The truth of these expressions in some way affects the working of the program.

(2) A set of effects. This is a set of states that the program moves into based upon a combination of causes. This set may include both output states as well as internal states.

(3) A relationship between the causes and effects.

The relationship between causes and effects is represented in terms of a diagram (formally called a *graph*). This diagram has one node for each of the causes and effects. Additional nodes as needed may be added to the diagram. The cause-effect relationships are represented by edges (or lines) that join a pair of nodes.

Once this cause-effect graph has been obtained, a systematic procedure can be used to obtain all the different cause combinations that result in different effect combinations. For each of these, one can generate a set of inputs to be used as test data. Hence, the test set has at least as many test data as the number of cause combinations generated from the cause-effect graph.

Let us consider an example. Suppose we wish to test a program module that finds $\max\{x, y, z\}$ when x, y, and z are distinct integers. Further, suppose that this module is to put out an error message whenever two or more of $\{x, y, z\}$ are the same. For this module, we can use the cause set:

C1 $x < y$

C2 $x < z$

C3 $y < x$

C4 $y < z$

C5 $z < x$

C6 $z < y$

C7 $x = y$

C8 $x = z$

C9 $y = z$

This cause set represents all possible relationships between pairs of inputs. The effect set consists of the four possible outputs from the modules. These are:

E1 x

E2 y

E3 z

E4 Input error

The cause-effect graph for the "max" problem defined above is shown in Figure 9.4. Before examining this graph, we state the following conventions for drawing cause-effect graphs:

(1) Nodes that represent causes are drawn in one column at the left end of the graph.

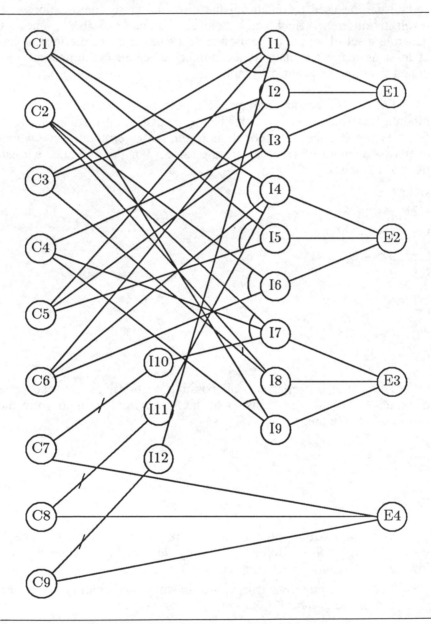

Figure 9.4 Cause-effect graph for "max" problem.

(2)   Nodes that represent effects are drawn in one column at the right end.

(3)   Intermediate nodes (nodes labeled I1-I12 in Figure 9.4), as needed, are drawn in between the cause and effect nodes. These are arranged in columns.

(4)   Each node (whether cause, intermediate, or effect) can be in one of two states: true and false. (Later, we shall introduce a third state. For now, these two states will suffice.) For example, a cause node is true iff the Boolean expression it represents is true. In our example, C1 is true iff $x < y$. An effect node is true iff the effect it denotes does, in fact, occur. Node E3 is true iff the output z is generated by the program.

(5)   Every edge connects a node in one column to a node in some column to its right.

(6)   The collection of edges that enters any node must be related in exactly one of the ways shown in Figure 9.5. The "identity" relation expressed by Figure 9.5(a) has the significance that node B is in the same state as node A. So, B is true iff A is. The "negation" relation of Figure 9.5(b) means that the state of A is different from that of B. If A is true, then B is false. If A is false, then B is true. The "or" relation of Figure 9.5(c) indicates that node Q is true iff at least one of A, B, ..., Z is true. Finally, the "and" relation of Figure 9.5(d) has the property that Q is true iff every one of A, B, ..., Z is true.

(7)   If a single edge comes into a node, then that node is either an *identity* or a *negation node*. Node "B" of Figure 9.5(a) is an identity node while node "B" of Figure 9.5(b) is a negation node. When all entering edges are related by the "or" ("and") relation, the node is an *"or" ("and") node*. Node "Q" of Figure 9.5(c) is an "or" node while in Figure 9.5(d), node Q is an "and" node.

Returning to our example and Figure 9.4, we see that I1 is true iff C3, C5, and I12 are true. But, I12 is true iff C9 is false. So, I1 is true iff $y < x$ and $z < x$ and $y \neq z$. I2 is true iff C3 and C6 are true. I.e., iff $y < x$ and $z < y$. I3 is true iff C4 and C5 are true. I.e., iff $y < z$ and $z < x$. Hence, when any one of I1, I2, and I3 is true, $x = \max\{x, y, z\}$. Furthermore, the conditions under which I1, I2 and I3 are true cover all conditions under which the program for the "max" problem is to output x. Since E1 is an "or" node, the graph of Figure 9.4 implies that the effect E1 occurs whenever any one (or more) of I1, I2, and I3 is true. Hence, the output x is produced

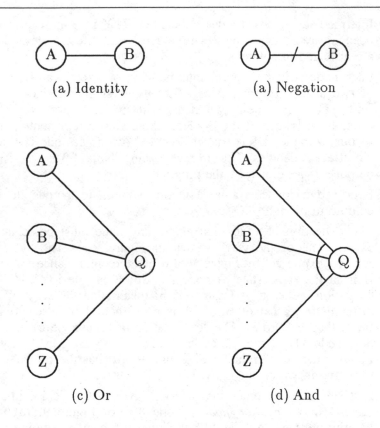

Figure 9.5 Relations for entering edges.

exactly when x is the maximum and x, y, and z are distinct.

A cause-effect graph is a formal representation of all the conditions under which a particular effect can occur. These conditions are represented as combinations of causes and may be extracted from the graph by working backwards from the effect nodes. To get all the conditions that can result in an effect Ej, we begin at the node Ej. This node is assigned the state: true. To determine all combinations of causes that result in a node being in a prespecified state, we use the following rules:

(1) If this is an identity node (Figure 9.5(a)) that is to be in the state true (false), we determine all conditions under which the node on its left is true (false).

(2) If this is a negation node that is to be in the state true, we determine all conditions under which the node on its left is false (true).

(3) In case this is an "and" node that is to be in the state true, we determine the conditions under which all the left nodes are true. If the "and" node is to be in the state false, then all combinations of states of the left nodes other than the combination having all left nodes true need to be explored. If there are n left nodes, then there are $2^n - 1$ combinations of states for the left nodes that will result in the "and" node having the state false. All combinations of causes leading to each of these $2^n - 1$ combinations of states need to be determined.

(4) In the case of an "or" node that is to be in the false state, we determine all conditions under which each of the left nodes is false. In case the "or" node is to be in the true state and there are n left nodes, then all cause combinations that result in any of the $2^n - 1$ combinations of states of the left nodes that imply the "or" node is in the true state are to be determined.

Let us use these rules to determine all conditions under which the effect E2 occurs. For clarity, Figure 9.4 has been redrawn in Figure 9.6. Only relevant nodes and edges have been retained.

E2 is an "or" node. Its state is set to true. This node has three left nodes: I4, I5, I6. For E2 to be in the true state, (I4, I5, I6) can be in any one of the seven state combinations:

(1) (true, true, true)

(2) (true, true, false)

(3) (true, false, true)

(4) (true, false, false)

(5) (false, true, true)

(6) (false, true, false)

(7) (false, false, true)

We need to determine the conditions under which each of the above seven state combinations occurs. Let us begin with the first. I4, I5, and I6 are "and" nodes. Hence, for I4 to be true, C1, C6, and

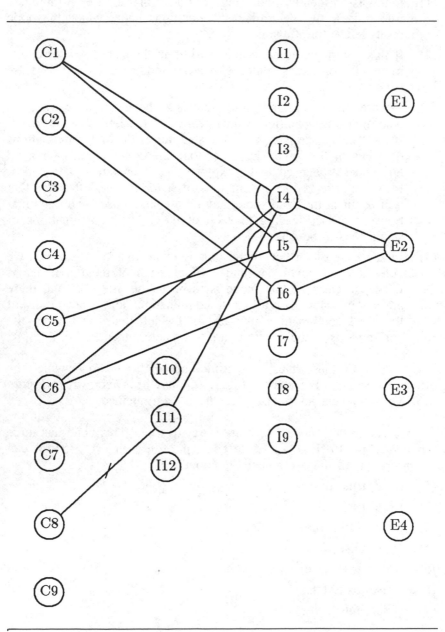

Figure 9.6 Portion of Figure 9.5

I11 must be true. Since I11 is a negation node, for I11 to be true, C8 must be false. For I5, C1 and C5 must be true. For I6, C2 and C6 must be true. So, the conditions under which I4, I5, and I6 have the state combination (true, true, true) are:

(C1 and C6 and (not C8)) and (C1 and C5) and (C2 and C6)
= C1 and C2 and C5 and C6 and (not C8)

This is the only set of conditions that results in the first of the seven state combinations listed above.

It is quite possible to have several sets of conditions that result in a given state combination. This, in fact, is the case with the second state combination (true, true, false). There are three possible state combinations of the left nodes, (C2, C6), of I6 that result in I6 having the state false. These are:

(1)   (true, false)

(2)   (false, true)

(3)   (false, false)

These are, respectively, represented by the cause combinations:

(1)   C2 and (not C6)

(2)   (not C2) and C6

(3)   (not C2) and (not C6)

Combining these with the conditions under which I4 and I5 are true, we get the following three conditions under which (I4, I5, I6) are in the state (true, true, false):

(C1 and C6 and (not C8)) and (C1 and C5) and (C2 and (not C6))
(C1 and C6 and (not C8)) and (C1 and C5) and ((not C2) and C6)
(C1 and C6 and (not C8)) and (C1 and C5) and ((not C2) and (not C6))

Generalizing from these two examples, we see that there are three different conditions that lead to the state combination (true, false, true); nine that lead to (true, false, false); seven that lead to (false, true, true); twenty one that lead to (false, true, false); and twenty one that lead to (false, false, true). In all there are 65 combinations of input conditions under which E2 can be in the state true. There are 65 for E1, 65 for E3, and 7 for E4. In all there are 202 combinations of the causes that result in one of the effects being true!

Some of these combinations may be the same and yet others may be impossible. Several combinations are impossible in our example. For instance, the cause combination

C1 and C2 and C5 and C6 and (not C8)

that results in the state (I4, I5, I6) = (true, true, true) is not possible. This is so as C2 = $x < z$ while C5 = $z < x$.

Even after the impossible combinations are weeded out and common combinations combined, the number of cause combinations that remain may be too large. In fact, because of the rules used for "and" nodes in the false state and for "or" nodes in the true state, the number of combinations grows exponentially as we move towards the left end of the graph. In an attempt to curb this explosive growth in the number of cause combinations that get generated, we suggest the following strategies:

(1) When considering an "and" ("or") node that is to be in the false (true) state generate only one of the many cause combinations that results in each of the $2^n - 1$ state combinations. This avoids further explosive growth in the number of generated conditions.

(2) When considering an "and" ("or") node that is to be in the false (true) state, consider at most n different left node state combinations. These should have the property that each of the left nodes is in the false (true) state in at least one of the state combinations and that no state combination is an impossible combination. To the extent possible, state combinations in which exactly one left node is in the false (true) state are to be preferred over those in which more than one left node is in the false (true) state. This cuts down the number of left node state combinations from $2^n - 1$ to at most n.

To see the difference between these two reduction strategies, consider the cause-effect graph of Figure 9.6. We have already determined that there are 65 cause combinations that result in E2 being true. If we use reduction strategy (1), then for each of the seven state combinations that result in E2 being true, we need to generate only one cause combination. The total number of cause combinations to generate is reduced from 65 to 7. If we use strategy (2), then for E2 we need to pick at most three state combinations for (I4, I5, I6) that are possible. The guidelines recommend the combinations (true, false, false), (false, true, false), and (false, false, true). Let us consider the first one. For the moment, assume that each of these is possible. The sole cause combination that results in I4 true is:

C1 and C6 and (not C8)

We have seen earlier that there are three state combinations for (C2, C6) that result in I6 being false. Under strategy (2), only two of these ((true, false) and (false, true)) need be considered. Similarly, there are two state combinations for (C1, C5) that need to be considered. In all, therefore, we will obtain four sets of cause conditions that result in (I4, I5, I6) having the state combination (true, false, false). By symmetry, we will obtain four combinations for each of the remaining two state combinations under consideration for (I4, I5, I6). Hence, the number of generated combinations reduces from 37 to 12.

The four combinations generated for (I4, I5, I6) = (true, false, false) are:
(1) (C1 and C6 and (not C8)) and (C1 and (not C5)) and (C2 and (not C6))
(2) (C1 and C6 and (not C8)) and (C1 and (not C5)) and ((not C2) and C6)
(3) (C1 and C6 and (not C8)) and ((not C1) and C5) and (C2 and (not C6))
(4) (C1 and C6 and (not C8)) and ((not C1) and C5) and ((not C2) and C6)

None of these is possible. (1) is not possible as it requires C6 to be both true and false. (3) and (4) are impossible for similar reasons. (2) requires that both C2 and C5 be false. But from the definition of C2 and C5, this implies that C8 be true. This contradicts the requirement in (2) that C8 is false. Since the state combination (true, false, false) is impossible, we can replace it by some other combination that has I4 = true. An examination of the remaining two state combinations being considered for (I4, I5, I6) reveals that neither is possible.

So, we need to consider some other state combinations. Since, whenever I5 or I6 is true, I4 is also true, the only possible combinations are (true, true, false) and (true, false, true). There is only one possible cause combination for each. These are:

(1) (C1 and C6 and (not C8)) and (C1 and C5) and ((not C2) and C6)
     = C1 and C5 and C6 and (not C2) and (not C8)
     = C1 and C5 and C6 (by definition of the C's)

(2) (C1 and C6 and (not C8)) and (C1 and (not C5)) and (C2 and C6)
     = C1 and C2 and C6 and (not C5) and (not C8)
     = C1 and C2 and C6 (by definition of the C's)

Similarly, for each of E1 and E3 exactly two cause combinations (which are not impossible) are generated. For E4, the guidelines for strategy (2) suggest the following cause combinations (C7, C8, C9): (true, false, false), (false, true, false), and (false, false, true). Each is possible. So, three cause combinations for E4 are generated. Hence, when strategy (2) is used we are left with 9 cause combinations.

The next step is to determine if these nine cause combinations result in any effects in addition to the one noted for each. To do this, we examine the cause combinations one at a time. The truth value of all causes in the combination is ascertained. For example, the cause combination for (I4, I5, I6) = (true, true, false) has C1, C5, and C6 true and C2 and C8 false. We begin by assigning these values to the cause nodes C1, C2, C5, C6, and C8. These truth values require that C3, C4, C7, and C9 be false. At this time, if there are any causes whose value is undetermined, these are assigned the value "?". In our example, no cause has an unassigned truth value. So, no "?"'s are introduced.

Next, we evaluate the states of the remaining nodes by moving left to right. The state of any node depends only on the states of the nodes on its left. So, its state may be evaluated using the node type information and the truth values of the nodes on its left. The following rules are used to handle the truth value "?":

(1) The truth value of an identity or negation node is "?" iff its left node has value "?".

(2) The truth value of an "or" node is true iff at least one of its left nodes have value true. It is false iff all its left nodes have value false. Otherwise, its value is "?".

(3)   An "and" node has value true iff all its left nodes have value true. It has value false iff at least one of its left nodes have value false. Otherwise, it has value "?".

Using these rules, the value of the effect nodes may be determined. For C1, C5, and C6 true and the remaining causes false, we get E1, E3, and E4 false and E2 true.

Let us consider another example. Consider the case E4 = true. As remarked earlier, when strategy (2) is used, only the following state combinations for (C7, C8, C9) are to be considered:

(1)   (true, false, false)

(2)   (false, true, false)

(3)   (false, false, true)

Consider the first of these. This requires C7 to be true and C8 and C9 to be false. When C7 is true, C1 and C3 must be false. The values of C2, C4, C5, and C6 are undetermined and set to "?". Using these truth values, the values of the effect nodes E1-E4 are, respectively, "?", "?", false, and true.

By repeating this process for each of the twelve cause combinations, we can determine the effects each is expected to produce. This cause-effect relationship may be tabulated in the form of a *decision table* as in Figure 9.7. A decision table has one row for each cause-effect combination. It contains one column for each cause and each effect. A "T" entry implies that the corresponding cause or effect is true (or present). An "F" entry implies that it is false (or absent). A blank entry signifies a value that is trivially determined from the other values and the cause-effect graph. It might evaluate to T, F, or "?".

For the example of Figure 9.4, there are 9 rows in the decision table. The first row of Figure 9.7, for example, states that when the causes C3, C4, and C5 are true (i.e., are present), the effect E1 is true. From the definitions of the causes C1-C9 and the specified truth values for C3, C4, and C5, we see that the remaining causes must be false. This results in E2, E3, and E4 having the value false. So, all the blanks in first row of the decision table correspond to the value false. For the last row of the table, C7 and C8 are false while C9 and E4 are true. This implies that C4 and C6 are false. The values of C1, C2, C3, and C5 are "?". This results in E1 false and E2 and E3 having value "?".

C1	C2	C3	C4	C5	C6	C7	C8	C9	E1	E2	E3	E4
		T	T	T					T			
		T		T	T				T			
T	T					T				T		
T				T	T					T		
T	T		T								T	
	T	T	T								T	
						T	F	F				T
						F	T	F				T
						F	F	T				T

Figure 9.7 Cause-effect decision table for Figure 9.4

Once a decision table has been constructed, it may be reduced using well known decision table reduction methods. We shall not go into these here. The effect of the reduction is to eliminate rows of the table that are subsumed by others. Following this reduction, a test set is devised so as to include at least one set of input data for each row of the reduced decision table. Since no row consists of an impossible set of cause conditions, there is at least one element in the input domain that satisfies the cause conditions of each of the rows. Because of the presence of don't cares in a decision table, it is possible for one input to satisfy the conditions of more than one row. So, the decision table doesn't result in a strict partitioning of the input domain. It does, however, come close to this.

From the table of Figure 9.7, we see that our test set for the "max" problem will include at least 9 test data. We need at least one test data for each of the following combination of causes:

(1) $y < x$, $y < z$, and $z < x$ (eg.: $x = 5$, $y = 3$, $z = 4$)

(2) $y < x$, $z < y$, and $z < x$ (eg.: $x = 5$, $y = 3$, $z = 2$)

(3) $x < y$, $x < z$, and $z < y$ (eg.: $x = 3$, $y = 8$, $z = 4$)

(4) $x < y$, $z < x$, and $z < y$ (eg.: $x = 5$, $y = 7$, $z = 2$)

(5) $x < y$, $x < z$, and $y < z$ (eg.: $x = 1$, $y = 3$, $z = 4$)

(6) $y < x$, $x < z$, and $y < z$ (eg.: $x = 2$, $y = 1$, $z = 4$)

(7) $x = y$, $x \neq z$, and $y \neq z$ (eg.: $x = 2$, $y = 2$, $z = 6$)

(8) $x \neq y$, $x = z$, and $y \neq z$ (eg.: $x = 2$, $y = 5$, $z = 2$)

(9) $x \neq y$, $x \neq z$, and $y = z$ (eg.: $x = 2$, $y = 6$, $z = 6$)

Comparing with the ad hoc I/O partitioning method used in the preceding section, we see that cause-effect graphing has led to 9 test data rather than 4.

9.3.3. White Box Methods

White box methods for test generation create test data based on an examination of the code to be generated. The weakest condition one can place on a test set is that it results in each program statement being executed at least once. This is called *statement coverage*. As an example, consider the program:

```
1 begin
2     max := a;
3     if max < b
4     then max := b;
5     if max < c
6     then max := c;
7 end
```

This program finds the maximum of the three numbers a, b, and c. Under the statement coverage requirement, the test set should result in each of the seven statements being executed at least once. The single test data ($a = 1$, $b = 2$, $c = 3$) causes each of the five statements to be executed and so results in full statement coverage. This test by itself isn't enough to give us confidence that the above program contains no errors. This is so as this test data exercises only one of the possible execution paths. The path exercised is (1, 2, 3, 4, 5, 6, 7). The program contains three other execution paths. These are (1, 2, 3, 5, 6, 7), (1, 2, 3, 4, 5, 7), and (1, 2, 3, 5, 7). Exercising these paths is accomplished by using three additional test data: (3, 1, 6), (4, 6, 1), and (8, 3, 2).

The execution paths of a program may be obtained from the *flow graph* of a program. This graph has one vertex for each statement in the program. There is a directed edge from vertex i to vertex j iff it is possible to execute statement j immediately after statement i. We shall limit ourselves to flow graphs that have exactly one vertex with no incoming edge and exactly one vertex with no outgoing edge. The single vertex with no incoming edge is called the *entry* vertex and the single vertex with no outgoing edge is called the *exit* vertex. Every execution path begins at the entry vertex and terminates at the exit vertex. The flow graph for the above "max" program is shown in Figure 9.8(a). From the flow graph, all execution paths are easily obtained.

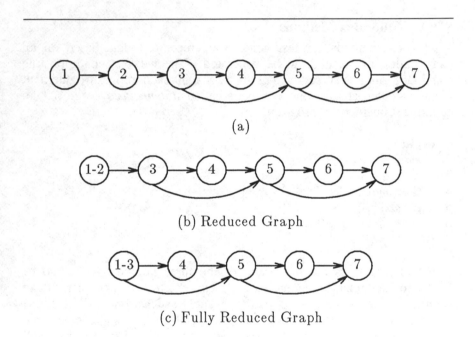

(a)

(b) Reduced Graph

(c) Fully Reduced Graph

Figure 9.8 Flow graphs for max program

Since the flow graph for a program contains as many vertices as edges, it is usually a very cumbersome graph to deal with. A *reduced flow graph* is obtained from a flow graph by repeatedly collapsing together pairs of vertices (i, j) with the following properties:

(1)   There is an edge from i to j.

(2)   There is no other edge that enters vertex j.

(3)   There is no other edge that leaves vertex i.

When two vertices i and j are collapsed, the edge from i to j is eliminated. Vertices 1 and 2 of Figure 9.8(a) can be collapsed to get the reduced graph of Figure 9.8(b). This graph can be reduced further to get the graph of Figure 9.8(c). The graph of Figure 9.8(c) cannot be reduced further.

The flow graphs for the quadratic roots program (Program 5.3), searching with **for** and **goto** statements (Program 5.11), and searching with a **while** loop (Program 5.12) are shown in Figures 9.9(a), 9.10(a), and 9.11(a), respectively. The corresponding reduced graphs are shown in Figures 9.9(b), 9.10(b), and 9.11(b). In Figure 9.10, the label 7a refers to the conditional part of line 7 of Program 5.11 while 7b refers to the statement **goto** 1.

From the reduced flow graph (Figure 9.9(b)) of the quadratic roots program, we see that this program has three execution paths: (1-8, 9-15, 28), (1-8, 16, 17-20, 28), and (1-8, 16, 21-27, 28). All the execution paths of this program can be tested using three test data; one for each of these execution paths. From Program 5.12 and its reduced flow graph Figure 9.11(b), we see that there are $n+1$ execution paths for any fixed n. These are given by the expression (3-4, $(5, 6)^j$, 5, 7-8) for $0 \le j \le n$. $(5, 6)^j$ is an abbreviation for 5, 6, 5, 6, ..., 5, 6 where the number of 5's (and hence of 6's) is j. While it is possible to test all execution paths for any fixed n, it is not possible to do so for all n. The same is true for Program 5.11.

When the number of iterations of a loop is a function of the input size (as in Programs 5.11 and 5.12), the number of execution paths is infinite. Even when we restrict ourselves to programs whose loops are iterated at most 10 or 1000 times, the number of execution paths may be very large. Further, even programs that contain no loops at all may have a very large number of execution paths. As an example, consider the flow graph of Figure 9.12. There are no loops in the program it represents. However, the number of execution paths is exponential in the number of vertices.

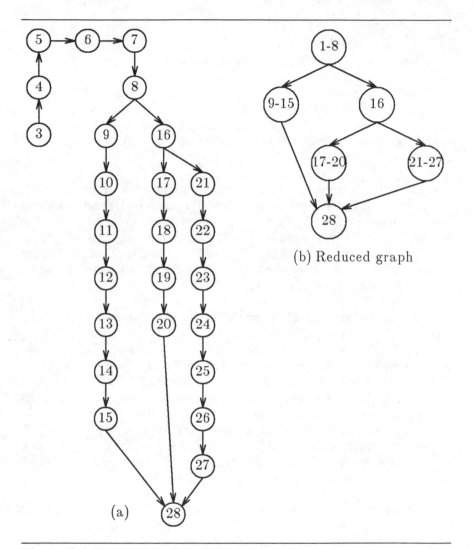

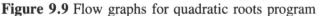

(b) Reduced graph

(a)

Figure 9.9 Flow graphs for quadratic roots program

While it would be nice to be able to use a test set that exercises each execution path in a program at least once, the size of such a test set will often be infinite or impractically large. Hence, it is necessary to lower our sights and develop criteria for an adequate test set whose coverage is somewhere between the two extremes of total statement coverage and total execution path coverage.

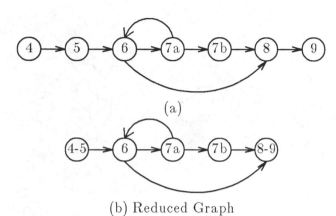

(a)

(b) Reduced Graph

Figure 9.10 Flow graphs for search program 5.11

One possibility is to require that each edge of the flow graph be traversed by the test set. This is called *edge* coverage. Note that if a reduced flow graph has at least one edge, then traversing all edges of the reduced flow graph results in traversing all edges of the full flow graph. If the reduced flow graph has no edges, then the empty test set provides a total edge coverage for the reduced flow graph but not for the full graph. Note that the full graph has at least one edge as it contains at least the two vertices: entry and exit. Hence, the edge coverage criterion may be applied to the reduced graph except in the case that this graph has no edges.

For the graph of Figure 9.8(c), two sets of test data suffice to obtain edge coverage. The test data $a = 6$, $b = 2$, $c = 3$ causes the edges (1-3, 5) and (5, 7) to be traversed. The data $a = 1$, $b = 2$, $c = 3$ causes the edges (1-3, 4), (4, 5), (5, 6), and (6, 7) to be traversed. Only two of the possible four execution paths are traversed using this test set.

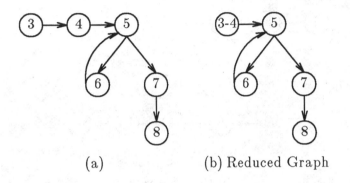

(a)   (b) Reduced Graph

Figure 9.11 Flow graphs for search program 5.12

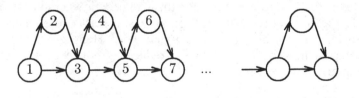

Figure 9.12 Loopless graph with many execution paths

For the graph of Figure 9.9(b), edge coverage requires all execution paths to be traversed. The edges of Figure 9.11(b) can be covered using a single execution path. In fact, every path of the form (3-4, (5, 6)^j, 5, 7-8) for $1 \leq j \leq n$ causes each edge to be traversed. Hence, edge coverage requires only one of the infinitely many execution paths to be tested.

An edge coverage of the graph of Figure 9.10(b) cannot be accomplished using a single test. Two tests will suffice. We need to traverse (for example) the paths: (4-5, 6, 7a, 6, 8-9) and (4-5, 6, 7a, 7b, 8-9). Generating the test data for each of these is quite straightforward.

The edge coverage criterion requires that all decisions in a program evaluate to both true and false (for two way decisions) during the test. For example, to traverse the edge (1-8, 9-15) in Figure 9.8(b), $x < 0$ must be true in Program 5.3. The edge (1-8, 16) can be traversed only if $x < 0$ is false; for edge (16, 17-20) to be traversed $x = 0$ must be true; and for edge (16, 21-27) to be traversed $x = 0$ must be false.

Decision coverage is a criterion that is closely related to edge coverage. In this criterion, we require that the test set cause each decision to take on all its possible values (true and false in case of a two way decision). For single entry single exit graphs, edge coverage implies decision coverage. However, decision coverage may not imply edge coverage. This is, in fact, the case when the flow graph has no decisions. Decision coverage results in an empty test set whereas edge coverage results in a test set with one test data. Note, however, that decision coverage together with statement coverage is equivalent to edge coverage.

The test criterion can be further strengthened to require that each condition of each decision take on all possible values. This is called *condition coverage*. A *condition* is formally defined to be a Boolean expression that contains no Boolean operator (i.e., **and**, **or**, **not**). Some examples are:

(1) $x > y$

(2) $x + y < y * z$

(3) c (where c is of type Boolean)

Consider the statement:

if ($C1$ **and** $C2$) **or** ($C3$ **and** $C4$) **then** S1
else S2

where $C1$, $C2$, $C3$, and $C4$ are conditions and S1 and S2 are statements. Under the edge or decision coverage criteria, we need to use one test set that causes ($C1$ **and** $C2$) **or** ($C3$ **and** $C4$) to be true and another that results in this decision being false. Condition coverage requires us to use a test set that causes each of the four conditions to evaluate to true at least once and to false at least once. This requires at least two data sets. Some of the possible pairs of truth value combinations for $C1-C4$ that satisfy the requirements of condition coverage are:

(1) (true, true, true, true), (false, false, false, false)

(2) (true, false, true, false), (false, true, false, true)

(3) (false, false, true, true), (true, true, false, false)

Each of the above requires two data sets. Note that both data sets for (2) result in the decision for the **if** being false while both data sets for (3) result in this decision being true. So, a test set that results in condition coverage need not result in decision coverage.

Note also that there may be no input data that corresponds to any of the above three pairs of truth value combinations. For example, there may be no data that results in $C1-C4$ being true simultaneously. Hence, condition coverage may require the use of more than two data sets. Two truth value combinations for $C1-C4$ that result in condition coverage and require three data sets are:

(1) (true, true, true, true), (true, true, false, false), (false, false, false, true)

(2) (true, false, false, true), (true, true, false, true), (false, true, true, false)

Condition coverage can be further strengthened to require that all combinations of condition values be tested for. In the above **if** example, this will require the use of 16 test data; one for each truth combination of $C1-C4$. Several of these combinations may not be possible. So, the number of test data will generally be smaller.

Of the test coverage criteria we have discussed so far, execution path coverage is generally the most demanding. A test set that results in total execution path coverage also results in statement and decision coverage. It may, however, not result in condition coverage. Total execution path coverage often requires an infinite number of test data or at least a prohibitively large number of test data. Hence, total path coverage is often impossible in practice.

It is often possible to use a test set that satisfies all three of the following:

(1)   statement coverage

(2)   decision coverage

(3)   all combinations condition coverage

The all combinations condition coverage requirement may result in too many test data. The number of test data can be reduced by changing this requirement to "condition coverage". A word of caution is in order for the reader who is going to program in a language other than Pascal. Several programming languages (but not Pascal) evaluate decisions in short circuit mode. In this mode, the evaluation of a decision terminates as soon as its value has been determined. For example, consider the statement:

if $(C1$ **and** $C2)$ **or** $(C3$ **and** $C4)$ **then** S1
else S2

If $(C1$ **and** $C2)$ evaluates to true, then $(C3$ **and** $C4)$ is not evaluated as regardless of its value, the decision is true. When this mode of decision evaluation is being used, it is necessary to strengthen condition coverage to *condition coverage and evaluation*. This requires that each condition actually be evaluated during the testing and that it take on the value true on at least one such evaluation and the value false on another. This is necessary as the evaluation of a condition may have side effects that impact the run time behavior of a program. For instance, a condition may involve a function invocation (say $f(x, y, z)$) that results in the values of x, y, and z being changed. To study the effects of this, the condition must be forced to evaluate.

In many cases, condition coverage and evaluation may be impossible. For example, suppose that the above **if** statement is evaluated as in the flow chart of Figure 9.13. There may be no input data that causes $C2$ to actually evaluate to false. This is so as $C2$ may be false only when $C1$ is. But, when $C1$ is false, $C2$ is not evaluated.

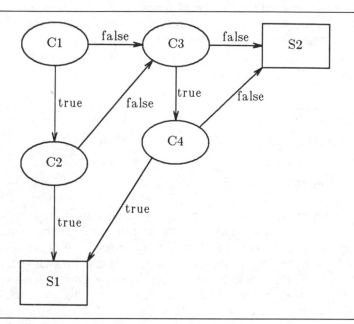

Figure 9.13 Flow chart for short circuit evaluation

9.3.4. Summary

When generating test data, one must keep in mind that the objective of testing is to expose the presence of errors. Generating a minimal test set that serves this purpose is a challenge. All too often, programmers rely on randomly generated test data. This is about the worst way to generate test data. We have discussed two functionally different approaches to the generation of test data: black box and white box. Both approaches aim at generating test data with maximum likelihood of exposing errors. To get a good test set, it is essential to use both the black and white box methods.

Test data obtained from black box methods can expose errors resulting from missing code segments, boundary conditions, numerical errors, interesting combinations of input conditions, etc. Test data obtained from white box methods may not detect such errors.

Test data obtained from white box methods will expose errors resulting from uninitialized variables, misspelled variable names, incorrect conditions (for example $x < y$ instead of $y < x$), unreachable code segments, etc. These errors may not be detected by the black box data.

The black and white box methods provide guidelines for a minimum test set. In practice, it may be possible to use more than a minimum test set. In this case, it is desirable to use additional tests in some uniform way. We would like to exercise all code segments uniformly. To accomplish this, one may use automatic program instrumentation aids. These aids provide statistics on the frequency of execution of each statement or flow graph edge. They can also record the number of times each decision took on a certain value, the number of times each condition had a certain evaluation, etc. Based on this information, one can devise additional tests to exercise those parts of the program that have not been sufficiently exercised. The interested reader is referred to the paper on program instrumentation by J. Huang that is cited in the references section of this chapter.

Program instrumentation is also useful in obtaining a test set that satisfies certain criteria. After a few test data have been used, the results from the program instrumentation can be used to determine what needs to be done to meet the test criteria. Additional test data to meet this end can now be obtained.

9.4. DEBUGGING

Testing exposes the presence of errors in a program. Once a test run produces a result different from the one expected, we know that something is wrong with the program. The process of determining and correcting the cause of this discrepency between the behavior as predicted by the specifications and that observed is called *debugging*. A thorough study of debugging methods is beyond the scope of this book. We simply provide some suggestions for debugging and refer the interested reader to the book by G. Myers that is cited in the references section.

(1) Use incremental testing so that the cause of the error is localized.

(2) Try to determine the cause of an error by logical reasoning. If this fails, then you may wish to perform a program trace to determine when the program started performing incorrectly. This becomes infeasible when the program executes many instructions with that test data. The program trace is too long to be examined manually. When this happens, testing must be refined to isolate the part of the code that is suspect and a trace of this part

obtained.

(3) Do not attempt to correct errors by creating exceptions. Soon, the number of exceptions will be very large. Errors should be corrected by first determining their cause and then redesigning your solution as necessary.

(4) When correcting an error, be certain that your correction does not result in errors where there were none before. Run your corrected program on the test data on which it worked alright before to be sure that it still works correctly on this data.

9.5. REFERENCES AND SELECTED READINGS

The text:

> *The art of software testing*, by G. Myers, John Wiley, New York, 1979

contains many dos and don'ts of program testing and debugging. It also contains chapters on walk-throughs, test design, and test generation tools. The terminology "big bang" is borrowed from this book.

The following papers discuss methods to generate test sets:

> Validation, verification, and testing of computer software, by W. R. Adrions, M. Branstad, and J. Cherniavsky, *ACM Computing Surveys*, Vol. 14, No. 2, June 1982, pp. 159-192.

> Static analysis and dynamic testing of computer software, by R. Fairley, *IEEE Computer*, April 1978, pp. 14-23.

> Hints on test data selection: Helpful for the practicing programmer, by R. DeMillo, R. Lipton, and F. Sayward, *IEEE Computer*, April 1978, pp. 34-41.

> Program instrumentation and software testing, by J. Huang, *IEEE Computer*, April 1978, pp. 25-32.

A system that generates test data and several references to other such systems can be found in the paper:

A system to generate test data and symbolically execute pro-grams, by L. Clarke, *IEEE Trans. On Software Engineering*, Sept. 1976, pp. 215-222.

9.6. EXERCISES

1. Describe two of the ways in which a top down incremental test-ing of the program of Figure 9.1 may proceed. In each case, state which stubs and drivers are needed.

2. Do the previous exercise for bottom up incremental testing.

3. List all the conditions under which (I4, I5, and I6) take on each of the following state combinations. See Figure 9.4. For each set of conditions determine whether it is an impossible condition.
   a. (true, false, true)
   b. (true, false, false)
   c. (false, true, true)
   d. (false, true, false)
   e. (false, false, true)

4. For the cause-effect graph of Figure 9.14, obtain all cause com-binations that result in each of the effects E1, E2, and E3. Present these in a decision table in which each different cause combination is represented by a single row. For each set of cause combinations, all effects should be marked T, F, or "?".

5. Do the previous exercise for the cause-effect graph of Figure 9.15.

6. You are to test a program that inputs the lengths of the three sides of a triangle and classifies the triangle into one of the categories:
   a. equilateral
   b. isosceles

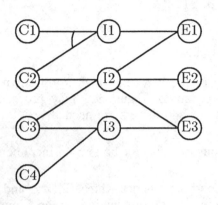

Figure 9.14

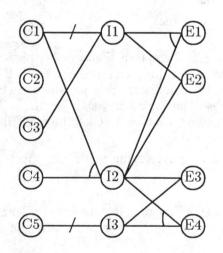

Figure 9.15

c.   scalene
Obtain a cause-effect graph for this problem. Next, obtain the complete decision table that contains the combination of causes that are to be tested for. Only possible combinations are to be included and the suggestions to reduce growth in the number of rows are to be used.

7.   Give an example of a program in which execution path coverage does not result in condition coverage.

8.   Do the following for Program 5.2.
   (a)   Obtain the full flow graph. Note that lines 1-6 are not executable statements. So, your graph should contain exactly 14 vertices.
   (b)   Reduce the flow graph obtained in (a).
   (c)   Show that when *TotalMonths* = 20, the number of execution paths is 1.

9.   Do the following for Program 5.13.
   (a)   Obtain the full flow graph.
   (b)   Reduce the flow graph obtained in (a).
   (c)   Determine the number of execution paths as a function of n.
   (d)   Obtain a test set that provides statement and decision coverage.

10.   Do the following for Program 5.16.
   (a)   Obtain the full flow graph.
   (b)   Reduce the flow graph obtained in (a).
   (c)   Determine the number of execution paths.
   (d)   Obtain a test set that provides statement and decision coverage.

11.   Obtain the reduced flow graph for Program 5.17. List all the execution paths.

12. Obtain the reduced flow graph for Program 6.2. How many execution paths are there?

13. Obtain the reduced flow graph for Program 6.11. List all the execution paths.

14. Obtain the full and reduced flow graphs for Program 6.13. How many execution paths are there for any given n?

15. Obtain the reduced flow graph for Program 6.14. Obtain test data that results in total execution path coverage.

16. Do the preceding exercise for Program 6.15.

17. Do the following for Program 7.11.
    (a) Obtain the reduced flow graph.
    (b) Determine the number of execution paths as a function of n.
    (c) Obtain a test set that results in statement and decision coverage.

CHAPTER 10

PERFORMANCE ANALYSIS

10.1. INTRODUCTION

In the preceding two chapters, we were concerned with establishing the correctness of a program. Once correctness has been established, we will be interested in knowing the amount of computer time and memory needed to run this program. *Performance analysis* is concerned with determining these two quantities. There are two approaches to determining the performance characteristics of a program. One is analytical, and the other experimental. This chapter is concerned solely with analytical methods. The next chapter deals with the experimental approach.

The *space complexity* of a program is the amount of memory it needs to run to completion. This is of interest to us for the following reasons:

1. If the program is to be run on a multiuser computer system, then we need to specify the amount of memory to be allocated to the program.

2. If the program is to run on a any system, then we would like to know in advance whether or not sufficient memory is available to run the program.

3.   We might have two or more alternate solutions to a problem. These may differ in their computer space requirements. For instance, one Pascal compiler for the IBM-PC might need only 27K of memory while another might need 128K. The 27K compiler is the only choice for persons with IBM-PCs that have less than 128K of memory. Even those who have the extra memory will prefer the smaller compiler if its capabilities are not significantly inferior to those of the bigger compiler. This is so as the smaller compiler leaves the user with more memory that can be used for other purposes (eg., electronic disk; print spooler, etc.). Also, it may be possible to compile larger programs as more memory is available for compilation when the smaller compiler is used.

4.   The space complexity can be used to estimate the size of the largest problem that can be solved in a given amount of memory. As an example, consider the rat in a maze problem introduced in Chapter 7. In addition to the space needed to store the program instructions, we need space to store the maze and the path. This space increases with the size of the maze and so limits the size of mazes that can be handled in a given amount of memory.

The *time complexity* of a program is the amount of computer time it needs to run to completion. We are interested in the time complexity of a program for the following reasons:

1.   Many computer systems require the user to provide an upper limit on the amount of time the program will run for. Once this upper limit has been reached, the program is aborted. An easy way out is to simply specify a time limit of a few thousand hours. This could result in serious fiscal problems if the program runs into an infinite loop caused by some discrepency in the data and you actually get billed for the computer time used. We would like to provide a time limit that is just slightly above the expected run time.

2.   The program we are developing might be required to provide a satisfactory real time response. This is so for all interactive programs. A text editor that takes a minute to move the cursor one page down or one page up will not be acceptable to many users. A spread sheet program that takes several minutes to reevaluate the cells in a sheet will be satisfactory only to very patient users. A database management system that requires its users to drink two cups of coffee while it is sorting a relation will not find too much acceptance. These are three examples of programs that are

designed for interactive use and which must provide satisfactory real time response. From the time complexity of the program or program module we can decide whether or not the response time will be acceptable. If not, we need to redesign the algorithm in use. If this cannot be done, then the target computer must be replaced by a faster one.

3. When the program is being run in batch mode, a real time response is not crucial. For instance, in the rat in a maze program of Chapter 7, the input module must provide satisfactory real time response as the user is entering and editing the rows of the maze one by one. The module that searches for a path isn't interactive and following the input of the maze, the user can probably attend to other tasks until the search for a path is complete. Similarly, when compiling a Pascal program using an interactive compiler, it is necessary that the compile time per statement be small. It is not so crucial that the compiled code run in real time (unless, of course, the program that was compiled is itself an interactive program).

   However, in batch mode too we would like the program to run in a reasonable amount of time. The user interested in finding a path in a maze cannot be expected to wait a few hundred years for the path finder to complete the search. We would like advance indication of the amount of time the program will run for.

4. In case we have alternate ways to solve a problem, then the decision on which to use will be based primarily on the expected performance difference amongst these alternate solutions. So, we will use some weighted measure of the space and time complexities of the alternate solutions.

10.2. SPACE COMPLEXITY

Function *abc* (Program 10.1) computes the expression $a+b+b*c+(a+b-c)/(a+b)+4.0$; function *sum* (Program 10.2) computes the sum $\sum_{i=1}^{n} a[i]$, where the $a[i]$'s are real numbers; and function *rsum* is a recursive program that computes $\sum_{i=1}^{n} a[i]$. The space needed by each of these programs is seen to be the sum of the following components:

```
function abc(a, b, c: real): real;
begin
  abc := a+b+b*c+(a+b-c)/(a+b)+4.0;
end; {of abc}
```

Program 10.1

```
line    function sum(a: ElementList; n: integer): real;
1       var s: real; i: integer;
2       begin
3         s := 0;
4         for i := 1 to n do
5           s := s + a[i];
6         sum := s;
7       end; {of sum}
```

Program 10.2

```
line    function rsum(a: ElementList; n: integer): real;
1       begin
2         if n<=0 then rsum := 0
3         else rsum := rsum(a, n-1) + a[n];
4       end; {of rsum}
```

Program 10.3

(a) *Instruction Space*
     This is the space needed to store the compiled version of the program instructions.

(b) *Data Space*
     This is the space needed to store all constant and variable values. We may divide this space into three components:

     1. Space needed by constants (for example, the numbers 0, 1, and 4.0 in Programs 10.1 - 10.3) and simple variables (such as a, b, c, i, etc. in Programs 10.1 - 10.3).

    2. Space needed by component variables such as the array *maze* and the lists *path* and *offset* in Program 7.7.

    3. Space needed by referenced variables such as variables of type *node* in Program 7.17.

(c) *Environment Stack*

Each time a procedure/function is invoked, it is necessary to save some information in order to commence the execution of the procedure/function and also to resume execution when the procedure/function terminates. At a minimum, this includes information about the program instruction to be executed following the termination of the procedure/function. This information is stored on an environment stack.

Instruction Space

The amount of instruction space that is needed depends upon such factors as:

(a) The compiler used to compile the program into machine code.

(b) The compiler options in effect at the time of compilation.

(c) The target computer.

The compiler used is a very important factor determining the space needed by the resulting code. Figure 10.1 shows three possible codes for the evaluation of $a+b+b*c+(a+b-c)/(a+b)+4.0$. All of these perform exactly the same arithmetic operations (i.e., every operator has the same operands) but each needs a different amount of space. The compiler in use determines exactly which code will be generated.

Even with the same compiler, the size of the generated program code can vary. For example, a compiler might provide the user with optimization options. These could include code size optimization as well as execution time optimization. In the example of Figure 10.1 for instance, the compiler might generate the code of Figure 10.1 (b) in non-optimization mode. In optimization mode, the compiler might use the knowledge that $a+b+b*c = b*c+(a+b)$ and generate the shorter and also more time efficient code of Figure 10.1 (c). The use of the optimization mode will generally increase the time needed to compile the program.

LOAD a	LOAD a	LOAD a
ADD b	ADD b	ADD b
STORE $t1$	STORE $t1$	STORE $t1$
LOAD b	SUB c	SUB c
MULT c	DIV $t1$	DIV $t1$
STORE $t2$	STORE $t2$	STORE $t2$
LOAD $t1$	LOAD b	LOAD b
ADD $t2$	MUL c	MUL c
STORE $t3$	STORE $t3$	ADD $t2$
LOAD a	LOAD $t1$	ADD $t1$
ADD b	ADD $t3$	ADD 4.0
SUB c	ADD $t2$	
STORE $t4$	ADD 4.0	
LOAD a		
ADD b		
STORE $t5$		
LOAD $t4$		
DIV $t5$		
STORE $t6$		
LOAD $t3$		
ADD $t6$		
ADD 4.0		
(a)	(b)	(c)

Figure 10.1 Three equivalent codes.

The example of Figure 10.1 brings to light an additional contribution to the space requirements of a program. Space is needed for temporary variables such as $t1$, $t2$, ... , $t6$.

Another option that can have a significant effect on program space is the overlay option. Here, space is assigned only to the program module that is currently executing. When a new module is invoked, it is read in from a disk (say) and the code for the new module overwrites the code of the old module. So program space corresponding to the size of the largest module is needed (rather than the sum of the module sizes).

The configuration of the target computer can also affect code size. If the computer has floating point hardware installed, then floating point operations will translate into one machine instruction per operation. If this hardware is not installed, then code to simulate floating point computations will be generated.

Data Space

For simple variables and constants, the space requirements are a function of the computer used and the size of the numbers involved. The reason for this is that we will normally be concerned with the number of words of memory required. Since the number of bits per word varies from computer to computer, the number of words needed per variable also varies. Also, it takes more bits to store the number 2^{100} than it does to store 2^3.

We shall make the simplifying assumption that all variables of type **integer** and **real** require one word each. All variables of type **boolean** require one bit each and all of type **char** require one byte each. Once we know the number of bits per byte (this is generally 8) and bytes per word in the target computer, the space needed by the simple variables and constants can be computed.

The space needed for component variables also depends on the above two factors. It also depends on the number of components in the variable. Each variable of type *position* (cf. Section 7.2) has two components *row* and *col*. Since each component is of type **integer**, each variable of type *position* requires two words (under the assumption that each integer requires one word).

The array *maze* of Section 7.2 is declared as:

var *maze*: **array** [1..*MaxRows*, 1..*MaxRows*] **of** 0..1;

This is an indexed variable that has $MaxRows^2$ components. Each component requires only one bit of space. So, the space needed for this array is $MaxRows^2$ bits. While only this many bits are needed, the actual space allocated to *maze* will depend on the particular compiler in use. Some compilers may simply allocate one byte or even one word for each component of *maze*. Others may allocate a whole number of bytes or words. So, if $MazeRows^2$ is 100, then 13 bytes may be allocated (in an 8 bit per byte computer) or 4 words in a 32 bit per word computer.

The variable *path* of Section 7.2 was declared as:

var *path*: **array** [1..*MaxPathLength*] **of** *position*;

This component variable has *MaxPathLength* components of type *position*. Each component of type *position* requires two words. So, the total space needed by *path* is 2*MaxPathLength* words. The data type *displacements* of Program 7.7 has two components. Each is in the range −1..1 and so needs only two bits. The array *offset* which is declared as:

var *offset*: **array** [1..4] **of** *displacements*;

needs a total of 16 bits of space.

The space needed by referenced variables depends on the space needed by each such variable and also on the number of such variables. Recall that referenced variables may be created dynamically during execution of a program using the procedure *new*. If we assume that each field that is a pointer (such as the field *link* in the data type *node* of Section 7.4) requires one word, then each variable of type *node* (Section 7.4) requires two words. The total space needed for variables of type *node* will depend on the number of such variables that get created.

Environment Stack

The space needed by the environment stack is often neglected by beginning performance analysts. This is so because one must first understand how procedures/functions (and in particular recursive ones) are invoked and what happens on termination. Each time a procedure or function is invoked the following data are saved on the environment stack:

1. the return address
2. the addresses of the variable actual parameters
3. the values of all local variables and value formal parameters in the procedure/function being invoked (this is necessary for recur-

It is worth noting that some Pascal compilers save the values of the local and value formal parameters for both recursive and non recursive procedures and functions. So, the compiler in use will have an effect on the amount of space needed by the environment stack.

In summary, the space needed by a program depends upon many factors. Some of these are not determined at the time the program is conceived or written (e.g., the computer to be used, the compiler that will be used, etc.). Until these factors have been determined, we cannot make an accurate analysis of the space requirements of a program.

We can, however, determine the contribution of those components which depend upon the characteristics of the problem instance to be solved. These characteristics typically include factors that determine the size of the problem instance (i.e., the number of inputs and outputs, magnitude of the numbers involved, etc.) being solved.

The size of the program space is relatively insensitive to the particular problem instance being solved.

The contribution of the constants and simple variables to the data space is also independent of the characteristics of the problem instance to be solved. An exception to this is when the magnitude of the numbers involved becomes too large for a word. At this time, we will probably have to rewrite the program using multiprecision arithmetic and then analyze the new program.

The space needed by some of the component variables may also be independent of the problem size. For example, the space needed by the array *offset* in Program 7.7 is 16 bits regardless of the size of the maze that is being searched. The space needed by other component variables depends on the size of the instance. For example, in the rat in the maze program the array maze must have at least $(n+1)^2$ positions in order to accommodate a maze with n rows together with the boundary wall of 1's. The space needed by each referenced variable and the number of such variables may also depend on the instance characteristics. For example, in Program 7.18, the number of variables of type *node* is twice the number of wires. The space needed by each node is, however, independent of the instance characteristics.

The space needed by the environment stack is generally independent of the instance characteristics unless recursive procedures and/or functions are in use. The truth of this statement rests on the assumption that the values of local and value formal parameters are not saved for non-recursive procedures and functions. When recursive procedures and/or functions are in use, the instance characteristics will generally (but not always) have an effect on the amount of space needed for the environment stack.

The amount of stack space needed by recursive procedures and functions is called the *recursion stack space*. For each procedure and function, this depends on the space needed by the local and value formal parameters and also on the number of variable formal parameters (as their addresses need to be stacked). In addition, this space depends on the maximum depth of recursion (this is the maximum number of nested recursive calls). For Program 10.3, recursive calls get nested until $n=0$. At this time, the nesting looks as in Figure 10.2. The maximum depth of recursion for this program is therefore $n+1$.

$$rsum(n)$$
$$rsum(n-1)$$
$$rsum(n-2)$$
$$.$$
$$.$$
$$.$$
$$rsum(1)$$
$$rsum(0)$$

Figure 10.2 Nesting of recursive calls for Program 10.3.

We may divide the total space needed by a program into two parts:

(a) A fixed part which is independent of the characteristics of the inputs and outputs. This part typically includes the instruction space (i.e., space for the code); space for simple variables and fixed size component variables; space for constants, etc.

(b) A variable part which consists of the space needed by component variables whose size is dependent on the particular problem instance being solved; space needed by referenced variables (to the extent that this depends on instance characteristics); and the recursion stack space (in so far as this space depends on the instance characteristics).

The space requirement $S(P)$, of any program P may therefore be written as $S(P) = c + S_P$(instance characteristics) where c is a constant.

When analyzing the space complexity of a program, we shall concentrate solely on estimating S_P (instance characteristics). For any given problem, we shall need to first determine which instance characteristics to use to measure the space requirements. This is very problem specific and we shall resort to examples to illustrate the various possibilities. Generally speaking, our choices are limited to quantities related to the number and magnitude of the inputs to and outputs from the program. At times, more complex measures of the interrelationships amongst the data items are used.

Example 10.1: For Program 10.1, the problem instance is characterized by the specific values of a, b, and c. Making the assumption that one word is adequate to store the values of each of a, b, c, and abc, we see that the space needed by function abc is independent of the instance characteristics. Consequently, S_P(instance characteristics) $= 0$. □

Example 10.2: The problem instances for Program 10.2 are characterized by n, the number of elements to be summed. Since, a and n are value formal parameters, space for these must be allocated. The space needed by the variable n is 1 word as it is of type **integer**. The space needed by a is the space needed by variables of type *ElementList*. This is at least n words as a must be large enough to hold the n elements to be summed. So, we obtain $S_{sum}(n) \geq n$.

Notice that if we change the formal parameter a from value to variable, only the address of the actual parameter gets transferred to the function and the space needed by the function is independent of n. In this case, $S_{sum}(n) = 0$.

So, even though the values of the individual components of a do not get changed by *sum*, it is desirable to make a a variable parameter in order to conserve space. As a variable parameter enough space to store a memory address is needed. This is typically just one or two words. □

Example 10.3: Let us consider the function *rsum*. As in the case of *sum*, the instances are characterized by n. The recursion stack space includes space for the formal parameters, the local variables, and the return address. Since a is a value formal parameter, the values of all its components get saved on the stack. Assume that the return address requires only one word of memory. Each call to *rsum* requires at least $(n + 3)$ words (including space for the values of n and s and the return address). More space is required if *ElementList* has been declared as an array $[1..MaxSize]$ where $MaxSize > n$. In this case, each call to *rsum* takes up $(MaxSize + 3)$ space.

Since the depth of recursion is $n+1$, the recursion stack space needed is $(n+1)(MaxSize+3)$ or $(n+1)(n+3)$ depending on whether or not the size of *ElementList* is changed whenever n changes.

Now that we realize the space cost of having a a value formal parameter, we see that *rsum* will fail when n is suitably large. For example, when $n = 1000$, at least $1001*1003 = 1,004,003$ words of memory are needed for the recursion stack space alone.

If we make a a variable parameter, then each call to *rsum* requires only 4 words of space. The recursion stack space becomes $4(n+1)$ or 4004 words when $n = 1000$. We can solve much larger instances now with a given amount of memory. Of course, we can do much better by not using recursion at all and sticking with the modified version of Program 10.2 in which a is a variable formal parameter. □

Example 10.4: Consider the rat in a maze problem of Chapter 7. Maze instances are characterized by the number of rows (*MazeRows*) in the maze. We could also characterize a maze by the number of maze positions ($MazeRows^2$); the number of blocked maze positions, the length of the shortest path (if any) from entrance to exit, etc. It is easiest to stay with *MazeRows* for now. The array *maze* needs $(MazeRows + 1)^2$ bits (including space for the boundary wall). The space needed by *path* is $2*MaxPathLength = 2*(MazeRows^2-1)$ words.

If the recursive version of procedure *FindPath* (Program 7.5) is used, then each invocation of *RealPathFinder* will cause the values of two parameters, three local variables, and a return address to get stacked. Since the maximum depth of recursion is $MazeRows^2$, $6*MazeRows^2$ words of recursion stack space are needed.

So, larger problem instances can be solved if the declared size of *maze* and *path* are changed as the number of rows changes. In this case, $S_{RatInAMaze}(MazeRows) = (MazeRows + 1)^2$ bits $+ 2*(MazeRows^2 - 1)$ words $+ 6*MazeRows^2$ words.

If the iterative version (Program 7.7) is used, then the needed space decreases significantly as no recursion stack space is needed.

Now, suppose that we wish to obtain the space complexity as a function of *MazeRows* and the number, u, of unblocked positions in the maze. The space needed for *maze* is unchanged. However, the space needed for *path* cannot exceed $2(u-1)$ words as only unblocked maze positions can be on the path (the -1 comes in as the exit is not put on *path*). One can easily construct a *maze* that will require this many positions in *path*. So, at least this much space must be allocated to *path*. The recursion stack space becomes $6*u$ words as the depth of recursion cannot exceed u. Hence, $S_{RatInAMaze}(MazeRows, u) = (MazeRows + 1)^2$ bits $+ 2(u - 1)$ words $+ 6*u$ words. $\square$

As our examples have pointed out, recursion and large value formal parameters are expensive in space. Hence, if we wish to minimize the space needs of our program, we should avoid the use of recursion and value parameters that are large. *Large parameters should be made variable parameters even if we do not wish to change any elements in them.*

In the examples considered thus far, the switch from recursion to iteration and the switch from value to variable parameters costs little in terms of loss in comprehensibility and increase in difficulty of program development. There will, however, be times when the penalty for following the above recommendation will be severe. In these situations, one needs to determine the degree to which it is necessary to optimize the space requirements. If the recursive program using large value parameters cannot run on the target computer for lack of space, then we have no choice but to expend the additional effort needed to develop a more space efficient version of the program.

Example 10.5: Program 10.4 is a recursive procedure that writes out all permutations of the elements in the array $a[k..n]$. Its correctness may be established by induction on $n-k$. The formal parameter a is a value parameter and the depth of recursion is n if the initial invocation of *perm* is $perm(a, 1, n)$.

We may attempt to change a to a variable parameter in order to reduce the amount of recursion stack space. For the procedure to still work correctly, it is necessary to explicitly save the elements $a[k+1..n]$. This introduces a degree of inelegance into the program. Additionally, if *ElementList* is of size n, then the space saving is only a factor of 2 and not a factor of n. To see this observe that when a is a value parameter, n^2 words of stack space are needed to save a n times (assuming one word per element of a). When we explictly save $a[k+1..n]$, $\sum_{k=1}^{n-2}(n-k) = n(n-1)/2 - 1$ words are needed.

Any simplistic attempt to eliminate the recursion results in an iterative procedure that simulates the recursion. This results in no saving of space. While it is possible to arrive at a space efficient iterative procedure to generate permutations, this takes considerably more effort than developing the recursive version (see the discrete mathematics text by S. Sahni cited in the references). □

```
procedure perm(a: ElementList; k,n: integer);
{generate all the permutations of a[k:n]}
var t: element;  {type of entries in a[]}
    i: integer;
begin
  if k = n
  then begin {output permutation}
          for i := 1 to n do
             write(a[i]);
          writeln;
       end
  else {a[k:n] has more than one permutation.
        Generate these recursively.}
     for i := k to n do
     begin
         {interchange a[k] and a[i]}
         t := a[k]; a[k] := a[i]; a[i] := t;
         perm(a, k+1, n); {all permutations of a[k+1..n]}
     end;
end; {of perm}
```

Program 10.4 Recursive procedure for permutations

10.3. TIME COMPLEXITY

The time complexity of a program depends upon all the factors that the space complexity depends on. A program will run faster on a computer capable of executing 10^8 instructions per second than on one that can execute only 10^6 instructions per second. The code of Figure 10.1(c) will require less execution time than the code of Figure 10.1(a). Some compilers will take less time than others to generate the corresponding computer code. Smaller problem instances will generally take less time than larger instances.

The time, $T(P)$, taken by a program P is the sum of the compile time and the run (or execution) time. The compile time does not depend on the instance characteristics. Also, we may assume that a compiled program will be run several times without recompilation. Consequently, we shall concern ourselves with just the run time of a program. This run time is denoted by t_P (instance characteristics).

Because many of the factors t_P depends on are not known at the time a program is conceived, it is reasonable to attempt to only estimate t_P. If we knew the characteristics of the compiler to be used, we could proceed to determine the number of additions, subtractions, multiplications, divisions, compares, loads, stores, etc. that would be made by the code for P. Having done this, we could present a formula for t_P. Letting n denote the instance characteristics, we might then have an expression for $t_P(n)$ of the form:

$$t_P(n) = c_a ADD(n) + c_s SUB(n) + c_m MUL(n) + c_d DIV(n) + \cdots$$

where c_a, c_s, c_m, c_d, etc., respectively, denote the time needed for an addition, subtraction, multiplication, division, etc. and ADD, SUB, MUL, DIV, etc. are functions whose value is the number of additions, subtractions, multiplications, divisions, etc. that will be performed when the code for P is used on an instance with characteristic n.

Obtaining such an exact formula is in itself an impossible task as the time needed for an addition, subtraction, multiplication, etc. often depends on the actual numbers being added, subtracted, multiplied, etc. In reality then, the true value of $t_P(n)$ for any given n can be obtained only experimentally. The program is typed, compiled, and run on a particular machine. The execution time is physically clocked and $t_P(n)$ obtained. Even with this experimental approach, one could face difficulties. In a multiuser system, the execution time will depend on system load: How many other programs are on the computer at the time program P is run? What are the characteristics of these other programs? etc.

Given the minimal utility of determining the exact number of additions, subtractions, etc. that are needed to solve a problem instance with characteristics given by n, we might as well lump all the operations together (provided that the time required by each is relatively independent of the instance characteristics) and obtain a count for the total number of operations. We can go one step further and count only the number of program steps.

A *program step* is loosely defined to be a syntactically or semantically meaningful segment of a program that has an execution time which is independent of the instance characteristics. For example, the entire statement:

$abc := a+b+b*c+(a+b-c)/(a+b)+4.0;$

of Program 10.1 could be regarded as a step as its execution time is independent of the instance characteristics (this statement isn't strictly true as the time for a multiply and divide will generally depend on the actual numbers involved in the operation).

The number of steps any program statement is to be assigned depends on the nature of that statement. The following discussion considers the various statement types that can appear in a Pascal program and states the complexity of each in terms of the number of steps:

(a) *Comments*
Comments are non-executable statements and have a step count of zero.

(b) *Declarative Statements*
This includes all statements of type **const**, **label**, **type**, and **var**. These are non-executable statements and so count as zero steps.

(c) *Expressions and Assignment Statements*
Most expressions have a step count of one. The exceptions are expressions that contain function calls. In this case, we need to determine the cost of invoking the functions. This cost can be large if the functions employ large value parameters as the values

of all actual parameters need to be assigned to the formal parameters. This is discussed further under procedure and function invocation. When the expression contains functions, the step count is the sum of the step counts assignable to each function invocation.

The assignment statement <variable> := <expr> has a step count equal to that of <expr> unless the size of <variable> is a function of the instance characteristics. In this latter case, the step count is the size of <variable> plus the step count of <expr>. For example, the assignment $a := b$ where a and b are of type *ElementList* has a step count equal to the size of *ElementList*.

(d) *Iteration Statements*
This class of statements includes the **for, while,** and **until** statements. These have the form:

for i := <expr> **to** <expr1> **by** <expr2> **do**
while <expr> **do**
until <expr>;

Each execution of a **while** and **until** statement will be given a step count equal to the number of step counts assignable to <expr>. The step count for each execution of the **for** statement is one unless the counts attributable to <expr>, <expr1>, and <expr2> are a function of the instance characteristics. In this latter case, the first execution of the **for** has a step count equal to the sum of the counts for <expr>, <expr1>, and <expr2> (note that these expressions are computed only when the loop is started). Remaining executions of the **for** have a step count of one.

(e) *Case Statement*
The statement **case** <expr> **of** is given a cost equal to that assignable to <expr>.

(f) *If-then-else Statement*
The if-then-else statement consists of three parts:

if <expr>
then <statements1>
else <statements2>;

Each part is assigned the number of steps corresponding to <expr>, <statements1>, and <statements2>, respectively.

Note that if the **else** clause is absent, then no cost is assigned to it.

(g) *Procedure and Function Invocation*
All invocations of procedures and functions count as one step unless the invocation involves value parameters whose size depends on the instance characteristics. In this latter case, the count is the sum of the sizes of these value parameters. In case the procedure/function being invoked is recursive, then we must also consider the local variables in the procedure or function being invoked. The sizes of local variables that are characteristic dependent need to be added into the step count.

(h) *Begin, End, With, and Repeat Statements*
Each **end** and **with** statement counts as one step. Each **begin** and **repeat** statement counts as zero steps.

(i) *Procedure and Function Statements*
These count as zero steps as their cost has already been assigned to the invoking statements.

(j) *Goto Statement*
This has a step count of 1.

With the above assignment of step counts to statements, we can proceed to determine the number of steps needed by a program to solve a particular problem instance. We can go about this in one of two ways. In the first method, we introduce a new variable, *count*, into the program. This is a global variable with initial value 0. Statements to increment count by the appropriate amount are introduced into the program. This is done so that each time a statement in the original program is executed, *count* is incremented by the step count of that statement.

Example 10.6: When the statements to increment *count* are introduced into Program 10.2 the result is Program 10.5. The change in the value of *count* by the time this program terminates is the number of steps executed by Program 10.2.

Since we are interested in determining only the change in the value of *count*, Program 10.5 may be simplified to Program 10.6. It should be easy to see that for every initial value of *count*, both Programs 10.5 and 10.6 compute the same final value for *count*. It is easy to see that in the **for** loop the value of *count* will increase by a total of $2n$. If *count* is zero to start with, then it will be $2n + 4$ on termination. So, each invocation of *sum* (Program 10.2) executes a total of $2n+4$ steps. □

```
function sum(a: ElementList; n:integer):real;
var s: real; i: integer;
begin
    s := 0;
    count := count +1; {count is global}
    for i := 1 to n do
    begin
        count := count +1; {for for}
        s := s +a[i];
        count := count +1;  {for assignment}
    end;
    count := count +1;  {for last time of for}
    sum := s;
    count := count +1;  {for assignment}
    count := count +1;  {for end}
end; { of sum}
```

Program 10.5

```
function sum(a: ElementList; n:integer):real;
var s: real; i: integer;
begin
    for i := 1 to n do
        count := count +2;
    count := count +4;
end; { of sum}
```

Program 10.6

Example 10.7: When the statements to increment count are introduced into Program 10.3, Program 10.7 is obtained. In this program, we have assumed that *ElementList* has a size n. It's size must be at least this much but it could be more. Let $t_{rsum}(n)$ be the increase in the value of *count* when Program 10.7 terminates. We see that $t_{rsum}(0)=3$. When $n>0$, *count* increases by $n+2$ plus whatever increase results from the invocation of *rsum* from within the **else** clause. From the definition of t_{rsum}, it follows that this additional increase is $t_{rsum}(n-1)$. So, if the value of *count* is zero initially, its value at the time of termination is $n+2+t_{rsum}(n-1)$, $n>0$.

When analyzing a recursive program for its step count, we often obtain a recursive formula for the step count (i.e., say $t_{rsum}(n) = n+2+t_{rsum}(n-1)$, $n>0$ and $t_{rsum}(0)=3$). As mentioned in Chapter 8, these recursive formulas are referred to as *recurrence relations*. We may solve this recurrence using the substitution method of Chapter 8 to obtain the solution $t_{rsum}(n) = (n+2)(n+3)/2$, $n\geq0$. So, the step count for procedure *rsum* (Program 10.3) is $(n+2)(n+3)/2$. This is significantly larger than that for the iterative version (Program 10.2). The n^2 term vanishes if a is made a variable parameter. When this is done, the step count becomes $3n+3$. □

```
function rsum(a: ElementList; n: integer): real;
begin
    count := count+1;  {for if conditional}
    if n<=0 then begin
                    rsum := 0;
                    count := count+1; {for assignment}
                end
    else begin
            rsum := rsum(a, n-1) + a[n];
            count := count+n; {for assignment}
        end;
    count := count+1;  {for end}
end; {of rsum}
```

Program 10.7

Comparing the step count of Program 10.2 to that of Program 10.3 with a changed to a variable parameter, we see that the count for Program 10.2 is less than that for Program 10.3. From this, we cannot conclude that Program 10.3 is slower than Program 10.2. This is so because a step doesn't correspond to a definite time unit. Each step of *sum* may take more time than every step of *rsum*. So, it might well be (though we don't expect it) that *sum* is slower than *rsum*.

The step count is useful in that it tells us how the run time for a program changes with changes in the instance characteristics. From the step count for *sum*, we see that if n is doubled, the run time will also double (approximately); if n increases by a factor of 10, we expect the run time to increase by a factor of 10; etc. So, we expect the run time to grow *linearly* in n. We say that *sum* is a linear program (the time complexity is linear in the instance characteristic n).

From the step count for Program 10.3, we expect the run time of *rsum* to increase by a factor of 4 if n is doubled. If n increases by a factor of 10, then the time will increase by a factor of about 100. *rsum* is a *quadratic* program as its time grows as the square of the instance characteristic. If the formal parameter a is made a variable parameter, then *rsum* becomes a linear program.

Example 10.8: [Matrix addition] Program 10.8 is a program to add two $m \times n$ matrices a and b together. Introducing the *count* incrementing statements leads to Program 10.9. Program 10.10 is a simplified version of Program 10.9 which computes the same value for *count*. Examining Program 10.10, we see that line 6 is executed n times for each value of i or a total of mn times; line 7 is executed m times; and line 9 is executed once. If *count* is zero to begin with, it will be $2mn + 2m + 2$ when Program 10.10 terminates.

From this analysis we see that if $m > n$, then it is better to interchange the two **for** statements in Program 10.8. If this is done, the step count becomes $2mn + 2n + 2$. Note that in this example the instance characteristics are given by m and n. □

```
line   procedure add(var a, b, c: matrix; m,n:integer);
 1       var i, j: integer;
 2       begin
 3         for i := 1 to m do
 4           for j := 1 to n do
 5             c[i,j] := a[i,j]+b[i,j];
 6       end; {of add}
```

Program 10.8 Matrix addition

```
procedure add(var a, b, c: matrix; m,n:integer);
var i, j: integer;
begin
  for i := 1 to m do
  begin
    count := count+1; {for for i}
    for j := 1 to n do
    begin
      count := count+1; {for for j}
      c[i,j] := a[i,j]+b[i,j];
      count := count+1; {for assignment}
    end;
    count := count+1; {for last time of for j}
  end;
  count := count+1; {for last time of for i}
  count := count+1; {for end}
end; {of add}
```

Program 10.9

```
line  procedure add(var a, b, c: matrix; m,n:integer);
 1     var i, j: integer;
 2     begin
 3       for i := 1 to m do
 4       begin
 5         for j := 1 to n do
 6           count := count+2;
 7         count := count+2;
 8       end;
 9       count := count+2;
10     end; {of add}
```

Program 10.10

The second method to determine the step count of a program is to build a table in which we list the total number of steps contributed by each statement to *count*. This figure is often arrived at by first determining the number of steps per execution of the statement and the total number of times (i.e., frequency) each statement is executed. By combining these two quantities, the total contribution of each statement is obtained. By adding up the contributions of all statements, the step count for the entire program is obtained.

There is an important difference between the step count of a statement and its steps per execution (s/e). The step count does not necessarily reflect the complexity of the statement. For example, the statement:

$x := sum(a,m)$;

has a step count of m (assuming that a is defined to be a size m array) while the total change in *count* resulting from the execution of this statement is actually m plus the change resulting from the the invocation of *sum* (i.e., $2m+4$). The steps per execution of the above statement is $m+2m+4 = 3m+4$. *The s/e of a statement is the amount by which count changes as a result of the execution of that statement.*

In Table 10.1, the number of steps per execution and the frequency of each of the statements in procedure *sum* (Program 10.2) have been listed. The total number of steps required by the program is determined to be $2n+4$. It is important to note that the frequency of line 4 is $n+1$ and not n. This is so as i has to be incremented to $n+1$ before the **for** loop can terminate.

line	s/e	frequency	total steps
1	0	0	0
2	0	0	0
3	1	1	1
4	1	$n+1$	$n+1$
5	1	n	n
6	1	1	1
7	1	1	1
Total number of steps =			$2n+4$

Table 10.1 Step table for Program 10.2.

Table 10.2 gives the step count for procedure *rsum* (Program 10.3). Line 2(a) refers to the **if** conditional of line 2 and line 2(b) refers to the statement in the **then** clause of the **if**. Notice that under the s/e (steps per execution) column, line 3 has been given a count of $n+t_{rsum}(n-1)$. This is the total cost of line 3 each time it is executed. It includes all the steps that get executed as a result of the invocation of *rsum* from line 3. The frequency and total steps columns have been split into two parts: one for the case $n = 0$ and the other for the case $n>0$. This is necessary as the frequency (and hence total steps) for some statements is different for each of these cases.

line	s/e	frequency		total steps	
		$n=0$	$n>0$	$n=0$	$n>0$
1	0	0	0	0	0
2(a)	1	1	1	1	1
2(b)	1	1	0	1	0
3	$n+t_{rsum}(n-1)$	0	1	0	$n+t_{rsum}(n-1)$
4	1	1	1	1	1
		Total number of steps		3	$n+2+t_{rsum}(n-1)$

Table 10.2 Step table for Program 10.3.

Table 10.3 corresponds to procedure *add* (Program 10.8). Once again, note that the frequency of line 3 is $m+1$ and not m. This is so as i needs to be incremented up to $m+1$ before the loop can terminate. Similarly, the frequency for line 4 is $m(n+1)$.

Program 10.11 transposes an $n \times n$ matrix a. Recall that b is the transpose of a iff $b[i,j] = a[j,i]$ for all i and j. The steps per execution are fairly easy to obtain (see Table 10.4). The frequency for each of lines 1, 2, 3, 5, and 8 is relatively easy to determine. Let us examine line 4. For each value of i, line 4 is executed $n-i+1$ times. So, the frequency for this line is $\sum_{i=1}^{n-1} (n-i+1) = (n+1)(n-1) - \sum_{1}^{n-1} i = (n+1)(n-1)-n(n-1)/2 = (n-1)(n+2)/2$. The frequency for each of lines 6 and 7 is $\sum_{i=1}^{n-1} (n-i) = n(n-1)/2$.

line	s/e	frequency	total steps
1	0	0	0
2	0	0	0
3	1	$m+1$	$m+1$
4	1	$m(n+1)$	$mn+m$
5	1	mn	mn
6	1	1	1
		Total	$2mn+2m+2$

Table 10.3 Step table for Program 10.7.

line	
	procedure *transpose*(**var** a: *matrix*; n: **integer**);
1	**var** i, j: **integer**; t: *element*;
2	**begin**
3	**for** $i := 1$ **to** $n-1$ **do**
4	**for** $j := i+1$ **to** n **do**
5	**begin**
6	$t := a[i,j]$; $a[i,j] := a[j,i]$; $a[j,i] := t$;
7	**end**;
8	**end**; {of *transpose*}

Program 10.11

In some cases, the number of steps per execution of a statement is not fixed. This is the case, for example, for line 4 of procedure *inef* (Program 10.12). Procedure *inef* is a very inefficient way to compute the sums $\sum_{i=1}^{j} a[i]$ for $j = 1,2,...,n$. *sum* is Program 10.2. The step count for *sum*(a, n) has already been determined to be $2n+4$. The number of steps per execution of line 4 of procedure *inef* is $3j+4$ (the additional n comes in as a corresponds to a value formal parameter). The frequency of this line is n. But, the total number of steps resulting from this line is not $(3j+4)n$. Instead, it is $\sum_{j=1}^{n} (3j+4) = 1.5n^2 + 5.5n$. Table 10.5 gives the complete analysis for this program.

line	s/e	frequency	total steps
1	0	0	0
2	0	0	0
3	1	n	n
4	1	$(n-1)(n+2)/2$	$(n-1)(n+2)/2$
5	0	0	0
6	3	$n(n-1)/2$	$3n(n-1)/2$
7	1	$n(n-1)/2$	$n(n-1)/2$
8	1	1	1
		Total	$(n-1)(5n+2)/2+n+1$

Table 10.4 Step table for Program 10.11.

line	
	procedure *inef*(**var** a, b: *ElementList*; n:**integer**);
1	**var** j: **integer**;
2	**begin**
3	**for** $j := 1$ **to** n **do**
4	$b[j] := sum(a, j)$;
5	**end**; {of *inef*}

Program 10.12

line	s/e	frequency	total steps
1	0	0	0
2	0	0	0
3	1	$n+1$	$n+1$
4	$3j+4$	n	$1.5n^2 + 5.5n$
5	1	1	1
		Total	$1.5n^2 + 6.5n + 2$

Table 10.5 Step table for Program 10.12.

Summary

The time complexity of a program is given by the number of steps taken by the program to compute the function it was written for. The number of steps is itself a function of the instance characteristics. While any specific instance may have several characteristics (e.g., the number of inputs, the number of outputs, the magnitudes of the inputs and outputs, etc.), the number of steps is computed as a function of some subset of these. Usually, we choose those characteristics that are of importance to us. For example, we might wish to know how the computing (or run) time (i.e., time complexity) increases as the number of inputs increase. In this case the number of steps will be computed as a function of the number of inputs alone. For a different program, we might be interested in determining how the computing time increases as the magnitude of one of the inputs increases. In this case the number of steps will be computed as a function of the magnitude of this input alone. Thus, before the step count of a program can be determined, we need to know exactly which characteristics of the problem instance are to be used. These define the variables in the expression for the step count. In the case of *sum*, we chose to measure the time complexity as a function of the number, n, of elements being added. For procedure *add* the choice of characteristics was the number, m, of rows and the number, n, of columns in the matrices being added.

Once the relevant characteristics $(n, m, p, q, r, ...)$ have been selected, we can define what a step is. A step is any computation unit that is independent of the characteristics $(n, m, p, q, r, ...)$. Thus 10 additions can be one step; 100 multiplications can also be one step; but n additions cannot. Nor can $m/2$ additions, $p+q$ subtractions etc. be counted as one step.

A systematic way to assign step counts was also discussed. Once this has been done, the time complexity (i.e., the total step count) of a program can be obtained using either of the two methods discussed.

The examples we have looked at so far were sufficiently simple that the time complexities were nice functions of fairly simple characteristics like the number of elements, and the number of rows and columns. For many programs, the time complexity is not dependent solely on the number of inputs or outputs or some other easily specified characteristic. Consider function *seqsearch* (Program 8.4). This program searches $a[1..n]$ for x. A natural parameter with respect to which one might wish to determine the step count is the number, n, of elements to be searched. I.e., we would like to know how the computing time changes as we change the number of elements n.

The parameter n is, however, inadequate. For the same n, the step count varies with the position of x in a. For example, when $n=4$, $a[1:4]= (12, 3, 26, 10)$, and $x = 10$, line 5 is executed zero times. When $x = 15$, line 5 is executed four times.

We can extricate ourselves from the difficulties resulting from situations when the chosen parameters are not adequate to determine the step count uniquely by defining two kinds of steps counts: worst case and average.

Let P be a program. Suppose we wish to determine its step count $t_{P(n_1,n_2,...,n_k)}$ as a function of the parameters n_1, n_2, ..., n_k. Let f be the function computed by P. For any instance I, let $STEP_{P(I)}$ be the number of steps needed by P to compute $f(I)$. Let $S(n_1,n_2,...,n_k)$ be the set

$\{I \mid I$ has the characteristics $n_1,n_2,...,n_k\}$.

The *worst case* step count of P, $t_P^{WC}(n_1,n_2,...,n_k)$, is a function of $n_1,n_2,...,n_k$ such that:

$$t_P^{WC}(n_1,n_2, \cdots ,n_k) = \max\{STEP_P(I) \mid I \in S(n_1,n_2,...,n_k)\}.$$

The *average* step count of P, $t_P^{AVG}(n_1,n_2,...,n_k)$, is a function of $n_1,n_2, \ldots ,n_k$ such that:

$$t_P^{AVG}(n_1,n_2, \cdots ,n_k) = \frac{1}{|S(n_1,n_2,...,n_k)|} \sum_{I \in S(n_1,...,n_k)} STEP_P(I)$$

Both t_P^{WC} and t_P^{AVG} are meaningful quantities to obtain as t_P^{WC} tells us the worst that can happen on a problem instance with characteristics n_1, n_2,..., n_k and t_P^{AVG} tells us how much time we would expect to spend on the average (or on a randomly chosen instance). The formulation for t_P^{AVG} assumes that all $I \in S$ are equally likely instances. If this is not the case then the equation needs to be modified to

$$t_P^{AVG}(n_1,n_2, \cdots ,n_k) = \sum_{I \in S(n_1,...,n_k)} p(I)STEP_P(I)$$

where p(I) is the normalized frequency (or probability) (frequency/ $S(n_1,n_2, \ldots ,n_k)$) with which instance *I* will be solved.

For *seqsearch* (Program 8.4), we see that the worst case is when *x* is not one of the $a[i]$s. The step count analysis for this case is given in Table 10.6.

line	s/e	frequency	total steps
1	0	0	0
2	0	0	0
3	2	1	2
4	1	$n+1$	$n+1$
5	1	n	n
6	1	1	1
7	1	1	1
		Total	$2n + 5$

Table 10.6 Worst case step count for Program 8.4

For the average case analysis, we assume that the *n* values in $a[1:n]$ are distinct and consider only the *n* values of *x* that are in $a[1:n]$. In addition, we assume that each $a[i]$ is searched for with the same probability. Under this assumption, the average step count for a successful search is the sum of the step counts for the *n* possible successful searches divided by *n*. To obtain this figure, we first obtain the step count for the case $x = a[n-i]$ where *i* is in the range [0, $n-1$]. This is done in Table 10.7. Now we obtain the average step count for successful searches as below:

$$t_{seqsearch}^{AVG}(n) = \frac{1}{n} \sum_{i=0}^{n-1}(2i+5)$$

$$= n + 4$$

This is a little more than half the step count for an unsuccessful search.

Now, suppose that successful searches will be made only 80% of the time. Each $a[i]$ still has the same probability of being searched for. The average step count for *seqsearch* is:

.8*(average count for successful searches) + .2*(count for an unsuccessful search)
$$= .8(n + 4) + .2(2n + 5)$$
$$= 1.2n + 4.2$$

line	s/e	frequency	total steps
1	0	0	0
2	0	0	0
3	2	1	2
4	1	$i+1$	$i+1$
5	1	i	i
6	1	1	1
7	1	1	1
		Total	$2i + 5$

Table 10.7 Step count for Program 8.4 when $x = a[n-i]$

10.4. ASYMPTOTIC NOTATION (O, Ω, Θ, o)

Our motivation to determine step counts is to be able to compare the time complexities of two programs that compute the same function and also to predict the growth in run time as the instance characteristics change.

Determining the exact step count (either worst case or average) of a program can prove to be an exceedingly difficult task. Expending immense effort to determine the step count exactly isn't a very worthwhile endeavour as the notion of a step is itself inexact. (Both the instructions $x := y$ and $x := y + z + (x/y) + (x*y*z - x/z)$ count as one step.) Because of the inexactness of what a step stands for, the exact step count isn't very useful for comparative purposes. An exception to this is when the difference in the step counts of two programs is very large as in $3n + 3$ vs $100n + 10$. We might feel quite safe in predicting that the program with step count $3n+3$ will run in less time than the one with step count $100n+10$. But even in this case, it isn't necessary to know that the exact step count is $100n+10$. Something like "it's about $80n$, or $85n$, or $75n$" is adequate to arrive at the same conclusion.

For most situations, it is adequate to be able to make a statement like $c_1n^2 \leq t_P^{WC}(n) \leq c_2n^2$ or $t_Q^{WC}(n,m) = c_1n+c_2m$ where c_1 and c_2 are nonnegative constants. This is so because if we have two programs with a complexity of $c_1n^2+c_2n$ and c_3n, respectively, then we know that the one with complexity c_3n will be faster than the one with complexity $c_1n^2+c_2n$ for sufficiently large values of n. For small values of n, either program could be faster (depending on c_1, c_2, and c_3). If $c_1=1$, $c_2 = 2$, and $c_3=100$ then $c_1n^2+c_2n \leq c_3n$ for $n \leq 98$ and $c_1n^2 + c_2n > c_3n$ for $n > 98$. If $c_1 = 1$, $c_2 = 2$, and $c_3 = 1000$ then $c_1n^2 + c_2n \leq c_3n$ for $n \leq 998$.

No matter what the values of c_1, c_2, and c_3, there will be an n beyond which the program with complexity c_3n will be faster than the one with complexity $c_1n^2 + c_2n$. This value of n will be called the *break even point*. If the break even point is 0 then the program with complexity c_3n is always faster (or at least as fast). The exact break even point cannot be determined analytically. The programs have to be run on a computer in order to determine the break even point. To know that there is a break even point it is adequate to know that one program has complexity $c_1n^2 + c_2n$ and the other c_3n for some constants c_1, c_2, and c_3. There is little advantage in determining the exact values of c_1, c_2, and c_3.

With the previous discussion as motivation, we introduce some terminology that will enable us to make meaningful (but inexact) statements about the time and space complexities of a program. In the remainder of this chapter, the functions f and g are nonnegative functions.

Definition: [Big "oh"] $f(n) = O(g(n))$ (read as "f of n is big oh of g of n") iff there exist positive constants c and n_0 such that $f(n) \leq cg(n)$ for all n, $n \geq n_0$. $\square$

Example 10.9: $3n + 2 = O(n)$ as $3n + 2 \leq 4n$ for all $n \geq 2$. $3n + 3 = O(n)$ as $3n + 3 \leq 4n$ for all $n \geq 3$. $100n + 6 = O(n)$ as $100n + 6 \leq 101n$ for $n \geq 10$. $10n^2 + 4n + 2 = O(n^2)$ as $10n^2 + 4n + 2$

$\leq 11n^2$ for $n \geq 5$. $1000n^2 + 100n - 6 = O(n^2)$ as $1000n^2 + 100n - 6 \leq 1001n^2$ for $n \geq 100$. $6*2^n + n^2 = O(2^n)$ as $6*2^n + n^2 \leq 7*2^n$ for $n \geq 4$. $3n + 3 = O(n^2)$ as $3n + 3 \leq 3n^2$ for $n \geq 2$. $10n^2 + 4n + 2 = O(n^4)$ as $10n^2 + 4n + 2 \leq 10n^4$ for $n \geq 2$. $3n + 2 \neq O(1)$ as $3n + 2$ is not less than or equal to c for any constant c and all n, $n \geq n_0$. $10n^2 + 4n + 2 \neq O(n)$. $\square$

As illustrated by the previous example, the statement $f(n) = O(g(n))$ only states that $g(n)$ is an upper bound on the value of $f(n)$ for all n, $n \geq n_0$. It doesn't say anything about how good this bound is. Notice that $n = O(n^2)$, $n = O(n^{2.5})$, $n = O(n^3)$, $n = O(2^n)$, etc. In order for the statement $f(n) = O(g(n))$ to be informative, $g(n)$ should be as small a function of n as one can come up with for which $f(n) = O(g(n))$. So, while we shall often say $3n + 3 = O(n)$, we shall almost never say $3n + 3 = O(n^2)$ even though this latter statement is correct.

From the definition of O, it should be clear that $f(n) = O(g(n))$ is not the same as $O(g(n)) = f(n)$. In fact, it is meaningless to say that $O(g(n)) = f(n)$. The use of the symbol "=" is unfortunate as this symbol commonly denotes the "equals" relation. Some of the confusion that results from the use of this symbol (which is standard terminology) can be avoided by reading the symbol "=" as "is" and not as 'equals'.

Theorem 10.1 obtains a very useful result concerning the order of $f(n)$ (i.e., the $g(n)$ in $f(n) = O(g(n))$) when $f(n)$ is a polynomial in n.

Theorem 10.1: If $f(n) = a_m n^m + \cdots + a_1 n + a_0$, then $f(n) = O(n^m)$.

Proof: $f(n) \leq \displaystyle\sum_{i=0}^{m} |a_i| n^i$

$$\leq n^m \sum_{0}^{m} |a_i| n^{i-m}$$

$$\leq n^m \sum_{0}^{m} |a_i|, \text{ for } n \geq 1.$$

So, $f(n) = O(n^m)$. $\square$

Definition: [Omega] $f(n) = \Omega(g(n))$ (read as "f of n is omega of g of n") iff there exist positive constants c and n_0 such that $f(n) \geq cg(n)$ for all n, $n \geq n_0$. □

Example 10.10: $3n + 2 = \Omega(n)$ as $3n + 2 \geq 3n$ for $n \geq 1$ (actually the inequality holds for $n \geq 0$ but the definition of Ω requires an $n_0 > 0$). $3n + 3 = \Omega(n)$ as $3n + 3 \geq 3n$ for $n \geq 1$. $100n + 6 = \Omega(n)$ as $100n + 6 \geq 100n$ for $n \geq 1$. $10n^2 + 4n + 2 = \Omega(n^2)$ as $10n^2 + 4n + 2 \geq n^2$ for $n \geq 1$. $6*2^n + n^2 = \Omega(2^n)$ as $6*2^n + n^2 \geq 2^n$ for $n \geq 1$. Observe also that $3n + 3 = \Omega(1)$; $10n^2 + 4n + 2 = \Omega(n)$; $10n^2 + 4n + 2 = \Omega(1)$; $6*2^n + n^2 = \Omega(n^{100})$; $6*2^n + n^2 = \Omega(n^{50.2})$; $6*2^n + n^2 = \Omega(n^2)$; $6*2^n + n^2 = \Omega(n)$; and $6*2^n + n^2 = \Omega(1)$. □

As in the case of the "big oh" notation, there are several functions $g(n)$ for which $f(n) = \Omega(g(n))$. $g(n)$ is only a lower bound on $f(n)$. For the statement $f(n) = \Omega(g(n))$ to be informative, $g(n)$ should be as large a function of n as possible for which the statement $f(n) = \Omega(g(n))$ is true. So, while we shall say that $3n + 3 = \Omega(n)$ and that $6*2^n + n^2 = \Omega(2^n)$, we shall almost never say that $3n + 3 = \Omega(1)$ or that $6*2^n + n^2 = \Omega(1)$ even though both these statements are correct.

Theorem 10.2 is the analogue of Theorem 10.1 for the omega notation.

Theorem 10.2: If $f(n) = a_m n^m + \cdots + a_1 n + a_0$ and $a_m > 0$, then $f(n) = \Omega(n^m)$.

Proof: Left as an exercise. □

Definition: [Theta] $f(n) = \Theta(g(n))$ (read as "f of n is theta of g of n") iff there exist positive constants c_1, c_2, and n_0 such that $c_1 g(n) \leq f(n) \leq c_2 g(n)$ for all n, $n \geq n_0$. □

Example 10.11: $3n + 2 = \Theta(n)$; $3n + 3 = \Theta(n)$; $10n^2 + 4n + 2 = \Theta(n^2)$; $6*2^n + n^2 = \Theta(2^n)$; and $10*\log n + 4 = \Theta(\log n)$. $3n + 2 \neq \Theta(1)$; $3n + 3 \neq \Theta(n^2)$; $10n^2 + 4n + 2 \neq \Theta(n)$; $10n^2 + 4n + 2 \neq \Theta(1)$; $6*2^n + n^2 \neq \Theta(n^2)$; $6*2^n + n^2 \neq \Theta(n^{100})$; and $6*2^n + n^2 \neq \Theta(1)$. □

The theta notation is more precise than both the "big oh" and omega notations. $f(n) = \Theta(g(n))$ iff $g(n)$ is both an upper and lower bound on $f(n)$.

Notice that the coefficients in all of the $g(n)$'s used in the preceding three examples has been 1. This is in accordance with practice. We shall almost never find ourselves saying that $3n + 3 = O(3n)$, or that $10 = O(100)$, or that $10n^2 + 4n + 2 = \Omega(4*n^2)$, or that $6*2^n + n^2 = \Omega(6*2^n)$, or that $6*2^n + n^2 = \Theta(4*2^n)$, even though each of these statements is true.

Theorem 10.3: If $f(n) = a_m n^m + \cdots + a_1 n + a_0$ and $a_m > 0$, then $f(n) = \Theta(n^m)$.

Proof: Left as an exercise. □

Definition: [Little "oh"] $f(n) = o(g(n))$ (read as "f of n is little oh of g of n") iff $\lim_{n \to \infty} f(n)/g(n) = 1$. □

Example 10.12: $3n + 2 = o(3n)$; $4n + 6 = o(4n)$; $3n + 2 \neq o(2n)$; $4n + 6 \neq o(8n)$; $10n^2 + 4n + 2 = o(10n^2)$; $10n^2 + 4n + 2 \neq o(12n^2)$; $6*2^n + n^2 = o(6*2^n)$; $6*2^n + n^2 \neq o(8*2^n)$. □

Theorem 10.4: If $f(n) = a_m n^m + ... + a_1 n + a_0$ and $a_m > 0$, then $f(n) = o(a_m n^m)$.

Proof: Left as an exercise. □

The following theorem is useful in computations involving asymptotic notation.

Theorem 10.5: The following are true for every real number x, $x > 0$ and every real ϵ, $\epsilon > 0$:

(1) There exists an n_0 such that $(\log n)^x < (\log n)^{x + \epsilon}$ for every n, $n \geq n_0$.

(2) There exists an n_0 such that $(\log n)^x < n$ for every n, $n \geq n_0$.

(3) There exists an n_0 such that $n^x < n^{x+\epsilon}$ for every n, $n \geq n_0$.

(4) For every real y, there exists an n_0 such that $n^x (\log n)^y < n^{x+\epsilon}$ for every n, $n \geq n_0$.

(5) There exists an n_0 such that $n^x < 2^n$ for every n, $n \geq n_0$.

Proof: Follows from the definition of the individual functions. □

Example 10.13: From Theorem 10.5, we obtain the following: $n^3 + n^2 \log n = \Theta(n^3)$; $2^n/n^2 = \Omega(n^k)$ for every natural number k; $n^4 + n^{2.5} \log^{20} n = \Theta(n^4)$; $2^n n^4 \log^3 n + 2^n n^4/\log n = \Theta(2^n n^4 \log^3 n)$. □

Table 10.8 lists some of the more useful identities involving the "big oh", omega, and theta notations. In this table, all symbols other than n are positive constants. Table 10.9 lists some useful inference rules for sums and products (see Section 8.1 for an explanation of the notation used).

	$f(n)$	Asymptotic
E1	c	$\oplus(1)$
E2	$\sum_0^k c_i n^i$	$\oplus(n^k)$
E3	$\sum_1^n j$	$\oplus(n^2)$
E4	$\sum_1^n j^2$	$\oplus(n^3)$
E5	$\sum_1^n j^k,\ k>0$	$\oplus(n^{k+1})$
E6	$\sum_0^n r^i,\ r>1$	$\oplus(r^n)$
E7	$n!$	$\oplus(\sqrt{n}\,(n/e)^n)$
E8	$\sum_{i=1}^n 1/i$	$\oplus(\log n)$

$\oplus$ can be any one of O, Ω, and Θ

Table 10.8 Asymptotic identities

I1 $\{f(n) = \oplus(g(n))\} \models \displaystyle\sum_{n=a}^{b} f(n) = \oplus(\sum_{n=a}^{b} g(n))$

I2 $\{f_i(n) = \oplus(g_i(n)), 1 \le i \le k\} \models \displaystyle\sum_{1}^{k} f_i(n) = \oplus(\max_{1 \le i \le k}\{g_i(n)\})$

I3 $\{f_i(n) = \oplus(g_i(n)), 1 \le i \le k\} \models \displaystyle\prod_{1}^{k} f_i(n) = \oplus(\prod_{1}^{k} g_i(n))$

I4 $\{f_1(n) = O(g_1(n)), f_2(n) = \Theta(g_2(n))\}$
$\models f_1(n) + f_2(n) = O(g_1(n) + g_2(n))$

I5 $\{f_1(n) = \Theta(g_1(n)), f_2(n) = \Omega(g_2(n))\}$
$\models f_1(n) + f_2(n) = \Omega(g_1(n) + g_2(n))$

I6 $\{f_1(n) = O(g(n)), f_2(n) = \Theta(g(n))\}$
$\models f_1(n) + f_2(n) = \Theta(g(n))$

Table 10.9 Inference rules for $\oplus \in \{O, \Omega, \Theta\}$

If you have studied Tables 10.8 and 10.9, then you are ready to see how asymptotic notation can be used to describe the time complexity (or step count) of a program. Let us reexamine the time complexity analyses of the previous section. For procedure *sum* (Program 10.2) we had determined that $t_{sum}(n) = 2n+4$. So, $t_{sum}(n) = \Theta(n)$. $t_{rsum}(n) = (n+2)(n+3)/2 = \Theta(n^2)$; $t_{add}(m,n) = 2mn + 2n + 2 = \Theta(mn)$; $t_{transpose}(n) = (n-1)(5n+2)/2 + 1 = \Theta(n^2)$.

We have already determined that $t_{seqsearch}^{WC}(n) = 2n + 5 = \Theta(n)$. From this, it follows that $t_{seqsearch}(n) = O(n)$. This last equality states that there exist positive constants c and n_0 such that the computing time of *seqsearch* is bounded by cn for all inputs of size n, $n \ge n_0$. Note that $t_{seqsearch}(n)$ is really a multivalued function as its value is different for different instances of size n. Also, $t_{seqsearch}(n) = \Omega(1)$ as the best situation is when $x = a[n]$. For this case, $t_{seqsearch}(n) = 4$. $t_{seqsearch}^{AVG}(n) = n+4 = \Theta(n)$.

While we might all see that the O, Ω, and Θ notations have been used correctly in the preceding paragraph, we are still left with the question: "Of what use are these notations if one has to first determine the step count exactly?". The answer to this question is that the asymptotic complexity (i.e., the complexity in terms of O, Ω, and Θ) can be determined quite easily without determining the exact step count. This is usually done by first determining the asymptotic complexity of each statement (or group of statements) in the program and then adding up these complexities. Tables 10.10 to 10.15 do just this for *sum*, *rsum*, *add*, *transpose*, *inef*, and *seqsearch*.

In the table for *rsum*, c is a constant. Note that in the table for *add*, lines 4 and 5 have been lumped together even though they have different frequencies. This lumping together of these two lines is possible because their frequencies are of the same order.

line(s)	s/e	frequency	total steps
1,2	0	0	$\Theta(0)$
3	1	1	$\Theta(1)$
4	1	$n+1$	$\Theta(n)$
5	1	n	$\Theta(n)$
6	1	1	$\Theta(1)$
7	1	1	$\Theta(1)$

$$t_{sum}(n) = \Theta(\max_{0 \le i \le 7}\{g_i(n)\}) = \Theta(n)$$

Table 10.10 Asymptotic complexity of *sum*.

In Table 10.13, there is an apparent misuse of notation. This is actually not the case because by the equality $\Theta(\sum_{i=1}^{n}(n-i)) = \Theta(n^2)$, we mean something different from when we say $f(n) = \Theta(g(n))$. Indeed, $\Theta(\sum_{1}^{n}(n-i))$ is not a function. By the equality $\Theta(g_1(n)) = \Theta(g_2(n))$ we mean that both $\Theta(g_1(n))$ and $\Theta(g_2(n))$ give the asymptotic frequency for lines 4, 6, and 7 (i.e., $f(n) = \Theta(g_1(n))$ iff $f(n) = \Theta(g_2(n))$). Another explanation can be provided by interpreting $O(g(n))$, $\Omega(g(n))$, and $\Theta(g(n))$ as being the sets defined below:

$$O(g(n)) = \{f(n) \mid f(n) = O(g(n))\}$$
$$\Omega(g(n)) = \{f(n) \mid f(n) = \Omega(g(n))\}$$
$$\Theta(g(n)) = \{f(n) \mid f(n) = \Theta(g(n))\}.$$

line	s/e	frequency		total steps	
		$n=0$	$n>0$	$n=0$	$n>0$
1	0	0	0	0	$\Theta(0)$
2(a)	1	1	1	1	$\Theta(1)$
2(b)	1	1	0	1	$\Theta(0)$
3	$2+t_{rsum}(n-1)$	0	1	0	$\Theta(2+t_{rsum}(n-1))$
4	1	0	0	0	$\Theta(0)$

$$t_{rsum}(n) = \begin{cases} c + t_{rsum}(n-1) & n>0 \\ 2 & n=0 \end{cases}$$

Table 10.11 Asymptotic complexity of *rsum*.

line(s)	s/e	frequency	total steps
1,2	0	0	$\Theta(0)$
3	1	$\Theta(m)$	$\Theta(m)$
4,5	1	$\Theta(mn)$	$\Theta(mn)$
6	1	1	$\Theta(1)$
		$t_{add}(m,n) =$	$\Theta(mn)$

Table 10.12 Asymptotic complexity of *add*.

Under this interpretation, it is meaningful to make statements such as $O(g_1(n))=O(g_2(n))$; $\Theta(g_1(n))=\Theta(g_2(n))$; etc. When using this interpretation, it is also convenient to read $f(n) = O(g(n))$ as "f of n is in (or is a member of) big oh of g of n", etc.

While the analyses of Tables 10.10 through 10.15 are actually carried out in terms of step counts, it is correct to interpret $t_P(n) = \Theta(g(n))$, or $t_P(n) = O(g(n)$ or $t_P(n) = \Omega(g(n))$ as a statement about the computing time of program P. This is so because each step takes only $\Theta(1)$ time to execute.

After you have had some experience using the table method, you will be in a position to arrive at the asymptotic complexity of a program by taking a more global approach. We elaborate on this method

line(s)	s/e	frequency	total steps
1,2,5	0	0	$\Theta(0)$
3	1	$\Theta(n)$	$\Theta(n)$
4,6,7	1	$\Theta(\sum_{i=1}^{n-1}(n-i))=\Theta(n^2)$	$\Theta(n^2)$
8	1	1	$\Theta(1)$
		$t_{transpose}(n) =$	$\Theta(n^2)$

Table 10.13 Asymptotic complexity of *transpose*

line(s)	s/e	frequency	total steps
1,2	0	0	$\Theta(0)$
3	1	$\Theta(n)$	$\Theta(n)$
4	$3j+4$	n	$\Theta(\sum_{1}^{n}(3j+4))=\Theta(n^2)$
5	1	1	$\Theta(1)$
		$t_{inef}(n) =$	$\Theta(n^2)$

Table 10.14 Asymptotic complexity of *inef*

line(s)	s/e	frequency	total steps
1,2	0	0	$\Theta(0)$
3	2	1	$\Theta(1)$
4	$\Theta(1)$	$\Omega(1), O(n)$	$\Omega(1), O(n)$
5	$\Theta(1)$	$\Omega(0), O(n)$	$\Omega(0), O(n)$
6	1	1	$\Theta(1)$
		$t_{seqsearch}(n) =$	$\Omega(1)$
		$t_{seqsearch}(n) =$	$O(n)$

Table 10.15 Asymptotic complexity of *seqsearch*

in the following examples.

Example 10.14: [*perm*] Consider procedure *perm* (Program 10.4). Assume that *a* is of size *n*. When $k = n$, we see that the time taken is $\Theta(n)$. When $k < n$, the **else** clause is entered. At this time, the **for** loop is entered $n-k+1$ times. Each iteration of this loop takes $\Theta(n + t_{perm}(k+1, n))$ time. So, $t_{perm}(k, n) = \Theta((n-k+1)(n+t_{perm}(k+1, n)))$ when $k < n$. Since, $t_{perm}(k+1, n)$, $k+1 \leq n$ is at least n, we get $t_{perm}(k, n) = \Theta((n-k+1)t_{perm}(k+1, n))$ for $k < n$. Using the substitution method, we obtain $t(1,n) = \Theta(n*n!)$, $n \geq 1$. $\square$

Example 10.15: [Binary search] Let us obtain the time complexity of the recursive binary search program Program 8.3. The instance characteristic that we shall use is the number *m* of elements in $a[i:n]$. Clearly, $m = n-i+1$. For any given *m*, the time complexity of *bsearch* varies with the actual values of *x* and the $a[j]$'s. So, let us obtain the worst case time complexity as a function of *m*. When $m = 0$, the worst case time complexity is $\Theta(1)$. When, $m > 1$, the worst case arises when $x > a[mid]$. At this time, we have to carry out a binary search on a segment of *a* that has about $m/2$ elements. Since the segment size decreases by about a factor of 2 on each invocation of *bsearch*, the worst case depth of recursion is $\Theta(\log m)$. The cost of each invocation is $\Theta(s)$ where *s* is the size of *ElementList*. Hence, the worst case time complexity of Program 8.3 is $\Theta(s \log m) = \Omega(m \log m)$ as *a* must have a size that is at least *m*.

If *a* is made a variable parameter, the cost of each invocation of *bsearch* becomes $\Theta(1)$ and the worst case time complexity becomes $\Theta(\log m)$. This is an impressive improvement in the run time needed especially when you consider that hardly any effort was needed to achieve it.

Next, consider the iterative version, Program 8.6, of binary search. Each iteration of the while loop takes $\Theta(1)$ time. We can show that the **while** loop is iterated at most $\lceil \log_2(n+1) \rceil$ times (see the book by S. Sahni cited in the references). Since an asymptotic analysis is being performed, we don't need such an accurate count of the worst case number of iterations. Each iteration except for the last results in a decrease in the size of the segment of *a* that has to be searched by a factor of about 2. So, this loop is iterated $\Theta(\log m)$ times in the worst case. As each iteration takes $\Theta(1)$ time, the overall worst case complexity of Program 8.6 is $\Theta(\log m)$. Note, however, that the actual complexity of using Program 8.6 is more than this as it takes $\Omega(m)$ time to invoke it (because a is a value parameter). □

Example 10.16: [Insertion sort] Program 7.11 sorts n elements using the insertion method. We shall analyze its time complexity using n and s (the size of each element in *ElementList*) as the instance characteristics. For each value of i, the **while** conditional is checked at most i times. Each iteration of the **while** loop has a time complexity of $\Theta(s)$. Hence, at most $\Theta(i*s)$ time is spent on iteration i of the **for** loop. As a result, the time complexity of Program 7.11 is *at most* $\Theta(\sum_{i=2}^{n} i*s + c) = \Theta(n^2 s)$. In other words, the time complexity is $O(n^2 s)$. The worst case time complexity is $\Theta(n^2 s)$ as the **while** conditional is checked i times for every i when $a[j].key = [n, n-1, n-2, ..., 1]$ initially. □

The asymptotic notation "o" is missing from our examples on asymptotic analysis. This notation is seldom used to analyze the time complexity (or even to obtain the step count) of a program as it is too precise a statement. The statement $t_P(n) = o(10n)$ means that program P needs $o(10n)$ time units to execute. Such a statement, of course, cannot be made until P is programmed and run on a machine and we determine the function that represents its computing time exactly. Even if this were done, we would have to say something like $t_P(n) = o(10n)$ when P is run on an IBM-PC using version 4.6 of the Turbo Pascal compiler! The "little oh" notation could be used for step counts. The step count for procedure *sum* is $2n+4 = o(2n)$. It is wasteful to use such a precise notation when counting an imprecise quantity such as a step.

The definitions of O, Ω, Θ, and o are easily extended to include functions of more than one variable. For example, $f(n,m) = O(g(n,m))$ iff there exist positive constants c, n_0 and m_0 such that $f(n,m) \leq cg(n,m)$ for all $n \geq n_0$ and all $m \geq m_0$.

10.5. PRACTICAL COMPLEXITIES

We have seen that the time complexity of a program is generally some function of the instance characteristics. This function is very useful in determining how the time requirements vary as the instance characteristics change. The complexity function may also be used to compare two programs P and Q that perform the same task. Assume that program P has complexity $\Theta(n)$ and program Q is of complexity $\Theta(n^2)$. We can assert that program P is faster than program Q for "sufficiently large" n. To see the validity of this assertion, observe that the actual computing time of P is bounded from above by n for some constant c and for all n, $n \geq n_1$ while that of Q is bounded from below by dn^2 for some constant d and all n, $n \geq n_2$. Since $cn \leq dn^2$ for $n \geq c/d$, program P is faster than program Q whenever $n \geq \max\{n_1, n_2, c/d\}$.

One should always be cautiously aware of the presence of the phrase "sufficiently large" in the assertion of the preceding discussion. When deciding which of the two programs to use, we must know whether the n we are dealing with is, in fact, "sufficiently large". If program P actually runs in $10^6 n$ milliseconds while program Q runs in n^2 milliseconds and if we always have $n \leq 10^6$, then program Q is the one to use.

To get a feel for how the various functions grow with n, you are advised to study Table 10.16 and Figure 10.3 very closely. As is evident from the table and the figure, the function 2^n grows very rapidly with n. In fact, if a program needs 2^n steps for execution, then when $n = 40$ the number of steps needed is approximately $1.1*10^{12}$. On a computer performing one billion steps per second, this would require about 18.3 minutes. If $n = 50$, the same program would run for about 13 days on this computer. When $n = 60$, about 310.56 years will be required to execute the program and when $n = 100$, about $4*10^{13}$ years will be needed. So, we may conclude that the utility of programs with exponential complexity is limited to small n (typically $n \leq 40$).

Programs that have a complexity that is a polynomial of high degree are also of limited utility. For example, if a program needs n^{10} steps, then using our one billion steps per second computer we will need 10 seconds when $n = 10$; 3,171 years when $n = 100$; and $3.17*10^{13}$ years when $n = 1000$. If the program's complexity had been n^3 steps instead, then we would need one second when $n = 1000$, 110.67 minutes when $n = 10,000$; and 11.57 days when $n = 100,000$.

Table 10.17 gives the time needed by a one billion instructions per second computer to execute a program of complexity $f(n)$

Time for f(n) instr. on a 10^9 instr/sec computer

n	f(n) = n	f(n) = nlog₂n	f(n) = n^2	f(n) = n^3	f(n) = n^4	f(n) = n^{10}	f(n) = 2^n
10	.01μs	.03μs	.1μs	1μs	10μs	10sec	1μs
20	.02μs	.09μs	.4μs	8μs	160μs	2.84hr	1ms
30	.03μs	.15μs	.9μs	27μs	810μs	6.83d	1sec
40	.04μs	.21μs	1.6μs	64μs	2.56ms	121.36d	18.3min
50	.05μs	.28μs	2.5μs	125μs	6.25ms	3.1yr	13d
100	.10μs	.66μs	10μs	1ms	100ms	3171yr	$4*10^{13}$yr
1,000	1.00μs	9.96μs	1ms	1sec	16.67min	$3.17*10^{13}$yr	$32*10^{283}$yr
10,000	10.00μs	130.3μs	100ms	16.67min	115.7d	$3.17*10^{23}$yr	
100,000	100.00μs	1.66ms	10sec	11.57d	3171yr	$3.17*10^{33}$yr	
1,000,000	1.00ms	19.92ms	16.67min	31.71yr	$3.17*10^7$yr	$3.17*10^{43}$yr	

μs = microsecond = 10^{-6} seconds
ms = millisecond = 10^{-3} seconds
sec = seconds
min = minutes
hr = hours
d = days
yr = years

Table 4.17

log n	n	$n \log n$	n^2	n^3	2^n
0	1	0	1	1	2
1	2	2	4	8	4
2	4	8	16	64	16
3	8	24	64	512	256
4	16	64	256	4096	65536
5	32	160	1024	32768	4294967296

Table 10.16

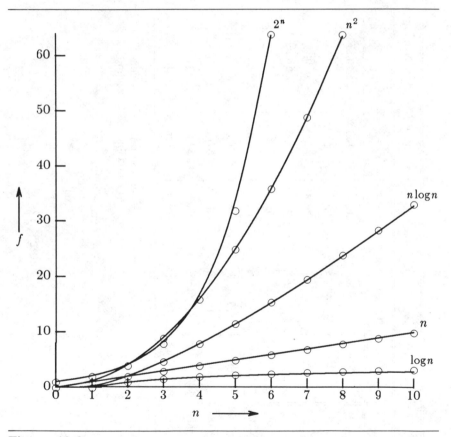

Figure 10.3

instructions. One should note that currently only the fastest computers can execute about one billion instructions per second. From a practical standpoint, it is evident that for reasonably large n (say $n > 100$) only programs of small complexity (such as n, $n\log n$, n^2, n^3, etc.) are feasible. Further, this is the case even if one could build a computer capable of executing 10^{12} instructions per second. In this case, the computing times of Table 10.17 would decrease by a factor of 1000. Now, when $n = 100$ it would take 3.17 years to execute n^{10} instructions, and $4*10^{10}$ years to execute 2^n instructions.

10.6. REFERENCES AND SELECTED READINGS

The study of programs and their performance analysis was given great impetus by Donald E. Knuth, most specifically in his projected seven volume work:

> *The art of computer programming*
> Volume 1, Fundamental Programs (1968)
> Volume 2, Seminumerical Programs (1969)
> Volume 3, Sorting and Searching (1973)
> Volume 4, Combinatorial Search and Recursion (to appear)
> Volume 5, Syntactical Programs (to appear)
> Volume 6, Theory of languages (to appear)
> Volume 7, Compilers (to appear)
> Addison-Wesley, Massachusetts.

Some entertaining articles on the analysis of programs are:

> *Algorithms*, by D. Knuth, Scientific American, April 1977.

> *Computer science and its relation to mathematics,* by D. Knuth, Amer. Math. Monthly, April, 1974.

Our definitions of O, Ω, and Θ are due to D. Knuth and appear in

> *Big omichron, big omega, and big theta*, by D. Knuth, SIGACT News, ACM, April 1971.

The following books contain several programs for which asymptotic analyses are also provided:

> *Fundamentals of computer algorithms*, by E. Horowitz and S. Sahni, Computer Science Press, Inc., Maryland, 1978.

> *Fundamentals of data structures in Pascal*, by E. Horowitz and S. Sahni, Computer Science Press, Inc., Maryland,

1984.

The design and analysis of computer algorithms, by A. Aho, J. Hopcroft, and J. Ullman, Addison-Wesley, Massachusetts, 1974.

Combinatorial algorithms, by E. Reingold, J. Nievergelt, and N. Deo, Prentice Hall, New Jersey, 1977.

and

Concepts in discrete mathematics, 2nd edition, by S. Sahni, Camelot Publishing Co., Fridley, Minnesota, 1985.

10.7. EXERCISES

1.   Obtain $S_P(n)$ for Program 8.1.

2.   Obtain $S_P(n)$ for Program 8.2.

3.   Obtain $S_P(n)$ for Program 8.3.

4.   Obtain $S_P(n)$ for Program 8.4.

5.   Obtain $S_P(n)$ for Program 8.5.

6.   Obtain $S_P(n)$ for Program 8.6.

7.   Obtain $S_P(n)$ for Program 7.12.

8.   Obtain $S_P(n)$ for Programs 7.18 and 7.19 together.

9.   (a)   Introduce statements to increment *count* at all appropriate points in Program 10.13.

     (b)   Simplify the resulting program by eliminating statements. The simplified program should compute the same value for *count* as computed by the program of (a).

```
procedure d(var x: list; n: integer);
var i: integer;
begin
    i := 1;
    repeat
        x[i] := x[i] + 2;
        i := i + 2;
    until (i > n);
    i := 1;
    while i <= (n div 2) do
    begin
        x[i] := x[i] + x[i+1];
        i := i + 1;
    end;
end; {of d}
```

Program 10.13

(c) What is the exact value of *count* when the program terminates? You may assume that the initial value of *count* is 0.

(d) Obtain the step count for Program 10.13 using the frequency method. Clearly show the step count table.

10. Do Exercise 9 parts (a)-(c) for procedure *transpose* (Program 10.11).

11. Do Exercise 9 parts (a)-(c) for procedure *inef* (Program 10.12).

12. Do Exercise 9 for Program 8.1. Obtain the worst case and average step counts. Repeat this with *a* a variable formal parameter.

13. Do Exercise 9 for Program 8.2. Obtain the worst case and average step counts.

14. Do Exercise 9 for Program 8.5. Obtain the worst case and average step counts.

15. Do Exercise 9 for Program 10.14. This program multiplies two
     $n \times n$ matrices a and b.

```
procedure mult(var a, b, c: matrix; n: integer);
var i, j, k: integer;
begin
  for i := 1 to n do
    for j := 1 to n do
    begin
      c[i,j] := 0;
      for k := 1 to n do
        c[i,j] := c[i,j] + a[i,k] * b[k,j];
    end;
end; {of mult}
```

Program 10.14

16. (a) Do Exercise 9 for Program 10.15. This program multiplies
          two matrices a and b where a is an $m \times n$ matrix and b is
          an $n \times p$ matrix.

```
procedure prod(var a, b, c: matrix; m, n, p: integer);
var i, j, k: integer;
begin
  for i := 1 to m do
    for j := 1 to p do
    begin
      c[i,j] := 0;
      for k := 1 to n do
        c[i,j] := c[i,j] + a[i,k] * b[k,j];
    end;
end; {of prod}
```

Program 10.15

(b) Under what conditions will it be profitable to interchange
     the two outermost **for** loops?

17. Show that the following equalities are correct. Do this by using the definitions of O, Ω, Θ, and o only. Do not use Theorems 10.1, 10.2, 10.3, Tables 10.8 and 10.9.
    (a) $5n^2 - 6n = \Theta(n^2)$
    (b) $n! = O(n^n)$
    (c) $2n^2 2^n + n\log n = \Theta(n^2 2^n)$
    (d) $\sum_{i=0}^{n} i^2 = \Theta(n^3)$
    (e) $\sum_{i=0}^{n} i^3 = \Theta(n^4)$
    (f) $n^{2^n} + 6*2^n = \Theta(2^{2^n})$
    (g) $n^3 + 10^6 n^2 = \Theta(n^3)$
    (h) $6n^3/(\log n + 1) = O(n^3)$
    (i) $n^{1.001} + n\log n = \Theta(n^{1.001})$
    (j) $n^{k+\epsilon} + n^k \log n = \Theta(n^{k+\epsilon})$ for all k and ϵ, $k \geq 0$, and $\epsilon > 0$.
    (k) $10n^3 + 15n^4 + 100n^2 2^n = o(100n^2 2^n)$

18. Show that the following equalities are incorrect:
    (a) $10n^2 + 9 = O(n)$
    (b) $n^2 \log n = \Theta(n^2)$
    (c) $n^2/\log n = \Theta(n^2)$
    (d) $n^3 2^n + 6n^2 3^n = O(n^3 2^n)$

19. Prove Theorems 10.2, 10.3, and 10.4.

20. Prove that equivalences E5 to E8 (Table 10.8) are correct.

21. Prove the correctness of inference rules I1 to I6 (Table 10.9).

22. Obtain the asymptotic time complexity of the following programs. Set up a frequency table similar to Tables 10.10 to 10.15.
    (a) Program 10.13
    (b) Program 10.14
    (c) Program 10.15
    (d) Program 7.6

CHAPTER 11

PERFORMANCE MEASUREMENT

11.1. INTRODUCTION

Performance measurement is concerned with obtaining the actual space and time requirements of a program. As noted in the preceding chapter, these quantities are very dependent on the particular compiler and options used as well as on the specific computer on which the program is run. Unless otherwise stated, all performance values provided in this book are obtained using the Turbo Pascal compiler; the default compiler options are used; and the computer used is an IBM-PC. By using this computer in single process mode, we avoid the difficulties encountered in measuring compute time on a time sharing computer.

In keeping with the discussion of the preceding chapter, we shall not concern ourselves with the space and time needed for compilation. We justify this by the assumption that each program (after it has been fully debugged) will be compiled once and then executed several times. Certainly, the space and time needed for compilation are important during program testing when more time is spent on this task than in actually running the compiled code.

We shall not explicitly consider measuring the run time space requirements of a program. This is so for the following reasons:

422

(1)   The size of the instruction and data space are provided by the compiler following compilation. So, no measurement techniques are needed to obtain these figures.

(2)   We can get a fairly accurate estimate of the recursion stack space and the space needed by referenced variables using the analytical methods of Chapter 10.

In order to obtain the computing (or run) time of a program, we need a clocking procedure. Most Pascal implementations provide such a procedure. Since Turbo Pascal does not do this, we need to write our own procedure. It is possible to do this only because Turbo Pascal provides a system call procedure *MsDos*. Program 11.1 is a Pascal procedure that reads the IBM-PC clock and returns the time of day in hours, minutes, seconds, and hundredths of a second. To time a program, we need merely read the clock before the program is begun and after it has terminated. The elapsed time is the run time of our program.

```
procedure time(var h, m, s, f : integer);
{time of day in hours, minutes, seconds, and seconds/100}
type     twobyte = record L, H: byte; end;
    DosFunction = record {Function registers}
                        AX,BX,CX,DX,DI,SI,DS,ES,FLAG: twobyte;
                  end;
var timer: DosFunction;
begin
    timer.AX.H := 44; {IBM DOS clock read function number}
    timer.AX.L := 0;
    MsDos(timer);
    h := timer.CX.H; m := timer.CX.L;
    s := timer.DX.H; f := timer.DX.L;
end; {of time}
```

Program 11.1 Time procedure for Turbo Pascal

In a time sharing environment, the elapsed physical time is generally not the run time of the program we are trying to time as the computer is working on several processes (or programs) and only a fraction of the elapsed time is spent on our program. In this environment, we need a timing procedure that keeps track of the amount of time spent on our program.

Suppose, we wish to measure the worst case performance of our iterative sequential search procedure (Program 8.4). Before we can do this, we need to:

(1) Decide on the values of n for which the times are to be obtained.

(2) Determine, for each of the above values of n, the data that exhibits the worst case behavior.

The decision on which values of n to use is to be based on the amount of timing we wish to perform and also on what we expect to do with the times once they are obtained. Assume that for Program 8.4, our intent is to simply predict how long it will take, in the worst case, to search for x given the size n of a. From the results of Chapter 10, we know that this time is $\Theta(n)$. So, we expect a plot of the times to be a straight line. Theoretically, if we know the times for any two values of n, the straight line is determined and we can obtain the time for all other values of n from this line. In practice, we need the times for more than two values of n. This is so for the following reasons:

(1) Asymptotic analysis only tells us the behavior for "sufficiently large" values of n. For smaller values of n the run time may not follow the asymptotic curve. To determine the point beyond which the asymptotic curve is followed, we need to examine the times for several values of n.

(2) Even in the region where the asymptotic behavior is exhibited, the times may not lie exactly on the predicted curve (straight line in the case of Program 8.4) because of the effects of low order terms that are discarded in the asymptotic analysis. For instance, a program with asymptotic complexity $\Theta(n)$ can have an actual complexity that is $c_1 n + c_2 \log n + c_3$ or for that matter any other function of n in which the highest order term is $c_1 n$ for some constant, c_1, $c_1 > 0$.

It is reasonable to expect that the asymptotic behavior of Program 8.4 will begin for some n that is smaller than 100. So, for $n > 100$ we shall obtain the run time for just a few values. A reasonable choice is $n = 200, 300, 400, \ldots, 1000$. There is nothing magical about this choice of values. We can just as well use $n = 500, 1000, 1500, \ldots, 10,000$ or $n = 512, 1024, 2048, \ldots 2^{15}$. It will cost us more in terms of computer time to use the latter choices and we will probably not get any better information about the run time of Program 8.4 using these choices.

For n in the range [0, 100] we shall carry out a more refined measurement as we aren't quite sure where the asymptotic behavior begins. Of course, if our measurements show that the straight line behavior doesn't begin in this range, we shall have to perform a more detailed measurement in the range [100, 200] and so on until the onset of this behavior is detected. Times in the range [0, 100] will be obtained in steps of 10 beginning at $n = 0$.

As noted in Chapter 10, Program 8.4 exhibits its worst case behavior when x is chosen such that it is not one of the $a[i]$s. For definiteness, we shall set $a[i] = i$, $1 \leq i \leq n$ and $x = 0$.

At this time, we envision using a program such as the one given in Program 11.2 to obtain the worst case times.

The output obtained from this program is given in Figure 11.1. The times obtained are too small to be of any use to us. Most of the times are zero indicating that the precision of our clock is inadequate. The nonzero times are just noise and not representative of the actual time taken.

In order to time a short event, it is necessary to repeat it several times and divide the total time for the event by the number of repetitions.

Since our clock has an accuracy of about one hundredths of a second, we should not attempt to time any single event that takes less than about one second. With an event time of at least one second, we can expect our observed times to be accurate to one percent.

A more reliable estimate of the length of the shortest event to time can be obtained experimentally. The repetition factor is chosen such that the measured time for each search is almost unchanged when a larger repetition factor is used. Figure 11.2 gives the times obtained for Program 8.4 using different repetition factors. $t1$ is event time and t the time per search. When a repetition factor of r is used, $t = t1/r$. As can be seen, the time per search stabilizes when the total event time is about 5 seconds. So, the repetition factors should be chosen such that the total search time for each n is at least 5 seconds. From

```
program TimeSearch(input,output);
{Time Program 8.4}
type ElementList = array [0..1000] of integer;
var z: ElementList;
    i, j, k, h, m, s, f, h1, m1, s1, f1, t1: integer;
    n: array [1..20] of integer;

{Procedure time and function seqsearch}
    .
    .
    .

begin {body of TimeSearch}
    for j := 1 to 1000 do {initialize z}
      z[j] := j;
    for j := 1 to 10 do  {values of n}
    begin
      n[j] := 10*(j−1); n[j+10] := 100*j;
    end;
    writeln('n':5,' ','time');
    for j := 1 to 20 do {obtain computing times}
    begin
      time(h, m, s, f); {get time}
      k := search(z, n[j], 0); {unsuccessful search}
      time(h1, m1, s1, f1); {get time}
      {time spent in hundredths of a second}
      t1 := (((h1−h)*60 + m1 − m)*60 + s1 − s)*100 + f1 − f;
      writeln(n[j]:5,' ',t1:5);
    end;
    writeln('Times are in hundredths of a second'};
end. {of TimeSearch}
```

Program 11.2 Program to time Program 8.4

Figure 11.2, we see a repetition factor of 700 will suffice (by extrapolation) when $n = 0$ or 10. A factor of 600 is adequate when $n = 20$, 30, 40, and 50. Between 60 and 100, we can use a factor of 500. We estimate that for $n := 200, 300, ..., 1000$ the repetition factors can, respectively, be 400, 400, 300, 300, 200, 200, 200, 200, and 200.

n	Time	n	Time
0	0	100	0
10	6	200	5
20	0	300	6
30	0	400	0
40	0	500	0
50	0	600	0
60	5	700	0
70	0	800	0
80	0	900	6
90	5	1000	5

Times are in hundredths of a second

Figure 11.1 Output from Program 11.2

The body of Program 11.2 needs to be changed to that of Program 11.3. In this program, $r[i]$ is the number of times the search is to be repeated when $n = n[i]$. Notice that rearranging the timing statements as in Programs 11.4 or 11.5 does not produce the desired results. For instance, from the data of Figure 11.1, we expect that with the structure of Program 11.4, the value output for $n = 0$ will still be 0. With the structure of Program 11.5, we expect the program to never exit the **while** loop when $n = 0$ (in reality, the loop will be exited as at times the measured time will turn out to be 5 or 6 hundredths of a second). Yet another alternative is to move the first call to *time* out of the **while** loop of Program 11.5, and change the assignment to t within the **while** loop to:

$$t := (((h1 - h)*60 + m1 - m)*60 + s1 - s)*100 + f1 - f;$$

This approach can be expected to yield satisfactory times. This approach cannot be used when the timing procedure available gives us only the time since the last invokation of *time*. Another difficulty is that the measured time includes the time to needed to read the clock. For small n, this time may be larger than the time to run *search*. This difficulty can be overcome by determining the time takem by the timing procedure and subtracting this time later. In further discussion, we shall use the explicit repetition factor technique.

$n \downarrow$	Number of Repetitions					
	100		200		300	
	$t1$	t	$t1$	t	$t1$	t
0	77	0.770	159	0.795	236	0.787
10	82	0.820	165	0.825	247	0.823
20	82	0.820	170	0.850	258	0.860
30	94	0.940	181	0.905	269	0.897
40	94	0.940	187	0.935	280	0.933
50	99	0.990	192	0.960	291	0.970
60	105	1.050	203	1.015	303	1.010
70	104	1.040	209	1.045	313	1.043
80	104	1.040	214	1.070	330	1.100
90	115	1.150	219	1.095	335	1.117
100	116	1.160	231	1.155	347	1.157

$n \downarrow$	Number of Repetitions					
	400		500		600	
	$t1$	t	$t1$	t	$t1$	t
0	314	0.785	390	0.780	466	0.777
10	324	0.810	412	0.824	488	0.813
20	341	0.852	429	0.858	511	0.852
30	362	0.905	451	0.902	533	0.888
40	373	0.932	466	0.932	560	0.933
50	390	0.975	489	0.978	582	0.970
60	401	1.002	505	1.010	610	1.017
70	418	1.045	522	1.044	627	1.045
80	434	1.085	544	1.088	654	1.090
90	451	1.127	560	1.120	670	1.117
100	461	1.152	582	1.164	698	1.163

Times are in hundredths of a second

Figure 11.2 Times per search using different repetition factors

The output from the timing program, Program 11.3, is given in Figure 11.3. The times for n in the range [0, 100] are plotted in Figure 11.4. The remaining values have not been plotted as this would lead to severe compression of the range [0, 100]. The linear dependence of the worst case time on n is apparent from this graph.

```
begin {body of TimeSearch}
   for j := 1 to 1000 do {initialize z}
      z[j] := j;
   for j := 1 to 10 do  {values of n}
   begin
      n[j] := 10*(j−1); n[j+10] := 100*j;
   end;

   {repetition factors}
   r[1] := 700; r[2] := 700; r[3] := 600; r[4] := 600; r[5] := 600;
   r[6] :=600; r[7] := 500; r[8] := 500; r[9] := 500; r[10] := 500;
   r[11] := 500; r[12] := 400; r[13] := 400; r[14] := 300; r[15] := 300;
   r[16] := 200; r[17] := 200; r[18] := 200; r[19] := 100; r[20] := 100;

   writeln('n':5,' ', 't1',' ','t');
   for j := 1 to 20 do {obtain computing times}
   begin
      time(h, m, s, f ); {get time}
      for b := 1 to r[j] do
         k := search(z, n[j], 0); {unsuccessful search}
      time(h1, m1, s1, f 1); {get time}
      {time spent in hundredths of a second}
      t1 := (((h1−h)*60 + m1 − m)*60 + s1 − s)*100 + f1 − f ;
      t := t1; t := t/r[j]; {time per search}
      writeln(n[j]:5,' ',t1:5, t:8:3);
   end;
   writeln('Times are in hundredths of a second'};
end. {of TimeSearch}
```

Program 11.3

The graph of Figure 11.4 can be used to predict the run time for other values of n. For example, we expect that when $n = 24$, the worst case search time will be 0.87 hundredths of a second. We can go one step further and get the equation of the straight line. The equation of this line is $t = c + mn$ where m is the slope and c the value for $n = 0$. From the graph, we see that $c = 0.78$. Using the point $n = 60$ and $t = 1.01$, we obtain $m = (t−c)/n = 0.23/60 = 0.00383$. So, the line of Figure 11.4 has the equation $t = 0.78 + 0.00383n$ hsec (hundredths of a second). From this, we expect that

```
t := 0;
for b := 1 to r[j] do
begin
    time(h, m, s, f);
    k := search(a, n[j], 0);
    time(h1, m1, s1, f1);
    t := t + (((h1 − h)*60 + m1 − m)*60 + s1 − s)*100 + f1 − f;
end;
t := t/r[j];
```

Program 11.4

```
t := 0; i := 0;
while t < DesiredTime do
begin
    time(h, m, s, f);
    k := search(a, n[j], 0);
    time(h1, m1, s1, f1);
    t := t + (((h1 − h)*60 + m1 − m)*60 + s1 − s)*100 + f1 − f;
    i := i +1;
end;
t := t/i;
```

Program 11.5

when $n = 1000$, the worst case search time will be 4.61 hsec and when $n = 500$, it will be 2.675 hsec. Comparing with the actual observed times of Figure 11.3, we see that these figures are very accurate!

An alternate approach to obtain a good straight line for the data of Figure 11.3 is to obtain the straight line that is the least squares approximation to the data (see Appendix A). The result is $t = 0.77747 + 0.003806n$ hsec. When $n = 1000$, and 500, this equation yields $t = 4.583$ and 2.680.

Now, we are probably ready to pat ourselves on the back for a job well done. This action is somewhat premature as our experiment

n	t1	t	n	t1	t
0	549	0.784	100	582	1.164
10	571	0.816	200	615	1.537
20	516	0.860	300	763	1.907
30	539	0.898	400	686	2.287
40	555	0.925	500	801	2.670
50	583	0.972	600	610	3.050
60	505	1.010	700	687	3.435
70	522	1.044	800	758	3.790
80	538	1.076	900	826	4.230
90	566	1.132	1000	922	4.610

Times are in hundredths of a second

Figure 11.3 Worst case run times for Program 8.4

is flawed. First, the measured time includes the time taken by the repetition **for** loop. So, the times of Figure 11.3 are excessive. This can be corrected by determining the time for each iteration of this statement. A quick test run indicates that 30,000 executions take only 65 hundredths of a second. So, subtracting the time for the **for** $b :=$ 1 **to** $r[j]$ **do** statement reduces the reported times by only 0.002. We can ignore this difference as from Figure 11.2 we see that the use of a higher repetition factor could well result in measured times that are lower by about 0.002 hsec per search. Our times are not accurate to a hundredth of a second and it is not very meaningful to worry about the two hundredths of a second spent on each repetition.

The second and more serious problem is caused by the fact that *ElementList* has been defined to be an array of size 1000. Consequently, each invocation of *seqsearch* begins by copying the 1000 values of the actual parameter z into the value formal parameter a. The measured times are therefore representative of the actual time to use *seqsearch* only when *ElementList* is of this size! If the size of *ElementList* is changed to 2,000 or 10,000, the measured times will change. The times when *ElementList* is defined to have a size of 2000 (i.e., **array** [0..2000] **of integer**] are given in Figure 11.5. A comparison with Figure 11.3 leads us to conclude that for small values of n a substantial part of the time reported in this figure is the time spent copying the 1000 elements of the actual parameter into the formal

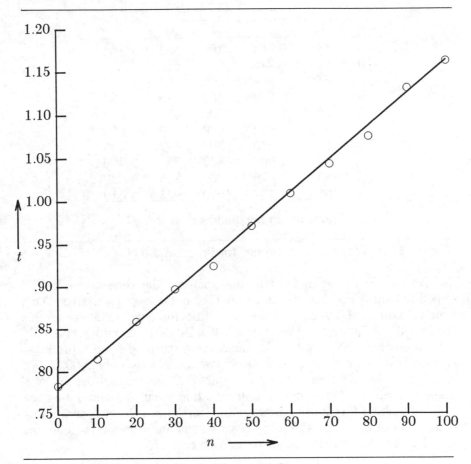

Figure 11.4 Plot of the data in Figure 11.3

parameter.

So, what constitutes a meaningful test for Program 8.4? The size of *ElementList* isn't known to us and yet, it is perhaps the most important factor. The realization that the worst case run time of Program 8.4 is a function of both n and s (the size of *ElementList*) motivates us to obtain the time for the body of Program 8.4 and that for its invocation separately. The former is independent of s and the latter is independent of n. The total time to use Program 8.4 is the sum of these two times.

n	t1	t	n	t1	t
0	1076	1.537	100	955	1.910
10	1104	1.577	200	917	2.292
20	972	1.620	300	1071	2.677
30	989	1.648	400	912	3.040
40	1010	1.683	500	1027	3.423
50	1038	1.730	600	764	3.820
60	879	1.758	700	835	4.175
70	901	1.802	800	912	4.560
80	918	1.836	900	494	4.940
90	939	1.878	1000	532	5.320

Times are in hundredths of a second

Figure 11.5 Times when *ElementList* has a size of 2000

To obtain the time for the body of Program 8.4, we place the timing loop directly into function *seqsearch* as in Program 11.6. This is preferable to placing the code of *seqsearch* directly into the body of *TimeSearch* as in Program 11.7. This is so as the strategy of Program 11.6 yields times that include the overhead of referencing parameters.

When Program 11.6 is used in place of Program 8.4, and the timing and repetition statements removed from Program 11.3, the times shown in Figure 11.6 are obtained. The total time spent on each *n* is less than 5 seconds (except when *n* is 500, 700, or 800). To get more accurate times, the repetition factors need to be increased. To get the time for $n = 0$ above 5 seconds requires an $r[0]$ that is larger than **maxint** on the IBM-PC (**maxint** = 32,767). Since, the time for $n = 0$ is quite close to the time required for each execution of the repetition **for** loop, it is unlikely that we will be able to determine this time very accurately. So, rather than set up two nested loops to get the number of repetitions up to the needed 60,000, we simply accept the times obtained with $r[1] = 32,000$. The values $r[2:20]$ can be estimated from Figure 11.6. It is seen that the set of values $r[2:20] =$ [12000, 6000, 5000, 4000, 3000, 2500, 2000, 2000, 1500, 1500, 800, 600, 500, 400, 300, 200, 200, 150, 150] will serve our purpose. When these values are used, the times of Figure 11.7 are obtained.

---

function *seqsearch* (*a*: *ElementList*; *n*,*x*:**integer**): **integer**;
var *i*, *k*: **integer**;
begin
  time(*h*, *m*, *s*, *f*); {get time}
  for *k* := 1 **to** *r*[*j*] **do** {*r*[*j*] is global}
  begin
    i := *n*; *a*[0] := *x*;
    while *a*[*i*] <> *x* **do**
      i := *i*−1;
    seqsearch := *i*;
  end; {of repetition **for**}
  time(*h*1, *m*1, *s*1, *f*1); {get time}
  {time spent in hundredths of a second}
  *t*1 := (((*h*1−*h*)*60 + *m*1 − *m*)*60 + *s*1 − *s*)*100 + *f*1 − *f*;
  t := *t*1; *t* := *t*/*r*[*j*]; {time per search}
  writeln(*n*[*j*]:5,' ',*t*1:5, *t*:8:3);
end; {of *seqsearch*}

Program 11.6 Timing the body of *seqsearch*

The time of 0.002 for each execution of the repetition **for** statement needs to be subtracted from the times of Figure 11.7. This subtraction has a material affect (i.e., at least 10%) only on the time for *n* = 0.

To time the invocation of Program 8.4 for different sizes *s* of *ElementList*, we delete all statements between the **begin** and **end** statements of Program 8.4 and run Program 11.3 for different values of *s*. The repetition factor needed varies with *s*. The observed times for various values of *s* are shown in Figure 11.8. Again, the time for the repetition **for** loop has not been subtracted. This does not materially affect the times shown.

The least squares straight line for the data of Figure 11.7 is $t = 0.008531 + 0.003785n$ hsec and that for Figure 11.8 is $t = 0.018009 + 0.000756s$. Adding these two contributions, we get $t = 0.02654 + 0.000756s + 0.003785n$. We can see how good this equation is in predicting actual run times by using it with $s = 1000$. The equation

```
writeln('n':5,'  ', 't1',' ', 't');
for j := 1 to 20 do
begin
  time(h, m, s, f); {get time}
  for b := 1 to r[j] do
  begin
    i := n; a[0] := x;
    while a[i] <> x do
      i := i-1;
    seqsearch := i;
  end; {of repetition for}
  time(h1, m1, s1, f1); {get time}
  {time spent in hundredths of a second}
  t1 := (((h1-h)*60 + m1 - m)*60 + s1 - s)*100 + f1 - f;
  t := t1; t := t/r[j]; {time per search}
  writeln(n[j]:5,'  ',t1:5, t:8:3);
end; {of for j}
writeln('Times are in hundredths of a second');
```

Program 11.7   Code of Program 8.4 placed into Program 11.3

n	t1	t	n	t1	t
0	6	0.009	100	193	0.386
10	33	0.047	200	308	0.770
20	49	0.082	300	456	1.140
30	76	0.127	400	455	1.517
40	93	0.155	500	571	1.903
50	121	0.202	600	455	2.275
60	121	0.242	700	533	2.665
70	132	0.264	800	604	3.020
80	154	0.308	900	340	3.400
90	176	0.352	1000	379	3.790

Times in hundredths of a second

Figure 11.6   Times for body of Program 8.4

n	t1	t	n	t1	t
0	275	0.009	100	583	0.389
10	560	0.047	200	610	0.762
20	511	0.085	300	687	1.145
30	610	0.122	400	764	1.528
40	643	0.161	500	758	1.895
50	594	0.198	600	686	2.287
60	593	0.237	700	527	2.635
70	544	0.272	800	609	3.045
80	626	0.313	900	511	3.407
90	522	0.348	1000	571	3.807

Times in hundredths of a second

Figure 11.7 Times for body of Program 8.4

s	r	time	time/r
10	30,000	769	0.026
20	30,000	999	0.033
30	30,000	1225	0.041
40	20,000	967	0.048
50	12,000	670	0.056
60	12,000	767	0.064
70	10,000	714	0.071
80	10,000	791	0.079
90	10,000	862	0.086
100	10,000	939	0.094
200	5,000	846	0.169
500	2,000	795	0.398
1000	1,000	774	0.774
5000	200	758	3.790
10,000	100	758	7.58

Times are in hundredths of a second

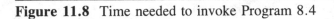

Figure 11.8 Time needed to invoke Program 8.4

becomes $t = 0.78254 + 0.003785n$. This is quite close to the least squares line for the data of Figure 11.3.

Summary

In order to obtain the run time of a program, we need to plan the experiment. The following issues need to be addressed during the planning stage:

(1) What is the accuracy of the clock? How accurate do our results have to be? Once the desired accuracy is known, we can determine the length of the shortest event that should be timed.

(2) For each instance size, a repetition factor needs to be determined. This is to be chosen such that the event time is at least the minimum time that can be clocked with the desired accuracy.

(3) Are we measuring worst case or average case performance? Suitable test data needs to be generated.

(4) What is the purpose of the experiment? Are the times being obtained for comparative purposes or are they to be used to predict actual run times? If the latter is the case, then contributions to the run time from such sources as the repetition loop and data generation need to be subtracted (in case they are included in the measured time). If the former is the case, then these times need not be subtracted (provided they are the same for all programs being compared).

(5) In case the times are to be used to predict actual run times, then we need to fit a curve through the points. For this, the asymptotic complexity should be known. If the asymptotic complexity is linear, then a least squares straight line can be fit; if it is quadratic, then a parabola is to be used (i.e., $t = a_0 + a_1n + a_2n^2$); etc. If the complexity is $\Theta(n\log n)$, then a least squares curve of the form $t = a_0 + a_1n + a_2n\log_2 n$ can be fit. The mathematics needed to fit a curve that is the least squares approximation to the observed data is developed in Appendix A. When obtaining the least squares approximation, one should discard data corresponding to "small" values of n as the program does not exhibit its asymptotic behavior for these n.

In the remainder of the chapter, we illustrate various timing techniques by means of examples. These examples also serve to bring to light the cost of various programming practices.

11.2. VARIABLE Vs VALUE PARAMETERS

From a purely aesthetic point of view, all formal parameters that do not transmit results back to the invoking program should be value parameters. What performance price, if any, do we pay for this programming style? The cost in data space is easily determined analytically. If we need to conserve space, then the use of large value formal parameters (e.g., a parameter of type *ElementList* when *ElementList* is of size 1000) should be avoided.

Let us concentrate on the relative effect variable and value parameters have on run time. We know that the values of all actual parameters that correspond to value formal parameters get copied into the formal parameters at the time the procedure/function is invoked. This penalty is negligible when the size of the parameter involved is small (e.g., for scalar and small component variables). What we haven't mentioned yet is that there is also a run time penalty associated with variable parameters. At the time a procedure/function is invoked, the address of each variable parameter is passed to it. The code for the procedure/function is generated without knowledge of this address. Consequently, all references to variable parameters within the procedure/function use a level of indirection that is one more than that used for value parameters, local variables, and non-parameter variables that are global to this procedure/function. Thus, a penalty is paid each time a variable parameter is referenced.

Sequential Search

Consider the iterative sequential search function given in Program 8.4. Assume that *ElementList* is of size 1000. The times for *a* being a value parameter and *ElementList* having this size have already been obtained (Figure 11.3). When *a* is changed to a variable parameter, some of the repetition factors used to obtain Figure 11.3 need to be changed. By first running the timing program using the old repetition factors, we estimate that the factors $r[1:12]$ need to be changed to [28000, 7000, 6000, 3000, 2400, 1800, 1500, 1500, 1500, 1000, 1000, 800]. The remaining factors need not be changed to get the time for their events up to 5 seconds. The times obtained using the new set of repetition factors are displayed in Figure 11.9.

n	time	n	time
0	0.025	100	0.615
10	0.084	200	1.194
20	0.143	300	1.785
30	0.201	400	2.363
40	0.258	500	2.947
50	0.321	600	3.545
60	0.377	700	4.120
70	0.436	800	4.720
80	0.495	900	5.270
90	0.555	1000	5.870

Times are in hundredths of a second

Figure 11.9 Times for Program 8.4 with a as a variable parameter

A comparison of Figures 11.3 and 11.9 reveals that having a as a value parameter becomes more efficient on time for a value of n between 300 and 400. The point at which one program becomes as fast as or faster than another is called the *break even* point. The break even point for our example can be found by plotting the two sets of times as in Figure 11.10 and determining the value of n at which the two graphs intersect. From Figure 11.10, we see that the break even point is close to 370.

The break even point can be found more accurately by experiment. We can search for the break even point using a binary search in the interval [300, 400]. The first point to check is $n = 350$. The measured times for the two cases a a value and a a variable parameter are 2.1 and 2.072 respectively. So, the break even point is between 350 and 400. The next value of n to examine is 375. The measured times are now 2.197 and 2.222. The break even point is therefore between 350 and 375. We must next try $n = 362$. The times are now 2.155 and 2.142. The next value of n to try is 368. The observed times are 2.170 and 2.185. For $n = 365$, both the times are the same (2.170). This is the break even point. We conclude that when *ElementList* has a size of 1000, using a variable parameter is faster (or at least as fast) so long as $n \le 365$. For n in the range [366, 1000], it is actually better to have a as a value parameter if run time is our primary concern.

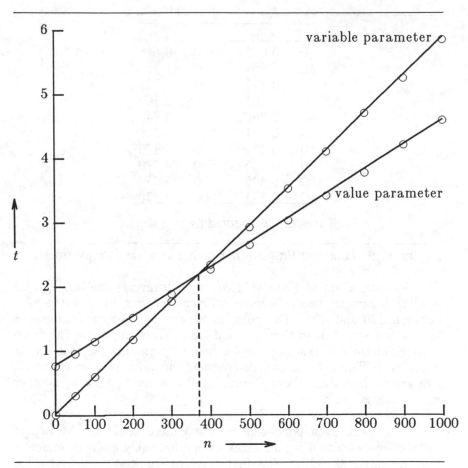

Figure 11.10 Graph for Figures 11.3 and 11.9

It is not too difficult to see that if the size of *ElementList* always equals n, then the worst case time performance of Program 8.4 is always better with a as a value parameter than with a a variable parameter. In fact, from the preceding results, it seems safe to conclude that whenever the number of references to a variable parameter is at least one third (or more accurately .365) the size of the parameter, the procedure or function will have a smaller run time if the parameter is a value parameter.

Binary Search

The asymptotic worst case complexity of the iterative binary search function (Program 8.6) was shown to be $O(\log n)$. However, the cost of invoking this function when a is a value parameter is $\Omega(n)$ as the size of *ElementList* is at least n. So, the actual cost of using this function is $\Omega(n)$. If a is changed to a variable parameter, then the cost of invoking the function becomes $\Theta(1)$ and the total cost of using it drops to $O(\log n)$. It can be shown that the asymptotic average complexity is also given by these functions. We shall concern ourselves only with measuring the average run time needed for a successful search (i.e., a search for an element x that is in $a[1..n]$).

Let us see what these analytical complexities translate to in terms of real run times. We shall make the assumption that in the target application it is not feasible to change the size of *ElementList* each time the number of elements changes. In particular, we may have different lists of different sizes and Program 8.6 is used to search in all of these. So, the size of *ElementList* has been fixed at the largest desired value (say 1000). In addition, we assume that the elements in a are distinct. Let $t_{value}(n)$ and $t_{var}(n)$, respectively, denote the average time to perform a successful binary search (including the invocation time) when a is a value and a variable parameter and the size of *ElementList* is 1000.

We wish to compare $t_{value}(n)$ and $t_{var}(n)$ for different values of n in the range [0, 1000]. Essentially the same values of n as used for *seqsearch* can be used here. The value $n = 0$ is replaced by the value $n = 1$ as no successful search is possible for $n = 0$.

To obtain the average times, we use Program 11.8. The repetition factors shown are for the case where a is a value parameter. These are obtained by first making an educated guess and running Program 11.8 with these guessed values. From the observed times, one can compute the repetition factors that will result in the time per event exceeding 5 seconds. The repetition factors for the case a is a variable parameter are obtained in the same way. The choice $r[1:20] =$ [14000; 800; 400; 200; 200; 200; 100; 100; 100; 100; 100; 20; 20; 20; 20; 20; 10; 10; 5; 5] serves our purpose. The measured times are shown in Figure 11.11.

```
begin {body of program to time binary search}
  for j := 1 to 1000 do {initialize z}
    z[j] := j;

  for j := 1 to 10 do  {values of n}
  begin
    n[j] := 10*(j−1); n[j+10] := 100*j;
  end;
  n[1] := 1;

  {repetition factors when a is a value parameter}
  r[1] := 700; r[2] := 70; r[3] := 60; r[4] := 30; r[5] := 15;
  r[6] :=15; r[7] := 15; r[8] := 10; r[9] := 10; r[10] := 10;
  r[11] := 10; r[12] := 10; r[13] := 2; r[14] := 2; r[15] := 2;
  r[16] := 1; r[17] := 1; r[18] := 1; r[19] := 1; r[20] := 1;

  writeln('n':5,' ', 't1',' ',' ','t');
  for j := 1 to 20 do {obtain computing times}
  begin
    time(h, m, s, f); {get time}
    for b := 1 to r[j] do
      for i := 1 to n[j] do  {search for each element}
        k := bsearch(z, n[j], i);
    time(h1, m1, s1, f1); {get time}
    {time spent in hundredths of a second}
    t1 := (((h1−h)*60 + m1 − m)*60 + s1 − s)*100 + f1 − f;
    t := t1; t := t1/r[j]/n[j]; {average time per search}
    writeln(n[j]:5,' ',t1:5, t:8:3);
  end;
  writeln('Times are in hundredths of a second'};
end. {of TimeSearch}
```

Program 11.8

From the times of Figure 11.11, we see that there is no value of
n for which it is more efficient to have a as a value formal parameter.
This result could have been anticipated from our experiments with
seqsearch. From these experiments, we concluded that when
ElementList has size 1000, about 365 references to a are needed to

n	value	variable	n	value	variable
1	0.809	0.048	100	0.874	0.132
10	0.823	0.080	200	0.887	0.149
20	0.842	0.094	300	0.897	0.161
30	0.849	0.102	400	0.906	0.167
40	0.852	0.110	500	0.906	0.172
50	0.864	0.115	600	0.915	0.178
60	0.867	0.118	700	0.910	0.184
70	0.871	0.122	800	0.920	0.187
80	0.865	0.127	900	0.921	0.189
90	0.872	0.130	1000	0.922	0.190

Times are in hundredths of a second

Figure 11.11 Average times for binary search

break even. The number of references to a in a binary search is at most $\lfloor \log n \rfloor + 1$. This is considerably fewer than 365 for $n \le 1000$.

The $\log n$ growth rate of the computing time is best seen by plotting it on a semi log paper as in Figure 11.12. We have plotted only the time for the case a is a variable formal parameter. On a semi log paper, the plot of $\log n$ vs n is a straight line.

11.3. GLOBAL VARIABLES Vs PARAMETERS

When coding a program we are often faced with the choice between making a certain variable a parameter or a global variable of a procedure or function. For instance, procedure *FindPath* (Program 7.6) has no parameters. We could just as well have written this procedure with a parameter list including the variables *maze*, *MazeRows*, and *path*. As far as program comprehensibility is concerned, the choice between global variables and parameters, in this case, is immaterial.

Is the comprehensibility of function *seqsearch* (Program 8.4) materially affected by making all its parameters global variables? While the answer to this is "No", the difficulty of using Program 8.4 may increase as a result of this. This is the case when we wish to use this program to search in different *ElementList*'s. Each time we change the element list, the new list has to be copied into the global list that

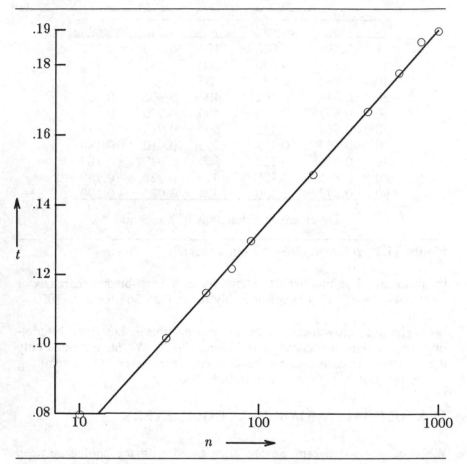

Figure 11.12 Plot of binary search times with *a* a variable parameter

Program 8.4 searches. Similarly, the size of the list has to be copied into the global variable *n*. If the element to be searched for isn't always in *x*, it too has to be copied into *x* before *seqsearch* can be invoked. In these situations, we will be simulating parameters and should instead use the parameter feature provided by Pascal.

Suppose that the environment in which Program 8.4 is to be used has only one element list whose size is *n*. However, the element to be searched for resides in different variables for different searches. So, we can let *a* and *n* be global variables but must leave *x* a parameter.

The heading for Program 8.4 is changed to:

function *seqsearch*(*x*: **integer**): **integer**;

The measured computing times for the values of *n* used earlier are shown in Figure 11.13. The repetition factors used are slightly larger than those used for the case when *a* is a variable parameter. Figure 11.13 also gives the percentage reduction in time with respect to the cases when *a* is a value parameter or a variable parameter. In both cases, *n* is a value parameter. The times for these cases are taken from Figures 11.3 and 11.9, respectively. We can explain the observed percentage reductions in the following way. When value parameters are used, the overhead of passing the actual parameters depends only on *MaxElements*. When *n* is small, this is a larger fraction of the total time than when *n* is large (i.e., close to *MaxElements*). Hence, we expect the percentage reduction in time from the use of global variables to decrease as *n* increases. When variable parameters are used, the additional cost (over global variables) is proportional to the number of references made to the variable parameters. For the worst case performance of *seqsearch*, this is linear in *n*. Since the worst case run time of this program is also linear in *n*, we expect the percentage reduction in time to be independent of *n*.

Binary Search

When *a* and *n* are made global variables, the average times for a successful binary search are as in Figure 11.14. This figure also presents the percentage reduction in the time from the cases when *a* is a value parameter and a variable parameter. In both these cases, *n* is a value parameter. The results can be explained as above.

11.4. RECURSION Vs ITERATION

In this section, we examine the performace penalty of using recursion in situations where it is easily eliminated (i.e., when the iterative version does not simulate the recursion using its own stack). As examples, we again consider sequential and binary search. We make the assumption that *a*, *n*, and *x* are required to be parameters. However, *a* is a variable parameter. This change in the status of *a* is necessary if we are to be able to run the recursive functions (Programs 8.1 and 8.3) using a reasonable amount of space.

n	time	% reduction from value	variable
0	0.018	98	28
10	0.058	93	31
20	0.096	89	33
30	0.136	85	32
40	0.176	81	32
50	0.214	78	33
60	0.255	75	32
70	0.294	72	33
80	0.332	69	33
90	0.373	67	33
100	0.410	65	33
200	0.804	48	33
300	1.195	37	33
400	1.594	30	33
500	1.977	26	33
600	2.380	22	33
700	2.775	19	33
800	3.160	17	33
900	3.570	16	32
1000	3.960	14	33

Times are in hundredths of a second

Figure 11.13 Times for Program 8.4 with a and n as global variables

Sequential Search

The measured times for the worst case performance of Program 8.1 with a as a variable parameter are given in Figure 11.15. This figure also gives the ratio of the times with recursion and without (i.e., $t_{recursion}/t_{iteration}$). When $n = 1000$, the recursive program took almost 93 times as much time as the iterative program.

Binary Search

The measured times for the average successful performance of Program 8.3 with a as a variable parameter are shown in Figure 11.16. The ratio of the time for this recursive program to that of the iterative

n	time	% reduction from	
		value	variable
1	0.042	95	13
10	0.067	92	16
20	0.079	91	16
30	0.085	90	17
40	0.092	89	16
50	0.097	89	16
60	0.100	88	15
70	0.104	88	15
80	0.107	88	16
90	0.109	88	16
100	0.112	87	15
200	0.126	86	15
300	0.136	85	16
400	0.141	84	16
500	0.144	84	16
600	0.150	84	16
700	0.154	83	16
800	0.157	83	16
900	0.159	83	16
1000	0.160	83	16

Times are in hundredths of a second

Figure 11.14 Average times for Program 8.6 with a and n as global variables

program is also given. The times for the iterative version (with a as a variable parameter) are given in Figure 11.11. The ratios for binary search are not as large as for sequential search as the number of recursive calls here is only $O(\log n)$.

11.5. RECURSION STACK SPACE

We can reduce the recursion stack space needed by Program 8.3 by recoding it as in Program 11.9. The function *rsearch* is the recursive part and has fewer parameters than does Program 8.3. As a result, the stack space needed is less. Program 11.9 is, however, somewhat slower than Program 8.3 as it takes more time to reference the

n	time	ratio	n	time	ratio
0	0.017	0.4	100	1.785	13.5
10	0.193	2.4	200	3.545	23.8
20	0.368	3.9	300	5.270	32.7
30	0.549	5.4	400	7.080	42.4
40	0.719	6.5	500	8.840	51.4
50	0.897	7.8	600	10.575	59.4
60	1.076	9.1	700	12.350	67.1
70	1.252	10.3	800	14.100	75.4
80	1.428	11.2	900	15.950	84.4
90	1.604	12.3	1000	17.600	92.6

Times are in hundredths of a second

Figure 11.15 Worst case times for Program 8.1

n	time	ratio	n	time	ratio
1	0.033	0.7	100	0.171	1.3
10	0.085	1.1	200	0.202	1.4
20	0.110	1.2	300	0.220	1.4
30	0.123	1.2	400	0.231	1.4
40	0.135	1.2	500	0.240	1.4
50	0.145	1.3	600	0.247	1.4
60	0.150	1.3	700	0.257	1.4
70	0.159	1.3	800	0.261	1.4
80	0.163	1.3	900	0.264	1.4
90	0.168	1.3	1000	0.269	1.4

Times are in hundredths of a second

Figure 11.16 Average times for recursive binary search

elements of a. The observed run times together with the percentage increase from those of Figure 11.16 are shown in Figure 11.17.

```
function bsearch(var a: ElementList; i, n, x:integer): integer;
function rsearch(i, n: integer): i teger;
{Real binary search function}
var mid: integer;
begin
    mid := (i+n) div 2;
    if i>n then rsearch := 0  {not found}
    else if x=a[mid] then rsearch := mid   {found}
        else if x<a[mid] then rsearch := rsearch(a, i, mid−1, x)
            else rsearch := rsearch(a, mid+1, n, x);
end; { of rsearch}


begin
    bsearch := rsearch(i, n);
end; (of bsearch}
```

Program 11.9 Recursive binary search

n	time	% Increase
1	0.045	36.4
10	0.100	17.6
20	0.125	13.6
30	0.138	12.2
40	0.152	12.6
50	0.159	9.7
60	0.167	11.3
70	0.174	9.4
80	0.180	10.4
90	0.186	10.7

Times are in hundredths of a second

Figure 11.17 Times for Program 11.9

11.6. PROCEDURES AND FUNCTIONS

How much does writing a piece of code as a procedure or function versus inserting it directly at needed points in the program cost? We measured the time needed to invoke and return from a procedure. The measured times are shown in Figure 11.18. As can be seen, the time depends on the number of parameters as well as on whether they are variable or value parameters. All parameters were of type integer in the experiment. These times, of course, do not include the overhead involved in referencing each variable parameter in the procedure/function.

Number of	Time	
Parameters	Variable	Value
0	0.010	0.010
1	0.011	0.011
2	0.012	0.012
3	0.013	0.013
4	0.014	0.014
10	0.018	0.017
20	0.027	0.024

Times are in hundredths of a second

Figure 11.18 Times for procedure invocation and return

11.7. BOUNDARY TESTS

Failure to take care of boundary conditions is a common source of errors in programs. Boundary conditions can be accounted for by either explicitly checking for a problem boundary and taking the appropriate action at the boundary (as in Programs 6.14 and 6.15) or by choosing the data representations so that these conditions are avoided. We took the latter approach in the rat in a maze program of Chapter 7. Here, we surrounded the maze by a wall of ones. This prevented us from ever reaching a maze position that has fewer than four neighbors. Also, in this program we avoided the need to test for stack full (i.e., too many positions in *path*) by making *path* large enough to accommodate the maximum number of positions that can possibly be on the path.

Manipulating the data representation so that boundary conditions cannot arise results in more elegant programs. What effect does this have on program performance? In the case of the rat in a maze problem, additional space is needed to accommodate the boundary wall of ones. For *path*, no additional space is needed. In the case of the insertion sort program (Program 7.11), an additional spot (position 0) is needed in the element list *a*. While the data space increases, the program space decreases. So, there may or may not be a space penalty associated with the increased elegance of the program. How about run time? Clearly, it will take less time to add positions to *path* as we no longer check to see if there is space in *path* for the position to be added. The boundary wall around the maze, however, causes positions on the original boundary to have additional neighbors that are to be examined. So, the expected savings from not explicitly checking for the maze boundary may be offset by the cost of examining the additional neighbors. Overall, we expect the rat in a maze programs of Chapter 7 to run faster than their counterparts that do not surround the maze with a boundary wall.

We shall quantify the expected benefits of avoiding explicit boundary checks by considering two examples.

Sequential Search

Program 8.4 avoids a boundary check by setting $a[0]$ equal to the element x that is being searched for. If, instead, we choose not to provide the additional spot $a[0]$ that is needed for this purpose, our program will take the form given in Program 11.10. In this program, we have made a a variable parameter. This is because we assume that in the environment in which our search program is to be used, n is generally much smaller than the size of *ElementList*.

The worst case run times for this program are shown in Figure 11.19. The percentage increase in time from the case when a boundary element is used (Figure 11.9) is also shown in this figure. We see that the performance penalty for not avoiding boundary checks is quite significant in the case of a sequential search.

```
function search(var a: ElementList; n,x: integer): integer;
var i: integer; NotDone: boolean;
begin
  NotDone := true; i := n;
  while NotDone do
  begin
    if i < 1 then
    begin
      search := 0; NotDone := false;
    end
    else if a[i] = x then
        begin NotDone := false; search := i; end;
    i := i-1;
  end;
end; {of search}
```

Program 11.10 Sequential search without boundary element

n	Time	% Increase	n	Time	% Increase
0	0.024	-4.0	100	0.879	42.9
10	0.109	29.8	200	1.740	45.7
20	0.196	37.1	300	2.580	44.5
30	0.281	39.8	400	3.460	46.4
40	0.366	41.9	500	4.285	45.4
50	0.449	39.9	600	5.192	46.5
60	0.538	42.7	700	5.990	45.4
70	0.627	43.8	800	6.920	46.6
80	0.708	43.0	900	7.750	47.1
90	0.797	43.6	1000	8.570	46.0

Times are in hundredths of a second

Figure 11.19 Worst case times for sequential search without boundary element

Insertion

Program 6.13 inserts x into a sorted sequence $a[1{:}n]$. It avoids check-ing for the left boundary of a by using the position $a[0]$. The check for the right boundary cannot be avoided unless $MaxListLength > n$ is guaranteed by the design. If the position $a[0]$ is not available, then the left boundary must also be checked for. Program 11.11 does this.

We have a difficulty experimenting with either Programs 6.13 or 11.11 as Turbo Pascal does not permit **goto** statements to exit the current block. This difficulty is easily circumvented as Turbo Pascal provides the non standard statement **halt** that terminates the program. This has the same effect as the **goto**.

```
procedure insert(var a: ElementList; n: integer; var x: integer);
var i: integer; NotDone: boolean;
begin
  if n = MaxListLength then begin
                         writeln('List too long');
                         goto 999; {end of program}
                       end;
  if n < 0 then n := 0;
  NotDone := true; i := n;
  while NotDone do
  begin
    if i = 0 then  NotDone := false
    else if a[i] <= x then  NotDone := false
         else begin a[i+1] := a[i]; i := i-1; end;
  end;
  a[i+1] := x; n := n+1;
end; {of insert}
```

Program 11.11 Insert without boundary element

Let us compare the worst case run times of Programs 6.13 and 11.11. The worst case data has $x < a[1]$. We use the same values of n as used for the sequential search program. The run times of the two programs are given in Figure 11.20.

Obtaining these times involves the use of a strategy slightly different from that used up to now. This is so as each insertion changes the element list and also increases the value of n. Consequently, it is necessary to restore the values of a and n following each invocation of *insert*. Our first attempt at modifying the timing strategy results in the timing loop of Program 11.12. Since, the time needed to restore the values is a significant part of the total measured time, this time must be subtracted from the results produced by this program.

```
for j := 1 to 20 do
begin
  time(h, m, s, f); {get time}
  for b := 1 to r[j] do
  begin
    for i := 1 to n[j] do {initialize z}
      z[i] := i;
    insert(z, n[j], 0);
    n[j] := n[j] − 1; {compensate for increase by insert}
  end;
  time(h1, m1, s1, f1); {get time}
end;
```

Program 11.12 Timing *insert*

An alternate to conducting an additional timing experiment to obtain the time needed to restore the values of a and n is to design the timing experiment so that there is no need to restore a and n. We can avoid having to restore a by decreasing the value of x by 1 for each successive repetition. Instead of increasing n by 1 in procedure *insert*, we can decrease x by 1. The time for the subtraction will almost balance the time for the addition. The additional change needed is to make x a variable parameter in place of n. Program 11.12 is now modified to Program 11.13. The times measured for the modified programs will be quite close to that for the original programs (in fact, the only difference is that between an addition and a subtraction, and the additional references to a variable parameter). The worst case times are shown in Figure 11.20. When explicit boundary checks are made, the time is about 16% larger.

```
for j := 1 to 20 do {obtain computing times}
begin
  for i := 1 to n[j] do  a[i] := r[j]+i;
  l := r[j];
  time(h, m, s, f );
  for b := 1 to r[j] do
    insert(a, n[j], l);
  time(h1, m1, s1, f1);
  t1 := (((h1 − h)*60 + m1 − m)*60 + s1 − s)*100 + f1 − f;
  t := t1; t := t/r[j];
  writeln(n[j]:5,' ',t1:5, t:6:3);
end;
```

Program 11.13 Timing program for *insert*

11.8. PROGRAMMING FOR EFFICIENCY

In the same way that we distinguish between a number and its representation, we can distinguish between an algorithm and its representation. As we have seen, the run time performance of an algorithm represented as a Pascal program is significantly affected by representational issues such as the choice amongst global variables, value parameters, and variable parameters; the choice between recursion and iteration; the use of procedures and functions, etc.

Some of these choices may affect the asymptotic complexity of a program. For instance, making a a variable parameter in the program for binary search (Program 8.6) changes the worst case time per search (including the time for invocation) from $\Theta(n)$ to $\Theta(\log n)$. Using the recursive version of Program 8.3, the worst case time becomes $\Theta(n \log n)$ and an additional $\Theta(n \log n)$ space is needed for the recursion stack.

Other choices change the run time by a constant factor. The change from a variable parameter to a global variable for example will speed the program by a constant factor.

Often, the decisions that result in efficient programs are different from those that follow so called "good programming practice". A good example of this is the choice between a value and variable formal

n	Time with $a[0]$	w/o $a[0]$	% Increase
0	0.038	0.033	-13.2
10	0.189	0.211	11.6
20	0.340	0.388	14.1
30	0.490	0.563	14.9
40	0.645	0.746	15.7
50	0.787	0.915	16.3
60	0.946	1.098	16.1
70	1.098	1.274	16.0
80	1.252	1.450	15.8
90	1.400	1.635	16.8
100	1.552	1.813	16.8
200	3.046	3.577	17.4
300	4.575	5.350	16.9
400	6.100	7.140	17.0
500	7.625	8.925	17.0
600	9.186	10.671	16.2
700	10.617	12.450	17.3
800	12.200	14.160	16.1
900	13.600	16.075	18.2
1000	15.200	17.767	16.9

Times are in hundredths of a second

Figure 11.20 Times for Programs 6.13 and 11.11

parameter. "Good" programming practice dictates that parameters whose values are not to be changed in a procedure or function are to be set up as variable parameters. Following this dictate on large parameters is quite expensive in terms of space. It is also very expensive in terms of time when only a small fraction of the components of the variable are referenced.

Similarly, a program that makes many references to a variable parameter can be speeded by copying the actual parameter into a local variable on entry to the procedure/function; replacing all references to the variable parameter by references to the local variable; and copying the local variable back into the actual parameter on exit. This results in a less elegant, but faster, program. *Caution:* This can change the outcome of the program in case two or more actual parameters are the same.

Consider the practice of modularizing a program. When the amount of work being done in a module is very small, the overhead of invoking the module may exceed or be comparable to the time spent in the module. If this module is very frequently used in the program, we can obtain a significant reduction in the run time of the program by coding the module directly at all places that would otherwise invoke the module.

As an example, consider the procedures *AddToStack* and *DeleteFromStack* (Programs 6.14 and 6.15). Each executes at most three statements. We expect the time needed to invoke each to be comparable to the time needed to execute each. So, by coding these directly into the programs that use them, the cost of using a stack will go down significantly. This action will, however, have an adverse affect on program readability and maintenance. The effect on readability can be mitigated by the use of a comment such as "{add to the stack}" or "{delete from the stack}". The effect on maintenance cannot be mitigated. Maintenance will have to be performed at all places where the code has been replicated rather than in just two modules. (This problem doesn't arise if we have a macro preprocessor for Pascal. In this case, macros to add to and delete from the stack may be defined once and used at several places. The preprocessor substitutes the macro definition at each place it is used in the program. Changes to the macro definition have to be made only at the place of definition.) The size of the program space will increase in case each procedure is invoked from more than one place.

Finally, note that even when our only concern is program efficiency, the goals of space and time efficiency may be in conflict. Avoiding boundary conditions often costs space but reduces run time. Using variable parameters saves space but can cause an increase in run time (this happens when many references to the variable parameter are made).

We can make the following recommendations for efficient programming. You must keep in mind that, in practice, it will be necessary to balance the desire to cut down on program development and maintenance time and the desire to obtain the most efficient representation of an algorithm.

(1) *Limit the number of parameters in each procedure/function.* For example, if we have only one stack, then don't make the name of the stack a parameter to the procedures to add to and delete from a stack. The stack name should be global. On the other hand, if more than one stack is in use, then the stack name should be a parameter.

(2) *Carefully evaluate the performance cost of making a parameter a value parameter versus a variable parameter.*

(3) *Don't use recursion in places where it is easily eliminated.* Whenever a recursive call is the last statement in the procedure or function, it can be replaced by a **goto** to the first statement in the program. Alternatively, a **while**, **repeat**, or **for** loop can be set up. Recursion can often be easily eliminated in other situations too. For instance, the two recursive calls in the recursive binary search function of Program 8.3 are easily replaced by a single **while** loop.

(4) *Try to speed up inner loops.* Significant savings in run time can be achieved by speeding statements that are executed often. Changing the statement $x := a*b + a*c$ to $x := a*(b + c)$ will have no noticeable effect on the run time if this statement is executed only once. If the statement is embedded in a loop and gets executed several thousand times, we will see an improvement in performance. Similarly, assignments to variables that do not change in a loop should be made outside the loop rather than inside. For example, the statement $x := 0$ should be moved out of the loop:

```
for i := 1 to 10000 do
begin
    x := 0;
    .
    .
    .
end;
```

if the value of x is not changed by any of the other statements in the **for** loop.

(5) Avoid functions and procedures that do little work.

(6) Avoid having to test for boundary conditions. Note that this is not to be done at the expense of program correctness. However, the data representations are to be modified so that there is no need to explicitly check for boundary conditions.

11.9. COMPARING ALGORITHMS

11.9.1. Introduction

When comparing the performance of several algorithms for the same task, it is essential that each is programmed using as similar programming styles as possible. Each should, to the extent possible, have the same set of value parameters, variable parameters, local and global variables, etc. The size of value parameters should not differ from one algorithm to the next.

For example, we can search for x in an element list a using either a sequential or a binary search. Suppose that we program the sequential search as a Pascal function which has no parameters (a, n, and x are global variables) and we program the binary search as a recursive function with a as a value parameter as in Program 8.3. Comparing the performance of these two programs will lead us to conclude that sequential search is superior to binary search. In fact, the worst case asymptotic run time of the recursive binary search program is $\Theta(n\log n)$ as it takes $\Theta(n)$ time to copy the values of the actual parameter for a (assuming that the size of *ElementList* is n) into the formal parameter on each invocation. $\Theta(\log n)$ invocations are made in the worst case. So, by adopting a particularly inefficient programming style for binary search, we have converted a very efficient search algorithm into a very inefficient program. The loss in efficiency isn't by just a constant factor but by a multiplicative function of n. The same is true of the space requirements. $\Theta(n\log n)$ additional space is needed to save the $\Theta(\log n)$ copies of a.

If we must use an inefficient programming style, then we must do so uniformly. So, the program for sequential search should also be recursive and declare a to be a value parameter. When comparing programs for different algorithms, the use of a different programming style for one algorithm biases the results of the comparison.

In addition to using the same (or at least similar) programming style(s) when programming the alternate algorithms, it is essential that the same assumptions be made about the form of the input data at the time the program is started and the form of all data (actual results as well as any other data that is useful for later work) after the program terminates.

Programs 8.4 and 8.6 represent similar programming styles. However, binary search requires the element list being searched to be in nondecreasing order of the key values. Comparing the times for the two programs isn't enough to conclude that binary search is better than sequential search as we haven't factored in the cost of sorting the elements. If the elements are known to be sorted to begin with, then this information can be used to obtain a more efficient sequential search program as in Program 11.14. Now, we can compare the two search strategies using Program 8.6 (with *a* changed to a variable parameter) and Program 11.14.

```
function search(var a: ElementList; n,x: integer): integer;
var i: integer;
begin
  i := n; a[0] := x;
  while a[i] > x do
    i := i-1;
  if a[i] = x then search := i
              else search := 0;
end; {of search}
```

Program 11.14 Sequential search for sorted lists

Figure 11.21 gives the average times for Program 11.14 for successful searches. This figure also reproduces the average times given in Figure 11.11 for binary search with *a* as a variable parameter. The difference in the rate of growth in the run times is best seen from the plot of Figure 11.22. From this plot, we see that the average performance of binary search is better than that of a sequential search when $n \geq 25$. The exact break even point can be determined by experimenting in the range 21 through 30.

n	seq	binary	n	seq	binary
1	0.035	0.048	100	0.318	0.132
10	0.057	0.080	200	0.615	0.149
20	0.086	0.094	300	0.907	0.161
30	0.115	0.102	400	1.195	0.167
40	0.145	0.110	500	1.494	0.172
50	0.174	0.115	600	1.785	0.178
60	0.203	0.118	700	2.079	0.184
70	0.231	0.122	800	2.376	0.187
80	0.261	0.127	900	2.661	0.189
90	0.293	0.130	1000	2.955	0.190

Times are in hundredths of a second

Figure 11.21 Average times for sequential and binary search

The worst case times for sequential and binary search are reported in Figure 11.23. The times for binary search might, at first, surprise you. The worst case times for $n = 20$ and 30 are the same. This is to be expected as the worst case number of iterations of the **while** loop of Program 8.6 is $\lceil \log_2(n+1) \rceil$. For both $n = 20$ and 30, this quantity is 5. Similarly, when $n = 40$, 50 and 60, the worst case number of iterations is 6. Hence the times for these n's are expected to be the same. The remaining apparent anomalies are explained in the same way.

The worst case search times have been plotted in Figure 11.24. The curve for binary search has been plotted as a step curve rather than as a continuous one. This reflects our knowledge of the stepwise nature of the worst case time. The steps are introduced at those values of n that are powers of 2. It is at these n's that the value of $\lceil \log_2(n+1) \rceil$ changes. To complete the graph, we need times for $n = 2$ and 4. From the graph, we see that the break even point for binary search (for worst case performance) is $n = 16$.

Summary

The following recommendations can be made for comparing the performance of several algorithms for the same problem:

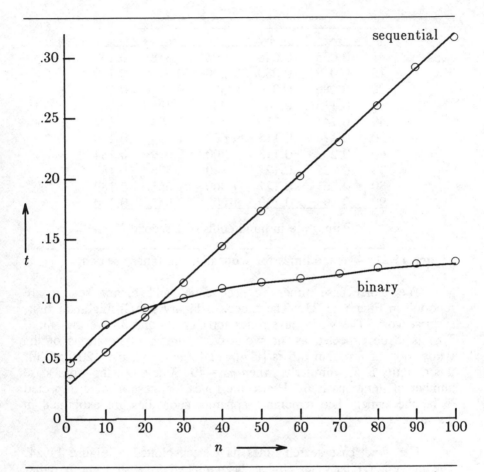

Figure 11.22 Plot of average times for binary and sequential search

1. Use the same programming style for each algorithm.
2. Make sure that the input/output assumptions for each are the same. In case these assumptions are different for different programs, be sure that the difference is acceptable for the application you have in mind. For instance, one algorithm may generate the output in sorted order while another may not. However, for the target application, unsorted output may be just as acceptable as sorted output.

n	seq	binary	n	seq	binary
0	0.030	0.022	100	0.620	0.167
10	0.088	0.104	200	1.208	0.187
20	0.148	0.126	300	1.777	0.209
30	0.205	0.126	400	2.380	0.209
40	0.266	0.147	500	2.964	0.209
50	0.325	0.145	600	3.536	0.231
60	0.381	0.147	700	4.136	0.229
70	0.439	0.166	800	4.704	0.228
80	0.499	0.167	900	5.320	0.228
90	0.560	0.166	1000	5.870	0.231

Times are in hundredths of a second

Figure 11.23 Worst case times for binary and sequential search

3. Plan your experiment. Determine the range in instance characteristics that you are going to use. Decide if worst case or average (or both) times are sought. Obtain suitable test data.

4. Know what to expect from the experiments. An asymptotic analysis can be very helpful for this. In case the results of your experiment do not agree with your expectations, examine your programs, test data, and asymptotic analysis to discover the cause of the inconsistency.

11.9.2. An Example: Insertion Sort Vs Bubble Sort

In Section 7.3, we developed a sorting procedure based on the insertion method. This sorting method is called insert sort. Let us develop another sort algorithm and code it as a Pascal procedure. The new sort algorithm is called *bubble sort*. The basic idea in this method is to scan the records from left to right *bubbling* records with large keys towards the right. An example will illustrate this.

Suppose we have four keys in the order [5, 3, 7, 1]. The 5 and the 3 are compared and the 5 bubbles to the right. The key sequence becomes [3, 5, 7, 1]. Next, the 5 and 7 are compared and no interchange takes place. Then, 7 and 1 are compared and the 7 bubbles right to get the sequence [3, 5, 1, 7]. This completes one pass of the

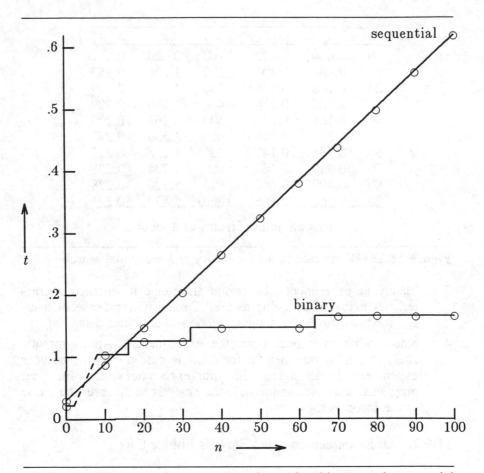

Figure 11.24 Plot of worst case times for binary and sequential search

bubble sort. At the end of this pass, we are assured that the record with the largest key is in position n.

Following the first pass of bubble sort, we are left with the problem of sorting the records in positions 1 through $n-1$. This can be done by using bubble sort recursively as in Program 11.15. The use of recursion in this program is easily replaced by a **for** loop as in Program 11.16. This program is to be preferred to Program 11.15 because of efficiency considerations.

```
procedure bubble(var a: ElementList; n: integer);
var j: integer; x: element;
begin
   for j := 1 to n−1 do
      if a[j].key > a[j+1].key then begin {bubble a[j] up}
                                   x := a[j];
                                   a[j] := a[j+1];
                                   a[j+1] := x;
                              end;
   {Now, the largest element is at a[n]}
   {Sort remaining n−1 elements}
   if n > 2 then bubble(a, n−1);
end; {of bubble}
```

Program 11.15 Recursive bubble sort

```
procedure bubble(var a: ElementList; n: integer);
var i, j: integer; x: element;
begin
   for i := 1 to n−1 do
      for j := 1 to n−i do
         if a[j].key > a[j+1].key then begin
                                   x := a[j];
                                   a[j] := a[j+1];
                                   a[j+1] := x;
                              end;
end; {of bubble}
```

Program 11.16 Iterative bubble sort

Let us analyze the time complexity of Program 11.16. The instance characteristics of interest are n, the number of elements and s the size of each element. We see that each execution of the **if** statement takes $\Theta(1)$ time when the **then** clause is not entered and $\Theta(s)$ time when it is. The number of times this statement is executed is $\sum_{i=1}^{n-1} n-i = \sum_{1}^{n-1} i = \Theta(n^2)$. This statement determines the overall complexity (except when n is 0 or 1). So, the complexity is $\Theta(n^2)$

when the **then** clause is never entered (this happens when the elements are initially in sorted order). The complexity is $\Theta(n^2 s)$ if the **then** clause is entered each time (this happens when $a[j].key > a[j+1].key$, $1 \le j < n$, initially).

Comparing the time complexities of Programs 7.11 (Example 10.16) and 11.16 for the case $s = 1$, we see that while Program 11.16 take n^2 time always, Program 7.11 needs this much time only in the worst case. In particular, when the records are already in sorted order Program 7.11 takes only $\Theta(n)$ time.

A close examination of Program 11.16 reveals that if the **then** clause of the **if** is not entered for some value of i, then the records are in sorted order and the remaining iterations of the outer loop need not be performed. This observation results in Program 11.17.

```
procedure bubble(var a: ElementList; n: integer);
var i, j: integer; x: element; done: boolean;
begin
  i := 1;
  repeat
    done := true;
    for j := 1 to n−i do
      if a[j].key > a[j+1].key then begin
                              done := false;
                              x := a[j];
                              a[j] := a[j+1];
                              a[j+1] := x;
                            end;
        i := i + 1;
    until done;
end; {of bubble}
```

Program 11.17 Early terminating bubble sort

We expect Program 11.17 to have a better average performance than Program 11.16. For instance, if the records are already in sorted order, then Program 11.17 will terminate as soon as i becomes 2. In fact, the time complexity of Program 11.17 for initially sorted data is $\Theta(n)$. The actual worst case run time of Program 11.17 is, however, expected to be larger than that of Program 11.16 as, in the worst case, all iterations up to $i = n-1$ are performed and in addition the overhead of using the variable *done* is incurred.

Whether Program 11.16 or 11.17 should be used depends on whether we wish to optimize worst case or average performance. Let us assume that in the environment in which the sort program is to be used, it is critical to have a sort program with good worst case behavior. So, Program 11.16 is preferred for this environment. We are left with determining which of Programs 7.11 and 11.16 to use. Since both have the same asymptotic complexity, we shall make this determination experimentally.

Comparing Programs 7.11 and 11.16, we see that both represent similar programming styles and both have the same parameters. The only difference is that Program 7.11 requires an additional position in the element list a (i.e., position 0). We see no reasonable way to use this additional position in the program for bubble sort. So, our experiments will not be biased by a difference in programming styles.

Before attempting to run the experiment, let us plan it. We need to be clear about the purpose of the experiment. Is it solely to determine which of the programs is faster or do we also want to use the results to predict actual computing times for various values of n? We shall see that the stated purpose of the experiment will affect its nature. For the time being, let us assume that we simply wish to determine which program has a smaller worst case time complexity.

Next, we need worst case test data. As stated earlier in Example 10.16, the worst case data for insertion sort has keys in the order $a[1].key < a[2].key < \ldots < a[n].key$. It is not too difficult to see that this data also represents the worst case for bubble sort.

It is a good idea to get a feel for the expected outcome of the experiment. Analyzing Programs 7.11 and 11.16 on this worst case data, we see that Program 7.11 makes $3n(n-1)/2$ element moves while Program 11.16 makes $(n+1)(n+2)/2 - 3$ moves. So, we expect Program 7.11 to outperform Program 11.16 for large values of n. However, for small values of n, Program 11.16 may be faster as it uses a simpler control structure.

We shall limit our experiment to values of n up to 500. The particular values of n we shall use are the same as in earlier experiments. The structure of the time measurement part of the program has to be changed from that given in Program 11.3 as the sort programs alter the input data. A possible solution is to make a a value parameter for the experiment. This can bias the experiment somewhat as the two sort programs make a different number of references to the variable a. So, we use the timing program shown in Program 11.18. A potential difficulty with this is that the initialization time for a is also measured. This time is the same for both sort programs. Consequently, for each value of n, the measured times are larger by the same amount for the two programs. This does not affect the comparison. However, if our objective is to predict actual run times, we can measure the initialization time for each n separately, and then subtract this from the times obtained using Program 11.18.

```
for j := 1 to 15 do {obtain computing times}
begin
  time(h, m, s, f);
  for b := 1 to r[j] do
  begin
    for l := 1 to n[j] do  a[l].key := n[j]−l+1;
    bubble(a, n[j]);
  end;
  time(h1, m1, s1, f1);
  t1 := (((h1 − h)*60 + m1 − m)*60 + s1 − s)*100 + f1 − f;
  t := t1; t := t/r[j];
  writeln(n[j]:5,' ',t1:5,'   ', t:9:3);
end;
```

Program 11.18 Timing program for bubble sort

The measured worst case times for insert sort and bubble sort (using Programs 7.11 and 11.16, respectively) are shown in Figure 11.25. As expected, the performance of insert sort is better than that of bubble sort except for some small values of n.

The exact value of n at which the worst case performance of insert sort becomes better than that of bubble sort is somewhere between 1 and 10. Given the significant difference in the times for n

n	bubble	insert	(bubble−insert)/insert*100
0	0.018	0.023	-21.7
10	1.743	1.036	68.2
20	7.140	3.705	92.7
30	16.117	8.050	100.2
40	28.800	13.960	106.3
50	44.750	21.550	107.7
60	65.200	30.967	110.5
70	88.308	41.760	111.5
80	115.375	54.200	112.9
90	146.500	68.583	113.6
100	180.200	84.000	114.5
200	725.000	333.000	117.7
300	1631.000	747.000	118.3
400	2900.000	1319.000	119.9
500	4531.000	2059.000	120.1

Times are in hundredths of a second

Figure 11.25 Worst case insert and bubble sort times

= 10, we expect the break even value of n to be closer to 1 than to 10. To determine this value, we need additional timing data. Since the range in which the break even point lies is small (at most from 1 to 10), we shall not use the binary search method used in Section 11.2. Instead, we shall just obtain the times for $n = 1, 2, 3, 4$, and 5. We expect this to be adequate. An alternate approach is to obtain the run times for $n = 1, 2, 3, ...$ and let the timing program terminate when the break even point has been found. The times for n in the range [1, 5] are shown in Figure 11.26. The break even point is $n = 3$.

The n^2 growth of the computing times is best seen from the plots of Figure 11.27. Another possibility is to plot the rate of change in the computing time as a function of n. For any value of n, this is defined to be $(t(n-d) - t(n))/d$, where d is a small positive integer (preferably 1). For a linear program, this should be constant; for a quadratic program, this should be linear; and for a cubic program, this should be quadratic. Figure 11.28 shows the rate of change in times for insert sort and bubble sort. The values shown in this figure are

n	bubble	insert
1	0.021	0.025
2	0.066	0.070
3	0.148	0.132
4	0.269	0.209
5	0.421	0.305

Times are in hundredths of a second

Figure 11.26 Times for narrowed range

computed using the data of Figure 11.25. The d values are therefore less than ideal, being 10 or 100 depending on the value of n. The rate of increase in the times for the two sort programs are plotted in Figure 11.29. The linear nature is evident.

11.10. GENERATING TEST DATA

Generating a data set that results in the worst case performance of a program isn't always easy. In fact, when we study merge sort in Chapter 14, we shall use a computer program to generate the worst case data. In some cases, even this is very difficult. In these cases, another approach to estimating worst case performance is taken. For each set of values of the instance characteristics of interest, we generate a suitably large number of random test data. The run times for each of these test data is obtained. The maximum of these times is used as an estimate of the worst case time for this set of values of the instance characteristics.

Suppose that we are unable to determine the worst case data for bubble sort. If we use the above approach, then for each value of n, we have to generate some number of random initial permutations of the keys in a. Our timing program takes the form shown in Program 11.19.

To generate a random permutation, we can use the procedure given in Program 11.20. This carries out $n-1$ random interchanges of the elements in a. An exercise examines the effectiveness of this approach to estimate worst case run times.

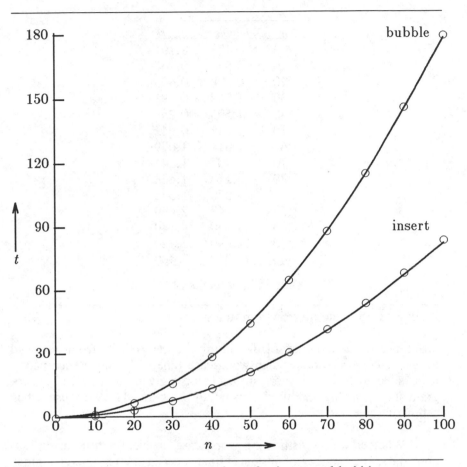

Figure 11.27 Plot of worst case times for insert and bubble sort

To measure average case times, it is usually not possible to average over all possible instances of a given characteristic. While it is possible to do this for sequential and binary search, it is not possible for a sort program. If we assume that all keys are distinct, then for any given n, $n!$ different permutations need to be used to obtain the average time.

Obtaining average case data is usually much harder than obtaining worst case data. So, we often adopt the strategy outlined above and simply obtain an estimate of the average time. An important

n	bubble	insert
0	0.173	0.101
10	0.540	0.267
20	0.898	0.435
30	1.268	0.591
40	1.595	0.759
50	2.045	0.942
60	2.311	1.079
70	2.707	1.244
80	3.112	1.438
90	3.370	1.542
100	5.448	2.490
200	9.060	4.140
300	12.690	5.720
400	16.310	7.400

Times are in hundredths of a second

Figure 11.28 Rate of growth in times

difference in the structure of the timing program results from our need to estimate average rather than worst case time. This difference makes it possible to try many more instances of a given characteristic. Program 11.21 is the modified version of Program 11.19 to use when estimating average time.

Whether we are estimating worst case or average time using random data, the number of instances that we can try is generally much smaller than the total number of such instances. Hence, it is desirable to analyze the algorithm being tested to determine classes of data that should be generated for the experiment. This is a very algorithm specific task and we shall not go into it here.

11.11. EXERCISES

1. Compare the run times of the recursive and iterative programs given in Chapter 7 to find a path in a maze. Do this for mazes of size 10, 20, 30, ..., 100. For each size, generate at least 10 sample mazes and compute the average time over the sample.

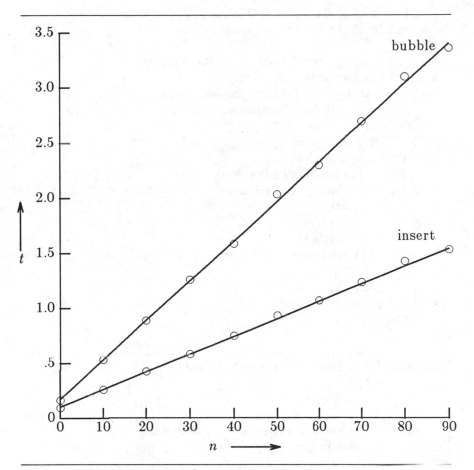

Figure 11.29 Plot of rate of growth of computing time

2. Modify the iterative program given in Chapter 7 to find a path in
    a maze so that it does not use a boundary wall of ones. Instead,
    you should explicitly check for the maze boundary. Obtain run
    times for the two versions of the program. These are to be
    obtained as described in the previous exercise. Compute the per-
    cent change resulting from using a boundary wall.

```
for j := 1 to 15 do {obtain computing times}
begin
   for i := 1 to n[j] do a[i].key := i; {Initialize a}
   tmax := 0; {maximum time so far}
   for i := 1 to p[j] do {for each permutation}
      permute(a, n[j]); {random permutation}
      time(h, m, s, f);
      for b := 1 to r[j] do
      begin
         {Set initial permutation for sort}
         for l := 1 to n[j] do z[l].key := a[l].key;
         bubble(z, n[j]);
      end;
      time(h1, m1, s1, f1);
      t1 := (((h1 - h)*60 + m1 - m)*60 + s1 - s)*100 + f1 - f;
      t := t1; t := t/r[j];
      if t > tmax then tmax := t;
   end; {of permutations loop}
   writeln(n[j]:5, ' ', tmax:9:3);
end;
```

Program 11.19 Timing program to estimate worst case run time

```
procedure permute(var a: ElementList; n:integer);
{Random permutation generator}
var i, j: integer; k: element;
begin
   for i := n downto 2 do
   begin
      j := random(i) + 1;  {j := random integer in the range [1, i]}
      k := a[j]; a[j] := a[i]; a[i] := k;
   end;
end; {of permute}
```

Program 11.20 Random permutation generator

```
for j := 1 to 15 do {obtain computing times}
begin
  {Initialize z}
  for i := 1 to n[j] do z[i].key := i;
  time(h, m, s, f);
  for b := 1 to r[j] do
  begin
    permute(z, n[j]); {new permutation to sort}
    bubble(z, n[j]);
  end;
  time(h1, m1, s1, f1);
  t1 := (((h1 − h)*60 + m1 − m)*60 + s1 − s)*100 + f1 − f;
  t := t1; t := t/r[j];
  writeln(n[j]:5, ' ', t:9:3);
end;
end.
```

Program 11.21 Estimating average time

3. Rewrite Program 8.1 using the strategy used to obtain Program 11.9 from Program 8.3. Measure the worst case times for the two recursive programs. Use the same values of n as used in Program 11.3. Compute the percent difference for each n.

4. Rewrite Program 6.13 so that it begins by copying the n values in a into a local variable b of type *ElementList*. Then, it sorts b. Finally, the sorted elements are copied from b into a. This reduces the worst case number of references to the variable parameter a from $\Theta(n^2)$ to $\Theta(n)$. Measure the worst case run times of the two programs for the values of n given in Program 11.3. What is the percent difference in the times?

5. Compare the average run times of Programs 11.16 and 11.17. Do this for suitable values of n in the range $[0, 100]$. For each value of n generate as many random sequences (use Program 11.20) to sort as is feasible. Your report must include a plan for the experiment as well as the measured times. These times are to be provided both in a table and as a graph. The table must show the percent difference in times. The graphs for both programs should be drawn on the same graph sheet.

6. Use the random permutation generator of Program 11.20 and the test Program 11.19 to estimate the worst case run times for insert sort. Use the same values of n as used in Figure 11.25. For each value of n, use 10 random initial permutations. Compare the worst case estimates obtained using this method to the times obtained using actual worst case data.

7. Repeat the previous exercise for average case times. The number of initial permutations to use is the larger of 10 and the number required to bring the event time up to the desired value for your computer and clock.

8. Use the random permutation generator of Program 11.20 and the test Program 11.19 to estimate the worst case run times for bubble sort. Use the same values of n as used in Figure 11.25. For each value of n, use 10 random initial permutations. Compare the worst case estimates obtained using this method to the times obtained using actual worst case data.

9. Repeat the previous exercise for average case times. The number of initial permutations to use is the larger of 10 and the number required to bring the event time up to the desired value for your computer and clock.

10. [Select sort] In a selection sort, the n elements to be sorted are examined and the one with largest key found. This element is exchanged with the element currently at position n. Now, we need to sort the first $n-1$ elements. This is done in a similar way.

    (a) Write a recursive procedure for selection sort. This should have the same parameters as the procedures for bubble and insert sort.

    (b) Transform the recursive procedure obtained in part (a) into an iterative one. Do this by replacing the recursion with a **while** loop.

    (c) Determine the worst case time complexity of your iterative sort procedure. Use n (number of elements) and s (size of an element) as the instance characteristics.

(d) What is the complexity if the input data is already sorted?

(e) What can you say about the relative performance of insert, bubble, and selection sort for worst case and average behavior?

(f) Compare the actual performance of the iterative versions of the three sort algorithms. Do this by using actual worst case data to measure worst case performance. Use the estimating technique for average case performance. What conclusions can you draw from your experiment?

11. Write a procedure to add two $n \times n$ matrices together. Assume that the data type matrix is defined as:

type *matrix* = **array** [1..*MaxSize*, 1..*MaxSize*] **of real**;

(a) What is the time complexity of your procedure?

(b) Obtain run times for $n = 1, 10, 20, ..., 100$.

(c) Plot the times obtained in part (b).

(d) Obtain the least squares quadratic approximation to your data. Compare the times computed from this equation to the observed times.

12. Do the previous exercise for matrix multiplication. This time obtain a cubic approximation to the data.

CHAPTER 12

DATA STRUCTURES

12.1. INTRODUCTION

A *data object* is a set of *instances* or *values*. Some examples are:
1. *Boolean* = {**true**, **false**}
2. *Digit* = {0, 1, 2, 3, 4, 5, 6, 7, 8, 9}
3. *Letter* = {A, B, C, ..., Z, a, b, ..., z}
4. *NaturalNumber* = {0, 1, 2, ...}
5. *Integer* = {0, ±1, ±2, ±3, ...}
6. *String* = {a, b, ..., aa, ab, ac, ...}

We may regard the individual instances of a data object as being either *primitive* (or *atomic*) or as being composed of instances of another (possibly the same) data object. In the latter case, we use the term *element* to refer to the individual components of an instance of an object.

For example, each instance of the data object *NaturalNumber* can be regarded as atomic. In this case, we are not concerned with a further decomposition of the instances comprising this data object. Another view is to regard each instance of a *NaturalNumber* as being composed of several instances of the data object *Digit*. In this view, the number 675 is composed of the elements 6, 7, and 5 (in that

478

order).

The data object *stack* is the set of all possible stack instances. Each instance of a stack is composed of elements. Three instances are shown in Figure 6.6. The instance of Figure 6.6(a) is composed of the four elements A, B, C, D. Each of these is an instance of the data object *Letter*. The instance of Figure 6.6(b) is composed of five elements while that of Figure 6.6(c) is composed of two elements. The instance *empty stack* is composed of zero elements.

The instances of a data object as well as the elements that compose individual instances are generally related in some way. For example, the natural number 0 is the smallest natural number, 1 is the next, 2 is the next, etc. In the natural number 675, 6 is the most significant digit, 7 is the next, and 5 is the least significant digit. In the stack instance of Figure 6.6(a), A is the bottom element and D the top. B is on top of A, C on top of B, and D on top of C. The instance of Figure 6.6(b) is obtained from that of Figure 6.6(a) by adding the element E. The instance of Figure 6.6(c) can be obtained from that of Figure 6.6(a) by deleting the elements D and C.

In addition to interrelationships, there is generally a set of functions associated with any data object. These functions may transform one instance of an object into another instance of that object, or into an instance of another data object, or into both. The function could simply create a new instance without transforming the instances from which the new one is created. For example, the function *add* defined on the natural numbers, creates a new natural number which is the sum of the two numbers to be added. The two numbers that get added are unaltered. The function *trunc* creates an integer instance obtained by truncating the provided real instance. The real instance is not modified. The function *DeleteFromStack* creates a new stack instance as well as an instance of the elements that compose the stack. The function *AddToStack* takes a stack instance and an instance of the composing elements and creates a new stack instance. Both stack functions transform the initial stack.

A *data structure* is a data object together with the relationships that exist amongst the instances and amongst the individual elements that compose an instance. These relationships are provided by specifying the functions of interest.

When we study data structures, we are concerned with the representation of data objects (actually of the instances) as well as the implementation of the functions of interest for the data objects. The representation of each data object should be such as to facilitate an efficient[1] implementation of the functions.

The most frequently used data objects together with the frequently used functions are already implemented in Pascal as a standard *data type*. The objects *Integer*, *Real*, etc., fall into this category. All other data objects can be represented using the standard data types and the grouping ability provided by the **record** and **array** features of Pascal.

Our study of data structures is in two parts. This chapter is organized by methods to represent data. The popular data structures: linear list, stack, queue, search table, and deque are used to illustrate the data representation methods. The next chapter is organized by data structures. In that chapter, we study additional data structures that have wide application.

12.2. Formula Based Representation

12.2.1. Introduction

In a *formula based* representation, an array is used to represent the instances of an object. Each position of the array is called a *cell* or *node*. Each cell is large enough to hold one of the elements that comprise an instance of the data object. In some cases, a separate array may be used for each instance while in other cases, all instances may be represented in the same array. Individual elements of an instance are located in the array using a mathematical formula.

---

1. The term efficient is used here in a very liberal sense. It includes performance efficiency as well as measures of the complexity of development and maintenance of associated software.

12.2.2. Linear Lists

Definition

A *linear list* is a data object whose instances are of the form $(a_1, a_2, ..., a_n)$ where n is a natural number. The a_i's are the elements of the list. These may be viewed as atomic as their individual structure is not relevant to the structure of the list. When $n = 0$, the list is *empty*. When $n > 0$, a_1 is the first element and a_n the last.   We say that a_1 comes before (or precedes) a_2, a_2 comes before a_3, etc. Other than this precedence relation, no other structure exists in a linear list.

The most common functions performed on a linear list are:
1.   Create a linear list.
2.   Determine the length of a list (i.e., the number of elements in it).
3.   Delete the kth element.
4.   Insert a new element before or after the kth.
5.   Search the list for an element with a particular characteristic.

Representation

In a formula based representation of a linear list, we can use one array for each list to be represented. We can, for instance, define the data type *LinearList* as below:

type *LinearList* = **array** [1..*MaxElements*] **of** *element*;

where *element* is the type of each element in the list and *MaxElements* is the largest number of elements any list can have. If we wish to maintain the five lists a, b, c, d, and e, then we need simply create these using the statement:

var a, b, c, d, e: *LinearList*;

Next, we need a mapping of the elements of a list to positions in the array used to represent it. Where does the first element reside? Where does the second reside? Etc. In a formula based representation, a mathematical formula determines the location of each element. The simplest formula to use is:

$$location(i) = i \qquad\qquad (12.1)$$

which simply states that the ith element of the list (if it exists) is in position i of the array. Figure 12.1(a) shows a five element list represented in the array a using this mapping. This figure assumes that each element is of type **char**. To completely specify the list, we also need to know the position of the last element. Let us use the variable $aLast$ for this purpose. When the list is empty, $aLast = 0$.

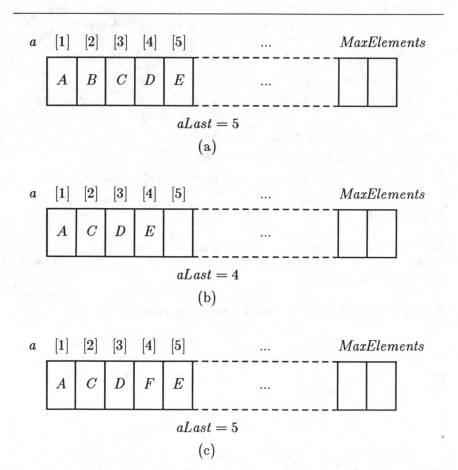

Figure 12.1 Linear lists

Functions

The length of a list x is readily seen to be the value of $xLast$. To delete the kth element from the list x, we need to first ascertain that the list contains a kth element and then delete this element. This deletion requires us to move elements $k+1$, $k+2$, ..., $xLast$ down one position and to reduce the value of $xLast$ by 1. For example, to delete the second element (B) from the list a of Figure 12.1(a), the elements C, D, and E have to be moved to positions 2, 3, and 4, respectively. The list following the deletion is shown in Figure 12.1(b). The value of $aLast$ following the deletion is 4.

Program 12.1 is a procedure that implements the delete function when linear lists are represented using formula (12.1). This procedure is written under the assumption that the deleted element is not to be returned. Notice the defenses introduced to guard against inappropriate values of k. Also, the invoking program is notified in case a delete could not be performed.

```
procedure DeleteFromList(var x: LinearList; var xLast: integer;
                         k: integer; var success: boolean);
{Delete the kth element in the linear list x}
var i: integer;
begin
  if (k < 1) or (k > xLast)
  then success := false {no kth element}
  else begin
        {Move elements k+1 through xLast one position down}
        for i := k+1 to xLast do
          x[i-1] := x[i];
        xLast := xLast - 1; success := true;
      end;
end; {of DeleteFromList}
```

Program 12.1 Deletion from a linear list

To insert a new element after the kth element in the list x, we need to first move elements $k+1$ through $xLast$ one position up and then insert the new element in position $k+1$. For example, inserting F after the third element of the list of Figure 12.1(b) results in the list of

Figure 12.1(c). The complete procedure for this is given in Program 12.2. Once again, notice the defenses against boundary errors.

---

procedure *InsertIntoList*(**var** *x*: *LinearList*; **var** *xLast*: **integer**;
  e: *element*; *k*: **integer**; **var** *success*: **boolean**);
{Insert element *e* after the *k*th element in list *x*}
var *i*: **integer**;
begin
  if ($k < 0$) **or** ($k > xLast$) **or** ($xLast = MaxElements$)
  then *success* := **false**
  else begin
      {Move elements $k+1$ through *xLast* one position up}
      for *i* := *xLast* **downto** $k+1$ **do**
        $x[i+1] := x[i]$;
      $x[k+1] := e$;
      xLast := *xLast* + 1; *success* := **true**;
    end;
end; {of *InsertIntoList*}

Program 12.2 Insertion into a linear list

A sequential search can be used to find elements that have any given characteristic. The required program is quite similar to Program 8.4. This requires an additional position 0 in each list. If we cannot afford this additional space, we can use the function given in Program 11.10. This, however, has a poorer time performance.

Performance Evaluation

Before accepting this representation of a linear list, let us reflect on its merits. Certainly, the functions to be performed on a linear list can be implemented as very simple Pascal programs. The programs to insert, delete, and search have a worst complexity that is linear in the size of the individual list. We might regard this as quite satisfactory (later, we shall see a representation that allows us to perform these operations faster).

A negative aspect of this representation is its usage of space. The amount of space allocated to each linear list is equal to the maximum amount needed by any list. If we have space available for at most 5,000 elements and we wish to maintain five lists, then no individual list can have more than 1,000 elements in it at any time. This is not very desirable when the five lists can be of very different size. If we know before hand that the lists will, respectively, have a maximum size of 200, 400, 500, 900, and 3000 elements, then we can allocate our available space accordingly. This will, however, require the use of five different data types.

The separate arrays for separate lists representation does not represent a satisfactory utilization of space. To see this, consider the following situation. We are to maintain three lists. We know that the three lists together will never have more than 5,000 elements in them at any time. However, it is quite possible for one to have 5,000 at one time and another to have 5,000 at another time.

To allow for this situation, it is necessary to represent all our lists in a single array using front and last pointers to tell us where each list begins and ends. Figure 12.2 shows three lists represented in the single array *list*. We adopt the convention that the lists are numbered 1 through m if there are m lists and that $first[i]$ is actually one less than the actual position of the first element in list i. This convention on $first[i]$ makes it easier to use the representation. $last[i]$ is the actual position of the last element in list i. Notice that with this convention, $last[i] > first[i]$ whenever the ith list is not empty. We shall have $first[i] = last[i]$ whenever list i is empty. So, in the example of Figure 12.2, list 2 is empty. The lists are represented in the array in the order 1, 2, 3, ..., m.

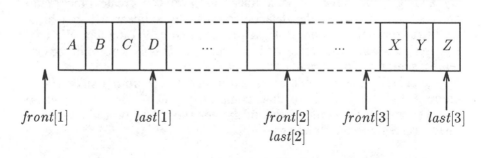

Figure 12.2 All lists in a single array

To avoid having to handle the first and last lists differently from others, we define two boundary lists 0 and $m+1$. The *first* and *last* values for these are: $first[0] = last[0] = 0$ and $first[m+1] = last[m+1] = MaxElements + 1$.

Suppose we wish to insert an element following the kth element of list i. We need to first create space for the new element. In case $last[i] = first[i+1]$, then there is no space between lists i and $i+1$ and we cannot move elements $k+1$ through the last one one position up. At this time, we can check if it is possible to move elements 1 through $k-1$ of the ith list one position down. This is so iff $last[i-1] < first[i]$. If this is not so, then we need to either shift some of the lists 1 through $i-1$ down or some of the lists $i+1$ through m up and create space for list i to grow. This is possible so long as the total number of elements in all the lists is fewer than *MaxElements*.

Program 12.3 is a pseudo Pascal version of the procedure to insert an element into list i. This may be refined into a Pascal procedure.

While all the lists in a single array representation uses space in a more efficient manner than used by the one list per array representation, insertions take more time in the worst case. In fact, a single insertion could require us to move *MaxElements* -1 elements. We shall later see other representations that avoid this difficulty.

12.2.3. Stacks

By adding more structure to a linear list, we can create other data objects. For example, the data object stack is a linear list in which additions and deletions are restricted to one end called the top. We can represent a stack in an array as in Chapter 6. This is a formula based representation. The formula to locate element i (provided $1 \le i \le top$) is (12.1). The procedures to add to and delete from a stack (Programs 6.14 and 6.15) have time complexity $\Theta(1)$. This is considerably better than the complexities of the corresponding procedures for a linear list represented in an array.

Two stacks can be efficiently represented in a single array $stack[1..MaxElements]$, by pegging the bottom of one stack at position 1 and the bottom of the other at position *MaxElements*. The two stacks grow towards the middle of the array (see Figure 12.3). When more

---

procedure *InsertIntoList*(*i*: **integer**; *e*: *element*; *k*: **integer**;
$\qquad\qquad\qquad\qquad$ **var** *success*: **boolean**);
{Insert element *e* after the *k*th element in list *i*}
{*first* and *last* are global}
var *j*, *n*: **integer**;
begin
$\quad$ *n* := *last*[*i*] − *first*[*i*]; {number of elements in list *i*}
$\quad$ **if** (*k* < 0) **or** (*k* > *n*) **then** *success* := **false**
$\quad$ **else begin**
$\qquad\qquad$ {Is there space on the right?}
$\qquad\qquad$ Find the least *j*, *j* ≥ *i* such that *last*[*j*] < *first*[*j*+1];
$\qquad\qquad$ If such a *j* exists, then move lists *i*+1 through *j*
$\qquad\qquad\qquad$ and elements *k*+1 through the last one of list *i* up one position
$\qquad\qquad\qquad$ and insert *e* into list *i*;
$\qquad\qquad$ This move should update appropriate *last* and *first* values;

$\qquad\qquad$ {Is there space on the left?}
$\qquad\qquad$ If no *j* was found above, then find the largest *j*, *j* < *i* such that
$\qquad\qquad\qquad$ *last*[*j*] < *first*[*j*+1];
$\qquad\qquad$ If such a *j* is found, then move lists *j* through *i*−1
$\qquad\qquad\qquad$ and elements 1 through *k*−1 of list *i* one position left
$\qquad\qquad\qquad$ and insert element *e*;
$\qquad\qquad$ This move should update appropriate *last* and *first* values;

$\qquad\qquad$ {Success?}
$\qquad\qquad$ If no *j* was found above set *success* to **false**, otherwise set it to **true**;
$\qquad\quad$ **end**;
end; {of *InsertIntoList*}

Program 12.3 Insertion in the many lists per array representation

than two stacks are to be represented, a scheme similar to that of Figure 12.2 may be used. When this is done, the worst case add time is O(*MaxElements*) rather than $\Theta(1)$. The delete time remains $\Theta(1)$.

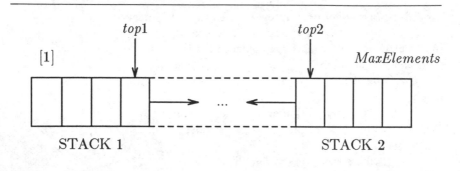

Figure 12.3 Two stacks in an array

12.2.4. Queues

Definition

A *queue* is a linear list in which additions take place at one end (called the *rear*) and deletions take place at the other end (called the front). So, a queue is a first-in-first-out (FIFO) list while a stack is a last-in-first-out (LIFO) list. We shall see some applications of queues in subsequent chapters.

Representation and Functions

We may represent a queue in an array using formula 12.1. Figure 12.4(a) shows a queue with three elements in it. The representation of Figure 12.4(b) results when one element is deleted from the queue of Figure 12.4(a). Adding an element to the queue of Figure 12.4(b) results in the queue shown in Figure 12.4(c).

The procedures to add to and delete from a queue that is represented in an array using formula (12.1) are simpler than the corresponding procedures for a linear list (Programs 12.1 and 12.2). However, the time complexity of the delete procedure is $\Theta(n)$ and that of the add procedure is $\Theta(1)$ where n is the number of elements in the queue. This is not quite as good as the complexities for a stack. We leave the writing of these procedures as an exercise.

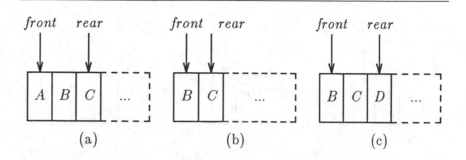

Figure 12.4 Queues using formula 12.1

A more efficient delete procedure results if we use the formula:

$$location(i) = location(1) + i - 1 \qquad (12.2)$$

When this formula is used, there is no need to shift the queue one position left each time an element is deleted from the queue. Instead, we simply increase *location*(1) by 1. Let us use the variables *front* and *rear* to keep track of the present location of the two ends of a queue. We adopt the convention that *front* = *location*(1) − 1 rather than *front* = *location*(1). This will simplify our add and delete procedures. Figure 12.5 shows the representation of the queues of Figure 12.4 that results when formula (12.2) is used in place of (12.1).

With the conventions stated above, a queue is empty iff *front* = *rear*. We may initialize these variables to zero. In this case, the first element to get inserted into the queue is placed in position 1.

As can be seen from Figure 12.5(b), each deletion causes *front* to move right by 1. Hence, there will be times when *rear* = *MaxElements* and *front* > 0. At these times, the queue is not full and there is space for additional elements at the left end of the array. To continue adding to the queue, we can shift all elements to the left end of the queue (as in Figure 12.6) and create space at the right end. This increases the worst case add time from $\Theta(1)$ when formula (12.1) is used to $\Theta(n)$ when formula (12.2) is used. So, the improved efficiency of a delete has been obtained at the expense of a loss of

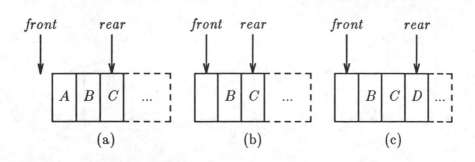

Figure 12.5 Queues using formula 12.2

efficiency for an addition.

Programs 12.4 and 12.5 are the add and delete programs that result when formula (12.2) is used and we opt to shift the queue to the left end when necessary. These handle unsuccessful additions and deletes differently from the corresponding procedures for a linear list. The particular application will determine whether failures should result in program termination or whether the invoking program should be notified of the failure.

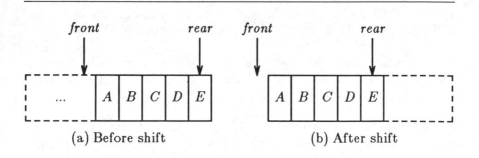

Figure 12.6 Shifting a queue

```
procedure  AddToQueue(x: element);
{Add to the global queue queue.  Formula (12.2) is used.}
var i: integer;
begin
  if rear = MaxElements
  then if front = 0 then begin
                          writeln('Queue Overflow');
                          goto 999; {end of program}
                       end
       else begin {shift queue left by front}
              for i := front+1 to rear do
                 queue[i−front] := queue[i];
              rear := rear−front; front := 0;
           end;
  rear := rear + 1;
  queue[rear] := x;
end; {of AddToQueue}
```

Program 12.4 Add to a queue

```
procedure DeleteFromQueue(var x: element);
{Delete when formula (12.2) is used}
begin
  if front = rear then begin {Queue empty}
                         writeln('Delete from an empty queue');
                         goto 999; {end of program}
                       end;
  front := front + 1;
  x := queue[front];
end; {of DeleteFromQueue}
```

Program 12.5 Delete from a queue

Some improvement in performance can be obtained by modifying procedure *DeleteFromQueue* so that following a deletion, it sets *front* = *rear* = 0 whenever the queue becomes empty. This will often reduce the number of times the add procedure has to shift the queue to the left end.

Circular Representation

The worst case add and delete times can both be made $\Theta(1)$ by using the formula:

$$location(i) = (location(1) + i - 2)\mathbf{mod}MaxElements + 1 \quad (12.3)$$

where $x\mathbf{mod}\, y$ is the remainder of x divided by y, $y \neq 0$.

   In this case, the array in which the queue is represented is regarded as circular (Figure 12.7). Adding an element to the queue of Figure 12.7(a) results in the queue of Figure 12.7(b). Deleting an element from the queue of Figure 12.7(b) results in the queue of Figure 12.7(c).

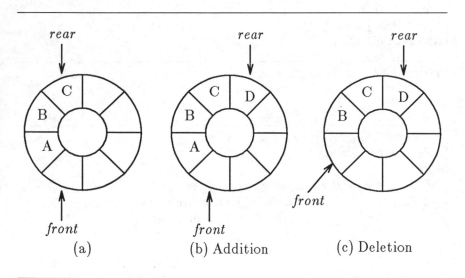

Figure 12.7 Circular Queues

   The variables *front* and *rear* are used with the same conventions as when formula (12.2) is used. A queue is empty iff *front* = *rear*. Initially, we have *front* = *rear* = 0. The remaining boundary condition needed is that for a full queue. If we add elements to the queue of Figure 12.7(b), until it gets full, the configuration of Figure 12.8 is obtained. This has *front* = *rear* which is the same condition as when the queue is empty! So, we cannot distinguish between an empty and a full queue. To avoid this difficulty, we shall not permit a queue to get full. Before adding an element to a queue, we verify if this addition will cause it to get full. If so, a queue full error is given. Hence, the maximum number of elements that can be in the queue is actually *MaxElements* − 1.

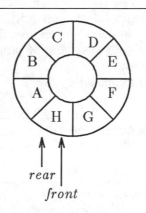

Figure 12.8 A circular queue with *MaxElements*

The procedures to add and delete are given in Programs 12.6 and 12.7. Both assume that *MaxElements* > 1. If this is not so, then the queue is always empty. Both procedures also assume that the program end statement has been assigned the label 999. Hence, the statement "**goto** 999" causes the program to terminate. These **goto** statements may be replaced by the nonstandard statement "**halt**" in case this is available in the Pascal implementation you are using. As can be seen, each procedure has a time complexity that is Θ(1). Also, note that each procedure leaves the global variables *front* and *rear* so that they satisfy the conventions for their values (except in the case of a queue overflow. This causes the program to terminate with an error message. At this time, it doesn't matter that the conventions are violated.).

```
procedure AddToQueue(x: element);
{Add x to the global circular queue queue. MaxElements > 1.}
var i: integer;
begin
   {move rear to position for add}
   if rear = MaxElements then rear := 1
                            else rear := rear +1;
   if front = rear then begin {queue gets full}
                            writeln('Queue Overflow');
                            goto 999; {end of program}
                        end;
   queue[rear] := x; {add to queue}
end; {of AddToQueue}
```

Program 12.6 Add to a circular queue

```
procedure DeleteFromQueue(var x: element);
{Delete from a circular queue. MaxElements > 1.}
begin
   if front = rear then begin {Queue empty}
                            writeln('Delete from an empty queue');
                            goto 999; {end of program}
                        end;
   {Move front clockwise}
   if front = MaxElements then front = 1
                            else front := front + 1;
   x := queue[front];
end; {of DeleteFromQueue}
```

Program 12.7 Delete from a circular queue

12.2.5. Search Table

Definition

A *search table* is a collection of elements. Each element has a field called *key* and no two elements in a table have the same *key* value. The functions to be performed on a search table are:

(1)   Insert an element with a specified key value.

(2)   Search the table for an element with a specified key value.

Representation

A search table can be maintained as a linear list $(e_1, e_2, ...)$ where e_i is the ith element inserted into the table. Additions to this list are made at one end. If formula (12.1) is used, an insertion into the table can be performed using the procedure to add to a stack (Program 6.14). A search can be performed using a sequential search as in Program 8.4. The time complexity of the insertion is $\Theta(1)$ and that of a search is $O(n)$ where n is the number of elements in the table at the time of the search.

An alternate way to represent a search table is as an ordered linear list. In this case, the elements are in increasing order of key values. I.e., $e_1.key < e_2.key < ... < e_n.key$. The formula used in this representation is (12.1). However, i is not the ith element inserted into the table, but is the element with the ith smallest key value.

When this representation is used, insertions can be performed as in procedure *insert* (Program 8.5) and searches as in function *bsearch* (Program 8.6). The time complexity of an insertion is now $O(n)$ while that of a search is $O(\log n)$. Hence, using an ordered list results in better performance than using an unordered list so long as the average number of searches per element is at least 1 or 2. This is so as each element is inserted only once. Note that the number of searches per element is generally guaranteed to be at least 1 as each insertion will normally be preceded by a search to verify that the key value of the new element is, in fact, different from those of existing elements.

Yet another possibility is to use *hashing*. Hashing utilizes a *hash function*. While several different hash functions are in use, hashing by division is most common. In this, the hash function has the form:

$$f(X) = X \bmod D \qquad (12.4)$$

where X is the key value of the element and D is the size of array in which the table is being maintained. When hashing is used, this array is called the *hash table*. The positions in the hash table table are

indexed 0 through *MaxElements* − 1 and *D* = *MaxElements*. Each position is called a *bucket*. In case the key values are not numeric, they
will need to be converted to numbers before $f(X)$ can be computed.
$f(X)$ is the *home bucket* for the element with key value *X*. Under
ideal circumstances, this is the location of the element with key value
X.

Functions

Figure 12.9(a) shows a hash table with 11 positions in it. These are
numbered 0 through 10 and the array name is *ht*. This table contains
three elements. The divisor *D* to use is 11. The 80 is in position 3 as
80 **mod** 11 = 3; the 40 is in position 40 **mod** 11 = 7; and the 65 is in
position 65 **mod** 11 = 10. Each element is in its home bucket. The
remaining buckets in the hash table are empty.

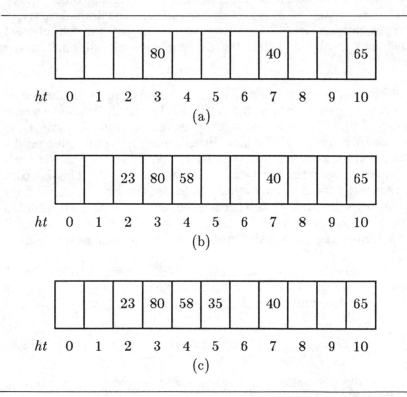

Figure 12.9 Hash tables

Now, suppose we wish to enter the value 58 into the table. The home bucket is $f(58) = 58 \bmod 11 = 3$. This bucket is already occupied by a different value. We say that a *collision* has occurred. In general, a bucket may contain space for more than one element so a collision may not create any difficulties. An *overflow* occurs in case there isn't place in the home bucket for the new element. Since each bucket of our table has space for only one element, collisions and overflows occur at the same time. Where shall we insert 58? The easiest thing to do is search the table for the next available bucket and place 58 into it. This method of handling overflows is called *linear open addressing*.

The 58 gets inserted into position 4. Suppose that the next value to be inserted is 23. $23 \bmod 11$ is 2. This bucket is empty and so the 23 is placed into it. Our hash table now has the form shown in Figure 12.9(b). Let us attempt to insert the value 35 into this table. Its home bucket (2) is full. Using linear open addressing, this value is placed in the next available bucket and the table of 12.9(c) results. As a final example, consider inserting 98 into the table. Its home bucket (10) is full. The next available bucket is 0 and the insertion is made into this bucket. So, the search for the next available bucket is made by regarding the table as circular!

Program 12.8 is the resulting function to search a hash table when linear open addressing is used. This function assumes that all buckets in the table are initialized to have a key value $-\mathbf{maxint}$ and that no legitimate element has this key value. In case the key value x is found in the table, *HashSearch* is the bucket that contains the element with this key. If no element with key x is in the table, *HashSearch* is the next available bucket or if there is no available bucket (i.e., the table is full) $ht(HashSearch).key \neq -\mathbf{maxint}$.

To insert an element into a hash table, we need to first verify that the table does not already contain an element with the same key. In addition, the table should not be full. The insert procedure is given in Program 12.9. The data type *outcome* is defined as:

type *outcome* $=$ (success, duplicate, full);

---

function *HashSearch*(*x*: **integer**): **integer**;
{Search the hash table, *ht*[0..*MaxElements* − 1]}
{Linear open addressing is used}
var *i*, *j*: **integer**; *done*: **boolean**;
begin
   i := *x* **mod** *MaxElements*; {home bucket}
   j := *i*; *done* := **false**;
   repeat
     if (*ht*[*j*].*key* = *x*) **or** (*ht*[*j*].*key* = −**maxint**)
     then *done* := **true**
     else *j* := (*j*+1) **mod** *MaxElements*; {next bucket}
   until (*j*=*i*) **or** *done*;
   HashSearch := *j*;
end; {of *HashSearch*}

Program 12.8 Searching a hash table

---

procedure *HashInsert*(*e*: *element*; **var** *result*: *outcome*);
{Insert element *e* into the hash table *ht*[0:*MaxElements* − 1]}
var *i*: **integer**;
begin
   i := *HashSearch*(*e*.*key*);
   if *ht*(*i*).*key* = − **maxint**
   then begin *ht*[*i*] := *e*; *result* := success; **end**
   else if *ht*[*i*].*key* = *e*.*key* **then** *result* := duplicate
      else *result* := full;
end; {of *HashInsert*}

Program 12.9 Inserting into a hash table

Performance Analysis

We shall analyze the time complexity only. The worst case insert and search time is $\Theta(n)$ when n elements are present in the table. This happens, for instance, when all n key values have the same home bucket. Comparing this to the previous two methods to maintain a search table, we see that the others are at least as good.

For average performance, however, hashing is considerably superior. Let U_n and S_n, respectively, denote the average number of buckets examined during an unsuccessful and a successful search. This average is defined over all possible sequences of n key values being inserted into the table. For linear open addressing, it can be shown that:

$$U_n \approx \frac{1}{2} \left(1 + \frac{1}{(1-\alpha)^2} \right)$$

$$S_n \approx \frac{1}{2} \left(1 + \frac{1}{1-\alpha} \right)$$

where $\alpha = n/MaxElements$ is the *loading factor*.

So, if α is 0.5, an unsuccessful search will examine 2.5 buckets on the average while an average successful search will examine 1.5 buckets. When $\alpha = 0.9$, these figures are 50.5 and 5.5. These figures, of course, assume that n is at least this large. When it is possible to work with small loading factors (say about 0.5), the average performance of hashing with linear open addressing is superior to that of the other two methods discussed.

Determining D

In practice, it is found that the performance of hashing is significantly affected by the choice of the divisor D (cf. (12.4)). Best results are obtained when D (and therefore *MaxElements*) is either a prime number or has *no prime factors less than 20*.

To determine D, we first determine what constitutes acceptable performance for unsuccessful and successful searches. Using the formulas for U_n and S_n, we can determine the largest α that can be used. From the value of n (or an estimate) and the computed value of α, we obtain the smallest permissible value for *MaxElements*. Next, the smallest integer that is at least as large as this value and which either is a prime or has no factors smaller than 20 is found. This is the value of D and *MaxElements* to use.

Example 12.1: We are to design a hash table for up to 1000 elements. Successful searches on the average should require no more than 4 bucket examinations and unsuccessful searches should examine no more than 50.5 buckets on the average. From the formula for U_n we obtain $\alpha \leq 0.9$ and from that for S_n, we obtain $4 \geq 0.5 + 1/(2(1-\alpha))$ or $\alpha \leq 6/7$. So, we require $\alpha \leq \min\{0.9, 6/7\} = 6/7$. Hence, *MaxElements* should be at least $\lceil 7n/6 \rceil = 1167$. *MaxElements* $= D = 37*37 = 1369$ is a suitable choice. □

Another way to compute D is to begin with a knowledge of the largest possible value for *MaxElements* (this is determined from the maximum amount of space available for the hash table). Now, we find the largest D no larger than this largest value that is either a prime or has no factors smaller than 20. For instance, if we can allot at most 530 buckets to the table, then $23*23 = 529$ is the right choice for D and *MaxElements*.

12.3. LINKED REPRESENTATION

12.3.1. Introduction

As in the case of a formula based representation, each element of an instance of a data object is represented in a cell or node. The nodes, however, need not be components of an array and no formula is used to locate individual elements. Instead, each node keeps explicit information about the location of other relevant nodes. This explicit information about the location of another node is called a *link*. When a linked representation is used, the node size is larger than when a formula based representation is used. This is so as each node must be able to hold both the data element and the links.

In standard Pascal, linked representations are supported by the procedures *new* and *dispose*. These, respectively, provide a new node and dispose of an old one. *pointer*s are used to represent links.

Some implementations of Pascal do not provide the procedure *dispose*. Instead, they provide the procedures *mark* and *release*. *mark(x)* records, in x, the current top of the *storage heap* and *release(x)* resets the current top of the storage heap to x. This, effectively, disposes of all nodes that were requested since the invocation *mark(x)*.

Yet other implementations provide both the *dispose* procedure as well as the *mark* and *release* procedures. Only one of these methods may, however, be used at once. Turbo Pascal (versions 2.0 and above) on the IBM-PC is an example.

12.3.2. Linear Lists

Chain Representation

Let $L = (a_1, a_2, ...,a_n)$ be a linear list. In one possible linked representation for this list, each element a_i is represented in a separate node. Each node has exactly one link field which is used to locate the next element in the linear list. So, the node for a_i links to that for a_{i+1}, $1 \leq i < n$. The node for a_n has no node to link to. This is represented by setting the link field for the corresponding node to **nil**. A pointer variable (say l) is used to locate the first node in the representation. We use the name of this variable to refer to the list. The statements "the list l" and "the list that l points to" are equivalent. The linked representation of list L is shown in Figure 12.10.

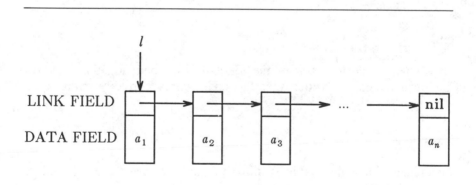

Figure 12.10 Chain representation of a linear list

There are many names for the linked structure of Figure 12.10. Since each node has exactly one link, it is called a *singly linked list*. Also, since the first node links to the second; the second to the third; ...; and the last has a **nil** link, the structure is called a *chain*.

The structure of Figure 12.10 can be created by first defining the data types *ListNode* and *ListPointer* as below:

type *ListPointer* = ↑ *ListNode*;
     ListNode = **record**
                    data: *element*;
                    link: *ListPointer*;
                end;

Then, the variables *l* and *x* are declared to be of type *ListPointer* as below:

var *l*, *x*: *ListPointer*;

The code:

```
l := nil;
for i := n downto 1 do
begin
   new(x);
   x ↑ .data := a_i;
   x ↑ .link := l;
   l := x;
end;
```

gets a new node for each of the a_is and links them together to form the desired chain. Notice that the code works correctly even when $n < 1$.

Functions

To create a linear list *l* that is initially empty, we need merely declare the variable *l* as below:

var *l*: *ListPointer*;

and initialize its value to **nil**.

To search the list *l* for an element with key value *x*, we begin at the first node and move down the list one node at a time. The key field of each node is compared with *x*. Program 12.10 implements this strategy. It returns **nil** if the search is unsuccessful, otherwise it returns a pointer to the node that has the key value x.

---

function *search*(l: *ListPointer*; x: **integer**): *ListPointer*;
{Search the linked list l for a node with key x}
var p: *ListPointer*; *NotFound*: **boolean**;
begin
   p := l; *NotFound* := **true**;
   while (p <>nil) **and** *NotFound* **do**
     if $p \uparrow .data.key = x$ **then** *NotFound* := **false**
     else p := $p \uparrow .link$;
   search := p;
end; {of *search*}

Program 12.10 Searching a linked list

     The complexity of Program 12.10 is seen to be $O(n)$ where n is the length of the list l (i.e., number of nodes on the list). In this program, we explicitly check for the right end of the list. This kind of check is avoided when a formula based representation (i.e., using (12.1)) is used by introducing a new element at position 0 (see Program 8.4). Can this be done for a chain representation? Consider the chain of Figure 12.10. We need to add a node immediately following the node for a_n and set the key value of this node to x. To find the other end of the list, we have to move down the list one node at a time. Once this end has been found, we can introduce a new node here. The time needed to do this is larger than the expected savings from eliminating the test p <> **nil** from Program 12.10.

Circular Representation

One way around this difficulty is to link the last node in the representation of Figure 12.10 to the first as in Figure 12.11(a). This converts the chain into a *circularly linked list* (or *circular list* for short). In addition, the convention for the list pointer l is changed so that it points to the last rather than the first node in the list.

     The search begins by introducing a new node at the front as in Figure 12.11(b). When the search is complete, the newly introduced node is deleted and disposed of. The details are spelled out in Program 12.11.

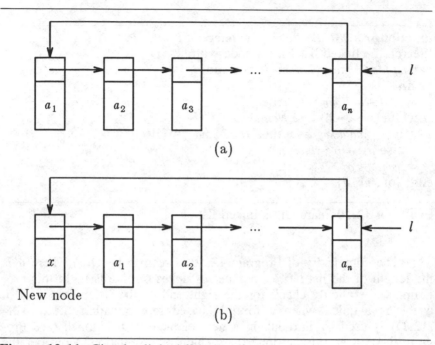

Figure 12.11 Circular linked lists

We can go one step further and require that each circular list have an extra node, called a *head node*, present at the front. The use of *head nodes* is a very common practice when linked lists are used. Their presence generally leads to simpler and faster programs. In addition, the test for a list being empty (**if** $l <>$ **nil**; cf. Program 12.11) is eliminated as each list has at least one node, the head node. Figure 12.12 shows two circular lists with head nodes. The first is an empty list and the second contains n, $n > 0$, elements.

The search program (Program 12.11) can now be simplified to Program 12.12. This returns a pointer to the head node (rather than **nil** in case the search is unsuccessful.

Delete

Next, let us consider the deletion function. We assume a chain representation with no head node. To delete the fourth node from the

---

function *search(l*: *ListPointer*; *x*: **integer**): *ListPointer*;
{Search the circularly linked list *l* for a node with key *x*}
var *p*: *ListPointer*;
begin
  if *l* <> **nil then** {list not empty}
  begin

      {Introduce new node at front of list}
      new(p); *p* ↑ *.data.key* := *x*;
      p ↑ *.link* := *l* ↑ *.link*; *l* ↑ *.link* := *p*;

      {search list}
      p := *p* ↑ *.link*; {first node for comparison}
      while *p* ↑ *.data.key* <> *x* **do**
        p := *p* ↑ *.link*;
      if *p* = *l* ↑ *.link*
      then *search* = **nil** {*p* is at front node}
      else *search* := *p*;

      {Delete front node}
      p := *l* ↑ *.link*; *l* ↑ *.link* := *p* ↑ *.link*; *dispose(p)*;
  end
  else *search* := **nil**; {list empty}
end; {of *search*}

Program 12.11 Searching a circularly linked list

list of Figure 12.13, we do the following:

(1) Locate the third and fourth nodes. To do this, we begin at the first node *l* and move down the list one node at a time until we reach the fourth.

(2) Link the third node to the fifth. The location of the fifth node is available from the link field of the fourth node.

(3) Dispose of the fourth node so that it becomes available for subsequent reuse.

We can generalize the above steps to obtain Program 12.13 which deletes the *k*th element from a linear list *l* that is represented as a chain.

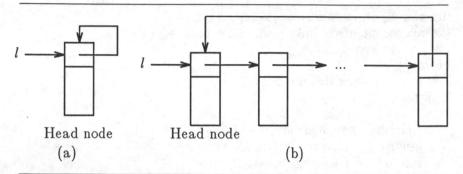

Head node
(a)

Head node
(b)

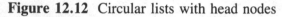

Figure 12.12 Circular lists with head nodes

---

function *search*(*l*: *ListPointer*; *x*: **integer**): *ListPointer*;
{Search a circularly linked list with head node for a node with key *x*}
var *p*: *ListPointer*;
begin
   l ↑ .*data.key* := *x*; {put *x* into head node}
   p := *l* ↑ .*link*; {first node for comparison}
   while *p* ↑ .*data.key* <> *x* **do**
     p := *p* ↑ .*link*;
   search := *p*;
end; {of *search*}

Program 12.12 Searching a circular linked list with head node

To check the correctness of this program, try it out on an initially empty list as well as on lists that contain at least one node. In addition, try out values of k such as $k \leq 0$, $k =$ list length, $k \geq$ list length, and $0 < k <$ list length. Modifying the insert program so that it works when l is a circular list with a head node is left as an exercise.

Insert

The final function we consider is that of insertion. To insert a new element immediately following the kth in a chain, we need to first locate the kth element and then insert a new node just after it. The link changes needed for the two cases $k = 0$ and $k \neq 0$ are shown in Figure 12.14. Program 12.14 performs an insertion.

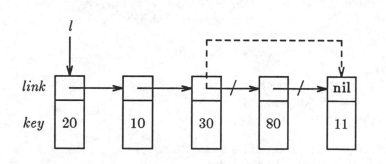

Figure 12.13 Deleting the fourth node

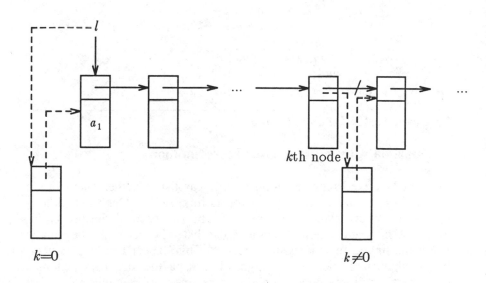

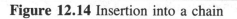

Figure 12.14 Insertion into a chain

---

procedure *DeleteFromList*(**var** *l*: *ListPointer*; *k*: **integer**;
                                var *success*: **boolean**);
{Delete the *k*th element in *l*}
var *p*, *q*: *ListPointer*; *NotDone*: **boolean**;
begin
  p := *l*; {present node}
  q := **nil**; {previous node}
  NotDone := **true**; *i* := 1;

  {Move *p* to *k*th node and *q* to *k*−1th node}
  while (*i* < *k*) **and** *NotDone* **do**
    if *p* = **nil then** *NotDone* := **false**
    else {move *p* and *q* one node right}
    begin *q* := *p*; *p* := *p* ↑ .*link*; *i* := *i*+1; **end**;

  if *NotDone* **then** *success* := **false** {no *k*th node}
            else begin
                  if *k* = 1 **then** *l* := *l* ↑ .*link*
                          else *q* ↑ .*link* := *p* ↑ .*link*;
                dispose(*p*);
                success := **true**;
            end;
end; {of *DeleteFromList*}

Program 12.13 Deletion from a chain

Comparison with formula based representation

The singly linked representation of a linear list (whether chain or circular) requires additional space for a link field. One link field is needed for every element in the list. The run time of the procedures to insert into and delete from a linear list will generally be smaller when the linked representation is used. This expectation is easily justified when each element is large. Let *s* be the size of an element (i.e., number of components) and *n* the number of elements in the list. The worst case insert and delete time complexity is $\Theta(ns)$ when formula (12.1) is used and $\Theta(n)$ when a chain or circular list is used.

    Even when *s* is small (say 1), the linked representation may outperform the formula based representation. The reason for this is that

---

procedure *InsertList*(**var** *l*: *ListPointer*; *x*:*element*;
　　　　　　　　k: **integer**; **var** *success*: **boolean**);
{Insert *x* after the *k*th node in the chain *l*}
var *p*, *q*: *ListPointer*; *i*: **integer**; *NotDone*: **boolean**;
begin
　if *k* >= 0 **then** {locate *k*th node}
　begin
　　NotDone := **true**; *i* := 1;
　　p := *l*; {*i*th node}

　　{Move *p* to *k*th node}
　　while (*i* < *k*) **and** *NotDone* **do**
　　　if *p* = **nil then** *NotDone* := **false**
　　　else begin *p* := *p* ↑ .*link*; *i* := *i* + 1; **end**;

　　if *NotDone* {list has at least *k* nodes}
　　then if *k*>0
　　　　then begin
　　　　　　new(*q*); *q* ↑ .*data* := *x*;
　　　　　　q ↑ .*link* := *p* ↑ .*link*; *p* ↑ .*link* := *q*;
　　　　　　success := **true**;
　　　　　end
　　　　else begin {insert at front}
　　　　　　new(*q*); *q* ↑ .*data* := *x*;
　　　　　　q ↑ .*link* := *l*; *l* := *q*;
　　　　　　success := **true**;
　　　　　end;
　end {of *k* >= 0}
　else *success* := **false**;
end; {of *InsertList*}

Program 12.14 Insertion into a chain

the overhead of referencing a variable parameter may be larger than that of following a link. This is particularly true if pointers are implemented as absolute memory addresses. We shall provide actual computer times in the next section.

The linked schemes adapt more readily to the case of many lists. In the case of the formula based representations, to utilize space efficiently we have to represent all lists in a single array. This results in more complex procedures for insertion and deletion. These procedures also have a significantly inferior worst case run time. No degradation in performance occurs whether we have one linked list or 100.

A formula based representation has the advantage that the k'th element of the list can be accessed in O(1) time. In a linked list, this operation requires O(k) time.

Summary

In this section the following important concepts have been introduced:

1. *Chain*. This is a singly linked list of nodes. Let l be a chain. l is empty iff $l = $ **nil**. If l is not empty, then l points to the first node in the chain. The first node links to the second; the second to the third; and so on. The link field of the last node is **nil**.

2. *Singly Linked Circular List*. This differs from a chain only in that the last node links back to the first. When the circular list l is empty, $l = $ **nil**.

3. *Head Node*. This is an additional node introduced into a linked list. The use of this additional node generally results in simpler programs as we can often avoid treating the empty list as a special case. When a head node is used, every list (including the empty list) has at least one node in it.

12.3.3. Performance Measurement

We shall compare the run time performance of two procedures to insert an element into a linear list that is ordered by key value. One procedure (Program 12.15) is for the case when the linear list is represented as a chain. This procedure assumes that the nodes are linked in non-increasing order of the key field and that the last node has the key −**maxint**. This last node is called a *tail node*. An example of such a list is given in Figure 12.15.

The other procedure (Program 12.16) is for the case when a formula based representation (formula (12.1)) is used. Since, Program 12.15 assumes that the list has a tail node, Program 12.16 is written under the assumption that position 0 is available and initialized to have the key −**maxint**.

Figure 12.15 Ordered chain with tail node

---

procedure *insert*(**var** *list*: *ListPointer*; *n*: **integer**; *x*: *ListPointer*);
{Insert node *x* into the ordered chain *list*}
var *i*: **integer**; *p*, *q*: *ListPointer*;
begin
  {Find position for *x*}
  p := *list*; *q* := **nil**;
  while *p* ↑ .*data.key* > *x* ↑ .*data.key* **do**
  begin
    q := *p*; *p* := *p* ↑ .*link*;
  end;

  {Insert *x* just before *p*}
  x ↑ .*link* := *p*;
  if *q* = **nil then** *list* := *x*
        else *q* ↑ .*link* := *x*;
end;

Program 12.15 Linked insertion with tail node

Program 12.17 is the timing program used to time the worst case performance of the linked insertion procedure on an IBM-PC. The observed times are reported in Figure 12.16. For the case of Program 12.16, we obtained worst case times using elements of different size *s*. These times are also reported in Figure 12.16. As can be seen, insertion into a linked list is faster even when the element size is just 1. Note that for small *s* using a linked list could be slower with certain Pascal compilers and on certain computers.

```
procedure insert(var a: ElementList; var n: integer; x: element);
var i:integer;
begin
  {Find position for x}
  i := n;
  while a[i].key > x.key do
  begin
    a[i+1] := a[i];
    i := i-1;
  end;

  {Insert x at i+1}
  a[i+1] := x; n := n+1;
end;
```

Program 12.16 Sequential insertion with $a[0].key = -\text{maxint}$

12.3.4. Stacks

Representation and Functions

A stack can be represented as a chain as in Figure 12.17 with the variable *top* pointing to the top node on the stack. We have a choice in terms of whether the nodes are to be linked from top to bottom(as in Figure 12.17(a)) or from bottom to top(as in Figure 12.17(b)). Rather than make this choice arbitrarily, we determine whether one direction of linkage is to be preferred. This is done by comparing the difficulty of performing stack functions with each choice.

Adding a new element to a linked stack involves getting a new node and linking it into the stack. The steps involved are shown by broken lines in Figures 12.18(a) and(b). As far as adding a new element to a stack is concerned, the direction of linkage is immaterial.

To delete an element from a stack, the top node must be removed. Figures 12.18(c) and(d) show the steps for the two linkage directions. It is difficult to delete when the linkage is bottom to top as there is no easy way to access the node immediately below the node being deleted. When the linkage is top to bottom, deletion is easy. So, this linkage direction is to be used.

```
begin
  for j := 1 to 10 do {values of n}
  begin
    n[j] := 10*(j−1);
    n[j+10] := 100*j;
  end;

  {Repetition factors}
  r[1] := 12000; r[2] := 6000; r[3] := 3000; r[4] := 2400; r[5] := 1500;
  r[6] :=1200; r[7] := 1000; r[8] := 1000; r[9] := 1000; r[10] := 800;
  r[11] := 800; r[12] := 350; r[13] := 240; r[14] := 200; r[15] := 160;
  r[16] := 140; r[17] := 120; r[18] := 100; r[19] := 80; r[20] := 60;

  writeln('n':5,'  ','time');
  for j := 1 to 20 do {obtain times}
  begin
    mark(HeapTop);  {save current top of space}
    new(y); y ↑ .link := nil; y ↑ .key := −maxint; {tail node}
    for i := 1 to n[j] do {Create initial list}
    begin
      new(x); x ↑ .key := r[j]+i;
      x ↑ .link := y; y := x;
    end;

    l := r[j]; new(x); x ↑ .key := l; {node to insert}
    time(h, m, s, f);
    for b := 1 to r[j] do
    begin
      insert(y, n[j], x);
      x := y; x ↑ .key := l−b; y := y ↑ .link;
    end;
    time(h1, m1, s1, f1);
    release(HeapTop); {Release all space used}
    t1 := (((h1−h)*60 + m1−m)*60 + s1−s)*100 + f1 − f;
    t := h1; t := t/r[j];
    writeln(n[j]:5,'  ',t:6:3);
  end;
end.
```

Program 12.17 Timing program for linked insertion

n	linked	sequential		
		$s=1$	$s=2$	$s=10$
0	0.044	0.032	0.033	0.044
10	0.127	0.209	0.222	0.359
20	0.209	0.385	0.410	0.681
30	0.293	0.563	0.599	0.998
40	0.377	0.737	0.792	1.318
50	0.457	0.915	0.980	1.647
60	0.539	1.088	1.164	1.956
70	0.626	1.274	1.350	2.264
80	0.708	1.440	1.548	2.592
90	0.789	1.620	1.730	2.910
100	0.872	1.797	1.922	3.240
200	1.711	3.577	3.829	6.411
300	2.537	5.317	5.725	9.617
400	3.380	7.140	7.580	12.860
500	4.225	8.850	9.475	15.925
600	5.029	10.671	11.386	19.286
700	5.867	12.350	13.283	22.333
800	6.700	14.060	15.160	25.720
900	7.550	15.925	17.025	28.800
1000	8.333	17.767	19.033	32.267

Times are in hundredths of a second

Figure 12.16 Worst case times for sequential and linked insertion

Before we can write the programs to add and delete elements, we need to know the initial and boundary values for *top*. The only boundary we need be concerned with is when a stack is empty. The stack can continue to grow so long as procedure *new* is successful. If it is unsuccessful, the program will abort and we don't have much control over this behavior.

Initially, the stack is empty. We would like our boundary condition for an empty stack to be the same as the initial value for *top*. Examining the steps involved in adding to and deleting from a stack, we see that *top* = **nil** is the right choice. With this choice, adding to an empty stack is no different from adding to a non-empty stack. Further, no extra work needs to be done when a deletion results in an

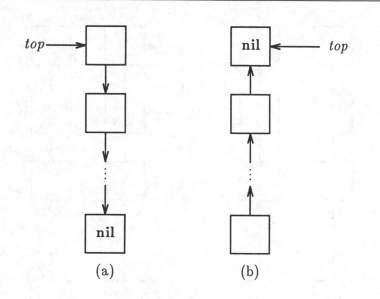

Figure 12.17 Linked stacks

empty stack and when it does not.

Programs 12.18 and 12.19 implement the add and delete schemes suggested by Figures 12.18(a) and (c). Both programs assume the node structure used for linear lists. You can verify that these programs work correctly on stacks that contain 0, 1, and many nodes. Each add and dclete takes $\Theta(1)$ time. As in the case of linear lists, no modifications are needed to handle several stacks. In fact, many stacks and linear lists can coexist. Each can grow until all collectively need more space than is available.

12.3.5. Queues

A queue, like a stack, can be represented as a chain. We need two variables *front* and *rear* to keep track of the two ends of a queue. As in the case of a stack, we have two possibilities for the direction of linkage. The nodes can be linked front to rear (Figure 12.19(a)) or

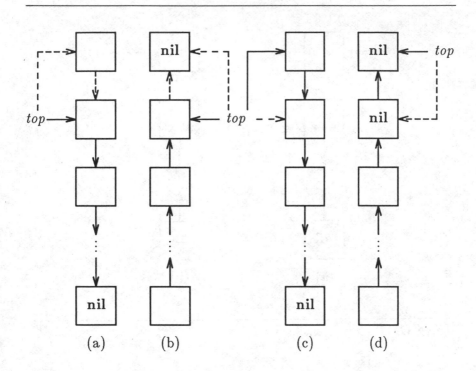

Figure 12.18 Adding to and deleting from a linked stack

```
procedure AddToStack(var top: ListPointer; x: element);
{Add x to the linked stack top}
var y: ListPointer;
begin
    new(y);
    y ↑ .data := x;
    y ↑ .link := top; {link to rest of stack}
    top := y;
end; {of AddToStack}
```

Program 12.18 Add to a linked stack

---

procedure *DeleteFromStack*(**var** *top*: *ListPointer*; **var** *x*: *element*);
{Delete from stack *top*. Return deleted element in *x*}
var *y*: *ListPointer*;
begin
  if *top* = **nil then begin**
                writeln('Deletion from an empty stack');
                goto 999; {end of program}
              end;
  x := *top* ↑ .*data*;
  y := *top*;
  top := *top* ↑ .*link*;
  dispose(*y*);
end; {of *DeleteFromStack*}

Program 12.19 Deletion from a linked stack

rear to front (Figure 12.19(b)). The direction of linkage is again determined by the relative difficulty of performing additions and deletions. Figures 12.20 and 12.21, respectively, illustrate the mechanics of an add and a delete. As can be seen, both linkage directions are well suited for additions. However, for deletions the front to rear linkage is more efficient. Hence, we shall link the nodes in a queue from front to rear.

The initial and boundary values for *front* and *rear* are arrived at following the same reasoning as used for a linked stack. The initial values *front* = *rear* = **nil** and the boundary value *front* = **nil** iff the queue is empty suffice.

Programs 12.20 and 12.21, respectively, implement the add and delete functions of a queue. You may wish to run through these by hand using an empty queue, a queue with one element, and a queue with many elements as examples. The complexity of each is seen· to be $\Theta(1)$. Further, no modifications are needed to handle several queues. In fact, several stacks, queues, and linear lists can coexist.

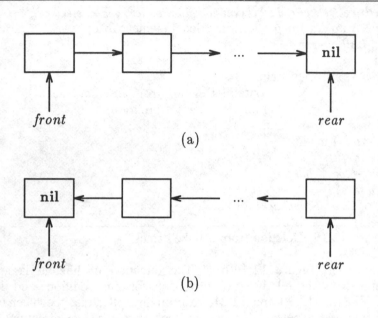

(a)

(b)

Figure 12.19 Linked queues

12.3.6. Deques

Definition

A *deque* is a double ended queue. Additions and deletions can be performed at either end of the linear list. Rather than call the two ends
front and rear as we do for a queue, we shall refer to the two ends of
a deque as the left and right ends. From our discussion on the linked
representation of a queue, we know that regardless of the direction of
linkage (left to right or right to left), additions can be performed at
either end efficiently. However, when a left to right linkage is used,
deletion from the right end is difficult. When a right to left linkage is
used, deletion from the left end is difficult. You may wish to try out
these deletions using Figure 12.19.

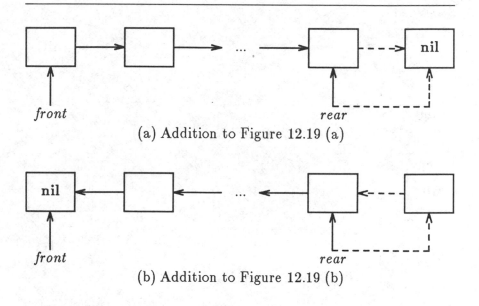

(a) Addition to Figure 12.19 (a)

(b) Addition to Figure 12.19 (b)

Figure 12.20 Additions to linked queues

Doubly Linked Representation

In order to delete efficiently from either end, we need links in both directions as in Figure 12.22. A linked list in which each node has exactly two link fields and in which the nodes are linked left to right as well as right to left is called a *doubly linked list*.

The node structure must now provide for two link fields. We may use the type definitions:

type *DequePointer* = ↑ *DequeNode*;
      DequeNode = **record**
                  data: *element*;
                  LeftLink, *RightLink*: *DequePointer*;
            end;

Figure 12.23 illustrates the mechanics of adding at and deleting from the right end of a deque that is represented as a doubly linked list.

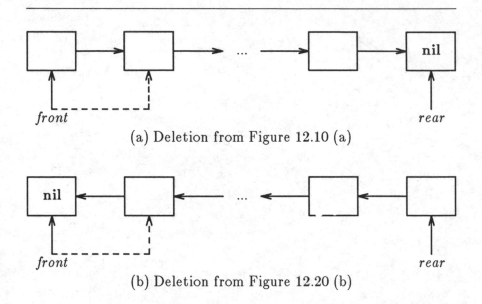

(a) Deletion from Figure 12.10 (a)

(b) Deletion from Figure 12.20 (b)

Figure 12.21 Deletions from linked queues

```
procedure AddToQueue(var front, rear: ListPointer; x: element);
{Add x to a linked queue}
var y: ListPointer;
begin
    new(y);
    y ↑ .data := x; y ↑ .link := nil;
    if front = rear then begin {empty queue}
                    front := y; rear := y;
                end
            else begin
                    rear ↑ .link := y; rear := y;
                end;
end; {of AddToQueue}
```

Program 12.20 Adding to a linked queue

procedure *DeleteFromQueue*(**var***front*, *rear*: *ListPointer*;
                          var *x*: *element*);
{Delete from a linked queue}
var *y*: *ListPointer*;
begin
   if *front* = *rear* **then begin**
                          writeln('Deletion from an empty queue');
                          goto 999; {end of program}
                       end;
   x := *front* ↑ .*data*;
   y := *front*;
   front := *front* ↑ .*link*;
   dispose(*y*);
end; {of *DeleteFromQueue*}

Program 12.21 Deletion from a linked queue

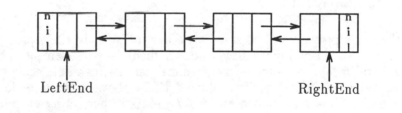

LeftEnd   RightEnd

Figure 12.22 A doubly linked list

We can use the initial condition *LeftEnd* = *RightEnd* = **nil** and the boundary condition *LeftEnd* = **nil** iff the deque is empty. The procedures for deque functions at the right end are given as Programs 12.22 and 12.23. The development of procedures for the left end are left as an exercise.

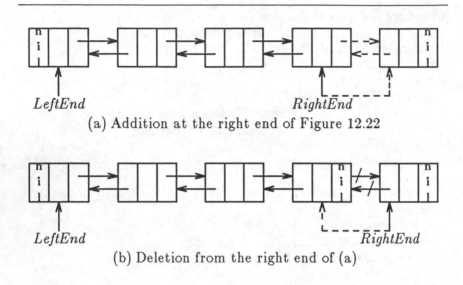

(a) Addition at the right end of Figure 12.22

(b) Deletion from the right end of (a)

Figure 12.23 Functions at right end of a deque

12.3.7. Search Table

Linked lists provide a good solution to the collision overflow problem that arises when hashing is used. Rather than place an element into a bucket other than its home bucket, we maintain chains of elements that have the same home bucket. Figure 12.24 shows a hash table in which overflows are handled by *chaining*. As in our earlier example, the hash function divisor is 11. In this hash table organization, each bucket has space for just a pointer to a node. All elements are kept on chains.

Since all elements in a hash table have distinct key values, each insertion must be preceded by a search to verify that the element to be inserted does indeed have a distinct key value. This search can, of course, be limited to the chain for the home bucket of the new element. As each insert is preceded by a search, it is less expensive to maintain the chains in ascending order of the key values (as in Figure 12.24) than in an unordered way.

```
procedure AddToRight(var LeftEnd, RightEnd: DequePointer;
                            x: element);
{Add x to the right end of a deque}
var y: DequePointer;
begin
    new(y); y ↑ .data := x; y ↑ .RightLink := nil;
    if LeftEnd = nil
    then begin {empty deque}
            y ↑ .LeftLink := nil;
            LeftEnd := y; RightEnd := y;
         end
    else begin {non-empty deque}
            y ↑ .LeftLink := RightEnd;
            RightEnd ↑ .RightLink := y;
            RightEnd := y;
         end;
end; {of AddToRight}
```

Program 12.22 Adding at the right end of a deque

```
procedure DeleteFromRight(var LeftEnd, RightEnd: DequePointer;
                                 var x: element);
{Delete from the right end of the deque}
var y: DequePointer;
begin
    if LeftEnd = nil then begin
                            writeln('Deletion from an empty deque');
                            goto 999; {end of program}
                          end;
    y := RightEnd; x := y ↑ .data;
    RightEnd := y ↑ .LeftLink;
    if RightEnd = nil then LeftEnd := nil {boundary condition}
                      else RightEnd ↑ .RightLink := nil;
    dispose(y);
end; {of DeleteFromRight}
```

Program 12.23 Delete from the right end of a deque

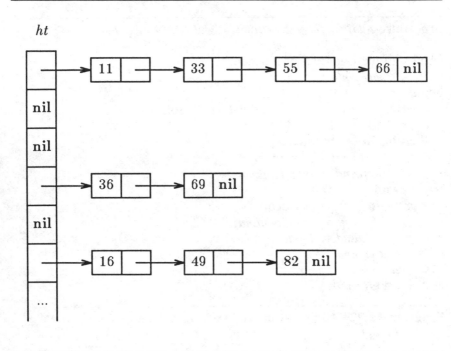

Figure 12.24 A chained hash table

For a chained hash table, we may use the same nodes as used earlier for linear lists, stacks, and queues (i.e., nodes of type *List-Node*). The hash table itself is created by the variable declaration:

var *ht*: **array** [0..*Dminus*1] **of** *ListPointer*

where *Dminus*1 is one less than the hash function divisor *D*. Initially, all entries in *ht* are **nil**. To search the table for an element with key value *x*, we need examine only the chain that begins at *ht*[*f*(*x*)] where *f* is the hash function. Further, since this chain is ordered, we need only go as far as the first element that has a key that is greater than or equal to *x*. Function *HashSearch* (Program 12.24) does this.

```
function HashSearch(x: integer): ListPointer;
{Search the chained hash table, ht, for an element with key x.}
{If there is no such element, return nil.}
{Otherwise, return a pointer y such that y ↑ .data.key = x.}
var i: integer; NotDone: boolean; y: ListPointer;
begin
    i := f (x); {home bucket}
    y := ht[i]; {start of chain}
    NotDone := true;
    while (y <> nil) and NotDone do
        if y ↑ .data.key < x then y := y ↑ .link
        else begin
                if y ↑ .data.key <> x then y := nil;
                NotDone := false;
            end;
        HashSearch := y;
    end; {of HashSearch}
```

Program 12.24 Searching a chained hash table

The search function can be made to run faster by placing a tail node at the end of each chain as in Figure 12.25. The key field in the tail node of each chain is set to **maxint**. Note that this works correctly even if a *key* with value **maxint** is in the table. The faster (and also simpler) search function is Program 12.25. The simplicity and speed of Program 12.25 is obtained at the cost of D tail nodes of space. In many applications it is not possible to provide this additional space, and Program 12.24 has to be used.

Let us turn our attention to the problem of inserting into a chained hash table. There are two cases that have to be considered. One is insertion at the front of a chain (Figure 12.26(a)). The other is insertion at any other position (Figure 12.26(b)). The first case can be eliminated if we have enough additional space to provide each chain with a head node. All insertions, then take place to the right of the head node. We leave the development of the insert procedure as an exercise.

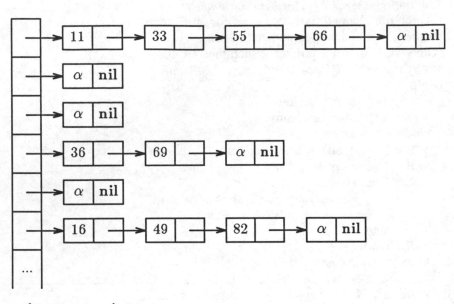

α denotes **maxint**

Figure 12.25 Hash table with tail nodes

Comparison With Linear Open Addressing

We shall explicitly compare linear open addressing with chaining for the case where the chains have neither a head nor a tail node. Let s be the space (in words) required by an element. Assume that each link requires one word of space. Further, assume that the hash table has b buckets and n elements. We first note that when linear open addressing is used, $n \leq b$. When chaining is used, n can have any value.

The space needed when linear open addressing is used is bs. When chaining is used, $b+n+ns$ words of space are needed. So,

---

```
function HashSearch(x: integer): ListPointer;
{Search the hash table for an element with key x.}
{If there is no such element, return nil.}
{Otherwise, return a pointer y such that y ↑ .data.key = x.}
{Each chain is assumed to have a tail node with key maxint.}
var i: integer;
begin
    i := f (x); {home bucket}
    y := ht[i]; {start of chain}
    while y ↑ .data.key < x do
        y := y ↑ .link;
    if (y ↑ .data.key <> x) or (y ↑ .link = nil) then HashSearch := nil
                                               else HashSearch := y;
end; {of HashSearch}
```

Program 12.25 Searching a chained hash table with tail nodes

whenever $n < b(s-1)/(s+1)$, chaining takes less space than does linear open addressing. When $s = 1$, chaining takes more space than does linear open addressing (except when $n = 0$). When $s > 1$, there are always values of n for which chaining is more space efficient. This is so despite the fact that in chaining space is being used for links!

As far as the worst case time complexities are concerned, a search can require the examination of all n elements in both cases. The average performance of a search when chaining is used can be derived in the following way. An unsuccessful search of an ordered chain with i nodes on it will examine either 1, 2, 3, ..., or i nodes, for $i \geq 0$. If each of these possibilities happens with equal probability, then the average number of nodes that get examined in an unsuccessful search is:

$$\frac{1}{i} \sum_{j=1}^{i} j = \frac{i(i+1)}{2i} = \frac{i+1}{2}$$

when $i \geq 1$. When $i = 0$, the average number of nodes examined is 0.

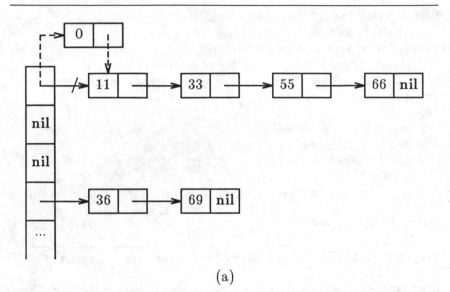

(a)

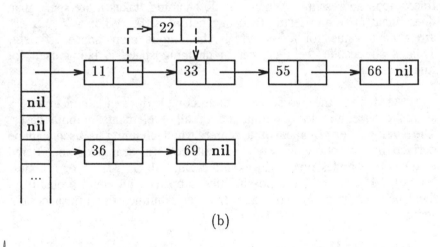

(b)

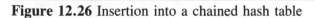

Figure 12.26 Insertion into a chained hash table

For chained hash tables, we expect the length of a chain to be $n/b = \alpha$ on the average. When $\alpha \geq 1$, we may substitute α for i in the above expression to get we get:

$$U_n \approx \frac{\alpha+1}{2}, \; \alpha \geq 1$$

When $\alpha < 1$, $U_n \leq \alpha$ as the average chain length is α and no search requires more than α nodes to be examined.

For S_n, we need to know the expected distance of each of the n identifiers from the head of its chain. To determine this, assume that the identifiers are inserted in increasing order. This assumption does not affect the positioning of identifiers on their respective chains. When the i'th identifier is inserted, its chain is expected to have a length of $(i-1)/b$. The i'th identifier gets added to the end of the chain as identifiers are inserted in increasing order. Hence, a search for this identifier will require us to examine $1 + (i-1)/b$ nodes. Note also that when identifiers are inserted in increasing order, their distance from the chain head does not change as a result of further insertions. Assuming that each of the n identifiers is searched for with equal probability, we get:

$$S_n = \frac{1}{n} \sum_{i=1}^{n} \{1 + (i-1)/b\} = 1 + \frac{n-1}{2b} \approx 1 + \frac{\alpha}{2}$$

Comparing these with the formulas for linear open addressing, we see that the expected performance of chaining is superior to that of linear open addressing. For instance, when $\alpha = 0.9$ a search in a chained hash table is expected to examine 0.95 elements when it is an unsuccessful search and .45 elements when it is successful. On the other hand, when linear open addressing is used 50.5 elements are expected to be examined if the search is unsuccessful and 5.5 in case it is successful!

12.4. INDIRECT ADDRESSING

The Method

Indirect addressing is a combination of a formula based and a linked representation. A formula is used to locate the position of a pointer to the desired element.

Figure 12.27 shows a linear list of five elements that is represented using the indirect addressing table t. $t[i]$ is a pointer to the ith element in the list.

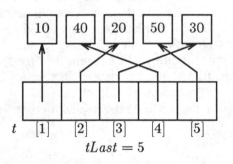

Figure 12.27 Indirect addressing

In comparing this scheme with the formula based scheme resulting from the use of formula (12.1), we see that this formula can be used to locate the pointer, in t, to the ith element in the list. However, this formula does not, in itself, locate the ith element. t provides one level of *indirection* in the addressing scheme for the elements of the list.

When the indirect addressing scheme of Figure 12.27 is compared with the linked representation of Figure 12.10, we see that both use pointer (or link) fields. In the linked scheme, the pointers are in each node. In the indirect addressing scheme, the pointers are in the table t. This is quite similar to an index in a book. To locate an item in a book, we first look in the index. The index tells us where the item is.

When indirect addressing is used to represent a linear list, the nodes are of type *element* (just as when a formula based scheme is used). The components of t are of type *ElementPointer* which is defined as:

type *ElementPointer* $= \uparrow$ *element*;

Functions on a Linear List

To delete the third element from the list of Figure 12.27, we need to move the pointers in $t[4..5]$ to $t[3..4]$, reduce *tLast* by 1, and dispose of the node used by the third element. Program 12.26 is the indirect addressing counterpart of the linear list deletion procedures given in Programs 12.1 and 12.13. For legal k, its complexity is $\Theta(n-k+1)$ where n is the length of the list. Recall that the complexity of Program 12.13 is $\Theta(k)$ while that of Program 12.1 is $\Theta((n-k)s+1)$ where s is the size of *element*.

Suppose we wish to insert the element x between the second and third elements of the list of Figure 12.27. We need to create the configuration shown in Figure 12.28. This requires us to move the pointers in $t[3:5]$ one position to the right, then insert a pointer to x at position 3 of t. Program 12.27 inserts an element just after element k of a linear list t. The worst case asymptotic complexity of this program is seen to be the same as that for Program 12.14 (insertion into a chain). I.e., it is $\Theta(n)$.

---

procedure *DeleteFromList*(**var** *t*: *LinearList*; **var** *tLast*: **integer**;
                          k: **integer**; **var** *success*: **boolean**);
{Delete the *k*th element in the linear list *t*}
{*t* is an indirect addressing table for the list}
var *i*: **integer**;
begin
  if ($k < 0$) **or** ($k > tLast$) **then** *success* := **false**
  else begin
       {Move pointers $k+1$ through *tLast* one position down}
       for $i := k+1$ **to** *tLast* **do**
          $t[i-1] := t[i]$;
       $tLast := tLast - 1$; *success* := **true**;
    end;
end; {of *DeleteFromList*}

Program 12.26 Deletion from a linear list using indirect addressing

---

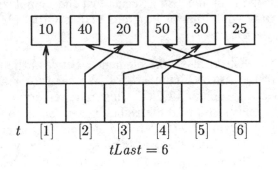

Figure 12.28 Insertion into an indirectly addressed list

---

procedure *InsertIntoList*(**var** *t*: *LinearList*; **var** *tLast*: **integer**;
        e: *ElementPointer*; *k*: **integer**; **var** *success*: **boolean**);
{Insert element *e* after the *k*th element in list *t*}
var *i*: **integer**;
begin
  if ($k > tLast$) **or** ($tLast = MaxElements$)
  then *success* := **false**
  else begin
       {Move pointers $k+1$ through *tLast* one position up}
       for $i := tLast$ **downto** $k+1$ **do**
         $t[i+1] := t[i]$;
       $t[k+1] := e$;
       $tLast := tLast + 1$; *success* := **true**;
    end;
end; {of *InsertIntoList*}

Program 12.27 Insertion into a linear list

12.5. A COMPARISON

The table of Figure 12.29 compares the asymptotic complexity of performing various functions on a linear list represented using each of three methods discussed in this chapter. Note that if the list is ordered by key value, then a search can be performed in $O(\log n)$ time when a formula based or indirect addressing scheme is used. When a linked representation is used, this takes $O(n)$ time.

12.6. SIMULATING POINTERS

In most applications, the desired linked and indirect addressing representations can be implemented using Pascal pointers. At times, however, the restrictions imposed by Pascal on the use of these pointers makes it necessary for us to implement our own pointers. This is done by replacing each field of type pointer by a field of type integer (or a range 0..*MaxNodes*).

For instance, the data type *ListNode* of Section 12.3.2 is now defined as:

	Function		
Representation	Locate kth	Delete kth	Insert after kth
Formula (12.1)	$\Theta(1)$	$\Theta((n-k)s + 1)$	$\Theta((n-k+1)s)$
Linked List	$\Theta(k)$	$\Theta(k)$	$\Theta(k+s)$
Indirect	$\Theta(1)$	$\Theta(n-k+1)$	$\Theta(n-k+1)$

Figure 12.29 Comparison of three representation methods

type *ListNode* = **record**
          data: *element*;
          link: **integer**;
      end;

Since the link field is of type **integer**, it is possible to perform arithmetic on it. It is also possible to write out link values and so save complex linked structures on a disk (say) for later use.

In order to use integer pointers, we need to collect all the nodes into an array. So, if we have enough space for *MaxNodes* number of nodes, we define the array *node* as below:

var *node*: **array** [1..*MaxNodes*] **of** *ListNode*;

This effectively indexes (or numbers) the nodes 1 through *MaxNodes*. The integer links, therefore, are simply index values into this array. So, if a chain, c, consists of nodes 10, 5, and 24 (in that order), we shall have $c = 10$ (pointer to first node on the chain); *node*[10].*link* = 5 (pointer to second node on chain); *node*[5].*link* = 24 (pointer to next node); and *node*[24].*link* = 0 (indicating that this is the last node on the chain). When drawing the chain, the links are drawn as arrows in the same way as when Pascal pointers are used (Figure 12.30).

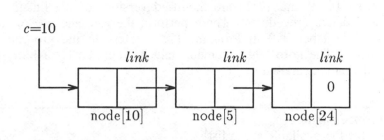

Figure 12.30   Chain using simulated pointers

To complete the simulation of pointers, we need to design our own procedures *new* and *dispose*. Nodes that are presently not in use will be kept in a *storage pool*. Initially, this pool contains all the nodes *node*[1..*MaxNodes*]. *new* takes nodes out of this pool, one at a time. *dispose* puts nodes into this pool one at a time. Hence, *new* and *dispose*, respectively, perform deletes and inserts on the storage pool. These functions are efficiently performed on a linked stack. So, we shall represent the storage pool as a linked stack.

The storage pool is a chain of nodes (as in Figure 12.31). This chain is called the *available space list*. It contains all nodes that are currently free. *avail* is an integer valued variable that points to the first node on this chain. Additions to and deletions from this chain are made at the front.

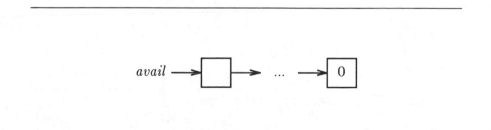

Figure 12.31   Available space list

Since all nodes are initially free, the available space list contains *MaxNodes* nodes. Program 12.28 initializes the available space list. Programs 12.29 and 12.30 are modified versions of the linked stack add and delete procedures. These perform the *new* and *dispose* functions. The label 999 in Program 12.29 refers to the program end statement. The **goto** 999 statement may be replaced by a **halt** statement if this is available.

```
procedure initialize;
{Initialize the available space list}
var i: integer;
begin
   for i := 1 to MaxNodes−1 do {link node i to i+1}
      node[i].link := i+1;
   node[MaxNodes].link := 0; {last node on chain}
   avail := 1; {first node on chain}
end; {of initialize}
```

Program 12.28 Initialize available space list

```
procedure new(var x: integer);
{Provide a free node}
begin
   if avail = 0 then begin {no node available}
                     writeln('No nodes available');
                     goto 999; {end of program}
                  end;

   {Provide a node}
   x := avail; avail := node[avail].link;
end; {of new}
```

Program 12.29 *new* with simulated pointers

Notice the defense introduced in Program 12.30 against the case $x = 0$. Also note that x is set to 0 to ensure that the program does not reference a returned node. We readily see that the three procedures have time complexity $\Theta(MaxNodes)$, $\Theta(1)$, and $\Theta(1)$,

---

procedure *dispose*(**var** *x*: **integer**);
{Put node *x* on available space list}
begin
  if *x*<>0 **then begin**
              node[*x*].*link* := *avail*;
              avail := *x*;
              x := 0; {remove reference to the disposed node}
        end;
end; {of *dispose*}

Program 12.30 *dispose* with simulated pointers

respectively.

    The initialization complexity can be reduced to $\Theta(1)$. To do this, we maintain two available space lists. One contains all free nodes that haven't been used yet. The second contains all free nodes that have been used at least once. Whenever a node is disposed, it is put onto the second list. When a new node is needed, we provide it from the second list in case this list is not empty. Otherwise, we attempt to provide it from the first list. Let *favail* and *avail*, respectively, point to the front of the first and second space lists. The procedure to dispose a node is unchanged from Program 12.30. The new initialization and *new* procedures are Programs 12.31 and 12.32.

---

procedure *initialize*;
begin
  favail := 1; {first unused node}
  avail := 0; {list of free used nodes is empty}
end; {of *initialize*}

Program 12.31 Initialization of dual available space list

    The dual available space list described above can be expected to provide better performance than the single list version in most applications. We make the following observations.

---

procedure *new*(**var** *x*: **integer**);
{Dual available space list}
begin
   if *avail* = 0 **then begin** {provide from first list}
                        if *favail* > *MaxNodes*
                    then begin
                          writeln('No free nodes');
                          goto 999; {end of program}
                      end
                    else begin *x* := *favail*; *favail* := *favail*+1; **end**;
                end
   else begin {give from linked list}
        x := *avail*; *avail* := *node*[*avail*].*link*;
      end;
end; {of *new*}

Program 12.32 Dual available space list version of *new*

1.   Program 12.32 takes the same time as does Program 12.29 except when the node is to be provided from the first list. This happens at most *MaxNodes* times. The extra time spent on these cases is balanced by the savings during initialization. In fact, it will often be the case that fewer than *MaxNodes* are needed at any time (especially during debugging runs and in software designed to handle problems with widely varying instance characteristics) and the dual scheme will be faster.

2.   The reduction in the initialization time from $\Theta(MaxNodes)$ to $\Theta(1)$ is very desirable in an interactive environment. The startup time for the program is significantly reduced.

3.   When the single list scheme is in use, chains can be built without explicitly setting the link fields in any but the last node. This is so as the appropriate link values are already present in the nodes (see Figure 12.31). This advantage can be incorporated into the dual list scheme by writing a procedure *get*(**var** *x*: **integer**; *n*: **integer**) which provides a chain with *n* nodes on it. This procedure will explicitly set links only when nodes are taken from the first list.

4. Chains can be disposed more efficiently using either of these schemes than when Pascal pointers are used. For instance, if we know the front, f, and end, e, of a chain, all nodes on it are freed by the statements:

    $node[e].link := avail$; $avail := f$;

5. If c is a circular list, then all nodes on it are disposed in $\Theta(1)$ time using Program 12.33. Figure 12.32 shows the link changes that take place.

```
procedure CircularDispose(var c: integer);
{Dispose the circular list c}
var i: integer;
begin
  if c <> 0 then
  begin {list not empty}
    i := node[c].link; {note, i = c if c has only one node}
    node[c].link := avail;
    avail := i;
    c := 0;
  end;
end; {of CircularDispose}
```

Program 12.33 Dispose a circular list

12.7. REFERENCES AND SELECTED READINGS

The following texts provide several additional examples of formula based, linked and indirect addressing representations:

Fundamentals of data structures in Pascal, by E. Horowitz and S. Sahni, Computer Science Press, Maryland, 1984.

and

The art of computer programming: Fundamental algorithms, by D. E. Knuth, Vol. 1, Second Edition, Addison Wesley, New York, 1973.

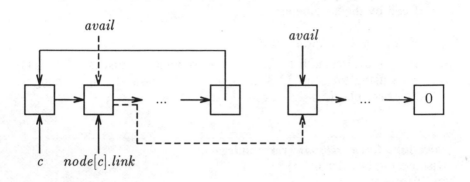

Figure 12.32 Disposing a circular list

Other hashing functions and methods to handle overflows can be found in the book by Horowitz and Sahni cited above as well as in the book:

The art of computer programming: Sorting and searching, by D. E. Knuth, Vol. 3, Addison Wesley, New York, 1973.

12.8. EXERCISES

1.   Refine Program 12.3 into a Pascal procedure.

2.   Write a procedure to insert an element after the kth element in list i. Assume that n lists are being represented in a single array. In case lists have to be moved to accomodate the new element, your procedure should first determine the amount of space that is available. The lists should be moved such that each has about the same amount of space available for future growth.

3.   Write a procedure to delete the kth element from list i. Assume that n lists are being represented in a single array.

4.   Assume that two stacks are represented in a single array
     stack[1..*MaxElements*] (Figure 12.3). The bottom of one is
     pegged at one end of the array and that of the other is pegged at
     the other end. The two stacks grow towards the middle of the
     array. Write procedures to add to and delete from a stack.
     These should be similar to Programs 6.14 and 6.15. You will
     need another parameter *i* which is 1 or 2 depending on which
     stack the function is to be performed on.

   (a)   What is the initial value of each of the top of stack
         pointers?

   (b)   What are the boundary conditions?

   (c)   What is the time complexity of each of your programs?
         The instance characteristic to use is the number of elements
         in the appropriate stack.

5.   Adapt the representation of Figure 12.2 to the case of many
     stacks. Assume that the first stack has its bottom pegged to
     position 1 while the last stack has it pegged to position *MaxEle-
     ments* as in Figure 12.3. The remaining stacks grow between
     these two. Write procedures to add to and delete from the *i*th
     stack. For the add procedure, begin with a pseudo Pascal ver-
     sion similar to Program 12.3 and refine it into a Pascal pro-
     cedure. What are the time complexities of the add and delete
     procedures? The instance characteristics to use are the size of
     the stack involved and *MaxElements*.

6.   Assume that a queue is being represented in an array using the
     formula (12.1). Write procedures to add to and delete from the
     queue. Let *n* be the number of elements in the queue. Show
     that the add procedure has time complexity $\Theta(1)$ and the delete
     procedure has time complexity $\Theta(n)$.

7.   A *deque* is a double ended queue. Additions and deletions can
     take place at either end. Use the circular array representation of
     a queue to represent a deque. Programs 12.6 and 12.7 can be
     used to add an element at one end of the deque and to delete
     from the other. Write corresponding procedures to add to and
     delete from the other ends. What are the time complexities of
     your procedures?

8. Suppose that we are to represent a linear list using formula (12.3). Assume that the variables *front* and *rear* have the same conventions as for a circular queue.

    (a) What should the initial values of *front* and *rear* be?

    (b) Given the values of *front* and *rear*, what is the number of elements in the linear list?

    (c) Write a procedure to insert an element following element k. What is its time complexity? Use the instance characteristics n, k, and the size, s, of the list.

    (d) Write a procedure to delete the kth element. What is its time complexity? Use the same characteristics as in part (c).

9. Program the three formula based representations for a search table. Assume that the elements are integers and that *MaxElements* is 961. Insert a randomly generated sequence of n distinct integers into the table and then search for each m times. These integers should be in the range [1, **maxint**]. Measure the average insertion and search times for different n's and m's. What conclusions can you draw from your experiment?

10. Obtain a suitable value for the hash function divisor D (and hence for *MaxElements*) when linear open addressing is used. Do this for each of the following situations:

    (a) $n = 50$, $S_n \leq 3$, $U_n \leq 20$.

    (b) $n = 500$, $S_n \leq 5$, $U_n \leq 60$.

    (c) $n = 10$, $S_n \leq 2$, $U_n \leq 10$.

11. For each of the following conditions, obtain a suitable value for the hash function divisor D. For this value of D determine S_n and U_n as a function of n.

    (a) *MaxElements* ≤ 530

    (b) *MaxElements* ≤ 130

    (c) *MaxElements* ≤ 150.

12. Suppose that in addition to searches and insertions, we wish to perform deletions from a search table. Assume that linear open addressing is used to handle overflows and that each bucket in the hash table has space for one element. One way to handle a delete is to require an additional bit *del*[*i*] to be available for each bucket *i*. *del*[*i*] is set to **true** initially for each bucket. Initially, all buckets have key value −**maxint**. Whenever an element is deleted from a bucket, its *del* bit is set to **true**. Whenever an element is inserted into a bucket, its *del* value is set to **false**. Write procedures to search, insert, and delete under these assumptions.

13. Repeat the previous exercise under the assumption that the *del* bits are unavailable and that Programs 12.8 and 12.9 are to work for searches and insertions. So, only a delete procedure needs to be written. This time, you will have to relocate some elements in the table. Try to minimize the number of elements that get relocated by your delete procedure.

14. Compare the run time performance of Programs 12.10 and 12.11. Do this for both worst case and average run times.

15. Modify Program 12.13 so that it works under the assumption that *l* is a circular list with a head node.

16. Modify Program 12.14 so that it works under the assumption that *l* is a circular list with a head node.

17. Assume that a queue is being represented as a singly linked circular list with *rear* a pointer to the last node in the queue. *rear* = **nil** iff the queue is empty. Write procedures to add to and delete from the queue. Your procedures must have complexity $\Theta(1)$. There is no explicit *front* pointer available.

18. The length of a *chain* is the number of nodes on it. Write a function to determine the length of the chain *c*. Nodes are linked together through the field *link*.

19. Do the previous exercise for a circular list c.

20. Let x and y be two ordered chains. Each node has the fields *link* and *key* (in addition to other fields). The nodes on the chains are in nondecreasing order of *key*. Write a procedure to merge these two chains into a single ordered chain z. Your procedure must not use any additional nodes. What is the time complexity of your procedure? Provide this as a function of the number of nodes in x and y.

21. Let c be a chain in which the nodes are in nondecreasing order of the field *key*. Write a procedure to change the order to nonincreasing. No additional nodes are to be used. When your procedure terminates, x should point to the first node in the newly ordered chain. How much time does your procedure take?

22. Program the insert sort algorithm for the case when the n elements to be sorted are in the chain l. Each node in this chain has the fields *key* and *link* (in addition to other fields). Your procedure should reorder the nodes in the chain so that they are in nondecreasing order of the field *key*. What is the worst case time complexity of your procedure? How much time does it need if the elements are already in sorted order?

23. Do the previous exercise for bubble sort.

24. Write procedures for the deque functions at the left end. Assume the doubly linked representation of Figure 12.22 and the initial and boundary values associated with it.

25. Write a procedure to insert an element x into a chained hash table *ht*. Assume that the chains have neither a head node nor a tail node.

26. Write a procedure to delete the element with key value x from a chained hash table *ht*. Assume that the chains have neither a head node nor a tail node.

27. Write a function to search a chained hash table for the element with key value x. Assume that the chains have both a head node and a tail node.

28. Write a procedure to insert an element x into a chained hash table ht. Assume that the chains have both a head node and a tail node.

29. Write a procedure to delete the element with key value x from a chained hash table ht. Assume that the chains have both a head node and a tail node.

30. Write a binary search function to search for an element with key x when a sorted list of n elements is represented using indirect addressing. Assume that $t[i]\uparrow.data.key \leq t[i+1]\uparrow.data.key$, $1 \leq i < n$.

31. Program the insert sort algorithm for the case when the n elements to be sorted are represented using indirect addressing. Initially, $t[i]$ is a pointer to the ith element. Your procedure should reorder the $t[i]$s such that $t[i]\uparrow.data.key \leq t[i+1]\uparrow.data.key$, $1 \leq i < n$ following the sort. The run time of your procedure should be independent of s, the size of each element. What is the worst case time complexity of your procedure? How much time does it need if the elements are already in sorted order?

32. Do the previous exercise for bubble sort.

33. Let *LeftEnd* and *RightEnd* point to the two ends of a doubly linked list. Assume the node structure of Section 12.3.6. Let x point to an arbitrary node in this list. Write a procedure to delete x from the list.

34. Obtain a representation for integers that is suitable for performing arithmetic on arbitrarily large integers. The arithmetic is to be performed with no loss of accuracy. Write Pascal procedures to input and output large integers and to perform the arithmetic operations: add, subtract, multiply, and divide. The procedure for division will return two integers: the quotient and the remainder. In addition to these procedures, you are to write a procedure to dispose of an integer. This procedure will free the space currently used by the integer being disposed.

CHAPTER 13

ADVANCED DATA STRUCTURES

13.1. BINARY TREES

13.1.1. Introduction

Trees were informally introduced in Chapter 1. A formal definition of a tree is provided below.

Definition: A *tree*, T, is a finite collection of n, $n>0$, elements. One of these is designated the *root* element. The remaining elements, if any, are partitioned into disjoint sets. These disjoint sets are themselves trees and are called the *subtrees* of the root. □

We have already seen several examples and applications of trees. Trees can be used to organize software design, menus, and program plans. The application of trees to software development does not stop here. In fact, trees find significant application in the organization of data. While many varieties of trees are used for this purpose, *binary trees* find most application.

Definition: A *binary tree*, T, is a collection of n, $n \geq 0$, elements. When $n = 0$, the binary tree is *empty*. When $n > 0$, there is one distinguished element called the *root*. The remaining elements (if any) are partitioned into two disjoint subsets which are themselves binary trees. One or both of these subsets may be empty. One subset is called the left subtree of T and the other is the right subtree of T. □

The essential differences between a binary tree and a tree are:

(1) A binary tree can be empty whereas a tree cannot.

(2) Each element in a binary tree has exactly two subtrees (one or both of these may be empty). Each element in a tree can have any number of subtrees.

(3) The subtrees of each element in a binary tree are ordered. I.e., we distinguish between the left and the right subtree. The subtrees in a tree are unordered.

Like a tree, a binary tree is drawn with its root at the top. The elements in the left (right) subtree of the root are drawn below and to the left (right) of the root. Between each element and its children, there is a line or edge.

Figure 13.1 shows some binary trees that represent arithmetic expressions. Each operator (+, −, *, /) may have one or two operands. The left operand (if any) is the left subtree of the operator. The right operand is its right subtree. The leaf elements in an expression tree are either constants or variables. Note that an expression tree contains no parentheses. One application of expression trees is in the generation of optimal computer code to evaluate an expression. While we shall not study algorithms to generate optimal code from an expression tree, we shall use these trees to illustrate some of the functions that are commonly performed on binary trees.

13.1.2. Properties

Property 1: The drawing of every binary tree with n elements, $n>0$, has exactly $n-1$ edges.

Proof: Every element in a binary tree (except the root) has exactly one parent. There is exactly one edge between each child and its parent. So, the number of edges is $n-1$. □

The *height* (or *depth*) of a binary tree is the number of levels in it. The binary tree of Figure 13.1(a) has a height of 3 while those of Figures 13.1(b) and (c) have a height of 4.

Property 2: A binary tree of height h, $h \geq 0$, has at least h and at most $2^h - 1$ elements in it.

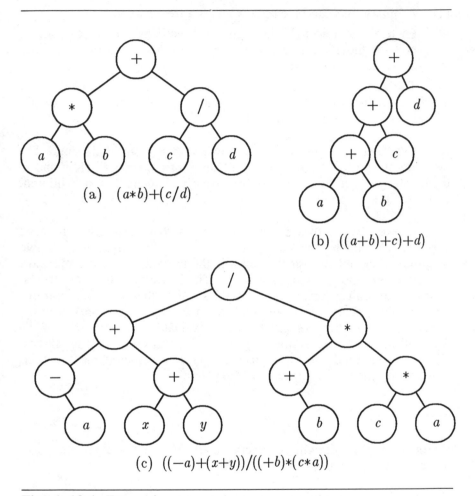

(a) $(a*b)+(c/d)$

(b) $((a+b)+c)+d$

(c) $((-a)+(x+y))/((+b)*(c*a))$

Figure 13.1 Expression trees

Proof: Since there must be at least one element at each level, the number of elements is at least h. As each element can have at most two children, the number of elements at level i is at most 2^{i-1}, $i>0$. For $h = 0$, the total number of elements is 0 which equals 2^0-1. For $h>0$, the number of elements cannot exceed $\sum\limits_{i=1}^{h} 2^{i-1} = 2^h-1$. □

Property 3: The height of a binary tree that contains n, $n\geq0$, elements is at most n and at least $\lceil \log_2(n+1) \rceil$.

Proof: Since there must be at least one element at each level, the height cannot exceed n. From Property 2, we know that a binary tree of height h can have no more than $2^h - 1$ elements. So, $n \leq 2^h - 1$. Hence, $h \geq \log_2(n+1)$. Since h is an integer, we get $h \geq \lceil \log_2(n+1) \rceil$. □

A binary tree of height h that contains exactly $2^h - 1$ elements is called a *full binary tree*. The binary tree of Figure 13.1(a) is a full binary tree of height 3. The binary trees of Figures 13.1(b) and (c) are not full binary trees. Figure 13.2 shows a full binary tree of height 4.

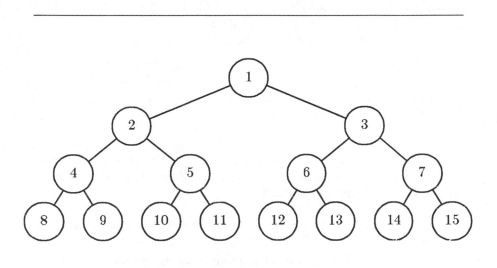

Figure 13.2 Full binary tree of height 4

Suppose we number the elements in a full binary tree of height h 1 through $2^h - 1$. This numbering is done beginning at level 1 and going down to level h. Within levels, the elements are numbered left to right. The elements of the full binary tree of Figure 13.2 have been numbered in this way. Now suppose we delete the k, $k \geq 0$, elements numbered $2^h - i$, $1 \leq i \leq k$ for any k. The resulting binary tree is called a *complete binary tree*. Some examples are given in Figure 13.3. Note that a full binary tree is a special case of a complete binary tree. Also, note that a complete binary tree that contains n elements has a height $\lceil \log_2(n+1) \rceil$.

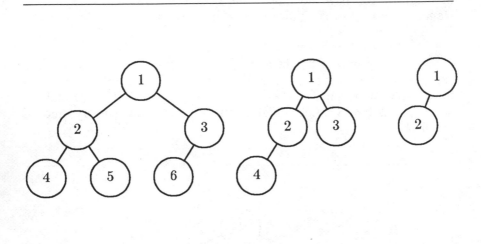

Figure 13.3 Complete binary trees

There is a very nice relationship amongst the numbers assigned to an element and its children in a complete binary tree. This relationship is given by the next property.

Property 4: Let i, $1 \leq i \leq n$, be the number assigned to an element of a complete binary tree. The following are true:

(1) If $i = 1$, then this element is the root of the binary tree. If $i > 1$, then the parent of this element has been assigned the number $\lfloor i/2 \rfloor$.

(2) If $2i > n$, then this element has no left child. Otherwise, its left child has been assigned the number $2i$.

(3) If $2i+1 > n$, then this element has no right child. Otherwise, its right child has been assigned the number $2i+1$.

Proof: Can be established by induction on i. □

13.1.3. Representation

Formula Based

The formula based representation of a binary tree utilizes Property 4. The binary tree to be represented is regarded as a complete binary tree with some missing elements. Figure 13.4 shows two example binary trees. The first has three elements (A, B, and C) and the second has five elements (A, B, C, D, and E). Neither is complete. The missing elements are shown by broken edges. All elements (including the missing ones) are numbered as described in the previous section.

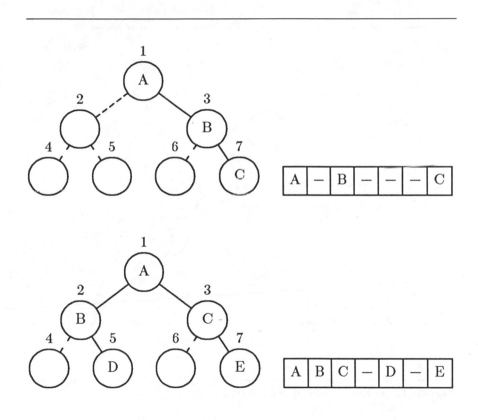

Figure 13.4 Incomplete binary trees

In a formula based representation, the binary tree is represented in an array by storing each element at the array position corresponding to the number assigned to it. The resulting representations for the binary trees of Figure 13.4 are also shown in this figure. Missing elements are represented by dashes. As can be seen, this representation scheme is quite wasteful of space when many elements are missing. In fact, a binary tree that has n elements may require an array of size up to $2^n - 1$ for its representation. This maximum size is needed when each element (except the root) of the n element binary tree is the right child of its parent. Figure 13.5 shows such a binary tree with four elements. Binary trees of this type are called *right skewed* binary trees.

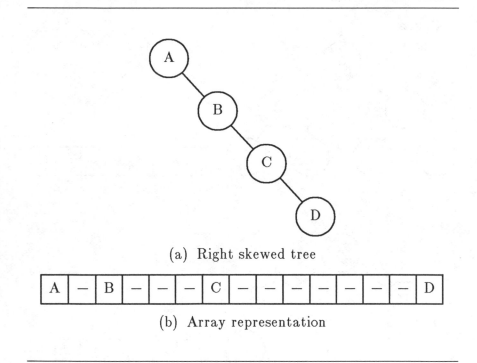

(a) Right skewed tree

| A | – | B | – | – | – | C | – | – | – | – | – | – | – | D |

(b) Array representation

Figure 13.5 Right skewed binary tree

The formula based representation is useful only when the number of missing elements is small.

Linked

The most popular way to represent a binary tree is as a linked list. Each element is represented by a node that has exactly two link fields. Let us call these *LeftChild* and *RightChild*. These are of type *TreePointer* which itself is a pointer to a node. In addition to these two link fields, each node has a field, *data*, of type *element*.

The type definitions needed are:

type *TreePointer* = ↑ *TreeNode*;
  TreeNode = **record**
       data : *element*;
       LeftChild : *TreePointer*;
       RightChild : *TreePointer*;
     end;

Each edge in the drawing of a binary tree is represented by a pointer from the parent node to the child node. This pointer is placed in the appropriate link field of the parent node. Since an n element binary tree has exactly $n-1$ edges, we are left with $2n - (n-1) = n+1$ link fields that have no value. These are set to **nil**. The linked representations of the binary trees of Figure 13.4 are shown in Figure 13.6.

A pointer variable (t in Figure 13.6) is used to keep track of the root of the binary tree. We use the name of this variable to refer to the root node as well as to the whole binary tree. So, we use the phrases "the root t" and "the binary tree" t. We can access all nodes in a binary tree t by starting at the root and following *LeftChild* and *RightChild* links.

The absence of a parent link from the linked representation of a binary tree generally causes no difficulties as most of the functions one performs on a binary tree do not require this link. In case some application needs this link, an additional link field may be added to each node.

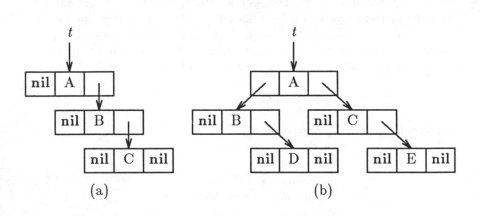

(a)   (b)

Figure 13.6 Linked representations

13.1.4. Functions

Some of the functions that are commonly performed on binary trees are:

(1) Determine the height.
(2) Determine the number of elements in it.
(3) Make a copy.
(4) Display the binary tree on a screen or on paper.
(5) Determine if two binary trees are identical.
(6) Dispose of it.
(7) If it is an expression tree, evaluate the expression.
(8) If it is an expression tree, obtain the parenthesised form of the expression.

All the functions listed above can be performed by traversing the binary tree in a systematic manner. In a binary tree *traversal*, each element is *visited* exactly once. It is during this visit that all action with respect to this element is taken. This action can include writing the element on a screen or on paper, evaluating the expression represented by the subtree of which this is the root, adding one to a running count of the number of elements in the binary tree, disposing the node used by this element, etc.

There are four common ways to traverse a binary tree. These are:

(1) Preorder

(2) Inorder

(3) Postorder

(4) Levelorder

The first three traversal methods are best described recursively as in Programs 13.1 - 13.3. These procedures assume that the binary tree being traversed is represented using the linked scheme of the previous section. We shall not present the procedures for the case of a formula based representation. The development of the traversal procedures for this representation is left as an exercise.

---

procedure *PreOrder*(*t*: *TreePointer*);
{Traverse the linked binary tree *t* in preorder}
begin
  if *t* <> **nil then** {tree not empty}
  begin
    visit(*t*);
    PreOrder(*t* ↑ .*LeftChild*); {traverse left subtree}
    PreOrder(*t* ↑ .*RightChild*); {traverse right subtree}
  end;
end; {of *PreOrder*}

Program 13.1 Preorder traversal

In the first three traversal methods, the left subtree of a node is traversed before the right subtree. The difference amongst the three orders comes from the difference in the time at which a node is visited. In the case of a preorder traversal, each node is visited before its left and right subtrees are traversed. In an inorder traversal, the root of each subtree is visited after its left subtree has been traversed but before the traversal of its right subtree begins. In a postorder traversal, each root is visited after its left and right subtrees have been traversed.

```
procedure InOrder(t: TreePointer);
{Traverse the linked binary tree t in inorder}
begin
   if t <> nil then {tree not empty}
   begin
      InOrder(t ↑ .LeftChild); {traverse left subtree}
      visit(t);
      InOrder(t ↑ .RightChild); {traverse right subtree}
   end;
end; {of InOrder}
```

Program 13.2 Inorder traversal

```
procedure PostOrder(t: TreePointer);
{Traverse the linked binary tree t in postorder}
begin
   if t <> nil then {tree not empty}
   begin
      PostOrder(t ↑ .LeftChild); {traverse left subtree}
      PostOrder(t ↑ .RightChild); {traverse right subtree}
      visit(t);
   end;
end; {of PostOrder}
```

Program 13.3 Postorder traversal

Figure 13.7 shows the output generated by Programs 13.1 - 13.3 when *visit*(*t*) is replaced by the statement:

write(*t* ↑ .*data*)

The input binary trees are those of Figure 13.1.

Obtaining iterative procedures for the three traversal methods of Programs 13.1 - 13.3 is quite a bit harder than doing the same for the recursive programs of Chapter 8. In fact, obtaining iterative versions that do not use a stack is very hard. We shall not attempt to provide iterative versions here. The interested reader is referred to the text

Preorder	$+*ab/cd$	$+++abcd$	$/+-a+xy*+b*ca$
Inorder	$a*b+c/d$	$a+b+c+d$	$-a+x+y/+b*c*a$
Postorder	$ab*cd/+$	$ab+c+d+$	$a-xy++b+ca**/$
	(a)	(b)	(c)

Figure 13.7 Elements of a binary tree listed in pre-, in-, and postorder

"Fundamentals of data structures in Pascal", by Horowitz and Sahni which is cited in the readings section. This text contains iterative traversal procedures that use a stack as well as procedures that do not use a stack to accomplish the traversal.

All functions listed earlier except that of displaying a binary tree can be performed efficiently using one of the tree traversal programs given above. The parenthesised form of an expression can be obtained by traversing an expression tree in inorder. The left operand of each operator is printed out first, then the operator, and then the right operand. The **then** clause of Program 13.2 needs to be changed to:

begin {write operand enclosed in parentheses}
   write('(');
   InOrder($t \uparrow$.*LeftChild*); {traverse left subtree}
   write($t \uparrow$.*data*);
   InOrder($t \uparrow$.*RightChild*); {traverse right subtree}
   write(')');
end;

To copy a binary tree, we can first copy the left subtree, then the right, and finally the root. When the root is being copied, its left and right subtrees have already been copied. This corresponds to a postorder traversal. An alternate way to copy a binary tree is to use preorder. We first get a new node, x, and copy the data from the root of the tree being copied into this new node. Then, a copy of the left subtree is made and $x \uparrow$.*LeftChild* set. Finally, the right subtree is copied and the pointer $x \uparrow$.*RightChild* is set. An exercise examines these two approaches. It is seen that using preorder is more space efficient.

To check if two binary trees are the same, we first compare the data in the two roots. If these are the same, then we determine if the two have the same left subtrees. If so, we check the two right subtrees. This corresponds to a preorder traversal. An expression tree can be evaluated using a postorder traversal. During the visit of a node that represents an operator, this operator is computed. The operands for this operator will have been computed by this time as the subtrees are traversed first in postorder.

While it is possible to display a binary tree on certain display devices by traversing it in one of the three orders discussed so far, it is generally desirable to provide the tree to the display device by levels. This is possible when the tree is traversed in levelorder. In this order, elements are visited by level top to bottom. Within levels, elements are visited left to right. It is quite difficult to write a recursive procedure for levelorder traversal as the correct data structure to use here is a queue and not a stack. Program 13.4 traverses a binary tree in levelorder. It makes use of a global circular queue. The elements of this queue are of type *TreePointer*. The procedure to add to the queue terminates the program in case there is no space for the addition. The procedure to delete an element returns **nil** in x in case the queue is empty. If the queue is not empty, it returns the pointer (i.e., the *TreePointer*) at the front of the queue.

```
procedure LevelOrder(t: TreePointer);
{Traverse the binary tree t in levelorder}
var x: TreePointer;
begin
    front := 0; rear := 0; {initialize queue}
    while x <> nil do
        visit(x);
        if x ↑ .LeftChild <> nil then AddToQueue(x ↑ .LeftChild);
        if x ↑ .RightChild <> nil then AddToQueue(x ↑ .RightChild);
        DeleteFromQueue(x);
    end;
end; {of LevelOrder}
```

Program 13.4 Levelorder traversal

Let n be the number of elements in a binary tree t. The space complexity of each of the four traversal programs is $O(n)$ and the time complexity is $\Theta(n)$.

13.2. HEAPS

Definition: A *max heap* is a complete binary tree. If the heap is not empty, each element has a field called *key* and the *key* value in the root is the largest (ties are broken arbitrarily) *key* value in the heap. The left and right subtrees of the root are also max heaps.

Definition: A *min heap* is a complete binary tree. If the heap is not empty, each element has a field called *key* and the *key* value in the root is the smallest (ties are broken arbitrarily) *key* value in the heap. The left and right subtrees of the root are also min heaps.

Some example max heaps are shown in Figure 13.8 and some min heaps are shown in Figure 13.9.

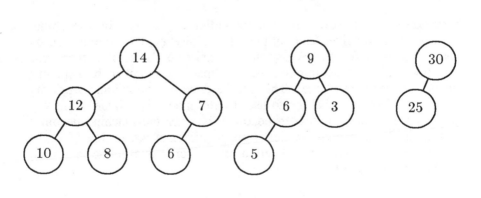

Figure 13.8 Max heaps

Heaps find application when a *priority queue* is to be maintained. In this kind of queue, the element to be deleted is the one with highest (or lowest) priority. At any time, an element with arbitrary priority

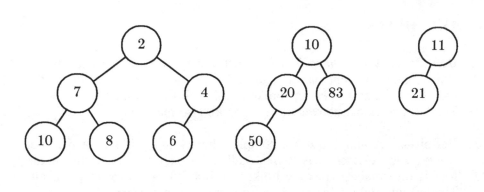

Figure 13.9 Min Heaps

can be inserted into the queue. In applications where an element with highest (lowest) priority is to be deleted each time, a max (min) heap may be used.

Example 13.1: Suppose that we are selling the services of a machine. Each user pays a fixed amount per use. However, the time needed by each user is different. We wish to maximize the returns from this machine under the assumption that the machine is not to be kept idle unless no user is available. This can be done by maintaining a priority queue of all persons waiting to use the machine. The value of the *key* field is the amount of time needed. Whenever the machine becomes available, the user with smallest time requirement is selected. Hence, a min heap is required. When a new user requests the machine, his/her request is put into the heap.

If each user needs the same amount of time on the machine but people are willing to pay different amounts for the service, then a priority queue on the amount of payment can be maintained. Whenever the machine becomes available, the user paying the most is selected. This requires a max heap. □

Example 13.2: Suppose that we are simulating a large factory. This factory has many machines and many jobs that require processing on some of these machines. An *event* is said to occur whenever a machine completes the processing of the job it is working on. When an event occurs, the job has to be moved to the queue for the next machine (if any) that it needs. If this queue is empty, the job can be assigned to the machine immediately. Also, a new job can be scheduled on the machine that has become idle (provided that its queue is not empty).

In order to determine the occurrence of events, a priority queue is used. This queue contains the finish time of all jobs that are presently being worked on. The next event occurs at the least time in the queue. So, a min heap can be used in this application. □

Before developing procedures to add to and delete from a heap, let us examine some other representations for a priority queue. We shall assume that each deletion removes the element with largest key value from the queue. The conclusions we draw are the same when the smallest element is to be deleted.

The simplest way to represent a priority queue is as an unordered linear list. Suppose that we have n elements each of size 1 in this queue. If formula (12.1) is used, then additions are most easily performed at the end of this list. Hence, the insert time is $\Theta(1)$. A deletion requires a search for the element with largest key followed by its deletion. Since it takes $\Theta(n)$ time to find the largest element in an n element unordered list, the delete time is $\Theta(n)$. If a chain is used, additions can be performed at the front of the chain in $\Theta(1)$ time. Each deletion takes $\Theta(n)$ time. An alternative is to use an ordered linear list. The elements are in nondecreasing order in case formula (12.1) is being used and in nonincreasing order in case an ordered chain is used. The delete time for each representation is $\Theta(1)$ and the insert time $O(n)$. When a max heap is used, both additions and deletions can be performed in $O(\log n)$ time.

A max heap with five elements is shown in Figure 13.10(a). When an element is added to this heap, the resulting six element heap must have the structure shown in Figure 13.10(b). This is so as a heap is a complete binary tree. If the element to be inserted has key value 1, it may be inserted as the left child of 2. If instead, the key value of the new element is 5, then this cannot be inserted as the left child of 2 (as otherwise, we will not have a max heap following the insertion). So, the 2 is moved down to its left child (Figure 13.10(c)) and we determine if placing the 5 at the old position of 2 results in a max heap. Since the parent element (20) is at least as large as the element (5) being inserted, it is alright to insert the new element at the position shown in the figure. Next, suppose that the new element has value 21 rather than 5. In this case, the 2 moves down to its left child as in Figure 13.10(c). The 21 cannot be inserted into the old position occupied by the 2 as the parent of this position is smaller than 21. Hence, the 20 is moved down to its right child and the 21 inserted in the root of the heap (Figure 13.10(d)).

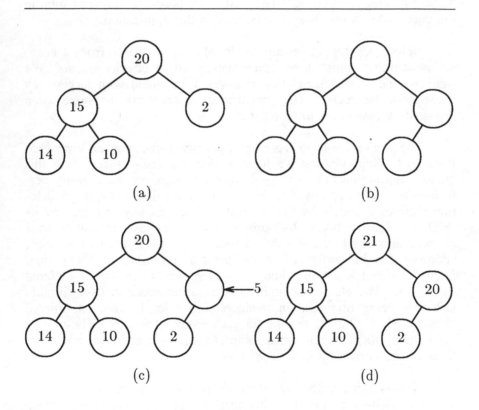

Figure 13.10 Insertion into a max heap

To implement the insertion strategy described above, we need to go from an element to its parent. If a linked representation is used, an additional *parent* field is to be added to each node. However, since a heap is a complete binary tree, the formula based representation can be used. Property 4 (Section 13.1.2) enables us to locate the parent of any element easily. Program 13.5 performs an insertion into a max heap that contains n elements. As a complete binary tree with n elements has a height $\lceil \log_2(n+1) \rceil$, the **while** loop of the insertion procedure is iterated $O(\log n)$ times.

```
procedure InsertMaxHeap (x: element);
{Insert x into the global max heap heap[1..MaxElements]}
{n is the present size of the heap}
var i: integer; NotDone: boolean;
begin
   if n = MaxElements then
   begin
      writeln('Heap full');
      goto 999; {end of program}
   end;
   n := n +1; i := n; NotDone := true;
   while NotDone do
      if i := 1 then NotDone := false {at root}
      else if x.key <= heap[i div 2].key then NotDone := false
         else begin {move from parent to i}
                 heap[i] := heap[i div 2];
                 i := i div 2;
              end;
   end;
   heap[i] := x;
end; {of InsertMaxHeap}
```

Program 13.5 Insertion into a max heap

When an element is to be deleted from a max heap, it is taken from the root of the heap. For instance, a deletion from the heap of Figure 13.10(d) results in the removal of the element 21. Since the resulting heap has only five elements in it, the binary tree of Figure 13.10(d) needs to be restructured to correspond to a complete binary tree with five elements. To do this, we remove the element in position 6. I.e., the element 2. Now, we have the right structure (Figure 13.11(a)) but the root is vacant and the element 2 is not in the heap. If the 2 is inserted into the root, the resulting binary tree is not a max heap. The element at the root should be the largest from amongst the

2 and the elements in the left and right children of the root. This element is 20. It is moved into the root thereby creating a vacancy in position 3. Since this position has no children, the 2 may be inserted here. The resulting heap is shown in Figure 13.10(a).

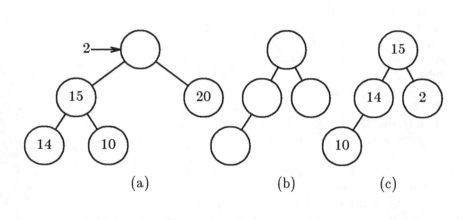

(a)   (b)   (c)

Figure 13.11   Deletion from a heap

Now, suppose we wish to perform another deletion. The 20 is to be deleted. Following the deletion, the heap has the binary tree structure shown in Figure 13.11(b). To get this structure, the 10 is removed from position 5. It cannot be inserted into the root as it is not large enough. The 15 moves to the root and we attempt to insert the 10 into position 2. This is, however, smaller than the 14 below it. So, the 14 is moved up and the 10 inserted into position 4. The resulting heap is shown in Figure 13.11(c).

Program 13.6 implements this strategy to delete from a heap. Once again, since the height of a heap with n elements is $\lceil \log_2(n+1) \rceil$, the **while** loop of this procedure is iterated $O(\log n)$ times. Hence the complexity of a deletion is $O(\log n)$.

```
procedure DeleteMaxHeap (var x: element);
{Delete from the max heap heap[1..MaxElements]}
{n is the current heap size}
var i, r, j: integer; k: element; NotDone: boolean;
begin
   if n = 0 then begin {heap empty}
                    writeln('Deletion from an empty heap');
                    goto 999; {end of program}
                 end;
   NotDone := true; x := heap[1]; k := heap[n]; n := n − 1;
   i := 1; j := 2; {j is left child of i}
   while (j <= n) and NotDone do
   begin
      if j < n then if heap[j].key < heap[j+1].key then j := j+1;
      {j points to larger child}
      if k.key >= heap[j].key then NotDone := false
                 else begin
                         heap[i] := heap[j]; {move child up}
                         {move i and j down}
                         i := j; j := 2*j;
                      end;
   end;
   heap[i] := k;
end; {of DeleteMaxHeap}
```

Program 13.6 Deleting from a max heap

Heap Sort

You might have already noticed that a heap can be used to sort n elements in $O(n\log n)$ time. We begin by inserting the n elements into an initially empty max heap. Then, elements are extracted from the heap one at a time. The elements appear in nonincreasing order of *key*. There are n insertions and n deletions. Each takes $O(\log n)$ time. So, the total time is $O(n\log n)$. This is better than the $O(n^2)$ time taken by a bubble or an insert sort.

We can perform a heap sort faster than by using the insert and delete procedures of Programs 13.5 and 13.6. As in the case of our procedures for insert and bubble sort, we assume that n integers are to be sorted. These are in the array $a[1..MaxElements]$. Suppose that n = 10 and $a[1:10]$ = [20, 12, 35, 15, 10, 80, 30, 17, 2, 1]. $a[1:10]$ corresponds to the complete binary tree of Figure 13.12(a). This is not a max heap.

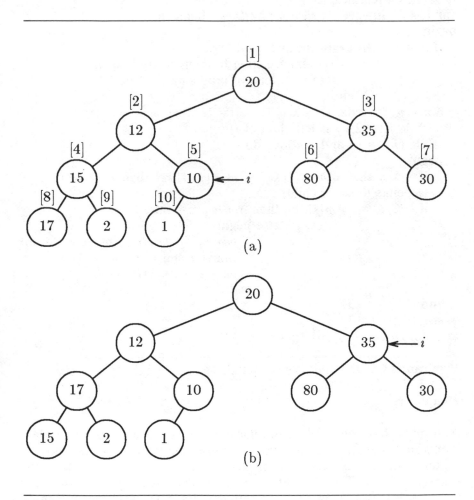

(a)

(b)

Figure 13.12 Creating a heap (Continued on next page)

To convert the complete binary tree of Figure 13.12(a) into a max heap, we begin with the first element that has a child (i.e., 10). This element is at position $i = \lfloor n/2 \rfloor$ of the array. If the subtree that this is a root of is a max heap, then no work is done here. If it is not,

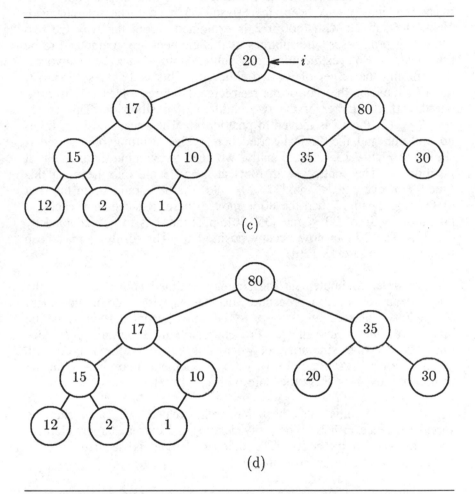

(c)

(d)

Figure 13.12 Creating a heap (Continued from previous page)

then we adjust the subtree so that it is a heap. Following this, we examine the subtree whose root is at $i-1$; then $i-2$; and so on until the root of the entire binary tree which is at 1 is examined.

Let us try this process on the binary tree of Figure 13.12(a). Initially, $i = 5$. The subtree with root at i is a max heap as $10 > 1$. Next, the subtree with root at 4 is examined. This subtree is not a max heap as $15 < 17$. To convert this subtree into a max heap, the 15 and 17 have to be interchanged. This gives us the tree of Figure

13.12 (b). The next subtree to examine has its root at position 3. To make this into a max heap, the 80 and 35 need to be interchanged. Next, the subtree with root at 2 is examined. From the way the restructuring progresses, the subtrees of this element are guaranteed to be max heaps. So, restructuring this subtree into a max heap involves determining the larger of its two children. This is 17. As $12 < 17$, the 17 should be the root of the restructured subtree. Next, 12 is compared with the larger of the two children of position 4. This is 15. As $12 < 15$, the 15 is moved to position 4. The vacant position 8 has no children and the 12 is inserted here. The resulting binary tree is shown in Figure 13.12(c). Finally, we need to examine the element at position 1. The subtrees with roots at 2 and 3 are max heaps at this time. However, $20 < \max\{17, 80\}$. So, the 80 should be in the root of the max heap. When the 80 is moved there, it leaves a vacancy at position 3. Since $20 < \max\{35, 30\}$, position 3 is to be occupied by the 35. The 20 can now occupy position 6. The resulting max heap is shown in Figure 13.12(d).

In order to implement the strategy outlined above to create the initial heap, we need a procedure that begins with a complete binary tree whose subtrees are known to be max heaps and converts the binary tree into a max heap. Procedure *adjust* (Program 13.7) does this. Notice the similarity between this procedure and procedure *DeleteMaxHeap* (Program 13.5). An n element max heap can be created by invoking this procedure with $i = \lfloor n/2 \rfloor$, ..., 1.

Once the initial max heap has been created, we can create the sorted sequence in a by repeatedly deleting the current largest element (i.e., the one in the root). The deleted element is inserted into the correct place in a as in Program 13.8.

Figure 13.13 shows the progress of the second **for** loop of Program 13.8 for the first few values of i. This loop begins with the max heap of Figure 13.12(d).

Complexity of Heap Sort

Procedure *adjust* takes $O(d)$ time where d is the height of the subtree to be adjusted. The first **for** loop of procedure *HeapSort* is executed for $i = n$ **div** 2, ..., 1. At most 2^{j-1} of these values denote elements at level j of the binary tree. j is in the range $[1, h-1]$ where $h = \lceil \log_2(n+1) \rceil$ is the height of the complete binary tree $a[1:n]$. The time

---

```
procedure adjust(var a: ElementList; i,n: integer);
{The subtree with root at i is converted into a max heap.}
{Initially, both its subtrees are max heaps.}
var j, r: integer; k: element; NotDone: boolean;
begin
    NotDone := true; k := a[i];
    j := 2*i;
    while (j <= n) and NotDone do
    begin
        if j < n then if a[j].key < a[j+1].key then j := j+1;
        if k.key >= a[j].key then NotDone := false
                             else begin
                                     a[j div 2] := a[j];
                                     j := 2*j;
                                 end;
    end;
    a[j div 2] := k;
end; {of adjust}
```

Program 13.7 Procedure *adjust*

to initialize the max heap is therefore: $O(\sum_{j=1}^{h-1} 2^{j-1}(h-j)) = O(n)$.

During the execution of the second **for** loop, $n-1$ invocations of *adjust* are made. Each has a cost of $O(\log n)$. So, the total cost of this loop is $O(n \log n)$. Hence, the overall time complexity of heap sort is $O(n \log n)$. This analysis assumes that n is the only instance characteristic of interest. In case we are interested in the complexity as a function of both n and the size, s, of *element*, the result is $O(ns \log n)$. This can be reduced to $O(n \log n)$ using indirect addressing.

Experimental Results

From the asymptotic analysis of Program 13.8, we know that there is an n_0 such that for every n, $n > n_0$, the maximum time needed by heap sort is less than the maximum time needed by insert sort (and also by bubble sort). While we have not proved this, this statement is also true for average times. On some specific initial permutations, however, insert sort will outperform heap sort. For instance, if the n

---

```
procedure HeapSort(var a: ElementList; n: integer);
{Sort a[1:n] using heap sort}
var i: integer; r: element;
begin
  {Create heap}
  for i := n div 2 downto 1 do
    adjust(a,i,n);

  {Create sorted sequence}
  for i := n-1 downto 1 do
  begin
    r := a[i+1]; a[i+1] := a[1]; a[1] := r;
    adjust(a, 1, i);
  end;
end; {of HeapSort}
```

Program 13.8 Heap Sort

elements are initially in sorted order, an insert sort will run for $\Theta(n)$ time while a heap sort will run for $\Theta(n\log n)$ time.

The value of n_0 for worst case and average times can be determined experimentally. Determining worst case and average case data for heap sort is quite difficult. So, for each n of interest, we obtain the run time for some number of random initial permutations. The maximum of these times is used as an estimate of the worst case time for this value of n. In order to accurately measure the time for each permutation, a suitable repetition factor is used. To obtain average times, each random permutation is sorted once. For each n, the time to sort a reasonable number of permutations is measured. The average of these times (total time / number of permutations) is used as an estimate of the actual average run time for this n.

The estimated average times obtained in this way are shown in Figure 13.14. In this figure, p is the number of random permutations used. The times were obtained on an IBM-PC using the Turbo Pascal compiler. Figure 13.14 also shows the estimated average times for insert sort. These times were obtained using the same permutations as used for heap sort. Because of the rapid growth in time needed by insert sort, times for this sort method were obtained only for values of

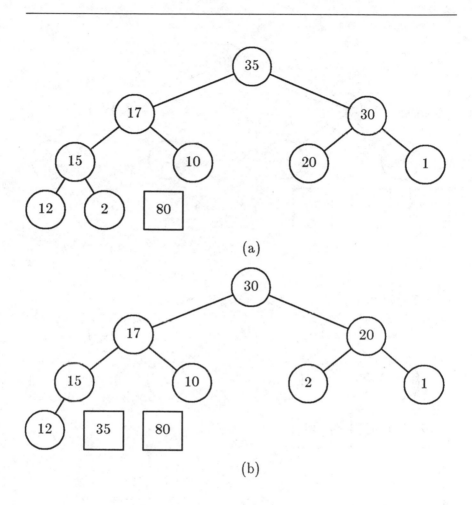

(a)

(b)

Figure 13.13 Heap Sort (Continued on next page)

n up to 500. All times in Figure 13.14 include the time needed to generate the random permutation using Program 11.20. Since this time is the same for heap and insert sort, the times of Figure 13.14 can be used for comparison of the two sort programs.

The average times of Figure 13.14 are plotted in Figure 13.15. As can be seen, for our implementation of the two sort algorithms, the

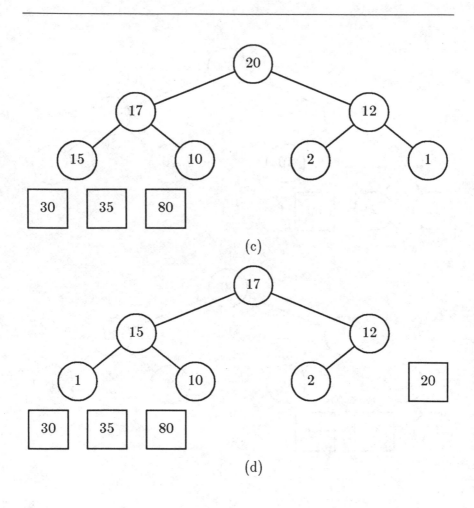

(c)

(d)

Figure 13.13 Heap Sort (Continued from previous page)

break even point for average performance is about $n = 55$. The exact break even point can be determined experimentally. From Figure 13.14, we know that this point is between 50 and 60.

n	p	heap	insert
0	800	0.034	0.032
10	800	1.482	0.775
20	300	3.680	2.253
30	300	6.153	4.430
40	200	8.815	7.275
50	120	11.583	10.892
60	75	14.427	15.013
70	75	17.427	20.000
80	60	20.517	25.450
90	60	23.717	31.767
100	40	26.775	38.325
200	40	60.550	148.300
300	35	96.657	319.657
400	35	134.971	567.629
500	30	174.100	874.600
600	30	214.400	
700	25	255.760	
800	25	297.480	
900	20	340.000	
1000	20	382.250	

Times are in hundredths of a second

Figure 13.14 Average times for heap and insert sort

13.3. BINARY SEARCH TREES

While a heap is well suited for applications that require priority queues, it is not suited for applications in which arbitrary elements are to be deleted from the element list. Deletion of an arbitrary element from an n element heap takes $O(n)$ time. This is no better than the time needed for arbitrary deletions from an unordered linear list that is represented using formula (12.1).

A *binary search tree* has a better performance than any of the data structures studied so far when the functions to be performed are: search, insert, and delete. In fact, with a binary search tree, these functions can be performed both by key value and by rank (i.e., find an element with key x; find the 5th smallest element; delete the

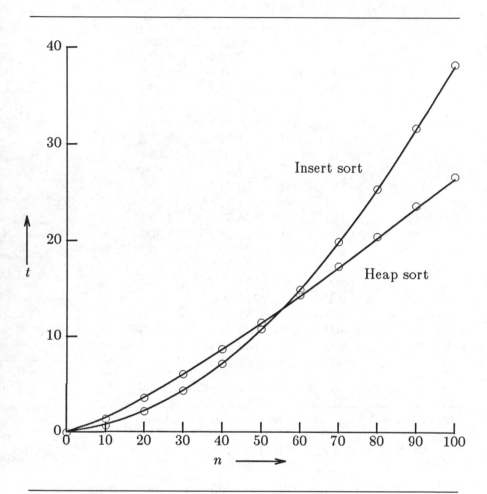

Figure 13.15 Plot of average heap and insert sort times

element with key x; delete the 5th smallest element; insert an element and determine its rank).

Definition: A *binary search tree* is a binary tree. It may be empty. If it is not empty then it satisfies the following properties:

(1) Every element has a key and no two elements have the same key. I.e., all keys are distinct.

(2)   The keys (if any) in the left subtree are smaller than the key in the root.

(3)   The keys (if any) in the right subtree are larger than the key in the root.

(4)   The left and right subtrees are also binary search trees.

There is some redundancy in the above definition. Properties (2), (3), and (4) together imply that the keys must be distinct. So, property 1 can be replaced by the property: The root has a key. The definition provided above is, however, clearer than the nonredundant version.

Some example binary trees in which the elements have distinct keys are shown in Figure 13.16. The tree of Figure 13.16(a) is not a binary search tree. This is so despite the fact that it satisfies properties (1), (2), and (3). The right subtree fails to satisfy property (4). This subtree is not a binary search tree as its right subtree has a key value (22) that is smaller than that in the subtrees' root (25). The binary trees of Figures 13.16(b) and (c) are binary search trees.

Searching a Binary Search Tree

Since the definition of a binary search tree is recursive, it is easiest to describe a recursive search method. Suppose we wish to search for an element with key x. We begin at the root. If the root is **nil**, then the search tree contains no elements and the search is unsuccessful. Otherwise, we compare x with the key in the root. If x equals this key, then the search terminates successfully. If x is less than the key in the root, then no element in the right subtree can have key value x and only the left subtree is to be searched. If x is larger than the key in the root, only the right subtree needs to be searched. The subtrees may be searched recursively as in Program 13.9. This function assumes a linked representation for the search tree. Each node has the three fields: *LeftChild*, *RightChild*, and *data*. *data* is of type *element* and has at least the field *key* which is of type **integer**. Notice the similarity between Program 13.9 and the recursive binary search function (Program 8.3).

The recursion of Program 13.9 is easily replaced by a **while** loop as in Program 13.10.

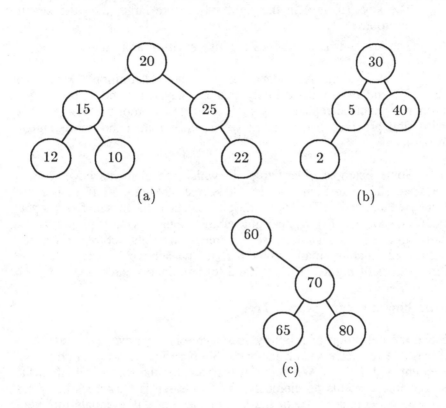

(a)

(b)

(c)

Figure 13.16 Binary trees

In case we wish to search by rank, each node should have an additional field *LeftSize* which is one plus the number of elements in the left subtree of the node. For the search tree of Figure 13.16(b), the nodes with keys 2, 5, 30, and 40, respectively, have *LeftSize* equal to 1, 2, 3, and 1. Program 13.11 searches for the kth smallest element.

As can be seen, a binary search tree of height h can be searched by key as well as by rank in $O(h)$ time.

---

function *search*(*t*: *TreePointer*; *x*: **integer**): *TreePointer*;
{Search the binary search tree *t* for an element with key *x*}
{Return a pointer to the element if it is found. Return **nil** otherwise.}
begin
  if *t* = **nil then** *search* := **nil**
  else if *x* = *t* ↑ .*data.key* **then** *search* := *t*
      else if *x* < *t* ↑ .*data.key* **then** *search* := *search*(*t* ↑ .*LeftChild*, *x*)
          else *search* := *search*(*t* ↑ .*RightChild*, *x*);
end; {of *search*}

Program 13.9 Recursive search of a binary search tree

---

function *search*(*t*: *TreePointer*; *x*: **integer**): *TreePointer*;
{Search the binary search tree *t* for an element with key *x*}
{Return a pointer to the element if it is found. Return **nil** otherwise.}
var *p*: *TreePointer*; *NotFound*: **boolean**;
begin
  p := *t*; *NotFound* := **true**;

  while (*p* <> **nil**) **and** *NotFound* **do**
    if *x* = *p* ↑ .*data.key* **then** *NotFound* := **false**
    else if *x* < *p* ↑ .*data.key* **then** *p* :=*p* ↑ .*LeftChild*
                      else *p* := *p* ↑ .*RightChild*;

  if *NotFound* **then** *search* := **nil**
              else *search* := *p*;
end; {of *search*}

Program 13.10 Iterative search of a binary search tree

Insert

To insert a new element *x*, we must first verify that its key is different
from those of existing elements. To do this a search is carried out. If
the search is unsuccessful, then the element is inserted at the point the
search terminated. For instance, to insert an element with key 80 into
the tree of Figure 13.16(b), we first search for 80. This search terminates unsuccessfully and the last node examined is the one with key

---

```
function search(t: TreePointer; k: integer): TreePointer;
{Search the binary search tree t for the kth smallest element}
{Return a pointer to the element if it is found.  Return nil otherwise.}
var p: TreePointer; NotFound: boolean; i: integer;
begin
    p := t; NotFound := true; i := k;

    while (p <> nil) and NotFound do
        if i = p ↑ .LeftSize then NotFound := false
        else if  i < p ↑ .LeftSize then p :=p ↑ .LeftChild
            else begin
                    i := i − LeftSize; {search for ith in right subtree}
                    p := p ↑ .RightChild;
                end;

    if NotFound then search := nil
                else search := p;
end; {of search}
```

Program 13.11 Searching a binary search tree by rank

40. The new element is inserted as the right child of this node. The resulting search tree is shown in Figure 13.17(a). Figure 13.17(b) shows the result of inserting the key 50 into the search tree of Figure 13.17(a).

Program 13.12 implements the insert strategy just described. In case nodes have a *LeftSize* field, then this is to be updated too. Regardless, the insertion can be performed in $O(h)$ time where h is the height of the search tree.

Delete

Deletion of a leaf element is quite easy. To delete 50 from the tree of Figure 13.17(b), the left child field of its parent is set to **nil** and the node disposed. This gives us the tree of Figure 13.17(a). To delete the 80, the right child field of 40 is set to **nil** obtaining the tree of Figure 13.16(b) and the node containing 80 disposed.

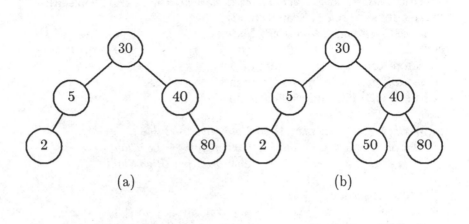

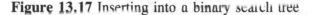

Figure 13.17 Inserting into a binary search tree

The deletion of a nonleaf element is accomplished by transforming it into the deletion of a leaf element. For instance, if we wish to delete the element with key 30 from the tree of Figure 13.17(b), then we find a suitable replacement for it. The 30 may be replaced by either the largest element in its left subtree or the smallest in its right subtree. Note that at least one of these subtrees contains an element as otherwise we are deleting a leaf element. Suppose we opt for the largest element in the left subtree. This has the key 5. It is moved into the root and the tree of Figure 13.18(a) obtained. Now we must delete the second 5. To do this, the 2 is moved up and the tree of Figure 13.18(b) obtained. The second 2 is in a leaf node and is easily deleted.

We leave the writing of the deletion procedure as an exercise. It should be evident that a deletion can be performed in $O(h)$ time if the search tree has a height of h.

Height of a Binary Search Tree

Unless care is taken, the height of a binary search tree with n elements can become as large as n. This is the case, for instance, when Program 13.12 is used to insert the keys [1, 2, 3, ..., n], in this order, into an initially empty binary search tree. It can, however, be shown

---

procedure *insert*(**var** *t*: *TreePointer*; *x*: *element*; **var** *success*: **boolean**);
{Insert *x* into the binary search tree *t*}
var *p*, *q*: *TreePointer*; *NotFound*: **boolean**;
begin
   {Search for *x.key*. *q* is parent of *p*}
   q := **nil**; *p* := *t*; *NotDone* := **true**;
   while (*p* <> **nil**) **and** *NotFound* **do**
      q := *p*; {save *p*}
      if *x.key* = *p* ↑ .*data.key* **then** *NotFound* := **false**
      else if *x.key* < *p* ↑ .*data.key* **then** *p* :=*p* ↑ .*LeftChild*
                       else *p* := *p* ↑ .*RightChild*;

   {Perform insertion}
   if *NotFound* **then** *success* := **false** {*x.key* already in *t*}
   else begin {insert into *t*}
        new(*p*);
        with *p* ↑ **do**
        begin
          LeftChild := **nil**; *RightChild* := **nil**; *data* := *x*;
        end;
        if *q* = **nil**
        then *t* := *q*
        else if *x.key* < *q* ↑ .*data.key* **then** *q* ↑ .*LeftChild* := *p*
                      else *q* ↑ .*RightChild* := *p*;
        success := **true**;
      end;
end; {of *insert*}

Program 13.12 Insertion into a binary search tree

that when insertions and deletions are made at random using the procedures given above, the height of the binary search tree is O(log *n*) on the average.

Search trees with a worst case height of O(log*n*) are called *balanced search trees*. Balanced search trees that permit searches, inserts, and deletes to be performed in O(*h*) time exist. Most notable amongst these are AVL and B trees. You are referred to the books by Knuth and Horowitz and Sahni that are cited in the readings section for a discussion of these balanced search trees.

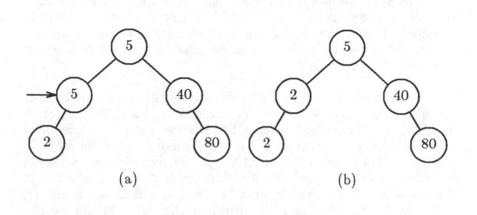

Figure 13.18 Deletion from a binary search tree

13.4. UNION-FIND TREES

In Chapter 6, we studied the problem of determining the nets in an electrical circuit. The solution provided there is very efficient. If the number of pins is n and the number of wires is e, the nets are found in $\Theta(n + e)$ time. This is the best asymptotic complexity one can hope for as it takes this much time to just read the input. The solution of Chapter 6 is, however, not well suited for an interactive environment. In this environment, the circuit designer sits at his/her computer/terminal and introduces wires one at a time. Before introducing a wire, the designer determines if the two end points (i.e., the two pins the wire will connect) are already in the same net. If so, the wire is not needed.

To solve the interactive net finding problem, we need a representation for the nets. The problem begins with a set of n pins numbered 1 through n and no wires. So, initially each pin is in a net of its own. Each time a wire is introduced, two nets are combined into one. The functions to be performed on the nets are:

(1) Determine the net that contains a particular pin i. This is used to determine if two pins are in the same net.

(2)   Combine two nets into one.

The first function is called *find* and the second *union*. At each time the nets are disjoint sets of pins. I.e., no two nets has a pin in common. Hence, the problem we are discussing is called the *disjoint set union-find* problem. Henceforth, we shall refer to the nets as sets and to the pins as elements.

A very good solution to the disjoint set union-find problem is obtained if the sets (or nets) are represented as trees. The degree of each tree is unconstrained. Figure 13.19 shows some sets represented as trees. Notice that each node that is not a root points to its parent in the tree. This is so as we intend to use the root element as the set identifier. Hence, we say that the elements 1, 2, 20, 30, etc. are in the set with root 20; the elements 11, 16, 25, and 28 are in the set with root 16; the element 15 is in the set with root 15; and the elements 26 and 32 are in the set with root 26 (or simply the set 26).

In our net example, the interactive designer may want to connect together pins 30 and 15. By performing two *find*s, he/she discovers that pin 30 is in the net 20 while pin 15 is in the net 15. So, the two pins are in different nets at this time and the wire (30, 15) may be used to connect these pins. If the designer wants to connect pins 1 and 3, he/she carries out a find on 1 and 3. Both are determined to be in the same net. So, they are already connected and an additional wire is not needed.

Representation

The solution to the union-find problem is a good example of the use of simulated pointers. A linked representation of the trees is needed. Each node must have a parent field. Children fields are, however, not needed. We also have a need to make direct access to nodes. To find the set containing element 10, we need to determine which node represents the element 10 and then follow a sequence of *parent* links to the root. This is best accomplished if the nodes are indexed 1 through n (the number of elements) and node i used to represent element i. When this is done, the parent field cannot be a Pascal pointer as it is to contain the index of another node. So, the parent field is of type **integer**. Figure 13.20 shows how the trees of Figure 13.19 are represented using this representation. The number inside a node is the

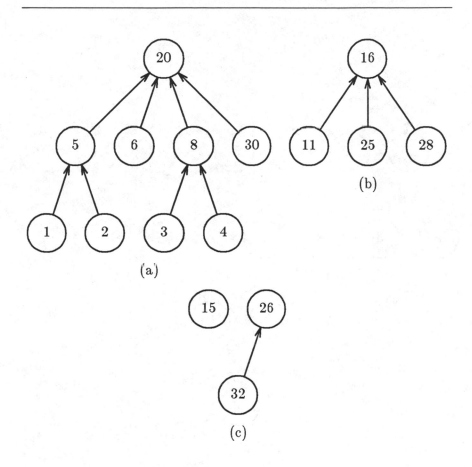

(b)

(a)

(c)

Figure 13.19 Tree representation of disjoint sets

value of its parent field. The number outside a node is its index. This is also the element it represents. The parent field for a root node is set to 0. Since there is no node with index 0, this is detected as a link to no node (or a null link).

Since each node has only one field, the declaration:

var *parent*: **array** [1..*MaxElements*] **of integer**;

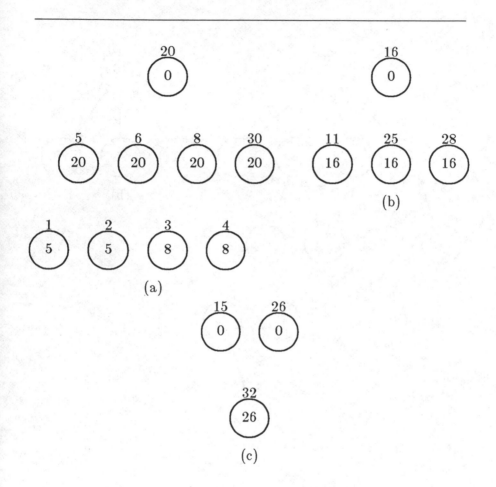

Figure 13.20 Representation of trees of Figure 13.19

suffices.

Functions

Assume that n, $n \leq MaxElements$, elements are present. Initially each is in a set of its own. To create the initial configuration, we need merely set $parent[1..n]$ to zero. Program 13.13 does this. This program assumes that the test $n \leq MaxElements$ is performed at the time n is input. Its complexity is $\Theta(n)$.

```
procedure initialize(n: integer);
{Initialize n sets each containing one of the elements i, 1≤i≤n}
var i: integer;
begin
   for i := 1 to n do
      parent[i] := 0;
end; {of initialize}
```

Program 13.13 Initialize sets

   To find the set that contains element i, we begin at node i and follow *parent* links until the root is reached. For instance, if $i = 4$ and the status of the sets is as in Figure 13.20(a), we begin at 4. The *parent* field gets us to node 8. Its *parent* field gets us to node 20 whose *parent* is 0. Hence 20 is the root and is therefore the set identifier. Program 13.14 implements the *find* function. This function assumes that the test $1 \le i \le n$ (i.e., i is a valid element) is performed at the time i is input. The complexity of *find* is $O(h)$ where h is the height of the tree that contains element i.

```
function find(i: integer): integer;
{Find set containing i}
var j: integer;
begin
   j := i;
   while parent[j] <> 0 do
      j := parent[j];
   find := j;
end; {of find}
```

Program 13.14 Find an clement

   The union of the sets with roots i and j, $i \ne j$, is obtained by making either i a subtree of j or j a subtree of i. For instance, if $i = 16$ and $j = 26$ (cf. Figure 13.19), the tree of Figure 13.21(a) results if i is made a subtree of j while the result is Figure 13.21(b) if j is made a subtree of i. Program 13.15 performs a union. It assumes that the check $i \ne j$ is performed before it is invoked. j is always made a subtree of i. The complexity of *union* is $\Theta(1)$.

---

procedure *union*(i, j: *integer*);
{Union sets with roots i and j, $i \neq j$}
begin
   parent[j] := i;
end; {of *union*}

Program 13.15 Combining two sets

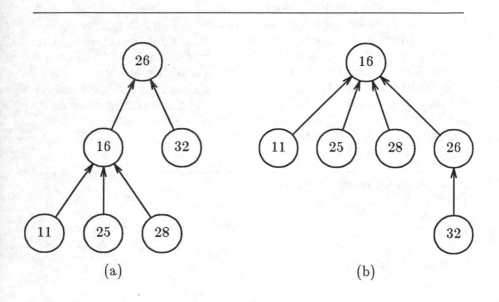

(a)   (b)

Figure 13.21 Union

Performance Evaluation

Assume that u unions and f finds are to be performed. Since each union is necessarily preceded by two finds, we may assume that $f >$ u. Each union takes $\Theta(1)$ time. The time required for each find depends on the height of the trees that get created. In the worst case, a tree with m elements can have a height of m. This happens, for instance, when the following sequence of unions is performed:

union(2,1), *union*(3,2), *union*(4,3), *union*(5,4), ...

Hence, each find can take as much as $\Theta(q)$ time where q is the number of unions that have been performed before the find. The average performance of a find is somewhat better. It can be shown (see *The Art Of Computer Programming: Sorting and Searching*, vol.3, by D. Knuth, Addison Wesley, 1973) that, on the average, a tree that is created by repeated use of procedure *union* has a height that is $O(\log p)$ where p is the number of elements in the tree. So, the average cost of a find is $O(\log q)$.

Weighting Rule

The worst case height of a tree with p elements can be controlled at $[\log_2 p] + 1$ by using the *weighting rule* during a union. This rule states that *the tree with fewer nodes is to be made a subtree of the other tree*. Ties are broken arbitrarily. The rationale behind this rule is easy to see. When a tree is made a subtree of another, the level number for each node in this tree increases by one. Hence, the cost of performing a find on each of these nodes increases by 1.

When the trees of Figures 13.19(a) and (b) are unioned, we should set *parent*[16] = 20. When trees (c) and (d) are unioned, we should set *parent*[15] = 26.

To incorporate the weighting rule into the procedure for a union, we add a **boolean** field *NotRoot* to each node. This field is false iff the node is presently a root node. The *parent* field of each root node is used to keep a count of the total number of nodes in the tree. For the trees of Figure 13.19, we have *NotRoot*[i] = **false** iff $i = 20$, 16, 15, or 26. Also, *parent*[i] = 9, 4, 1, and 2 for $i = 20$, 16, 15, and 26, respectively. The remaining *parent* fields are unchanged.

The initialization and union procedures now take the form given in Programs 13.16 and 13.17. These assume that *NotRoot* has been declared as another array as below:

var *NotRoot*: **array** [1..*MaxElements*] **of boolean**;

In addition, we need to change the conditional of the **while** of function *find* (Program 13.13) to *NotRoot*[j].

```
procedure initialize(n: integer);
{Initialize n sets each containing one of the elements i, 1≤i≤n}
var i: integer;
begin
   for i := 1 to n do
      begin parent[i] := 0; NotRoot[i] := false; end;
end; {of initialize}
```

Program 13.16 Initialize sets

```
procedure union(i, j: integer);
{Union sets with roots i and j, i≠j}
{The weighting rule is used}
begin
   if parent[i] < parent[j]
   then begin {make i a subtree of j}
           parent[j] := parent[i] + parent[j];
           NotRoot[i] := true;
           parent[i] := j;
        end
   else begin {make j a subtree of i}
           parent[i] := parent[i] + parent[j];
           NotRoot[j] := true;
           parent[j] := i;
        end;
end; {of union}
```

Program 13.17 Combining two sets using the weighting rule

The Collapsing Rule

Further improvement in the worst case performance is possible by using the collapsing rule. This rule is used during a find. It requires us to collapse all nodes on the path from i (the element being searched) to the root so that these nodes point directly to the root.

As an example, consider the tree of Figure 13.22 (a). When a *find*(10) is performed, the nodes 10, 15, and 3 are determined to be on the path from 10 to the root. Their parent fields are changed to 2 and the tree of Figure 13.22(b) obtained (since node 3 already points to 2, its field doesn't have to be changed; when writing the program it turns out to be easier to include this node in the set of nodes whose parent field is to be changed).

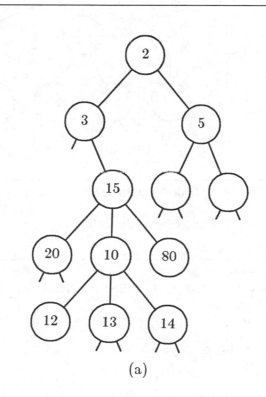

(a)

Figure 13.22 Collapsing nodes (Continued on next page)

While this collapsing of nodes may increase the time needed for an individual find, it reduces the cost of future finds. For instance, finding the elements in the subtrees of 10 and 15 is quicker in the collapsed tree of Figure 13.22(b). In fact, it can be shown that when both the collapsing and weighting rules are in use, the worst case time for u unions and f finds, $f > u$ is almost linear in f. For a proof of this fact, you are referred to the paper by Tarjan cited in the readings

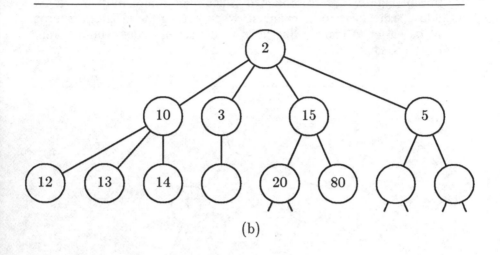

(b)

Figure 13.22 Collapsing nodes (Continued from previous page)

section. Program 13.18 implements the collapsing rule.

```
function find(i: integer): integer;
{Find set containing i.  Incorporate collapsing rule.}
var j, k, l: integer;
begin
    j := i;
    while NotRoot[j] do {find root}
        j := parent[j];
    k :=i;
    while NotRoot[k] do {collapse nodes}
    begin
        l := parent[k];
        parent[k] := j;
        k := l;
    end;
    find := j;
end; {of find}
```

Program 13.18 Find an element

13.5. GRAPHS

13.5.1. Definition

A *graph* $G = (V, E)$ is an ordered pair of finite sets V and E. The elements of V are called *vertices* (vertices are also called *nodes* and *points*). The elements of E are called *edges* (edges are also called *arcs* and *lines*). Each edge in E joins two distinct vertices in V. A graph is generally displayed as a figure in which the vertices are represented by circles and the edges by lines. Some examples are given in Figure 13.23.

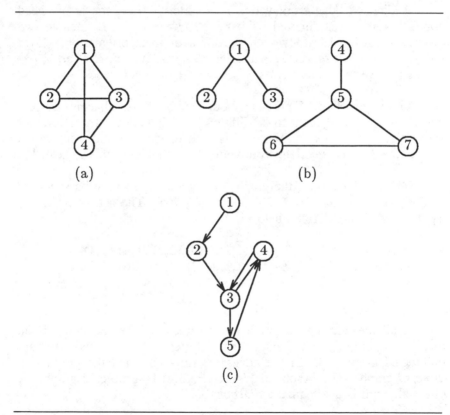

Figure 13.23 Some example graphs

Some of the edges in Figure 13.23 have arrow heads on them while others do not. An edge with an arrow head is called a *directed* edge while one without an arrow head is called an *undirected* edge. An undirected edge that joins vertices i and j is denoted (i, j). The edges (i, j) and (j, i) are the same. Let (i, j) be an edge in a graph. i and j are said to be *adjacent* and the edge (i, j) is *incident* on the vertices i and j.

In Figure 13.23(a), vertices 1 and 2 are adjacent. So also are vertices 1 and 3; 1 and 4; 2 and 3; and 3 and 4. This graph has no other pairs of adjacent vertices. The edge $(1,2)$ is incident on the vertices 1 and 2; edge $(2,3)$ is incident on the vertices 2 and 3; etc.

A directed edge from vertex i to vertex j (i.e., the arrow head points towards j) is denoted $<i, j>$. $<i, j>$ and $<j, i>$ denote two different edges. These two edges differ in their orientation. Edge $<i, j>$ is *incident to* vertex j and *incident from* vertex i. Vertex i is *adjacent to* vertex j and vertex j is *adjacent from* vertex i.

In the graph of Figure 13.23(c), vertex 2 is adjacent from 1 while vertex 1 is adjacent to 2. Edge $<1,2>$ is incident from vertex 1 and incident to vertex 2. Vertex 4 is both incident to and from vertex 3. Edge $<3,4>$ is incident from vertex 3 and incident to vertex 4.

Using set notation, the graphs of Figures 13.23 may be specified as $G_1 = (V_1, E_1)$, $G_2 = (V_2, E_2)$, $G_3 = (V_3, E_3)$. The sets V_1, V_2, V_3, E_1, E_2, and E_3 are defined below:

$V_1 = \{1,2,3,4\};$ $E_1 = \{(1,2),(1,3),(2,3),(1,4),(3,4)\}$
$V_2 = \{1,2,3,4,5,6,7\};$ $E_2 = \{(1,2),(1,3),(4,5),(5,6),(5,7),(6,7)\}$
$V_3 = \{1,2,3,4,5\};$ $E_3 = \{<1,2>,<2,3>,<3,4>,<4,3>,$
$<3,5>,<5,4>\}$

If all the edges in a graph are undirected, then the graph is an *undirected* graph. The graphs of Figures 13.23(a) and (b) are undirected graphs. If all the edges are directed, then the graph is a *directed* graph. The graph of Figure 13.23(c) is a directed graph. A directed graph is also called a *digraph*.

By definition, a graph does not contain multiple copies of the same edge. For an undirected graph this means that there can be at most one edge between any pair of vertices. In the case of a directed graph there can be at most one edge from vertex i to vertex j and one from j to i. Also, we require that a graph contain no *self edges* (i.e., no edges of the form (i,i) or $<i,i>$). A self edge is also called a *loop*.

13.5.2. Applications

Graphs have found application in a variety of situations. They are used in the analysis of electrical networks, the study of the molecular structure of chemical compounds (particularly hydrocarbons), the representation of airline routes, the representation of communication networks, planning projects, genetic studies, in statistical mechanics, in social sciences, etc. In this section, we formulate some problems as problems on graphs.

Example 13.3: [Path Problems] Consider a city with many streets. Each intersection may be regarded as a vertex in a graph. Each segment of a street that is between two adjacent intersections is represented by an edge. The edge is undirected if the street segment is two way and directed if it is a one way segment. Figure 13.24 shows a hypothetical street map and the corresponding graph.

A sequence of vertices $P = i_1, i_2, ..., i_k$ is an i_1 to i_k *path* in the graph $G = (V, E)$ iff the edge (i_j, i_{j+1}) or the edge $<i_j, i_{j+1}>$ is in E for every j, $1 \leq j < k$. There is a path from intersection i to intersection j iff there is a path from vertex i to vertex j in the corresponding graph. In the graph of Figure 13.24(b), 5, 2, 1 is a path from 5 to 1. There is no path from 5 to 4 in this graph.

With each edge in a graph, we may associate a *length*. The length of a path is the sum of the lengths of the edges on the path. The shortest way to get from intersection i to intersection j is obtained by finding a shortest path from vertex i to vertex j in the corresponding graph. □

Example 13.4: [Interpreters] Suppose that you are planning an international convention. All the speakers at this convention know English only. The remaining participants know one of the languages {L1, L2, L3, ..., Ln}. You have available a set of interpreters who can translate between English and some of the other languages. Your task is to select the fewest number of interpreters needed.

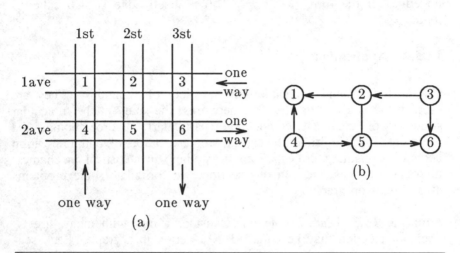

Figure 13.24 Street map and corresponding graph

The problem can be formulated as a graph problem. The graph has two sets of vertices. One corresponds to interpreters and the other to languages (Figure 13.25). There is an edge between interpreter i and language Lj iff interpreter i can translate between English and this language. Interpreter i is said to *cover* language Li iff there is an edge connecting the interpreter and the language. We are interested in finding a smallest subset of the interpreter vertices that covers the language vertices. □

Example 13.5: [Spanning Trees] Let $G = (V, E)$ be an undirected graph. G is *connected* iff there is a path between every pair of vertices in G. The undirected graph of Figure 13.23(a) is connected while that of Figure 13.23(b) is not. Suppose that G represents a possible communication network with V being the set of cities and E the set of communication links. It is possible to communicate between every pair of cities in V iff G is connected.

Suppose that G is connected and that each link has the same construction cost. We wish to construct the fewest number of links that will enable us to communicate between every pair of cities. If G is the graph of Figure 13.23(a), then it suffices to construct the links (1,2), (1,3), and (1,4).

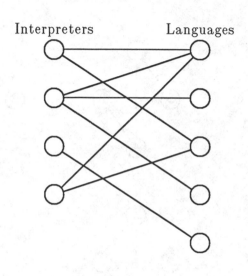

Figure 13.25 Interpreters and languages

A graph *H* is a *subgraph* of another graph *G* iff its vertex and edge sets are subsets of those of *G*. A *cycle* is a path with the same start and end vertex. For example, 1, 2, 1 is a cycle in the graph of Figure 13.23(a). A connected undirected graph that contains no cycles is called a *tree*. A subgraph of *G* that contains all the vertices of *G* and is a tree is called a *spanning tree* of *G*. The spanning trees of Figure 13.23(a) are shown in Figure 13.26.

It can be shown that if we wish to construct the fewest number of links in a communication graph, then all links on any one spanning tree are to be constructed. Further, if the links have different (but nonnegative) costs then the links on a minimum cost spanning tree (the cost of a spanning tree is the sum of the costs of the edges on it) are to be constructed. Figure 13.27 shows a graph and two of its spanning trees. The spanning tree of Figure 13.27(b) can be shown to be of minimum cost. □

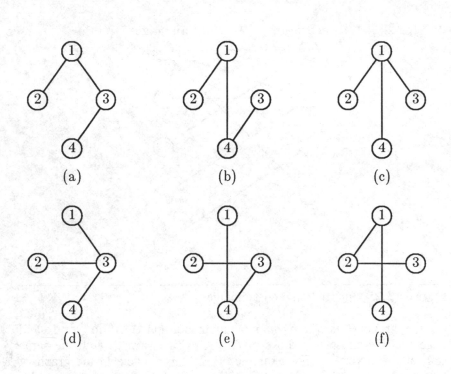

Figure 13.26 Spanning trees of Figure 13.23 (a)

13.5.3. Properties

Let G be an undirected graph. The *degree* d_i of vertex i is the number of edges incident on vertex i. For the graph of Figure 13.23(a), $d_1 = 3$; $d_2 = 2$; $d_3 = 3$; and $d_4 = 2$.

Property 1: Let $G = (V, E)$ be an undirected graph. Let $|V| = n$, $|E| = e$, and d_i = degree of vertex i.

(a) $0 \leq e \leq n(n-1)/2$

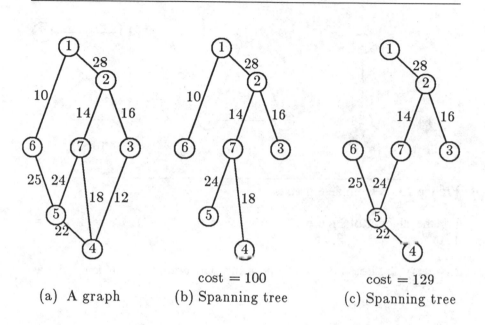

(a) A graph   (b) Spanning tree   (c) Spanning tree

cost = 100   cost = 129

Figure 13.27 Connected graph and two of its spanning trees

(b) $\sum_{i=1}^{n} d_i = 2e$

Proof: (a) follows from the observation that the degree of each vertex is between 0 and $n-1$. To prove (b), we note that each edge in an undirected graph is incident on exactly two vertices. Hence, the sum of the degrees of the vertices equals two times the number of edges. □

An n vertex graph with $n(n-1)/2$ edges is called a *complete graph*. The complete graphs for the cases $n = 1, 2, 3,$ and 4 are given in Figure 13.28. The complete graph on n vertices is denoted K_n.

Let G be a digraph. The *in-degree*, d_i^{in}, of vertex i is the number of edges incident to i (i.e., the number of edges coming into this vertex). The *out-degree*, d_i^{out}, of vertex i is the number of edges incident from this vertex (i.e., the number of edges leaving vertex i).

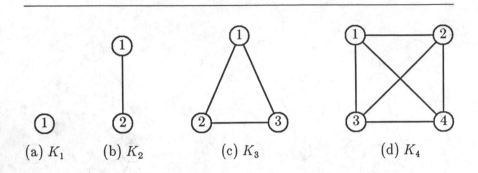

(a) K_1 (b) K_2 (c) K_3 (d) K_4

Figure 13.28 Complete graphs

For the digraph of Figure 13.23(c), $d_1^{in} = 0$, $d_1^{out} = 1$, $d_2^{in} = 1$, $d_2^{out} = 1$, $d_3^{in} = 2$, $d_3^{out} = 2$, etc.

Property 2: Let $G = (V, E)$ be a directed graph. Let n and e be as in Property 1.

(a) $0 \le e \le n(n-1)$

(b) $\sum_{i=1}^{n} d_i^{in} = \sum_{i=1}^{n} d_i^{out} = e$

Proof: Left as an exercise. $\square$

A *complete* digraph on n vertices contains exactly $n(n-1)$ directed edges. Figure 13.29 gives the complete digraphs for $n = 1$, 2, 3, and 4.

13.5.4. Representation

There are many good ways to represent a graph within a computer. The most frequently used representation schemes are adjacency based: adjacency matrices, packed adjacency lists, and linked adjacency lists.

Adjacency Matrix

The *adjacency matrix* of an n vertex graph $G = (V,E)$ is an $n \times n$ array $a[1..n, 1..n]$ of type *bit*. *bit* is a 0/1 valued data type defined as:

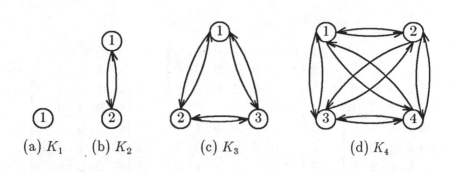

Figure 13.29 Complete digraphs.

type *bit* = 0..1;

We shall assume that $V = \{1, 2, ..., n\}$. If G is an undirected graph, then the elements of a are defined as:

$$a[i,j] = \begin{cases} 1 & \text{if } (i,j) \in E \text{ or } (j,i) \in E \\ 0 & \text{otherwise} \end{cases} \qquad (13.1)$$

If G is a digraph, then the elements of a are defined as:

$$a[i,j] = \begin{cases} 1 & \text{if } <i,j> \in E \\ 0 & \text{otherwise} \end{cases} \qquad (13.2)$$

The adjacency matrices for the graphs of Figures 13.23 are given in Figure 13.30.

The validity of the following statements is an immediate consequence of (13.1) and (13.2):

$$
\text{(a)}\quad
\begin{array}{c}
\\
1\\
2\\
3\\
4
\end{array}
\begin{array}{c}
1\ 2\ 3\ 4\\
\left[\begin{array}{cccc}
0 & 1 & 1 & 1\\
1 & 0 & 1 & 0\\
1 & 1 & 0 & 1\\
1 & 0 & 1 & 0
\end{array}\right]
\end{array}
$$

$$
\text{(b)}\quad
\begin{array}{c}
\\
1\\
2\\
3\\
4\\
5\\
6\\
7
\end{array}
\begin{array}{c}
1\ 2\ 3\ 4\ 5\ 6\ 7\\
\left[\begin{array}{ccccccc}
0 & 1 & 1 & 0 & 0 & 0 & 0\\
1 & 0 & 0 & 0 & 0 & 0 & 0\\
1 & 0 & 0 & 0 & 0 & 0 & 0\\
0 & 0 & 0 & 0 & 1 & 0 & 0\\
0 & 0 & 0 & 1 & 0 & 1 & 1\\
0 & 0 & 0 & 0 & 1 & 0 & 1\\
0 & 0 & 0 & 0 & 1 & 1 & 0
\end{array}\right]
\end{array}
$$

$$
\text{(c)}\quad
\begin{array}{c}
\\
1\\
2\\
3\\
4\\
5
\end{array}
\begin{array}{c}
1\ 2\ 3\ 4\ 5\\
\left[\begin{array}{ccccc}
0 & 1 & 0 & 0 & 0\\
0 & 0 & 1 & 0 & 0\\
0 & 0 & 0 & 1 & 1\\
0 & 0 & 1 & 0 & 0\\
0 & 0 & 0 & 1 & 0
\end{array}\right]
\end{array}
$$

Figure 13.30 Adjacency matrices for the graphs of Figure 13.23

(1) $a[i,i] = 0$, $1 \le i \le n$ for all n vertex graphs.

(2) The adjacency matrix of an undirected graph is symmetric. I.e., $a[i,j] = a[j,i]$, $1 \le i \le n$, $1 \le j \le n$.

(3) For an n vertex undirected graph, $\sum_{j=1}^{n} a[i,j] = \sum_{j=1}^{n} a[j,i] = d_i$
(recall that d_i is the degree of vertex i).

(4) For an n vertex digraph, $\sum_{j=1}^{n} a[i,j] = d_i^{out}$, $1 \le i \le n$ and

$$\sum_{i=1}^{n} a[i,j] = d_j^{in}, \ 1 \le j \le n.$$

Since every entry in a is either 0 or 1, it takes n^2 bits to store the adjacency matrix of an n vertex graph in a computer. The space requirement can be reduced to $n^2 - n$ by not explicitly storing the diagonal of a. All diagonal entries are known to be zero. For undirected graphs the adjacency matrix is symmetric. So, only the elements above (or below) the diagonal need to be stored explicitly. Hence only $(n^2 - n)/2$ bits are needed. When adjacency matrices are used, $\Theta(n)$ time is needed to determine the set of vertices adjacent to or from any given vertex. $\Theta(n^2)$ time is needed to determine the number of edges in the graph. However, a new edge can be added or an old one deleted in $\Theta(1)$ time.

Packed Adjacency Lists

In the *packed adjacency list* representation of a graph $G = (V,E)$ with $|V| = n$ and $|E| = e$, we use two one dimensional arrays $h[1..n+1]$ and $l[1..x]$ where $x = e$ if G is a digraph and $x = 2e$ if G is an undirected graph. First, all vertices adjacent from vertex 1 are put into l; then all vertices adjacent from 2 are put into l; then all vertices adjacent from 3 are put into l; and so on. (If i and j are adjacent vertices in an undirected graph, then i is adjacent from j and j is adjacent from i). h is set up so that the vertices adjacent from vertex i are in positions $l[h[i]]$, $l[h[i]+1]$, ..., $l[h[i+1]-1]$ if $h[i] < h[i+1]$. If $h[i] \geq h[i+1]$ then there are no vertices adjacent from i. We say that $l[h[i]]$, $l[h[i]+1]$, ..., $l[h[i+1]-1]$ is the packed adjacency list for vertex i. The order in which vertices appear in this list is not important. Figure 13.31 gives the packed adjacency lists corresponding to the graphs of Figure 13.23.

For an undirected graph, the values of h are in the range 1 to $2e+1$. As this range represents only $2e+1$ distinct values, each $h[i]$ need be at most $\lceil \log(2e+1) \rceil$ bits long. The l entries are each in the range 1 to n. Hence, each of these need be at most $\lceil \log n \rceil$ bits long. The total number of bits needed to store the packed adjacency lists of an undirected n vertex e edge graph is therefore at most $(n + 1)\lceil \log(2e+1) \rceil + 2e\lceil \log n \rceil = O((n + e)\log n)$.

When e is much less than n^2, the space needed by packed adjacency lists is less than that needed by an adjacency matrix. If G is an undirected graph, the degree of vertex i is simply $h[i+1] - h[i]$ and the number of edges in G is $(h[n+1] - 1)/2$. So, it is easier to determine these quantities when adjacency lists are used than when adjacency matrices are used. The addition of a new edge or the deletion of an old one, however, requires $O(n+e)$ time (see the exercises).

Linked Adjacency Lists

In the case of linked adjacency lists, each adjacency list is maintained as a chain. Each node on such a chain has the two fields *vertex* and *link*. The data type definitions are:

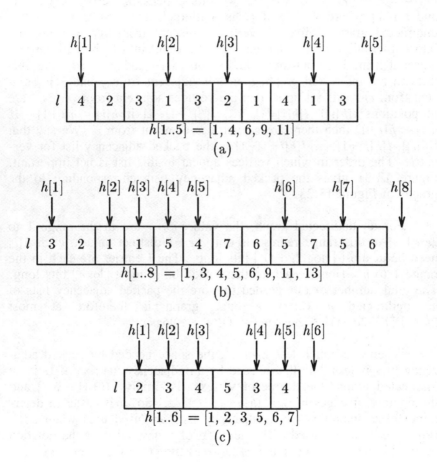

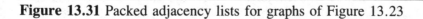

Figure 13.31 Packed adjacency lists for graphs of Figure 13.23

type *pointer* = ↑ *node*;
    node = **record**
               vertex : **integer**;
               link : *pointer*;
        end;

In addition, an array, h, of head nodes is used to locate these adjacency lists. This array is declared as:

var h : **array**[1..*MaxVertices*] **of** *pointer*;

Figure 13.32 gives the linked adjacency list representations for the graphs of Figure 13.23.

To arrive at a comparative space requirement for this representation, it is useful to consider a three array representation in which the pointers are simulated by integers. Assume we use the three arrays: $h[1..n]$, $v[1..x]$, and $link[1..x]$. Each array is of type **integer**, $x = 2e$ for an undirected graph, and $x = e$ for a directed graph. $h[i]$ is the head node for the adjacency list of vertex i, $1 \leq i \leq n$ and it points to the location in v where the first vertex in the adjacency list for i is stored. The only change needed in Figure 13.32 is to replace all occurrences of **nil** by a 0. The total number of bits needed for the linked adjacency lists representation of a graph is at most $(n+x)\log x + x \log n$ where $x = 2e$ if G is undirected and $x = e$ if G is directed. In either case, the number of bits needed is $O((n+e)\log n)$.

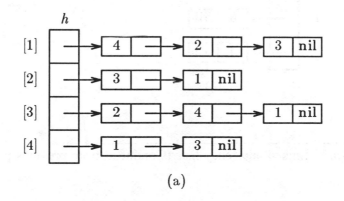

(a)

Figure 13.32 Linked adjacency lists (Continued on next page)

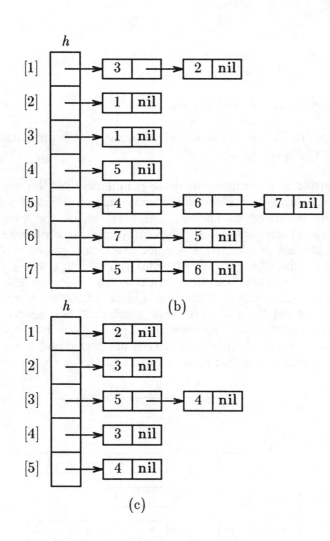

(b)

(c)

Figure 13.32 Linked adjacency lists (Continued from previous page)

Linked adjacency lists permit easy addition and deletion of edges. The time needed to determine the number of vertices on an adjacency list is proportional to the number of vertices on that list.

13.5.5. Functions

The number of functions that one can perform on a graph are too numerous to list here. We have already seen some (e.g., find a path, find a spanning tree, is the undirected graph connected?) and shall see some others in the next chapter. Many of the functions that one performs on a graph require us to visit all vertices that can be reached from a given start vertex. There are two standard ways to search for these vertices: breadth first search and depth first search.

Breadth First Search

Let $G = (V,E)$ be a graph (either directed or undirected). Let $i \in V$ and $j \in V$ be two distinct vertices. Vertex j is *reachable* from i iff there is a path from i to j in G. Consider the directed graph of Figure 13.33(a). One way to determine all the vertices reachable from vertex 1 is to first determine the set of vertices adjacent from 1. This set is {2,3,4}. Next, we determine the set of new vertices (i.c., vertices not yet reached) that are adjacent from vertices in {2,3,4}. This set is {5,6,7}. The set of new vertices adjacent from vertices in {5,6,7} is {8,9}. There are no new vertices adjacent from a vertex in {8,9}. So, {1,2,3,4,5,6,7,8,9} is the set of vertices reachable from vertex 1.

This method of starting at some vertex in a graph and searching it for all vertices reachable from that vertex is called *breadth first search*. A formal specification of this search method is provided by procedure *BreadthFirstSearch* (Program 13.19). This procedure assumes that *reached*(1..n) is initialized to **false**. When the procedure terminates, *reached*(i) = **true** iff vertex i is reachable from vertex v.

If procedure *BreadthFirstSearch* is used on the graph of Figure 13.33(a) with $v = 1$, then vertices 2, 3, and 4 will get added to *queue* (assume that they get added in this order) in the **for** loop. Following this, 2 is removed from *queue* (by definition, vertices are removed from a queue in the order they were added to it). The next iteration of the **for** loop results in vertex 5 getting added to *queue*. Next, 3 is deleted from *queue* and no new vertices are added. Then, 4 is deleted and 6 and 7 added. 5 is deleted next and 8 added. Then 6 is deleted

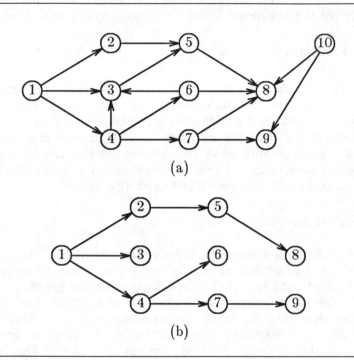

(a)

(b)

Figure 13.33

and nothing added. Next, 7 is deleted and 9 added. Finally, 8 and 9 are deleted and *queue* becomes empty. The procedure terminates and vertices 1 through 9 have been marked as reached. Figure 13.33(b) shows the subgraph formed by the edges used to reach the nodes that get visited.

Theorem 13.1: Let G be an arbitrary graph. Let v be any vertex of G. Procedure *BreadthFirstSearch* sets *reached*(i) = **true** for all vertices that are reachable from vertex v (including vertex v).

Proof: Left as an exercise. $\square$

Observe that if G is a connected undirected graph, then all vertices in G are reachable from all others. So, *BreadthFirstSearch* will mark all vertices no matter what the start vertex is. Consequently, G is connected iff a call to *BreadthFirstSearch* results in *reached*(i) = **true**

```
procedure BreadthFirstSearch(v: integer);
{Breadth first search of an n vertex graph G.}
{Search begins at vertex v.}
var w: integer; NotDone: boolean;
begin
    x := v; reached(v) := true; NotDone := true;
    initialize queue to be an empty queue;
    while NotDone do
    begin
        for all vertices w adjacent from x do
            if not reached(w) then begin
                                  reached(w) := true;
                                  add w to queue;
                              end;
        if queue is empty then NotDone := false
                          else delete a vertex x from queue;
    end;
end; {of BreadthFirstSearch}
```

Program 13.19 Breadth first search

for all $v \in V$. Hence, *BreadthFirstSearch* can be used to determine if an undirected graph is connected.

The time complexity of *BreadthFirstSearch* depends on whether adjacency matrices or lists are used to represent G. If an adjacency matrix is used and if G has n vertices, then $\Theta(n)$ time is needed to determine all the vertices adjacent from any vertex x. If a total of p vertices get marked, then x takes on p different values and $\Theta(pn)$ time is spent just to determine the vertices adjacent from all the x's. Since all vertices other than v that get reached get added to *queue*, $\Theta(p-1)$ time is spent in the **for** loop (assuming that each addition to *queue* takes $\Theta(1)$ time). The total time spent in *BreadthFirstSearch* is $\Theta(pn)$. In the worst case, $p = n$ and the time complexity becomes $O(n^2)$.

When adjacency lists (whether packed or linked) are used, the time needed to determine all the vertices adjacent from x is $\Theta(d_x^{out})$ in the case of a directed graph and $\Theta(d_x)$ in the case of an undirected graph. Thus the total time needed for the search is $\Theta(\sum_x (1 + d_x^{out}))$ or $\Theta(\sum_x (1 + d_x))$ where the sum is taken over all values assigned to x in

BreadthFirstSearch. In the worst case, x takes on all values 1, 2, 3, ..., n and the time complexity of *BreadthFirstSearch* is therefore $O(n+e)$ where e is the number of edges in G.

As far as the space complexity is concerned, n bits of space are needed for *reached*. If p vertices get marked, then at most $p-1$ vertices can be in *queue* at any one time. So, the space needed for *queue* is $O(p) = O(n)$. In addition, space is needed to store the graph G.

If a breadth first search is carried out starting from any vertex in a connected graph with $| V | = n$, then from Theorem 13.1 we know that all vertices will get marked. Exactly $n-1$ of these will get reached in the **for** loop of *BreadthFirstSearch*. When a new vertex w is reached in this loop, the edge used to reach this previously unreached vertex is (x,w). The set T of edges used in this way is such that $| T | = n-1$. Since this set of edges contains a path from v to every other vertex in the graph, it defines a connected subgraph which is a spanning tree of G.

Consider the graph of Figure 13.34(a). If a breadth first search is started at vertex 1, then $T = \{(1,2), (1,3), (1,4), (2,5), (4,6), (4,7), (5,8)\}$. This set of edges corresponds to the spanning tree of Figure 13.34(b).

A *breadth first spanning tree* is any spanning tree obtained in the manner described above from a breadth first search. One may verify that the spanning trees of Figures 13.34 (b), (c), and (d) are all breadth first spanning trees of the graph of Figure 13.34 (a) ((c) and (d) are, respectively, obtained by starting at vertices 8 and 6).

Depth First Search

Depth first search is an alternate to breadth first search. Starting at a vertex v, a depth first search proceeds as follows. First, the vertex v is marked as reached. Next, an unreached vertex w adjacent from v is selected. If such a vertex does not exist, the search terminates. Assume that a w as described exists. A depth first search from w is now initiated. When this search is completed, we select another unreached vertex adjacent from v. If there is no such vertex, then the search terminates. If such a vertex exists, a depth first search is initiated from this vertex, and so on. Program 13.20 is a formal recursive specification of depth first search. As in the case of breadth first

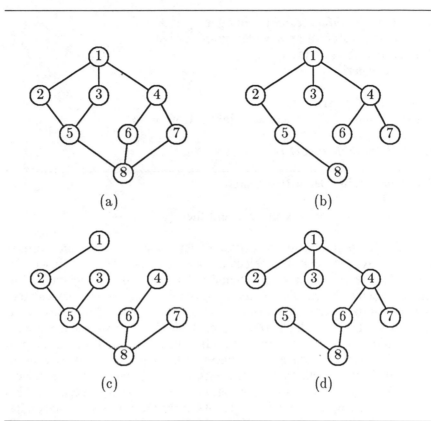

(a)

(b)

(c)

(d)

Figure 13.34 A graph and some of its breadth first spanning trees

search, it is assumed that *reached*(*i*) = **false**, $1 \le i \le n$, at the time of initial call to *DepthFirstSearch*.

Let us try out procedure *DepthFirstSearch* on the graph of Figure 13.33(a). If $v = 1$, then vertices 2, 3, and 4 are the candidates for the first choice of w in the **for** loop of *DepthFirstSearch*. Suppose that the first value assigned to w is 2. The edge used to get to 2 is <1,2>. A depth first search from 2 is now initiated. Vertex 2 is marked as reached. The only candidate for w this time is vertex 5. The edge <2,5> is used to get to 5. A depth first search from 5 is initiated. 5 is marked as reached. Using the edge <5,8>, vertex 8 is reached and marked. From 8 there are no unreached adjacent vertices. So, the algorithm backs up to vertex 5. There are no new candidates

---

procedure *DepthFirstSearch*(*v*: **integer**);
{Depth first search of an *n* vertex graph *G*.}
{Search begins at vertex *v*.}
var *w*: **integer**;
begin
    reached(*v*) := **true**;
    for all unreached vertices *w* adjacent from *v* **do**
        DepthFirstSearch(*w*);
end; {of *DepthFirstSearch*}

Program 13.20 Depth first search

for *w* here. So, we back up to 2 and then to 1.

At this point, there are two candidates for *w*. These are vertices 3 and 4. Assume that 4 is selected. Hence, edge <1,4> is used. A depth first search from 4 is initiated. 4 is marked as reached. 3, 6, and 7 are now the candidates for *w*. Assume that vertex 6 is selected. When *v* = 6, vertex 3 is the only candidate for *w*. Edge <6,3> is used to get to 3. A depth first search from 3 is initiated and vertex 3 gets marked. No new vertices are adjacent from 3 and we back up to vertex 6. No new vertices are adjacent from here. So, we back up to 4. From here a depth first search with *w* = 7 is initiated. Next, vertex 9 is reached. From 9 there are no new adjacent vertices. This time, we back up all the way to 1. As there are no new vertices adjacent from 1, the algorithm terminates.

During the above depth first search, vertices 1, 2, 3, ..., and 9 are marked. Figure 13.35 shows the subgraph consisting of only those edges that were used to reach a new vertex. The numbers outside each vertex give the order in which the vertices are reached. This number is called the *depth first number*. Note that the depth first number of a vertex is not unique. It depends on the starting vertex and also on the order in which the vertices *w* are selected in the **for** loop of procedure *DepthFirstSearch*.

For procedure *DepthFirstSearch*, one may prove a theorem analogous to Theorem 13.1. I.e., *DepthFirstSearch* marks vertex *v* and all vertices reachable from *v*.

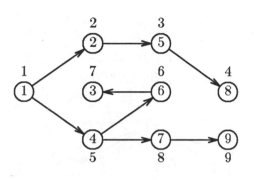

Figure 13.35

Theorem 13.2: Let G be an arbitrary graph. Let v be any vertex of G. Procedure *DepthFirstSearch* sets *reached*(i) = **true** for all vertices (including v) that are reachable from vertex v.

Proof: Left as an exercise. □

One may also verify that *DepthFirstSearch* has the same time and space complexities as does *BreadthFirstSearch* (see the exercises). However, the graphs for which *DepthFirstSearch* takes maximum space (i.e., stack space for the recursion) are the ones on which *BreadthFirstSearch* takes minimum space (i.e., *queue* space). The graphs for which *BreadthFirstSearch* takes maximum space are the ones for which *DepthFirstSearch* takes minimum space. Figure 13.36 gives the best case and worst case graphs for *DepthFirstSearch* and *BreadthFirstSearch*. One may readily verify the truth of the statements just made.

For undirected graphs, *DepthFirstSearch* has the same properties as does *BreadthFirstSearch*. All vertices are marked reachable when a *DepthFirstSearch* is initiated from any vertex in the graph G iff G is connected. If G is connected then exactly $n-1$ edges are used to reach new vertices. The subgraph formed by these edges is a spanning tree of G. A spanning tree obtained in this manner from a depth first search is called a *depth first spanning tree*. Figure 13.37 shows some of the depth first spanning trees of the graph of Figure 13.34(a).

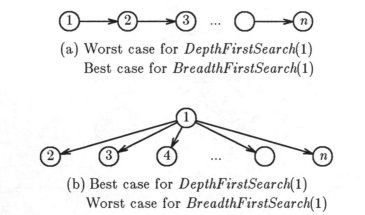

(a) Worst case for *DepthFirstSearch*(1)
Best case for *BreadthFirstSearch*(1)

(b) Best case for *DepthFirstSearch*(1)
Worst case for *BreadthFirstSearch*(1)

Figure 13.36 Worst case and best case space complexity graphs

13.6. REFERENCES AND SELECTED READINGS

The following texts provide an in depth study of data structures:

> *Fundamentals of data structures in Pascal*, by E. Horowitz and S. Sahni, Computer Science Press, Maryland, 1984.

and

> *The art of computer programming: Fundamental algorithms*, by D. E. Knuth, Vol. 1, Second Edition, Addison Wesley, New York, 1973.

An alternate to heaps as a data structure for event lists is examined in the paper:
> A comparison of heaps and the TL structure for the simulation event set, by W. Franta and K. Maly *Communications of ACM*, Vol. 21, No. 10, October 1978, pp. 873-875.

For an analysis of the weighting and collapsing rules, see the paper:
> *Efficiency of a good but not linear set union algorithm*, by R. Tarjan, *JACM*, Vol. 22, No. 2, April 1975, pp. 215-225.

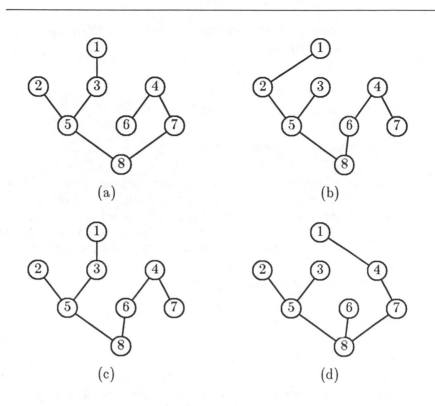

Figure 13.37 Some depth first spanning trees of Figure 13.34(a)

Additional material on graphs can be found in the books:

> *Concepts in discrete mathematics*, by Sartaj Sahni, 2nd Edition, 1985, Camelot Publishing Company, Minnesota.

and

> *Graph algorithms*, by Shimon Even, Computer Science Press, Maryland, 1979.

13.7. EXERCISES

1. Draw the binary expression trees corresponding to each of the following expressions:
    a) $(a+b)/(c-d*e)+e+g*h/a$
    b) $-x-y*z+(a+b+c/d*e)$
    c) $((a+b)>(c-e))$ **or** $a<f$ **and** $(x<y$ **or** $y>z)$

2. Prove Property 4 of Section 13.1.2.

3. Write a procedure to perform a preorder traversal on a binary tree represented using the formula based scheme. Assume that the elements of the binary tree are stored in the array $t[1..MaxElements]$ and that $t[i] = 0$ iff there is no element at position i. What is the time complexity of your procedure?

4. Do Exercise 3 for inorder.

5. Do Exercise 3 for postorder.

6. Do Exercise 3 for levelorder.

7. Write a Pascal procedure to make a copy of a binary tree represented using the formula based scheme.

8. Write two recursive Pascal functions to copy a binary tree t that is represented using the linked representation. The first of these should traverse the tree in postorder and the second in preorder. What is the difference (if any) in the recursion stack space needed by these two functions?

9. Write a recursive procedure to evaluate an expression tree t. Assume that each node has a field *value* that may be used by your procedure. The value field for nodes representing constants and variables contains the appropriate numeric value.

10. Write a recursive procedure to erase a binary tree t. Assume that t is a linked tree and that the nodes are to be returned to the free space list using the Pascal procedure *dispose*.

11. Write an iterative procedure to traverse a linked binary tree in inorder. Your procedure may utilize a formula based stack. Make your procedure as elegant as possible. How much stack space is needed for the traversal? This should be given as a function of the number of nodes, n, in t.

12. Do Exercise 12 for preorder.

13. Do Exercise 12 for postorder.

14. Compare the worst case run times of heap sort and insert sort. For heap sort, use some number of random permutations to estimate the worst case run time. At what value of n does the run time of heap sort become less than that of insert sort?

15. Write a procedure to list the elements in a binary search tree in increasing order of the key field. What are the time and space complexities of your procedure?

16. Do the previous exercise for decreasing order of the key field.

17. Write a procedure to insert an element x into a linked binary search tree. Assume that each node has the field *LeftSize* in addition to the other fields. Your procedure should run in $O(h)$ time.

18. Write a procedure to delete an element with key x from a linked binary search tree. Assume that the field *LeftSize* is not present. Your procedure must run in $O(h)$ time where h is the height of the search tree.

19. Do the previous exercise under the assumption that each node has a *LeftSize* field.

20. Generate a random permutation of the integers 1 through n. Insert the keys 1 through n into an initially empty binary search tree. Perform the insertion in the order specified by the random permutation. Measure the height of the resulting search tree. Repeat this for several random permutations and compute the average of these heights. Compare this figure with $\lceil \log_2(n+1) \rceil$. For n, use the values 10, 50, 100, 150, 200, 250.

21. Prove that when the weighting rule is used, the height of a tree with p elements is at most $\lfloor \log_2 p \rfloor + 1$. [Hint: use induction on p.]

22. Compare the average performance of Programs 13.13 - 13.15 with that of Programs 13.16 - 13.18. Do this for different values of n. For each value of n generate a random sequence of pairs $(i \ j)$. Replace each pair by two finds (one for i and the other for j). If the two are in different sets, then a union is to be performed. Repeat the experiment using many different random sequences. Measure the total time taken over these sequences. It is left to you to take this basic description of the experiment and plan a meaningful experiment to compare the average performance of the two sets of programs. Write a report that describes your experiment and the conclusions that can be drawn. Include program listings; a table of average times, and graphs in your report.

23. For each of the graphs of Figure 13.38, determine the following:
    (a) The in-degree of each vertex.
    (b) The out-degree of each vertex.
    (c) The set of vertices adjacent from vertex 2.
    (d) The set of vertices adjacent to vertex 1.
    (e) The set of edges incident from vertex 3.
    (f) The set of edges incident to vertex 4.
    (g) All directed cycles and their lengths.

24. Prove Property 2 of Section 13.5.3.

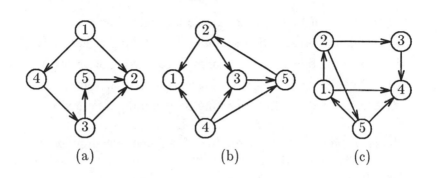

Figure 13.38 Digraphs

25. Obtain the following representations for the graphs of Figure 13.37.
    (a) Adjacency matrix.
    (b) Compact adjacency lists.
    (c) Linked adjacency lists.

26. Let G be any undirected graph. Show that the number of vertices with odd degree is even.

27. Let G be an n vertex e edge undirected graph. What is the least value of e for which the adjacency matrix representation of G uses less space than used by the packed adjacency lists representation?

28. Do the previous exercise for the case of a directed graph G.

29. Write an algorithm to delete an edge (i,j) from the packed adjacency list representation of the undirected graph G. What is the complexity of your algorithm?

30. Do the previous exercise for the case of edge insertion (i.e., a new edge (i,j) is to be added to the graph).

31. For the graph of Figure 13.23(a), do the following:
    (a) Obtain a breadth first spanning tree starting at vertex 1.
    (b) Obtain a breadth first spanning tree starting at vertex 3.
    (c) Obtain a depth first spanning tree starting at vertex 1.
    (d) Obtain a depth first spanning tree starting at vertex 3.

32. Obtain a procedure to determine if an undirected graph $G = (V,E)$ contains a cycle.
    (a) Prove the correctness of your procedure.
    (b) Obtain the time and space complexities of your procedure.

33. For each of the depth first spanning trees of Figure 13.37, determine a possible start vertex and a sequence of depth first numbers.

34. Let $G = (V, E)$ be a connected graph with $|V| > 1$. Show that G contains either a vertex of degree 1 or a cycle (or both).

35. Let $G=(V, E)$ be a connected graph that contains at least one cycle. Let $(i,j) \in E$ be an edge that is on at least one cycle of G. Show that the graph $h = (V, E-\{(i,j)\})$ is also connected.

36. Prove the following:
    (a) For every n there exists a connected undirected graph containing exactly $n-1$ edges, $n \geq 1$.
    (b) Every n vertex connected undirected graph contains at least $n-1$ edges. You may use the results of the previous two exercises.

37. A digraph is *strongly connected* iff it contains a directed path from i to j and from j to i for every pair of distinct vertices i and j.

(a)   Show that for every n, $n \geq 2$, there exists a strongly connected digraph that contains exactly n edges.

(b)   Show that every n vertex strongly connected digraph contains at least n edges, $n \geq 2$.

(c)   Write a procedure to determine whether or not the digraph G is strongly connected.

(d)   Analyze the time complexity of your procedure for the case when G is represented as an adjacency matrix as well as for the case of a linked adjacency list representation.

38.   Prove Theorem 13.1.

39.   Prove Theorem 13.2.

40.   A subgraph $G_1 = (V_1, E_1)$ of the undirected graph G is a *connected component* iff G_1 is a connected graph and G contains no connected subgraph that properly contains G_1 (i.e., there is no connected subgraph $G_2 = (V_2, E_2)$ of G such that $V_1 \subseteq V_2$ and $E_1 \subset E_2$). Write a procedure to find the connected components of G. What is its time complexity?

CHAPTER 14

ALGORITHM DESIGN METHODS

14.1. INTRODUCTION

While the design of a good algorithm for any given problem is more an art than a science, there are some design methods that have proved effective in the solution of many problems. These methods are studied in this chapter. When posed with a problem for computer solution, you can apply these methods and see how good the resulting algorithm is. Generally, it will be necessary to fine tune the resulting algorithm to get acceptable performance. In some cases, this fine tuning will not be possible and you will have to think of some other way to solve the problem.

Many of the examples used in this chapter are *optimization problems*. In an optimization problem we are given a set of *constraints* and an *optimization function*. Solutions that satisfy the constraints are called *feasible solutions*. A feasible solution for which the optimization function has the best possible value is called an *optimal solution*.

Example 14.1: [Loading Problem] A large ship is to be loaded with cargo. The cargo is containerized and each container has the same size. Different containers may have different weight. Let w_i be the weight of the ith container, $1 \le i \le n$. The cargo capacity of the ship is c. We wish to load the ship with the maximum number of containers.

620

This problem can be formulated as an optimization problem in the following way. Let x_i be a variable whose value can be either 0 or 1. If we set x_i to 0, then container i is not to be loaded. If x_i is 1, then it is to be loaded. We wish to assign values to the x_is that satisfy the constraints:

$$\sum_{i=1}^{n} w_i x_i \le c$$

and

$$x_i \in \{0, 1\}, \ 1 \le i \le n$$

The optimization function is:

$$\sum_{i=1}^{n} x_i$$

Every set of x_is that satisfies the constraints is a feasible solution. Every feasible solution that maximizes $\sum_{i=1}^{n} x_i$ is an optimal solution. $\square$

Example 14.2: [Thirsty Baby] This problem was introduced in Example 2.3. The constraints are:

$$\sum_{i=1}^{n} x_i = t$$

and

$$0 \le x_i \le a_i$$

The optimization function is:

$$\sum_{i=1}^{n} s_i x_i$$

Every set of x_is that satisfies the constraints is a feasible solution. Every feasible solution that maximizes $\sum_{i=1}^{n} s_i x_i$ is an optimal solution.

$\square$

Example 14.3: [Minimum Cost Communication Network] We introduced this problem in Example 13.5. The set of cities and possible communication links can be represented as an undirected graph. Each edge has a cost (or weight) assigned to it. This is the cost of constructing the link it represents. Every connected subgraph that includes all the vertices represents a feasible solution. Under the assumption that all weights are nonnegative, the set of feasible solutions can be narrowed to the set of spanning trees of the graph. An optimal solution is a spanning tree with minimum cost. □

14.2. THE GREEDY METHOD

In the greedy method we attempt to construct an optimal solution in stages. At each stage, we make a decision that appears to be the best (under some criterion) at this time. Since this decision cannot be changed at a later stage, the decision should be such that feasibility is assured.

Loading Problem

The terminology is from Example 14.1. The greedy method to load the ship is to first select the container that has least weight, then the one with the next smallest weight, and so on until either all containers have been loaded or there isn't enough capacity for the next one.

Suppose that $n = 8$, $w[1:8] = [100, 200, 50, 90, 150, 50, 20, 80]$, and $c = 400$. Using the greedy algorithm outlined above, the containers are considered for loading in the order 7, 3, 6, 8, 4, 1, 5, 2. Containers 7, 3, 6, 8, 4, and 1 together weigh 390 units. This leaves us with a capacity of 10 units. This is inadequate for any of the remaining containers. In the greedy solution, we have $x[1:8] = [1, 0, 1, 1, 0, 1, 1, 1]$ and $\sum x[i] = 6$.

The optimality of the solution produced by the greedy algorithm above may be established in the following way. Let $x[1:n]$ be the solution produced by the greedy algorithm. Let $y[1:n]$ be any feasible solution. We shall show that $\sum_{i=1}^{n} x[i] \geq \sum_{i=1}^{n} y[i]$. Without loss of generality, we may assume that the containers have been ordered so that $w[i] \leq w[i+1]$, $1 \leq i \leq n$. We shall transform y, in several steps, into x. Each step of the transformation will produce a new y that is feasible and for which $\sum_{i=1}^{n} y[i]$ is no smaller than before the transformation. As a result, $\sum_{i=1}^{n} x[i] \geq \sum_{i=1}^{n} y[i]$ initially.

From the way the greedy algorithm works, it follows that there is a k in the range $[0, n]$ such that $x[i] = 1$, $i \leq k$ and $x[i] = 0$, $i > k$. Find the least integer, j, in the range $[1, n]$ such that $x[j] \neq y[j]$. If no such j exists, then $\sum_{i=1}^{n} x[i] = \sum_{i=1}^{n} y[i]$. If such a j exists, then $j \leq k$ as otherwise y is not a feasible solution. Since, $x[j] \neq y[j]$ and $x[j] = 1$, it follows that $y[j] = 0$. Set $y[j]$ to 1. If the resulting y denotes an infeasible solution, there must be an l in the range $[j+1, n]$ for which $y[l] = 1$. Set $y[l]$ to 0. As $w[j] \leq w[l]$, the resulting y is feasible. Also, the new y has at least as many 1's as the old one.

By repeatedly using this transformation several times, y may be transformed into x. As each transformation produces a new y that has at least as many ones as the previous one, it follows that x has at least as many ones as does the y we started with.

A pseudo Pascal version of the greedy algorithm for the loading problem is given in Program 14.1. Since the sort can be carried out in $O(n \log n)$ time and the remainder of the algorithm takes $O(n)$ time, its overall time complexity is $O(n \log n)$.

0/1 Knapsack Problem

This is a generalization of the loading problem to the case where the profit earned from each container is different. The problem formulation is:

maximize $\sum_{i=1}^{n} p[i] x[i]$

subject to the constraints:

$$\sum_{i=1}^{n} w[i] x[i] \leq c$$

and

---

procedure *LoadingProblem*(**var** *x*: *answers*; *w*: *weights*;
$\qquad\qquad\qquad\qquad$ *c*: *capacity*; *n*: **integer**);
{Greedy algorithm for the loading problem}
var *t*: **array** [1..*MaxContainers*]; *i*: **integer**; *NotDone*: **boolean**;
begin
$\quad$ Sort *w*[1..*n*] using the indirect addressing table *t*. Following
$\qquad$ the sort, *w*[*t*[*i*]] ≤ *w*[*t*[*i*+1]], 1≤*i*<*n*.
$\quad$ *i* := 1; *NotDone* := **true**;
$\quad$ Set *x*[1:*n*] to 0;
$\quad$ **while** (*i* <= *n*) **and** *NotDone* **do**
$\quad\quad$ **if** *w*[*t*[*i*]] <= *c* **then begin** {it fits}
$\qquad\qquad\qquad\qquad$ *x*[*t*[*i*]] := 1;
$\qquad\qquad\qquad\qquad$ *c* := *c*−*w*[*t*[*i*]];
$\qquad\qquad\qquad\qquad$ *i* := *i*+1;
$\qquad\qquad\qquad$ **end**
$\qquad\qquad\qquad$ **else** *NotDone* := **false**; {no more fit}
end; {of *LoadingProblem*}

Program 14.1 Pseudo-Pascal code for greedy loading algorithm

$x[i] \in \{0,1\}$, $1 \le i \le n$

$\qquad$ Several greedy strategies for this problem are possible. We may
load our ship by being greedy on profit. The container with the largest *p* is loaded first (provided enough capacity is available); then the
one with next largest *p*, and so on. This strategy does not guarantee
an optimal solution. For instance, consider the case *n* = 3, *w*[1:3] =
[100, 10, 10], *p*[1:3] = [20, 15, 15], and *c* = 105. When we are
greedy on profit, the solution *x*[1:3] = [1, 0, 0] is obtained. The total
profit from this solution is 20. The optimal solution is [0, 1, 1]. This
solution has profit 30.

$\qquad$ An alternative is to be greedy on weight. Load the ship in nondecreasing order of weight. While this yields an optimal solution for
the above instance, it does not do so in general. Consider the
instance: *n* = 2, *w*[1:2] = [10, 20], *p*[1:2] = [5, 100], and *c* = 25.
When we are greedy on weight, we obtain the solution *x*[1:2] = [1,
0]. This is inferior to the solution [0, 1].

Yet another possibility is to be greedy on profit density. This is the ratio $p[i]/w[i]$. Load the ship by considering the containers in nondecreasing order of the profit density. This strategy does not guarantee optimal solutions either. To see this, simply consider the instance $n = 3$, $w[1:3] = [20, 15, 15]$, $p[1:3] = [40, 25, 25]$, and $c = 30$.

The moral of this example is that there exist problems for which it is quite easy to formulate greedy algorithms that generate feasible solutions. However, *it is necessary to prove that these algorithms generate an optimal solution.* It will often be the case that what appears to be a promising algorithm actually does not guarantee optimality.

Minimum Cost Spanning Trees

This problem was introduced in Examples 13.5 and 14.3. We can construct a minimum cost spanning tree by selecting the tree edges one at a time. Each time an edge is to be added, we add one that has the least cost from amongst those that retain feasibility. Feasibility can be assured by ensuring that the set of selected edges contains no cycle. An example will illustrate the resulting greedy algorithm.

Consider the network of Figure 14.1(a). We begin with no edges selected. Figure 14.1(b) shows the current state of affairs. Edge (1,6) is the first edge picked. It is included into the spanning tree that is being built. This yields the graph of Figure 14.1(c). Next, the edge (3,4) is selected and included into the tree (Figure 14.1(d)). The next edge to be considered is (2,7). Its inclusion into the tree being built does not create a cycle. So, we get the graph of Figure 14.1(e). Edge (2,3) is considered next and included into the tree (Figure 14.1(f)). Of the edges not yet considered, (7,4) has the least cost. It is considered next. Its inclusion into the tree results in a cycle. So, this edge is discarded. Edge (5,4) is the next edge to be added to the tree being built. This results in the configuration of Figure 14.1(g). The next edge to be considered is the edge (7,5). It is discarded as its inclusion creates a cycle. Finally, edge (6,5) is considered and included into the tree being built. This completes the spanning tree (Figure 14.1(h)). The resulting tree has cost 99.

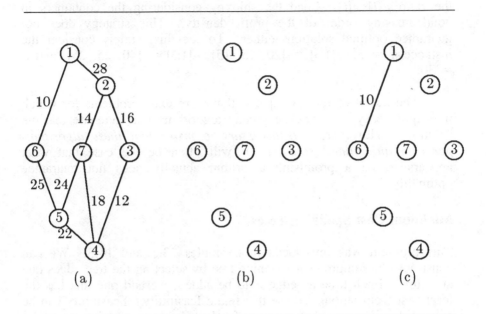

Figure 14.1 Constructing a minimum cost spanning tree
(Continued on next page)

The greedy algorithm described above is known as Kruskal's method. A pseudo Pascal version of this algorithm is given in Program 14.2.

To select edges in nondecreasing order of cost, we can set up a min heap and extract edges one by one as needed. When there are e edges in the graph, it takes $\Theta(e)$ time to initialize the heap and $O(\log e)$ time to extract each edge.

The edge set T together with the vertices of G define a graph that has up to n connected components. Let us represent each component by the set of vertices in it. These vertex sets are disjoint. To determine if the edge (u, w) creates a cycle, we need merely check if u and w are in the same vertex set (i.e., in the same component). If so, then a cycle is created. If not, then no cycle is created. Hence, two *find*s on the vertex sets suffice. When an edge is included in T, two components get combined into one and a *union* is to be performed on the two sets. The set operations *find* and *union* can be carried out

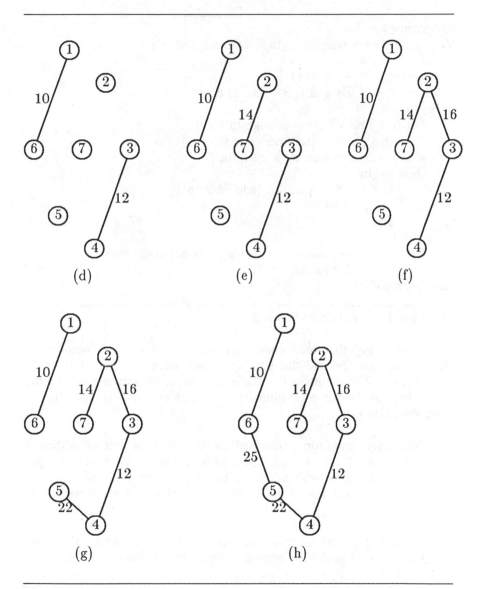

Figure 14.1 Constructing a minimum cost spanning tree
(Continued from previous page)

```
procedure Kruskal;
{G is an n vertex weighted graph with edge set E}
begin
    T := ∅; i := 0; {i = |T|}
    while (E <> ∅) and (i <> n−1) do
    begin
        Let (u,w) be a least cost edge in E;
        E := E - {(u,w)}; {remove edge from E}
        if (u,w) does not create a cycle in T
        then begin
                T := T + {(u,w)}; {add edge to T}
                i := i+1;
            end
    end;
    if i <> n−1 then success := false {G is not connected}
                else success := true;
end; {of Kruskal}
```

Program 14.2 Kruskal's method

efficiently using the tree scheme of Section 13.4. The number of *find*s is at most $2e$ and the number of *union*s at most $n-1$ (exactly $n-1$ in case G is connected). Including the initialization time for the trees, this part of the algorithm has a complexity that is just slightly more than $O(n+e)$.

The only operation performed on the set T is that of adding a new edge to it. T may be implemented as a Pascal set or more simply as an array of edges with additions being performed at one end. At most $n-1$ edges get added to T. So, the total time for operations on T is $O(n)$.

Summing up the various components of the computing time, we get $O(n + e \log e)$ as the asymptotic complexity of Program 14.2.

Correctness Proof

We may prove that the greedy algorithm of Program 14.2 always constructs a minimum cost spanning tree by using the transformation technique used for the loading problem. We need to establish the following:

(a) Kruskal's method results in a spanning tree whenever a spanning tree exists.

(b) The spanning tree generated is of minimum cost.

   From the discussion of Section 13.5, we know that an undirected graph G has a spanning tree iff it is connected. Further, the only edges that get discarded in Kruskal's method are those that are currently on a cycle. The deletion of a single edge that is on a cycle of a connected graph results in a graph that is also connected. Hence, if G is initially connected, the set of edges in T and E always form a connected graph. Consequently, if G is initially connected, the algorithm cannot terminate with $E = \varnothing$ and $i < n-1$.

   Now, let us proceed to establish that the constructed spanning tree, T, is of minimum cost. Since G has a finite number of spanning trees, it must have at least one of minimum cost. Let U be such a minimum cost spanning tree. Both T and U have exactly $n-1$ edges. If $T = U$, then T is of minimum cost and we have nothing to prove. So, assume that $T \neq U$. Let k, $k > 0$, be the number of edges in T that are not in U. Note that k is also the number of edges in U that are not in T.

   We shall show that T and U have the same cost by transforming U into T. This transformation will be done in k steps. At each step, the number of edges in T that are not in U will be reduced by exactly 1. Further, the cost of U will not change as a result of the transformation. As a result, U after k steps of transformation will have the same cost as the initial U and will consist of exactly those edges that are in T. This implies that T is of minimum cost.

   Each step of the transformation involves adding to U one edge from T and removing one edge, f, from U. The edges e and f are selected in the following way:

(a) Let e be the least cost edge in T that is not in U. Such an edge must exist as $k > 0$.

(b) When e is added to U, a unique cycle is created. Let f be any edge on this cycle that is not in T. Note that at least one of the edges on this cycle is not in T as T contains no cycles.

From the way e and f are selected, it follows that $V = U + \{e\}$ $- \{f\}$ is a spanning tree and that T has exactly $k-1$ edges that are not in V. We need to show that the cost of V is the same as that of U. Clearly, the cost of V is the cost of U plus the cost of the edge e minus the cost of the edge f. The cost of e cannot be less than the cost of f as otherwise the spanning tree V has a smaller cost than the tree U. This is impossible. If e has a higher cost than f, then f is considered before e by Kruskal's algorithm. Since it is not in T, Kruskal's algorithm must have discarded this edge at this time. Hence, f together with edges in T having a cost less than or equal to the cost of f must form a cycle. By the choice of e, all these edges are also in U. Hence, U must also contain a cycle. But, it does not as it is a spanning tree. So, the assumption that e is of higher cost than f leads to a contradiction. The only possibility that remains is that e and f have the same cost. Hence, V has the same cost as U.

14.3. DIVIDE-AND-CONQUER

The Method

The divide-and-conquer methodology is very similar to the modularization approach to software design. To solve a large problem, we divide it into some number of smaller problems; solve each of these; and combine these solutions to obtain the solution to the original problem.

Often, the subproblems generated are simply smaller instances of the original and may be solved using the divide-and-conquer strategy recursively.

Towers of Hanoi

The "Towers of Hanoi" puzzle is fashioned after the ancient Tower of Brahma ritual. According to legend, at the time the world was created there was a diamond tower (labeled A) with sixty four golden disks. The disks were of decreasing size and were stacked on the tower in decreasing order of size bottom to top. Besides this tower there are two other diamond towers (labeled B and C). Since the time of creation, Brahman priests have been attempting to move the disks from tower A to tower B using tower C for intermediate storage. As the disks are very heavy, they can be moved only one at a time. In addition, at no time can a disk be on top of a smaller disk. According to legend, the world will come to an end when the priests have completed their task.

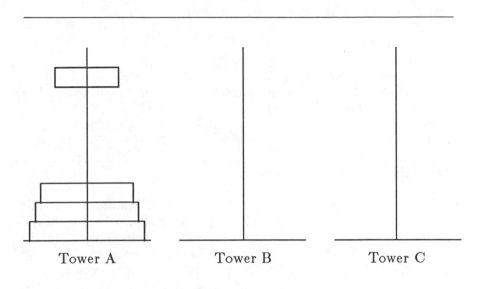

Figure 14.2 Towers of Hanoi

You may wish to attempt a solution to this problem before reading further. A very elegant solution results from the use of the divide-and-conquer method described above. In describing this solution, we assume that the number of disks is n, $n > 0$. To get the largest disk to the bottom of tower B, we move the remaining $n-1$ disks to tower C and then move the largest to tower B. Now, we are left with the task of moving the disks from tower C to tower B. To do this we have available the towers A and B. The fact that B has a disk on it can be ignored as this disk is larger that the disks being moved from C and so any disk can be placed on top of it. The recursive nature of the solution is apparent from the Pascal procedure given in Program 14.3. Observe that our solution for an n disk problem is formulated in terms of solutions to two $n-1$ disk problems. Divide-and-conquer coupled with recursion has provided us a very elegant solution to a rather difficult problem.

---

procedure *TowersOfHanoi* (*n*: **integer**; *x*, *y*, *z*: *tower*);
{Move the top *n* disks from tower *x* to tower *y*}
begin
  if *n* > 0 **then**
  begin
    TowersOfHanoi (*n* − 1, *x*, *z*);
    writeln('Move top disk from tower ', *x*, ' to top of tower ', *y*);
    TowersOfHanoi (*n* − 1, *z*, *y*);
  end;
end;

Program 14.3 Towers of Hanoi

The correctness of Program 14.3 is easily established. Let $t(n)$ be the time taken by Program 14.3. We see that $t(n)$ is proportional to the number of lines of output generated. This is equal to the number of disk moves performed. Examining Program 14.3, we obtain the following recurrence for the number of moves, *moves*(*n*):

$$moves(n) = \begin{cases} 0 & n=0 \\ 2moves(n-1) + 1 & n>0 \end{cases}$$

This recurrence may be solved using the substitution method of Chapter 8. The result is $moves(n) = 2^n - 1$. One can show that this is, in fact, the least number of moves in which the disks can be moved. So, it will take the Brahman priests quite a few years to finish their task. From the solution to the above recurrence, we also obtain $t(n) = \Theta(2^n)$.

Merge Sort

The divide-and-conquer method can be used to arrive at a sort algorithm that has the same asymptotic complexity as does heap sort (i.e., $O(n \log n)$). Experimental results will show this new sort algorithm to be superior to heap sort.

Suppose that *n* elements are to be sorted into nondecreasing order of the field *key*. The divide-and-conquer method suggests that we divide the sort instance into two or more smaller instances, sort these independently, and finally combine the sorted sequences into one

sorted sequence. To develop this strategy further, we need to determine the number of smaller instances to be created as well as the size
of each.

Assume that we decide on a division into two smaller instances.
If one is of size $i = n$ **div** k, then the other is of size $n-i$. We may
simply decide that the instance of size i consists of the first i elements. The remaining $n-i$ elements comprise the other instance.
These two instances may be sorted recursively. The two sorted
sequences obtained may be combined into a single sorted sequence by
merging the two.

As an example, consider the 8 elements with keys [10, 4, 6, 3,
8, 2, 5, 7]. If we pick $k = 2$, then [10, 4, 6, 3] and [8, 2, 5, 7] are
to be sorted independently. The result is [3, 4, 6, 10] and [2, 5, 7,
8]. To merge these two sorted sequences, we begin at the front of
each. The smaller element (2) is moved to the result sequence. Next,
3 and 5 are compared and 3 moved to the result sequence. Then 4
and 5 are compared and 4 placed in the result sequence. Next, 6 and
5 are compared and so on.

If we pick $k = 4$, then the sequences [10, 4] and [6, 3, 8, 2, 5,
7] are to be sorted. The result of sorting these independently is [4,
10] and [2, 3, 5, 6, 7, 8]. When these sorted sequences are merged,
the desired eight element sorted sequence is obtained.

Program 14.4 is a pseudo-Pascal version of the divide-and-
conquer sort algorithm that results when the number of smaller
instances created is 2.

From our brief description of merge, it is evident that n elements
can be merged in $O(n)$ time. Let $t(n,k)$ be the worst case time of the
divide-and-conquer sort algorithm (Program 14.4). We obtain the following recurrence for t:

$$t(n) = \begin{cases} d & n \leq 1 \\ t(n \textbf{ div } k) + t(n - n \textbf{ div } k) + cn & n > 1 \end{cases}$$

where c and d are constants. $t(n)$ is minimum when n **div** $k \approx$
$n - n$ **div** k. I.e., when the two smaller instances are of approximately the same size. This happens when we set $k = 2$. This is a
common requirement for optimal performance of a divide-and-conquer

---

```
procedure sort(var a: ElementList; n: integer);
{Sort the n elements in a.  k is global}
var b, c: ElementList; i, j: integer;
begin
   if n>1 then
   begin
      i := n div k; j := n − i;
      Let b consist of the first i elements in a;
      Let c consist of the remaining j elements in a;
      sort(b, i);
      sort(c, j);
      merge(b, c, a, i, j); {merge from b and c into a}
   end;
end; {of sort}
```

Program 14.4 Divide-and-conquer sort

algorithm. *The smaller instances created should be of approximately the same size.*

Setting $k = 2$ in the recurrence for $t(n)$, we get:

$$t(n) = \begin{cases} d & n \le 1 \\ t(\lceil n/2 \rceil) + t(\lfloor n/2 \rfloor) + cn & n > 1 \end{cases}$$

The presence of the floor and ceiling operators makes this recurrence difficult to solve. This difficulty is overcome if we decide to solve the recurrence only for values of n that are a power of 2. In this case, the recurrence takes the simpler form:

$$t(n) = \begin{cases} d & n \le 1 \\ 2t(n/2) + cn & n > 1 \end{cases}$$

This can be solved using the substitution method. The result is $t(n) = O(n \log n)$. While the recurrence that was solved is valid only when n is a power of 2, the asymptotic bound obtained is valid for all n as we know that $t(n)$ is a nondecreasing function of n.

Let us now proceed to refine Program 14.4 into a Pascal procedure to sort *n* elements. The easiest way to do this is to let *ElementList* be a linked list of *n* elements. In this case, dividing *a* into two roughly equal lists is accomplished by moving down to the (*n* **div** 2)th node and breaking the list here. The merge procedure should be capable of merging two sorted linked lists together. We shall not complete the refinement using linked lists. This is because we wish to compare the performance of the resulting Pascal code with that of heap and insert sort. Neither of these was coded using a linked representation for *a*.

To be compatible with our earlier sort procedures, we require that the merge sort procedure begin with the elements in an array and return the sorted sequence in the same array. With this requirement, the refinement of Program 14.4 takes the following course. When *a* is divided into two, we can avoid copying the two halves into *b* and *c* and simply keep track of the left and right ends of each half. The merge will then be performed with the sequences to be merged in *a* initially. From here, they can be merged into a new array *b* and then copied back into *a*. The refined version of Program 14.4 is given in Program 14.5.

```
procedure MergeSort(var a: ElementList; left, right: integer);
{Sort the elements in a[left..right]}
var b: ElementList; i: integer;
begin
   if left < right then
   begin {at least 2 elements}
      i := (left + right) div 2; {mid point}
      MergeSort(a, left, i);
      MergeSort(a, i+1, right);
      merge(a, b, left, i, right); {merge from a into b}
      copy(b, a, left, right); {put sorted sequence back into a}
   end;
end; {of MergeSort}
```

Program 14.5 Divide-and-conquer sort refinement

Much can be done to improve the performance of Program 14.5. First, the recursion is easily eliminated. If we examine this program carefully, we see that the recursion simply divides the element list repeatedly until we are left with segments of size 1. The merging that takes place after this is best described for the case when n is a power of 2. The segments of size 1 are merged together to get sorted segments of size 2. These are then merged to get sorted segments of size 4. The merge process is repeated until we are left with a single sorted sequence of size n. Figure 14.3 shows the merging (and copying) that takes place when $n = 8$. Square brackets are used to denote the start and end of sorted segments.

---

initial segments [8] [4] [5] [6] [2] [1] [7] [3]

merge to b [4 8]   [5 6]   [1 2]   [3 7]

copy to a [4 8]   [5 6]   [1 2]   [3 7]

merge to b [4 5 6 8]   [1 2 3 7]

copy to a [4 5 6 8]   [1 2 3 7]

merge to b [1 2 3 4 5 6 7 8]

copy to a [1 2 3 4 5 6 7 8]

Figure 14.3

An iterative version of merge sort begins by merging together pairs of adjacent segments of size one, then it merges together pairs of adjacent segments of size two, and so on. Virtually all of the copying from b to a can be eliminated by alternately merging from a to b and from b to a. The iterative merge sort algorithm takes the form given in Program 14.6.

```
procedure MergeSort(var a: ElementList; n: integer);
{Sort the n elements in a}
var s: integer; b: ElementList;
begin
    s := 1; {s is current segment size}
    while s < n do
    begin
        MergePass(a, b, s); {merge pairs of adjacent segments of size s}
        s := 2*s; {segment size is doubled after the merge}
        MergePass(b, a, s); {merge from b to a}
        s := 2*s;
    end;
end; {of MergeSort}
```

Program 14.6 Iterative merge sort

To complete our sorting procedure, we need to specify the procedure *MergePass*. We shall develop this as two modules. The first will simply determine the left and right ends of the segments to be merged. The second will perform the actual merge. The two modules are given in Programs 14.7 and 14.8.

The procedures *MergePass* and *Merge* are physically placed within procedure *MergeSort* (i.e., between the **var** and first **begin** statement in *MergeSort*). Note that the sort will work even if x is made a value parameter in procedure *MergePass*. This is, however, not recommended as *MergePass* itself references at most s elements of x (this is done in the **for** loop). Since s will generally be much smaller than *ElementList*, making x a value parameter will result in a loss in performance.

In procedure *Merge*, the elements of c are unchanged and the correct answers are produced even if c is made a value parameter. Doing this has a disastrous effect on the performance of this procedure. When $s = 1$, this procedure is invoked about $n/2$ times from *MergePass*. The cost of these $n/2$ invocations will be $n*MaxElements/2$. Since *MaxElements* is at least n, we can expect to perform worse than an $O(n^2)$ algorithm such as insert sort.

---

procedure *MergePass* (**var** *x*, *y*: *ElementList*; *s*: **integer**);
{Merge together adjacent segments of size *s*.}
{*n* is global to this procedure.}
var *i*, *j*: **integer**;
begin
  i := 1;
  while *i* <= (*n*−2*∗s*+1) **do**
  begin {merge two adjacent segments of size *s*}
    Merge(*x*, *y*, *i*, *i*+*s*−1, *i*+2*∗s*−1);
    i := *i* + 2*∗s*;
  end;
  {Fewer than 2*∗s* elements remain}
  if (*i*+*s*−1) < *n* **then** *Merge*(*x*, *y*, *i*, *i*+*s*−1, *n*)
  else for *j* := *i* **to** *n* **do** {copy last segment to *y*}
      y[*j*] := *x*[*j*];
end; {of *MergePass*}

Program 14.7 Merge pass

To get reasonable performance from *MergeSort*, it is *essential* that *x* and *c* be variable parameters. *y* and *d* cannot be made value parameters as these transmit results back to the invoking procedures.

The average run time of *MergeSort* can be obtained using the same technique as used for heap sort in Chapter 13. The times obtained on an IBM-PC are shown in Figure 14.4. The corresponding times for heap and insert sort are reproduced from Figure 13.14. As can be seen, the break even point between merge sort and insert sort is between 40 and 50. Merge sort becomes faster than heap sort for some value of *n* between 20 and 30.

Quick Sort

It is interesting that we can arrive at another totally different sort method using the divide and conquer approach. This new method is called *quick sort*. In this method the *n* elements to be sorted are divided into three groups A, B, and C. B contains exactly one element. No element in A has a key larger than the key of the element in B and no element in C has a key that is smaller than that of the element in B. As a result, the elements in A and C can be sorted

---

```
procedure Merge(var c, d: ElementList; left, middle, right: integer);
{Merge c[left:middle] and c[middle+1:right] to d[left:right]}
var i, j, k, l: integer;
begin
    i := left; j := middle + 1; k := left;
    while (i <= middle) and (j <= right) do
        if c[i].key <= c[j].key
        then begin
                d[k] := c[i];
                k :=k + 1; i := i + 1;
            end
        else begin
                d[k] := c[j];
                k :=k + 1; j := j + 1;
            end;
    {Take care of left overs}
    if i > middle
    then for l := j to right do
            d[k+l-j] := c[l]
    else for l := i to middle do
            d[k+l-i] := c[l];
end; {of Merge}
```

Program 14.8 Merge

independently. No merge needs to be performed following this. The sort method is described more precisely by the code of Program 14.9.

Consider the element list [4, 8, 3, 7, 1, 5, 6, 2]. Suppose we pick the element with key 6 for B. Then, 4, 3, 1, 5, and 2 are in A and 8 and 7 are in C. When A has been sorted, the keys are in the order 1, 2, 3, 4, 5. When C has been sorted, its keys are in the order 7, 8. Putting the elements in C after the element in B and those in A before the one in B, we get the sorted sequence [1, 2, 3, 4, 5, 6, 7, 8].

The partitioning of the element list into A, B, and C can be done in place as in the refinement of Program 14.10. In this refinement the element for B is always the one at position *left*. Other choices that result in improved performance are possible. One such choice is

n	Merge	Heap	Insert
0	0.027	0.034	0.032
10	1.524	1.482	0.775
20	3.700	3.680	2.253
30	5.587	6.153	4.430
40	7.800	8.815	7.275
50	9.892	11.583	10.892
60	11.947	14.427	15.013
70	15.893	17.427	20.000
80	18.217	20.517	25.450
90	20.417	23.717	31.767
100	22.950	26.775	38.325
200	48.475	60.550	148.300
300	81.600	96.657	319.657
400	109.829	134.971	567.629
500	138.033	174.100	874.600
600	171.167	214.400	
700	199.240	255.760	
800	230.480	297.480	
900	260.100	340.000	
1000	289.450	382.250	

Times are in hundredths of a second

Figure 14.4 Average times for merge, heap, and insert sort

discussed in the exercises. Note that a could have been made global to *qSort* rather than made a parameter. From our experiments of Chapter 11, we know that this will result in a less efficient quick sort procedure.

Program 14.10 remains correct when the $>=$ and $<=$ in the conditionals of the **until** statements are, respectively, changed to $>$ and $<$. Experimental evidence suggests that the average performance of quick sort is better when it is coded as in Program 14.10. All attempts to eliminate the recursion from this procedure result in the introduction of a stack. The last recursive call can, however, be eliminated without the introduction of a stack. We leave this as an exercise.

---

procedure *QuickSort*(**var** *a*: *ElementList*; *n*: **integer**);
{Sort *a*[1:*n*] using quick sort}
begin
   Select an element from *a*[1:*n*] for B;
   Partition the remaining elements into A and C so that no element
     in A has a key larger than that of the element in B and no
     element in C has a key smaller than that of the element in B;
   QuickSort A;
   QuickSort C;
   The answer is A followed by B followed by C;
end; {of *QuickSort*}

Program 14.9 Quick sort

Program 14.10 requires $O(n)$ recursion stack space. This can be reduced to $O(\log n)$ by simulating the recursion using a stack. In this simulation, the smaller of the two partitions A and C is sorted first. The boundaries of the other partition are put on the stack.

The worst case computing time for quick sort is $\Theta(n^2)$. This happens, for instance, when A is always empty. The average time can be shown to be $\Theta(n \log n)$ (see, for example, the text by Horowitz and Sahni that is cited in the readings section). The table of Figure 14.5 compares the average and worst case complexities of the sort methods developed in this book.

method	worst	average
insert	n^2	n^2
bubble	n^2	n^2
heap	$n \log n$	$n \log n$
merge	$n \log n$	$n \log n$
quick	n^2	$n \log n$

Figure 14.5 Comparison of sort methods

---

procedure *QuickSort*(**var** *a*: *ElementList*; *n*: **integer**);

procedure *qSort*(**var** *a*: *ElementList*; *left*, *right*: **integer**);
{Sort *a*[*left*:*right*]}
var *y*: *element*; *k*: *KeyType*; *i*, *j*: **integer**;
begin
  if *left* < *right* **then**
  begin {at least 2 elements}
    i := *left*; *j* := *right* + 1;
    k := *a*[*i*].*key*; {element for B}

    {Create A on the left end and C on the right}
    repeat
      repeat {search for an element at the left end to move to the right}
        i := *i* + 1;
      until *a*[*i*].*key* >= *k*;

      repeat {search for an element at the right end to move to the left}
        j := *j* − 1;
      until *a*[*j*].*key* <= *k*;

      y := *a*[*i*]; *a*[*i*] := *a*[*j*]; *a*[*j*] := *y*; {exchange}
    until *i* >= *j*;

    y := *a*[*i*]; *a*[*i*] := *a*[*j*]; *a*[*j*] := *a*[*left*]; *a*[*left*] := *y*;
    qSort(*a*, *left*, *j*−1); {sort A}
    qSort(*a*, *j*+1, *right*); {sort B}
  end; {of **if**}
end; {of *qSort*}

begin {body of *QuickSort*}
  a[*n*+1].*key* := **maxint**; {boundary condition}
  qsort(*a*, 1, *n*);
end; {of *QuickSort*}

Program 14.10 Quick sort

The observed average times for procedure *QuickSort* are shown in Figure 14.6. This figure includes the times for merge, heap, and insert sort. The data of this figure for $n \leq 100$ is plotted in Figure 14.7. As can be seen, quick sort outperforms the other sort methods for suitably large n. We see that the break even point between insert and quick sort is around 20. The exact break even point can be found experimentally. Let the exact break even point be *nBreak*. For average performance, insert sort is the best sort method to use when $n <$ *nBreak* and quick sort is the best when $n \geq$ *nBreak*.

n	quick	merge	heap	insert
0	0.041	0.027	0.034	0.032
10	1.064	1.524	1.482	0.775
20	2.343	3.700	3.680	2.253
30	3.700	5.587	6.153	4.430
40	5.085	7.800	8.815	7.275
50	6.542	9.892	11.583	10.892
60	7.987	11.947	14.427	15.013
70	9.587	15.893	17.427	20.000
80	11.167	18.217	20.517	25.450
90	12.633	20.417	23.717	31.767
100	14.275	22.950	26.775	38.325
200	30.775	48.475	60.550	148.300
300	48.171	81.600	96.657	319.657
400	65.914	109.829	134.971	567.629
500	84.400	138.033	174.100	874.600
600	102.900	171.167	214.400	
700	122.400	199.240	255.760	
800	142.160	230.480	297.480	
900	160.400	260.100	340.000	
1000	181.000	289.450	382.250	

Times are in hundredths of a second

Figure 14.6 Average times for sort methods

We can improve on the performance of quick sort for $n \geq$ *nBreak* by composing insert and quick sort into a single sort procedure as in Program 14.11. The performance measurement of this procedure is left as an exercise. Further improvement in performance may be possible by replacing *nBreak* by a smaller value (see the Exercises).

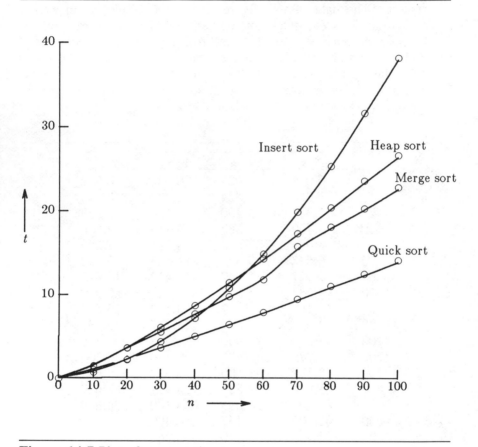

Figure 14.7 Plot of average times

For worst case behavior, most implementations will show merge sort to be best for $n \geq c$ where c is some constant. For $n < c$, insert sort has the best worst case behavior. The performance of merge sort can be improved by composing insert sort into merge sort. This is examined in the Exercises.

---

procedure *QuickSort*(**var** *a*: *ElementList*; *n*: **integer**);

procedure *qSort*(**var** *a*: *ElementList*; *left*, *right*: **integer**);
{Sort *a*[*left*:*right*]}
var *y*: *element*; *k*: *KeyType*; *i*, *j*: **integer**;
begin
  if *left* <= (*right* − *nBreak*) **then**
  begin {at least *nBreak* elements}
    i := *left*; *j* := *right* + 1;
    k := *a*[*i*].*key*; {element for B}

    {Create A on the left end and C on the right}
    repeat
      repeat {search for an element at the left end to move to the right}
        i := *i* + 1;
      until *a*[*i*].*key* >= *k*;

      repeat {search for an element at the right end to move to the left}
        j := *j* − 1;
      until *a*[*j*].*key* <= *k*;

      y := *a*[*i*]; *a*[*i*] := *a*[*j*]; *a*[*j*] := *y*; {exchange}
    until *i* >= *j*;

    y := *a*[*i*]; *a*[*i*] := *a*[*j*]; *a*[*j*] := *a*[*left*]; *a*[*left*] := *y*;
    qSort(*a*, *left*, *j*−1); {sort A}
    qSort(*a*, *j*+1, *right*); {sort B}
  end; {of **if**}
  else *InsertSort*(*a*, *left*, *right*);
end; {of *QuickSort*}

begin {body of *QuickSort*}
  a[*n*+1].*key* := **maxint**; {boundary condition}
  qSort(*a*, 1,*n*);
end; {of *QuickSort*}

Program 14.11 Quick sort

Divide-and-Conquer Recurrence Equations

The complexity of many divide-and-conquer algorithms is given by a recurrence of the form:

$$t(n) = \begin{cases} t(1) & n=1 \\ a*t(n/b)+g(n) & n>1 \end{cases} \qquad (14.1)$$

where a and b are known constants. We shall assume that t(1) is known and that n is a power of b. Using the substitution method, it can be shown that

$$t(n) = n^{\log_b a}[t(1)+f(n)]$$

where $f(n) = \sum_{j=1}^{k} h(b^j)$ and $h(n) = g(n)/n^{\log_b a}$.

Figure 14.8 tabulates the asymptotic value of $f(n)$ for various values of $h(n)$. This table allows one to easily obtain the asymptotic value of $t(n)$ for many of the recurrences one encounters when analyzing divide-and-conquer algorithms.

$h(n)$	$f(n)$
$O(n^r)$, $r<0$	$O(1)$
$\Theta((\log n)^i)$, $i\geq 0$	$\Theta(((\log n)^{i+1})/(i+1))$
$\Omega(n^r)$, $r>0$	$\Theta(h(n))$

Figure 14.8 $f(n)$ values for various $h(n)$ values

Let us consider some examples using this table. The recurrence for binary search when n is a power of 2 is:

$$t(n) = \begin{cases} t(1) & n=1 \\ t(n/2)+c & n>1 \end{cases}$$

Comparing with (14.1), we see that $a=1$, $b=2$, and $g(n) = c$. So, $\log_b(a) = 0$ and $h(n) = g(n)/n^{\log_b a} = c = c(\log n)^0 = \Theta((\log n)^0)$. From Figure 14.8, we obtain: $f(n) = \Theta(\log n)$. So, $t(n) = n^{\log_b a}(c+\Theta(\log n)) = \Theta(\log n)$.

For the merge sort recurrence, we obtain $a = 2$, $b = 2$, and $g(n) = cn$. So, $\log_b a = 1$, and $h(n) = g(n)/n = c = \Theta((\log n)^0)$. Hence, $f(n) = \Theta(\log n)$ and $t(n) = n(t(1) + \Theta(\log n)) = \Theta(n \log n)$.

As another example, consider the recurrence:

$t(n) = 7t(n/2) + 18n^2$, $n \geq 2$ and n a power of 2

we obtain: $a = 7$, $b = 2$, and $g(n) = 18n^2$. So, $\log_b a = \log_2 7 \approx 2.81$ and $h(n) = 18n^2/n^{\log_2 7} = 18n^{2-\log_2 7} = O(n^r)$ where $r = 2-\log_2 7 < 0$. So, $f(n) = O(1)$. The expression for t(n) is:

$$t(n) = n^{\log_2 7}(t(1)+O(1))$$

$$= \Theta(n^{\log_2 7})$$

as t(1) is assumed to be a constant.

As a final example, consider the recurrence:

$t(n) = 9t(n/3)+4n^6$, $n \geq 3$ and a power of 3.

Comparing with (14.1), we obtain $a = 9$, $b = 3$, and $g(n) = 4n^6$. So, $\log_b a = 2$ and $h(n) = 4n^6/n^2 = 4n^4 = \Omega(n^4)$. From Figure 14.7, we see that $f(n) = \Theta(h(n)) = \Theta(n^4)$. So,

$$t(n) = n^2(t(1)+\Theta(n^4))$$

$$= \Theta(n^6)$$

as t(1) may be assumed constant.

14.4. DYNAMIC PROGRAMMING

The Method

Dynamic programming bears much resemblence to divide-and-conquer. The solution to a large problem instance is obtained from the solutions to smaller (or at least simpler) problem instances. Unlike divide-and-conquer, the smaller problem instances are not solved recursively. This is so because when the division process is repeated on the smaller instances, many of the new problem instances that are created are the same. To get a good run time performance, each smaller instance is solved only once and its solution used as often as needed.

Shortest Paths

Let G be a directed graph in which each edge has a cost (or length) assigned to it. The cost (length) of any directed path in this graph is the sum of the costs (lengths) of the edges on this path. For any pair of vertices (i, j), there may be several paths from vertex i to vertex j. These paths may differ in their costs. A path from i to j that has the minimum cost from amongst all i to j paths is called a *shortest i to j path*.

As an example, consider the digraph of Figure 14.9. Some of the paths from vertex 1 to vertex 3 are:

(1)   1, 2, 5, 3

(2)   1, 4, 3

(3)   1, 2, 5, 8, 6, 3

(4)   1, 4, 6, 3

The lengths of these paths are, respectively, 10, 28, 9, 27. By inspecting the graph, we see that path (3) is the shortest 1 to 3 path in this graph.

Let us consider the problem of finding a shortest path between every pair of vertices in a directed graph G. I.e., for every pair of vertices (i, j), we are to find a shortest path from i to j as well as one from j to i. In all, $n(n-1)$ shortest paths are to be found for an n vertex graph. This problem is called the *all pairs shortest paths*

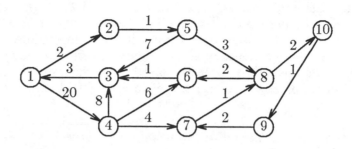

Figure 14.9 An example graph

problem. We shall assume that G contains no cycles that have a negative length. Under this assumption, for every pair of vertices (i, j), there is always a shortest path that contains no cycles.

Let the n vertices of G be numbered 1 through n. Let $c[i,j,k]$ denote the length of a shortest path from i to j that has no intermediate vertex larger than k. Hence, $c[i,j,0]$ is the length of the edge $<i, j>$ in case this edge is in G. It is 0 if $i = j$ and **maxint** (or ∞) otherwise. $c[i,j,n]$ is the length of a shortest path from i to j.

For the graph of Figure 14.9, $c[1,3,k] =$ **maxint** for $k = 0, 1,$ 2, 3; $c[1,3,4] = 28$; $c[1,3,k] = 10$ for $k = 5, 6, 7$; $c[1,3,k] = 9$ for $k = 8, 9, 10$. Hence, the shortest 1 to 3 path has length 9.

How can we determine $c[i,j,k]$ for any k, $k>0$? There are two possibilities for a shortest i to j path that has no intermediate vertex larger than k. This path may or may not have k as an intermediate vertex. If it does not, then its length is $c[i,j,k-1]$. If it does, then its length is $c[i,k,k-1] + c[k,j,k-1]$. $c[i,j,k]$ is the smaller of these two quantities. So, we obtain the recurrence:

$$c[i,j,k] = \min\{c[i,j,k-1], c[i,k,k-1] + c[k,j,k-1]\}, k>0$$

The above recurrence formulates the solution for one k in terms of the solutions for $k-1$. Obtaining solutions for $k-1$ should be easier than obtaining those for k directly. If the above recurrence is solved recursively, the complexity of the resulting procedure is excessive. Let $t(k)$

be the time needed to solve the recurrence recursively for any i, j, k combination. From the recurrence, we see that $t(k) = 2t(k-1) + c$. Using the substitution method, we obtain $t(n) = O(2^n)$. So, the time needed to obtain all the $c[i, j, n]$ values is $O(n^2 2^n)$. The values $c[i, j, n]$ may be obtained far more efficiently by noticing that some $c[i, j, k-1]$ values get used several times in the computations for k. We shall solve the recurrence in a systematic manner; never recomputing a value that has already been computed. The values of c may be computed in the order $k = 1, 2, ..., n$ as in Program 14.12.

```
procedure ShortestLengths(var a, l: CostMatrix; n: integer);
{Find the lengths of the shortest paths.}
var c: array [1..MaxElements, 1..MaxElements, 1..MaxElements]
        of integer; i, j, k: integer;
begin
  for i := 1 to n do
    for j := 1 to n do
      c[i,j,0] := a[i,j]; {initialize}
  for k := 1 to n do {compute c[i,j,k]}
    for i := 1 to n do
      for j := 1 to n do
        if (c[i,k,k-1] + c[k,j,k-1]) < c[i,j,k-1]
        then c[i,j,k] := c[i,k,k-1] + c[k,j,k-1]
        else c[i,j,k] := c[i,j,k-1];
  for i := 1 to n do
    for j := 1 to n do
      l[i,j] := c[i,j,n];
end; {of ShortestLengths}
```

Program 14.12

We can actually do away with the three dimensional array c. Observe that $c[i,k,k] = c[i,k,k-1]$ and that $c[k,i,k] = c[k,i,k-1]$ for all i. As a result, Program 14.12 may be rewritten as Program 14.13. This produces exactly the same results.

The time complexity of Program 14.13 is readily seen to be $\Theta(n^3)$. To construct the shortest paths, we need to record the last value of k when each $c[i,j]$ was updated. This requires us to change the **then** clause of Program 14.13 to:

```
procedure ShortestLengths (var a, c : CostMatrix; n: integer);
var i, j, k: integer;
begin
  for i := 1 to n do
    for j := 1 to n do
      c[i,j] := a[i,j]; {initialize}
  for k := 1 to n do {compute c[i,j,k]}
    for i := 1 to n do
      for j := 1 to n do
        if (c[i,k] + c[k,j]) < c[i,j]
          then c[i,j] := c[i,k] + c[k,j];
end; {of ShortestLengths}
```

Program 14.13 Computing shortest path lengths

```
begin
  c[i,j] := c[i,k] + c[k,j];
  kay[i,j] := k;
end;
```

Additionally, *kay* is added to the parameter list of the procedure and is initialized to zero.

A sample cost matrix a is shown in Figure 14.10(a). Figure 14.10(b) gives the c matrix computed by Program 14.13 and Figure 14.10(c) gives the *kay* values. From these *kay* values, we see that the shortest path from 1 to 5 is the shortest path from 1 to $kay[1,5] = 4$ followed by the shortest path from 4 to 5. The shortest path from 4 to 5 has no intermediate vertex on it as $kay[4,5] = 0$. The shortest path from 1 to 4 goes through $kay[1,4] = 3$. Repeating this, we determine that the shortest 1 to 5 path is 1, 2, 3, 4, 5. This path finding process can be written as a recursive procedure. The shortest path from i to j can be determined in $O(n)$ time using the *kay* values.

14.5. BACKTRACKING

The Method

Backtracking is a systematic way to search for the solution to a problem. The solution provided in Chapter 7 for the rat in a maze problem

0	1	4	4	8		0	1	2	3	4		0	0	2	3	4
3	0	1	5	9		3	0	1	2	3		0	0	0	3	4
2	2	0	1	8		2	2	0	1	2		0	0	0	0	4
8	8	9	0	1		5	5	3	0	1		5	5	5	0	0
8	8	2	9	0		4	4	2	3	0		3	3	0	3	0
		(a)						(b)						(c)		

Figure 14.10

utilized this technique. We begin by defining a *solution space* for the problem. This must include at least one (optimal) solution to the problem. In the case of the rat in a maze problem, we may define the solution space to consist of all paths from the entrance to the exit. For the case of the 0/1 knapsack problem with n containers, a reasonable choice for the solution space is the set of 2^n 0/1 vectors of size n. When $n = 3$, this is the set $\{(0,0,0), (0,1,0), (0,0,1), (1,0,0), (0,1,1), (1,0,1), (1,1,0), (1,1,1)\}$. This set represents all possible ways to assign the values 0 and 1 to $x[1:n]$.

The next step is to organize the solution space so that it can be searched easily. The typical organization used is either a graph or a tree. Figure 14.11 shows a graph organization for a 3×3 maze. All paths from the vertex labeled (1,1) to the one labeled (3,3) define an element of the solution space for a 3×3 maze. Depending on the placement of obstacles, some of these paths may be infeasible.

A tree organization for the three container 0/1 knapsack solution space is shown in Figure 14.12. All paths from the root to a leaf define an element of the solution space. Depending on the values $w[1:3]$ and c, some or all of these paths may define infeasible solutions. The path from the root to the leaf labeled H defines the solution $x[1:3] = [1,1,1]$.

The solution space is searched beginning at a start node (the entrance node (1,1) in the rat in a maze problem or the root node in the case of the 0/1 knapsack problem). This node is called a *live* node. From this live node, an attempt is made to move to a new node. The node from which we are trying to move is called the $E-node$ (expansion node). If we can move to a new node from the

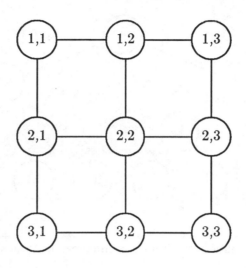

Figure 14.11 Solution space for a 3×3 maze

current E-node, then we do so. The new node becomes a live node and also becomes the new E-node. If we cannot move to a new node, the current E-node dies and we move to the nearest live node that remains. This becomes the new E-node. The search terminates when we have found the answer or when we run out of live nodes to back up to.

Rat In A Maze

Consider the 3×3 rat in a maze instance given by the matrix of Figure 14.13(a). We shall search this maze using the solution space graph of Figure 14.11.

Every path from the entrance of the maze to the exit corresponds to a path from vertex (1,1) to vertex (3,3) in the graph of Figure 14.11. However, some of the (1,1) to (3,3) paths in this graph do not correspond to entrance to exit paths in the example maze. The search begins at position (1,1). This is the only live node at this time. It is also the E-node. To avoid going through this position again, we set

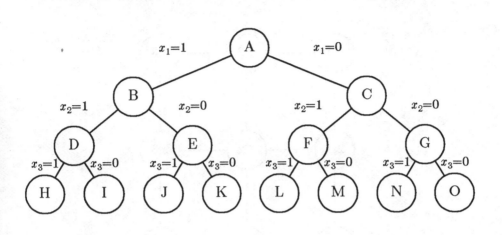

Figure 14.12 Solution space for a 3 container knapsack

0	0	0	1	1	0	1	1	1
0	1	1	0	1	1	0	1	1
0	0	0	0	0	0	0	0	0
	(a)			(b)			(c)	

Figure 14.13 Mazes

maze[1,1] to 1. From this position, we can move to either (1,2) or (2,1). For the particular instance we are dealing with, both moves are feasible as the maze has a zero at each position. Suppose we choose to move to (1,2). *maze*[1,2] is set to 1 to avoid going through here again. The status of *maze* is as in Figure 14.13(b). At this time we have two live nodes (1,1), and (1,2). (1,2) becomes the E-node. From the current E-node, there are three moves possible in the graph of Figure 14.11. Two of these are infeasible as *maze* has a 1 in these positions. The only feasible move is to (1,3). This position is blocked and the *maze* of Figure 14.13(c) obtained. The graph of Figure 14.11 indicates two possible moves from (1,3). Neither of these is feasible. So, the E-node (1,3) dies and we back up to the nearest live node which is (1,2). No feasible moves from here remain and this node dies too. The only remaining live node is (1,1). This becomes the E-node again. From here, there is an untried move. This gets us to position (2,1). The live nodes now are (1,1), and (2,1). Continuing in this way, the position (3,3) is reached. At this time, the list of live nodes is (1,1), (2,1), (3,1), (3,2), (3,3). This is also the path to the exit.

As noted in Chapter 7, the list of live nodes is maintained as a stack.

0/1 Knapsack

Consider the knapsack instance $n = 3$, $w[1:3] = [20, 15, 15]$, $p[1:3] = [40, 25, 25]$, and $c = 30$. We search the tree of Figure 14.12 beginning at the root. This is the only live node at this time. It is also the E-node. From here, we can move to either B or C. Suppose we move to B. The live nodes now are A and B. B is the current E-node. At node B, the remaining capacity, r, is 10 and the profit earned, p, is 40. From B we can move to either D or E. The move to D is infeasible as the the capacity needed to move there is $w[2] = 15$. The move to E is feasible as no capacity is used in this move. E becomes the new E-node. The live nodes at this time are A, B, and E. At node E, $r = 10$, and $p = 40$. From E, there are two possible moves (i.e., to nodes J and K). The move to node J is infeasible while that to K is not. Node K becomes the new E-node. Since this is a leaf, we have a feasible solution. This solution has $p = 40$. The values of x are determined by the path from the root to K. This path is also the live node sequence at this time, i.e., A, B, E, K. Since we cannot expand K further, this node dies and we back up to E. This cannot be expanded further and it dies too. Next, we back up to B which also dies. A becomes the E-node again. It can be expanded further and node C is reached. At this node, $r = 30$, and $p = 0$. From C, we can move to either F or G. Suppose we move to F. This becomes the new E-node. The live nodes are A, C, and F. At F, $r = 15$, and $p = 25$. From F we can move to either L or M. Suppose a move to L is made. At this node $r = 0$, and $p = 50$. Since L is a leaf and it represents a better feasible solution than the best found so far (i.e., the one at node K), we remember this as the best solution. Node L dies and we back up to node F. Continuing in this way, the entire tree is searched. The best solution found during the search is the optimal one.

The search for an optimal solution can be speeded by determining whether or not a newly reached node can possibly lead to a solution better than the best found so far. If it cannot, then we might as well kill it. A simple strategy to use is to just see if (p + (sum of remaining $p[i]$'s)) is bigger than the profit from the best solution found so far. If it isn't, then expanding the current E-node is unnecessary and it is killed. Strategies such as this that are used to kill live nodes are called *bounding functions*. A more effective strategy is discussed in the text by Horowitz and Sahni that is cited in the readings section.

14.6. BRANCH-AND-BOUND

Branch-and-bound is another way to systematically search a solution space. It differs from backtracking primarily in the way an E-node is expanded. Each live node becomes an E-node exactly once. At this time, all new nodes that can be reached using a single move are generated. Those of these that cannot possibly lead to a (optimal) feasible solution are killed. The remaining nodes are added to the list of live nodes. From the list of live nodes, one is selected to become the next E-node. This node is extracted from the list of live nodes and expanded. This expansion process is continued until either the answer is found or the list of live nodes becomes empty.

There are three common ways to select the next E-node. These are:

1. *FIFO (First-in-first-out)*
    In this scheme, nodes are extracted from the list of live nodes in the same order as they are put into it. The live node list behaves as a queue.

2. *LIFO (Last-in-First-Out)*
    Here the list of live nodes behaves as a stack.

3. *Least Cost or Max Profit*
    In this scheme, a cost or profit is associated with each node. If we are searching for a solution with least cost, then the list of live nodes can be set up as a min heap. If a solution with maximum profit is sought, this list can be set up as a max heap.

Rat In A Maze

Consider the rat in a maze instance of Figure 14.13(a) and the solution space organization of Figure 14.11. In a FIFO branch-and-bound, we begin with (1,1) as the E-node. The list of live nodes is empty and the maze position (1,1) set to 1. (1,1) is expanded and the nodes (1,2) and (2,1) added to the queue (i.e., the list of live nodes). Positions (1,2) and (2,1) are set to 1 in the maze to prevent moving to these positions again. The maze now is as in Figure 14.14(a).

1	1	0	1	1	1	1	1	1
1	1	1	1	1	1	1	1	1
0	0	0	0	0	0	1	0	0
	(a)			(b)			(c)	

Figure 14.14

Node (1,2) is removed from the queue and expanded. Its three neighbors (Figure 14.11) are examined. Only (1,3) represents a feasible move and it is added to the queue. This maze position is set to 1 and the status of *maze* is as in Figure 14.14(b). Node (1,2) is killed. The next E-node is extracted from the queue. It is (2,1). When this is expanded, node (3,1) is added to the queue, *maze*[3,1] is set to 1, and node (2,1) killed. *maze* is as in Figure 14.14(c) and the queue has the nodes (1,3) and (3,1) on it. (1,3) becomes the next E-node. This does not get us to any new nodes. It is killed and (3,1) becomes the new E-node. At this time, the queue is empty. (3,1) gets us to (3,2). This is added to the queue and (3,1) killed. (3,2) is the next E-node. Expanding this, we reach the exit (3,3) and the search terminates.

A FIFO search of a maze has the desirable property that the path found (if any) is a shortest path from the entrance to the maze. This is not the case for a path found by backtracking.

0/1 Knapsack

We shall carry out a maximum profit branch-and-bound on the knapsack instance $n = 3$, $w[1:3] = [20, 15, 15]$, $p[1:3] = [40, 25, 25]$, and $c = 30$. The search begins at the node A (Figure 14.12). This is the initial E-node and the max heap of live nodes is empty. Expanding this node yields the nodes B and C. Both are feasible and are inserted into the heap. A is killed and B becomes the next E-node as its profit value (40) is larger than that of C. When B is expanded, the nodes D and E are generated. D is infeasible and killed. E is added to the heap. E becomes the next E-node as its profit value is 40 while that of C is 0. When E is expanded, the nodes J and K are generated. J is infeasible and killed. K represents a feasible solution. This solution is recorded as the best found so far and K killed. Only one live node remains. This is node C. It becomes the new E-node. Nodes F and G are generated and inserted into the max heap. F has a profit of 25 and becomes the next E-node. Nodes L and M are generated. Both are killed as they are leaf nodes. The solution corresponding to L is recorded as the best found so far. Finally, G becomes the E-node and the nodes N and O generated. Both are leaves and are killed. Neither represents a solution that is better than the best found so far. So, no solution update takes place. The heap is empty and there is no next E-node. The search terminates with J representing the optimal solution.

As in the case of backtracking, the search for an optimal solution can be speeded by using a bounding function. This function places an upper bound on the maximum profit that can possibly be obtained by expanding a particular node. If a node's bound isn't larger than the profit of the best solution found so far, it may be killed without expansion. Further, nodes may be extracted from the heap in nonincreasing order of the profit bound rather than by the actual profit for the node.

You are referred to the text by Horowitz and Sahni that is cited in the readings section for further information on the use of bounding functions in the solution of the 0/1 Knapsack and other problems.

14.7. HEURISTIC METHODS

14.7.1. Introduction

Webster's third new international dictionary defines the word heuristic as: *providing aid and direction in the solution of a problem but otherwise unjustified or incapable of justification.*

There are two kinds of heuristics that are used in computer algorithms. The first kind is used to improve the time and space requirements of an algorithm. This kind fits Webster's definition quite well. The heuristic is used to provide the algorithm with direction. If it is a good heuristic, it will result in the algorithm taking less time (and or space) on many instances. There will, however, be instances on which the algorithm performs better without the heuristic. The heuristic has no effect on the quality of the solution produced by the algorithm. In other words, with or without the heuristic, the algorithm produces a solution of the same quality.

The bounding functions used in backtracking and branch-and-bound algorithms are a good example of heuristics employed to improve the time complexity. While these do not reduce the worst case time complexity of the algorithm (in fact, the worst case asymptotic complexity is often less without the heuristic), the average performance is significantly improved. The rationale behind a least cost or maximum profit branch-and-bound itself is heuristic. Intuitively, we expect to find an optimal solution quicker when E-nodes are selected in this way than when they are selected at random or by the FIFO or LIFO discipline.

The second kind of heuristic employed in a computer algorithm affects the quality of the solution produced by the algorithm. These heuristics are the focus of this section. They are typically used in the solution of problems for which there is no efficient algorithm that finds an optimal solution. The heuristic algorithm generally finds a good solution quickly. At times it is possible to bound the quality of the solution generated by the heuristic. For instance a heuristic may guarantee feasible solutions with value within 10% of the value of an optimal solution. When this is the case, the heuristic is, in fact, an approximation algorithm for the problem. Generally, no such guarantee is provided by a heuristic. At times the solution value is very close to optimal and at times very far from it. The value of a heuristic lies in its ability to produce acceptable solutions most of the time.

14.7.2. Greedy Heuristics

As remarked earlier, it is often easy to devise a greedy algorithm for an optimization problem. Often, the algorithm will not guarantee optimal solutions. However, intuition suggests that the algorithm will work well most of the time. Let us examine some greedy heuristics.

0/1 Knapsack Problem

Loading a knapsack by considering the objects in nondecreasing order of the ratio $p[i]/w[i]$ is an intuitively appealing approach. While we have already seen that this does not guarantee optimal solutions, we can expect the method to perform well in practice. In fact, we expect it to produce solutions that are very close to optimal most of the time. The results of an experimental evaluation of this heuristic were reported by the author in the Journal of the ACM. Of 600 randomly generated knapsack instances, the greedy heuristic generated optimal solutions for 239. For 583 instances the generated solution had a value within 10% of optimal. All 600 solutions were within 25% of optimal. Quite an impressive performance by an algorithm that runs in $O(n\log n)$ time.

We may ask whether the greedy heuristic guarantees solutions that have a value that is within $x\%$ of the optimal value for some x, $x<100$. The answer is no. To see this, consider the instance $n = 2$, $w[1:2] = [1,y]$, $p[1:2] = [10, 9y]$, and $c = y$. The greedy solution is $x[1:2] = [1,0]$. This solution has value 10. For $y\geq10/9$, the optimal solution has value $9y$. So, the value of the greedy solution is $(9y-10)/(9y)*100\%$ away from the optimal value. For large y, this approaches 100%.

The greedy heuristic can be modified to provide solutions within $x\%$ of optimal for $x<100$. This is done at the expense of run time. First, a subset of at most k objects is placed into the knapsack. If this subset has weight greater than c, it is discarded. Otherwise the remaining capacity is utilized using the greedy strategy described above. The best solution obtained considering all possible subsets with at most k objects is the solution generated by the heuristic.

Example 14.5: Consider the knapsack instance $n = 4$, $w[1:4] = [2, 4, 6, 7]$, $p[1:4] = [6, 10, 12, 13]$, and $c = 11$. When $k = 0$, the knapsack is filled in nonincreasing order of profit density. First, object 1 is put into the knapsack, then object 2. The capacity that remains at this time is 5. None of the remaining objects fits and the solution $x[1:4] = [1, 1, 0, 0]$ is produced. The profit earned from this solution is 16.

Let us now try the greedy heuristic with $k = 1$. The subsets to begin with are {1}, {2}, {3}, and {4}. The subsets {1} and {2} yield the same solution as obtained above with $k = 0$. When the subset {3} is considered, $x[3]$ is set to 1. 5 units of capacity remain and we attempt to utilize this by considering the remaining objects in nonincreasing order of density. Object 1 is considered first. It fits and $x[1]$ is set to

1. At this time only 3 units of capacity remain and none of the remaining objects can be added to the knapsack. The solution obtained when we begin with the subset {3} in the knapsack is $x[1{:}4]$ = [1, 0, 1, 0]. The profit earned from this is 18. When we begin with the subset {4}, the solution $x[1{:}4]$ = [1, 0, 0, 1] that has a profit value of 19 is produced. The best solution obtained considering subsets of size 0 and 1 is [1, 0, 0, 1]. This is the answer produced by the greedy heuristic when $k = 1$.

If $k = 2$, then in addition to the subsets considered for $k < 2$, we need to consider the subsets {1, 2}, {1, 3}, {1, 4}, {2, 3}, {2, 4}, and {3, 4}. The last of these represents an infeasible starting point and is discarded. For the remaining, the solutions obtained are [1, 1, 0, 0], [1, 0, 1, 0], [1, 0, 0, 1], [0, 1, 1, 0], and [0, 1, 0, 1]. The last of these has the profit value 23. This is higher than that obtained from the subsets of size 0 and 1. This solution is therefore the solution produced by the heuristic. □

The solution produced by the modified greedy heuristic is $k-optimal$. I.e., if we remove up to k objects from the solution and put back up to k, the new solution is no better than the original one. Further, solutions obtained in this manner can be shown to have value within $100/(k+1)\%$ of optimal. When $k = 1$, the solutions are guaranteed to have value within 50% of optimal, when $k = 2$, they are guaranteed to have value within 33.33% of optimal, and so on. The run time of the heuristic increases with k. The number of subsets to be tried is $O(n^k)$ and $O(n)$ time is spent on each. So, the total time taken is $O(n^{k+1})$ when $k > 0$.

The observed performance is far better than suggested by the worst case bounds. The results of 600 random tests are summarized in Figure 14.15.

Bin Packing

In the bin packing problem, we are given n objects. Object i has a nonnegative size $s[i]$. These objects are to be packed into bins of size c. The objective is to find a packing that uses the fewest number of bins. Several greedy algorithms come to mind. Some of these are:

	Percent Deviation				
k	0	1%	5%	10%	25%
0	239	390	528	583	600
1	360	527	598	600	
2	483	581	600		

Figure 14.15 Number of solutions within $x\%$ out of 600

1. *First Fit (FF)*
   Objects are considered for packing in the order 1, 2, ..., n. We assume a large number of bins arranged left to right. Object i is packed into the left most bin into which it fits.

2. *Best Fit (BF)*
   Let $cAvail[j]$ denote the capacity available in bin j. Initially, this is c for all bins. Object i is packed into the bin with the least $cAvail$ that is at least $s[i]$.

3. *First Fit Decreasing (FFD)*
   This is the same as FF except that the objects are first reordered so that $s[i] \geq s[i+1]$, $1 \leq i < n$.

4. *Best Fit Decreasing (BFD)*
   This is the same as BF except that the objects are reordered as for FFD.

You should be able to show that none of these methods guarantee optimal packings. All four are intuitively appealing and can be expected to perform well in practice.

Let I be any instance of the bin packing problem. Let $b(I)$ be the number of bins used by an optimal packing. In the paper by Johnson et al. cited in the readings section, it is shown that the number of bins used by FF and BF never exceeds $(17/10)b(I) + 2$ while that used by FFD and BFD does not exceed $(11/9)b(I) + 4$.

Example 14.6: Four objects with $s[1:4] = [3, 5, 2, 4]$ are to be packed in bins of size 7. When FF is used, object 1 goes into bin 1 and object 2 into bin 2. Object 3 fits into the first bin and is placed there. Object 4 does not fit into either of the two bins used so far and a new bin is used. The solution produced utilizes 3 bins and has objects 1 and 3 in bin 1, object 2 in bin 2, and object 4 in bin 3.

When BF is used, objects 1 and 2 get into bins 1 and 2, respectively. Object 3 gets into bin 2 as this provides a better fit than does bin 1. Object 4 now fits into bin 1. The packing obtained uses only two bins and has objects 1 and 4 in bin 1 and objects 2 and 3 in bin 2.

For FFD and BFD, the objects are packed in the order 2, 4, 1, 3. In both cases a two bin packing is obtained. Objects 2 and 3 are in bin 1 and objects 1 and 4 in bin 2. □

Board Permutation

The board permutation problem arises in the design of large electronic systems. The classical form of this problem has n circuit boards that are to be placed into slots in a cage (Figure 14.16). Each permutation of the n boards defines a placement of the boards into the cage. Let $B = \{b_1, \ldots, b_n\}$ denote the n boards. A set $L = \{N_1, \ldots, N_m\}$ of m nets is defined on the boards. Each N_i is a subset of B. These subsets need not be disjoint. Each net is realized by running a wire through the boards that comprise the net.

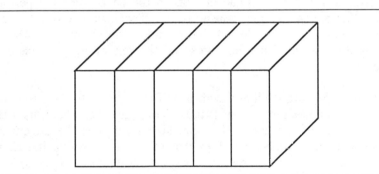

Figure 14.16 Cage with slots

Example 14.7: Let $n = 8$, and let the boards and nets be as given below.

$$B = \{b_1, b_2, b_3, b_4, b_5, b_6, b_7, b_8\}$$
$$L = \{N_1, N_2, N_3, N_4, N_5\}$$
$$N_1 = \{b_4, b_5, b_6\}$$
$$N_2 = \{b_2, b_3\}$$
$$N_3 = \{b_1, b_3\}$$
$$N_4 = \{b_3, b_6\}$$
$$N_5 = \{b_7, b_8\}$$

Figure 14.17 shows a possible permutation for the boards. The edges denote the wires that have to be run between the boards. □

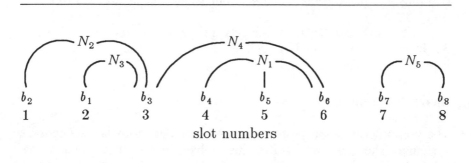

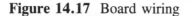

slot numbers

Figure 14.17 Board wiring

Let $p[1{:}n]$ denote a board permutation. Board $p[i]$ is placed into slot i of the cage when the placement is done using permutation $p[i]$. *density*(p) is defined to be the maximum number of wires that cross the gap between any pair of adjacent slots in the cage. For the permutation of Figure 14.17, the *density* is 2. Two wires cross the gaps between slots 2 and 3, slots 4 and 5, and slots 5 and 6. The gap between slots 6 and 7 has no wires and the remaining gaps have one wire each.

Card cages are designed with a uniform gap size (i.e., the space between adjacent slots is the same). This gap size therefore determines the size of the cage. The gap size itself must be adequate to accommodate the number of wires that must pass through it. Hence, the gap size (and in turn the cage size) is determined by *density*(p).

The objective of the board permutation problem is to find a permutation of the boards that has least *density*.

Let a be a set of boards and let $s[a]$ be the union of the nets in the boards of a. I.e., $s[a] = \bigcup_{i \in a} N_i$. A possible greedy heuristic for this problem is to build the permutation left to right. Boards are added to the permutation in an order that keeps the current *density* minimum. This order is described by Program 14.14.

---

procedure *LeftToRight*(**var** *p*: *permutation*; *n*: **integer**);
{Construct a greedy left to right permutation}
var *q*: *SetOfBoards*; *i*, *b*: **integer**;
begin
    q := {1, 2, ..., *n*};
    for *i* := 1 **to** *n* **do**
    begin
        Select a board *b* from *q* that minimizes the size of
        $s[\{p[1{:}i-1]\} + \{b\}] \cap s[q - \{b\}]$
        p[*i*] := *b*; {*b* is the next board in the permutation}
        q := *q*−{*b*};
    end;
end; {of *LeftToRight*}

Program 14.14

Another possibility is to construct the permutation inwards from the two ends as in Program 14.15. Yet another possibility is to consider the boards in some order *r* (*r* is a permutation of {1, 2, ..., *n*}) and construct the desired board permutation as in Program 14.16. When Program 14.16 is used, we can obtain solutions using several different orders *r* and then pick the best of these solutions.

One can construct instances for which all three of the greedy heuristics developed above generate permutations with density *m* while an optimal permutation has density 2. Since all three construct optimal solutions with density 1 whenever such a solution exists, the maximum value for the ratio of a greedy permutation density to an optimal density is $m/2$. The only way to determine which of the three greedy heuristics is to be preferred is through experimentation. We delay this experimentation until we have studied some other heuristics for the board permutation problem.

14.7.3. Exchange Methods

In an exchange heuristic for an optimization problem, we generally begin with a feasible solution and change parts of it in an attempt to improve its value. This change in the feasible solution is called a *perturbation*. The initial feasible solution may be obtained using some other heuristic method (such as the greedy method) or may be any

---

procedure *EndsIn*(**var** *p*: *permutation*; *n*: **integer**);
{Construct a greedy ends in permutation}
var *q*: *SetOfBoards*; *i*, *b*: **integer**;
begin
   q := {1, 2, ..., *n*};
   for *i* := 1 **to** *n* **div** 2 **do**
   begin
      Select a board *b* from *q* that minimizes the size of
        s[{*p*[1:*i*−1]} + {*b*}] ∩ *s*[{*p*[*n*−*i*+2:*n*]} + *q* − {*b*}];
      p[*i*] := *b*; {*b* is the next board at the left end
                           of the permutation}
      q := *q*−{*b*};

      Select a board *b* from *q* that minimizes the size of
        s[{*p*[1:*i*]} + *q* − {*b*}] ∩ *s*[{*p*[*n*−*i*+2:*n*]} + {*b*}];
      p[*n*−*i*+1] := *b*; {*b* is the next board at the right end
                              of the permutation}
      q := *q*−{*b*};
end;
if *n* is odd **then**
  p[*n* **div** 2 + 1] := last board in *q*;
end; {of *EndsIn*}

Program 14.15

randomly obtained solution.

    Suppose that we wish to minimize the objective function $h(i)$ subject to the constraints C. Here, i, denotes a feasible solution (i.e., one that satisfies C). Classical exchange heuristics follow the steps given in Program 14.17. This assumes that we start with a random feasible solution. As remarked earlier, we may at times start with a solution constructed by some other heuristic.

    The quality of the solution obtained using Program 14.17 can be improved by running this program several times. Each time, a different starting solution is used. The best of the solutions produced by the program is used as the final solution.

```
procedure OrderDirected(var p, r: permutation; n: integer);
{Construct a greedy permutation using the permutation r}
var t, q: permutation; cost, i, j, k: integer;
begin
  for i := 1 to n do {find best place for r[i]}
  begin
    for j := 1 to i−1 do t[j+1] := p[j];
    t[1] := r[i]; {trial place for r[i]}
    cost := density(t, i);
    for j := 1 to i−1 do {try other places for r[i]}
    begin
      q[1:i] := (p[1:j], r[i], p[j+1:i−1]);
      k := density(q, i);
      if k < cost then begin cost := k; t := q; end;
    end;
    p := t;
  end;
end; {of OrderDirected}
```

Program 14.16

Step 1   Let i be a random feasible solution (i.e., $C(i)$ is satisfied) to the given problem.

Step 2   Perform perturbations (i.e., exchanges) on i until it is not possible to improve i by such a perturbation.

Step 3   Output i.

Program 14.17 General form of an exchange heuristic

We illustrate two popular exchange methods by considering the knapsack and board permutation problems as examples.

0/1 Knapsack

Let $x[1:n]$ be a feasible solution to the given knapsack instance and let k be an integer. In a k exchange heuristic for the 0/1 knapsack problem, k of the objects that are presently in the knapsack (i.e., k of the objects with $x[j] = 1$) are removed from the knapsack. The objects not in the knapsack (these include the k just removed) are considered for inclusion into the knapsack in nonincreasing order of profit density. If the new solution is better than the previous one the exchange process is continued with this new solution. If the present solution cannot be improved by such an exchange, the exchange heuristic terminates.

Board Permutation

Let r be an initial board permutation. In a single exchange heuristic, we attempt to get a permutation with lesser density by moving one of the boards from its present position to another position. The details are provided in Program 14.18.

```
procedure SingleExchange (var p , r: permutation; n: integer);
{Single exchange heuristic for the board permutation problem.}
var cost, MinCost, i, j: integer;
begin
    cost := density(r, n);
    repeat
        p := r; {update best permutation found so far}
        MinCost := cost; {MinCost is density of p}
        i := 0;
        repeat {try to reduce density}
            i := i + 1;
            j := 0;
            repeat {try all positions for p[i]}
                j := j + 1;
                {insert p[i] at position j shifting others to make room}
                r := insert(p, i, j);
                cost := density(r, n);
            until (j=n) or (cost < MinCost);
        until (i=n) or (cost < MinCost);
    until cost >= MinCost; {until no reduction is possible}
end; {of SingleExchange}
```

Program 14.18 Single exchange heuristic

A *pairwise* exchange heuristic for the board permutation problem begins with a permutation *r* and attempts to produce a permutation with lesser *density* by interchanging the positions of exactly two boards. The process is continued until no further improvement can be obtained by making a pairwise exchange. Program 14.19 describes the process.

---

procedure *PairwiseExchange* (**var** *p*, *r*: *permutation*; *n*: **integer**);
{Pairwise exchange heuristic for the board permutation problem.}
var *cost, MinCost, i, j*: **integer**;
begin
   cost := *density* (*r*, *n*);
   repeat
      p := *r*; {update best permutation found so far}
      MinCost := *cost*;
      i := 0;
      repeat {try to reduce density}
         i := *i*+1;
         j := *i*;
         while (*j* < *n*) **and** (*cost* >= *MinCost*) **do**
         begin
            j := *j* + 1;
            r := *interchange* (*p*, *i*, *j*); {swap *p*[*i*] and *p*[*j*]}
            cost := *density* (*r*, *n*);
         end;
      until (*i*=*n*) **or** (*cost* < *MinCost*);
   until *cost* >= *MinCost*; {until no reduction is possible}
end; {of *PairwiseExchange*}

Program 14.19 Pairwise exchange heuristic

For both of these exchange heuristics, the worst case ratio of heuristic *density* to optimal is also *m*/2.

14.7.4. Performance Measurement

In measuring the relative performance of the heuristics designed for the board permutation problem, we shall consider only the density of the permutation produced. The heuristics developed were used on 150 randomly generated board permutation instances. The instances had between 5 to 30 boards. The exchange heuristics were run five times for each instance. Each time, a different starting permutation was used. The best of the five solutions produced was used for comparison with other heuristics. Figure 14.18 gives the number of times each heuristic produced the best permutation. The total exceeds 150 as often two or more heuristics tied with the best solution. As can be seen, the *LeftToRight* heuristic had the best performance and the two exchange heuristics were close behind.

Number Of Times In 150 Trials A Heuristic Produces A Solution With Minimal Density With Respect To Other Heuristics		
No.	Heuristic	Total
1	*LeftToRight*	69
2	*EndsIn*	29
3	*OrderDirected*	32
4	*SingleExchange*	56
5	*PairwiseExchange*	58

Figure 14.18

14.7.5. A Monte Carlo Improvement Method

In practice, the quality of the solution produced by an exchange heuristic is enhanced if the heuristic occasionally accepts exchanges that produce a feasible solution with increased $h()$ (recall that h is the function we wish to minimize). This is justified on the grounds that a bad exchange now may lead to a better solution later.

In order to implement this strategy of occasionally accepting bad exchanges, we need a probability function $prob(i, j)$ which provides us the probability with which an exchange that transforms solution i into the inferior solution j is to be accepted. Once we have this probability function, the Monte Carlo improvement results in exchange heuristics taking the form given in Program 14.20. This form was proposed by Metropolis in 1953. The variables *counter* and n are used to stop the procedure. If n successive attempts to perform an exchange on i are rejected, then an optima with respect to the exchange heuristic is assumed to have been reached and the algorithm terminates.

Step 1	Let i be a random feasible solution to the given problem. Set *counter* = 0.
Step 2	Let j be a feasible solution that is obtained from i as a result of a random perturbation.
Step 3	If $h(j) < h(i)$, then [$i = j$, update best solution found so far in case i is best, *counter* = 0, go to Step 2].
Step 4	[$h(j) \geq h(i)$] If *counter* = n then output best solution found and stop. Otherwise, r = random number in the range (0, 1); If $r < prob(i, j)$ then [$i = j$, *counter* = 0] else [*counter* = *counter* + 1]. go to Step 2.

Program 14.20 Metropolis Monte Carlo Method

Several modifications to the basic Metropolis scheme have been proposed. One of these is to use a sequence of different probability functions. The first in this sequence is used initially, then we move to the next function, and so on. The transition from one function to the next may be done whenever sufficient computer time has been spent at one function or when a sufficient number of perturbations have failed to improve the current solution. When the sequence of probability functions used is of the form $e^{(h(i)-h(j))/Y_q}$ for $q = 1, 2, 3, \ldots$, the method is called *simulated annealing*. The number of Y_q's to use and their values need to be determined experimentally.

Another modification to the scheme of Program 14.20 is to accept bad exchanges only when no good exchanges are possible. Another way to state this is that instead of using a sequence of unrelated starting solutions as suggested at the end of Section 14.7.3, let the next starting solution be obtained from the best solution obtained so far by performing a random exchange on it. This translates into the strategy of Program 14.21.

We may combine the strategies of Programs 14.20 and 14.21 into a single strategy as in Program 14.22. Here, we attempt to make good perturbations only. However, if n attempts to do this fail, then a

---

Step 1   Let i be a random feasible solution to the given problem. Set *counter* $= 0$.

Step 2   Perform perturbations (i.e., exchanges) on i until it is not possible to improve i by such a perturbation.

Step 3   Update the best solution found so far in case i is best; If *counter* $= n$ then output best solution found and stop. Otherwise, set *counter* $=$ *counter* $+ 1$; Make a random perturbation to i; go to Step 2.

Program 14.21

Step 1   Let i be a random feasible solution to the given problem. Set *counter* 1 and *counter* 2 to 0.

Step 2   Let j be a feasible solution that is obtained from i as a result of a random perturbation.

Step 3   If $h(j) < h(i)$, then [set $i = j$, update best solution found so far in case i is best, set *counter* 1 $= 0$, go to Step 2].

Step 4 $[h(j) \geq h(i)]$ If *counter* 1 $= n$ and *counter* 2 $= m$ then output best solution and stop. Otherwise, if *counter* 1 $= n$ then [set *counter* 1 $= 0$, *counter* 2 $=$ *counter* 2 $+ 1$, and $i = j$, go to Step 2]. Otherwise, [set *counter* 1 $=$ *counter* 1 $+ 1$, go to Step 2].

Program 14.22 Combination of Programs 14.20 and 14.21

bad perturbation is made.

Program 14.22 is appealing. It is easier to use than Program 14.20 as no probability function is to be designed. It may be faster than 14.21 as we do not wait till a local optima is found before accepting a bad exchange.

An experiment involving 30 board permutation instances was performed. In this experiment, n was set to 18 in Program 14.22. This program was allowed the same amount of computer time as required by the procedure *LeftToRight* (Program 14.14). This was accomplished by first timing Program 14.14. Next, Program 14.22 was modified by changing the terminating condition from (*counter*1 = n and *counter*2 = m) to (time used $\geq$ time allowed). The solutions produced by Program 14.22 were slightly better than those obtained by Program 14.14. Recall that Program 14.14 produces slightly better solutions than the simple exchange heuristics of Programs 14.18 and 14.19.

Dramatic improvements in the performance of simple exchange heuristics are observed for other problems. For example, consider the traveling salesperson problem. In this problem, we are given a complete digraph. There is a cost associated with each edge of this digraph. We are required to find a minimum cost cycle that begins at vertex 1, goes through every other vertex exactly once, and returns to vertex 1.

It is easy to develop single exchange and pairwise exchange heuristics for the traveling salesperson problem. Every permutation of the vertices {2, 3, 4, ..., n} defines a feasible solution (the complete solution is obtained by adding "1" at the front and end of the permutation). Experiments with this problem show that the Monte Carlo improvement of Program 14.22 yields solutions that are significantly better than those obtained by Program 14.17. However, the solutions are not as good as those that can be obtained using some of the sophisticated heuristics that have been developed for this problem.

14.8. SELECTED READINGS AND REFERENCES

The correctness proof for Kruskal's algorithm can be found in:

> *Concepts in discrete mathematics*, by Sartaj Sahni, 2nd Edition, Camelot Publishing Company, Fridley, Minnesota, 1985.

Additional examples of the design methods given in this chapter appear in the book:

> *Fundamentals of computer algorithms*, by S. Sahni and E. Horowitz, Computer Science Press, Maryland, 1978.

Details of the experiment involving greedy heuristics for the 0/1

Knapsack problem can be found in the paper:

> Approximate algorithms for the 0/1 Knapsack problem, by S. Sahni, *JACM*, 22, pp. 115-124, 1975.

The analyses for the bin packing heuristics appear in the paper:

> Performance bounds on simple one dimensional bin packing algorithms, by D. Johnson, A. Demers, J. Ullman, M. Garey, and R. Graham, *SIAM Jr. on Computing*, vol. 3, no. 4, pp. 299-325, 1974.

Our discussion of the heuristics for the board permutation problem are based on the paper:

> Heuristics for the board permutation problem, by J. Cohoon and S. Sahni, Proceedings, 1983 IEEE ICCAD Conference, Santa Clara, CA. A detailed version of this paper appears as report 82-16, 1982, of the Computer Science Department, University of Minnesota, Minneapolis, MN 55455.

The left to right greedy heuristic for the board permutation problem is due to Goto et al. and appears in the paper:

> Suboptimal solution of the backboard ordering with channel capacity constraint, IEEE Trans. Circuits and Systems, by S. Goto, I. Cederbaum, and B. Ting, pp. 645-652, Nov. 1977.

Additional material on the Metropolis Monte Carlo method and on simulated annealing can be found in the following papers. The paper by Nahar et al. provides experimental results for the traveling salesperson problem as well as for other problems.

> Optimization by simulated annealing, S. Kirkpatrick, C. Gelatt, and M. Vecchi, Science, vol. 220, pp. 671-680, 1983.

> Experiments with simulated annealing, by S. Nahar, S. Sahni, and E. Shragowitz, University of Minnesota, Technical Report, 1984.

> Heuristics for the circuit realization problem, by J. Cohoon

and S. Sahni, 1983 IEEE Design Automation Conference, Miami.

and

Global wiring by simulated annealing, by M. Vecchi and S. Kirkpatrick, IEEE Trans. On CAD, vol. 4, pp. 215-222, 1983.

A fairly sophisticated and successful heuristic for the traveling salesperson problem appears in the paper:

An effective heuristic for the traveling salesman problem, by S. Lin and B. Kernighan, *Operations Research*, vol. 21, pp. 498-516, 1973.

14.9. EXERCISES

1. Extend the greedy solution of Section 14.2 to the loading of two ships. Does the algorithm generate optimal solutions always?

2. Consider the continuous 0/1 knapsack problem that is defined as:

$$\text{maximize } \sum_{i=1}^{n} p[i]x[i]$$

subject to the constraints:

$$\sum_{i=1}^{n} w[i]x[i] \le c$$

and

$0 \le x[i] \le 1,\ 1 \le i \le n$

(a) Show that feasible solutions obtained by being greedy on profit aren't necessarily optimal.

(b) Show that feasible solutions obtained by being greedy on weight aren't necessarily optimal.

    (c)   Show that feasible solutions obtained by being greedy on the profit density $p[i]/w[i]$ are always optimal.

    (d)   Write a greedy algorithm using the strategy of (c). Your algorithm should have a worst case time complexity that is $O(n\log n)$. Show that this is so.

3.   Refine Program 14.2 into a Pascal procedure. Experiment with this and obtain average times to find minimum cost spanning trees in connected graphs with n vertices.

4.   Refine Program 14.4 into a Pascal procedure under the assumption that *ElementList* is a linked list of elements. Compare the run time of this procedure to that of the iterative merge sort procedure obtained in the text for the case when *ElementList* is an array.

5.   What are the essential differences between the way Program 14.6 accomplishes a sort and the way Program 14.5 does this?

6.   Compare, experimentally, the average case run times of Programs 14.10 and 14.11.

7.   Replace the last recursive call to *qSort* in procedure *qSort* (Program 14.10) by a **while** loop. Compare the average run time of the resulting sort procedure with that of Program 14.10.

8.   Rewrite Program 14.10 using a stack to simulate the recursion. The new procedure should stack the boundaries of only the smaller of A and C.

    (a)   Show that the stack space needed is $O(\log n)$.

    (b)   Compare the average run time of Program 14.10 with that of the new procedure.

9.   Show that the worst case time complexity of procedure *QuickSort* is $\Theta(n^2)$. Give an example of a data set on which this much time is taken.

10. When the element at position *left* is selected as the partitioning element in quick sort, it is possible for A or C to be empty. This possibility can be eliminated by comparing the keys at the positions *left*, *right*, and (*left*+*right*) **div** 2 and using the median (i.e., middle value) for partitioning. When this is done, both A and C must have at least one element in them. This selection rule is called the *median of three* rule. Compare the worst case and average times of Program 14.10 when the median of three rule is used to that when it is not used.

11. Program 14.11 is obtained by composing together two sort methods: quick sort and insertion sort. The composite algorithm is essentially a quick sort that reverts to an insertion sort when the size of a subfile is less than or equal to *ChangeOver* = *nBreak*. Could a faster composite algorithm be obtained by using a different value for *ChangeOver*? Why? Experiment with different values of *ChangeOver* and see what happens. Determine the best value of *ChangeOver* for the case of average performance.

12. In this exercise, we shall develop a sort procedure with best worst case performance.

    (a) Compare the worst case run times of insert, heap, merge, and quick sort. The worst case input data for insert and quick sort is easy to generate. For merge sort, write a program to generate the worst case data. This program will essentially unmerge a sorted sequence of *n* elements. For heap sort, estimate the worst case time using random permutations.

    (b) Use the results of part (a) to obtain a composite sort procedure that has the best worst case performance. More likely than not, your composite procedure will include only merge and insert sort (see previous exercise).

    (c) Obtain the worst case run time of your composite procedure. Compare the performance with that of the original sort procedures.

    (d) Plot the worst case times of the five sort procedures on a single graph sheet.

13. Write a recursive procedure to determine the shortest path from i to j. Your procedure may utilize the already computed values $kay[1:n, 1:n]$. What is the time complexity of your procedure?

14. Consider the 0/1 Knapsack instance: $n = 4$, $w[1:4] = [20, 25, 15, 35]$, $p[1:4] = [40, 49, 25, 60]$, and $c = 62$.

    (a) Draw the solution space tree for 0/1 knapsack instances when $n = 4$.

    (b) Trace the working of a backtracking algorithm on this tree (use the above instance). Clearly label the nodes in the order in which the backtrack algorithm first reaches them. Identify the nodes that do not get reached.

    (c) Do part (b) for the case of a FIFO branch-and-bound.

    (d) Do part (b) for the case of a max profit branch-and-bound.

15. In the n queens problem we wish to find a placement of n queens on an $n \times n$ chessboard such that no two queens attack. Two queens are said to attack iff they are in the same row, column, diagonal, or antidiagonal of the chess board. Hence, we may assume that in any feasible solution, queen i is placed in row i of the chess board. So, we are interested only in determining the column placement of each queen. Let $c[i]$ denote the column that queen i is placed in. If no two queens attack, then $c[1:n]$ is a permutation of $(1, 2, ..., n)$. The solution space for the n queens problem can therefore be limited to all permutations of $(1, 2, ..., n)$.

    (a) Organize the n queens solution space as a tree.

    (b) Write a backtracking procedure to search this tree for a feasible placement of the n queens.

16. Write a procedure to find a path in a maze. Use a FIFO branch-and-bound.

17. Show that the path (if any) found by a FIFO search of a maze is a shortest length path. Show that this is not necessarily true for a path found using backtracking.

18. Generate four bin packing instances. The first should have the property that the solution produced by FF uses fewer bins than that used by the solutions produced by BF, FFD, and BFD. The second should have the property that the solution produced by BF uses fewer bins than that used by the solutions produced by FF, FFD, and BFD. The third should have the property that the solution produced by FFD uses fewer bins than that used by the solutions produced by FF, BF, and BFD. The fourth should have the property that the solution produced by BFD uses fewer bins than that used by the solutions produced by FF, BF, and FFD.

19. Write a Pascal program for the bin packing problem (Section 14.7.2). Use the first fit method. Your program should have a time complexity $O(n \log n)$.

20. Write a Pascal program for the bin packing problem (Section 14.7.2). Use the best fit method. Your program should have a time complexity $O(n \log n)$.

21. Write a Pascal program for the bin packing problem (Section 14.7.2). Use the first fit decreasing method. Your program should have a time complexity $O(n \log n)$.

22. Write a Pascal program for the bin packing problem (Section 14.7.2). Use the best fit decreasing method. Your program should have a time complexity $O(n \log n)$.

23. Refine procedure *LeftToRight* (Program 14.14) into a Pascal procedure whose time complexity is $O(n^2 m)$ where n is the number of boards and m the number of nets.

24. Refine procedure *EndsIn* (Program 14.15) into a Pascal procedure. What is the time complexity of your procedure?

25. Refine procedure *OrderDirected* (Program 14.16) into a Pascal procedure. What is the time complexity of your procedure?

26. Refine procedure *SingleExchange* (Program 14.18) into a Pascal procedure. What is the time complexity of your procedure?

27. Refine procedure *PairwiseExchange* (Program 14.19) into a Pascal procedure. What is the time complexity of your procedure?

28. Obtain three elegant Pascal procedures for the pairwise exchange heuristic for the board permutation problem. Your procedures should incorporate the Metropolis improvement strategies of Program 14.20-14.22; one strategy per program. Experiment with these three programs using randomly generated board permutation instances. Your experiments should allow each program to run for the same amount of time.

29. Write two Pascal procedures for the traveling salesperson problem. Both of these should begin with a random solution and use the pairwise exchange heuristic to improve this solution. One of these should incorporate the Monte Carlo scheme of Program 14.22 and the other should be based on Program 14.17. Experiment with these two programs under the assumption that both must work in the same amount of time. Use randomly generated problem instances.

APPENDIX A

CURVE FITTING

In this appendix, we consider the problem of fitting a curve through a set of points. For simplicity, we restrict our discussion to the case when the curve is a polynomial. You are referred to one of the texts cited in Chapter 6 for a discussion of curve fitting using more general functions.

Let P be a program that sorts n records. Suppose that we wish to determine a function $t(n)$ such that $t(n)$ is the worst case run time of P. This function is to be used to predict the worst case run time of P for different values of n. Assume that an asymptotic analysis of this program has revealed that its worst case run time is $O(n^2)$. This isn't sufficient information to predict the actual worst case run time of P on an IBM-PC (say) for any value of n.

In order to get actual run times, an experiment is conducted. Suppose that the worst case run times are measured for m values of n. Let these m values be n_1, n_2, ..., n_m. Let q_i be the observed worst case time for $n = n_i$, $1 \leq i \leq m$. Having obtained these times, we can proceed to obtain $t(n)$ using one of two possible strategies.

The first strategy is to obtain a polynomial $t(n)$ with the property $t(n_i) = q_i$, $1 \leq i \leq m$. A polynomial with this property is called the *interpolating polynomial*. It can be shown that such a polynomial is unique and has degree at most m. In the case of our sort program, an interpolating polynomial is undesirable because the observed times are in error. Some of the possible causes for inaccuracy in the observed times are:

(1) Clock inaccuracy.

(2) The observed times probably include overheads associated with the time measurement process. For instance, the q_i's probably include the time needed to read the clock and the time taken by the repetition **for** loop.

(3) The data used to get the q_i's may not be worst case data. Perhaps the worst case data is too difficult to generate and some method to estimate the worst case run times has been used.

As a result of the inaccuracy in the observed times q_i, we can conclude that $t(n_i) \neq q_i$, $1 \leq i \leq m$. Because of this, we expect the interpolating polynomial to have a degree higher than 2. This is so despite our knowledge that the asymptotic run time is $O(n^2)$.

The second approach to fitting a polynomial through the observed points is to use our knowledge of the asymptotic complexity ($O(n^2)$) and determine a polynomial of degree 2 that best approximates these times. Such a polynomial is called an *approximating polynomial*. This approach is a more reasonable one to take when the observed data are known to be in error and when the degree of the polynomial we seek is known from other considerations. While in the case of our sort program we seek an approximating polynomial of degree 2, in other cases we may seek a polynomial of any known degree k.

Let $t(n)$ denote the approximating polynomial for the observed points (n_i, q_i), $1 \leq i \leq m$. Let $d_i = t(n_i) - q_i$ denote the difference between the value of the approximating polynomial and the observed value for $n = n_i$, $1 \leq i \leq m$. In determining the approximating polynomial $t(n)$, we may require that $t(n)$ minimize one of the following:

(1) $\max\limits_{i}\{|d_i|\}$

(2) $\sum\limits_{i=1}^{m} |d_i|$

(3) $\sum\limits_{i=1}^{m} d_i^2$

Minimizing either of the first two conditions is rather difficult as they lead to nonlinear equations. So, it is customary to minimize the third condition. An approximating polynomial that minimizes $\sum_{i=1}^{m} d_i^2$ is called a *least squares approximating polynomial.* Let us see how such a polynomial of degree k may be found.

The least squares approximating polynomial of degree k has the form:

$$t(n) = \sum_{j=0}^{k} a_j n^j$$

where the a_i's are constants whose values are to be determined using criterion (3) and the experimental data.

From criterion (3) and the definition of the d_i's, we see that the a_j's are to be chosen so that:

$$\sum_{i=1}^{m} (\sum_{j=0}^{k} a_j n_i^j - q_i)^2$$

is minimized. This requires that the partial derivative of the above expression with respect to each of the a_j's be zero. (Strictly speaking, when the partial derivatives are all zero, the above expression is either minimized or maximized. However, one can argue that the following development will always yield a_j's that minimize this expression.)

The partial derivative of the least squares criterion with respect to a_p for any p in the range $[0, k]$ is:

$$2 \sum_{i=1}^{m} (\sum_{j=0}^{k} a_j n_i^j - q_i) n_i^p$$

Setting the partial derivative to zero yields:

$$\sum_{i=1}^{m} \sum_{j=0}^{k} a_j n_i^{j+p} = \sum_{i=1}^{m} q_i n_i^p$$

Letting p take on the $k+1$ values $\{0, 1, .., k\}$ gives us $k+1$ linear equations that have to be solved for the $k+1$ constants a_i, $0 \le i \le k$. This can be done using standard methods to solve systems of linear

equations. Once again, you are referred to any of the texts on numerical methods that are cited in Chapter 6.

Let us develop the form of this system of linear equations for the
cases $k = 1$, and 2. When $k = 1$, the above equation becomes:

$$a_0 \sum_{i=1}^{m} n_i^p + a_1 \sum_{i=1}^{m} n_i^{p+1} = \sum_{i=1}^{m} q_i n_i^p$$

The possible values for p are 0 and 1. Substituting these into the
above equation yields the two equations:

$$a_0 m + a_1 \sum_{i=1}^{m} n_i = \sum_{i=1}^{m} q_i$$

$$a_0 \sum_{i=1}^{m} n_i + a_1 \sum_{i=1}^{m} n_i^2 = \sum_{i=1}^{m} q_i n_i$$

When $k=2$, the equation for the partial derivative with respect to
a_p becomes:

$$a_0 \sum_{i=1}^{m} n_i^p + a_1 \sum_{i=1}^{m} n_i^{p+1} + a_2 \sum_{i=1}^{m} n_i^{p+2} = \sum_{i=1}^{m} q_i n_i^p$$

The possible values for p are 0, 1, and 2. Substituting these into the
above equation yields the three equations:

$$a_0 m + a_1 \sum_{i=1}^{m} n_i + a_2 \sum_{i=1}^{m} n_i^2 = \sum_{i=1}^{m} q_i$$

$$a_0 \sum_{i=1}^{m} n + a_1 \sum_{i=1}^{m} n_i^2 + a_2 \sum_{i=1}^{m} n_i^3 = \sum_{i=1}^{m} q_i n_i$$

$$a_0 \sum_{i=1}^{m} n_i^2 + a_1 \sum_{i=1}^{m} n_i^3 + a_2 \sum_{i=1}^{m} n_i^4 = \sum_{i=1}^{m} q_i n_i^2$$

Example A.1: Let's find the least squares approximating polynomial
of degree 1 for the three points $\{(1,2), (2,5), (3,7)\}$. For this data set,
$\sum_{i=1}^{3} n_i = 6$, $\sum_{i=1}^{3} n_i^2 = 14$, $\sum_{i=1}^{3} q_i = 14$, and $\sum_{i=1}^{3} q_i n_i = 33$. The two
equations involving the a_i's are:

$3a_0 + 6a_1 = 14$
$6a_0 + 14a_1 = 33$

Solving for a_0 and a_1, we get: $a_0 = -1/3$, and $a_1 = 5/2$. So, the approximating polynomial of degree 1 is:

$t(n) = 5n/2 - 1/3$

We readily see that $t(n_i) - q_i$ is $1/6$, $-1/3$, and $1/6$ when $i = 1, 2$, and 3, respectively. The least squares error is $\sum_{i=1}^{3} (t(n_i) - q_i)^2 = 1/6$.

□

Example A.2: For the experimental data of Figure 11.7 which corresponds to the worst case times for a sequential search (body of Program 8.4), we have: $m = 20$, $\sum_{i=1}^{m} n_i = 5950$, $\sum_{i=1}^{m} n_i^2 = 3{,}878{,}500$, $\sum_{i=1}^{m} q_i = 22.692$, and $\sum_{i=1}^{m} q_i n_i = 14{,}731.29$. Substituting these values into the two equations for the case $k = 1$, yields:

$20a_0 + 5950a_1 = 22.692$
$5950a_0 + 3878500a_1 = 14731.29$

Solving these for a_0 and a_1 gives us $a_0 = .008531$ and $a_1 = .003785$. Hence, the least squares approximating polynomial for the body of Program 8.4 is $t(n) = .003785n + .008531$. □

Example A.3: For the experimental data of Figure 11.8 which corresponds to the invokation time for Program 8.4 for different sizes s of *ElementList*, we have: $m = 15$, $\sum_{i=1}^{m} s_i = 17250$, $\sum_{i=1}^{m} s_i^2 = 1.263285 * 10^8$, $\sum_{i=1}^{m} q_i = 13.309$, and $\sum_{i=1}^{m} q_i n_i = 95795.94$. Substituting these values into the two equations for the case $k = 1$, yields:

$15a_0 + 17250a_1 = 13.309$
$1.725a_0 + 12632.85a_1 = 9.579594$

Solving these for a_0 and a_1 gives us $a_0 = .018009$ and $a_1 = .000756$. Hence, the least squares approximating polynomial for the data of Figure 11.8 is $t(s) = .000756s + .018009$. □

APPENDIX B

TRADE MARKS

The following registered trade marks have been referenced in this book:

123
Bandit
Cosmic Crusaders
dBase II
Donkey
Freeware
Frenzy
IBM
IBM-PC
Lotus
Pac Man
Paratroopers
PC-TALK III
Spider
Turbo Pascal
Wordstar
Wumpus

INDEX